T0213943

Communications in Computer and Information Science 1201

Commenced Publication in 2007
Founding and Former Series Editors:
Simone Diniz Junqueira Barbosa, Phoebe Chen, Alfredo Cuzzocrea,
Xiaoyong Du, Orhun Kara, Ting Liu, Krishna M. Sivalingam,
Dominik Ślęzak, Takashi Washio, Xiaokang Yang, and Junsong Yuan

More information about this series at http://www.springer.com/series/7899

Vladimir Sukhomlin · Elena Zubareva (Eds.)

Modern Information Technology and IT Education

13th International Conference, SITITO 2018
Moscow, Russia, November 29 – December 2, 2018
Revised Selected Papers

 Springer

Editors
Vladimir Sukhomlin (iD)
Moscow State University
Moscow, Russia

Elena Zubareva (iD)
Moscow State University
Moscow, Russia

ISSN 1865-0929   ISSN 1865-0937 (electronic)
Communications in Computer and Information Science
ISBN 978-3-030-46894-1   ISBN 978-3-030-46895-8 (eBook)
https://doi.org/10.1007/978-3-030-46895-8

This Springer imprint is published by the registered company Springer Nature Switzerland AG
The registered company address is: Gewerbestrasse 11, 6330 Cham, Switzerland

Preface

This CCIS volume, published by Springer, contains the proceedings of the 13th International Conference on Modern Information Technologies and IT-Education (SITITO 2018), which took place during November 29 – December 2, 2018, at the Lomonosov Moscow State University, Faculty of Computational Mathematics and Cybernetics. The Lomonosov Moscow State University was founded in 1755 and was the first university in Russia. It currently hosts more than 50,000 students. The Lomonosov Moscow State University is one of the major traditional educational institutions in Russia, offering training in almost all branches of modern science and humanities. By providing up-to-date infrastructure, convenient logistics, as well as historical and natural attractions, the venue allowed for the organization of the SITITO 2018 conference to ensure a high standard.

SITITO 2018 was designed to integrate the efforts of the academic community and experts from different countries in order to improve the efficiency of research and development of scientific and technological potential of IT in science, technology, economics, and training of scientific personnel.

SITITO 2018 was attended by hundreds of the most active in research and teaching representatives of higher-education teaching personnel, undergraduate and graduate students, representatives of the IT industry. The SITITO conference series has gathered a rich collection of scientific works from conference participants that reflects the history of the development of IT and IT-education system. Currently the conference is widely known both in Russia and abroad. The number of its participants is growing, and the quality of research papers is enhancing. This volume contains 33 contributed papers selected from 118 full paper submissions. Each submission was reviewed by at least three Program Committee members, with the help of external reviewers, and the final decisions took into account the feedback from a rebuttal phase. We wish to thank all the authors who submitted to SITITO 2018, the Program Committee members, and the external reviewers.

A plenary report on "Teaching Programming and Design-by-Contract" was delivered by Manuel Mazzara, Director of the Institute for Software Technology and Development, Head of the Laboratory of Software Architecture and Software Development Models, Innopolis University. His speech summarized his experience and innovative solutions for teaching the programming of bachelors and masters in computer science and software engineering at Innopolis University, as well as conducting research work with students in these areas. Considerable attention was paid to the experiment with the implementation of an innovative method of teaching programming, which focuses on the conceptual foundations of programming languages, the development of abstraction skills and design methodology, the acquisition of extensive long-term intellectual skills to continue a successful career for several decades, and ultimately the development skills in the programming language range (e.g., Java, C #, C, C ++, Python). The methodological basis of the author's approach was the training in formal methods and construction correctness, as well as the contract design method (DbC), implemented successively from the first steps of programming training.

A plenary report entitled "Alt Platform for Educational Institutions: a Tool in Teaching and Studying Informatics" was made by Associate Professor Tatyana Gubina from the company Basalt SPO. Her speech noted the acute relevance of the problem of imports phase-out in the field of software for the country's security. One of the basic solutions to this problem is the creation and widespread implementation of the Alt Linux national operating system (OS) in the national economy, for which the company Basalt SPO is to be held responsible. The rapporteur reviewed the Alt OS distributions and hardware platforms. The report focused on the educational distribution on the Alt platform and the company's cooperation with universities, including: the preparation of training and teaching materials for training courses; collection and dissemination of information on the development of universities on the basis of free software to automate the educational process and scientific work; conducting a cycle of classes with students on the development of free software; and holding the annual conference Free Software in Higher Education. The report further considers a project for the creation a typical domestic module for studying Internet technologies, whose software and hardware complex is being created on the basis of computer technology using domestic processors and software. It provided an overview of the complex of laboratory works for the formation of practical skills in the development and implementation of domestic hardware and software tools that implement Internet technologies, as well as a set of teaching materials for use in training courses on the study of Internet technologies in universities. Finally, attention has been given to the issues of methodological support of software solutions based on Alt distributions for higher and secondary schools.

A plenary report entitled "Methods of Creating Digital Doubles Based on Neural Network Modeling" was made by Dmitry Tarkhov, Professor of the Department of Higher Mathematics of the Institute of Applied Mathematics and Mechanics, Peter the Great St. Petersburg Polytechnic University. The report was devoted to the development of methods and tools for the implementation of the concept of digital twins, in which each complex technical system at all stages of its operation (from design and creation to scrapping and disposal) must be accompanied by an adequate adaptive mathematical model (digital double). The rapporteur examined the advantages of such an approach and substantiated the need to develop a methodology for creating digital doubles of complex technical objects with the active introduction of artificial intelligence methods. Further, the Unified Process of constructing doubles of real objects, developed by the authors, based on the use of the neural network apparatus, was considered. In particular, the class of neural network models of systems with interval specified parameters was examined in detail.

A plenary report entitled "D-Link Solutions for Organizing the Educational Process in the Field of Info-Communications and Telecommunications Infrastructure of Data Processing Centers" was made by Pavel Romasevich, D-Link, Volgograd. The study was carried out in collaboration with Smirnova Elena Viktorovna, D-Link, Moscow. The report's review modern hardware and software solutions of D-Link in the field of network technologies, as well as the company's infrastructure for the promotion of network technologies in Russia. A considerable part of the company's work is concerned with training in network technologies based on D-Link technical solutions. For this purpose, a distance learning portal has been created, training centers have been deployed in large cities, and close cooperation with universities has been carried out. D-Link employees together with high school teachers created and published a series of textbooks on network technologies and network security. In conclusion, the hardware and software of the new product line, designed to deploy data centers with a complex architecture, were reviewed.

A plenary report entitled "Developing the Skills of the Staff of the Research Center to Solve Actual Research Problems" was made by Evgeny Gavrin, Head of the Compilation Department of the Samsung Research Center. His speech focused on the problem of staff training for research projects conducted by Samsung. In particular, there was an analysis of the tasks, the requirements for theoretical and practical training of researchers and developers in the form of sets of basic and advanced competencies. Also, an overview of the target months-long curriculum for candidates for research projects implemented on the basis of Innopolis University was made.

SITITO 2018 was attended by about 350 people. The Program Committee reviewed 164 submissions and accepted 118 as full papers, 20 as short papers, 2 as posters, and 1 a demo; 26 SITITO 2018 submissions were rejected. According to the conference program, these 140 oral presentations (of the full and short papers) were structured into 8 sessions, including IT-Education: Methodology, Methodological Support, E-learning and IT in Education, Educational Resources and Best Practices of IT-Education, Research and Development in the Field of New IT and their Applications, Scientific Software in Education and Science, School Education in Computer Science and ICT, and Economic Informatics, Innovative Information and Pedagogical Technologies in IT-Education.

The conference was attended by leading experts and teams from research centers, universities, the IT industry, institutes of the Russian Academy of Sciences, Russian high-tech companies, and from countries abroad.

SITITO 2018 was further supported by the following associations and societies: Federal Educational-Methodical Association in higher education for the enlarged group of specialties and areas of training 02.00.00 Computer and Information Sciences, Fund for Promotion of Internet Media, IT Education, Human Development League Internet Media, Federal Research Center Computer Science and Control of the Russian Academy of Sciences, Russian Transport Academy, Samsung Research Center, D-Link Corporation, and BaseALT.

March 2019   Vladimir Sukhomlin
                                                     Elena Zubareva

Organization

General Chair

Evgeny Moiseev   RAS, Lomonosov Moscow State University, Russia

Program Committee Co-chairs

Igor Sokolov   Federal Research Center Computer Science
and Control of RAS, Russia

Vladimir Sukhomlin   Lomonosov Moscow State University, Russia

Organizing Committee Co-chairs

Evgeny Moiseev   RAS, Lomonosov Moscow State University, Russia

Vladimir Sukhomin   Lomonosov Moscow State University, Russia

Organizing Committee

Leonid Dmitriev   Lomonosov Moscow State University, Russia
Mikhail Fedotov   Lomonosov Moscow State University, Russia
Dmitry Gouriev   Lomonosov Moscow State University, Russia
Evgeniy Ilyushin   Lomonosov Moscow State University, Russia
Sergey Lozhkin   Lomonosov Moscow State University, Russia
Mikhail Lugachyov   Lomonosov Moscow State University, Russia
Vassily Lyubetsky   Kharkevich Institute for Information Transmission
Problems, RAS, Lomonosov Moscow State
University, Russia
Evgeniy Morkovin   Lomonosov Moscow State University, Russia
Dmitry Namiot   Lomonosov Moscow State University, Russia
Mikhail Posypkin   Computing Center of A. A. Dorodnicyn, Federal
Research Center Computer Science and Control
of RAS, Lomonosov Moscow State University,
Russia
Alexander Razgulin   Lomonosov Moscow State University, Russia
Vasiliy Tikhomirov   Lomonosov Moscow State University, Russia
Alexander Tomilin   Lomonosov Moscow State University, Russia
Evgeniy Zakharov   Lomonosov Moscow State University, Russia
Elena Zubareva   Lomonosov Moscow State University, Russia

Program Committee

Sergei Andrianov	Saint Petersburg State University, Russia
Sergei Avdonin	University of Alaska Fairbanks, USA
Esen Bidaibekov	Abai Kazakh National Pedagogical University, Kazakhstan
Yousef Daradkeh	Prince Sattam bin Abdulaziz University, Saudi Arabia
Alekzander Emelianov	National Research University - Moscow Power Engineering Institute, Russia
Yuri Evtushenko	Federal Research Center Computer Science and Control of RAS, Russia
Victor Gergel	Lobachevsky State University of Nizhni Novgorod, Russia
Luis Gouveia	University Fernando Pessoa, Portugal
Sava Grozdev	IHEAS, Institute of Mathematics and Informatics, BAS, Bulgaria
Tatyana Gubina	BaseALT, Russia
Dmitry Izmestiev	LANIT Group of Companies, Russia
Evgeniy Khenner	Russian Academy of Education, Perm State National Research University, Russia
Alekzander Kim	The Institute of Electronic Control Computers, Russia
Alexander Klimov	Russian University of Transport (MIIT), Russia
Vladimir Korenkov	Joint Institute for Nuclear Research, Laboratory of Information Technologies, Russia
Sergey Kramarov	Surgut State University, Russia
Tok Ling	National University of Singapore, Singapore
Alexander Misharin	Russian Railways, Russian University of Transport (MIIT), Russia
Valentin Nechaev	MIREA - Russian Technological University, Russia
Diethard Pallaschke	Karlsruhe Institute of Technology, Germany
Oleg Pokusaev	Russian University of Transport (MIIT), Russian Transport Academy, Russia
Gennady Ryabov	RAS, Lomonosov Moscow State University, Russia
Konstantin Samouylov	Peoples Friendship University of Russia, Russia
Manfred Schneps-Schneppe	Ventspils University College, Latvia
Alexey Smirnov	BaseALT, Russia
Leonid Sokolinsky	South Ural State University, Russia
Margarita Sotnikova	Saint Petersburg State University, Russia
Vladimir Sukhomlin	Lomonosov Moscow State University, Russia
Dmitry Tarkhov	Peter the Great St. Petersburg Polytechnic University, Russia
Mourat Tchoshanov	University of Texas at El Paso, USA
Andrey Terekhov	Saint Petersburg State University, Russia
Alexander Vasilyev	Peter the Great St. Petersburg Polytechnic University, Russia
Evgeny Veremey	Saint Petersburg State University, Russia

Vladimir Voevodin	RAS, Lomonosov Moscow State University, Russia
Dmitry Volkov	Institute for Applied Mathematics of the RAS, Open Systems Publishing House, Russia
Alexander Yazenin	Tver State University, Russia
Victor Zakharov	Federal Research Center Computer Science and Control of RAS, Russia
Alexey Zhabko	Saint Petersburg State University, Russia
Yuri Zhuravlev	Federal Research Center Computer Science and Control of RAS, Russia
Elena Zubareva	Lomonosov Moscow State University, Russia

Contents

Educational Resources and Best Practices of IT-Education

Research and Development in the Field of New IT and Their Applications

Scientific Software in Education and Science

School Education in Computer Science and ICT

Economic Informatics

IT-Education: Methodology, Methodological Support

Analytical Review of the Current Curriculum Standards in Information Technologies

Vladimir Sukhomlin and Elena Zubareva

Lomonosov Moscow State University, Leninskie Gory, 1, GSP-1, 119991 Moscow, Russia
sukhomlin@mail.ru, e.zubareva@cs.msu.ru

Abstract. The article provides us with an analytical overview of the current state (the beginning of 2018) of the curriculum system for undergraduate and graduate programs in computing (computing is the academic name of the field of Information Technology or IT), inter alia it considers: definition of the concept of curriculum, modern architecture of the curriculum system, construction principles and content of relevant curricula of the last decade, including the following documents: CC2005, CS2013, CE2016, SE2014, GSwE2009, IS2010, MSIS2016, IT2017, CSEC2017. The article provides a comparative analysis of curricula in terms of methodological solutions in describing educational content and learning objectives, highlighting the minimum required part of the curriculum knowledge (core), composition and methods of using didactic parameters for describing pedagogical emphasis on curricula and learning outcomes. The article will be useful for methodologists-developers of curricula and educational standards, in particular for comparing the domestic educational regulatory and methodological base with international experience in standardizing curricula in the field of training IT personnel. The information presented in the article can also be useful to students and graduate students to understand the international structure of the methodological foundations of the modern IT education system.

Keywords: Curriculum · International educational standards · Computing · IT-education

1 Introduction

The authors have been following the process of developing curriculum standards in the field of computing for many years (computing is the academic name of the field of Information Technology or IT) [1–7]. This approach is not new; it has long celebrated its half-century anniversary. The draft of the first curriculum standard for Computer Science (CS) was published by ACM in 1965 [8], and in 1968, after being finalized, it was published in its final form, known as Curriculum 68 [9]. The history of the curricular standardization of computing is described in detail by Perekatov V.I. [10, 11].

First of all, let's clarify what is meant by the term "curriculum". This is a teaching material in the form of a teacher's manual, designed to develop curricula in specific areas of training, which includes determining the set of expected characteristics of graduates and the requirements for pre-training for applicants to the curriculum, a description of

V. Sukhomlin and E. Zubareva (Eds.): SITITO 2018, CCIS 1201, pp. 3–41, 2020.
https://doi.org/10.1007/978-3-030-46895-8_1

the architecture of the body of knowledge of the curriculum, a detailed specification of the elements of the code knowledge, determination of learning outcomes/competencies, and also includes teaching materials with recommendations on methods for training programs, practices and laboratory work, the requirements in the final work, adapt to different institutional environments, etc. As a rule, another important component of such guidelines is the description of examples of curricula and examples of training courses implemented by well-known universities. Unfortunately, the authors cannot offer the term Russian language adequate to this concept. Therefore, we are forced to use the English term.

The goal of the activity under examination is to standardize at the international level the curricula of the IT education system in various areas of IT staff training. Curriculum standardization proved to be the most important methodological tool which contributed to the creation of a modern IT education system. The relevance of standardization of educational programs of IT education, due to the processes of globalization of the world economy and the widespread spread of IT with universal digitalization, is constantly growing.

It is the development of international standards/recommendations in the field of IT education, which have a high level of consensus in the professional environment and serve as a guideline for universities and universities, provides an opportunity to systematize and unify the practice requirements for relevant educational programs and for university graduates, and timely take into account the achievements and trends in the development of science and technology, to generalize and use the best educational practice, to increase the effectiveness of developing current educational programs and thus makes it possible to create a common space in the field of IT education, to provide high mobility of IT specialists. The leading international professional organizations such as the Association of Computer Engineering[1] and the Computer Community of the Institute of Electronics and Electrical Engineers[2] have responsibility for solving the problem of forming such guidelines-recommendations in the form of standardized curricula or curriculums.

Since the beginning of this century, the process of curriculum standardization has taken a systemic, continuous character. By the middle of the first decade of the current century, a holistic approach to building a curriculum standards system was developed, as it was reflected in Computing Curricula 2005 (CC2005) [12], and a set of curricula was created that describe typical curriculum models for the main profiles/areas of IT training. In subsequent years, as part of this process, all the curricula of the first five years were revised and published in new editions. The frequency of revision of curriculum standards is approximately five years.

The article considers the current state (at the beginning of 2018) of the curriculum system for undergraduate and graduate programs, in particular, the content and principles of constructing relevant curriculums of the last five years are examined, their comparative analysis is given in terms of methodological solutions, educational characteristics, and the use of didactic parameters.

---

[1] Association for Computing Machinery, http://www.acm.org.
[2] IEEE Computer Society, http://www.computer.org.

1.1 Systematic Approach to Curriculum Development

The main conceptual document of the curriculum system for IT education is the document SS2005 [12] mentioned above, defining the architecture of the curriculum system and describing the most important methodological principles underlying the curriculum approach.

In particular, CC2005 includes:

- a description of the curriculum system architecture and professional characteristics of the basic profiles/areas of training;
- a description of the characteristic areas of activity for different basic training profiles using a graphical model of the task space;
- a comparative analysis of basic profiles on the thematic content of training using a scaled tabular form for key technologies common to all profiles;
- a description of the outgoing professional characteristics of graduates of basic profiles;
- general principles for the development of the curricula, ensuring their conceptual integrity, etc.

An important outcome of CC2005 is the differentiation of the main areas of training IT specialists in accordance with the nature of their activities, as well as the definition of the appropriate architecture of the curriculum system. In particular, the following basic profiles are defined (SS 2005 also calls them as subdisciplines):

- Computer Science – CS;
- Computer Engineering – CE;
- Information Systems – IS;
- Information Technology – IT;
- Software Engineering – SE.

Figure 1 illustrates the architectural model of the curriculum system defined in CC2005. The figure demonstrates that this model is open, i.e. it can expand if new IT training profiles are developed. One of the candidates for expanding of this model was the Cybersecurity direction after the Curriculum Guidelines for Post-Secondary Degree Programs in Cybersecurity appeared in 2017 [20]. A distinct feature of this curriculum is that it determines the amount of knowledge and competence for the preparation of bachelors in cybersecurity, while it is assumed that this body of knowledge is the development of one of the main training profiles. This curriculum will be considered in more detail below.

Of the principles of curriculum development defined in CC2005, we note two aspects:

- the emphasis on the design, systematization and structuring of relevant collections of knowledge (explicit or implicit, through competencies), as well as the design of the associated learning outcomes/competencies system for various areas of training IT specialists,

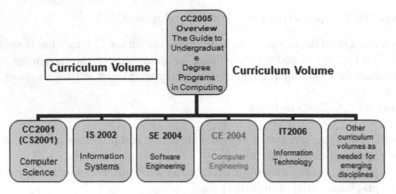

Fig. 1. Architectural model of the curriculum system defined in CC2005.

– the concept of the core of the body of knowledge - the allocation in the body of knowledge of the minimum necessary content (and the corresponding learning outcomes/competencies) for all curricula of a particular profile in the interest of supporting the integrity of the educational space, student mobility, guaranteeing a given level of quality of basic training.

The contents of this document were considered in more detail in previous works of the authors.

In the last five years, almost all the curricula for the above training profiles have been revised and released in new editions.

The modern stack of computing curricula for the training of bachelors and masters, including the main methodological document CC2005, consists of the following documents:

1. Curricula Computing 2005 (CC2005) [12];
2. Computer Science 2013 (CS2013) [13];
3. Computer Engineering 2016 (CE2016) [14];
4. Software Engineering 2014 (SE2014) [15];
5. Graduate Software Engineering 2009 (GSwE2009) [16];
6. Information Systems 2010 (IS2010) [17];
7. Global Competency Model for Graduate Degree Programs in Information Systems (MSIS2016) [18];
8. Information Technology. Curricula 2017 (IT2017) [19];
9. Cybersecurity. Curricula 2017 (CSEC2017) [20].

Figure 2 shows the architecture structure of a modern curriculum system.

Let's look at the main content and characteristics of the above current curriculum standards for each of the basic profiles (areas of training) with an emphasis on the principles of building a Body of Knowledge and CBoK core, as well as determining the learning outcomes and the ones used for them descriptions of didactic parameters.

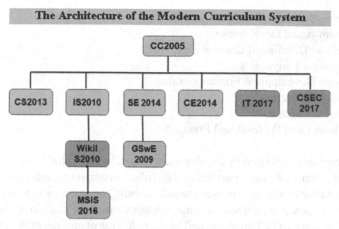

Fig. 2. The architecture of the modern curriculum system.

2 Actual Curricula of Undergraduate and Graduate Programs. Key Features

2.1 Profile Computer Science (CS)

For the CS profile, the latest version of the curriculum standard is CS2013: Curriculum Guidelines for Undergraduate Programs in Computer Science 2013 - a comprehensive revision of the previous edition of the curriculum (CS2008). CS2013 is designed to develop undergraduate CS-programs.

The main attention in the preparation of CS2013 was given to the following points: a thorough review of the body of knowledge, rethinking the core of the body of knowledge, clarification of the characteristics of graduates of CS programs, methodological aspects of training computer scientists in various institutional contexts. CS 2013 also includes a description of examples of CS programs and a significant pool of descriptions of the courses themselves for individual computing disciplines. The document contains more than 500 pages.

Let's take a closer look at CS2013.

In CS2013, the entire amount of top-level professional knowledge is divided into the following 18 subject areas:

- AL Algorithms and Complexity
- AR Architecture and Organization
- CN Computational Science
- DS Discrete Structures
- GV Graphics and Visualization
- HCI Human-Computer Interaction
- IAS Information Assurance and Security
- IM Information Management
- IS Intelligent Systems
- NC Networking and Communications

- OC Operating Systems
- PBD Platform-based Development
- PD Parallel and Distributed Computing)
- PL Programming Languages
- SDF Software Development Fundamentals
- SE Software Engineering
- SF Systems Fundamentals
- SP Social Issues and Professional Practice

CS2013 captures important IT development trends. In particular, this is the increased importance of system solutions, parallel and distributed computing, information security services, and platform-oriented software developments. The attention is again focused on network technologies, in which revolutionary changes are taking place in connection with the advent of the Internet of Things era and the introduction of new network technologies.

Characteristics of the CS2013 Curriculum Standard

1. The basis of this curriculum is the definition of a body of knowledge CS BoK and Learning Outcomes associated with its didactic units. The CS BoK architecture is a four-level hierarchical structure:

   - at the top level of the hierarchy are subject areas (area - disciplinary subfields) - 18 areas;
   - subject areas are divided into thematic modules (units) - 163 modules;
   - modules are divided into topics, revealing the contents of the modules, and they, in turn, can be divided into subtopics.

2. When describing the modules, a list of mandatory topics is highlighted, that is, those topics which make up the core. A two-level core design is proposed, which, for technological reasons, is divided into two parts - two layers (tiers). The core volume, measured in lecture hours, is approximately 300 lecture hours (300 * 4 = 1200 - total hours, taking into account the independent work of students). The first layer of the core includes a list of unconditionally binding topics; for topics in the second layer, some variation is allowed, when it is difficult for universities to implement a complete list of core topics. Module topics can be marked as belonging to the core or be topics of choice (Electives).

3. Learning outcomes are defined at the level of knowledge modules. Thus, a set of topics and sets of learning outcomes are associated with each knowledge module. Result sets can relate to the first layer of the core (Core-Tier1), to the second layer (Core-Tier1), or be unrelated to core themes. In total, 1111 learning outcomes were determined, 562 of which relate to core modules.

4. Each record of the learning outcome is clearly associated with a level of cognition or mastery (level of mastery). Classification of cognitive levels is a simplified Bloom classification/taxonomy model [21]. CS2013 uses a three-level skill assessment scale: Familiarity, Usage, Assessment. From examples of the use of other didactic parameters, the hourly volume (in lecture hours) of the core material (used at the level of knowledge modules), as well as a sign of the presence of optional topics in the module, should be noted.

2.2 Profile Computer Engineering (CE)

For the CE profile, the latest revision of the curriculum is CE2016: Computer Engineering Curricula 2016, a revised version of the previous standard - CE2004, in which the developers tried to reflect the achievements of the last decade in the Computer Technology. CE2016 is designed to develop undergraduate programs.

The introductory part of CE2016 defines the basic principles of its development. The very first is the principle of the continuity of the curriculum updating process, that is, providing the continuous updating of its individual components, taking into account the dynamics of the development of computer technology. The student learning strategy for lifelong learning (LLL) is declared to be an important principle.

CE2016 focuses on building a body of knowledge (CEBoK) in a three-tier architecture. The upper level of the CEBoK hierarchy consists of subject areas (areas), which are divided into basic (core) or additional (supplementary) knowledge modules (units). The lower level of the CEBoK hierarchy (at the topic level) contains learning outcomes associated with the modules and revealing their contents.

The total material of the fields of knowledge is approximately 50% of the total study load in a typical four-year CE bachelor's degree program.

One of the main tasks of CE2016 is the selection and specification of the basic component – the professional knowledge core, which contains the most important concepts and methods of the CE area, which should be included in any CE bachelor's program, which, as has already been pointed out, supports student mobility, guaranteed curriculum compilation, guaranteed level of training quality, flexibility in the development of individualized curricula.

An undoubtedly important part of CE2016 should include a description of the set of laboratory works, both mandatory and optional (about 20 in total), without which it is impossible to train qualified engineers, as well as a description of the requirements for practice and design activities.

The main chapters of CE2016 include the second and third chapters. Chapter 2 defines the characteristics of the graduate, and Chapter 3 describes the architecture of the body of knowledge and its core.

- CE2016 contains 12 subject areas, including:
- CE-CAE Circuits and Electronics
- CE-CAL Computing Algorithms
- CE-CAO Computer Architecture and Organization
- CE-DIG Digital Design
- CE-ESY Embedded Systems
- CE-NWK Computer Networks
- CE-PPP Preparation for Professional Practice
- CE-SEC Information Security
- CE-SGP Signal Processing
- CE-SPE Systems and Project Engineering
- CE-SRM Systems Resource Management
- CE-SWD Software Design

The core of CE2016 also includes four mathematical disciplines, namely:

- CE-ACF Analysis of Continuous Functions
- CE-DSC Discrete Structures
- CE-LAL Linear Algebra
- CE-PRS Probability and Statistics.

Additionally, the minimum set of mathematical areas and modules is determined; they are presented in Table 1 with the minimum required amount of lecture hours [14, p. 27].

Table 1. The minimum set of mathematical fields and modules including the minimum number of lecture hours, required for the study.

Mathematics knowledge areas and units	
CE-ACF analysis of continuous functions [30 core hours]	CE-DSC discrete structures [30 core hours]
CE-ACF-1 History and overview [1] CE-ACF-2 Relevant tools and engineering applications [1] CE-ACF-3 Differentiation methods [4] CE-ACF-4 Integration methods [6] CE-ACF-5 Linear differential equations [8] CE-ACF-6 Non-linear differential equations [3] CE-ACF-7 Partial differential equations [5] CE-ACF-8 Functional series [2]	CE-DSC-1 History and overview [1] CE-DSC-2 Relevant tools and engineering applications [1] CE-DSC-3 Functions, relations, and sets [6] CE-DSC-4 Boolean algebra principles [4] CE-DSC-5 First-order logic [6] CE-DSC-6 Proof techniques [6] CE-DSC-7 Basics of counting [2] CE-DSC-8 Graph and tree representations and properties [2] CE-DSC-9 Iteration and recursion [2]
CE-LAL linear algebra [30 core hours]	CE-PRS probability and statistics [30 core hours]
CE-LAL-1 History and overview [1] CE-LAL-2 Relevant tools and engineering applications [2] CE-LAL-3 Bases, vector spaces, and orthogonality [4] CE-LAL-4 Matrix representations of linear systems [4] CE-LAL-5 Matrix inversion [2] CE-LAL-6 Linear transformations [3] CE-LAL-7 Solution of linear systems [3] CE-LAL-8 Numerical solution of non-linear systems [4] CE-LAL-9 System transformations [3] CE-LAL-10 Eigensystems [4]	CE-PRS-1 History and overview [1] CE-PRS-2 Relevant tools and engineering applications [2] CE-PRS-3 Discrete probability [5] CE-PRS-4 Continuous probability [4] CE-PRS-5 Expectation and deviation [2] CE-PRS-6 Stochastic processes [4] CE-PRS-7 Sampling distributions [4] CE-PRS-8 Estimation [4] CE-PRS-9 Hypothesis tests [2] CE-PRS-10 Correlation and regression [2]

The bulk of the material in CE2016 is presented in two appendices. Appendix A provides a detailed description of the fields and modules of knowledge, together with the associated learning outcome requirements.

Characteristic features of CE2016 structure

1. The main part of CE2016 is the description of the body of knowledge (CEBoK) in the form of a three-level hierarchical structure. The upper level of decomposition of this hierarchy is made up of subject areas (arrears); a purpose (thematic scope) and a set of knowledge modules (units) - obligatory (core), i.e. constituting the core, and additional (supplementary) are defined. At the lowest level in the CEBoK architecture, a set of learning outcomes is defined for each module. The entire volume of professional knowledge is divided into 12 areas plus 4 mathematical areas, 135 modules plus 37 mathematical modules. For the modules of professional fields of knowledge, 923 learning outcomes were identified, 754 of which belong to the core.
2. The core volume is determined by the set of mandatory CEBoK modules. The total academic workload for the professional part of the core is 420 lecture hours, which is significantly higher than the core volume for CS direction (about 300 h), in addition, the CE2016 core also includes modules of mathematical disciplines in the amount of (minimum) 120 lecture hours. (Compared to the previous edition of CE2004, the volume of the mathematical part of the kernel is almost doubled, while the authors of CE2016 admit that 120 h is clearly not enough for training CE-professionals, noting that, as a rule, CE programs give significantly more hours for the mathematical education of engineers).
3. Each level of learning is associated with a learning outcome, which varies from basic abilities, such as understanding and defining concepts, to advanced abilities, such as participating in synthesis and evaluation. Learning outcomes are divided into Core Learning Outcomes and Elective Learning Outcomes.
4. The level of training is determined implicitly using the semantics of the verbs used to describe the learning outcomes and generally corresponding to Bloom's taxonomy, while the learning outcomes provide a mechanism for describing not only knowledge and relevant practical skills, but also personal and transferable skills.

2.3 Profile Software Engineering (SE)

Among the SE documents, two documents are currently relevant:

- SE2014: Curriculum Guidelines for Undergraduate Degree Programs in Software Engineering 2014 – it is a revised version of the previous curriculum SE2004 and is focused on undergraduate studies;
- GswE2009: Curriculum Guidelines for Graduate Degree Programs in Software Engineering 2009 – It is intended to train masters in software engineering.

Let's take a closer look at them.

Curriculum SE2014

This document is a revision of the curriculum SE2004. The new edition largely repeats the structure of the previous version, however, the contents of the original document underwent a thorough revision, starting from the first chapters. In particular, a detailed understanding of the discipline of software engineering is given, taking into account its development over the past decade (Chapter 2), the results of student training on SE programs and the principles on which the SE2014 itself (Chapter 3) is based are rewritten in a more consolidated form. The main contents of the document are:

- The specification of the SEEK knowledge set (The Software Engineering Education Knowledge), which SE graduates should own, with the allocation of a core (Chapter 4), i.e. minimum required amount of knowledge for all bachelor programs in SE profile.
- The core is defined by a set of essential topics (essentials), which are marked with a sign (E - Essential). Topics not marked as E are considered desirable (D - Desirable).
- Methodological aspects determining:

  - methods of studying the body of knowledge and the acquisition of practical skills, guidelines for the development of curricula and plans, possible pedagogical strategies (Chapter 5);
  - ways of organizing curricula and the procedure for learning material from the body of knowledge, requirements for a graduation project (Capstone Project) (Chapter 6);
  - issues of adaptation to various institutional environments (Chapter 7);
  - issues of the implementation and evaluation of training programs (Chapter 8).

- Description of examples of curricula (Appendix A).
- Description of an extensive collection of sample courses (Appendix A).

As already noted, the overall structure of SEEK in Chapter 4 has remained virtually the same as in SE2004, but the contents of the body of knowledge have undergone a full revision and adjustment.

The following 10 subject areas comprise the upper level of the hierarchy of knowledge volume SE2004:

1. Computing essentials – CMP.
2. Mathematical and engineering fundamentals – FND.
3. Professional practice – PRF.
4. Software modeling and analysis – MAA.
5. Requirements analysis and specification – REQ.
6. Software design – DES.
7. Software verification & validation – VAV.
8. Software process – PRO.
9. Software quality – QUA.
10. Security – SEC.

It is important to note that SE2014 in terms of structure and content is harmonized with document SWEBOK v3 [22] - a kind of gospel for software developers and practitioners, which makes it easier for curriculum developers to detail the content of topics for individual courses.

SE2014 presents the logical and semantic relationship of the above subject areas, illustrated in Fig. 3.

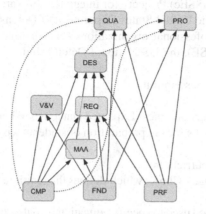

Fig. 3. Relationship between subject areas [15, p. 53].

The main features of SE2014 are:

1. The basis of this curriculum is the definition of the body of knowledge - Software Engineering Education Knowledge - SEEK. SEEK architecture is a three-level hierarchical structure: the top level is subject areas (areas – disciplinary subfields), subject areas are divided into thematic modules (units), modules are divided into topics (topics). In total - 10 areas, 37 modules, 213 topics.
2. The structuring of subject areas into modules is described with the use of tables containing, for each module, the minimum number of contact hours required for study. The structuring of modules on topics is also presented in tabular form, indicating for each topic whether it is mandatory (Essential ©) or desired (Desirable (D)), as well as indicating the minimum level of cognitive development of this topic.
3. The training results give the names of topics with the minimum level of cognitive skill (skill) corresponding to the topic indicated for each topic. The scale of cognitive levels is a simplified model of Bloom's taxonomy and includes three values: k (Knowledge) - Knowledge, c (Comprehension) - Understanding, a (Application) - Application.
4. The total hourly load for studying SEEK core material is 467 h.

Curriculum GswE2009 (*Graduate Software Engineering 2009: Curriculum Guidelines for Graduate Degree Programs in Software Engineering*).

In 2009, a curriculum for the preparation of masters in software engineering - Graduate Software Engineering 2009 (GswE2009) appeared. It represented an example of the transfer to the magistracy of curriculum development technology based on curriculums with their characteristic features - a clear description of the goals and learning outcomes, a detailed specification the volume of knowledge of vocational training, the allocation of a mandatory set of knowledge (core) for all curricula, the definition of an approximate list of relevant areas of specialization.

GswE2009 was created as part of the iSSEc project (Integrated Software & Systems Engineering Curriculum (iSSEc) Project - for integrated software and systems engineering). Its main sponsor is the United States Department of Defense. An active role in the project was played by professional organizations - the International Council for Systems Engineering (INCOSE), the US National Defense Industry Association (NDIA), IEEE-CS, ACM, etc.

GswE2009 includes a description:

– a set of expected learning outcomes (Expected Outcomes When a Student Graduates);
– a set of input requirements for the preparation of students wishing to study under the GswE2009 programs;
– architectural model of curriculum;
– Core Body of Knowledge - CboK, which defines the required body of knowledge for GswE2009 programs;
– a modified Bloom method used to specify educational goals when studying the volume of knowledge;
– training courses containing CboK material, supplementing the SWEBOK knowledge base, taken as the basis for the content of CboK, etc.

The scope of knowledge of GswE2009 (and CboK) is built in the form of a three-level hierarchical system of structural elements (didactic units), including:

– subject areas at the highest level of the hierarchy,
– knowledge modules (second level),
– topics (third and fourth levels, respectively).

Each didactic unit is associated with a certain index that determines the necessary level of mastering of this unit by students and is scaled using the modified Bloom method.

Let's look at the architectural model of the curriculum, shown in Fig. 4.

The curriculum architecture presented includes:

– preparatory material, the possession of which is necessary upon admission to the GswE2009 programs;
– core materials, i.e. CboK;
– university-specific materials;
– elective materials;
– mandatory capstone experience, the figure shows that below it extends the space of professional activity of the master.

In the list of outgoing requirements for graduates under the GswE2009 programs, the first is the requirement for mastery level knowledge in CboK, formed on the basis of the SWEBOK knowledge body, supplemented by a number of topics in systems engineering, information security, training, a human-machine interface, and engineering economics risk management, software quality.

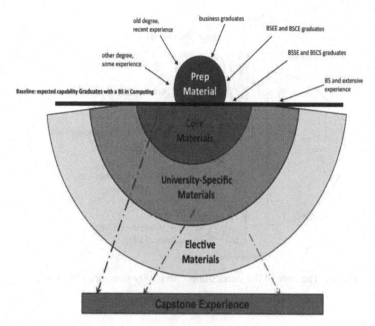

Fig. 4. Architectural model of the curriculum of master's programs in SE profile [16, p. 27]

The core volume is estimated at 200 classroom hours or contact hours needed to study it (i.e., the total hours are four times as much as 800), which is equivalent to 5 semester study courses of 40 classroom hours per semester (160 general hours for each course).

The core structure is shown in Fig. 5 as a right semicircle consisting of sectors corresponding to the nuclear part of a certain subject area of knowledge, while the size of the sector corresponds to the percentage of this part in percent relative to the entire curriculum.

In total, the kernel includes modules from 11 subject areas, taken mainly from SWEBOK:

1. Ethics and Professional Conduct,
2. System Engineering,
3. Requirements Engineering,
4. Software Design,
5. Software Construction,
6. Testing,
7. Software Maintenance,
8. Configuration Management (CM),
9. Software Engineering Management,
10. Software Engineering Process,
11. Software Quality.

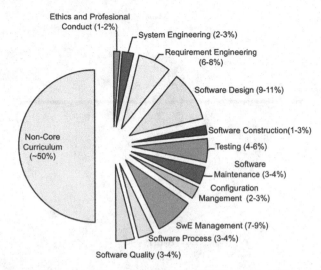

Fig. 5. The core of the curriculum GswE2009 structure [16, p. 46].

Characteristic features of SE2014 are:

1. The body of knowledge GswE2009 (and therefore CboK) is built in the form of a three-level hierarchical system of structural elements (didactic units), including:

   – subject areas at the highest level of the hierarchy (11 areas),
   – knowledge modules - second level, 53 modules,
   – topics/subtopics of knowledge modules - third level, more than 200 topics.

2. The affiliation of the didactic unit (region/module) to the core is indicated both for the regions (in this case, all the modules of the region are considered to be part of the core) and for the modules. SWEEBOK is used to form the content of topics in the body of knowledge
3. A certain didactic parameter is associated with each module. The parameter determines the necessary level of mastering of this unit by the student and is scaled using the modified Bloom method. In particular, the following scale is used to determine the cognitive level of the knowledge module:

   • Knowledge (K)
   • Understanding ©
   • Application (AP)
   • Analysis (AN).

4. The amount of mandatory material in CboK at 200 class hours seems to be very significant. This is essentially about 50% of the entire curriculum.

5. The CboK analysis shows the extremely important importance that GswE2009 devotes to the study of modern international standards, especially in the field of system and software engineering, including: SWEBOK, CMMI, ISO/IEC 12207, ISO/IEC 15288, IEEE software engineering standards package (about 40)
6. Knowledge and systems of educational standards of computing is required of masters.
7. 10 Outcomes of a high level are identified. They are related to the educational program as a whole. The level of development of educational material (didactic parameter) is determined for the modules. The final results of the mastery of the module material are more than 200 topics.

2.4 Information Systems

For the IS profile, the following documents are relevant:

– IS2010 Curriculum Update: The Curriculum Guidelines for Undergraduate Degree Programs in Information Systems – It focuses on the training of IS bachelors, it is developed in the form of two technically equivalent manuals - in the form of a traditional document, as well as in the form of a Wiki resource - IS Curriculum Wiki.
– MSIS2016: Global Competency Model for Graduate Degree Programs in Information Systems – Global competency model for master's programs in information systems.

IS2010

The development of IS2010 aims at displaying significant changes in this area, including: standardization of IS design processes, the widespread adoption of web technologies, the creation of new architectural paradigms, the extensive use of large-scale ERP systems, the extensive use of mobile computers and gadgets, and the extensive use of infrastructure frameworks (such as ITIL, COBIT, ISO 17799), etc.

IS2010 defines the highest level outcome expectations, and the graduate must be able to do the following:

• Improving organizational processes
• Harnessing the power of technological innovations
• Understanding and resolving information requirements
• Design and management of enterprise architecture
• Identification and evaluation of solutions and sources of alternatives
• Securing data and infrastructure and
• Understanding, managing and controlling IT risks.

The body of knowledge IS BoK, described in Appendix 4 of IS2010, is traditionally built in the form of a three-four-level hierarchy - at the top level there are areas divided into units of knowledge (units), which, in turn, are represented as sets of topics/subtopics (topics). IS BoK contains 20 subject areas, divided into four categories, as shown in Table 2 [17, p. 82].

Table 2. The structure of subject areas (areas) of the IS BoK knowledge base.

Areas of the IS BoK knowledge base	
General computing knowledge areas (details from CS 2008)	Programming Fundamentals Algorithms and Complexity Architecture and Organization Operating Systems Net Centric Computing Programming Languages Graphics and Visual Computing Intelligent Systems
Information Systems Specific Knowledge Areas	IS Management and Leadership Data and Information Management Systems Analysis & Design IS Project Management Enterprise Architecture User Experience
Professional Issues in Information Systems	Foundational Knowledge Areas Leadership and Communication Individual and Organizational Knowledge Work Capabilities
Domain-related Knowledge Areas	General models of the domain Key specializations within the domain Evaluation of performance within the domain

The category of general subject areas of computing uses the corresponding amount of knowledge from CS2008 (now from CS2013).

The category of areas specific to this profile is structured into knowledge modules as shown in Table 3 [17, pp. 83–84].

For IS2010, the following features of its construction are characteristic:

1. A structural model of the curriculum is introduced. It consists of core courses and elective courses, which include descriptions of the body of knowledge and learning outcomes. The latter are associated with courses (core courses or additional courses), and not with BoK didactic units.
2. Two categories of courses are used here: - core courses and optional courses or electives. The core courses contain the topics necessary for all tracks of vocational training, and the electives contain the topics from which the profiling of training or tracks of vocational training are built.

Table 3. IS BoK-specific areas for this profile.

Information Systems Specific Knowledge Areas	
IS Management and Leadership	Information Systems Strategy
	Information Systems Management
	Information Systems Sourcing and Acquisition
	Strategic Alignment
	Impact of Information Systems on Organizational Structure and Processes
	Information Systems Planning Role of IT in Defining and Shaping Competition
	Managing the Information Systems Function
	Financing and Evaluating the Performance of Information Technology Investments and Operations
	Acquiring Information Technology Resources and Capabilities
	Using IT Governance Frameworks
	IT Risk Management
	Information Systems Economics
Data and Information Management	Basic File Processing Concepts
	Data Structures
	Data Management Approaches
	Database Management
	Systems Data and Information Modeling at Conceptual and Logical Levels
	Physical Database Implementation
	Data Retrieval and Manipulation with Database Languages
	Data Management and Transaction Processing
	Distributed Databases
	Business Intelligence and Decision Support
	Security and Privacy
	Policies and Compliance
	Data Integrity and Quality
	Data and Database Administration
Systems Analysis & Design	Systems Analysis & Design Philosophies and Approaches
	Business Process Design and Management
	Analysis of Business Requirements
	Analysis and Specification of System Requirements
	Configuration and Change Management
	Different Approaches to Implementing Information Systems
	High level System Design Issues
	Identification of Opportunities for IT-enabled Organizational Change
	Realization of IT-based Opportunities with Systems Development Projects
	System Deployment and Implementation
	System Verification and Validation
IS Project Management	Project Management Fundamentals
	Managing Project Teams
	Managing Project Communication
	Project Initiation and Planning
	Project Execution & Control
	Project Closure
	Project Quality
	Project Risk
	Project Management Standards
Enterprise Architecture Enterprise	Architecture Frameworks
	Component Architectures
	Enterprise Application
	Service Delivery Systems
	Integration Content
	Management Interorganizational
	Architectures Processes for Developing
	Enterprise Architecture
	Architecture Change Management
	Implementing Enterprise Architecture
	Enterprise Architecture and Management Controls

(*continued*)

Table 3. (*continued*)

Information Systems Specific Knowledge Areas	
User Experience	Usability Goals and Assessment
	Design Processes
	Design Theories and Tradeoffs
	Interaction Styles
	Interaction Devices
	Information Search
	Information Visualization
	User Documentation and Online Help
	Error Reporting and Recovery
	Professional Issues in Information Systems
	Societal Context of Computing
	Legal Issues
	Ethical Issues
	Intellectual Property
	Privacy
	IS as a Profession

Such an approach for the architectural construction of IS2010 is illustrated in Fig. 6.

Implemented Curriculum Architecture

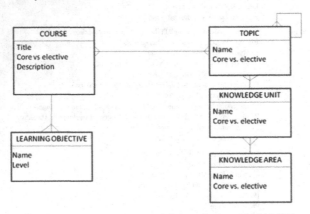

Fig. 6. The implemented structure of the curriculum IS2010 [17, p. 24].

Curriculum includes 7 core courses:

- Information Systems,
- Data and Information Management,
- Enterprise Architecture,
- Project Management,
- IT Infrastructure,
- System Analysis and Design,
- Strategy, Management and Acquisition of Information Systems.

Figure 7 shows the composition of core courses and their relationship to each other.

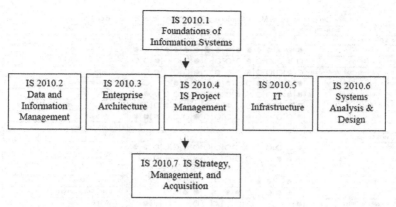

Fig. 7. IS 2010 Core Courses [17, p. 27].

An illustrative list of elective courses includes the following courses:

- Application Development,
- Business Process Management,
- Corporate Systems,
- Introduction to Human-Machine Interaction,
- Audit and Management in It,
- IP Innovations and New Technologies,
- IT Security and Risk Management.

3. There is a novel tool for diversifying programs by presenting educational content in the form of a set of courses in a tabular form, shown in Fig. 8. In these tables the rows correspond to basic or optional courses, and the columns are specialization tracks. A black or white circle is placed at the intersection of the rows and columns of the table. If the circle is black then it is believed that the course should be delivered in full scale, if the circles is white then it may not fully cover the course topics. In total, 17 specialization tracks were developed:

- Application Developer
- Business Analyst
- Business Process Analyst
- Information Technology Management Analyst
- Database Administrator
- Database Analyst
- E-Business Manager
- ERP Specialist
- Information Audit and Data Compatibility Specialist
- Information Technology Developer

Structure of the IS Model Curriculum:Information Systems specific courses

Career Track:	A	B	C	D	E	F	G	H	I	J	K	L	M	N	O	P	Q
Core IS Courses:																	
Foundations of IS	●	●	●	●	●	●	●	●	●	●	●	●	●	●	●	●	●
Enterprise Architecture	○	●	○	○	○	●	○	○	○	○	●	○	○	○	●	○	○
IS Strategy, Management and Acquisition	○	●	○	○	○	●	○	○	●	○	●	○	○	○	●	○	○
Data and Information Management	●	○	○	●	●	○	○	●	●	○	●	○	●	○	○	○	○
Systems Analysis & Design	●	●	●	○	○	●	○	○	○	○	○	○	○	●	●	●	●
IT Infrastructure	○	○	○	●	○	●	○	○	●	●	○	●	●	●	○	○	○
IT Project Management	●	○	○	○	○	●	○	○	○	○	●	○	○	○	●	●	●
Elective IS Courses:																	
Application Development	●	○	○	○	○	○	○	○	○	○	○	○	○	○	○	●	●
Business Process Management		●	●			○	○	○		○	●			○			
Collaborative Computing						○					○			○			
Data Mining / Business Intelligence		●		●	●	○	○	○	●		○	○	○	○		○	
Enterprise Systems		●	●	○	○	○	●	●	○		●	●	○	○			
Human-Computer Interaction	●					○	○			○				●			
Information Search and Retrieval		○		○	●					○				●			
IT Audit and Controls	○		●	○	○	○	○	●		●	○		○	○	○		○
IT Security and Risk Management	○			○	○	○	○	●	●	○	○		●	●	○		○
Knowledge Management		●		○		○	○			○							
Social Informatics											○		○				

Key:
● = Significant Coverage
○ = Some Coverage
Blank Cell = Not Required

Legend:
A = Application Developer
B = Business Analyst
C = Business Process Analyst
D = Database Administrator
E = Database Analyst
F = e-Business Manager
G = ERP Specialist
H = Information Auditing and Compliance Specialist
I = IT Architect
J = IT Asset Manager
K = IT Consultant
L = IT Operations Manager
M = IT Security and Risk Manager
N = Network Administrator
O = Project Manager
P = User Interface Designer
Q = Web Content Manager

Fig. 8. Tracks for the training of bachelors IS [17, p. 26].

- Information Resources Processing Manager
- IT Consultant
- Information Technology Operations Manager
- Information Technology Risk and Security Manager
- Network Administrator
- Project Manager
- Web Content Manager

4. Courses are described as follows:

   - Catalog description
   - Learning objectives
   - Topics
   - Discussion.
   In this way, learning outcomes are described in terms of learning objectives and are associated with courses. There are 161 results in total, 95 of them belong to the IS BoK core.

5. A parameter of a depth metric is associated with each learning objective. This level is implicitly set using the verbs used to describe the learning objectives. The document provides a table of correspondence of such verbs and values of depth of knowledge. As a scale for knowledge levels, a simplified Bloom taxonomy is used (1 - Awareness, 2 - Literacy, 3-Concept/Use, 4 Detailed, 5 Advanced).

MSIS2016

MSIS2016 provides a competency model and curriculum development guide for an IS degree. This joint effort of AIS and ACM is based on previous curriculum standards for IS profile.

The main feature of MSIS2016 is that in it the content of training is not set using the specification of the body of knowledge, it is set indirectly through a structured competency system for graduates of master's programs in the direction of IS.

The overall structure of the MSIS2016 competency framework is shown in Fig. 9.

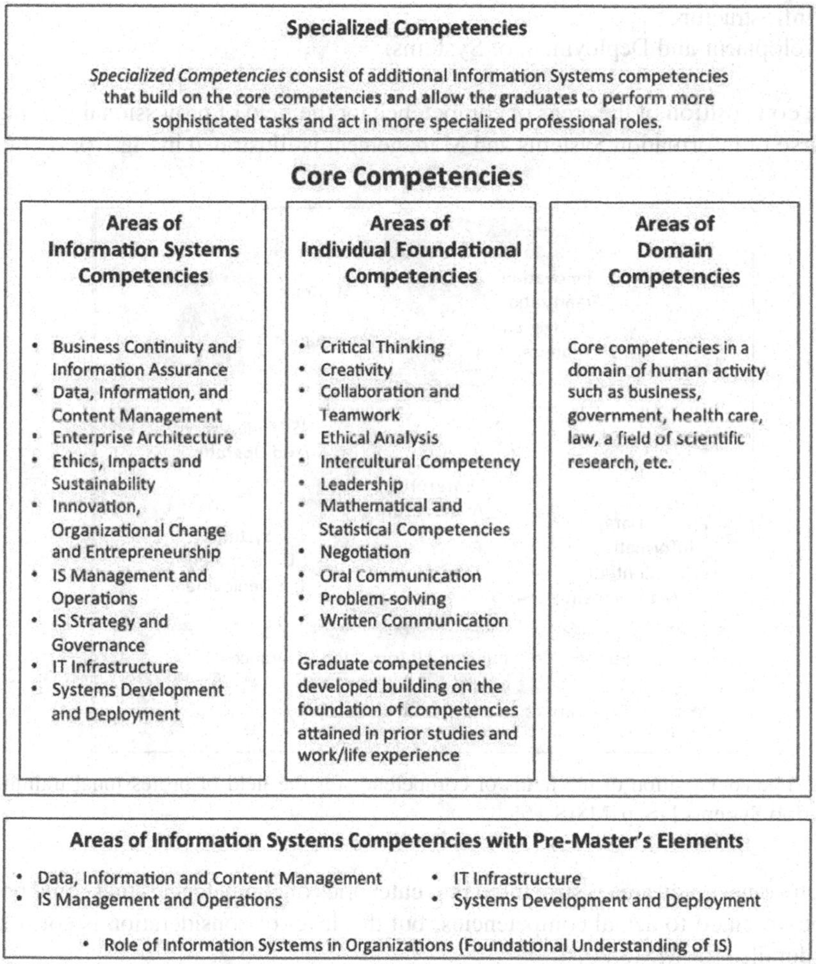

Specialized Competencies

Specialized Competencies consist of additional Information Systems competencies that build on the core competencies and allow the graduates to perform more sophisticated tasks and act in more specialized professional roles.

Core Competencies

Areas of Information Systems Competencies	Areas of Individual Foundational Competencies	Areas of Domain Competencies
• Business Continuity and Information Assurance • Data, Information, and Content Management • Enterprise Architecture • Ethics, Impacts and Sustainability • Innovation, Organizational Change and Entrepreneurship • IS Management and Operations • IS Strategy and Governance • IT Infrastructure • Systems Development and Deployment	• Critical Thinking • Creativity • Collaboration and Teamwork • Ethical Analysis • Intercultural Competency • Leadership • Mathematical and Statistical Competencies • Negotiation • Oral Communication • Problem-solving • Written Communication Graduate competencies developed building on the foundation of competencies attained in prior studies and work/life experience	Core competencies in a domain of human activity such as business, government, health care, law, a field of scientific research, etc.

Areas of Information Systems Competencies with Pre-Master's Elements

• Data, Information and Content Management	• IT Infrastructure
• IS Management and Operations	• Systems Development and Deployment

• Role of Information Systems in Organizations (Foundational Understanding of IS)

Fig. 9. The competency structure of MSIS 2016 [18, p. MSIS-v].

The figure shows that MSIS 2016 includes nine areas of competence in the field of information systems:

1. Business Continuity and Information
2. Data, Information and Content Management
3. Enterprise Architecture
4. Ethics, Consequences and Sustainability
5. Innovation, Organizational Change and Entrepreneurship
6. IP Management and Operations
7. IP Strategy and Management
8. IT Infrastructure
9. Development and Deployment of Systems.

The composition of the areas of competence for the field of professional training on the course of Information Systems and Management is illustrated in Fig. 10.

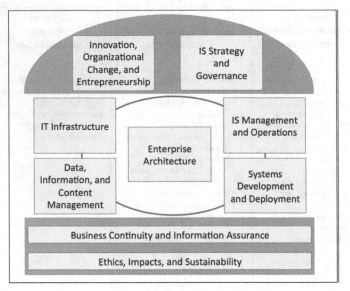

Fig. 10. The composition of the fields of competence for the field of professional training on Information Systems [18, p. MSIS-15].

Each competency area is structured into categories of competencies that could potentially be specified to actual competencies, but this level of consideration is considered overly detailed for MSIS 2016.

MSIS2016 also includes the following areas of individual core competencies: critical thinking, creativity, cooperation and collaboration, ethical analysis, intercultural competence, leadership, mathematical and statistical competencies, negotiations, oral communication, problem solving and written communication.

Another area of competence is competencies in the application area in which IS masters have to work. They identify key areas of competence related to the field of real practice that a particular master's program focuses on. This may be business, healthcare, law, government, education, etc.

Thus, the competency model defined in MSIS2016 is considered as initial data for the design of specific master's programs in the direction of IS, while at the methodological level, an instrument for the transition from competencies to the implemented master's IS-program is considered.

This approach is illustrated in Fig. 11.

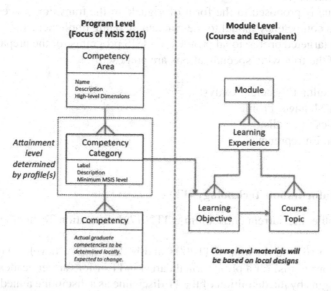

Fig. 11. The MSIS2016 approach involving the design of master's programs based on the competency model of curricula defined in this document for the direction of IS [18, p. MSIS-8].

The main features of building MSIS 2016 are:

1. The integrative nature of the direction of MSIS master's training, aimed at integrating competencies in the field of information systems, a specific applied field of activity and individual basic competencies.
2. The central component of this recommendation contains specifications for the hierarchy of areas of competence and categories of competencies related to technological aspects and management in the field of information systems. The specification of the competency model is two-level.
3. First, a description of the areas of competence at the upper level of abstraction (the level of areas) is given, and then for each area of competence, the competencies of the categories are determined in tabular form with an indication of the minimum acceptable level of their mastery. At this level, there are 88 competencies for technologies and management in the field of information systems, which are considered mandatory, i.e. related to the core BoK.
4. Moreover, category competencies are detailed to 314 competencies. There is also a description of the required areas of individual fundamental competencies

(11 competencies) and examples of areas of competence in the applied sphere (at least 4).

5. Four levels of mastering by each graduate of each competency category are determined: Awareness level, Novice level, Supporting (role) level and Independent (contributor level). For each competency of the category, the minimum acceptable level of its development is set explicitly. The competencies of the category class and the levels of their achievement form the basis for determining the modules (courses and their equivalents).

6. A technique is proposed in the form of a guide to the transition process from the MSIS2016 competency model to the curriculum being implemented.

7. Models of targeted professional profiles of MSIS programs for the preparation of IS masters of the following specializations are proposed:

   - IT Consultant/Systems Analyst
   - Project Manager Profile
   - Analytics Specialist
   - Start-up Entrepreneur.

2.5 Profile Information Technology (IT)

For the IT profile, the current curriculum is IT2017: Information Technology Curricula 2017.

IT2017 is a revised version of IT2008 and is designed to develop IT bachelor's programs (IT programs) for a professional career in IT or for further academic studies.

IT2017 begins by the definition of the IT discipline as a discipline aimed at studying systemic approaches to the selection, development, application, integration and administration of secure computing technologies that allow users to fulfill their personal, organizational and social goals.

Unlike most of the curricula of ACM and IEEE organizations, this document is developed using a competency-based approach in which the content and principles of training are implicitly determined using a structured competency system rather than explicitly defined by a set of professional knowledge. Competencies also determine the results of training the necessary skills that allow graduates of IT programs to successfully perform integrative tasks, apply systemic approaches to the development and administration of safe technological solutions and support users to achieve their ultimate goals.

IT2017 also reflects the need to develop students' personal qualities corresponding to three dimensions: knowledge, skills and dispositions/relationships. In particular, IT2017 proposes a working definition of the concept of competence as an entity linking knowledge, skills and dispositions into a single category. These three related dimensions have the following meanings.

- Knowledge requires knowledge of the basic concepts and content of IT, as well as the ability to learn in new situations.
- Skills relate to opportunities and strategies that develop in practice when interacting with other people and the world around us.

- Dispositions cover socio-emotional skills, behavior and relationships, including responsibility, adaptability, flexibility, self-direction and self-motivation, as well as self-confidence, integrity and self-control, tolerance, perseverance in dealing with complex problems, enthusiasm, innovation, energy, self-generation, respectfulness or resilience.

The competency system structuring is carried out by breaking it into domains covering the main field of activity and knowledge of IT profile graduates. In this case, the domains are divided into essential (essential), which are mandatory, and additional (supplemental).

Essential domains include:

1. Information Management
2. Integrated Systems Technology
3. Platform Technologies
4. System Paradigms
5. User Experience Design
6. Cybersecurity Principles
7. Global Professional Practice
8. Networking
9. Software Fundamentals
10. Web and Mobile Systems.

Essential domains cover those competencies that all students in all IT programs must master. Essential domains represent the minimum amount of competency that should be part of a complete educational IT program.

Additional domains cover competencies, where students perform more specialized work in accordance with the objectives of the program. Additional domains give IT programs more choice and flexibility. They include:

1. Cybersecurity Emerging Challenges
2. Social Responsibility
3. Applied Networks
4. Software Development and Management
5. Mobile Applications
6. Cloud Computing
7. Data Scalability and Analytics
8. Internet of Things
9. Virtual Systems and Services

IT2017 suggests that in the implemented IT programs, approximately 40% of their volume will be significant domains, 20% - additional, and the remainder - specialization domains.

The domain-specific part of the curriculum is determined as a percentage for each domain. The program model with domain weights, expressed as a percentage, is shown in Fig. 12.

IT Domains	Essential Percent	Supplemental Percent
Essential Only (5)		
Information Management	6%	0
Integrated Systems Technology	3%	0
Platform Technologies	1%	0
System Paradigms	6%	0
User Experience Design	3%	0
Subtotal:	**19%**	**0**
Essential + Supplemental (5+5)		
Cybersecurity Principles / Cybersecurity Emerging Challenges	6%	4%
Global Professional Practice / Social Responsibility	3%	2%
Networking / Applied Networks	5%	4%
Software Fundamentals / Software Development and Management	4%	2%
Web and Mobile Systems / Mobile Applications	3%	3%
Subtotal:	**21%**	
Supplemental Only (4)		
Cloud Computing	0	4%
Data Scalability and Analytics	0	4%
Internet of Things	0	4%
Virtual Systems and Services	0	4%
Subtotal:	**0**	
IT2017 TOTAL:	**40.0%**	

Fig. 12. Model IT program with domain weights, expressed as a percentage [19, p. 48].

Essential and additional domains are structured into subdomains, and a didactic parameter is associated with each subdomain - the level of learning engagement.

Three levels are introduced - L1, L2 and L3, determining the nature of training for domain material. L2 level includes L1 level, and L3 level - L2 level, where L1 level corresponds to the first function of the spiral curriculum model, and L2 and L3 levels correspond to the second level [23]. The L1 level used in the subdomain indicates the minimum degree of development related to skills training, the L2 and L3 levels indicate an average and high degree of participation in training.

Another significant domain is mathematical. It includes the following subdomains:
ITM-DSC Discrete Structures:

- ITM-DSC-01 Perspectives and impact [L1]
- ITM-DSC-02 Sets [L1]
- ITM-DSC-03 Functions and relations [L1]
- ITM-DSC-04 Proof techniques [L1]
- ITM-DSC-05 Logic [L1]
- ITM-DSC-06 Boolean algebra principles [L1]
- ITM-DSC-07 Minimization [L1]
- ITM-DSC-08 Graphs and trees [L2]
- ITM-DSC-09 Combinatorics [L1]
- ITM-DSC-10 Iteration and recursion [L1]
- ITM-DSC-11 Complexity Analysis [L1]
- ITM-DSC-12 Discrete information technology applications [L1].

A typical design is used to describe each domain. It includes the following components:

1. Title, for example: ITE-CSP Domain: Cybersecurity Principles
   General description (purpose) of a domain or Scope, for example, **Scope**

   - A computing-based discipline involving technology, people, information, and processes to enable assured operations.
   - A focus on implementation, operation, analysis, and testing of the security of computing technologies.
   - Recognition of the interdisciplinary nature of the application of cybersecurity including aspects of law, policy, human factors, ethics, and risk management in the context of adversaries.
   - The practice of assuring information and managing risks related to the use, processing, storage, and transmission of information or data and the systems and processes used for those purposes.
   - Measures that protect and defend information and information systems by ensuring their availability, integrity, authentication, confidentiality, and non-repudiation

2. Domain level competencies, for example, **Competencies**:

   - Evaluate the purpose and function of cybersecurity technology identifying the tools and systems that reduce the risk of data breaches while enabling vital organization practices. (*Cybersecurity functions*)
   - Implement systems, apply tools, and use concepts to minimize the risk to an organization's cyberspace to address cybersecurity threats. (*Tools and threats*)
   - Use a risk management approach for responding to and recovering from a cyber-attack on system that contains high value information and assets such as an email system. (*Response and risks*)
   - Develop policies and procedures needed to respond and remediate a cyber-attack on a credit card system and describe plan to restore functionality to the infrastructure. (*Policies and procedures*).

3. A list of subdomains indicating the level of training, for example, **Subdomains**:

   - ITE-CSP-01 Perspectives and impact [L1]
   - ITE-CSP-02 Policy goals and mechanisms [L1]
   - ITE-CSP-03 Security services, mechanisms, and countermeasures [L2]
   - ITE-CSP-04 Cyber-attacks and detection [L2]
   - ITE-CSP-05 High assurance systems [L2]
   - ITE-CSP-06 Vulnerabilities, threats, and risk [L2]
   - ITE-CSP-07 Anonymity systems [L1]
   - ITE-CSP-08 Usable security [L1]
   - ITE-CSP-09 Cryptography overview [L1]
   - ITE-CSP-10 Malware fundamentals [L1]

- ITE-CSP-11 Mitigation and recovery [L1]
- ITE-CSP-12 Personal information [L1]
- ITE-CSP-13 Operational issues [L2]
- ITE-CSP-14 Reporting requirements [L1]

The document presents a model of the IT bachelor's curriculum, structured in the form of tapestry fabric, in which the processes of studying the material of significant domains, depicted by straight lines, going from left to right, are stitched with classes on additional domains, forming a structure resembling a tapestry structure. Such a model is illustrated in Fig. 13.

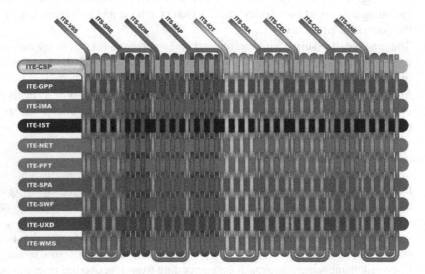

Fig. 13. Tapestry IT program paradigm [19, p. 65].

Appendix B provides a detailed description of the domains, in which for each subdomain a list of competencies corresponding to it is determined. In particular, more than 460 competencies are defined for material domains.

The use of competency of both the domain level and the subdomain implies the association with it of a cognitive parameter called "the learning transfer".

The learning transfer level scale includes the following values:

- **Explain** - students explain the essence of the issue in their own words (with support), use appropriate analogies; they are able to teach others.
- **Interpret** - students understand the meaning, provide a disclosure of the historical or personal dimension of ideas, data and events; they provide a convincing and consistent theory.
- **Apply** - students use what they learn in diverse and unique situations; they go beyond the context in which they learned new topics, courses, and situations.

– **Demonstrate Perspective** - students see the big picture, know and consider different points of view; they take a critical and selfless attitude; they avoid bias in how positions are formulated.
– **Show Empathy** - students are sensitive; they can "walk in someone else's shoes", find potential value in what others may find strange, alien, or implausible.
– **Have Self-Knowledge** - students demonstrate metacognitive awareness of motivation, confidence, responsibility, and honesty; the importance of new learning and experience; they can recognize prejudices and habits that both form and impede their own understanding.

However, when describing competencies in explicit form, this scale is not used. Its implementation is carried out implicitly using a fixed list of Performance Verbs, corresponding in meaning to the considered values of the scale of learning transfer levels.

The main features of IT2017 are:

1. The basis of the document is the definition of the content of educational programs for the preparation of IT bachelors by developing a hierarchical system of competencies. Therefore, this approach to building a curriculum is called competency-based. Competencies are defined at two levels of abstraction: at the domain level (10 substantive subject areas and 14 additional; a total of 80 competencies at this level, including 47 essential) and at the subdomain (module) level - a total of 164 modules, including 83 essential and 12 mathematical), for which defined competencies in the form of actions (Performances) - more than 460 essential (mandatory), and about the same number of additional competencies.
2. Two didactic parameters are defined:

    – the minimum allowable part of the general program volume required to study the material of each substantial and additional domain (determined as a percentage in relation to the volume of the curriculum);
    – for each subdomain, the level of learning engagement is determined - level L1 indicates the minimum degree of load in the development of the corresponding skill, levels L2 and L3 indicate the average and high degree of training load.

3. For each competency, one of six character scenarios of its development, called the level of learning transfer with a scale: Explain, Interpret, Apply, Demonstrate Perspective, Show Empathy, Have Self-Knowledge, is implied.
4. In the competencies wording (both for domains and for subdomains), activity verbs are used, which allows not to explicitly use the parameter level of learning transfer.
5. A tapestry paradigm for organizing IT training programs is proposed to provide a higher degree of integration and interconnectivity of domain material. Also, the authors of the document return to the concept of spiral curriculum [23].

2.6 Cybersecurity. CSEC

For CSEC discipline, Cybersecurity Curricula 2017 has been developed. Curriculum Guidelines for Post-Secondary Degree Programs in Cybersecurity. (CSEC2017).

The construction of cybersecurity as an independent educational discipline is due to the growing dependence of society on the global cyber infrastructure and the digital socio-economic ecosystem, as well as the increasing demand for training highly qualified specialists in a number of work roles related to ensuring the security of system operations, including the creation, operation, protection, analysis and testing of secure computer systems.

Cybersecurity as an educational discipline has extensive and deep educational content that covers many areas of knowledge, including mathematics, cryptography, software development, computer networking, database management, web technologies, automated manufacturing, smart cities, as well as aspects of law, politics, human factors, ethics, risk management, etc.

All this has led to the emergence of internationally standardized recommendations for the development of training programs for specialists in the field of cybersecurity, namely, Cybersecurity Curricula 2017. Curriculum Guidelines for Post-Secondary Degree Programs in Cybersecurity. (CSEC2017).

The development of this document was aimed at the following:

– to develop a comprehensive and flexible curriculum for university education in cybersecurity
– to create educational content, structuring the content of the cybersecurity discipline to develop training programs for training of human resources.

The development of CSEC2017 JTF leads to the expansion of the architecture of computing curricula, introduced in CC2005, the introduction of cybersecurity as another discipline/profile of computing.

Since cybersecurity is an interdisciplinary discipline based on computer and information technologies, the implementation of the academic programs of cybersecurity specialists can develop on the basis of any bachelor's degrees in computer science, but this requires the inclusion of the necessary aspects of law, politics, human factors, ethics and management risks. The cybersecurity architecture presented in Fig. 14 shows these features.

The criteria for the development of CSEC2017 were the following objectives and provisions:

• The foundation for cybersecurity is one of the areas of computing (for example, computer science or information systems),
• The use of cross-category concepts that permeate all areas of cybersecurity knowledge (for example, hostility of the environment in the field of activity)
• Creating a body of knowledge containing the most essential knowledge and skills in the field of cybersecurity,
• Direct connection with a range of specializations that meet the requirements of the relevant sector of the labor market.

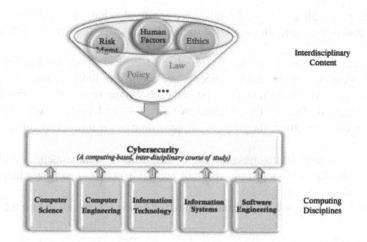

Fig. 14. The structure of cybersecurity as an academic discipline [20, p. 18].

- Focus on ethical behavior and professional responsibility.

When developing this document, we used some abstract cybersecurity model (CSEC thought model), then just a CSEC model, shown in Fig. 15.

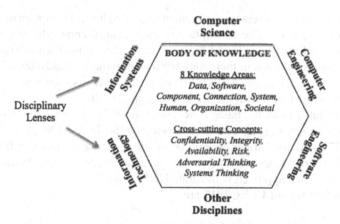

Fig. 15. CSEC- model [20, p. 20].

As you can see from the figure, the main component of the CSEC model is the amount of knowledge covering the security of such entities as data, software, components, systems, organizations, society, and is built on the basis of the concepts of confidentiality, integrity, accessibility, risk, a hostile environment, systematic thinking.

The body of knowledge CSEC is designed in a traditional way. It represents a three-level hierarchical structure. At the top level, its organizational basis is knowledge areas (KAs). Collectively, the fields of knowledge represent the full body of knowledge of the cyber security discipline. Areas of knowledge are divided into knowledge units (KUs) - thematic groups covering many related topics that describe the necessary content for each KU.

Each area of expertise includes a number of critical concepts that are critical to all cybersecurity content. Such concepts are called the fundamentals or the main themes/concepts (essentials)/It is assumed that each student should master them regardless of the direction of the CSEC program. A total of 44 such basic concepts have been identified. In a real program, they can be implemented in the form of modules or topics of educational content.

Learning outcomes (outcomes) are the descriptions of what students should know or be able to do after studying topics in their area of expertise. Learning outcomes are associated with basic concepts (!).

In total, 8 areas of knowledge fundamental for cybersecurity are identified:

- *Data Security*
- *Software Security*
- *Component Security*
- *Connection Security*
- *System Security*
- *Human Security*
- *Organizational Security*
- *Societal Security*

The description of all cybersecurity content is divided into a description of the content for each area of expertise. The description of each field of knowledge is given in two tables. The first table defines a list of basic concepts, then a list of knowledge modules for which the topics included in their composition are indicated, and a description of its content is given for each topic. An example of such a table (its fragment) for the "Data Security" area is illustrated with the Table 4 [20, pp. 24–30].

The second table links the basic concepts of the field of knowledge with learning outcomes. An example of such a table is shown with the Table 5 [20, pp. 30–31].

CSEC2017 also demonstrates an approach to linking learning outcomes from a CSEC program with competencies (Competence = Knowledge, Skills, and Abilities (KSA)) of the workplace. This approach is illustrated in Fig. 16.

The main features of CSEC2017 are:

1. The basis of the document is the definition of the content of educational programs for the training of cybersecurity specialists, as well as the definition of learning outcomes. The amount of knowledge is traditionally determined in the form of a three-layer architecture: knowledge areas (KAs), knowledge units (KUs), topics (topics).
2. For each field of knowledge, a set of critical concepts that are of fundamental importance for the formation of cybersecurity specialists is determined. Such concepts are called fundamentals or basic concepts (essentials), and they serve as the core of the volume of knowledge - the minimum required amount of knowledge. In CSEC programs, the basics can be implemented using stand-alone modules or themes. A

Table 4. Knowledge area "Data Security".

Units	Topics	Topic description
Cryptography	Basic concepts	• Encryption/decryption, sender authentication, data integrity, non-repudiation, • Attack classification (ciphertext-only, known plaintext, chosen plaintext, chosen ciphertext), • Secret key (symmetric), cryptography and public key (asymmetric) cryptography, • Information-theoretic security (one-time pad, Shannon Theorem), and • Computational security
	Advanced concepts Mathematical background	• Advanced protocols: - Zero-knowledge proofs, and protocols, - Secret sharing, - Commitment, - Oblivious transfer, Secure multiparty computation, • Advanced recent developments: fully homomorphic encryption, obfuscation, quantum cryptography, and KLJN scheme, • Modular arithmetic, • Fermat, Euler theorems, • Primitive roots, discrete log problem, • Primality testing, factoring large integers, • Elliptic curves, lattices and hard lattice problems, • Abstract algebra, finite fields, and • Information theory
Digital Forensics	...	...
Data Integrity and Authentication	...	...
Access Control		
Secure Communication Protocols		
Cryptanalysis		
Data Privacy		
Information Storage Security		
Digital Forensics		

total of 44 concepts and about 140 compulsory learning outcomes associated with them are identified.

3. Learning outcomes in the form of outcomes are associated with essentials.
4. Didactic parameters are not used explicitly.
5. The general approach to linking curricula with the skills required for a particular workplace for roles that are directly related to cybersecurity is discussed.

3 Curriculum Analysis

Let us briefly analyze the material discussed above.

1. The most important component of curricula is the description of educational content. The following solutions are possible:

   – direct construction in the form of a Body of Knowledge or BoK, as a rule, in the form of a hierarchical structure - areas, modules, themes/subtopics.

Table 5. Learning outcomes.

Essentials	Learning outcomes
Basic cryptography concepts	Describe the purpose of cryptography and list ways it is used in data communications Describe the following terms: cipher, cryptanalysis, cryptographic algorithm, and cryptology, and describe the two basic methods (ciphers) for transforming plaintext in ciphertext Explain how public key infrastructure supports digital signing and encryption and discuss the limitations/vulnerabilities Discuss the dangers of inventing one's own cryptographic methods Describe which cryptographic protocols, tools and techniques are appropriate for a given situation
Digital forensics	Describe what a digital investigation is, the sources of digital evidence, and the limitations of forensics Compare and contrast variety of forensics tools
End-to-end secure communications	*[See also Connection Security KA for related content, p. 32.]*
Data integrity and authentication	Explain the concepts of authentication, authorization, access control, and data integrity Explain the various authentication techniques and their strengths and weaknesses Explain the various possible attacks on passwords
Information storage security	Explain the concepts of authentication, authorization, access control, and data integrity Explain the various authentication techniques and their strengths and weaknesses Explain the various possible attacks on passwords
Data erasure	Describe the various techniques for data erasure

CS2013, CE2016, IS2010, MSIS2006, GSwE2009, SE2014, CSEC2017.
   − Implicit definition of BoK through the description of competencies (competency-based approach): MSIS2016, IT2017.

2. Another important task is to determine the BoK core (CoreBoK - CBoK):

   − direct build BoK:
   − at the area level - CSEC2017 (main topics, critical oblast topics)
   − at the course level - IS2010, course topics
   − at the module level - GSwE2009
   − at the topic level - CS2013, CE2016,

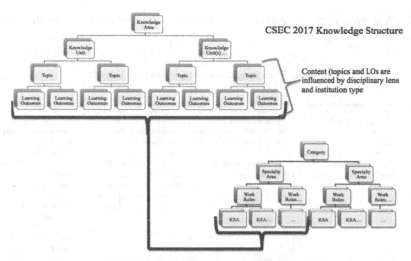

Fig. 16. Establishing the relationship between the learning outcomes of a certain CSEC program with the competencies of the workplace, while competency is understood as a set of knowledge, skills, abilities (Competence = Knowledge, Skills, and Abilities (KSA)) [20, p. 83].

- implicit through the description of competencies (competency-based approach): MSIS2016 (competencies of the categories of areas included in the core - 88, detailed to 314 competencies), IT2017 (significant domains of competencies - more than 460),

3. Definition of learning objectives:

- in the form of learning outcomes - SE2014 (at the topic level), CE2016 (for each topic), GSwE2009 (program level)
- in the form of learning objectives - IS2010 (at the level of courses), MSIS2006 (at the level of courses), CS2013 (at the level of modules),
- in the form of competencies - MSIS2016 (at the level of categories of regions), IT2017 (at the level of domains and subdomains).

4. Didactic parameters:

- the minimum amount of training load necessary to study the material of the didactic unit of educational content (area/domain, module/subdomain, topic) - hours, credits, percent of the total curriculum volume. We will denote it by DEV (Didactic Element Volume);
- level of learning engagement or LLE - the intensity of teaching a didactic unit;
- the level of training, the level of cognition or the level of learning transfer - the minimum allowable part of the total program volume necessary to study the material of each significant and additional domain (in percentage terms), the corresponding part of the curriculum;
- for each subdomain, the level of learning engagement.

Table 6 summarizes the listed above properties of the above curriculum standards in the IT field.

Table 6. The curriculum standards in the IT field.

Curriculum	Body of Knowledge (BoK)	Core BoK	Outcomes	Didactic parameters
CS2013	CSBoK hierarchical structure: - areas - units, - topics, (subtopics) Total 18 areas, 163 modules	Core BoK - approximately 300 (280--308) contact hours, they are defined at the module level A two-level core formation mechanism is used	Learning outcomes are defined explicitly, they are tied to knowledge modules, a total of 1111 learning outcomes, of which 562 relate to core modules. Modules and themes are marked as belonging to the core or as optional (Electives)	• The minimum number of hours to study the part of the core related to the core. Module parameter • Each record of the learning outcome is clearly associated with a level of mastery (a simplified Bloom model): Familiarity, Usage, Assessment • An indication of the presence of optional topics in the module
CE2016	BoK - hierarchical structure: - areas, - units, - learning outcomes. In total there are 12 areas plus 4 math, 135 modules plus 37 math modules	Core BoK 420 plus 120 - mathematics	Learning outcomes are defined when describing modules as mandatory (core related) or optional (elective). There are about 1000 (923) total learning outcomes related only to professional areas, of which 754 are CEBoK core	Levels of learning for learning outcomes are determined implicitly by the semantics of the verbs used. Bloom's taxonomy is the source
SE2014	Body of Knowledge - Software Engineering Education Knowledge (SEEK). The SEEK architecture is a three-level hierarchical structure: areas (area - disciplinary subfields), modules (units), topics (topics), In total - 10 areas, 37 modules, 213 topics	The core is defined by a set of essential topics (essentials), which are marked with a sign (E - Essential). Topics not marked as E are considered desirable (D - Desirable). The total hourly load for studying SEEK core material is 467 h	Expected Student Outcomes - Learning outcomes are measured using the topics themselves by indicating for each topic the minimum level of cognitive skill corresponding to the topic. 213 topics are identified	The scale of cognitive levels is a simplified model of Bloom's taxonomy and includes three values: k (Knowledge), c (Comprehension), a (Application). For each topic, it is indicated whether it is mandatory (Essential - E) or desired (Desirable - D), as well as indicating the minimum level of cognition. Lecture hours are indicated for modules
GSwE2009	The scope of knowledge of GSwE2009 (and, accordingly, CBoK is built in the form of a three-level hierarchical system of structural elements including: - subject areas (11 areas), - knowledge modules (53 modules), - topics (over 200)	The affiliation of a didactic unit (region/module) to the core is indicated both for the regions (in this case, all the modules of the region are considered to be part of the kernel) and for the modules The core volume is estimated at 200 lecture hours, which corresponds to 5 semester courses The core includes a significant portion of the SWEBOK material	10 high level outcomes are defined. The educational material level of learning is determined for each module. The final results are topics with a didactic parameter - (more than 200 topics)	Each module is associated with a parameter that determines the level of development of the material of the module. Bloom's simplified taxonomy is used: • Knowledge (K) • Understanding (C) • Application (AP) • Analysis (AN) For modules, the SYS attribute is used, indicating that the module topics belong to the core

(continued)

Table 6. (*continued*)

Curriculum	Body of Knowledge (BoK)	Core BoK	Outcomes	Didactic parameters
IS2010	The Body of Knowledge IS BoK described in Appendix 4 is traditionally built in the form of a three-level hierarchy: - areas, - knowledge modules (units), - topics/subtopics. IS BoK contains 20 areas divided into 4 categories A curriculum structural model is introduced, it consists of 7 core courses (core courses) and 7 elective courses, which include topics/subtopics of the body of knowledge and learning outcomes	The core consists of core, courses. Volume - 280 h	Learning outcomes are described in terms of Learning objectives and are associated with courses In total of 161 results were determined, 95 of which belong to the IS BoK core	Each learning outcome is associated with a depth of knowledge metric parameter. This level is implicitly set with the verbs used to describe the learning outcome. The document provides a table of correspondence of such verbs and values of depth of knowledge. A slightly simplified Bloom taxonomy is used as a scale for levels (1 - Awareness, 2 - Literacy, 3-Concept/Use, 4 Detailed, 5 Advanced - 6)
MSIS2016	The content of training is set indirectly through a structured system of competencies for graduates of master's programs in the direction of IS: - competence areas, - competency categories	All 88 competencies of the category level belong to the core of MSIS, therefore all MSIS programs should provide the opportunity for graduates to master them, at least at the level of awareness	The competency specification is two-level: - at the level of areas of competence - at the level of categories of areas of competencies, a total of 88 competencies of this level for the IS are defined. Competencies of categories are detailed to 314 competencies	Four levels of mastering by each graduate of each competency category are defined: Awareness level, Novice level, Supporting (role) level and Independent (contributor level). For each category competency, the minimum acceptable level of its development is explicitly set
IT2017	The definition of BoK is implicit; it is made through a hierarchical system of competencies. 10 essentials, i.e. Mandatory, domains and 14 additional (Supplemental) domains of competencies spitting mathematical domain	The core is determined by the content of the essential domains of competencies, which determine the competencies that the graduate should receive. Is defined 10 essential domains. The total amount of core material is estimated at 15% of the entire bachelor's program (18 US credits)	Learning outcomes are defined as competencies at two levels: at the level of domains (subject areas) and at the level of subdomains (subdomains or modules). In total, there are 80 domain level competencies, including 47 essential ones), and at the subdomain level, which is only 164, including 83 essential and 12 mathematical ones), more than 460 competences in the form of actions (Performances), and about the same number of additional competencies	Two didactic parameters are defined: 1) DEV - as a percentage of the entire BoK, for substantial and additional domains. 2) LLE: levels L1, L2 and L3. They are used for subdomains. 3) Each competency corresponds to one of six levels of learning transfer: Explain, Interpret, Apply, Demonstrate Perspective, Show Empathy, Have Self-Knowledge. 4) Learning transfer levels are implicitly determined through Performance verbs
CSEC2017	CSEC BoK has a three-level hierarchical structure: Knowledge areas (KAs) - knowledge units (KUs) - topics (topics); thematic groups, which cover many related topics that describe the necessary content for each KU. A total of 8 subject areas are identified	Each area includes a number of critical topics, called essentials, which form the core of the content of a CSEC program. A total of 44 such frameworks are identified.	Learning outcomes in the form of outcomes relate to the basics of areas. A total of about 140 compulsory learning outcomes are defined for 44 foundations	Didactic parameters not used

4   Conclusion

The article attempts to provide an analytical review of the current state (at the beginning of 2018) of the curriculum system for undergraduate and graduate programs in the field of computing, with an emphasis on the study of the principles of building curricula, studying their content, methods for specifying educational content and the minimum required amount of knowledge (core) in training programs, methods for determining learning outcomes, as well as methods for applying didactic parameters to describe the pedagogical emphasis of training programs and learning outcomes. The work examined the entire set of relevant curricula of the last decade, including the following documents: CC2005, CS2013, CE2016, SE2014, GSwE2009, IS2010, MSIS2016, IT2017, CSEC2017.

The article will be useful to methodologists-developers of curricula and educational standards, in particular for comparing the domestic educational regulatory and methodological base with international experience in standardizing curricula in the field of training IT personnel. The material presented in the article can also be useful to students and graduate students to represent the international structure of the methodological bases of the modern system of IT education.

References

1. Sukhomlin, V.A.: Open system of IT- education as a tool to enhance digital skills. Strateg. Priorities **1**(13), 70–81 (2017). https://elibrary.ru/item.asp?id=29432623. (in Russian)
2. Sukhomlin, V.A., Zubareva, E.V.: Standardization of it-education based on curriculums at the present stage. Mod. Inf. Technol. IT-Educ. **12**(3–1), 40–46 (2016). https://elibrary.ru/item. asp?id=27411973. (in Russian)
3. Sukhomlin, V.A., Zubareva, E.V.: Curriculum paradigm - the methodological basis of modern education. Mod. Inf. Technol. IT-Educ. **11**(1), 54–61 (2015). https://elibrary.ru/item.asp?id= 25024558. (in Russian)
4. Sukhomlin, V.A.: The analysis of the international standards of a master's of education in the field of information technologies. Vestnik St. Petersburg University Appl. Math. Comput. Sci. Control Process. (1), 95–105 (2013). https://elibrary.ru/item.asp?id=18894706. (in Russian)
5. Sukhomlin, V.A., Andropova, E.V.: Diversification of professional development programs in terms of international education standards in the IT area. The Moscow University Bulletin. Series 20. Pedagogical Educ. (1), 73–86 (2013). https://elibrary.ru/item.asp?id=18958025. (in Russian)
6. Sukhomlin, V.A.: Analysis of international educational standards in the field of information technology. Syst. Means Inf. **22**(2), 278–307 (2012). https://elibrary.ru/item.asp?id= 18270050. (in Russian)
7. Sukhomlin, V.A.: Educational standards in the field of information technologies. Appl. Inf. **1**(37), 33–54 (2012). https://elibrary.ru/item.asp?id=17363662. (in Russian)
8. Conte, S.D., Hamblen, J.W., Kehl, W.B., Navarro, S.O., Rheinboldt, W.C., Young Jr., D.M., William, F.: Atchinson: an undergraduate program in computer science – preliminary recommendations. Commun. ACM **8**(9), 543–552 (1965). https://doi.org/10.1145/365559. 366069
9. Atchison, W.F., et al.: Curriculum 68: recommendations for academic programs in computer science: a report of the ACM curriculum committee on computer science. Commun. ACM **11**(3), 151–197 (1968). https://doi.org/10.1145/362929.362976

10. Perekatov, V.I.: Computer disciplines in the view of US professional societies: milestones of an academic legend. J. Inf. Technol. Comput. Syst. **1**, 1–29 (2002). (in Russian)
11. Perekatov, V.I.: Computer disciplines in the view of US professional societies: the latest curriculum? J. Inf. Technol. Comput. Syst. (4) (2002). (in Russian)
12. Shackelford, R., McGettrick, A., Sloan, R., Topi, H., Davies, G., Kamali, R., Cross, J., Impagliazzo, J., LeBlanc, R., Lunt, B.: Computing curricula 2005: the overview report. In: Proceedings of the 37th SIGCSE Technical Symposium on Computer Science Education, SIGCSE 2006, pp. 456–457. ACM, New York (2006). https://doi.org/10.1145/1121341.1121482
13. Task Force Joint: Computer Science Curricula 2013: Curriculum Guidelines for Undergraduate Degree Programs in Computer Science. ACM, New York (2013). https://doi.org/10.1145/2534860
14. Computer Engineering Curricula 2016: Curriculum Guidelines for Undergraduate Degree Programs in Computer Engineering. ACM & IEEE, New York (2016) https://doi.org/10.1145/3025098
15. The Joint Task Force on Computing Curricula: Software Engineering 2014. Curriculum Guidelines for Undergraduate Degree Programs in Software Engineering. Technical report. ACM, New York (2015)
16. Adcock, R., Alef, E., et al.: Curriculum guidelines for graduate degree programs in software engineering. Technical report. ACM, New York (2009)
17. Topi, H., Kaiser, K.M., Sipior, J.C., Valacich, J.S., Nunamaker Jr., J.F., de Vreede, G.J., Wright, R.: Curriculum guidelines for undergraduate degree programs in information systems. Technical report. ACM, New York (2010)
18. Topi, H., et al.: MSIS 2016: Global Competency Model for Graduate Degree Programs in Information Systems. Technical report. ACM, New York (2017)
19. Information Technology Curricula 2017: Curriculum Guidelines for Baccalaureate Degree Programs in Information Technology. ACM, New York (2017)
20. Cybersecurity Curricula 2017: Curriculum Guidelines for Post-Secondary Degree Programs in Cybersecurity. A Report in the Computing Curricula Series Joint Task Force on Cybersecurity Education. ACM, IEEE, AIS, IFIP, USA (2017). https://doi.org/10.1145/3184594
21. Bloom, B.S., Krathwohl, D.R.: Taxonomy of educational objectives: the classification of educational goals. In: Handbook I: Cognitive Domain. By a Committee of College and University Examiners. Longmans, Green, New York (1956)
22. Bourque, P., Fairley, R.E.: Guide to the Software Engineering Body of Knowledge (SWEBOK(R)): Version 3.0, 3 edn. IEEE Computer Society Press, Los Alamitos (2014)
23. Bruner, J.S.: The Process of Education. Vintage, New York (1960)

Engineering Education and a New Paradigm of Project Thinking

Elena Vasilieva$^{(\boxtimes)}$ (iD)

Financial University under the Government of the Russian Federation,
49 Leningradsky Prospekt, GSP-3, 125993 Moscow, Russia
evvasileva@fa.ru

Abstract. In the article the author substantiates the importance of the approach of project thinking in the training and education of future professionals for the digital economy. Development of entrepreneurial abilities, creative thinking, ability to work in a project team, to make decisions in unusual situations - all these important competencies must be obtained during the training of students at the University. The article presents the experience of design seminars, especially the use of popular tools of design thinking to create projects of Internet entrepreneurship, recommendations for the introduction of the approach of design thinking (DT) in engineering education. The author describes in detail one of his cases "Search for sources of ideas". DT can redirect from the usual ways of judgment about the object to the unconventional solution. They help develop an innovation that is based on empathy for the pain of the consumer, including one that is still unconscious to prevent his hidden needs and create a breakthrough product for him. It is important to learn how to accept even the most ridiculous at first glance the ideas of their colleagues, which can trigger your best idea. In the case we used tools of design thinking, such as random stimulus technique, the technique of personal ideas, World café, "good and bad ideas", etc. Each point of the case contains comments on how the new idea was developed, what difficulties arose with this or that tool, what ways we found to get the team out of the deadlocks.

Keywords: IT education · New educational technologies · Human centered design · Personnel training · Technological entrepreneurship · Design thinking · Competencies · Soft skills

1 Introduction

Design Thinking is often associated solely with the discipline of design and is considered as the tool of creativity, which involves a huge amount of magical manipulation of cards multi-colored post-it (Brautigam 2017). However, an outstanding scientist, Nobel laureate Herbert Simon, whose developments are in demand today by specialists in various technical fields (engineers, system technicians, programmers), in 1969 he first wrote about the importance of the development of human thinking through empirical rules, experience, the ability to adapt to conditions of high uncertainty of the environment (Simon 1996). His analysis of the nature of organized complexity is the basis of research

© Springer Nature Switzerland AG 2020
V. Sukhomlin and E. Zubareva (Eds.): SITITO 2018, CCIS 1201, pp. 42–51, 2020.
https://doi.org/10.1007/978-3-030-46895-8_2

in the field of artificial intelligence, information processing, complex systems. Today, many design researchers believe that Herbert Simon is the founder of the philosophy of design thinking.

The Soviet scientist and inventor Heinrich Altshuller also studied the problem of teaching people to build thought processes so that every person who is engaged in creative work can find non-standard solutions to complex unusual problems. The first publication of the principles of the organization of "creative solution of a new technical problem" (Altshuller and Shapiro 1956), which formed the Basis of the Theory of Inventive Problem Solving (TRIZ), contained conclusions about the importance of studying and experimental study of the growth opportunities of research potential, "mental processes of technical creativity". We can continue the list of scientists that studies the features of development of creative abilities of the person calling the Shchedrovitsky (Shchedrovitsky 2012), Bekhtereva (Bekhtereva 2007), Khryascheva (Khryascheva 2001), Michalko (Michalko 1998), de Bono (de Bono 1999, 2010), etc.

Creativity in the era of the progress of digital technologies and robotics, which creates new challenges for humanity, is perhaps one of the main features that is needed today to become successful, to stand in the race for leadership in any professional activity. Methods of design thinking approach allow to improve and hone creative abilities through the formation of response processes, teamwork, game mechanics, visualization and inspiration, teach "to be more flexible in the application of their knowledge" (de Bono 1999), develop emotional intelligence and empathy, structure information, help to see connections and relationships in complex systems.

2 Design Thinking Is an Approach to Designing Innovative Solutions Focused on Human

2.1 The Philosophy of Design Thinking

In 2004, David Kelly, founder of IDEO design Agency, and Hasso Plattner, co-founder of SAP, formulated a philosophy of creating innovative Design Thinking solutions, which combines various developments in the field of development of human creative skills, study of client behavior, generation of ideas, visualization (Kelley and Kelley 2013; Liedtka and Ogilvie 2011). Such an integrated design iterative and research approach is aimed at creating breakthrough ideas based on the processing of implicit knowledge and empathy, which is important in the context of the trend of orientation of modern business to people. The key steps of the process - empathy, focus (Poin-of-Vew, POV), generation, selection, prototyping and testing – are supported by different variations of a variety of tools.

2.2 The Value of Design Thinking to Different Fields

The developer of software products and services will find in the design thinking tools to find sources for new ideas (random stimulus method, SCAMPER, World café), testing (Customer Journey Map, included observation, "Wizard of Oz"), prototyping and evaluation of project goals.

The Manager will find a basis for changing the corporate culture of the organization. Discussion of important tasks in an informal setting at a round table with the help of various design thinking techniques will help to maximize the potential and ideas of their employees for business development, involve staff in the problem and increase their responsibility for change. The company's skills in the use of design thinking tools can be used in meetings, strategic sessions, brainstorming (Ertel and Solomon 2014).

This approach is necessary when it is necessary to understand the conflicting demands and expectations of customers (empathy map, guerrilla Ethnography, POV-question). When your competitors have made a breakthrough, and you have nothing to quickly respond to their challenge (method triads, the matrix of positive and negative customer experience). Design thinking forces "to leave office" (Blank 2014), helps to learn to cooperate with others and to be inspired by others ideas, to discover new points of view and unexpected opportunities, to be able to direct the creative abilities to the solution of problems.

2.3   The Possibility of Introducing Design Thinking in Engineering Education

We have been implementing the Design Thinking approach since 2015, trying out different tools in conducting scientific events and hackathons for students, in professional development programs. We use design thinking techniques at design seminars and practical training courses:

1. "Internet entrepreneurship". Eric Rees calls design thinking-one of the basic principles of the approach "Lean Start-up" (Ries 2013).
2. "Information technology marketing". Philip Kotler in recent books reveals the value of research unconscious motives of consumers in the context of globalization of proposals, where the empathy of an entrepreneur to their potential buyers – is its key success factor (Kotler et al. 2010), and emphasizes the need to include lateral thinking in the development of a unique trade (value) proposal (de Bono 2010; Ries 2013).
3. "Information technologies and transformation of business models". T. Clark, A. Osterwalder and Y. Pigneur devoted in his book a separate Chapter to the possibilities of using design thinking in building a business model (Clark et al. 2012).

Classes based on Design Thinking involve project work in the team (Vasilieva 2018), when its participants explore the customer experience of interaction with a product, service or process, develop business ideas, create prototypes of products or services. Participants in these design workshops gain the skills of empathy, systems analysis and project experience. Communication and cooperation in the team, readiness for innovation and proactivity arise among designers, develop their creative abilities and social intelligence.

3   Case "Search of Sources of Ideas Using Design Thinking"

How to come up with a new idea? If we apply any of the techniques of generating ideas of design thinking, we can abandon the usual ways of thinking about the object, but to develop an innovation that solves the problem (pain of the consumer). We were able to focus on this pain during the study of the target audience, when we built an empathy map, conducted interviews, applied methods of guerrilla Ethnography, etc., tested a prototype with the user, formulated a POV question (Vasilieva 2018). Important: we must learn to accept even the most ridiculous at first glance ideas of our colleagues, which can be a trigger for our best idea. And together we can create a breakthrough innovation. This is the secret to success.

3.1   The Conditions and Tools for Conducting a Design Workshop

Duration of teamwork - from 2 h to 2.5 h. It is important that we follow the schedule clearly. Time limit allows you to provoke creativity and start the process of generating more promising ideas. In this case, we presented the tools of design thinking, such as random stimulus technique, the technique of personal ideas and method of grouping and filling, Empathy Map, Person model, Customer Journey Map, POV-formula, World café, method of good and bad ideas, and Matrix "Force - Effects" (Vasilieva 2018).

Description of the Case

Step 1: the explanation of the rules of the World café and a description of the course assignments case study (5 min). Technique "World cafe" involves the discussion of hypotheses put forward by participants of all teams participating in the design seminar. First, each team starts working on one problem. After 20 min, one project team moves on to another problem (changing tables). The captains of the team ("master table"), taking new participants at their table, quickly obliged them to explain the essence of the problem previously formulated hypotheses, record their concerns and new ideas. Changing tables the project team takes place in three stages every 20, 15 and 10 min respectively.

Step 2: select random stimulus (5 min). Teams are invited to choose 3 cards (random incentives (Michalko 1998)) from the previously compiled list of technological trends, current problems of society and the world, or any other concepts. Each of the team members within 5 min should record 5–7 associations, which he will have when thinking about the resulting combination of random stimuli (quiet brainstorming or technique of personal ideas (Vasilieva 2018). Then, when discussing each participant can explain why there were certain associations. This option allows you to create an atmosphere of trust, and the associations discussed leave an information trail, which may be the basis for the generation of new ideas.

Step 3: Brainstorming. The more ideas we can generate at this step, the more likely the result will be achieved. Even the most ridiculous ideas can be the basis for breakthrough innovation, if they are tested for compliance with the three main limitations of design thinking: desirable for the consumer, implementable using existing technology, profitable for business.

During brainstorming, the project team formulates 3–5 possible solutions to the problem. Priorities are arranged as: the best, worst, reserve ideas (a method of grouping and filling).

Step 4: Empathy and focus on the problem. At this step, an Empathy map is compiled to examine the hidden needs of a potential consumer and a POV-question is formulated (the focus stage on the "Point of View" problem) in the format: "How can we help _ _ _ to solve the _ _ problem and surprise _ _ _" (Vasilieva 2018).

The Empathy map (Liedtka and Ogilvie 2011; Clark et al. 2012; Vasilieva 2018) reflects the characteristic features of a particular character ("Person-model"), which is given a name, determine its age, features, artifacts. Designers reflect and record on the verge of "What does he hear?" those with whom he can communicate, who is for him an authority. They describe on the brink of "That he sees?" what surrounds him. They describe on the brink of "That he thinks and feels?" his achievements and fears. They describe on the brink of "That he says and makes?" his actions, attitude to others. Based on the experience of design workshops, we note that sometimes helps to select one of the team members to create a portrait of the target consumer based on his interviewing. It can also help to prove the value of conducting in-depth interviews or participant observation for the life of the real representatives of the target group at the stage of Customer Discovery Customer Development approach (Blank 2014), and show the design of the workshop, how far we are in his hallucinations about the user of his product under development even in cases when trying to describe a person of his age category and social group.

We presented the process of mapping empathy with the use of Customer Journey Map (CJM) (Fig. 1). A team of students at the hackathon of the International Scientific Student Congress (MNSK), regularly held at the Faculty of Applied Mathematics and Information Technology of the Financial University, received the trigger words: "Internet of things", "Construction", "Ecology". Quiet brainstorming led to three associations, which were repeated in the responses of participants and were selected as priorities for discussion: cleaning dogs while walking, watering flowers, sorting garbage. The Empathy map was drawn from a team member who described one day in his life, where all the stories that involve waste requiring special disposal were sequentially selected from the daily routine: headphones, glass, tin and plastic cans and bottles, batteries, torn sneakers, etc. Then they formulated a POV question (the stage of focusing on the problem of "Point of View"): "How can we help Vovochka to solve the problem of sorting and recycling garbage and surprise everyone?».

The generation of hypotheses allowed to create the concept of mobile service, the task of which is to motivate people to sort garbage. Eco-Project "#In_The_Trash" included elements of gamification. In the application, for each individual scenario of garbage collection and disposal, developers offer points that turn into prizes from recycled materials (books from paper, shale from plastic waste, Christmas toys from recycled glass). Information is also recorded on the portal "Active citizen" (https://ag.mos.ru), on social networks, reminders and penalties for overdue events have been introduced. In General, the proposal developed by the team is aimed at increasing social responsibility of people and solving the complex problem of the big city.

Fig. 1. Project "#In_The_Trash".

In Fig. 2 we presented another example of the problem analysis with the empathy map. As triggers, the project team received the words: "beauty industry", "Robotics", "Track Hubit". Related hypotheses have led to the idea of a mobile voice assistant to motivate a healthy lifestyle (HLS) and a personal schedule optimizer. The concept of a mobile application with voice assistant function controls health indicators, calories consumed, diet, exercise, emotional level; optimizes the schedule; reminds and advises. The information is aggregated and analyzed from the indicators of fitness trackers, photos of food consumption and purchase barcodes, statistics of author's emoticons in correspondence, transmitting the mood, schedules of transport and the working day of a person. Mobile service with an epic name "Avatar BIG BROTHER" gives recommendations and posts achievements in social networks.

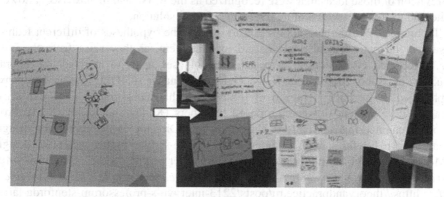

Fig. 2. The grouping of associations and a map of empathy.

Empathy map helped the project team to understand the interests characteristic of young people, to agree on the problems that are most important for them and need to be addressed.

Steps 5 & 6: «World café». This steps are two consecutive transitions of the team (in 15 and 10 min) to the new table. "The host of the table" formulates the problems and reads the hypotheses proposed earlier to the new team. In Fig. 3, the ideas of different teams were recorded on post-it notes of different colors.

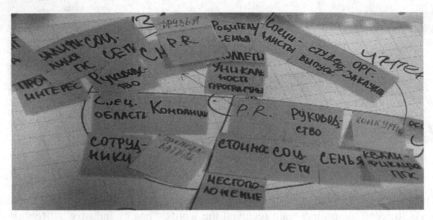

Fig. 3. Collect information on multi-colored stickers.

Step 7: evaluation of the prospects of ideas (5 min). Each team groups all formulated hypotheses, distributing them to the best, reserve and worst. The best ideas are put off, and from the list of the worst one is selected for discussion.

Step 8: the development of unpromising ideas (25 min). Brainstorming is conducted to finalize a bad idea. If in the allotted time the new solution of the studied problem turns out to be less interesting than the previously formulated best, the team returns to work on its best hypothesis (Silig 2009). In two of the three cases, as our practice has shown, it is the revision of those ideas that were recognized as the worst, and then revised, allowed in the end to come up with a more interesting design solution.

Technique "World cafe" allows you to discuss the hypotheses of different teams, to subject them to critical analysis and look at them, as they say, "from the outside." Repeated consideration of rejected hypotheses helps to manifest the lateral thinking (de Bono 2010). Tom Kelly, General Manager of IDEO design company, emphasized in the book "The Art of Innovation" that breakthrough ideas can arise from the development of ideas proposed by others (Kelley and Kelley 2013). Professor of engineering at Stanford University and Director of the center for design research Larri Leyfer said in an interview with the British higher school of design in Moscow: "Design Thinking is a talent to use other people's ideas" *[Interview prof. Larri Leyfer: «Design Thinking — it's a talent to use other people's ideas» [on-line]. URL:* https://theoryandpractice.ru/posts/2213-intervyu-s-professorom-stenforda-larri-leyferom-design-thinking–eto-talant-ispolzovat-chuzhie-idei/ *(Accessed: 14.06.2011)]*. In addition, the participation of all members of the project team in the evolution of the idea creates a sense of their personal contribution, makes it more valuable, causes a desire to support it in the implementation process.

Step 9: prototyping and testing (20 min). The prototype can be made using the technology of business origami (figures made of cardboard). During the work on the prototype, elements of functional fullness of the product and its presentation are discussed and worked out (Fig. 4). To describe the idea of this process is best suited metaphor David Kelly: "think with your hands" (Kelley and Kelley 2013).

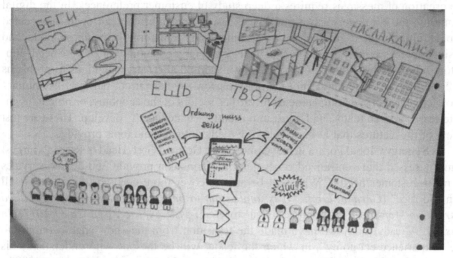

Fig. 4. Presentation of the project voice assistant "Avatar - BIG BROTHER".

The matrix of evaluation of ideas "Efforts and effects" can be constructed. Then the team move to create a prototype of key ideas that received the maximum score by the criterion of efficiency and the minimum of the criterion of costs. Each of the steps of the case suggests that the designers, having tested the hypothesis, at any time can make "pivot" (Blank 2014; Ries 2013) to other ideas.

Result: selection of the most successful creative ideas related to the solution of strategic tasks (Fig. 5).

Fig. 5. Presentation of the project "#In_The_Trash".

4 Conclusion

Today, the company has access to a huge amount of information, which means that the creation of messages requires a deep study of customer preferences. In the digital economy, the competencies of employees are in demand, who can open unexpected opportunities in the digital markets and competently transform the business model and business processes of the organization under them. Organizations of the future need innovators who are able to think outside the box and find alternative solutions to problems in conditions of uncertainty, not having a narrow specialization, but interdisciplinary knowledge and broad competencies in various sectors of the economy, be able to negotiate, work in open teams, and, most importantly, – to constantly develop. These are just a few of the features that Design Thinking methodologies and tools provide.

At Synergy Global Forum in November 2017, German Gref, Head of Russia's largest Bank, stressed that centralized ecosystem platforms can provide 360-degree services to meet customer needs. "Who will be able to cover more needs of the client – will win the race" [German Gref: "It is unpleasant to be in the center of what is called disruption" [on-line]. URL: https://rb.ru/story/gref-synergy/ (accessed: 28.11.2017) (In Russ.)]. Already today we have made the transition from the knowledge economy to the "experience economy", in which the leader will be the one who understands his consumer and his thoughts and desires, who shows him empathy (Nussbaum 2005). Empathy is at the heart of most Design Thinking techniques. The Design Thinking approach primarily makes pay more attention in the study of the context, to explore the ecosystem to identify the most hidden needs of consumers that open the digital value to the business. Understanding the consumer's experience, feelings and sensations is aimed at further filling the innovative product with emotions that are understandable to the consumer. And intuitive and creative thinking opens up prospects for the future "imagination economy" for the company (Bidshahri 2018).

References

Altshuller, G., Shapiro R.: On the psychology of inventive creativity. Questions Psychol (6), 37–49 (1956). (in Russian). https://www.altshuller.ru/triz/triz0.asp
Bekhtereva, N.: Magic of the Brain and Labyrinths of Life. AST, Moscow (2007). (in Russian)
Bidshahri, R.: These are the Most Exciting Industries and Jobs of the Future (2018) https://singularityhub.com/2018/01/29/these-are-the-most-exciting-industries-and-jobs-of-the-future. Accessed 12 Oct 2018
Blank, S.: The Four Steps to the Epiphany: Successful Strategies for Products that Win. Quad/Graphics, Sussex (2014)
Brautigam, B.: How Using Design Thinking Will Fix Design Thinking (2017) https://thenextweb.com/2017/04/27/design-thinking-will-fix-design-thinking/#.tnw_BZYUrgPF. Accessed 12 Oct 2018
Clark, T., Osterwalder, A., Pigneur, Y.: Business Model You: A One-Page Method For Reinventing Your Career. Wiley, Hoboken (2012)
de Bono, E.: Six Thinking Hats. Penguin Books, Limited, Toronto (1999)
de Bono, E.: Lateral Thinking: A Textbook of Creativity. Penguin Adult, London (2010)
Ertel, C., Solomon, L.: Moments of Impact: How to Design Strategic Conversations That Accelerate Change. Simon & Schuster, New York (2014)

Kelley, T., Kelley, D.: Creative Confidence Unleashing the Creative Potential Within Us All. Barnes & Noble, New York (2013)

Khryascheva, N.: Psihogimnastiki in the Training. Rech, Sankt-Peterburg (2001). (in Russian)

Kotler, P., Kartajaya, H., Setiawan, I.: Marketing 3.0: From Products to Customers to the Human Spirit. Wiley, Hoboken (2010)

Liedtka, J., Ogilvie, T.: Designing for Growth: A Design Thinking Toolkit for Managers. Columbia University Press, New York (2011)

Michalko, M.: Cracking Creativity: The Secrets of Creative Genius. Ten Speed Press, Berkeley (1998)

Nussbaum, B.: The Empathy Economy, Business Week (2005). http://www.businessweek.com/bwdaily/dnflash/mar2005/nf2005037_4086.htm. Accessed 12 Oct 2018

Ries, E.: The Lean Start-up: How Today's Entrepreneurs Use Continuous Innovation to Create Radically Successful Businesses. Crown Business, New York (2013)

Shchedrovitsky, G.: A Guide to the Methodology of Organization, Management and Administration. Alpina Publisher, Moscow (2012). (in Russian)

Silig, T.: What I Wish I Knew When I was 20 A Crash Course on Making Your Place in the World. HarperCollins Publishers, New York (2009)

Simon, H.: The Sciences of the Artificial. MIT Press, Cambridge (1996). (in Russian)

Vasilieva, E.: Design thinking: a little bit about the approach and a lot about the tools of creative thinking, learning client requests and creating ideas: monograph. RU-SCIENCE (2018). (in Russian)

Esthetic Education in Mathematics Lessons with the Use of Software Products

Aibek Dautov[1] , Kaiyrzhan Kozhabaev[1] , Alimbubi Aktayeva[1](✉) ,
Nadezhda Gagarina[1] , and Ludwig Van Graan[2]

[1] Sh. Ualikhanov Kokshetau State University, 76, Abay Street, Kokshetau 475003, Kazakhstan
d.abeke@mail.ru, labdid_2008@mail.ru, aaktaewa@list.ru,
gagarina_08@mail.ru
[2] Abay Myrzakhmetov Kokshetau University, 189 Auzoeva Street, Kokshetau 020000,
Kazakhstan
vangraan@mail.ru

Abstract. The article deals with the possibilities of information-communication technologies (ICT) for the process of aesthetic education of future specialists teaching natural sciences, including mathematics. This paper makes a compelling case for the inclusion of the aesthetic in the teaching and learning of mathematics. Using a provocative set of philosophical, psychological, mathematical, technological, and educational insights, illuminates how the materials and approaches we use in the mathematics classroom can be enriched for the benefit of all learners. In this paper offered specific recommendations to help teachers evoke and nurture their students' aesthetic abilities, includes examples of mathematical inquiry in a software-based learning environments, revealing some of the roles they play in supporting students' aesthetic inclinations. The result ours research electronic textbook "Mathematics" allows fully opens up all intellectual and creative opportunities for future experts, develops their imagination and broadens their horizons in the use of innovative computer technologies. The experimental design provides a basis for understanding whether software products improve achievement. While the study worked to ensure that teachers received appropriate training on using products and that technology infrastructures were adequate and that teachers would like to use electronic textbook "Mathematics" more or use them differently. Because of this feature of the study, the results relate to conditions of use that high schools would face if they were developing the electronic textbook "Mathematics" or provide the software service using internal resources products on their own.

Keywords: Esthetic education · Mathematical education · Information and communication technologies · Software product

1 Introduction

To form a harmoniously developed personality, the aesthetic education of future specialists must take an important place. Because of its enormous potential, It is difficult to overestimate the role of mathematics in aesthetic education Mathematics is very rich

V. Sukhomlin and E. Zubareva (Eds.): SITITO 2018, CCIS 1201, pp. 52–58, 2020.
https://doi.org/10.1007/978-3-030-46895-8_3

in beautiful formulas and proofs, and you can specify whole sections, for example: trigonometry, the golden section, symmetry, algebra and number theory, and Boolean algebra, etc.

To efficiently disclose the esthetic potential of mathematics, one must assumes the full perception of mathematical beauty, the development of esthetic senses and taste, an ideal of figurative thinking and logical culture, to orientate person in his/her aspirations. According to like Zhokhova A.L., Vygotsky L.S., Dzhems V., Kozhabayeva K.G., Kornilov K.N., Peters E., Dalinger V.A. education by beauty and through beauty is, on the one hand, an important development tool of motivation of the doctrine, and on the another a source for becoming an emotional person as one of the main components of his/her esthetic culture [1–5].

It is a major problem to form an esthetic relation to mathematics as part of culture a when forming the outlook of a person [1:184]. He/she has to and can learn to perceive and feel the beauty of mathematical expressions and theoretical designs, to estimate mathematical designs and works of mathematical culture from the esthetic positions inherent in the subject when studying it [6]. Disclosing the beauty of mathematics will enable the preparation of future professionals, who will use special methods to get creativity in the classroom, for life under modern conditions.

The development of the modern ICT does not eradicate the need for creativity, but on the contrary, demands higher and higher levels of common cultural development, education, creativity and activity. Modern information technologies open new didactic opportunities in realizing the goals of aesthetic education in mathematics classes [7:49]. These classes should be used to add the teaching of aesthetic tastes and experiences to the beauty of mathematics, as well as to develop multimedia tools through methods related to computer graphics and animation, etc.

The electronic textbook "Mathematics", developed by us, can positively influence the formation of aesthetic qualities, increase interest in studying mathematics and informatics subjects, as well as increase the level of mathematical knowledge with the use of the latest digital technologies and the level of development of the thinking activity of future specialists.

This electronic textbook was designed for 3 credits, was created with the use of innovative information and communication technologies, and is intended for experts. In the course of training, it is supposed to be used for laboratory and practical work together with software products like Mathematica, Mathcad, Mathlab, Compass-3D, and Maple and for working in the online and offline modes.

The electronic textbook "Mathematician" developed by us has the following sections:

1. introduction;
2. symmetry;
3. numerical approximations;
4. algebraic calculations;
5. golden ratio;
6. processing image and analysis;

7. geometrical calculations;
8. an electronic library;
9. glossary;
10. test tasks;
11. typical solutions of problems.

The purpose and tasks of the electronic textbook are:

1. Identifying the relationship of mathematics with different areas of human activity and phenomena occurring in nature.
2. Expanding the horizons in the application of mathematics.
3. Formation of common and mathematical culture of the person.
4. Esthetic development of the person.
5. Development of logical and figurative thinking in future experts.
6. Development of skills in working with information and communication technologies.
7. Development of skills in the development of modern electronic textbooks in the field of natural sciences.

According to us, it is the most appropriate to use the above-stated software products in the process of illustrative and demonstrative work integration in the lessons of mathematics and computer science, as well as in the disciplines of the natural sciences. The interdisciplinary approach is one of the priority areas in modern pedagogical science [8:96]. According to Russian scholars [7, 9, 10], "the mathematical apparatus and mathematical methods can be used in the study of qualitatively different fragments of reality, ...promote disclosure of their unity and thus indicate new ways of integrating new knowledge ..." [11].

The interdisciplinary approach allows future specialists to understand the subject communication more fully, learn to apply new innovative ICT capabilities, and to feel the aesthetic appeal of the sections of mathematics.

The practical part of the electronic textbook is built in the course of performing laboratory, practical tasks in software products.

The practical part of the electronic textbook was built during the implementation of laboratory and practical tasks in software like Mathematica, Mathcad, Mathlab, Compass-3d, Maple, as well as in on-line and off-line modes.

Studying the fundamentals of the above tools of software products unite in themselves all innovative communication technologies. They represent the opportunity to experiment and conduct experiments on modeling with various solutions to problems, and to analyze and synthesize any kind of information.

The computational and multifunctional system of the electronic textbook "Mathematics" is known as the most powerful research and mathematical platform. Many examples show how it can be applied in various fields of the natural sciences (see Fig. 1).

```
In[n]:= Multicolumn[primes, Alignment → {Center, Center}, Spacings → {1, 1},
        Frame → All, FrameStyle → Directive[Orange, Dashing[Small]]]
```

2	53	127	199	283	383	467	577	661	769	877	983	1087	1193	1297
3	59	131	211	293	389	479	587	673	773	881	991	1091	1201	1301
5	61	137	223	307	397	487	593	677	787	883	997	1093	1213	1303
7	67	139	227	311	401	491	599	683	797	887	1009	1097	1217	1307
11	71	149	229	313	409	499	601	691	809	907	1013	1103	1223	1319
13	73	151	233	317	419	503	607	701	811	911	1019	1109	1229	1321
17	79	157	239	331	421	509	613	709	821	919	1021	1117	1231	1327
19	83	163	241	337	431	521	617	719	823	929	1031	1123	1237	1361
23	89	167	251	347	433	523	619	727	827	937	1033	1129	1249	1367
29	97	173	257	349	439	541	631	733	829	941	1039	1151	1259	1373
31	101	179	263	353	443	547	641	739	839	947	1049	1153	1277	1381
37	103	181	269	359	449	557	643	743	853	953	1051	1163	1279	1399
41	107	191	271	367	457	563	647	751	857	967	1061	1171	1283	1409
43	109	193	277	373	461	569	653	757	859	971	1063	1181	1289	1423
47	113	197	281	379	463	571	659	761	863	977	1069	1187	1291	1427

Fig. 1. Generated list of exponents of the Mersenne prime number.

The software product Mathlab is a high-level interpreted programming language, has a wide range of functions, an integrated development environment, object-oriented capabilities and interfaces with programs written in other programming languages (see Fig. 2). Programs written in Mathlab come in two types; functions and scripts. The main feature of the Mathlab language is its wide possibilities for working with matrices, which the creators of the language expressed in the slogan "Think vectorized".

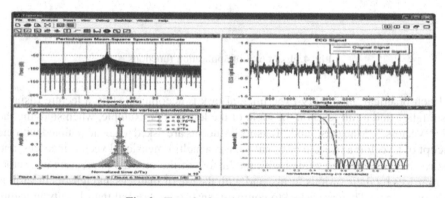

Fig. 2. Transfer function of ideal filters

The next package of application programs, Mathcad, allows you to create corporate and industry-specific means of certified calculations in various branches of science and technology, including mathematics, providing a unified methodology for natural aesthetic perception to illustrate the solution of various mathematics (see Fig. 3).

Maple is a powerful and versatile system that has become the standard of three-dimensional design, thanks to the simple mastery and wide possibilities of mathematical modeling of various objects (see Fig. 4).

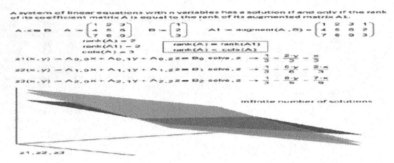

Fig. 3. A linear algebraic solution is an infinite number of solutions.

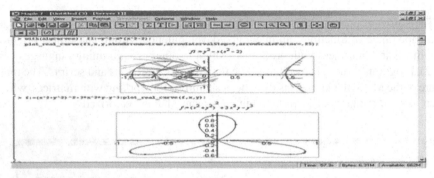

Fig. 4. Examples of application functions.

Each practical, laboratory-experimental task is accompanied by a lecture (using a presentation and a full text) on the topic of the lesson. For example, when studying the topic "Vectors," "Matrixes," and "Tensors," students are asked to get acquainted with the concept of a vector, a one-dimensional vector, a multidimensional vector, matrices, and tensor. They also get acquainted with the history of the origin and creation of vectors and matrices by their various forms, and with the use of matrices and tensors in various fields of science. They are asked to compare, analyze and reveal their beauty in nature and life. Vectors and matrices with their various kinds, the initial information about the complex plane and complex numbers are involved in the classes on programming and the construction of algebraic computations.

It is then suggested that students do several practical exercises on the subject in various programs, to construct various images of matrixes and vectors and also a tensor, and their compositions, to design an n-dimensional image with multimedia. While they perform these tasks they can use the possibilities of any program (graphics, animation, multimedia, programming use of Script).

Let's show how Mathcad allows you to build and create matrix objects. As an example, let us consider the process of solving a system of a linear-algebraic equation (SLAE) using the Gauss method. Consider the system of linear equations:

We write the system in the matrix form: $A \cdot x = b$, where

A – is the matrix of the coefficients; b – the right side of the constraints; x is the vector of variables that you want to find.

Where $Rang(A) = p$. The process of solving SLAE on Mathcad is as follows (see Fig. 5).

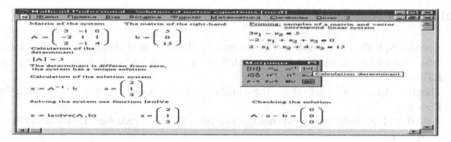

Fig. 5. Process of the decision by SLAE method of Gauss on Mathcad

Having received the image, it is possible to emphasize its beauty with various special effects of the program. To transform it to even more interesting form see Fig. 6 [11].

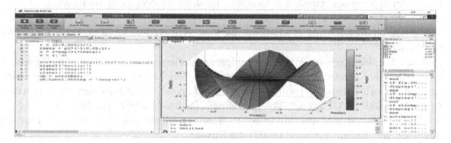

Fig. 6. The process of solving the problem on Mathlab

2 Conclusion

Proceeding from the above research of scientists, it can be concluded that aesthetic education occupies an important place in the process of personality development.

If we use modern information and communication technologies, whose capabilities allow us to show the beauty of mathematical objects, and the harmony of the shapes of geometric bodies, we can achieve even greater results in both aesthetic education and in mathematical education.

One of the best tools for constructing and studying aesthetic objects of mathematics is packages with the use of software products, such as: Mathematica, Mathcad, Mathlab, Compass-3d, and Maple. They allow us to fully discover all the intellectual and creative abilities of individuals, to develop their imagination, and to broaden the horizons of ICT.

Thus, the use of the innovative technology of the above software products makes it possible to increase interest in learning, to develop the information and technological culture and logical thinking of the future specialist to form an optimal analysis of the task in its solution.

References

1. Kozhabaev, K.G.: Educational and Developmental Training in Mathematics, and the Preparation for the Future Teacher: Textbook. Izd. Sh. Ualikhanov KSU, Kokshetau (2009). (in Russian)
2. Zhokhov, A.L.: How to help shape the world outlook of schoolchildren. Samara (1995). (in Russian)
3. Vygodsky, L.S.: Pedagogical Psychology. Davydov, V.V. (ed.) Pedagogika, Moscow (1991). (in Russian)
4. James, B.: Is there a Consciousness? New Ideas in Philosophy. St. Petersburg 4 (1913). (in Russian)
5. Kornilov, K.N.: The Doctrine of Human Reactions. Moscow (1924). (in Russian)
6. Peters, E.: School Full of Life. Moscow (1912). (in Russian)
7. Dalinger, V.A.: Cognitive-visual approach and its features in teaching mathematics. In: Mathematics and Informatics: Science and Education: Interuniversity Collection of Scientific Proceedings: Yearbook. Omsk: Ed. OmGPU, no. 4, pp. 48–55 (2004). (in Russian)
8. Zhokhov, A.L.: Cognition of Mathematics and the Foundations of a Scientific World Outlook: Worldview on the Direction of Mathematics. Proc. Help. Izd-vo YAGPU, Yaroslavl (2008). (in Russian)
9. Smirnov, E.I.: Unified mathematics in problems as an element of integration of mathematical knowledge. In: Smirnov, E.I. (ed.) Problems in Teaching Mathematics: Theory, Experience, Innovations. All-Russia. Scientific-Practical. Conf., cons. 115 Anniversary of Corporative Cor. APN USSR P. A. Larichev. Vologda, Russia, pp. 68–77 (2007). (in Russian)
10. Smirnova, E.I. (ed.): Visual Modeling in Teaching Mathematics: Theory and Practice: Textbook. IPC Indigo, Yaroslavl (2007). (in Russian)
11. Rozin, V.M.: Methodology: Formation and Modern State. The Moscow Psychological and Social Institute, Moscow (2005). Tutorial. (in Russian)

Designing Anticipation Activity of Students When Studying Holomorphic Dynamics Relying on Information Technologies

Valeriy Sekovanov$^{(\boxtimes)}$ ⓘ, Vladimir Ivkov ⓘ, Aleksey Piguzov ⓘ, and Yelena Seleznyova ⓘ

Kostroma State University named after N.A. Nekrasov,
1-st of May Street 14, Kostroma 156961, Russia
sekovanovvs@yandex.ru, ivkov_wa@mail.ru, piguzov@ksu.edu.ru,
lena_selez@mail.ru

Abstract. In this paper, we consider the design of anticipatory activities aimed at development of students creativity at a higher education institution when studying holomorphic dynamics. Interpretation of anticipation as an ability to put forward hypotheses, that are subject to verification by means of analytical methods, has been specified. The connection between Mandelbrot set and the accompanying Julia sets has been noted. Using information and communication technologies, students put forward hypotheses related to Julia sets' visualisation, and then use the analytical methods to identify the main frames of these sets. First, special cases are considered, then the obtained results are generalised. By analogy, other tasks are formed and their solutions are analysed. In our opinion, this approach makes it possible to organise students' creative mathematical activity, develops their intuition, flexibility and critical thinking.

Keywords: Anticipation · Intuition · Creativity · Information and communication technologies · Holomorphic dynamics · Julia set · Mandelbrot set · Creative activity · Creative quality

1 Introduction

Designing anticipatory activity aims at development of students' creativity. In the modern rapidly changing world, anticipatory skills are of great interest. They define success and development of personality.

On the basis of the analysis of psychological and pedagogical literature [1–8, 15, 16], one can draw a conclusion that development of creativity, including intuition development, is the main priority under conditions of professional education at all grade levels.

From Latin, "anticipation" means predetermination, prescience, pre-guessing of events; an idea of something made in advance, ability of a person to imagine possible result of an act before it is done. Pyotr Anokhin offered "anticipatory reflection" of a concept which he understood as ability of the brain to put the card before the

© Springer Nature Switzerland AG 2020
V. Sukhomlin and E. Zubareva (Eds.): SITITO 2018, CCIS 1201, pp. 59–68, 2020.
https://doi.org/10.1007/978-3-030-46895-8_4

horse, to look to the future, in response to an incentive which works only in the present [1]. Anticipation represents a special case or, more precisely, a form of the advancing reflection.

It should be noted that anticipatory activity influences development of students' creativity because it aims at hypothesising and at hypotheses' checking. It is considered that hypothesising develops intuitive ideation and contributes to the development of creative work.

Hence, what is made the cornerstone of anticipatory activity is an ability to hypothesesise, because anticipation is by definition "an ability (in the broadest sense) to work and make these or those decisions with certain anticipation of expectations, of future events in time and in space". In mathematical activity it includes: hypothesising and hypotheses' checking; formation of a mathematical operation's acceptor [5]; solving tasks on the basis of intuitive ideation [5–8, 16], solving tasks strictly by logical method [4].

For designing students' anticipatory activity, the scenario of visualisation of Julia sets by students with use of information and communication technologies (ICTs) which promote hypothesesing as well as hypotheses' checking and which contribute to the development of other types of creative mathematical activity, has been worked out.

This scenario can be presented in the form of the scheme which defines the sequence of steps when solving a task:

1. problem definition is the purpose;
2. process:
   - hypothesising
   - resolution of contradiction
3. checking of the hypothesis is the result.

The scenario represents the system of rules of an optimum combination of a pedagogical technique based on identification of a hypothesis and on searching of decision.

Designing student's anticipatory activity is offered to be carried out by means of solving tasks when using modern mathematical methods and the ICTs. There are various techniques [3], when studying the discipline. Relying on investigations in the works [9–14], let us consider the holomorphic dynamics studying technique, which aims at development of the major creative quality – an intuition, – in this article. This technique within a mathematical problem allows hypothesising, arguing by analogy, mastering selection of methods, receptions and tools as well as mastering management of creative mathematical activity in the course of tasks solution. What plays a large role when studying holomorphic dynamics, is iterative method.

It should be noted that the iterative method occurs quite often when studying higher mathematics. It is first of all the nonlinear equations' solution by tangent method, by contracting mapping theorem proving, etc. In the modern mathematics – in dynamic systems, in fractal geometry, in chaos theory – process of iteration of functions is crucial. However iterated functions' systems are not studied in a higher educational institution individually.

The iterative method will aim at studying of Julia sets and Mandelbrot sets in our work. Julia sets and Mandelbrot sets are important mathematical objects used when creating models of various processes and phenomena of the real world. Investigations in the works [5–14] are devoted to these sets.

Let us insert definitions and designations.

Say z_0 is the entry point, $z_1 = f(z_0), \ldots, z_n = f(z_{n-1}), \ldots$ Sequence $\{z_n\}_{n=0}^\infty = \{f^{(n)}(z_0)\}_{n=0}^\infty$ is called orbit of the point z_0, where $f^{(n)}(z) = f(f \ldots (f(z_0)))$.

Julia set for a polynomial of complex variable $f(z)$, designated as $J(f)$, is defined as $J(f) = \partial\{z : f^{(n)}(z) \to \infty, n \to \infty\}$, where ∂ is the boundary of domain of attraction of infinity, while $f^{(n)}(z) = f(f^{(n-1)}(z)), n = 1, 2, \ldots$.

What is called the filled-in Julia set, is an ensemble of points each orbit of which, is bounded.

Julia sets (boundary of the filled-in Julia set) have a larger variety depending on the choice of parameter c. At certain values c Julia sets are tie sets – while at other values, Julia sets are scattered as "dust". What allows defining the form of Julia set, is Mandelbrot set.

What we will understand as Mandelbrot set M_p, is a set of points c of complex plane at which, orbit of function zero $f(z) = z^p + c$ is bounded.

Mandelbrot set consists of a leading part and the infinite number of its parts of the smaller size which are called points.

In this case students are offered by us to make computer experiments at first for the case $p = 2$, that is we investigate the case when $f(z) = z^2 + c$ (Figs. 1 and 2).

The program below establishes connection between Mandelbrot set and Julia set. This program specifies construction of Julia sets on the basis of chosen points from Mandelbrot set or on the basis of chosen points outside the latter set.

```
var a,b,Nx,Ny,M,k:Integer;
Xk,Yk,Xk1,Yk1,Xmin,Xmax,Ymin,Ymax,dX,dY,P,Q,r,f,l:Real;
    W,E,s:BYTE;
    Bmt:TBitmap;
begin
    Bmt:=TBitmap.Create;
    Bmt.Width:=ClientWidth;
    Bmt.Height:=ClientHeight;
    Form1.Canvas.FillRect(Rect(0,0,Form1.Width,Form1.Height));
    s:=0;
    w:=0;
    e:=0;
    a:=ClientWidth;
    b:=ClientHeight;
    P:=X0;
    Q:=Y0;
    Xmin:=-2;
    Ymin:=-1.2;
    Xmax:=2;
    Ymax:=2;
    dX:=(Xmax-Xmin)/(a-1);
```

```
for Nx:=0 to a-1 do
   for Ny:=0 to b-1 do
      begin
      Xk:=Xmin+Nx*dX;
      Yk:=Ymin+Ny*dX;
      k:=0;
         While k<20 do
            begin
               Inc(K);
               Xk1:=sqr(Xk)-sqr(Yk)+P;
               Yk1:=2*Xk*Yk+Q;
               Xk:=Xk1;
               Yk:=Yk1;
               if sqr(Xk)+sqr(Yk)>=4 then k:=20;
            end;
               if (sqr(Xk)+sqr(Yk))<4 then
                  begin
                  inc(m);
                  Bmt.Canvas.Pixels[Nx,Ny]:=clBlack;
                  end;
      end;
   form2.Canvas.Draw(0,0,Bmt);
   finally
      Bmt.Free;
   end;
end;
```

Construction of the graph splits up into a number of stages:

1. sizing of construction area;
2. checking if the point c belongs to Mandelbrot set;
3. Mandelbrot set construction;
4. creation of filled-in Julia set when iterating the function $f(z) = z^2 + c$, where c belongs to Mandelbrot set, occurs on the chosen point (parameter c) in Mandelbrot set.

Boundary of filled-in Julia set will represent Julia set. On Figs. 1 and 2, arrows specify which Julia sets correspond to the allocated c points, located in Mandelbrot set.

When making computer experiments, students come to a conclusion that if the point c belongs to the leading part of Mandelbrot set, then the accompanying filled-in Julia will be a deformed circle. At that the function $f(z) = z^2 + c$ has only one attracting fixed point in only case when the point c belongs to the leading part of Mandelbrot set.

If the c point does not cease to be located in Mandelbrot set, then the accompanying Julia set is deformed, but remains a connected set. However, if the point c goes beyond Julia set, then the accompanying Julia set becomes discontinuous and thus non-connected.

Further students state a hypothesis that the leading part of Mandelbrot set will be a cardioid. And they confirm its correctness by proving the following:

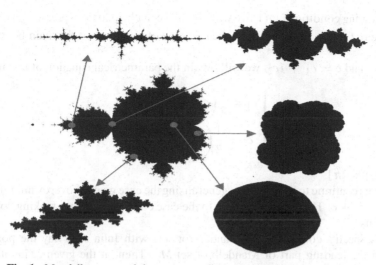

Fig. 1. Mandelbrot set and the corresponding connected filled-in Julia sets.

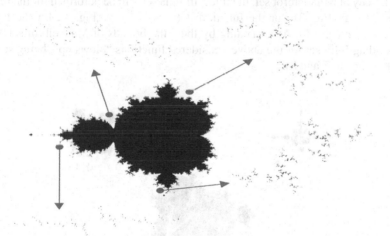

Fig. 2. Mandelbrot set and corresponding non fully-connected Julia sets.

Say z it is an attracting fixed point. Then two conditions are satisfied:

1. $f_c(z) = z^2 + c = z;$
2. $\left| f_c'(z) \right| = |2z| < 1.$

What follows from the condition 2, is that points of the boundary satisfy the ratio $2|z| = 1$. Or else $|z| = \frac{1}{2}$. Then variable z can be written down as

$$z = \frac{1}{2} e^{it}, \tag{1}$$

where $t \in [0;\ 2\pi]$.

Considering conditions 1, (1) we will obtain the mathematical expression $c = \frac{1}{2}e^{it} - \frac{1}{4}e^{2it}$ (where $t \in [0; \ 2\pi]$), which is the equation of boundary of the main body of the set M_2.

Having laid $c = c_1 + ic_2$, we will obtain the parametrical equation of this line:

$$\begin{cases} c_1 = \frac{1}{2}\left(\cos t - \dfrac{\cos 2t}{2}\right), \\ c_2 = \frac{1}{2}\left(\sin t - \dfrac{\sin 2t}{2}\right), \end{cases}$$

where $t \in [0; \ 2\pi]$.

Students continue to hypothesise, generalising the case given above, examining functions $f_p = z^p + c$. They notice analogy to the case considered above, making computer experiments.

Let us specify connection of Mandelbrot sets with Julia sets. Say the point c is located in the leading part of Mandelbrot set M_p. Then, at the given c, iterating the function $f_c(z) = z^p + c$, Julia set will be a deformed circle. When moving the c along the black body of Mandelbrot set, the filled-in Julia set will be deformed for the function $f_c(z) = z^4 + c$ (Fig. 3), for the function $f_c(z) = z^5 + c$ (Fig. 4), for the function $f_c(z) = z^6 + c$ (Fig. 5). At exceeding by the c the bounds of Mandelbrot set M_p the corresponding Julia set for the above-considered functions "blows up", being scattered as "dust" (Figs. 6, 7 and 8).

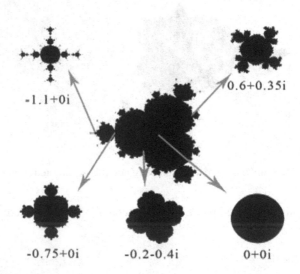

Fig. 3. Mandelbrot set and the corresponding connected filled-in Julia sets.

Let us note the most important properties of Mandelbrot set: Mandelbrot set serves as the indicator of Julia sets when iterating the function $f_c(z) = z^p + c$.

Computer experiments show that Mandelbrot set M_p generated by the polynomial $f_c(z) = z^p + c$, $p \geq 2$, consists of the dominating area made of adjoining areas

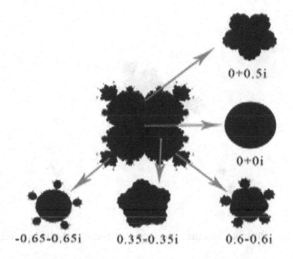

Fig. 4. Mandelbrot set and the corresponding connected filled-in Julia sets.

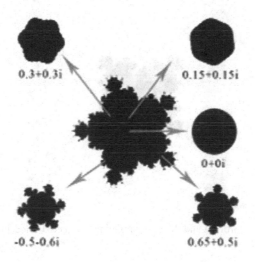

Fig. 5. Mandelbrot set and the corresponding connected filled-in Julia sets.

numbering $p - 1$ (for $p = 4$ Fig. 3, for $p = 5$ Fig. 4, for $p = 6$ Fig. 5). Let us note that the interior of this area corresponds to the points c for which the accompanying filled-in Julia set has the single attracting fixed point. Let us reveal the equation of boundary of this area.

Say z is an attracting fixed point. Then, two conditions are satisfied:

1. $f_c(z) = z^p + c = z$;
2. $\left| f_c'(z) \right| = \left| p z^{p-1} \right| < 1$.

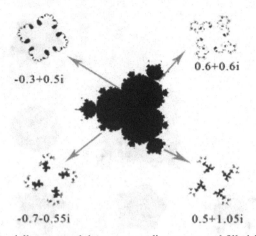

Fig. 6. Mandelbrot set and the corresponding connected filled-in Julia sets.

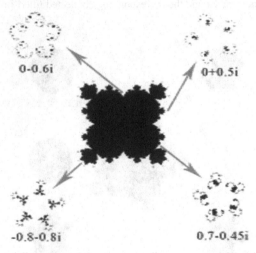

Fig. 7. Mandelbrot set and the corresponding connected filled-in Julia sets.

What follows from the condition 2, is that points of the boundary satisfy the ratio $p|z|^{p-1} = 1$. Or else $|z| = \frac{1}{p-\sqrt[1]{p}}$. Then variable z can be written down as

$$z = \frac{1}{p-\sqrt[1]{p}}e^{it}, \tag{2}$$

where $t \in [0; 2\pi]$.

Considering conditions 1, (2) and $z^p = \frac{e^{ipt}}{p-\sqrt[1]{p^p}} = \frac{e^{ipt}}{p\,p-\sqrt[1]{p}}$, we will obtain the mathematical expression

$$c = \frac{1}{p-\sqrt[1]{p}}e^{it} - \frac{1}{p-\sqrt[1]{p}}e^{pit} = \frac{1}{p-\sqrt[1]{p}}\left(e^{it} - \frac{e^{pit}}{p}\right)$$

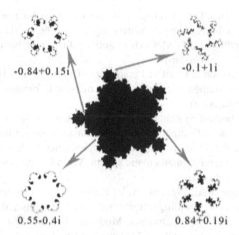

Fig. 8. Mandelbrot set and the corresponding connected filled-in Julia sets.

(where $t \in [0; \ 2\pi]$, $p \geq 2$), which is the equation of boundary of the main body of the set M_p.

Having laid $c = c_1 + ic_2$, we will obtain the parametrical equation of this line:

$$\begin{cases} c_1 = \dfrac{1}{p\sqrt[p]{p}}\left(\cos t - \dfrac{\cos pt}{p}\right) \\ c_2 = \dfrac{1}{p-\sqrt[p]{p}}\left(\sin t - \dfrac{\sin pt}{p}\right) \end{cases},$$

where $t \in [0; \ 2\pi]$, $p \geq 2$.

2 Conclusion

Thus, using information technologies and possibilities of evident modelling, students hypothesise and, confirming their hypotheses on the basis of analytical methods, they obtain general results, that positively affects development of their intuition which is the most important creative quality of the personality.

Acknowledgements. The research has been executed at the expense of a grant of the Russian scientific fund (project # 16-18-10304).

References

1. Anokhin, P.K.: Cybernetics of functional systems. In: Sudakov, K.V. (ed.) Selected Works. Medicine, Moscow (1998). (in Russian)
2. Lomov, B.F., Surkov, E.N.: Anticipation in Structure of Activity. Science Publisher, Moscow (1980). (in Russian)

3. Matytsina, T.N., Gladkova, E.A.: On one of the aspects of teaching theory of limits. Int. Sci. Rev. **7**(8), 8–10 (2015). https://elibrary.ru/item.asp?id=24209349. (in Russian)
4. Natyaganov, V.L., Luzhina, L.M.: Methods of Solving Tasks with Parameters: Manual. MSU Press, Moscow (2003). (in Russian)
5. Sekovanov, V.S.: Formation of Creative Personality of a Student of a Higher Education Institution When Studying Mathematics on the Basis of New Information Technologies. KSU, Kostroma (2004). (in Russian)
6. Sekovanov, V.S.: Methodical System of Formation of a University Student's Creativity in the Process of Teaching Fractal Geometry. KSU, Kostroma (2006). (in Russian)
7. Sekovanov, V.S.: Using new information technologies when designing anticipatory activity of university students attending mathematic syllabi. Vestnik Nekrasov Kostroma State Univ. **6**(1), 21–26 (2001). (in Russian)
8. Sekovanov, V.S., Ivkov, V.A., Piguzov, A.A., Fateev, A.S.: Execution of mathematics and information multistep task "Building a fractal set with L-systems and information technologies" as a means of creativity of students. Mod. Inf. Technol. IT-Educ. **12**(3-1), 118–125 (2016). https://elibrary.ru/item.asp?id=27411983. (in Russian)
9. Sekovanov, V., Pastukhov, A., Pikulev, A., Shestakov, A.: On Julia and Mandelbrot sets. Topical issues of teaching information and natural history disciplines. In: Materials of the XII All-Russia Scientific and Methodical Conference, pp. 102–107. KSU, Kostroma (2018). (in Russian)
10. Sekovanov, V.S.: Elements of the Theory of Discrete Dynamical Systems Theory: Manual. Lan Publishing, Saint Petersburg (2017). (in Russian)
11. Sekovanov, V.S.: Elements of the Theory of Fractal Sets, 2nd edn. KSU, Kostroma (2006). (in Russian)
12. Sekovanov, V.S., Ivkov, V.A.: Multi-stage mathematic and information task "Strange attractors". Vestnik Nekrasov Kostroma State Univ. **19**(5), 155–157 (2013). https://elibrary.ru/item.asp?id=20935969. (in Russian)
13. Sekovanov, V.S.: Elements of the Theory of Fractal Sets, 3rd edn. KSU, Kostroma (2010). (in Russian)
14. Sekovanov, V.S.: Elements of the Theory of Fractal Sets, 4th edn. KSU, Kostroma (2012). (in Russian)
15. Sekovanov, V. S.: On some discrete nonlinear dynamic systems. Fundam. Appl. Math. **21**(3), 185–199 (2016). https://elibrary.ru/item.asp?id=36548986. (in Russian)
16. Sergienko, E.A.: Anticipation in Early Human Ontogenesis. Nauka, Moscow (1992). (in Russian)
17. Smirnov, E.I.: Technology of Teaching Mathematics Utilising Visual Model. Ushinsky Yaroslavl State Pedagogical Unversity, Yaroslavl (1998). (in Russian)

Information and Communication Technologies as a Phenomenon and Its Impact on Goals and Quality of Education

Magomed Abdurazakov[1](✉) ⓘ, Tatyana Fomicheva[2] ⓘ, Alibek Dzamyhov[1] ⓘ,
Marina Dzamyhova[3] ⓘ, and Ekaterina Tumbasova[4] ⓘ

[1] Karachay-Cherkess State University UD Aliyev, Lenin St. 29, Karachaevsk 369202, Russia
abdurazakov@inbox.ru, dzamyhov63@mail.ru
[2] Financial University under the Government of the Russian Federation,
Leningradsky Prospekt 49, Moscow 125993, Russia
tatlfom@mail.ru
[3] North-Caucasian Federal University, Pushkin St. 1, Stavropol 355017, Russia
sgu.marishka@mail.ru
[4] Nosov Magnitogorsk State Technical University, Lenin Ave. 38, Magnitogorsk 455000, Russia
kate6979@yandex.ru

Abstract. One of the most important factors for improving the quality of education and the successful achievement of modern educational results is the use of innovative forms and means of education in the educational process. The work notes that fundamentally new educational results, relevant to the needs of the modern education system, can be achieved only by new educational activities and support of new types of educational activities of subjects of education. Interaction of subjects of education in information and educational environment is a feature of contemporary training prosses.

Being a social and cultural phenomenon, Internet-, Web-, Smart- technologies as a result of the development of information and communication technology, are becoming increasingly significant in modern information society changes, have a huge impact on the formation and development of the information and educational space. In this regard, the article deals with qualitative changes in education in the information society under the influence of modern information and communication technologies, media technologies, SMART technologies.

The phenomenon of media culture (personal media culture of a subject of education) is relatively new for the analysis of cultural aspects of the information society in the information digital era and the range of discussion issues goes well beyond this paper. However, it should be emphasized that the influence of media culture leads to the formation of a particular type of mass consciousness in society - mass media consciousness. In this perspective, the issues of the formation of modern media culture, the awareness of which will help to preserve humanistic ideals in the age of digital technology, are outlined. All these circumstances encouraged the authors to express their opinion in this paper and discuss issues related to the expansion of educational opportunities and the didactic potential of information technologies and the degree of their impact on goals and quality of education, educational activities of subjects of education.

© Springer Nature Switzerland AG 2020
V. Sukhomlin and E. Zubareva (Eds.): SITITO 2018, CCIS 1201, pp. 69–77, 2020.
https://doi.org/10.1007/978-3-030-46895-8_5

Keywords: Media environment · Communication · Social culture · SMART-education

1 Introduction

In the modern understanding, education is a teaching process and its results, where the process involves educating and development of an individual, his instruction and parenting. That is, education is the transfer, assimilation and personal "adoption" of experience, knowledge, skills, culture of previous generations by a new generation for its subsequent use and expansion in accordance with the goals of society and its development requirements. In this regard, the following *educational goals* can be identified:

- maintenance of the continuity of the society reproduction in its new subjects formed in the education system and the objects of the social environment;
- historical security of the society – continuous existence and development: the resources and knowledge of society lose their value without being acquired by new generation;
- the formation of an individual who is capable and directed at solving socially significant issues and problems;
- the formation of a harmoniously developed personality, capable of perceiving and developing social culture, intellectual and spiritual values of society;
- formation of the subject's ability to adapt to changing environmental conditions, to orient in the sphere of social, economic, scientific, educational, industrial and other relations.

Education is in the stage of updating and the development of content and methodology, conditioned by the objective grounds:

- Change of epochs and social economic structure, resulting in change of conditions and priorities, change of culture, worldview.
- Change in the state of the subject of education under the influence of the environment, the general social cultural and scientific and educational development of modern society.
- Changing the environment under the influence of global informatization, which has become the medium of the postindustrial society.
- Changing the content and methodology of education in accordance with changing its conditions.

Along with the growing need for continuous education, there is a growing trend towards the formation of *international educational systems* of various types and various goals. There is a process of internationalization of education, not only in content, but also in teaching methods and organizational forms.

2 Problem Statement

In the information-digital era, information and pedagogical technologies are being integrated into education, which enables the adaptation and formation of the educational process of the student. In particular, UNESCO [1] documents state that *digital pedagogy* [2] (we would call it instrumental didactics) is becoming the key to effective and efficient use of ICT, involving critical use of electronic components and open educational resources [3] in order to improve the efficiency of education and achieve the proper quality of learning results.

In particular, the UNESCO document notes that the key to effective and efficient use of ICT is becoming a digital pedagogy, which implies the critical use of electronic components and to improve the efficiency of education and achieve quality learning outcomes.

Naturally, the task becomes complex and difficult and at the same time extremely relevant. It becomes the subject of discussions [4–11].

There is a need to study the degree of influence of ICT on goals and quality of education, the formation of the personal culture of the student and problems of media education, media competence and media culture of subjects of education.

3 Research Issue

The topic of the discussion is the process of integration of information and pedagogical technologies, the practice of implementation and development of digital pedagogy in education. The problem is the definition and differentiation of sources and the degree of influence of IT-technologies on the goals and quality of education.

There are also *significant issues* on the characteristic feature of the information society *"social culture, information culture"*. A complex, system-based formation of the information culture of subjects of education is required. It has not been formulated (as a social and educational factor) in the system of information education and it has not been maintained by the content and means of teaching computer science.

4 Research Questions

Educational resources, information, electronic educational resources (EER) should be viewed from the standpoint of *informatization of education* as a purposeful and specific projection of the informatization of society on the education sector. First of all, it is necessary to:

1. Consider information educational resources (IER) in an integrated relationship, systematized; to classify them according to uniformity and specification.
2. Describe information educational resources as products of creative labor, information products in the aspect of its production and consumption, in the aspect of separation of information and pedagogical work, in the aspect of information rights, duties, responsibilities.
3. Determine the place of IER as an integrated information and educational resource in the system of information education.

5 Research Methods

The following *methodological approaches* are used: systemic, informational, sociocultural, personal, ontological.

6 Findings

Education becomes an instrument of interpenetration not only of knowledge and technology, but also of capital, an instrument for competition for the market, solving geopolitical tasks. This is the result and inevitable consequence of the introduction and implementation of a system information approach in the field of education. This is the development of the *"ontological dimension of education"* [12].

Informatization of society (the world community) has become a global phenomenon, changing the way of life, culture and world vision of peoples, science and manufacture, reflected in the nature of relationships, communication and interaction, in social norms and law. Global information exchange and interaction in a unified information environment, formed under the influence of information, create favorable conditions for the development of integration processes. Inter-system interaction is supplemented by the interaction of national information systems.

Informatization in the social (sociocultural) aspect is an objective factor in the development of society and its social and information environment, caused by the rapid development of the scientific and cognitive sphere, computer science and its applied field, computerization. It is focused on the development of society, its resources and productive forces, the nature of its activities, culture. It is oriented towards informatization (in its objective and fundamental meaning) of cognition processes and is itself being implemented in these processes.

The consequence of informatization in the social aspect is not only a change in production, but also *social cultural relations*. A new stage in the development of society and the whole of civilization, a new stage in the development of culture - the *information culture* has started.

Social and cultural informatization is a complex of naturally interrelated subjects and objects, processes and relationships, i.e. an open and evolving social and information system. This system is an objective factor of the social environment, developed in accordance with its conditions and itself significantly modifying these conditions.

Therefore, the informatization of education is not only the informatization of the educational environment and the educational infrastructure, but also, first of all, the solution of all problems of information cognitive activities, information interaction of subjects of education, which implies its penetration into all pores of the educational process and the sphere it forms.

The following definition has special significance for the suggested research:

Informatization is a "systemic activity process of acquiring information as a resource of management and development with the help of computer science tools with the goal of creating an information society and on this basis" maintaining the progress of civilization", [13].

Following this definition, informatization of education can be understood as a universal means of its *modernization*, development, improvement with the goal of transforming it into a state corresponding to the *information society*. This level of education is often called *noospheric*.

As a consequence, the *quality of education is determined by the degree of its relevance to the information society*. Due to the fact that, like any other correspondence, it involves the implementation of direct and inverse links, it should be considered in the following aspects:

- Education should inherit the characteristic features of the information society and, firstly, in regard to knowledge and cognition, as its determining properties, its social culture, as well as its resource and technological equipment and infrastructure.
- Education must meet the requirements of the development of the information society, go slightly ahead and, developing itself, develop society.
- That is, the information society and its formation are mutually defined and mutually express each other:
- The Information Society is a scientific, technological and socio-cultural base that ensures the noospheric development of education.
- Education predetermines the state of society as an information society and develops it during its own development.

The information sphere of the society is not only the informatization industry, it is also the social-information interaction in which all information processes are fulfilled. Optimization of this sphere involves availability not only of a system of legal norms and the corresponding organization, but also of a high level of *information culture* of subjects of interaction, including their legal culture.

The culture of the information society is determined by its information worldview, the level of intellectual development, knowledge and technology; spiritual culture - information morality, the state of the humanitarian sphere.

It is the high level of the information and legal culture of the society and its subjects that characterizes the state of society as an information society. This is not only another formation, but also a *new level of civilization*. "The concept of the information society reflects, in our opinion, not a formational, but a civilizational aspect of social development, [14]. We still aspire to this level, the society aspires, therefore, education aspires.

The information society with the accelerating growth of knowledge and technology change, has received the most important task of generational change, educating people able to perceive the experience and knowledge of mankind, provide further development. The higher the level of informatization, the greater the investment of resources, intellectual forces, knowledge into the education system.

The Information Society requires a comprehensive, systemically interconnected subject teaching, a logically complete information education.

Education must become qualitatively different:

Firstly, modern education should be *continuous*, providing for the possibility of continuing education and self-education "of the individual throughout the economically active life, synchronized with production tasks and changing in the course of life by the needs of the individual in self-development, [15]. The main result of general education (secondary and higher) is the development of the individual, the ability of a person to self-education and self-instruction.

Secondly, the requirement for the continuity of human education means that it is not the specific knowledge and skills (they can quickly become obsolete in the developing information environment), in the forefront, but super-subject, general scientific knowledge, general educational skills and competencies, knowledge of universal methods of activities and the ability to implement them. Therefore, general education, especially higher education, should become *universal*, while remaining specialized, and therefore fundamental. It must provide a person not only with opportunities for adaptation in a wide range of activities, but also, if necessary, the ability to work in the related field of personal activity, professional development, retraining.

Global informatization itself poses many problems for society, which together with its development also become global and difficult to solve. They are problems of information and legal culture, regulation of information relationships on the principles of law and universal morality, the problem of information security and its provision. A declaration of the right, along with a control system and appropriate repressive measures to solve these problems is insufficient.

The development of the informatization industry entails an increase in the role of automated intellectual systems, artificial intelligence systems with bases of formal knowledge. There is a convergence of natural and artificial intelligence knowledge, which has both positive and negative impact (elements of technological development and robotization of thinking).

The information society is characterized not only as a *knowledge society*, but primarily as a cognition society, where "the labor processes are merged into a single whole, new knowledge is obtained for solving production problems and generating new knowledge,… the cognitive activity of man becomes the determining factor of development… Personality becomes the bearer of a unique "set" of knowledge, skills and abilities", [15].

This statement leads to the conclusion that knowledge is not only a starting point, a means and a product of cognition, but also the object of production in the industry of the society (information and general). Therefore, cognition appears as an integrated process of *consumption of knowledge* (as a result of its acquisition, assimilation) and the *knowledge production* (in the processes of research, processing in artificial intelligence systems). This increases the social significance of knowledge and cognition as social phenomena.

Since the main characteristic of the information society is "knowledge", then the corresponding education should inherit this property, specifically express it in its quality. Knowledge is the main and most important resource of education, a means of its development. But the main task of education is not the production, but the reproduction of knowledge in personal systems, in the efficient and rational transfer of knowledge and its absorption and "appropriation" of the recipients of this transfer.

Consequently, the quality of education is determined by the *quality of its cognition by the subjects*:

– Cognition of the world, nature, society, methods and means of this knowledge.
– Cognition of man as an element of the world and a member of society.

– Self-knowledge of man as a subject, individual, personality in the context of his socialization.

The information society with the accelerating growth of knowledge and technology change, has received the most important task of generational change, educating people able to perceive the experience and knowledge of mankind, provide further development. The higher the level of informatization, the greater the investment of resources, intellectual forces, knowledge into the education system.

Another important characteristic of the information society, without which the society does not exist, is "social culture", expressed in personal culture, information culture, in the personal development of its subjects. Consequently, the quality of education is also expressed by this characteristic. It manifests itself in the results of the formation and development of personal culture, information culture, as well as the personal *culture of knowledge and culture of cognition* as expressions of integrated quality combined with the characteristics of "knowledge", "cognition", "socioculture".

The information society and the corresponding noospheric education are also characterized by a high level of development of information and communication technologies or information and communication technologies, since these two characteristics of technologies form a coherent logical whole in it. An *information educational environment* (EEE) is gaining an increasingly important role in education, where information, including electronic educational resources of open access and technologies that provide this access, as well as its organization and management are concentrated. This is an expansion of educational interaction up to information and educational interaction through communication technologies.

The main objective of the information educational environment is its positive impact on education and subjects of education, the result of which should be their compliance with the state and requirements of the information society. That is, the goals of education are inherited by its information educational environment and are achieved in an indirect way.

Modern information cognitive environment mostly includes *media technologies* and electronic media resources, as well as means of their reproduction, display, and perception support. All together they create a *media environment* for society and education. As a result, media education and media education, media competence and media culture of its subjects have become qualitative signs of noospheric education.

Media education is the formation of media competence and personal media culture. Media education includes media teaching and education through media environment on the basis of media competence and media culture of subjects received in media education. In fact, media education is a new form, a media level of education.

Products of the new technological wave on the basis of nano, cyber and other innovative technologies have become Smart technologies, Smart devices, Smart resources integrated in *Smart systems*, [16–20]. These systems are based on "smart" devices with their own built-in artificial intelligence, which transform interaction in the media environment into an intellectual one. They "smart" devices with their own built-in artificial intelligence, transforming the interaction in the media space.

That is, Smart-environment, generated by these "smart" devices and systems, is a Smart-representation of the media environment. Smart technologies allow "to use an individual training schedule, to maintain a constant contact of the student with the teacher, to achieve a lasting assimilation of knowledge," [18].

Smart-systems have had such a significant impact on society and education that the terms "Smart-society" and "Smart-education" came into use, meaning their new types, new quality levels. However, this is not quite true: it is just an expression of the qualitative level of technology in society and in education, but not their expression. The society remained informational, education - corresponding, in its new development state. That is, SMART-education is a state of *media education*, and an educational SMART-resource is a kind of media electronic-educational resource.

Smart-technologies and Smart-systems determine the opportunities for the transition of the educational and training process to a new quality, but they themselves do not create this transition. They only contribute to the acquisition of new qualities by education, as well as by society.

Even the best and highest level information and communication technologies, media technologies, Smart technologies are just a "quantity" that can "turn to quality", or rather, with the appropriate growth and perfection create the opportunity to transition to a new quality. This, of course, does not attribute lesser importance for education and its media environment, as well as their impact on the personal development of subjects of education.

7   Conclusion

Thus, a qualitative expression of the impact of information and communication technologies on education is:

– Information content, media content of education.
– A relatively large personal orientation, an orientation toward the socialization of the subject of education as a person, as a subject of the informative cognitive social cultural environment, the development of personal information culture.
– Focus on self-organization, self-management of the subject in information and educational interaction, self-development.

SMART-education allows expanding opportunities for the development of personality in solving these problems in the changing world. It forms the creative potential of the future specialist, so vital in modern conditions [17, p. 21].

References

1. Daniel, S.J.: ICTs in Global Learning/Teaching/Training: Policy Brief. UNESCO Institute for Information Technologies in Education, Moscow (2012). http://iite.unesco.org/publications/3214713
2. Moscow International Education Fair 2018, MMCO-EXPO 2018, 19–21 April 2018. (in Russian). http://mmco-expo.ru

3. World Open Educational Resources (OER) Congress: 2012 Paris OER Declaration, Paris, 20–22 June 2012. UNESCO, Paris (2012). http://www.unesco.org/new/fileadmin/MULTIMEDIA/HQ/CI/CI/pdf/Events/English_Paris_OER_Declaration.pdf
4. Abdurazakov, M.M., Aziyev, R.A.-S., Muhidinov, M.G.: The principles of constructing a methodical system for teaching computer science in general educational school. Espacios **38**(40), 2 (2017)
5. Bruner, J.S.: The Culture of Education. Harvard University Press, Cambridge (2006)
6. Lapchik, M.P. (ed.): Contemporary problems of informatization of education. OmGPU, Omsk (2017). (in Russian)
7. Colin, K.K.: Information technologies in the system of global safety: new priorities. Mod. Inf. Technol. IT-Educ. **11**(1), 14–21 (2015). (in Russian). https://elibrary.ru/item.asp?id=25024552
8. Korotenkov, Yu.G.: Training in informatics and ICT in modern education. In: Sukhomlin, V.A. (ed.) Modern Information Technology and IT-Education, pp. 43–49. MSU, Moscow (2016). (in Russian). https://elibrary.ru/item.asp?id=28413000
9. Tikhomirov, V.P., Dneprovskaya, N.V.: Smart education as main paradigm of development of information society. Mod. Inf. Technol. IT-Educ. **11**(1), 9–13 (2015). (in Russian). https://elibrary.ru/item.asp?id=25024551
10. Kudryavtseva, M.E. (ed.): Humanitarian aspects of education, creativity and personal freedom. Direct Media, Moscow (2014). (in Russian)
11. Guidelines for working with open educational resources (OER) in higher education. The UNESCO Institute for information technologies in education (2013). (in Russian). https://iite.unesco.org/ru/news/639152-ru
12. Birich, I.A.: Synergetical tasks of education. Philos. Sci. (1), 39–54. Gumanitary, Moscow (2010). (in Russian)
13. Ursul, A.D.: Informatization of society and the transition to sustainable development of civilization. Inf. Soc. (1–3), 35–45 (1993). (in Russian). http://emag.iis.ru/arc/infosoc/emag.nsf/BPA/bae746f66def051bc32576b100308172
14. Sokolova, I.V.: Social Informatics and Sociology: Problems and Prospects of Interconnection. Soyuz, Moscow (1999). (in Russian)
15. Karpenko, M.P.: Education for innovative economy. In: Intellectual Economy - The Basis of Sustainable Development of Russia. Inforizdat, Moscow (2010). (in Russian)
16. Abdurazakov, M.M., Korotenkov, Yu.G, Muhidinov, M.G.: Educational space representation in cyberspace. SHS Web Conf. **29**, 01001 (2016). https://doi.org/10.1051/shsconf/20162901001
17. Gonick, I.L., et al.: Innovative modernization of Russia and the new mission of universities in the Russian conditions of globalization of educational space. VolgGTU, Volgograd (2013). (in Russian)
18. Tikhomirov, V.P.: World on the way to Smart education. New opportunities for development. Open Educ. (3), 22–28 (2011). (in Russian). https://elibrary.ru/item.asp?id=17092157
19. Zavrazhin, A.V., et al.: SMART: the contents and features of the penetration in modern society. Macy's, Moscow (2015). (in Russian)
20. Skills for Smart Industrial Specialisation and Digital Transformation. Interim Report. Publications Office of the European Union, Luxembourg (2018). https://doi.org/10.2826/822644

Fuzzy Models of Educational Process Management: Digital Transformation

Sergey Kramarov[1]([✉]) [iD], Vladimir Khramov[2] [iD], and Valeriya Bezuevskaya[1] [iD]

[1] Surgut State University, Lenin Ave. 1, Surgut 628412, Russia
maoovo@yandex.ru
[2] Southern University (IMBL), M. Nagibin Ave. 33a/47, Rostov-on-Don 344068, Russia

Abstract. The approach to the formation of a multidimensional digital model of the learning environment using the mathematical unit of differential equations of the first order, implemented on the system of systems principle is considered. It is shown that within the framework of digitalization of the main components of this environment, bifurcation analysis can be carried out to detect fuzzy and under-defined learning results that do not depend directly on either the teachers or the learner. In other words, it has been found the source of the strange attractors of the learning environment as a complex nonlinear open system, which essentially depends on the initial conditions. Such situations may arise while simultaneous using old, well-established teaching methods and some new digital tools to form knowledge of learners. The results of modeling of such situations are discussed, approaches to neutralize this kind of fuzziness are considered.

Keywords: Digital transformation · Knowledge · Self-organization · System of Systems

1 Introduction

Digital transformation of education is based on modern digital information resources, that is translated into digital code information in the form of data, databases and software products, which is processed using computer technology [1, 2].

The purpose of creating the architecture of the digital school is creation and implementation of a model of the educational process, which will not only provide the opportunity to design and build knowledge of students, long-term forecast of learning results, but also the formation of some other important characteristics of this knowledge.

The instruments of digital transformation of the modern school are, first of all, technologies in the field of data processing: artificial intelligence, fuzzy and hazy computing, quantum and supercomputer technologies, cross-cutting, image recognition and identification, blockchain technology, artificial neural systems and also mathematical modeling.

From a mathematical point of view, digital models of educational process control lead to nonlinear differential equations (or their systems), the study of which, recently, is paid more attention [6, 9]. Quite serious results have already been obtained in this direction [7, 10, 11].

© Springer Nature Switzerland AG 2020
V. Sukhomlin and E. Zubareva (Eds.): SITITO 2018, CCIS 1201, pp. 78–85, 2020.
https://doi.org/10.1007/978-3-030-46895-8_6

2 Modeling of the Educational Process on the Principles of Self-organization

Considering that the educational process is a very complex and difficult to formalize phenomenon, one group of authors limited its verbal description [3, 11], the other one [12] considers the performance of students in high school depending on the school training and psychophysical characteristics of the student, while using regression models to determine the dependence of performance on indicators such as test data, data on school performance, etc. In a number of works [for example, 5, 8–10] the general cybernetic model of process of interaction of the teacher and the student is applied.

In this model, the learning process is represented as the interaction of the control system of the teacher (S_t) and the controlled system-student (Ss) in the conditions of random interactions (x_i) and various types of control (a_J), and the purpose of control is to select such control actions (z_k), which would provide the student's reaction to the control action (y_m) in given area Y. The process is considered on a small period of time. However, the requirements of this model, such as pre-obtaining of the necessary parameters and its complication, as a result of generalization, often lead to difficulties in its using.

Even a brief analysis of the papers that have appeared recently [12] makes it is possible to draw the following conclusion: despite the rather large number of externally diverse models, there is still no sufficiently universal model, or a system of interrelated models that would allow to describe the educational process at the University with an acceptable degree of reliability, analyze and predict it, check and evaluate possible management decisions.

3 Models as Objects of Cognitive Space

The term *Cognitive space*, which originally appeared in linguistics, is used in other subject areas, including, even in the first place, in the systems of knowledge formation. At the same time, cognitive space is "an operational self-generating and self-regulating system in which human communicative experience is formed, developed and transformed" [1].

The term *Cognitive space* can be used for the interests of ensuring cognitive interoperability in the formation of information educational environment. The concept of cognitive space allows to take into account the multifactorial nature of the interaction of the individual systems being studied and researched in the organization and management of the educational process [12, 14], the concept of *SoS* (System of Systems) for which the system of reference, thought processes, quantitative analysis, tools and design methods are incomplete and/or illegible.

Systems of systems [16] is a branch of system engineering, dealing with such a system, individual parts of which one can exist independently, as a rule, have been developed independently of each other, and thus represent a complete target system. However, from these autonomous and independent systems it is necessary to make a system with useful emergent properties. However, from these autonomous and independent systems it is necessary to make the system with useful emergent properties.

Regarding the systems of knowledge formation, we note the prospects of the following types of SoS:

– *directed*, where there is a dominant moderator who has the right to issue orders to the component systems and manage their resources (for example, the Ministry of education at different levels);
– *acknowledged*, where although there is a dominant moderator, but having the opportunity to only recommend the component systems to self-change according to the chosen architecture (for example, the system of private educational institutions);
– *collaborative*, where the systems coordinate their actions with each other on each emerging problem, but there is no single moderator, project manager or similar dedicated management body [14].

This approach complements the term *Cognitive space* with the aspect of situational response to search for coordinated images of the information they operate in the course of their activities.

3.1 The Uncertainty of the Basic Information

Considering the problem of uncertainty at the main levels of obtaining and processing information for each type of uncertainty, it is necessary to implement:

– search for the appropriate mathematical description and representation of a particular type of uncertainty;
– choice of mathematical apparatus, with which it is possible to control (adjust parameters) model with the selected type of uncertainty;
– finding an effective way to measure real uncertainty in any situation under analysis;
– development of a methodology of generation of adequate models for real objects and monitoring processes to select the uncertainty indicators that can be calculated.

4   Mathematical Modeling and Self-organization

In a brief preface to his book "From existing to emerging" [13] I. Prigozhin characterizes the current state of mathematical modeling from different sides. He describes the main reason for the new approach in modeling, gives a new look at the problem of time and related problems of modeling non-equilibrium processes of emergence and development. Without going into more detail on the general problems discussed in [3], we note that the new modeling that has arisen at the intersection of science, primarily in biology and chemistry, from a mathematical point of view, leads to the solution of the equation of the form [7, 11]

$$\frac{\partial X_i}{\partial t} = V(X_1, X_2, \dots X_N) + \frac{\partial^2 X_i}{\partial r^2}, \quad i = \overline{1, N} \tag{1}$$

Where X_i, for example, in the study of chemical reactions, is the concentration of the component. Moreover, the dependence (1) is equally effectively applied, both in the modeling in mechanics and in the modeling of social, biological and other processes, thus being an evolutionary principle of development.

It is obvious that the comments made here should be taken into account when modeling the educational process, because they are of a General nature.

5   Computer Modeling of the Functioning of Private Educational Institution

In many cases, the behavior of the training system, close to the instability points, may depend on the behavior of very few variables, even it is possible to say that the behavior of individual parts of the system is simply determined by these few factors [6, 8]. These factors, called order parameters, play a dominant role in the concept of synergetics. They "subordinate" separate parts, i.e. determine the behavior of these parts. The relationship between the order parameters and the individual parts of the system implements the principle of subordination. Instead of describing the behavior of a complex system by describing individual parts of it, it is possible to have deal only with order parameters. Thus, a huge information compression is provided.

As an illustration, we consider a typical educational institution, forming an ergatic system, the process of functioning, in the first approximation, which can be described by three parameters of the order: X_1 – number of employees (including teachers and managers), X_2 – the number of tasks to be solved (for the training of specialists at all levels), X_3 – the number of (technical) instruments at the disposal of the enterprise. The main proportions of the problem can be briefly described as follows:

1. The rate of increase in the number of staff X_1 is proportional to the number of tasks minus a certain percentage α retired ones, and also taking into account the share of work γ, performed by automatic (automated) means.
2. The rate of X_2 tasks receipt, solved by private educational institution, is proportional to its importance, related to X_1 staff and X_3 technical equipment, and can be reduced considering the influence of promotional activities θ.
3. The rate of replacement (modernization) of equipment of technical means X_3 is proportional to the solved tasks (their quantity and quality, complexity and commercial attractiveness) X_2 and the number of employees X_1, using this equipment, taking into account the share μ dismantled (written off) equipment. Then the system of differential equations describing the life cycle of the enterprise [9, 13] can have the form (1):

$$\frac{\partial X_1}{\partial t} = - \alpha X_1 + \beta X_2 - \gamma X_3;$$

$$\frac{\partial X_2}{\partial t} = \eta X_1 X_3 - \theta \sin \lambda t; \qquad (2)$$

$$\frac{\partial X_3}{\partial t} = \rho(X_1 + X_2) - \mu X_3;$$

The results of the numerical research of this system of equations by instruments of the Maple package are shown in Fig. 1. It turned out that private educational institution, as the system, is quite sensitive to the dynamics of the market, is forced to flexibly change both its ergatic and technical components. At the same time, there are conditions under which sustainable work is possible, achieved already in several production cycles (Fig. 1a, b, c, g, h). However, it is possible that the conditions under which private educational institution either works unstable, "falls into chaos" (Fig. 1e, f), becomes unprofitable and forced to curtail production - degrades (Fig. 1d).

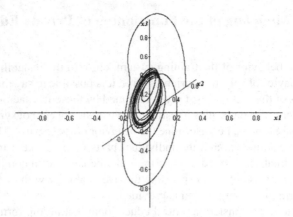

Fig. 1a. Attractors of the system (2) with $\alpha, \beta, \gamma, \eta, \rho = 0.1, \theta = 0.2, \ \lambda = 0.7, \ \mu = 0.2.$

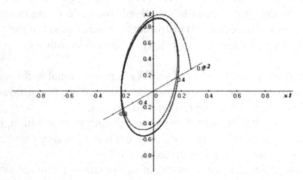

Fig. 1b. Attractors of the system (2) with $\alpha, \beta, \gamma, \eta, \rho = 0.1, 0 \leq \theta \leq 0.1, \ \lambda = 0.7, \ \mu = 0.2.$

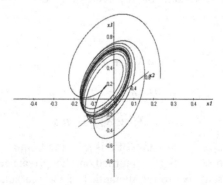

Fig. 1c. Attractors of the system (2) with $\alpha, \beta, \gamma, \eta, \rho = 0.1, \theta = 0.2, \ \lambda = 0.6, \ \mu = 0.2.$

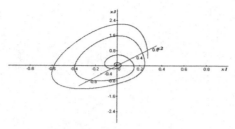

Fig. 1d. Attractors of the system (2) with $\alpha, \beta, \gamma, \eta, \rho = 0.1, \theta \leq 0, \lambda = 0.7, \mu = 0.2$.

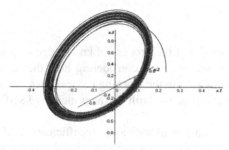

Fig. 1e. Attractors of the system (2) with $\alpha, \beta, \gamma, \eta, \rho = 0.1, \theta = 0.2, \lambda = 0.5, \mu = 0.2$.

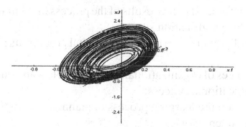

Fig. 1f. Attractors of the system (2) with $\alpha, \beta, \gamma, \eta, \rho = 0.1, \theta = 0.2, \lambda = 0.49, \mu = 0.2$.

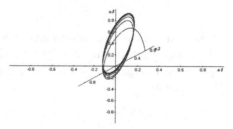

Fig. 1g. Attractors of the system (2) with $\alpha, \beta, \gamma, \eta, \rho = 0.1, \theta = 0.2, \lambda = 0.5, \mu \geq 0.3$.

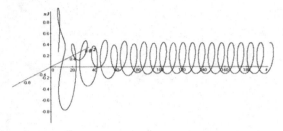

Fig. 1h. Attractors of the system (2) with $\alpha, \beta, \gamma, \eta, \rho = 0.1, \theta = 0.1, \lambda = 0.7, \mu = 0.2$.

6 Conclusion

The main mathematical model of the process of knowledge acquisition and estimation of residual knowledge of the learners, considering how the accumulation of knowledge trainees and their scattering in the learning process, were presented. The proposed mathematical models of this process, built on the principle of self-organization, allow:

- with proper selection of empirical indicators (coefficients) and with sufficient reliability of the initial information about the educational process to obtain information about the process of assimilation and dispersion of knowledge by students during the semester, month, week, etc.;
- implement long-term forecast of the results of the process of assimilation of knowledge at the beginning of the examination session;
- to assess the degree of organization of the educational process, its intensity, uniformity, etc.;
- predict the consequences of organizational, methodological and other decisions related to changes in the educational process;
- to analyze the impact on the learning process of planned and unplanned separation of students from independent work;
- to optimize the educational process according to its main indicators: the volume of educational information, time of independent work, the degree of self-organization, etc.

The information about the educational process obtained with the help of a mathematical model enables the management to make the right decisions to eliminate the shortcomings made in its planning, to organize the educational process in accordance with the tasks and to predict its results.

References

1. Fedinskiy, Y.: Great Regulatory and Technical Dictionary: 15000 Terms. Astrel, AST, Moscow (2007). (in Russian)
2. Kramarov, S.: System approach in solution of the problems of informatization of the regional education system. In: Papers of Southern (Rostov) Branch of Informatization of Education, pp. 15–27. Rostov State Pedagogical University, Rostov-on-Don (2006). (in Russian)

3. Gurevich, L.: Cognitive Space of Metacommunication. Publisher of IGLU, Irkutsk (2009). (in Russian)
4. Prigozhin, I.: From Existing to Emerging. KomKniga, Moscow (2006). (in Russian)
5. Cvetkova, M.: SMART education as a perspective for systemic change of the school in the digital era. Prof.-Oriented Sch. **4**(2), 18–21 (2016). https://doi.org/10.12737/19621. (in Russian)
6. Solodova, E.: Problems of education and new models of educational processes, Moscow (2016). (in Russian). http://spkurdyumov.ru/education/problemy-obrazovaniya-i-novye-modeli-obrazovatelnyx-processov
7. Khramov, V., Vitchenko, O., Tkachuk, E.: Intellectual methods, models and algorithms of educational process organization in technical University. RGUPS, Rostov-on-Don (2015). (in Russian)
8. Khramov, V.: Information support of meaning-forming technologies in the university. In: The Materials of Scientific and Practical Conference "Informatization of Education - 2010", pp. 323–327. KSU, Kostroma (2010). (in Russian). https://elibrary.ru/item.asp?id=36338280
9. Abakumova, I., Khramov, V.: The architecture of the personal-semantic space and psychoenergetically description of the process of self-organization. North-Caucasian Psychol. Bull. **5**(2), 5–10 (2007). (in Russian). https://elibrary.ru/item.asp?id=36304772
10. Khramov, V.: Information aggregating as a problem of personal self-orginazation. Russ. Psychol. J. **4**(4), 9–21 (2007). (in Russian). https://elibrary.ru/item.asp?id=16974213
11. Khramov, V., Golubenko, E., Smolina, O.: Synergetic approach to the formation of research and teaching staff of the university. In: The Collection Contains Materials of Scientific and Practical Conference "Achievements of High School – 2013" (2013). Collection of papers, Sophia, Bulgaria **21**: 58–63
12. Khramov, V.: Theory of information processes and systems: educational manual. RGUPS, Rostov-on-Don (2011). (in Russian)
13. Andrews, J.G., McLone, R.L.: Mathematical Modelling. Butterworth-Heinemann, London (1976)
14. Jamshidi, M.: System of Systems Engineering: Innovations for the Twenty-First Century. Wiley, Hoboken (2008)

E-learning and IT in Education

Model Shaper Competencies Trainees on the Basis of Block Alternative Networks

Valentin Nechaev[✉] (iD) and Alisa Bogoradnikova (iD)

MIREA - Russian Technological University, Vernadsky Prospekt 78, Moscow 119454, Russia
nechaev@mirea.ru, its.kafedra@yandex.ru

Abstract. The report considers the task of organizing a set of competencies defined by the FSES HE, the University, as well as the employer. This approach makes it possible to consider the needs of key stakeholders in the training of young professionals. Various purposefully formed categories of competencies are considered as a multidimensional complex, and each aspect is represented by attributes, as well as their qualitative and quantitative values. The General architecture of the complex of competencies is formed in the form of a tree of competencies, isostructural corresponding to the tree of content of the discipline. To solve this problem, we propose to use the method of block alternative networks. According to this method, each aspect of competencies is represented in the form of a network block, and the set of blocks forms a complete network – abbreviated BAN. The formation of individual competencies is carried out in the form of a route to the BAN in accordance with the individual learning path, synthesized or given a priori. Applicability theoretical provisions are considered on the example of the embodiment of the synthesis of individual competence trajectory (TIC) of the discipline of the working curriculum, implementing the FSES HE the direction of training 09.03.04 "Software engineering" (bachelor level) in the profile "Engineering of intelligent software systems and complexes".

Keywords: Individual learning paths · Competence · Educational content · Block alternative network · Elementary block of alternatives

1 Introduction

The task of improving the quality of training has a number of difficulties associated with the modernization of education, the transition to a two-level system (bachelor and master) and the requirements of the Federal state educational standards of higher education (FSES HE). The practical implementation of these requirements includes the problem of individualization of the educational process based on the competence approach.

Research and development of methods focused on the individualization of learning using the competence approach, therefore, is an urgent task. The content of the report reflects some of the results of the author's work aimed at solving the above problems, as well as the corresponding structuring of educational and teaching materials in the system of information educational resources.

© Springer Nature Switzerland AG 2020
V. Sukhomlin and E. Zubareva (Eds.): SITITO 2018, CCIS 1201, pp. 89–97, 2020.
https://doi.org/10.1007/978-3-030-46895-8_7

2 Competence Approach

There are many interpretations of the concept of competence. Some define competencies as personal characteristics, others as willingness and ability to perform tasks, and others as areas of responsibility or performance.

Competence (specialist) – is the ability and willingness to carry out activities in certain professional conditions, an integrated characteristic of the individual, one of the components of which is a professional qualification.

Competence – «knowledge in action», the designation of the educational result, expressed in readiness for the real possession of methods and means of activity, the possession of such a form of combination of knowledge, skills and abilities that can successfully achieve this goal.

Let consider the structure of competencies that the UNIVERSITY should form as part of training specialists in a given area of training. Mandatory are the competence of the educational standard, as well as the competence determined by the University because of its specificity. The needs of the employer complement and adjust the General core competencies laid by the Ministry of education and science of the Russian Federation and the Scientific and methodological Council of the University, form the area of targeted training, designated by the employer (Fig. 1). Accordingly, we present the General core of competencies:

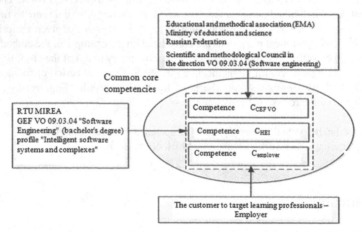

Fig. 1. The scheme of sources of competencies that determine the content of educational content

$$K_{ЯДР} = K_{ФГОС} + K_{ВУЗ} + K_{РАБ} \tag{1}$$

In view of the above, the structure of competencies will be determined by three basic components.

2.1 Model of Competence Formation

Consider the modular representation of the electronic training course (discipline). Module—a complete set of competencies (skills, knowledge, relationships and experience) to be mastered, presented in the form of requirements that the student must meet upon completion of the module. Module competencies is professionally important for the world of work. Each module is evaluated and certified.

Specific modules are formed as a structural unit of the working curriculum of the specialty (for example, one credit equals to 36 h); as the organizational-methodological and interdisciplinary structure, in the form of a set of topics from different disciplines that are grouped thematically according to the basic component, or as an organizational-methodical structural unit in the framework of the discipline.

Consequently, the academic discipline can be represented as a set of different modules, for example, the module of knowledge (MK); module of skills (MS); module of competencies (MC). The modules of the training course are connected to each other in a meaningful and logical way (Fig. 2). On the basis of the module of knowledge (MK), the module of competencies (MC) should be formed. Module skills (MS) forms and or expanded module of competencies (MK).

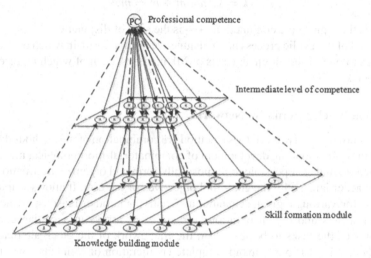

Fig. 2. Geometric 3 - dimensional model of the structure of professional competencies.

On the basis of modules of formation of knowledge and abilities the intermediate level forming professional competences is formed.

2.2 Combinatorial-Morphological Approach to Solving the Problem of Synthesis of Competencies

The morphological approach is based on the combinatorial principle of finding solutions. The procedure of morphological analysis allows purposefully, systematically lay in the morphological solutions of a large number of analogues of technical solutions. At the stage of morphological analysis is formed not a plan for solving the problem, and the so-called morphological set of solutions, that is, description of all potential solutions to the problem. With different morphological methods, the stage of morphological analysis and the stage of morphological synthesis are implemented in different ways. But at the stage of analysis, they always build a set of acceptable solutions, in other layers, carry out full or partial coverage of the field of possible solutions, that is, options for multidimensional alternatives, and so on. Completeness is understood in the normative sense - as the construction of all solutions that meet the conditions of the problem.

2.3 Method "Count AND-OR" for the Decision of Tasks of Synthesis of Competencies

Consider the synthesis of training routes based on the graph «AND-OR» [1]. The synthesis of training routes begins with the choice of a set of target and initial concepts. This choice is made by the teacher, focusing on the individual characteristics of the student and/or the curriculum of the course. Next, a cyclic process of selecting modules for each target concept is performed. The following rules are used when forming routes:

$$k * k = k, \ a * m + m = m, \tag{2}$$

where $*$ – is the sign of the conjunction, $+$ – is the sign of disjunction.

At the end of the cyclic process has a disjunctive normal form, in which each disjunct corresponds to one of the alternative sets of Mk modules, each of which represents one training route.

2.4 Method Block Alternative Networks

The block alternative networks (BAN) method is a combination of the methods discussed above and the corresponding development of combinatorial-morphological methods [2–4]. This method makes it possible to purposefully form and organize information arrays and data in accordance with the goals and objectives of the user. It allows you to group information for various logical, semantic, associative and other reasons; create named information arrays and organize various sequences of arrays in accordance with the requirements of the tasks to be solved. In the framework of the block alternative network method, it is possible to avoid complete enumeration of elements when they are combined by cutting off unnecessary paths at each step of passing through the network and, therefore, to ensure a relatively fast convergence of solutions.

2.5 Competency Formation Model (CFM)

The CFM consists of a common core of competencies and a common core of disciplines. In turn, the core of disciplines is formed from a list of disciplines listed in the FSES HE and university disciplines in the curriculum.

To solve the problem of automated synthesis of the structure of competencies, focused on the use in the system of individual training, the block alternative networks (BAN) method has been proposed and used.

Algorithm of Formation of Competencies
Consider the algorithm for the formation of competencies on the basis of academic disciplines according to the FSES HE 09.03.04 "Software Engineering" - "Bachelor".

1. At the entrance of the system through the user interface enters a list of academic disciplines, on the basis of which the synthesis of competencies will be made.
2. Each selected discipline is entered into an array. The result is an array of N academic disciplines.
3. In order to form competencies according to an individual learning path, it is necessary to select competencies for the received list of academic disciplines. Thus, for each of the N disciplines, a pattern is searched for such competencies that are associated with this discipline. Competences are recorded for future reference.
4. At the final stage, in order to eliminate duplication, those that are used repeatedly are removed from the generated list of competencies.
5. The generated competencies are displayed to the user through the system interface.

2.6 The Implementation of the Model

To implement the process of forming specialist competencies, the block alternative networks (BAN) method described earlier is used. In the structure of the block of alternatives, the function of choice of alternative (FCA) should be implemented under the condition of the multiple existence of alternative values. A similar function is realized in the environment of the elementary block of alternatives (EBA), which contains in its structure three basic components: meaningful (ky), reversible (R) and transit (T) vertices presented in the diagram (Fig. 3).

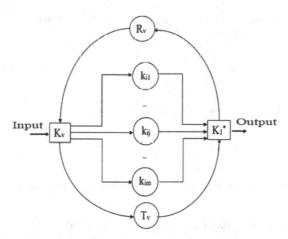

Fig. 3. Graph diagram of the elementary block alternatives.

The transit vertex is used in cases when none of the alternatives in the General solution is involved, and in the particular case can act as a limiter for recursive search of alternatives, that is, when no alternative value of the attribute (competence) is used, it is possible to pass from the entrance to the exit through the transit vertex T_i. If the search for alternative A_i attributes continues, the path lies through the reverse vertex R_i. In other words, a reversible vertex is used when it is necessary to solve the problem of finding an alternative value on an array of alternatives, i.e. organize a cyclic process.

3 Formation of Competence BAN

BAN is formed from EBA, each of which is determined by the corresponding type of competence. Consider the procedures for the formation of the EBA.

3.1 Representation of General Cultural Competences in the Form of EBA

The set of General cultural competences (CC) is determined by a set of alternative values of ca_{1m1}, the totality of which is represented by:

$$A_1 = \{ok_{11}, \ldots, ok_{1j}, \ldots, ok_{1m1}\}, j = 1, 2, \ldots, m_1 \tag{3}$$

The variable m_1 defines the number of competencies used in FSES HE, $m_1 \in N$.

The type of the elementary block of such network for the choice of alternative General cultural competences is presented in Fig. 4.

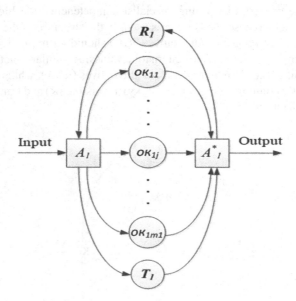

Fig. 4. Elementary block of alternatives for the choice of General cultural competences.

Symbols in Fig. 4: A_1 – block name; A_1^* – closure of alternatives.

The A_1 attribute can take one of the set of values $\{ок_{ji}\}$, the set of which represents alternative vertices of the EBA.

3.2 Representation of Professional Competences in the Form of EBA

At the next stage professional competences corresponding to the chosen disciplines are considered. At the same time, the set of professional competences A_2 is represented by a formal record of alternative values $nк_{m2}$:

$$A_2 = \{nk_{11}, \ldots, nk_{1j}, \ldots, nk_{1m2}\}, j = 1, 2, \ldots, m_2 \tag{4}$$

The variable m_2 determines the number of professional competencies that will be involved in the formation of an individual learning path, based on the FSES HE, $m_2 \in N$.

The elementary block of alternatives for the choice of professional competences is shown in Fig. 5.

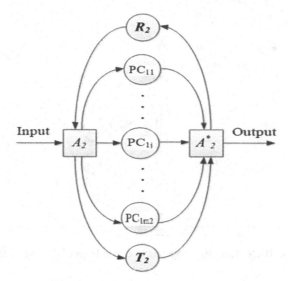

Fig. 5. Elementary block of alternatives for the choice of professional competencies.

3.3   The Process of Formation of BAN

Based on the EBA presented above, we will form a block alternative network of competencies. The set of elements for building an individual trajectory includes: $Q = (A_1, A_2)$. The combination of different $\{A_i\}$ attributes forms the M_K^D route on the block alternate network. The route is chosen purposefully, in accordance with the original disciplines.

On the network we get a set of routes $M_K^D = \{M_K^D\}$, where D – disciplines, K – variant of the route for the discipline; $M_K^D = (ok_{1j}, nk_{1j})$ (Fig. 6).

Generated routes:

$$M_1^1 = (OK_1, PC_{14}, PC_{26})$$
$$M_2^2 = (OK_6, PC_2, PC_{27})$$
$$M_3^3 = (OK_{13}, PC_1 PC_{13}).$$

According to FSES HE 09.03.04 we will receive the following competences for each route:reinforced routes:

M_1^1: knowledge of the culture of thinking, the ability to generalize, analyze, perceive information, setting goals and choosing ways to achieve it (OK-1); the ability to create

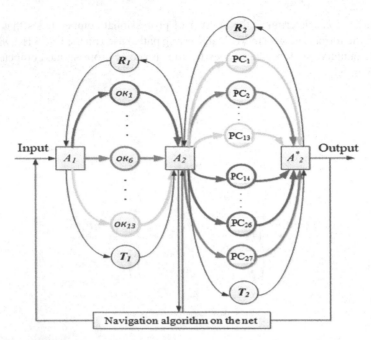

Fig. 6. BAN synthesis competences on the basis of the FSES HE.

software interfaces (PC-14); understanding the basic concepts and models of evolution and maintenance of software (PC-26);

M_2^2: aspiration to self-development, improvement of the qualification and skill (OK-6); ability to formalization in the subject area taking into account restrictions of the used research methods (PK-2); ability to formalization understanding of features of evolutionary activity, both from the technical point of view, and from the point of view of business (work with the inherited systems, return design, reengineering, migration and refactoring) (PK-27).

M_3^3: possession of means of independent, methodically correct use of methods of physical education and health promotion, readiness to achieve the proper level of physical fitness to ensure full social and professional activity (OK-13); understanding of the basic concepts, principles, theories and facts related to computer science (PC-1); ability to assess the time and capacitive complexity of software (PC-13).

4 Conclusion

In the report the model of synthesis of competences on BAN focused on development of the corresponding content of educational material of individual trajectories of training with use of a method of block alternative networks is considered. The proposed approach makes it possible to use BAN for the formation of both competencies and content of educational material on the example of the curriculum of the FSES HE the direction of training 09.03.04 "Software engineering" (bachelor's level).

References

1. Norenkov, I.P., Sokolov, N.K.: Creation of individual learning routes in ontology education systems. Inf. Technol. (3), 74–77 (2009). (in Russian). https://elibrary.ru/item.asp?id=11746766
2. Nechaev, V.V.: Synthesis of control questions in interactive learning systems. In: New Methods in Learning Environments. Issues of Increasing the Educational Process Evectivity, vol. 2, pp. 104–114. MIREA, Moscow (1981). (in Russian)
3. Nechaev, V.V.: Presentation of data in problems of automated synthesis of structures by the block alternative network method. In: Mathematical and Software in Modeling Problems in SAPR, vol. 24. MEI, Moscow (1984). (in Russian)
4. Nechaev, V.V., Bogoradnikova, A.V.: Block-alternative network as an information-algorithmic tool for the preparation and formation of multifactorial integrated solutions. In: Scientific Deposit VINITI RAN 71-V2018, pp. 1–15 (2017). (in Russian)
5. Baidenko, V.I.: Competency-based approach to the design of state educational standards of higher professional education. Research Center for Quality Problems of Training Specialists, Moscow (2005). (in Russian)

Biometric Methods of Identification and Verification in the Systems of Tele-Education

Valentin Nechaev[1]([✉]) [iD] and Konstantin Markelov[2] [iD]

[1] MIREA – Russian Technological University, Vernadsky Prospekt 78, Moscow 119454, Russia
nechaev@mirea.ru
[2] Joint Stock Company "Central Research Institute of Economics, Informatics and Control Systems", Tverskoi Bul. 7, Moscow 2906017, Russia
kosmar89@mail.ru

Abstract. The paper considers the problem of identification of students in problem-oriented distance learning systems (tele-education). The use of biometric technologies in tele-education systems is becoming the most effective solution to the problem of adequate identification of the student. However, the problem of choosing the most appropriate biometric methods still remains unsolved. In this paper the solution of selecting appropriate biometric identification and verification methods of identity of students is encouraged to implement on the basis of a unified system of biometric classification. The basis of this classification are systemic and comprehensive approach, and corresponding to this approach, system-integrated analysis (SI-analysis). To present a general and ordered biometric image, a unified classification system is suggested, which is based on a system-integrated analysis. The suggested system-complex classification is based on aspect, component, attributive and parametric analysis. Biometric identification and verification methods are classified according to the types of biometric identifiers, determined by anatomical, physiological factors, as well as psychological (behavior) and psychophysical characteristics of a person. For a reliable identification of personality in tele-education systems multimodal biometrics methods (MBM) are offered, i.e. based on several mutually agreed biometric methods. On the basis of SI-analysis are highlighted biometric methods which are the most appropriate to the tasks of personal identification in tele-education systems. Examples of specific methods oriented to use in computer and telecommunication training systems are given in this paper.

Keywords: Biometrics · Biometric methods · Biometric parameters · Classification · Distance education · Tele-education

1 Introduction

Modern information technologies as well as technical and software-algorithmic tools have fundamentally changed the possibilities to individualize not only learning, but also the educational process as a whole. Thanks to modern problem-oriented educational software and hardware complexes (SHC), both information and methodological

V. Sukhomlin and E. Zubareva (Eds.): SITITO 2018, CCIS 1201, pp. 98–109, 2020.
https://doi.org/10.1007/978-3-030-46895-8_8

as well as didactic opportunities for education and self-education have been significantly expanded. Through personal computers, remote real-time communication has become possible, i.e. *tele-dialogue*, between teacher and students, as well as between student and computer.

Note that the term tele-communication in the context of this work is similar to the term *tele-education* proposed by Professor Karpenko [1], but in its essence it is similar to the concept of "distance learning". In the following, we will use the term tele-education.

Modern telecommunications facilities and educational SHC provide an opportunity to expand the range of educational services and improve their quality and efficiency, to move to a new technological level of educational activities – i.e. to tele-education. Tele-education has already passed a long way of development; it is rapidly developing at the moment and will undoubtedly develop in the future. However, in addition to the existing problems, in the process of development of distance learning new challenges appear, in particular, following ones are highly relevant:

- effective identification of a person or a group of people during a learning session;
- the problem of monitoring homework or tests;
- the impact of costs on the implementation of the identification system and of the cost of education in general.

One of the possible approaches to resolve the situation by identifying students is the introduction of biometric methods and technologies in the educational process to solve the problems of identification and verification of the individual in the learning process.

Biometric identification (BMI) is a complex information technology which includes automated methods for processing information, identifying and verifying a person, as well as methods for authenticating a person, based on his anatomical, physiological and/or behavioral characteristics. Identification and authentication are very similar processes, but with certain differences. *Identification* is carried out in the process of matching or comparison of *the original information portrait biological individual identifier number of characteristics* saved templates (samples) in the database, with the subsequent delivery of information about the extent of probable proximity (pattern recognition). *Authentication* is a process initiated by the specific person asserting or claiming that it is he or she, and not anyone else.

The use of biometric technologies is becoming the most effective solution to the problem of determining the identity of the student in tele-education systems. However, the problem of choosing the most appropriate biometric methods still remains unsolved. Biometrics has a wide range of applications. Deciding which method of BMI should be used in the educational field to solve various tasks seems to be challenging. The majority of domestic and foreign publications consider specific identification methods and represent the classification pattern only by a limited part of all existing methods. For a general introduction to the ordered pattern of biometrics method is offered *a single clas-*

sification system, based on the system-integrated approach. The classification system under consideration is based on aspectual, componential, attributive, and parametrical analysis. It is the system-complex classification of biometric methods of personal identification that is relevant for use in practical applications.

2   The Classification System of Biometric Methods

The systemic organization of biometric methods of personal identification is based on the identification of the grounds and levels of classification, according to which the structure of the classification system is formed. It is represented by the corresponding clusters, as well as examples of specific methods assigned to one or another group. When considering the human body as an object of biometric identification, some of its parts or features that have unique properties and are defined as biological identifiers (BI) are distinguished. That BI are the subject of research to solve the problem of identification. For example, eyes, face, fingers, and other parts of the body can act as BI. Each BI is characterized by certain properties — the attributes and values of these attributes — by biometric parameters. Such parameters make it possible to determine some unique characteristics about the object in question - the person. For example, a person has unique patterns on the skin of his fingers — papillary patterns. The prints of these patterns are characterized by certain properties, and each property by corresponding values - parameters. There is a whole direction in the study of fingerprints called fingerprinting. Along with the fingerprinting can specify a number of other examples, in particular the identification of the retina and iris recognition, hand geometry and arrangement of veins in the arm and etc. However, there are such unique features of a person that are impossible to describe through BI, as well as measure them. For example, voice or gait. Such identifiers are also unique. They can be regarded as psychophysiological and attributed to the group of behavioral biometric identifiers (BPI). Thus, biometric methods of identification and verification can be classified according to the types of BI, determined by anatomical and physiological factors, as well as by types of BPI, determined by the psychological (behavior) and psycho-physiological properties of a person.

2.1   Classification Groups

The first group of methods of BMI will be determined by a set of anatomical BI. It includes the methods presented by the classification scheme (Fig. 1).

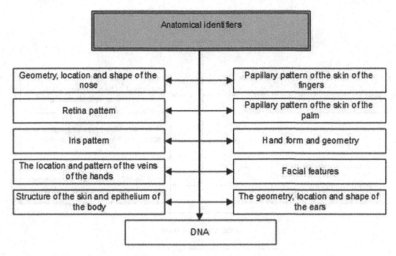

Fig. 1. Classification scheme of BMI, determined by anatomical identifiers.

The second group of methods of BMI is formed on the basis of physiological BI. The methods of BMI corresponding to physiological identifiers are shown in the classification scheme (Fig. 2).

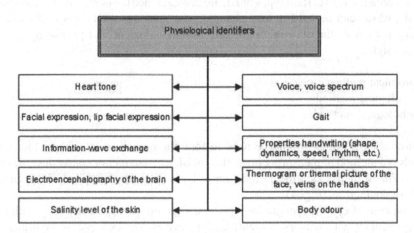

Fig. 2. Classification scheme of BMI, determined by physiological identifiers.

The third group of methods of BMI is determined by psychological identifiers and is presented in Fig. 3.

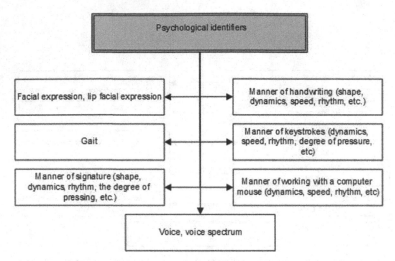

Fig. 3. Classification scheme of BMI, defined by psychological identifiers.

In accordance with the types of BI defined above and methods of BMI, can be determined biometric identification methods that are most appropriate (convenient, efficient and economically feasible) for use in tele-learning systems.

In accordance with certain types of BI, are distinguished the corresponding biometric methods, which can be used in tele-education (for anatomical BI - iris of the eye and papillary pattern of the skin of the finger; for physiological and psychological BI - keyboard style):

- Anatomical methods;
- Physiological methods;
- Psychological methods.

Another basis which should be used to form the classification scheme biometrics methods is a method of measuring properties of BI, e.g., *contact* or *contactless*. Existing methods for biometric identification, in general, can be attributed to one of two classes: contact or contactless (Fig. 4).

In the case of contact recognition systems, a person has to directly (physically and tactilely) contact with sensors of identification devices. For example, leave prints on a glossy surface, or touch the electrodes to measure galvanic parameters of the skin. In this case, the main problem is compliance with sanitary standards - after each measurement session, it is necessary to clean and sanitize the contact surfaces of the sensors or use disposable components of such sensors. All this reduces greatly the operational characteristics of such devices, especially when it is necessary to carry out mass measurements with a large flow of people.

Obviously, contactless recognition systems are free from such problems. However, contactless biometrics methods are not possible for any measurement methods (fingerprinting, measurement of electro-galvanic characteristics of the skin, etc.) [3].

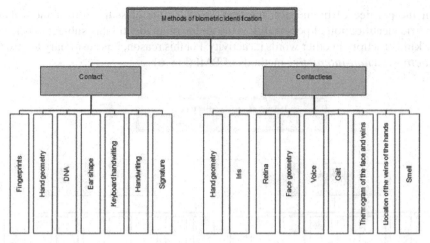

Fig. 4. Classification scheme of methods of biometric identification by the method of measuring the properties of BI.

Usually, when forming classification schemes of biometric identification methods, two classification groups are distinguished according to the method of changing or fixing the properties (characteristics) of BI depending on their behavior in time.

The first group of methods is based on the *static* properties of BI, for example, fingerprints, hand geometry, retina, etc.

The second group of methods is based on the use of the *dynamic* properties of BI, for example, the dynamics of reproduction of a signature or a handwritten keyword, voice, etc. The classification scheme reflecting the methods of BMI for the considered reasons is presented in Fig. 5.

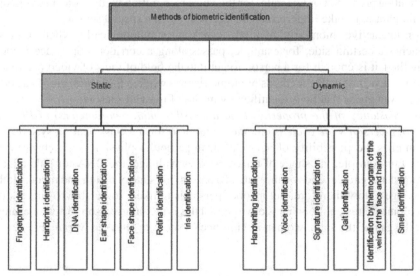

Fig. 5. Classification scheme of methods of biometric identification by the method of changing the properties of BI in the course of time.

In the practice of biometrics, the basis used for the classification of methods of biometric identification of personality is the ability of an identifiable subject to perform some kind of action, in other words its activity. For this reason, it is customary to discern *interactive* and *non-interactive* methods of BMI (Fig. 6).

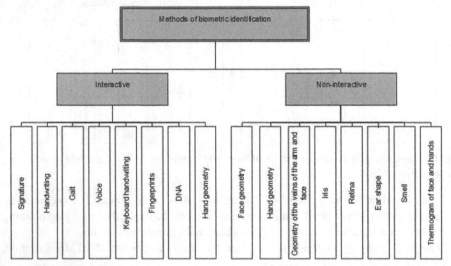

Fig. 6. Classification scheme of methods of biometric identification by the criterion of the activity of an identifiable subject.

Interactive methods of BMI require the individual to perform certain actions in the identification process. For example, for the voice recognition method one needs to utter a certain phrase, to take fingerprints one needs to touch a special sensor.

Non-interactive biometric methods can trigger automatically when a person approaches a certain side, for example, passes along a corridor. For a face recognition method, it is enough for a person to get into the field of view of video equipment. Therefore, non-interactive methods of biometrics can work in the stealth mode - a person may not even guess that he is identified by means of masked sensors.

The constancy of the properties (characteristics and/or parameters) of BI in the course of a person's life cycle is one more reason to form a classification system. This basis implies the possibility of age-related, in particular physiological, changes in a person. For example, the shape of a face changes with age, the DNA formula remains unchanged, the gait depends on the state of a person (his state of health and mood, clothes chosen, age). Now therefore, not a sober person is unlikely to be able to successfully pass a biometric test, although it is obvious that this is the same person. Another example is that the gait of the same woman in high-heeled shoes or sneakers varies (Fig. 7).

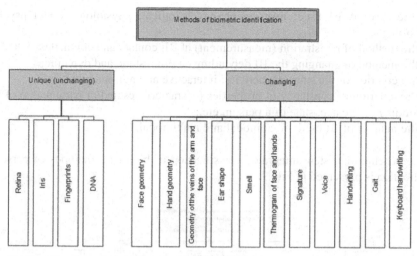

Fig. 7. Classification scheme of methods of biometric identification by age constancy of BI.

Multimodal biometrics. When solving practical problems of BMI, which require a high level of reliability of the result, the integration of the methods of BMI, discussed above, is used. This approach is called *multimodal biometrics* (*MMB*). MMB implies the selection and registration (measurement) of properties of several mutually agreed BI. At the same time, on the basis of allocated BI, the solution of the BMI problem is carried out in several stages. For example, a person's voice and papillary patterns of the skin of a person's finger can be a combined pair of dedicated BIs, along which BMI occurs. Such multimodal systems have high efficiency and are successfully used, for example, on sensitive sites (Fig. 8).

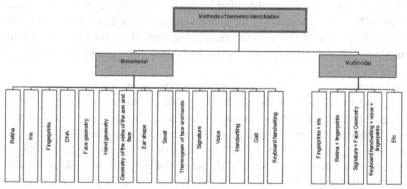

Fig. 8. Classification scheme of biometric identification methods according to the number of BI used.

Concluding consideration of the systemic organization of the BI system and the corresponding classification of biometric person identification methods, we will form the final classification scheme for all reasons discussed above, namely:

- by the type of BI used: anatomical, psychological, physiological and psycho-physiological;
- by the method of registration (measurement) of BI: contact and contactless;
- by the method of changing the BI depending on time: static and dynamic;
- by the criterion of the subject's activity: interactive and non-interactive;
- by the criterion of constancy of properties (characteristics and/or parameters) of BI: depending on the age, state of a person, etc.;
- by the number of BI used, monomodal and multimodal.

The scheme of system-integrated classification of biometric methods of personal identification is presented in Fig. 9.

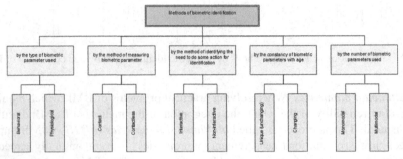

Fig. 9. Scheme of the system-complex classification of methods for biometric identification of a person.

The system for classifying the methods of BMI of a person discussed above makes it possible to solve problems of analysis, assessment and informed choice of methods of BMI of learners. Such a system is intended for use in tele-training software and hardware complexes (SHC). As an example, let us consider some of them, the most promising from the point of view of the authors. In tele-learning SHC, for example, BI such as finger papillary patterns (fingerprinting), iris and facial shape can be used to identify the student.

Dactylography is the most common method of biometric identification. The method is based on the uniqueness of the pattern of papillary patterns of the fingers of each person. Figure papillary pattern is formed in the final form in the process of intrauterine development and from birth to death of a person remains unchanged.

In each fingerprint, you can define two types of signs - global and local. *Global signs* include those that can be seen with the naked eye. If you look at the structure of the skin on the fingers, you can notice the presence of a complex relief pattern (the so-called *papillary pattern*), formed by alternating rollers (0.1–0.4 mm high and 0.2–0.7 mm wide) and grooves - deepenings (0.1–0.3 mm wide). Despite the diversity of the structure of papillary patterns, they are amenable to a clear classification, ensuring the process of their individualization and identification. All papillary patterns are divided into three main types: arc, loop and curl. These types of patterns form the basis of their classification.

Another type of trait is *local*. They are called *minutiae*. Minutiae are unique for each fingerprint signs, defining points for changing the structure of papillary lines (ending, bifurcation, rupture, etc.), orientation of papillary lines and coordinates at these points. Each print contains up to 70 minutiae. Practice shows that the fingerprints of different people may have the same global signs, but it is absolutely impossible to have the same minutiae. Therefore, global attributes are used to divide the database into classes at the authentication stage. At the second stage of recognition, local features are used. The fingerprint image obtained with the help of a special scanner is converted into a digital code (convolution) and compared with the previously entered pattern (reference) or a set of templates (if process is identification) [2].

Fingerprint identification is the most common, reliable and effective biometric technology. Due to the versatility of this technology, it can be used in tele-education tasks to identify trainees.

Another unique for each individual BI is the iris of the eye. The uniqueness of the iris pattern is due to the personality's genotype. Significant differences in the iris are observed even in twins. The method is based on the uniqueness of the iris pattern. To implement the method, a special camera and corresponding software are needed, that allows to isolate the iris pattern from the resulting image, on which the digital code is built. This method of identification is based on the analysis of the colored iris surrounding the pupil. This feature is also unique. Samples of the irises are available through video systems. Such systems will be able to identify a person, even if this person is wearing glasses or contact lenses. This identification system is also user-friendly and does not require personal contact with the scanner. Iris identification is used to verify the student's identity [2].

The cost of implementing the method is one of the most limiting factors of the widespread introduction of the technology in question. However, in recent years iris identification systems have become more and more accessible. Proponents of this method claim that iris recognition will very soon become a common identification technology in various fields.

Monitoring the learning process can be provided by tracking the dynamics of typing on the keyboard or by tracking the configuration of the face. In the method of identification, a 2D or 3D image of a person's face is constructed using the shape of a face. Using the camera and specialized software on the image, the outlines of the eyes, eyebrows, nose, lips, etc. are highlighted, and the distances between them are calculated. According to these data for further comparison an image is constructed to be converted into digital form.

Identification of a person by the face can be done in various ways, for example, by fixing the image in view of sight with a conventional video camera or based on the use of a thermal face pattern. Recognition of a lit face consists in highlighting of certain most characteristic features. Using a large number of cameras, the system analyzes the features of the resulting image, which do not change throughout life. This ignores surface characteristics such as facial expression or hair. Some face recognition systems require a fixed position of the identifiable person in order to get the most identical image. However, along with the above, there are such systems that work in real time to capture the image and recognize the face automatically. This method of identification is one of the fastest developing ones. It is fully suitable for monitoring and controlling the work of a student in the process of performing any control tasks or tests [2].

In the field of biometric systems, authentication systems based on keyboard handwriting are very promising today. Studies have shown that the keyboard handwriting of a particular user is stable. This feature allows a high degree of accuracy to identify the user working with the keyboard. Not many people know that in dealing with the computer appears the individuality of users on such aspects as the speed of the character set, the habit to use either primary or secondary side of the keyboard, the manner of "double" and "triple" keystrokes in the favorite methods of computer management, etc. There is nothing surprising. Such features are similar to the ability of music lovers to distinguish pianists playing the same melody or telegraphists using Morse code [2]. The listed features of keyboard handwriting can be used indeed for mass tracking and control of students' activities in tele-education systems.

3 Conclusion

The introduction of biometric technologies in the educational process has become a reality long ago. The faster the methods of biometric identification develop becoming more accessible, the more widely will be used biometric technologies in tele-education systems. For example, in 2006, a biometric fingerprint scanning system was installed at Holland Park School in London. The school has a database of student fingerprints, which was supposed to be included in the national UK database. Similar biometric systems are installed in Jefferson County High School, in the Rainer School in Portland, in the Kowloon Elementary School in Hong Kong, in some elementary schools in Shanghai, etc. In 2005, the cafeteria at Madras Secondary School installed two fingerprint scanners. Previously, the school used the card system. To get breakfast, the student had to scan his card. There were not rare cases when schoolchildren either forgot to draw their card or used someone else's card. After installing the biometric system, these problems disappeared [4].

Thus, the use of biometric technology is no longer just a topic for discussion. Existing developments allow to use biometric tools to identify individuals in tele-education. Biometrics allows you to solve many problems through the establishment and authentication of the identity of the student and through the possibility of substitution or loss of standard authorization tools (PIN codes, identification cards, etc.). Biological identifiers are always with a person, and the corresponding biometric information portraits are stored in biometric data banks (BDB).

The above classification system of biometric methods makes it possible in the future to make a choice and decide on the applicability of a particular method in specific practical conditions. Therefore, to ensure the authenticity of the identification, it is necessary to know which methods are most suitable for the purposes in question, and how a particular method can be used in dependence to the necessary security or authentication conditions. It should be noted that in this article not only well-known methods of biometric identification are considered, but also less well-known promising methods. All considered methods are summarized in a single classification system. In foreign and domestic publications the system-integrated approach is rarely used to assess the applicability of various methods. In the overwhelming majority of cases, specific methods are considered without providing a general picture. Thus, taking into account the above, it can be concluded that the use of biometric technologies in distance education will allow:

- to carry out a reliable monitoring of the learning process at all stages;
- to increase confidence in the performance of tele-education systems in relation to each student;
- to reduce the cost of the entire distance education, since it is not necessary to issue additional identification cards and not to think about the identification process itself;
- to increase the accessibility of the tele-education system infrastructure and make the educational process more comfortable.

References

1. Karpenko, M.P.: Tele-education. SGA Publictions, Moscow (2008). (in Russian)
2. Nechaev, V.V., Markelov, K.S.: Biometric information technology: actual and perspective methods. Inf. Telecommun. Technol. **18**, 24–41 (2013) https://elibrary.ru/item.asp?id=19000115. (in Russian)
3. Kashyap, R.: Biometric Authentication Techniques and E-Learning. In: Kumar, A. (ed.) Biometric Authentication in Online Learning Environments, pp. 236–265, IGI Global, Hershey. https://doi.org/10.4018/978-1-5225-7724-9.ch010
4. Martemyanov, I.S.: The problem of biometric identification in distance education. In: Workshop of the Department Applied Mathematics and Computer Science, State Technical University, Orel (2008). http://www.abashin.ru/conference/students/2008/Martemiianov.pdf. (in Russian)
5. Markelov, K.S., Nechaev, V.V.: Biometrics identification and verification of man in the system tele education. Inf. Telecommun. Technol. **20**, 50–61 (2013). https://elibrary.ru/item.asp?id=21228935. (in Russian)
6. Markelov, K.S.: Development of mathematical methods, algorithms and software for biometric identification of a person according to fingerprinting data. Ph.D. (Engineering), MIREA, Moscow (2015). (in Russian)

Interdisciplinary Aspects of Development and Software Implementation of Electronic Textbooks for Students of Technical Universities

Georgiy Mkhitaryan(✉) ⓘ, Andrei Kibzun ⓘ, Yanina Martyushova ⓘ, and Evgeniy Zharkov ⓘ

Moscow Aviation Institute (National Research University), Volokolamskoe Shosse 4, Moscow 125993, Russia
grgmkn@mail.ru

Abstract. The emergence of electronic textbooks as a means of teaching in the real educational process of the school and university necessitates scientific research in the field of their design and application. These scientific researches, which are currently conducted in didactics, psychology, information technology, computational mathematics, are inherently polydisciplinary, since didactic problems are solved by means of other scientific directions. At the same time, there are all prerequisites for conducting interdisciplinary research, the subject of which can be an electronic textbook. The purpose of this article is to substantiate the need for interdisciplinary research in the field of building electronic textbooks. In the main part of the work, the specific mathematical algorithms implemented in practice in the programming of the e-textbooks of the learning management system of the Moscow Aviation Institute are described. New mathematical approaches to designing an electronic textbook, in particular, a graph-oriented approach, are proposed. The model of forming a time-limited test is considered, where the weighted convolution of the normalized values is carried out by an optimization criterion: deviations of the test complexity from a given level and quantiles of the test execution time. The modern software technologies are used in the development of mathematical algorithmic module. In conclusion, we described the effectiveness of the joint research of specialists from different scientific fields, which has been confirmed by the practical implementation of this project.

Keywords: Electronic textbook · Information and Communication Technologies (ICT) · Electronic textbook usage scenarios · Structure of the electronic textbook · The construction of an electronic textbook

1 Introduction

The changes to modern society are inevitably reflected in the field of education. A student of the 21st century from early childhood lives in the digital information environment. The living conditions of the modern student have changed as well as the student himself. This gave rise to a new problem in the pedagogy, which is extremely difficult to resolve within the frameworks and methods of one pedagogical science. There is a need for research

V. Sukhomlin and E. Zubareva (Eds.): SITITO 2018, CCIS 1201, pp. 110–120, 2020.
https://doi.org/10.1007/978-3-030-46895-8_9

in which representatives of different branches of knowledge take part, the result of such research belongs not only to one science, but to several. This is particularly evident in the process of creating of such learning tool as a textbook, and not the textbook in its usual print form, but an electronic textbook with a number of additional didactic possibilities.

The process of electronic textbooks constructing is often considered by researchers in the field of pedagogy in connection with the study of the general problem of using information and communication technologies (ICT) in education, as well as the creation of various software products designed to improve the efficiency of the educational process. Informatization of education is the subject of research of many modern scientists, among which are: S.A. Beshenkov, B.S. Berenfeld, K.L. Butiagin, E.O. Ivanova, V.P. Kulagin, V.V. Neykhanov, B.B. Ovezov, I.M. Osmolovskaya, I.V. Robert and others. In the works of these authors it was noted that the most efficiency of ICT can be achieved in combination with the advantages of individualization and differentiation, which is facilitated by the presence of a whole range of software tools.

Despite the fact that the electronic textbook is considered as a subject of pedagogical research, there has been a clear differentiation of the concepts of «electronic textbook» and «electronic form of textbook», and these differences are now reflected in government documents. The main difference between an electronic textbook and an electronic form of a textbook is its interactivity, as well as the possibilities of individualization and differentiation of instruction which are noted above. When creating electronic textbook, additional tasks appear, while the electronic form of a textbook fully corresponds to the printed edition on a set of didactic tasks. A modern electronic textbook (ET) is «an educational electronic publication containing a systematic and complete presentation of the subject or its part in accordance with the program, supporting all parts of the didactic cycle of the learning process, which is an important component of an individualized actively-effective educational environment» [1, p. 8]. The electronic textbook can define the individual trajectory of the educational process for each student.

The purpose of this article is to substantiate the need for interdisciplinary research in the field of constructing electronic textbooks as a result of solving a multitasking problem in the field of didactics, psychology, computer science and requiring the use of algorithms developed by means of computational mathematics. The results of the use of mathematical algorithms provide an objective assessment of the effectiveness of solving didactic problems and allow you to enter a variety of learning trajectories, solving the problem of individualization and differentiation of learning process. This article describes specific mathematical algorithms implemented in practice when constructing textbooks of the distance learning management system (DLMS) of the Moscow Aviation Institute, as well as the specific features of the DLMS architecture from the standpoint of building it as a software product.

2 Main Part

An electronic textbook, like any other textbook, is addressed to the students; it can be used to organize students' independent work, accompanying it with individual dosed pedagogical assistance, to provide it with the means of the usual print edition. By using a modern electronic textbook a teacher can conduct full-time and part-time monitoring of students' knowledge, and dynamically analyze the statistics of their work. The process of automatic control and test assignments, taking into account the level of complexity and the time limit for their implementation, are also included in the scenarios for the use of ET by the teacher. Creating a set of scenarios for the use of an electronic textbook is necessary to determine the functional units of its structure at the design stage [2, 3].

In most scenarios, a block of statistical information is used, which includes grades and the time for students to complete tasks, their activity during the semester, the results of control measures and attendance (for full-time students). But a full-fledged, high-quality implementation of all the mentioned scenarios is impossible without the set of evaluation tools. Its functions include an assessment of the complexity of each task based on statistical information about the number of students who completed it correctly, and the time spent on the solution; assessment of the level of knowledge of the user, based on the same parameters; obtaining a preliminary rating corresponding to the GEF rating control form. The use of statistical methods for processing information about users' work allows you to organize feedback and give the electronic textbook adaptive properties, that is, to give the ability to automatically change the content set and adjust the usage scenario depending on the identified level of knowledge and abilities of the student.

The need for a textbook design process involves not only specialists in a narrow subject-matter field, an electronic textbook should be the product of teamwork of specialists in the field of didactics, psychology and, importantly, the teams of programmers responsible for the final implementation of the project, as well as specialists in the field of computing mathematics.

The essence of the electronic textbook is dual initially, perhaps also for this reason there are many definitions, depending on the specialist in which field of knowledge it is formulated. By appointment, purpose of use, an electronic textbook is a means of learning, and, like any textbook, a carrier of educational content, but also it is a software product. That is, the electronic textbook since its invention is the subject of didactic research, and the result of research in the field of information technology and mathematical algorithms.

Currently, research related to the process of creating an electronic textbook is poly-disciplinary [4], since the electronic textbook, as well as the process of its construction and use in practice, are studied simultaneously by several scientific disciplines: didactics, psychology, computer science, and computational mathematics. At the same time, there are prerequisites for conducting interdisciplinary research and projects that combine the efforts of not only teachers and psychologists, psychophysiologists, but also specialists in information technology and applied mathematics, whose achievements are currently being used for didactic purposes.

Interdisciplinary projects in education have been carried out in European countries and USA with the support of scientific foundations since the early 2000s, and the review of the basic principles of their organization and implementation was made by Tagunova [5]. In Russia, such an example could be the project "Modern Digital Educational Environment in the Russian Federation" [6].

At the university level, the subject of interdisciplinary research can be an electronic textbook from the problem of its design to use. The form and sequence of presentation of educational material is subject to didactic and psychological patterns; the presentation of information on the screen is determined by the laws of perception; the creation of software occurs with the use of information technology, which requires the construction of various kinds of mathematical models [7].

It is necessary to structure the educational material in more detail than when divided into functional units, in particular, to facilitate the program implementation, to give the textbook adaptive properties and ensure the possibility of generating individual educational trajectories. This can help graph-oriented approach.

Graph-oriented approach [3] to the structuring of educational material allows you to build individual learning paths, use a student-centered approach to learning, that is, take into account the personal characteristics of students, their level of training and psychology.

The essence of the graph-oriented approach lies in the possibility of presenting various training scenarios and course trajectories in the form of a directed weighted graph. At the vertices of the graph are content elements (tasks, tests of various kinds, theoretical positions, creative tasks, etc.), the direction of the arcs determines the sequence of passing these elements, and branch points adapt the learning process to the learner's personality.

Using mathematical graph theory, we solve the following didactic problems:

1. the construction of individual sets of tasks of the required level of difficulty to control the formation of user training competencies (in this case, the difficulty of tasks is used as the weights of the arcs of the graph);
2. the construction of individual learning trajectories of users, allowing for the most effective assimilation of educational material (the choice of arc graph is carried out interactively, depending on the response of the student);
3. content adaptation of an electronic textbook for a specific audience of users (recalculation of the weights of task difficulty is carried out, weights are introduced related to educational competencies, test time, etc.).

Other aspects of the use of graph theory are possible, including, inter alia, the technical implementation of the project.

Let us consider in more detail the software and algorithmic tools used for solving formulated didactic problems by the example of a series of electronic textbooks on mathematical disciplines developed at the Moscow Aviation Institute. These textbooks are used in the distance learning system (DLS) MAI CLASS.NET [8].

Content adaptation of LMS MAI CLASS.NET satisfies the concept of CAT (computerized adaptive testing), the main idea of which is the formation of current tasks for the user based on the history of the previous ones. In this paradigm, test generation algorithms have been developed with a restriction on execution time and without restrictions [9, 10]. In the case where there is a restriction on the time the test is performed by the user, prioritization may occur between the difficulty of the test and the execution time. Consider, for example, the mathematical model used to solve the problem of generating a time-limited test.

The problem of determining a certain set of tasks approximately equal in total difficulty was considered in [9, 10] and looks as follows.

Let there is a set $Z = (z_1, \ldots, z_I)$ of I tasks divided into M different types, I_M is the number of tasks of the m-th type, then $\sum_{m=1}^{M} I_m = I$, $m = 1, \ldots, M$. Each task belongs only to one type, and to denote the belonging of a task to a certain type, we introduce a matrix A of dimension $I \times M$:

$$A = \|a_i^m\|, a_i^m = \begin{cases} 1, z_i \in Z_m \\ 0, z_i \notin Z_m \end{cases}$$

This matrix determines the assignment of the task z_i to the set of tasks of the type $Z_m, m = 1, \ldots, M$, if $a_i^m = 1$.

Each of the tasks has a certain difficulty, which, for example, can be determined using the maximum likelihood method applied to the Rasch model in [7]. We introduce a vector $u \in R^I$ (hereinafter the vector means the column vector), the coordinates of which $u_i, i = 1, \ldots, I$, denote the belonging of the task i to the generated set in such a way that

$$u_i = \begin{cases} 1, \text{ if task } i \text{ is in the task set,} \\ 0, \text{ if task } i \text{ is not in the task set.} \end{cases}$$

The test set will be considered k tasks for which $u_i = 1$. Suppose that for each task its difficulty is known. We introduce the vector $w \in R^I$, the i-th coordinate of which is the difficulty of the i-th task and will be denoted as w_i.

The problem is to generate a set of individual test of k tasks belonging to different types, given that $k \geq M$. In this case, the total difficulty of the test is initially specified, denoted by c, which is determined on the basis of expert judgment. We assume that there may be a deviation from the given required total difficulty for any small number, up or down. We denote such a number by ε.

Let N users participate in testing. Let T_n^i a random time, which will require the user $n, n = 1, \ldots, N$, to solve the problem $i = 1, \ldots, I$. Consider an $N \times I$ matrix T:

$$T = \left\| T_n^i \right\|$$

Suppose, in contrast to the model obtained in [10], the total time for the test is unknown. Denote it by φ. Then, in order for all students to perform a given test version with a given probability α for a certain optimal time, consider the quantile function:

$$\Phi_\alpha(u) \triangleq \min\left\{ \varphi \in R^1 : P\left\{ \max_{n=1.N} T_n u \leq \varphi \right\} \geq \alpha \right\}, \tag{1}$$

where T_n is the n-th row of the matrix T.

Based on the described model and the introduced notation, we formulate the quantile optimization problem:

$$u_\alpha = \arg \min_{u \in \{0;1\}^I} \left(\frac{\gamma |c - w^T u|}{\varepsilon} + \frac{(1 - \gamma)\Phi_\alpha(u)}{2700} \right), \tag{2}$$

$$\varphi_\alpha = \min_{u \in \{0;1\}^I} \left(\frac{\gamma |c - w^T u|}{\varepsilon} + \frac{(1 - \gamma)\Phi_\alpha(u)}{2700} \right), \tag{3}$$

$$c - w^T u \leq \varepsilon, \tag{4}$$

$$w^T u - c \leq \varepsilon, \tag{5}$$

$$A^T u \geq e_M, \tag{6}$$

$$e_I^T u = k, \tag{7}$$

where $(\cdot)^T$ - transposition, $e_I \in R^I$, $e_I = (1, \ldots, 1)^T$, $e_M \in R^M$, $e_M = (1, \ldots, 1)^T$, $\alpha \in (0, 1)$- predetermined confidence level, $\gamma \in (0, 1)$ - weight coefficient.

The criterion function of the problem in (2) is the sum of two normalized dimensionless quantities. The first term is a deviation from a predetermined test difficulty level c, the normalized maximum permissible deviation level ε. The second term is the test execution time, which cannot be exceeded with a given level of confidence probability α. This time is normalized by the maximum permissible test response time.

Such a criterion seems to be a universal flexible test generation tool. Using the weight coefficient γ, we can adjust the importance of each term of the criterion. Constraints (4) and (5) regulate the choice of a set of tasks in the test, the total difficulty of which must differ from the level of difficulty set by the expert by no more than ε value. Constraint (6) is responsible for ensuring that among all the tasks in the test there is at least one task of each type, since this problem is solved provided that $k \geq M$. The constraint (7) means that there must be exactly k tasks in the set.

The solution of the formulated problem of stochastic programming is carried out by modern methods and algorithms developed by the authors team of the CLASS.NET system [11–15].

Using these algorithms, the DLMS can generate unique personal task sets based on user abilities and task difficulty. In turn, the difficulty of the task is calculated algorithmically, based on the previous statistics on the solution of tasks by users of the DLMS [12], which allows you to adapt the content of the system to a changing contingent of users.

CLASS.NET MAI distance learning system allows to analyze not only the user experience, but also to carry out continuous operation of the modification of the system content that is primarily determined by the theoretical and practical teaching materials. For this, the following indicators are analyzed:

- the number of hits of content items in individual tasks generated by the system to the user;
- the number of correct and incorrect answers;
- the number of attempts to solve one task;
- the number of hyperlinks usage within the section with the theory;
- correlations between the above indicators, etc.

Such an approach allows studying the content from different sides and further modifying it for users, for example, removing any tasks or replacing them with new ones. Some tasks may turn out to be "difficult" for this category of users, for example, due to the lack of skills necessary for its solution, which may not be included in the standard of this specialty. In this case, as a result of statistical analysis of the solution of this task by a specific group of users, obtained by the methods of recalculating user ratings and the task difficulty level, the assigned task difficulty level can be so high that it automatically stops falling into individual task sets with a total equal level of difficulty and will be recognized worthless. There is a need to delete the task or replace it.

The futility of the task may not be the only reason for removing content from the system. As users communicate with each other, some tasks may be compromised. Accordingly, the problem of identifying such tasks arises, and the system can automatically identify the compromised tasks, i.e. those that were most likely resolved by the user with assistance or with an answer known in advance, thanks to the prediction of the time to response the task and comparison with the actual time.

According to the results of the users passing the test or solving individual tasks, an integral rating is formed and the task difficulties are corrected. At the same time, the automatic rating formed in the DLMS can be used as a complete objective assessment of user work in the system or as a component of a certain overall assessment, taking into account the indicators of full-time work at practical classes and full-time tests [18, 19].

All the problems described above have rigorous mathematical formulations. Algorithms for solving these problems were implemented in the framework of the module of mathematical support for the DLMS MAI CLASS.NET, which is responsible for processing user data and adapting the system to users in real time. Implementations of algorithms are quite demanding on the resources of the DLMS, since involve the processing of a large amount of different data and constant new calculations or partial recalculations. On this basis, this module is isolated from the main software modules responsible for the standard functionality of the system. Within the framework of this module, the process of interaction of submodules responsible for each computational algorithm was developed (see Fig. 1).

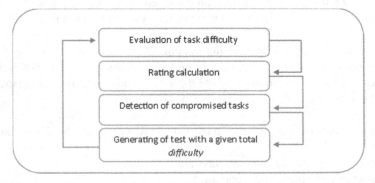

Fig. 1. The process of interaction of algorithmic submodules inside the module of mathematical support.

The specified algorithmic module of mathematical support for the operation of the DLMS must be organically and optimally integrated into the electronic control shell. The principles of building an electronic control shell are the subject of research by specialists in modern IT technologies. Most modern web applications are based on the MVC architecture (Model-View-Controller), whose main task is to divide the application into separate layers in such way that changing one layer has minimal impact on the other layers. The main components of the MVC architecture are:

- model - provides access to data;
- view - defines what data to receive and how to display it;
- controller - selects a view based on user input.

This approach at building web applications allows you to strictly separate the boundaries of each module and maintain low Coupling [8] of the application.

Of the modern web application development tools, the most effective is the Django framework, due to its simplicity and scalability. This framework closely follows the MVC architecture, but with a few changes, namely, it is based on the MTV (Model-Template-View) architecture. Main components of MTV architecture are:

- Model - A data access layer. Checks them, knows how they are connected and how to work with them.
- Template - The data presentation layer. This layer makes decisions about the presentation of data: how and what should be displayed on the page or in another type of document.
- View - a layer of logic. Provides access to models and applies the appropriate template. In other words, it is a bridge between models and patterns.

Thus, «Views» in Django are «controllers, and «Templates» are «Views». Templates are HTML markup, within which special variables and template tags are used.

As an advantage to Django, you can also highlight the built-in support for object-relational mapping (ORM), which allows you to associate a database management layer with objects of the described models. This technology allows you to effectively maintain the integrity and consistency of data, which makes it easy for developers to upgrade the model, change the data structure without affecting the rest of the application.

There is the basic structure of a distance learning management system (DLMS) based on the Django framework (see Fig. 2). The basic principle of operation is as follows: incoming HTTP requests are processed by the DLMS MAI server. The security and integrity of the data is checked, as well as the current server load [16]. After that, the HTTP request is processed by the web server and goes to the router (urls.py), which, using the specified URL pattern, transmits the current request to the controller (views.py). The controller, in turn, determines which logic should be applied to the models, as well as which patterns should be used to form the correct answer. The HTTP response is sent back to the web server, which sends the response back to the user.

The basic DLMS application can easily be extended with the help of external application modules, regardless of the language and development platform. All requests coming to the web server are processed using a Django router (urls.py), which allows you to

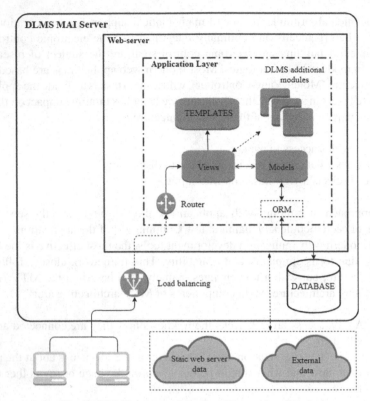

Fig. 2. DLMS structure based on *Django* framework.

quickly create your own web service based on the RESTful architecture (Represen-
tational State Transfer) [17] and provide integration with any application capable of
transmitting HTTP requests and data in XML or JSON format.

The advantage of REST web services is scalability and improved performance due
to the fact that the HTTP request includes all the data needed by the server to generate
a response. Thus, the server does not need to synchronize data with other external
applications. Application state management is provided by the client (browser).

This approach allowed us to move the mathematical support module to a new external
server, removing the restriction of used technologies to ensure the best performance of
the developed mathematical algorithms. Data exchange with the main DLMS application
is carried out using the developed REST interface of the service using the HTTP protocol.

3   Conclusion

The process of constructing electronic textbooks for students of technical universities
is currently the object of multidisciplinary research, which in the future may turn into
interdisciplinary cooperation, which has all the prerequisites. At present, the results
obtained by representatives of various scientific fields in the field of designing electronic

textbooks are considered separately, within the framework of each scientific discipline. At the same time, in the long term, the emergence of new integrated scientific fields is possible, the results of studies of which will find general acceptance. The paper presents an example of joint research of specialists in the field of optimization theory, IT-technologies and pedagogy, the result of which was the system MAI CLASS.NET, effectively used at the present time for teaching mathematical disciplines at the Moscow Aviation Institute.

References

1. Leibovich, A.N., et al.: Electronic Textbooks: Recommendations for the Development, Implementation and use of a New Generation Of Interactive Multimedia Electronic Textbooks for General Education Based on Modern Mobile Electronic Devices. Federal Institute for the Development of Education, Moscow (2012). (in Russian)
2. Martyushova, Y.G.: Scenario approach to the development and use of learning management system in universities. Psychol. Sci. Educ. **22**(6), 45–55 (2017). https://doi.org/10.17759/pse.2017220604. (in Russian)
3. Martjushova, Y.G.: Application of a graph-oriented approach to the design of an electronic textbook. In: Proceedings of the XII International Conference on Applied Mathematics and Mechanics in Aero Space Industry (NPNJ 2018), pp. 734–736. MAI, Moscow (2018). (in Russian)
4. Tagunova, I.A.: Some Aspects of interdisciplinary research in the sphere of education. Otechestvennaja i Zarubezhnaja Pedagogika **1**(6), 27–41 (2017). https://elibrary.ru/item.asp?id=32850715. (in Russian)
5. Osmolovskaya, I.M.: Development of didactic knowledge in cross-disciplinary researches. Hum. Educ. **9**(1), 89–96 (2018). https://elibrary.ru/item.asp?id=32741548
6. National Project: Modern Digital Educational Environment. http://neorusedu.ru. (in Russian)
7. Rasch, G.: Probabilistic Models for Some Intelligence and Attainment Tests. The University of Chicago Press, Chicago (1980)
8. Distance Learning Management System MAI CLASS.NET. http://217.9.86.154. (in Russian)
9. Naumov, A.V., Inozemtsev, A.O.: The algorithm for generating the individual tasks in distance learning. Her. Comput. Inf. Technol. **6**(108), 46–51 (2013). https://elibrary.ru/item.asp?id=19113375. (in Russian)
10. Naumov, A.V., Mkhitaryan, G.A.: On the problem of probabilistic optimization of time-limited testing. Autom. Remote. Control. **77**(9), 1612–1621 (2016). https://doi.org/10.1134/S0005117916090083
11. Naumov, A.V., Mhitarjan, G.A., Cherygova, E.E.: About the task of quantile optimization of time-limited testing for one user. In: Proceedings of the XII International Conference on Applied Mathematics and Mechanics in Aerospace Industry (NPNJ 2018), pp. 736–738. MAI, Moscow (2018). https://elibrary.ru/item.asp?id=35651981. (in Russian)
12. Kibzun, A.I., Zharkov, E.A.: Two algorithms for estimating test complexity levels. Autom. Remote. Control. **78**(12), 2165–2177 (2017). https://doi.org/10.1134/S0005117917120050
13. Naumov, A.V., Mkhitaryan, G.A., Rybalko, A.A.: Software set of intellectual support and security of LMS MAI CLASS.NET. Bull. South Ural. State Univ. Ser. Math. Model. Program. Comput. Softw. (Bull. SUSU MMCS) **9**(4), 129–140 (2016). https://doi.org/10.14529/mmp160412
14. Kibzun, A.I., Naumov, A.V., Norkin, V.I.: On reducing a quantile optimization problem with discrete distribution to a mixed integer programming problem. Autom. Remote. Control. **74**(6), 951–967 (2013). https://doi.org/10.1134/S0005117913060064

15. Naumov, A.V., Ivanov, S.V.: On stochastic linear programming problems with the quantile criterion. Autom. Remote. Control. **72**(2), 353–369 (2011). https://doi.org/10.1134/S0005117911020123
16. McConnell, S.: Code Complete: A Practical Handbook of Software Construction, 2nd edn. Microsoft Press, Redmond (2004)
17. Alarcon, R., Wilde, E., Bellido, J.: Hypermedia-driven RESTful service composition. In: Maximilien, E.M., Rossi, G., Yuan, S.-T., Ludwig, H., Fantinato, M. (eds.) ICSOC 2010. LNCS, vol. 6568, pp. 111–120. Springer, Heidelberg (2011). https://doi.org/10.1007/978-3-642-19394-1_12
18. Martyushova, Y.G., Lykova, N.M.: Organization of reflexive-evaluative activity of university students by using the learning management system. Psychol. Educ. Stud. **10**(2), 125–134 (2018). https://doi.org/10.17759/psyedu.2018100211. (in Russian)
19. Martiushova, Ia.G., Meshcheryakov, Ye.A., Mkhitaryan, G.A.: Organization of the automated rating control type in LMS MAI ClASS.NET. Modern Information Technology and IT-Education. In: Sukhomlin, V.A. (ed.) Proceeding of Scientific Papers of the XII International Scientific and Practical Conference, pp. 133–138 (2017). https://elibrary.ru/item.asp?id=32661952

Simulation Tools for E-Learning in Microelectronics and Nanoelectronics at the University

Tatyana Demenkova[✉] ⓘ, Valery Indrishenok ⓘ, and Evgeny Pevtsov ⓘ

MIREA - Russian Technological University, Vernadsky Prospekt 78, 119454 Moscow, Russia
{demenkova,indrishenok,pevtsov}@mirea.ru

Abstract. In work results of researches in the area of simulation of electrical characteristics of the AlGaN/GaN field-effect transistor are provided. The considerable difference of transport processes in case of the strong and feeble electrical polarization is shown. The role of capture of centers in volume of a buffer layer GaN is analyzed and it is shown that deep interruptions can influence considerably on distribution of electrostatic potential and density of electrons in a buffer layer. In case of high concentration of interruptions there is a sharp lowering of density of the free electrons with increase of distance from the channel, the current density in the depth of a buffer layer decreases. The received scientific results have allowed to use the scientific software for disciplines on the automated design in electronics, automation of an experiment and for design and modeling micro and nanosystems within the direction of microelectronics and nanoelectronics for training of masters at the university. Software systems are designed for mathematical simulation of semiconductor manufacturing processes, their electrical, optical, thermal, and other characteristics. A significant advantage is the possibility of establishing a relationship between the devices characteristics and the manufacturing technology and design parameters, without involving costly experimental studies, based on their physical implementation. The software is used to develop devices and elements of integrated circuits, to study device properties in various operating modes when exposed to various external factors.

Keywords: E-learning · Microelectronics · Nanoelectronics · Simulation tools

1 Introduction

Training in problem solving based on modern simulation programs, the automation of technical and scientific experiments, as well as monitoring of physical and technological processes is a necessary component of training engineers and researchers in the field of solid state physics and modern solid-state electronics. It should be noted that the Russian Technology University (RTU MIREA) was one of the first Russian universities included in the development program of the electronic component base in order to create a specialized design center equipped with computer-aided design and simulation software. As a result, the university has been equipped with licensed software products from

© Springer Nature Switzerland AG 2020
V. Sukhomlin and E. Zubareva (Eds.): SITITO 2018, CCIS 1201, pp. 121–133, 2020.
https://doi.org/10.1007/978-3-030-46895-8_10

Cadence Design Systems, Synopsys, Keysight technologies, and other leading CAD manufacturers for electronics. The specificity of these software packages is their wide versatility and, accordingly, a relatively large amount of material for studying in order to use their tools in practice with limited material and time resources. Generalization of many years of experience accumulated by the Department of Nanoelectronics of the Physics and Technology Institute resulted in the creation of an integrated methodology for teaching the basic principles of designing the electronic component base, the main component of which is the independent and individual implementation of practical tasks. The necessary knowledge is acquired by students in the course of studying the basic course in "Computer-Aided Design Systems in Electronics", whereas their skills are fixed when implementing course projects in related disciplines of the Department. The modern e-learning technology is best suited to the implementation of such methods, as, in this case, a personal approach is applied, taking into account the individual abilities and capabilities of each student in terms of the pace of mastering the material and acquiring the skills for working with CAD tools. The education quality indicator is solving specific problems as part of research activities and graduation design projects. This paper describes an example of simulating the electrical characteristics of a field effect microwave transistor, which served as the basis for launching the development of an integrated e-learning methodology using modern EDA tools [1–7].

GaN field-effect heterojunction transistors became the main type of high-power semiconductor microwave devices. Large band-gap width of gallium nitride (3.4 eV) and low collisional ionization coefficient enable operation of devices with high bias voltages. AlGaN/GaNheterojunction transistors provide quite high electron density in the channel (about 10^{13} cm^{-2}), which taking into account large value of saturated electron velocity ($2.7 \cdot 10^7$ cm/s) may provide drain current of several amperes per millimeter of channel width.

At present, a number of publications are dedicated to aspects of instrumental-technological modeling of GaN-based transistor structures (see, for example, [8–10], but the results obtained in these publications are not sufficiently complete. Within the framework of this paper, we propose methods for modeling effects associated with existence of deep centers and polarization and their influence on performance of microwave transistors and present corresponding numerical calculations.

2 Formulation of the Problem

Mechanisms of high electron density appearance in the channel were considered in [10–12]. These mechanisms are associated with the effects of spontaneous and piezoelectric polarization in nitride semiconductor materials with wurtzite type crystal lattice. Hexagonal wurtzite lattice has no center of symmetry, and interatomic bond contains a considerable proportion of ionic component. Therefore, spontaneous polarization P_{SP} occurs in such crystals. P_{SP} vector is parallel to axis c of the lattice and is directed opposite to the direction of normal to crystal face, on the surface of which cations (Ga, Al) are located. Polarization value depends on chemical composition of the material. In $Al_xGa_{1-x}N$ P_{SP} value is approximately linearly dependent on Al content, and at x = 1 it is three times higher than in GaN. Piezoelectric polarization P_{PE} depends on deformation of crystal lattice under mechanical stresses. Relationship between P_{PE} value and direction with tensor of mechanical stresses is determined by tensor of piezoelectric coefficients [13, 14].

Polarization pattern in heterostructure typical of gallium nitride transistors is shown in Fig. 1.

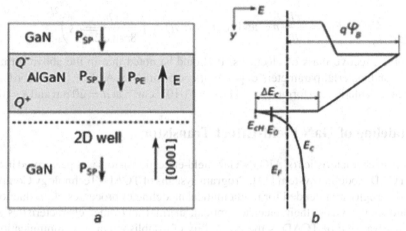

Fig. 1. Location of layers (a) and dependence of energy of Ec conductivity band bottom on distance from the surface (b) in the structure of field-effect transistor. Energy diagram corresponds with thermodynamic equilibrium condition and presence of metal electrode on the surface.

Structure oriented along the crystal axis [0001] consists of thick lower GaN layer, AlGaN layer and thin upper GaN layer. Spontaneous polarization P_{SP} occurs in each of these layers. Due to difference in lattice parameter a in AlGaN and GaN, middle layer is exposed to extension, so piezoelectric polarization P_{PE} coincident in direction with spontaneous polarization occurs in it. In upper rather thin GaN layer piezopolarization is insignificant due to relaxation. Condition for continuity of electrical induction in the presence of difference in polarization values in different sides of heterojunction is taken into account by introducing Q^+ and Q^- charges on corresponding heterointerfaces. Surface density of Q^+ charges may exceed surface density of $qN_D d$ donors in $Al_x Ga_{1-x}N$ layer with thickness d. As calculated in [4], $Q^+/q = 1.4 \times 10^{13}$ cm^{-2} at x = 0.25; where q – value of elementary charge [13].

Positive charge on heteroboundary pulls free electrons and, as illustrated in Fig. 1b, potential well with surface electron density n_S is formed on the surface of lower buffer layer. Value of this electron density may be determined using formula given in [11], which defines the change of Ec on the thickness of middle barrier layer assumed that there are no charges in it,

$$\frac{dq^2}{\varepsilon\varepsilon_0}\left(\frac{Q^+}{q} - n_s\right) = q\phi_B - \Delta E_c + (E_F - E_{cH}), \tag{1}$$

where ε_0 – electrical permittivity of vacuum, ε – material relative permeability, $q\phi_B$ – potential barrier height, ΔE_c – discontinuity of E_c on the boundary, $E_F - E_{cH}$ – distance between Fermi level and conduction band bottom of buffer layer on the boundary. The latter value may be represented in the following form $E_F - E_{cH} = (E_F - E_0) + (E_0 - E_{cH})$, where E_0 – absolute value of energy of the bottom of lower subband in two-dimensional quantum well of triangular profile. Energy intervals included in the latter equation may be expressed in terms of n_S:

$$(E_F - E_0) = \frac{\pi \hbar^2}{m} n_S \text{ and } (E_0 - E_{cH}) = \left(\frac{9\pi \hbar q^2}{8\varepsilon\varepsilon_0\sqrt{2m}} n_S \right)^{2/3}, \qquad (2)$$

where m – effective mass of electrons. It should be noted that in the above formulas variables and material parameters depend on composition of $Al_xGa_{1-x}N$. According to numerical calculation performed in [11] $n_S = 1 \cdot 10^{13}$ cm^{-2} at $d = 20$ nm and $x = 0.25$.

3 Modeling of GaN Field-Effect Transistor

Modeling of characteristics of AlGaN/GaN field-effect transistors was performed in Sentaurus TCAD modeling system [14]. Program systems of TCAD (Technology Computer Assisted Design) are intended for mathematical modeling of processes of production of semiconductor devices, their electric, optical, thermal and other characteristics. The essential advantage of TCAD is the possibility of establishment of communication of characteristics of devices with manufacturing techniques and parameters of a design, without resorting to the expensive experimental researches based on their physical realization. TCAD is applied to development of devices and elements of integrated circuits, researches of properties of devices in various operating modes at various external influences.

The TCAD tools allow even until direct production at silicon factory to execute modeling and optimization of technological operations and verification of characteristics of the developed device therefore the quantity of batches is reduced and considerable saving time and resources of development is reached. Moreover, modeling of Sentaurus TCAD provides important data on behavior of the designed semiconductor devices which can lead to the new concept of the device [15–19]. Among the main advantages of Sentaurus TCAD it is also necessary to note:

– the expeditious prototyping of schemes and devices providing the fullest testing of functions and characteristics of the designed devices;
– optimization of a wide range of technologies micro and a nanoelectronics on the basis of the modern description of physical processes of formation of the designed device and the principles of its work;
– representation of the physical phenomena by means of the self-coordinated multi-dimensional modeling of functions and characteristics of devices therefore the high quality of design, profitability of the carried out developments and their reliability is reached;
– the integrated and user-friendliest environment of design providing the full 3-D description of routes of design and modeling of technical processes;
– application of progressive methods of creation of grids and techniques of numerical calculations.

In the Sentaurus TCAD system physical models of both technological processes, and the mechanical, thermal, optical, electric phenomena which important part is transfer of carriers of a charge in semiconductor structures are completely presented. The numerical decision of the equations is passed, generally, by a finite element method. Spatial sampling is made by means of special program modules. There is a possibility of the choice of solvers of the matrix equations. In a number of tasks the statistical approach based on pair interactions of particles Monte Carlo method is used. Characteristics of materials and parameters of models contain in the databases which are also a part of a software package. The possibility of entering into files of these databases of necessary changes and additions is provided. In programs of visualization and the analysis results of modeling can be presented in the form of images of a design, a grid and fields of distributions of the counted variables and also in the form of schedules of dependences of these variables.

Modeling begins with creation of geometrical model of the device with the indication of materials of elements of a design and their parameters. Technological modeling assumes that the design of the device is created in result of consecutive modeling of processes of his production. In terms of programming the complex of modeling of operations of production of the device represents a stream of consistently carried out macroes which are independently created by the user and/or taken from libraries of system. The output data of technological modeling represents the description of a design of the device − his geometry and distribution of the alloying impurity. These data are analyzed by means of visualization tools and can serve as entrance data for instruments of modeling characteristics of the device.

Modeling of characteristics consists in a task (in the simplest case, the choice of the built-in databases) physical models of the processes and the phenomena defining the interesting properties of the device, the indication of methods of numerical calculations, an algorithm of performance of tasks and a type of the output data [20–26]. The received results can be subjected to additional processing and are presented in the form of schedules. Structural components of the considered transistor are shown in Fig. 2. Source/drain contacts are buried, so that they overlap the thickness of channel area of buffer layer. Distance between source and drain is 5 μm, gate length is 0.8 μm, drain is 3 μm away from the gate.

Modeling of structures with heterojunctions and corresponding calculations in particular are based on generalization of Shockley diode theory (Anderson model) and special models of charge transfer process in heterojunctions, which take into account recombination of carriers through surface states, tunneling and both effects simultaneously. At initial stage we investigated dependence of states of spontaneous and piezoelectric polarization of $AlXGa1-XN$ barrier layer on aluminum content in its composition and the way it affects characteristics of such devices. According to model proposed in [11] at pseudomorphic growth of AlGaN on GaN with AlGaN barrier layer thickness of more than 15 nm, carriers concentration is in quadratic dependence on Al molar content in AlGaN. However, spontaneous polarization is determined not by the absolute value of dipole moment averaged by volume, but by difference of polarization in two different system states, at that the value of macroscopic polarization is also determined by piezoelectric polarization arising due to mismatch of the lattice parameters on heterointerfaces.

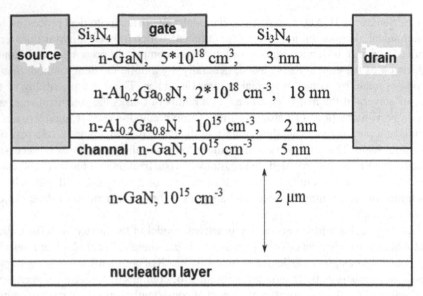

Fig. 2. Field-effect transistor structure.

The analysis of results of experiments allows to understand influence of those concrete parameters of technical process, a design and properties of materials on characteristics of a designed project of modeling in particular, to make their manual optimization.

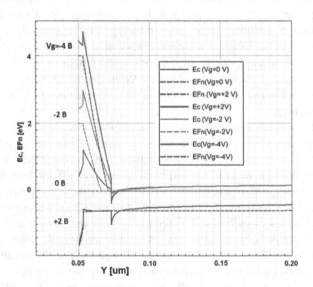

Fig. 3. Band diagrams in section passing through the middle of the gate length at different voltages Vgs on it and at voltage on drain Vds = 0.

Polarization effects considered in the program – batch file of characteristics modeling, may be seen in band diagrams and space-charge density distributions shown in Fig. 3 and 4.

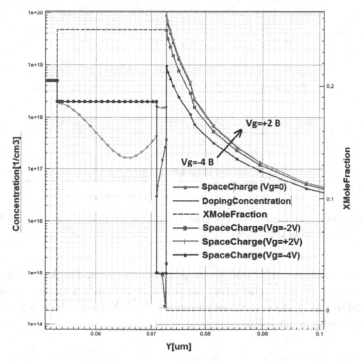

Fig. 4. Space-charge density distributions in section passing through the middle of the gate length at different voltages Vgs on it and at voltage on drain Vds = 0.

Increase of negative voltage on the gate reduces electron density n_S in the channel; however, permanence of Q^+ polarization charge causes the intensity of electric field in the barrier to increase, and almost all V_{gs} voltage falls on the barrier layer. At positive V_{gs}, n_S increases and voltage on barrier layer decreases. With further growth of V_{gs}, accumulation of n_S is limited due to electrons pass to the gate through ΔE_c permanent barrier.

Fermi quasi-level shift in buffer layer is shown in Fig. 3 and is probably related to the use of quasi-ohmic contacts (barrier type) to source/drain regions in initial program.

Output current-voltage characteristics $I_d(V_d)$ are shown in Fig. 5.

This figure shows the decrease of current increment and, consequently, the decrease of transmittance at positive gate bias, which is connected with the above-mentioned dependence of n_S on V_{gs}. Maximum value of transmittance in transistor without traps is 3.7 S/mm.

Properties of transistors depend on presence of deep power levels of the traps located in various parts of structure of the device [27–31]. In order to clarify the role of traps in GaN-buffer they were included in batch file for modeling of device characteristics.

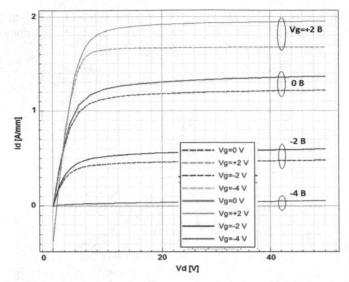

Fig. 5. Families of output current-voltage characteristics of the model without (solid lines) and with (dashed lines) traps in GaN layer.

Specified concentration is 10^{16} cm^{-2}, energy position is located in the middle of band-gap, electrons and holes capture cross section is 10^{-18} cm^2. Simulation results also are presented in Fig. 5. As can be seen from Fig. 5, such traps reduce drain current in saturation region by about 10%.

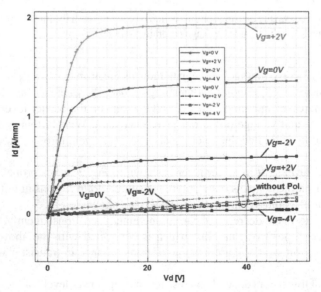

Fig. 6. Output characteristics without (dashed lines) and with (solid lines) taking into account polarization.

Of particular interest is the comparison of modelling results with and without taking into account polarization effects, for which purpose polarization models call commands were excluded from the program. Design and material parameters remained the same. The simulation results are showed in Fig. 6 and 7.

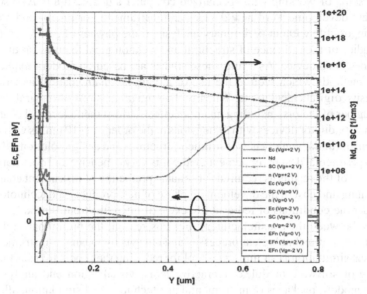

Fig. 7. Energy diagrams, distribution of electron density and space charge density in section passing through the middle of the gate length at various V_{gs} and at $V_{ds} = 0$.

Absence of polarization results in sharp decrease of drain current and change of characteristics of charge carrier transfer in the channel. Insufficient concentration of donors in barrier layer cannot provide high surface electron density in the channel quantum well even at $V_{gs} = 0$ (see Fig. 6 and 7).

At negative gate voltage the well is emptied and electric field penetrates into the depth of buffer layer. At $V_{gs} = -2$ V, thickness of depletion region takes significant part of this layer. Drain current is determined by transfer of electrons through non-depleted part of the buffer.

4 Conclusion

The authors believe that the following provisions and results are new in this paper. Modeling of electrical characteristics of AlGaN/GaN field-effect transistor was performed. Significant difference in transfer of charge carriers in case of strong and weak electric polarization in structural elements is shown. In the absence of polarization effects, localization of current in the region of quantum well is noticeably reduced. Consideration of the role of trapping centers in the volume of GaN buffer layer showed that deep traps may significantly affect distribution of electrostatic potential and electron density in the volume of buffer layer. In case of high concentration of traps, their capture of electrons results in sharper decrease of free electron density with increasing distance from the channel, current density in the depth of buffer layer becomes smaller.

The practice of introducing information technology in engineering processes, which is being intensively developing now, determines the relevance of creating textbooks to master the skills of working with specialized computer-aided design (CAD) software. Most modern developments of new devices and instruments for micro- and nanoelectronics is impossible without preliminary analysis of the physics of their operation and without studies of the influence of structural and technological features on the properties of the designed device. As a rule, these studies are based on modern mathematical simulation methods which require the use of a complex mathematical apparatus and labor-intensive digital calculations. When scaling the dimensions of integral devices, a growing number of factors, including quantum effects, affect their electrical characteristics. For semiconductor devices with dimensions of the order of 1–10 nm, as well as in the development of fundamentally new instrument structures and design solutions, the application of experimental design refinement methods is very expensive and does not provide high accuracy of the results as required for reliable prediction of instrument characteristics. The timing and cost of the development phase of new products and technologies are crucial under the conditions of reduced life cycle of microelectronics products and the competition between their manufacturers. For this reason, the preliminary refinement and optimization of technological processes and designs by means of instrumental and technological simulation is an important tool for reducing the production startup phase.

The use of software modules, interactive tools, visualization and analysis tools, included in modern packages of instrumental and technological simulation, allows for:

– exploring new manufacturing operations and optimizing their features and design parameters, based on the calculations of the impurities distribution profiles and electrophysical characteristics of structures;
– simulating the sequences of manufacturing operations, i.e. the total manufacturing route and for implementing a preliminary optimization of manufacturing parameters, manufacturing routes, the elements dimensions in order to obtain the preset characteristics of the product;
– based on digital simulation, exploring the electrical, optical, electromagnetic, and other characteristics of semiconductor structures;
– based on the electrical characteristics of the device, designing circuit fragments and extracting its circuit parameters into other CAD systems.

The software, that is applied in this work, is used to simulate the operation of a wide range of devices, including nanoscale CMOS transistors, vertical field effect transistors, CMOS image sensors, flash memory, large powerful transistors, silicon germanium bipolar heterotransistors, high electron mobility transistors, high cy transistors, light emitting diodes, lasers, as well as new devices based on silicon, silicon-germanium, silicon carbide, gallium arsenide, and other semiconductor compounds of the A3B5 group, both triple and quaternary solid solutions.

Having the skills of working with the latest software of instrumental and technological simulation is a prerequisite for professional activities of engineers specializing in microelectronics and solving the problems of designing the electronic component base. The information provided in this manual is just an introduction, the main purpose of which is providing the initial skills of working with the environment and overcoming the psychological barrier that arises when mastering a new CAD package, creating the basis for further professional growth in the field of designing new devices for microelectronics instruments. At the same time, we should remember that a significant drawback, inevitably accompanying all such CAD systems, is a very poor information about the original physical models that formed the basis for calculations. This necessitates the continuous knowledge improvement in the field of physics of the designed instruments operation. On a concrete example it is shown that for training in bases of use of modern tools of a professional CAD for microelectronics the most optimal solution is application of techniques of e-learning that is confirmed also by publications on similar subject.

Acknowledgments. This work was supported by Ministry of Education and Science of Russian Federation (project No. 8.5098.2017/8.9).

References

1. Suhomlin, V.A.: Educational standards in the field of information technologies. Appl. Inform. **1**(37), 33–54 (2012). https://elibrary.ru/item.asp?id=17363662. (in Russian)
2. Suhomlin, V.A., Zubareva, E.V.: Standardization of IT-education based on curriculums at the present stage. Mod. Inf. Technol. IT-Educ. **12**(3–1), 40–46 (2016). https://elibrary.ru/item.asp?id=27411973. (in Russian)
3. Nechaev, V.V., Panchenko, V.M., Komarov, A.I.: Interdisciplinary "system-forming" basis of educational process organization according to studies direction. Open Educ. **5**, 70–77 (2012). https://elibrary.ru/item.asp?id=18359809. (in Russian)
4. Nechayev, V.V.: Configurational Modeling: Part I. Theoretical Aspects. MIREA, Moscow (2007). (in Russian)
5. Nechayev, V.V., Bashirov, A.S., Lebedeva, N.I., Fedin, M.A.: Adaptation of software systems to user tasks based on the method of configuration modeling. Mod. Inf. Technol. IT-Educ. **14**(2), 317–324 (2018). https://doi.org/10.25559/SITITO.14.201802.317-324
6. Demenkova, T.A., Tomashevskaya, V.S., Shirinkin, I.S.: Mobile applications for tasks of distance learning. Russ. Technol. J. **6**(1), 5–19 (2018). https://elibrary.ru/item.asp?id=32466033. (in Russian)
7. Golovanova, N.B., Rogova, V.A.: Implementation of the practically-oriented approach in the specialists training on radio engineering and communication systems. Russ. Technol. J. **6**(2), 5–19 (2018). https://rtj.mirea.ru/upload/medialibrary/19b/RTZH_2_2018_5_19.pdf
8. Radchenko, D., Sbitnev, K., Maleev, N.: Modeling of a microwave transistor based on epitaxial heterostructure (HEMT) using Synopsys Sentaurus TCAD. Prod. Electron. (7–8), 57–61 (2009). http://www.russianelectronics.ru/engineer-r/review/2327/doc/48316. (in Russian)
9. Haijun, G., et al.: Analytical model of AlGaN/GaN HEMTs with a partial GaN cap layer. Superlattices Microstruct. **123**, 210–217 (2018). https://doi.org/10.1016/j.spmi.2018.07.031
10. Vinichenko, A.N., Vasilevskii, I.S.: Pseudomorphic HEMT quantum well AlGaAs/InGaAs/GaAs with AlAs:δ-Si donor layer. In: AMNST2015. IOP Conference Series: Materials Science and Engineering, vol. 151. no. 1, p. 012037 (2016). https://doi.org/10.1088/1757-899x/151/1/012037

11. Ashok, A., Vasileska, D., Goodnick, S.M., Hartin, O.L.: Importance of the gate-dependent polarization charge on the operation of GaN HEMTs. IEEE Trans. Electron Devices **56**(5), 998–1007 (2009). https://doi.org/10.1109/TED.2009.2015822

12. Ambacher, O., et al.: Two-dimensional electron gases induced by spontaneous and piezo-electric polarization charges in N- and Ga-face AlGaN/GaNheterostructures. J. Appl. Phys. **85**(6), 3222–3233 (1999). https://doi.org/10.1063/1.369664

13. Ambacher, O., et al.: Two dimensional electron gases induced by spontaneous and piezoelectric polarization in undoped and doped AlGaN/GaN hetero-structures. J. Appl. Phys. **87**(1), 334–344 (2000). https://doi.org/10.1063/1.371866

14. Synopsys. https://www.synopsys.com/

15. Korolev, M.A., Krupkina, T.Yu., Reveleva, M.A.: Technology, designs and methods of modeling of silicon integrated chips. In: Chaplygin, Yu.A. (ed.) Part 1: Technological Processes of Production of Silicon Integrated Chips and Their Modeling. BINOM, Moscow (2007). (in Russian)

16. Korolev, M.A., Krupkina, T.Yu., Reveleva, M.A.: Technology, designs and methods of modeling of silicon integrated chips. In: Chaplygin, Yu.A. (ed.) Part 2: Elements and Routes of Production of Silicon Integrated Circuits and Methods of their Mathematical Modeling. BINOM, Moscow (2009). (in Russian)

17. Tikhomirov, V.G., Zemlyakov, V.G., Volkov, V.V., et al.: Optimization of the parameters of HEMT GaN/AlN/AlGaN heterostructures for microwave transistors using numerical simulation. Semiconductors **50**(2), 244–248 (2016). https://doi.org/10.1134/S1063782616020263

18. Farameher, S., Kalna, K., Igic, K.: Drift-diffusion and hydrodynamic modeling of current collapse in GaN HEMTs for RF power application. Semicond. Sci. Technol. **29**(2), 25007–25017 (2014). https://doi.org/10.1088/0268-1242/29/2/025007

19. Yachmenev, A.E., Ryzhii1, V.I., Maltsev, P.P.: GaAs PHEMT performance increase using delta-doping in the form of nanowires of tin atoms. Russ. Technol. J. **5**(2), 40–46 (2017). https://elibrary.ru/item.asp?id=29711757. (in Russian)

20. Vimala, P., Vidyashree, L.: Modeling and simulation of unilateral power gain for GaN/AlGaN HEMT. Int. J. Adv. Eng. Glob. Technol. **04**(04), 2105–2109 (2016)

21. Parveen, M., Bhattacharya, M., Jogi, J.: Modeling of InAlAs/InGaAs/InAlAs DG-HEMT mixer for microwave application. IOSR J. Electron. Commun. Eng. **10**(4-II), 21–27 (2015). https://doi.org/10.9790/2834-10422127

22. Parveen, et al.: Intrinsic admittance parameter for separate gate InAlAs/InGaAs DG-HEMT for 100 nm Gate length. In: 2013 IEEE Conference on Information & Communication Technologies, Thuckalay, Tamil Nadu, India, pp. 750–754 (2013). https://doi.org/10.1109/cict.2013.6558194

23. Agarwal, A., Goswami, A., Sen, S., Gupta, R.S.: Capacitance-voltage characteristics and cut-off frequency of pseudomorphic (AlGaAs/InGaAs) modulation-doped field-effect transistor for microwave and high-speed circuit applications. Microw. Opt. Technol. Lett. **23**(5), 312–318 (1999). https://doi.org/10.1002/(SICI)1098-2760(19991205)23:5<312::AID-MOP16>3.0.CO;2-S

24. Ahlawat, A., Pandey, M.: Microwave analysis of 70 nm InGaAs pHEMT on InP substrate for nanoscale digital IC application. Microw. Opt. Technol. Lett. **49**(10), 2462–2470 (2007). https://doi.org/10.1002/mop.22779

25. Vitanov, S., Palankovski, V., Murad, S., Rodle, T., Quay, R., Selberherr, S.: Predictive simulation of AlGaN/GaN HEMTs. In: 2007 IEEE Compound Semiconductor Integrated Circuits Symposium, Portland, Oregon, USA, pp. 1–4 (2007). https://doi.org/10.1109/csics07.2007.31

26. Swain, R., Jena, K., Lenka, T.R.: Model development for current–voltage and transconductance characteristics of normally-off AlN/GaN MOSHEMT. Semiconductors **50**(3), 384–389 (2016). https://doi.org/10.1134/S1063782616030210

27. Uren, M.J., Moreke, J., Kuball, M.: Buffer design to minimize current collapse in GaN/AlGaN HFETs. IEEE Trans. Electron Devices **59**(12), 3327–3333 (2012). https://doi.org/10.1109/TED.2012.2216535
28. Latrach, S., et al.: Trap states analysis in AlGaN/AlN/GaN and InAlN/AlN/GaN high electron mobility transistors. Curr. Appl. Phys. **17**(12), 1601–1608 (2017). https://doi.org/10.1016/j.cap.2017.09.003
29. Ubochi, B., Ahmeda, K., Kalna, K.: Buffer trap related knee walkout and the effects of self-heating in AlGaN/GaN HEMTs. ECS J. Solid State Sci. Technol. **6**(11), S3005–S3009 (2017). https://doi.org/10.1149/2.0021711jss
30. Uren, M.J., Kuball, M.: GaN transistor reliability and instabilities. In: The Tenth International Conference on Advanced Semiconductor Devices and Microsystems, Smolenice, pp. 1–8 (2014). https://doi.org/10.1109/asdam.2014.6998665
31. Fiorenza, P., Greco, G., Iucolano, F., Patti, A., Roccaforte, F.: Slow and fast traps in metal-oxide-semiconductor capacitors fabricated on recessed AlGaN/GaN heterostructures. Appl. Phys. Lett. **106**(14), 142903 (2015). https://doi.org/10.1063/1.4917250

Approach for Personalizing the Education Content Based on Data Mining for a Cloud Platform

Veronika Zaporozhko[1] , Denis Parfenov[2]([⊠]) , Vladimir Shardakov[3] ,
Igor Parfenov[2] , and Larisa Anciferova[3]

[1] Department of Informatics, Orenburg State University,
Pobeda Ave., 13, 460018 Orenburg, Russia
`zaporozhko_vv@mail.osu.ru`
[2] Department of Applied Mathematics, Orenburg State University,
Pobeda Ave., 13, 460018 Orenburg, Russia
`prmat@mail.osu.ru`
[3] Faculty of Distance Learning Technologies, Orenburg State University,
Pobeda Ave., 13, 460018 Orenburg, Russia
`fdotinfo@mail.osu.ru`

Abstract. Cloud-based learning environments, one of the main components of which are massive open online courses, have enormous collections of Big data. Rapid growth of the volumes of collected and stored information allows using methods of Data Mining. One of the main directions for further improvement of the online courses is to provide complex personalization. The need for personalization of learning is a reflection of the natural for mankind desire for an individual approach to personal needs, preferences and opportunities. A serious disadvantage of the online courses is the lack of an individual and differentiated approach to each student due to a pre-determined learning route in typical courses. We have developed a heuristic algorithm that implements methods of intellectual management of individual educational trajectories. The developed algorithm allows building an optimal individual learning route for each student, providing the widest possible opportunities and comfortable conditions for personalized learning. Using the proposed algorithm will dynamically development and correct the individual educational trajectory of each student within the course. The algorithm takes into account a variety of parameters: age, diagnostic questionnaire results, tests score, features of perception and memorization of the material.

Keywords: Cloud computing · Big data · Data mining · Online course · Massive open online course · MOOC · Personalization · Personalized learning · Adaptive learning · Individual educational trajectory · Individual learning route · Evolutionary algorithms

1 Introduction

Intellectual processing of large amounts of data (Big data) in a branch such as education is becoming more and more in demand [1]. Researchers are searching for algorithms that

V. Sukhomlin and E. Zubareva (Eds.): SITITO 2018, CCIS 1201, pp. 134–145, 2020.
https://doi.org/10.1007/978-3-030-46895-8_11

allow efficient processing of such data to extract useful information and make decisions. This is especially important for the further development and improvement of online learning. This approach can be used to design and create an intelligent cloud-based learning environment in which conditions must be realized to maximize the personal potential (self-realization) of each learner. This is quite achievable due to the intellectual management of individual educational trajectories with the provision of complex personalization in massive open online courses (MOOCs).

The work is organized as follows. Section 2 provides an overview of the researches on Educational Data Mining/Learning analytics (EDM/LA). Section 3 presents the architecture of an intelligent cloud-based learning environment, describes the functionality of the hybrid MOOC Intelligent System, which provides personalization in online courses. Section 4 shows the genetic algorithm on the basis of which an individual educational trajectory is generated within the online course. Further directions of our research are described in Sect. 5.

2 Existing Approaches

In this section, we will consider the Educational Data Mining/Learning analytics in MOOCs.

Researcher Baker believes that in the field of "Education" data mining and analytics also have a huge transformational potential: the discovery of how people learn, predict learning and understand the real behavior of learning. Achieving these goals, EDM can be used to develop more advanced and intelligent learning technologies and to better inform students and educators [2].

MOOC provides more information on how a large number of students interact with educational platforms and interact with the offered courses. This vast amount of data provided by MOOCs regarding information about the use of students is the gold mine for EDM [3]. According to Romer, Ventura, EDM can help solve the following problems in MOOC: predicting students at risk of dropout; adapting learning and making recommendations; grading, assessing, and providing feedback to students; analyzing students' interactions.

Scientists from Spain have reviewed many different methods and techniques adapted from other disciplines or specifically designed for the analysis of educational data [3]. These include, for example, social network analysis, knowledge tracing, text mining, process mining, distillation of data for human judgment [4, 5].

Mukala and others suggested conducting an analysis of students' behavior on the basis of trails of click events that they generated. The data obtained allowed to improve both the quality and delivery of MOOCs [6].

Researchers from New Zealand predicted the progress of students through the tracks that they leave during the MOOC. Algorithms for data mining, but for machine learning, were applied to weekly generated student data, as students progressed at the rate to predict which students were at risk of failing to meet the requirements of the course, or were likely to fail [7].

Erman Yukselturk and others studied the possibility of predicting the dropout of students from MOOC with the help of such methods of intelligent data analysis as k-Nearest Neighbor, Decision Tree, Naive Bayes and Neural Network [8].

3   Intellectual Management of the Individual Educational Trajectory in the Online Course

The self-organizing cloud-based learning environment, in which complex personalization is realized, is characterized by high dynamism, complexity, uncertainty and handling of huge data flows. The architecture of this multi-dimensional, holistic environment is shown in Fig. 1.

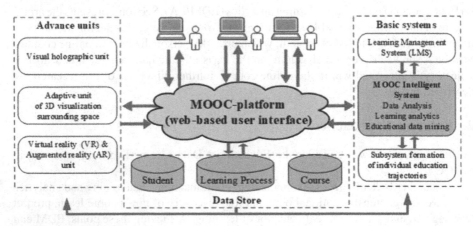

Fig. 1. The architecture an intelligent cloud-based learning environment.

The functioning of this cloud-based learning environment is carried out on the basis of processing and analysis of Big data using the methods of Data Analysis, Learning Analytics, Educational Data Mining.

The hybrid MOOC Intelligent System allows solving the task of providing complex personalization in the cloud-based learning environment, using a whole arsenal of methods for simulating the intellectual activity of a person. For example, at the level of the MOOC platform, neural network technologies are used to dynamically space-time the individual educational trajectories of students. To solve this problem, the Kohonen network is built, since it most efficiently performs clustering and classification of objects [9]. This network consists of many neurons and is trained without a teacher on the basis of self-organization. A neural network based on knowledge of the learner determines an acceptable plan of learning activities, taking into account the level of readiness for the development of educational programs, learning objectives, a list of specific competencies and the components of their planned learning outcomes, academic achievements). In this way, an individual curriculum for the study of various disciplines, modules or electives is built up, taking into account their interdisciplinary integration and time boundaries.

Thanks to cluster analysis, the following functionalities are implemented [10, 11]:

– differentiation of the listeners of the online course for the organization of purposeful collaborative work (the discovery of students with similar psychological, physiological, behavioral and intellectual characteristics);

– issuance of personal (individual) step-by-step recommendations on the development of additional educational facilities (video lessons, workshops, assessment assignments, etc.) in the online course;
– identification of students who are a risk group for academic achievement in the online course (used to prevent the early dropout from the online course or to identify students who may not be able to cope with the final exam/test).

Within the framework of a specific course, based on the genetic algorithm [12], an acceptable (optimal) individual learning route is formed, which is a sequence of elements of the learning activity (learning objects) of the particular learner at some fixed stage of mastering the online course. This algorithm allows you to dynamically build and adjust the individual educational trajectory of each student, depending on the set of parameters: learning objectives, age and gender, input questionnaire data, learning style, and tests score. Thus, for each learner, adaptive electronic learning content is formed within a certain online course.

4 Forming of an Individual Educational Trajectory in MOOC

In this research to solve the problem of forming an individual educational trajectory in MOOC we will use a genetic algorithm.

4.1 Genetic Algorithm

The practical task of forming the optimal individual educational trajectory in MOOC is complex and multicriteria. Multicriteria optimization consists in finding the best (acceptable, optimal) solution, satisfying several criteria that are not reducible to each other. Traditional algorithms and methods for optimizing the solution of the desired problem do not give the desired result. The following reasons are identified: the need to determine a large number of criteria for the search task, an extensive search area. Therefore, it is expedient in this case to use genetic algorithms.

«Genetic algorithms are search algorithms based on the mechanics of natural selection and natural genetics» (Goldberg) [13].

Prior research has shown [13, 14] that the problem of finding the optimal solution based on genetic algorithms is effectively solved if:

1. It is necessary to operate with a set of parameters simultaneously, that is, carry out multicriteria search.
2. An extensive search is given. This is important especially when it is infinite, or changes in time, or has a multiple local optimum.
3. Parallel processing of a number of alternative solutions is desirable.
4. There is no need for a strict search for a global optimum, but it is enough to find an acceptable, most suitable solution in a short time.

The solution of multicriteria problems is not the only optimal solution, but the set of compromise solutions known as Pareto-optimal (effective solutions).

4.2 Algorithm of Generating Initial Data for Forming an Individual Educational Trajectory in MOOC

One way to implement an individual educational trajectory in MOOC is to form an individual learning route, consisting of learning objects (LO) of the discipline, module or elective. The individual learning route is a varied set of LO of different types. A LO can be a video, a presentation, a quiz, an audio, an ebook or any other kind of document or multimedia objects you use to create course content for online learning. Their list is compiled on the basis of the received primary information and is subsequently corrected in real time. You will recall that a learning objects in MOOC is considered as a separate structural element of electronic learning content, corresponding to a specific learning goal and contributing to the overall goal of the course [15]. The number of possible individual learning routes in the course depends on the number of selected LOs.

To determine the characteristics of students' perception and memorization of information (learning style), we will use the diagnostics of the dominant perceptive modality – VARK (authors: Fleming and Mills1992) [16]. The VARK method shows how a person perceives information. The acronym VARK stands for Visual (V), Aural (A), Read-write (R), and Kinesthetic (K) sensory modalities that are used for learning information. In the framework of this VARK model, researchers identify four types of students [17]:

1. Visual learners (information to arrive in the form of graphs, charts, and flow diagrams).
2. Aural learners (information exchange as speech that arrives at the learner's ear).
3. Read-write learners (reading and writing are their preferred modes for receiving in information).
4. Kinesthetic learners (concrete, multi-sensory experiences in their learning).

To construct an optimal individual learning route, we have developed an algorithm for generating initial data. Conditionally, the algorithm can be represented as the following sequence of actions:

Step 1. Identify the possible types of electronic learning content specific to any course. To match VARK, we combine them into four generalized groups (Table 1). The first group consisted of the content types most suitable for students with the dominant «Visual» modality. The second group is for students with the dominant modality «Aural». The third group is for students with the dominant modality «Read-write». The fourth group is for students with the dominant modality «Kinesthetic».

Table 1. Composition of four generalized groups of different types of content.

Type of electronic educational content	Dominating learning styles	The designation of the type of content	The attribute value coefficient	Relative attribute weight (b)
Group 1. Types of content most suitable for students with the dominant modality «Visual» (G_1)				
Presentations (slides), textbooks with diagrams, flowcharts, pictures, etc.	V	LO_1	μ_1	1
Infographics (mind maps, charts, diagrams, etc.), illustrations (pictures, posters)	V	LO_2		
Webinars (video online meetings)	V	LO_3		
Video lessons, recording screencasts, animated video clips (2D &3D animation)	V	LO_4		
Group 2. Types of content most suitable for students with the dominant modality «Aural/Auditory» (G_2)				
Audio conferencing and online meetings	A	LO_5	μ_2	1
Audio notes	A	LO_6		
Audio lessons (recordings)	A	LO_7		
Workbooks audio	A	LO_8		
Group 3. Types of content most suitable for students with the dominant modality «Read/write» (G_3)				
Glossaries (thesaurus, dictionaries)	R	LO_9	μ_3	2
Reading (lecture notes, ebooks, tutorials, manuals, reports, articles, interactive textbooks, documents)	R	LO_{10}		
Quizzes (or tests)	R	LO_{11}		
Assignments (self-reports, tasks, essays, exercises, project works, mini action researches)	R	LO_{12}		

(*continued*)

Table 1. (*continued*)

Type of electronic educational content	Dominating learning styles	The designation of the type of content	The attribute value coefficient	Relative attribute weight (b)
Group 4. Types of content most suitable for students with the dominant modality «Kinesthetic» (G_4)				
Games (educational games, including simulation video games, virtual worlds)	K	LO_{13}	μ_4	2
Virtual laboratories (interactive training systems)	K	LO_{14}		
Interactive learning models	K	LO_{15}		
Workshops	K	LO_{16}		

Step 2. Introduce the standard course as a set of interrelated units, each of which must contain a certain set of learning objects of different types (Fig. 2). The data for each course is stored in the «Data Store Course» [18].

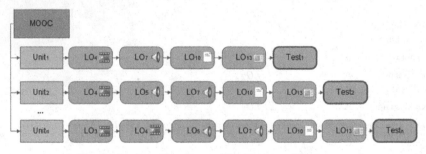

Fig. 2. An example of a possible structure of the course.

Step 3. Identify the dominant learning style of each student's when he or she registered and enrolled in specific online course. To do this, you must use the VARK questionnaire. The list of questions is presented on the official website (http://vark-learn.com/the-vark-questionnaire/). So 15,457 people of different gender and age groups participated in the questionnaire survey, which ensured the representativeness of the research.

The generation of certain types of content for each course student takes place in accordance with the dominant learning style. For example, for Visual learners, it's more logical to add as many LOs as possible to the course of the first group, and for Aural learners – LOs of the second group. Nevertheless, research scientists have shown that the combination of different channels of information perception makes the learning process more successful. In addition, most learners can have mixed models. For example,

Willingham states that «It is true that some people have especially good visual or auditory memories» [19].

Therefore, we proposed to generate the course with different types of content, but at the same time taking into account the revealed dominant modality as much as possible. In this case, we believe that learning in the cloud-based learning environment will be personalized and most successful.

Based on the results of the survey, we will determine the ratio of different types of content in a specific online course for each type of student (Table 2). Then the sum of the content types ratio of the different groups for each type of learner should be equal to one ($\mu_1 + \mu_2 + \mu_3 + \mu_4 = 1$). Varying the ratio of μ_1, μ_2, μ_3 and μ_4 in the overall content structure gives different sets of LOs in the individual learning route.

Table 2. The ratio of different types of content in the course.

Types of students (by VARK)	The weight of each type of content in the course structure			
	G_1	G_2	G_3	G_4
	μ_1	μ_2	μ_3	μ_4
Visual learners	0.31	0.21	0.26	0.22
Aural learners	0.25	0.31	0.22	0.22
Read-write learners	0.24	0.18	0.34	0.24
Kinesthetic learners	0.22	0.23	0.24	0.31

Step 4. Extract the information stored in the datastore, which characterizing each student. Some of the data was received by the course attendee while filling in the profile, and the other part of the data was obtained from the results of the questionnaire (Table 3). Such characteristics included such as gender, age and learning style.

Step 5. During the learning on the MOOC platform, the data of the student's learning process is recorded in the «Data Store Learning Process» in real time. The datastore contains a set of different characteristics that describe the learning process (progress of learners) based on a specific online course. The value of these characteristics is constantly changing in the learning process. Such a characteristic includes the scores for evaluated final test in each unit.

4.3 A Model for the Formation of the Individual Educational Trajectory in MOOC

Let us present the initial data for solving the claimed problem with the help of the mathematical tools of the genetic algorithm. Having analyzed the subject area of the

Table 3. Characteristics and values of attributes for a set of students.

Attribute name	Attribute (parameter)	Possible attribute values	The attribute value coefficient	Relative attribute weight (v)
a_1	Gender	Female	$a_{1,1}$	1
		Male	$a_{1,2}$	
a_2	Age group	Under 18	$a_{2,1}$	2
		19–25	$a_{2,2}$	
		26–34	$a_{2,3}$	
		35–44	$a_{2,4}$	
		45–54	$a_{2,5}$	
		55+	$a_{2,6}$	
a_3	Learning style	Visual learners	$a_{3,1}$	3
		Aural learners	$a_{3,2}$	
		Read-write learners	$a_{3,3}$	
		Kinesthetic learners	$a_{3,4}$	

task, we have identified the following tuple, characterizing the formation process of the individual educational trajectory (IET).

$$IET = \{S, C, P\}, \tag{1}$$

where $S = \{s_k\}$ – the set of students learning a particular MOOC, k – number of students, $k \in N$; $C = \{Unit_x\}$ – MOOC, located in a cloud-based learning environment and consisting of units, x – number of units in a particular course, $x \in N$.

Each unit of the MOOC contains a specific set of content groups. Then let $G = \{g_1, ..., g_n\}$ – the set of generalized content type groups, где n – number of these groups, $n = 4$. Each group contains a certain set of learning objects $g_i = \{LO_{i,j}\}$, where $LO_{i,j}$ – the set of LOs in each unit, belonging to the selected generalized group g_i (Table 1). $Unit_x = \{G_1, ..., G_4\}$. Then $P = \{P_1, ..., P_n\}$ is a valid set of individual routes for each student. Each individual learning route should consist of a specific set of $LO_{i,j}$ different types (according to the Table 1). Each learning object $LO_{i,j}$ can take part in the formation of an individual learning route with its mandatory entry into a generalized group g_i. For the purposes of formalization, we introduce the Boolean variables 0 or 1, which describe alternatives to the selection of learning objects, i.e. $LO_{i,j} = \{0,1\}$.

Each object of the sets G and S can be represented as a set of attributes that numerically characterize these objects. Attributes are defined on a limited set of positive values. The definition of characteristics and values of attributes (parameters) for the identified sets is presented in Tables 1 and 3, respectively. The task of determining the value of the attribute coefficient and the relative weight of the attribute is solved using empirical data, obtained as a result of the questionnaire, and expert estimates. To identify the relative weights of these attributes, experts were asked who ranked attribute values in order of increasing importance.

The weight of each unit in the course is determined by the following formula:

$$W_{Unit_x} = \prod_{h=1}^{D} (\mu_{h,s_k})^{b_h}, \qquad (2)$$

where μ_{h,s_k} – attribute coefficient value μ_h for unit x depending on the particular type of student s_k, b_h – relative weight of attribute g_h for unit x (Table 1).

To select an individual learning route in MOOC, you also need to find the weight of the student. The weight of each student is determined by the following formula:

$$W_{s_k} = \prod_{y=1}^{Z} (a_{y,s_k})^{v_y}, \qquad (3)$$

where a_{y,s_k} – attribute coefficient value a_y for student s_k, v_y – relative weight of attribute a_y (Table 3).

In the process of optimization under consideration, the parameter space under study is sufficiently large. The task does not require a strict global optimum, so it is sufficient to find an acceptable, most suitable (effective) solution in a short time. To find an acceptable (optimal) individual learning route P in a cloud-based learning environment (depending on parameters $a_1 \ldots a_3$, $\mu_1 \ldots \mu_4$), we use the genetic algorithm. Flowchart of the genetic algorithm is shown in Fig. 3.

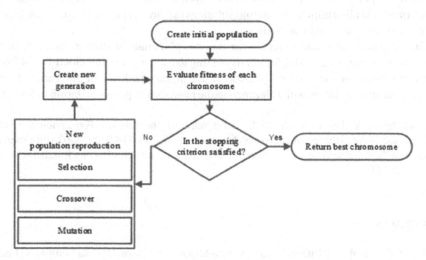

Fig. 3. A genetic algorithm flow chart.

As part of the organization of the genetic algorithm and its subsequent implementation, we define the following concepts.

The objective function numerically characterizes the result of selecting an individual educational trajectory in MOOC by the following formula:

$$F(P) = F(P)\text{max} - \sum_1^x \left(W_{Unit_x} \cdot W_{s_k} \cdot T_x(S_k) \cdot Z(P_x)\right), \tag{4}$$

where P – vector of selection of individual learning route; W_{unit_x} – the weight of each unit in the course; W_{s_k} – the weight of each student; $T_x(S_k)$ – student test score in each unit; $F(P)_{max}$ – maximum value of the objective function; $Z(P_x)$ – function of formation a set of LOs.

Population is a collection of several vectors P. The size of the population is set before the genetic algorithm begins work. The individual is one element of the vector P. The gene is an element of $LO_{i,j}$ from the vector P. The criteria for termination of the genetic algorithm are as follows: obtaining a solution of the required quality; the solution falls into a deep local optimum of the objective function; search time expired.

5   Conclusion

For the task of intellectual management of individual educational trajectories in MOOC, various methods Data Mining of solving it have been identified. This paper has described a genetic algorithm that allows in real time to create and adjust the optimal individual learning route for each student, taking into account his preferences, educational opportunities and needs. We have tested the proposed algorithm on the example of two online courses for students of the faculty of distance education technologies. The results showed that the proposed algorithm is able to find solutions that are very close to optimal solutions and in most cases are identical to them.

This research has found several area that has potential for further research. In the future, we will present a model for personalizing the self-organizing cloud-based learning environment. We will investigate other intelligent methods of Educational Data Mining/Learning analytics with reference to the provision of personalization in MOOCs.

Acknowledgments. The research work was funded by the Russian Foundation for Basic Research, according to the research projects No. 16-29-09639, 18-37-00400,18-07-01446 and the President of the Russian Federation within the grant for state support of young Russian scientists (MK-860.2019.9).

References

1. Baker, R.S., et al.: Educational data mining: a MOOC experience. In: Data Mining and Learning Analytics: Applications in Educational Research, pp. 55–66. Wiley Blackwell (2016). https://doi.org/10.1002/9781118998205.ch4
2. Baker, R.S.: Educational data mining: an advance for intelligent systems in education. IEEE Intell. Syst. **29**(3), 78–82 (2014). https://doi.org/10.1109/MIS.2014.42
3. Romer, C., Ventura, S.: Educational data science in massive open online courses. WIREs Data Min. Knowl. Discov. **7**(1), e1187 (2017). https://doi.org/10.1002/widm.1187

4. Calvet, L., Perez, J.: Educational data mining and learning analytics: differences, similarities, and time evolution. Int. J. Educ. Technol. High. Educ. **12**(3), 98–112 (2015). https://doi.org/10.7238/rusc.v12i3.2515
5. Merceron, A.: Educational data mining learning analytics: methods, tasks and current trends. In: Proceedings of DeLFI Workshops 2015 Co-located with 13th e-Learning Conference of the German Computer Society (DeLFI 2015), pp. 101–109, München, Germany (2015). http://ceur-ws.org/Vol-1443/paper22.pdf
6. Mukala, P., Buijs, M., Aalst, P.: Exploring students' learning behaviour in MOOCs using process mining techniques. BPM reports, vol. 1510, p. 25. BPMcenter. org (2015)
7. Umer, R., Susnjak, T., Mathrani, A., Suriadi, S.: On predicting academic performance with process mining in learning analytics. J. Res. Innov. Teach. Learn. **10**(2), 160–176 (2017). https://doi.org/10.1108/JRIT-09-2017-0022
8. Yukselturk, E., Ozekes, S., Turel, Y.K.: Predicting dropout student: an application of data mining methods in an online education program. Eur. J. Open, Distance E-Learning **17**(1), 118–133 (2014). https://doi.org/10.2478/eurodl-2014-0008
9. Hagan, M.T., Demuth, H.B., Beale, M.H., Jesús, O.D.: Neural Network Design, 2nd edn. Academic Press, New York (1995)
10. Aldenderfer, M.S., Blashfield, R.K.: Cluster Analysis. Sage Press, Beverly Hills (1984)
11. Everitt, B.S., Landau, S., Leese, M.: Cluster Analysis, 4th edn. Arnold, London (2009)
12. Koehn, P.: Combining Genetic Algorithms and Neural Networks. The Encoding Problem (1994)
13. Goldberg, D.E.: Genetic Algorithms in Search, Optimization, and Machine Learning. Addison-Wesley, Boston (1989)
14. Holland, J.H.: Adaptation in Natural and Artificial Systems. An Introductory Analysis with Applications to Biology, Control, and Artificial Intelligence. MIT Press, Cambridge (1992)
15. Zaporozhko,, V., Parfenov, D., Parfenov, I., Approaches to the description of model massive open online course based on the cloud platform in the educational environment of the university. In: SEEL: International Conference on Smart Education and Smart e-Learning 2017: Conference Proceedings, 21–23 June 2017, vol. 75, pp. 177–187, Vilamoura, Portugal (2017)
16. Fleming, N.D., Mills C.: Helping Students Understand How They Learn. The Teaching Professor, vol. 7, issue 4. Magma Publications, Madison (1992)
17. Zapalska, A., Brozik, D.: Learning styles and online education. Procedia Campus Wide Inf. Syst. **23**(5), 325–335 (2006)
18. Parfenov, D., Zaporozhko, V.: Developing SMART educational cloud environment on the basis of adaptive massive open online courses. In: EMIT 2018 Internationalization of Education in Applied Mathematics and Informatics for HighTech Applications: Proceedings of the Workshop, 27–29 March 2018, vol. 2093, pp. 35–41, Leipzig, Germany (2018)
19. Willingham, D.T.: Why Don't Students Like School? A Cognitive Scientist Answers Questions About How the Mind Works and What It Means for Your Classroom. Jossey-Bass, San Francisco (2009)

Educational Resources and Best Practices of IT-Education

Creating a Unified Educational Environment for Training IT Specialists of Organizations of the JINR Member States in the Field of Cloud Technologies

Nikita Balashov[1] , Alexander Baranov[1] , Ruslan Kuchumov[1,2] ,
Nikolay Kutovskiy[1] , Yelena Mazhitova[1,3](✉) , Igor Pelevanyk[1] ,
and Roman Semenov[1,4]

[1] Joint Institute for Nuclear Research,
Joliot-Curie St. 6, 141980 Dubna, Moscow Region, Russia
emazhitova@jinr.ru
[2] Saint Petersburg State University, Universitetskaya nab. 7/9, 199034 Saint Petersburg, Russia
[3] Institute of Nuclear Physics, Ibragimov Str. 1, 050032 Almaty, Kazakhstan
[4] Plekhanov Russian University of Economics, Stremyannyj per. 36, 115093 Moscow, Russia

Abstract. Modern science heavy relies on the usage of information technologies (IT). It is important to organize knowledge transfer from IT specialists to non-IT and to less educated and/or skilled IT ones. Nowadays a speed of IT development (as well as achievements of the results these IT are used for) can be sufficiently increased by joining efforts and resources of cooperating organizations, which solve similar tasks. An important aspect of such cooperation is an experience exchange and knowledge transfer, which can be obtained by participating in conferences, seminars, workshops, master classes, etc. That article provides information on the activities around a cloud infrastructure created at the Laboratory of Information Technologies of the Joint Institute for Nuclear Research (JINR). It describes a purpose of its creation, implemented features, use-cases and training events it is used in. A relevance of the JINR and its Member State organizations clouds integration based on the DIRAC middleware is described too. Particular attention is paid to a process of knowledge transfer from JINR colleagues to fellows of other participating institutions through the organizing and holding of seminars, schools, conferences, round tables as well as semestrial training courses for students.

Keywords: Cloud computing · OpenNebula · Virtualization · Virtual machine · Clouds integration · DIRAC · Training · VMware

1 Introduction

An informatization of the society is a global social process one of the key characteristic of which is that mainstreamed activity in the sphere of social production is data acquisition, accumulation, processing, transfer and usage as well as a production of information with

V. Sukhomlin and E. Zubareva (Eds.): SITITO 2018, CCIS 1201, pp. 149–162, 2020.
https://doi.org/10.1007/978-3-030-46895-8_12

the help of modern computing devices and various means of informational interactions and exchange [1].

Information technologies play an important role in modern science, which is tightly related with a necessity to manage huge date volumes and analyze them.

Apart from other duties the Laboratory of Information technologies (LIT) is responsible for supplying network, computing and storage resources as well as mathematical support for wide range of scientific projects the JINR and its Member State organizations participate in. A hardware support of such LIT's responsibility is realized on the basis of Multifunctional Information and Computing Complex (MICC) [2].

One of the MICC component is a JINR cloud infrastructure [3] (hereinafter referred to as "JINR cloud service", "JINR cloud", "cloud"). It was created in order to manage LIT IT services and servers more efficiently using modern technologies, to increase the efficiency of hardware utilization and services reliability, to simplify access to application software and to optimize proprietary software usage as well as to provide a modern computing facility for JINR users, a local private cloud infrastructure was created. Apart from listed above tasks the JINR cloud resources are actively used for various trainings on grid, cloud and Big Data technologies. More details on that service are provided below.

2   The JINR Cloud Infrastructure

The LIT JINR cloud is based on OpenNebula software [4]. It consists of the several major components:

- OpenNebula core,
- OpenNebula scheduler,
- MySQL database back-end,
- user and API interfaces,
- cloud worker nodes (CWNs) where KVM-based virtual machines (VMs) or OpenVZ containers (CTs) are running.

A schema of the JINR cloud architecture is shown on the Fig. 1.
There are the following types of servers:

- Cloud worker nodes (CWNs) which host virtual machines (VMs) and containers (CTs) are marked on the figure by numeral "1" in a grey square;
- Cloud front-end nodes (CFNs) where all core OpenNebula services including database, scheduler and some other ones are deployed (such hosts are marked on the figure by black numeral "2" inside the same color square);
- Cloud storage nodes (CSNs) based on Ceph SDS for keeping VMs' and CTs' images as well as users' data (marked by black numeral "3" inside the same color square).

Following the OpenNebula documentation recommendations the JINR cloud has odd number of the front-end nodes – three ones which provides a fault-tolerance for 1 node.

All these servers are connected to the same set of networks:

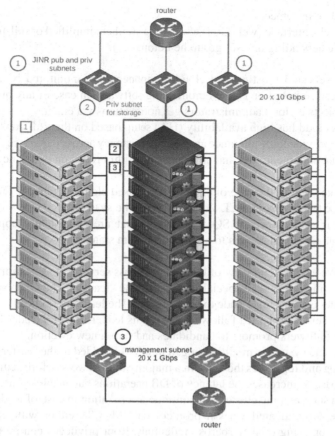

Fig. 1. The schema of the JINR cloud Raft HA architecture.

- JINR public and private subnets (they are marked on the figure by blue lines near which the numeral "1" is placed in the same color circle and signed as "JINR pub and priv subnets");
- An isolated private network dedicated for a SDS traffic (dark green lines with numeral "2" in a circle of the same color and signed as "Priv subnet for storage");
- Management network (black lines with numeral "3" in a circle of the same color singed as "management subnet").

All network switches excluding those which are for the management network have 48 ports with 10 GbE each as well as four 40 Gbps SPF-ports for uplinks.

All cloud resources are splitted into few clusters depending on virtualization (KVM or OpenVZ) type and scientific experiment resources are used by. In case of KVM its virtual instance is called "virtual machine" or "VM" whereas in case of OpenVZ it is "container" or "CT".

The JINR cloud service provides two user interfaces:

- command line interface;
- graphical web-interface (web-GUI) «Sunstone» (either simplified or full-featured one are possible depending on user group he belongs to).

Cloud servers and most critical cloud components are monitored by a dedicated monitoring service based on Nagios monitoring software. In case of any problem with monitored objects a cloud administrators get notifications via email.

The JINR cloud has high availability (HA) setup based on the Raft consensus algorithm [5, 6] to provide fault-tolerance and state consistency across its services. According to OpenNebula documentation that consensus algorithm relies on two concepts:

- System State what in the case of OpenNebula-based clouds means the data stored in the database tables (users, ACLs, or the VMs in the system);
- Log what is a sequence of SQL statements that are consistently applied to the OpenNebula DB in all servers to evolve the system state.

To preserve a consistent view of the system across servers, modifications to system state are performed through a special node called the "leader". The OpenNebula cloud front-end nodes elect a single node to be the leader. The leader periodically sends heartbeats to the other CFNs called followers to keep its leadership. If a leader fails to send the heartbeat followers promote to candidates and start a new election.

Whenever the system is modified (e.g. a new VM is added to the cluster), the leader updates the log and replicates the entry in a majority of followers before actually writing it to the database. It increases the latency of DB operations but enables a safe replication of the system state and the cluster can continue its operation in case of leader failure.

Users are authenticated via ssh protocol on VMs/CTs either with help of their {rsa,dsa}-key or using own Kerberos credentials. Root privileges can be gained with help of sudo tool. The authentication in the cloud web-GUI is based on Kerberos credentials too. SSL encryption is enabled to make more secure information exchange between web-GUI and users' browsers.

All CFNs and CWNs are connected through 10 GbE network interfaces to the corresponding rack switches which in their turn are connected to the backbone router.

At the moment of writing that article the JINR cloud has about 1600 CPU cores and 8.1 TB of RAM.

Apart from the locally deployed CWNs the JINR cloud has some amount of external resources from the partner organizations of JINR Member State (see below for more details).

3   Ceph-Based Software Defined Storage

Another key component of the JINR cloud infrastructure is a software-defined storage (SDS) based on Ceph [7]. It delivers object, block and file storage in one unified system. According to Ceph documentation, each ceph server can play a single or few roles, which are the following:

- Monitor (mon). It maintains maps of the cluster state, including the monitor map, manager map, the OSD map, and the CRUSH map. These maps are critical cluster state required for Ceph daemons to coordinate with each other. Monitors are also responsible for managing authentication between daemons and clients. At least three monitors are normally required for redundancy and high availability;
- Manager (mgr). It is responsible for keeping track of runtime metrics and the current state of the Ceph cluster, including storage utilization, current performance metrics, and system load. The Ceph Manager daemons also host python-based plugins to manage and expose Ceph cluster information, including a web-based dashboard and REST API. At least two managers are normally required for high availability;
- Object storage daemon (OSD). It stores data, handles data replication, recovery, rebalancing, and provides some monitoring information to Ceph Monitors and Managers by checking other Ceph OSD Daemons for a heartbeat. At least 3 Ceph OSDs are normally required for redundancy and high availability;
- Metadata Server (MDS). It stores metadata on behalf of the Ceph Filesystem. Ceph MDSs allow POSIX file system users to execute basic commands (like ls, find, etc.) without placing an enormous burden on the Ceph Storage Cluster.

Apart from these daemons, there is RADOS gateway (RGW) which provides interfaces for interacting with the storage cluster.

The JINR Ceph-based SDS deployment schema as well as each server roles are shown on the Fig. 2.

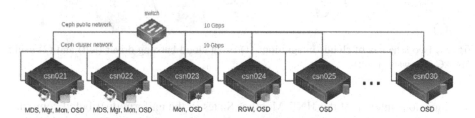

Fig. 2. The schema of the Ceph-based software-defined storage deployed at LIT JINR.

At the moment of writing that article total amount of raw disk space in that SDS is about 1 PB. Due to triple replication, an effective disk space available for users is about 330 TB.

4 Clouds Integration

A necessity to process and analyze huge data volumes as well as a luck of computing and storage resources in a single place for such kind of tasks led to development of worldwide distributed information and computing infrastructures which integrates resources all over the world.

The JINR also participates in the large number of research projects in many of which computing infrastructures play important role in obtaining meaningful scientific results.

In that connection, an integration of JINR Member State organizations resources in uniform distributed information and computing environment (DICE) is an important and topical task, the solution of which would significantly accelerate a scientific research [8].

Each organization participating in joining its local computational resources created or being creating a private cloud infrastructure for effective utilization of resources.

Initially a driver for clouds integration following so called "cloud bursting" model [9] was developed by the fellows of the LIT JINR. That driver had been successfully used during several years as a tool for joining clouds from such the JINR Member State organizations as Plekhanov Russian University of Economics (Moscow, Russia), Bogolyubov Institute for Theoretical Physics (Kiev, Ukraine) and the Institute of Physics of the National Academy of Sciences of Azerbaijan (Baku, Azerbaijan).

A scheme of the clouds integration following the "cloud bursting" model is shown on the Fig. 3, left.

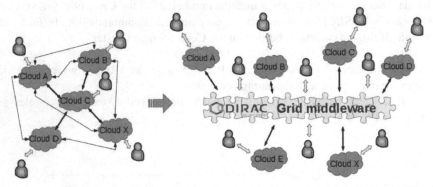

Fig. 3. Two schemas of clouds integration: (1) using cloud bursting driver (left) and (2) using DIRAC interware (right).

Enormous interest of the JINR Member States in the uniform distributed computational environment has led to the growing number of its participants. That revealed a low scalability of approach used due to sufficiently increased complexity of such infrastructure maintenance (every new cloud integration requires changes in configuration files of every integrated cloud as well as appropriate services restart). That is why research work was started to evaluate possible alternatives.

Among existing software platforms for distributed computing and data management a DIRAC (Distributed Infrastructure with Remote Agent Control) [10] one was chosen because of the following reasons:

- it provides the whole needed functionality including both job and data management;
- cloud as a computational back-end support (although an appropriate plugin required some development);
- easier services deployment and maintenance in comparison with other platforms with similar functionality (e.g. EMI).

A schema of clouds integration using DIRAC grid middleware is shown on the Fig. 3, right.

Such approach also allows to share resources of each cloud between external grid users and local non-grid ones.

The services of the DIRAC platform itself are deployed in the JINR cloud, which, together with the clouds of the organizations of the JINR Member States, provides computing resources for the grid environment.

DIRAC is a software framework for distributed computing providing a complete solution to one (or more) user community requiring access to distributed resources.

DIRAC builds an intermediate layer between the users and the resources offering a common interface to a number of providers of heterogeneous resources.

The Workload Management System with Pilot Jobs introduced by the DIRAC project is now widely used in various grid infrastructures. This concept allows one to aggregate in a single system the computing resources of different source and nature, such as computational grids, clouds or clusters, transparently for the end users.

Unlike the "cloud bursting" model, the DIRAC platform allows one to use different computing resources with the help of pilot tasks.

There is already built-in mechanism in DIRAC for interaction with clouds, which is based on the usage of one of the implementation of Open Cloud Computing Interface (OCCI) – for example rOCCI, which is ruby-written one. Since clouds integration with help of cloud bursting driver also relied on the utilization of rOCCI-servers locally deployed at each partner cloud then adding clouds into DIRAC-based infrastructure required much less extra efforts.

Due to pretty limited set of operations client is capable to perform with a cloud via rOCCI it was decided to develop DIRAC module (named "VMDIRAC") which should be able to interact with OpenNebula-based clouds using their native XML-RPC API.

Such module was developed [11] and successfully validated for usage in production DIRAC release.

In order to test the possibility of such use of cloud resources, a series of tests were conducted, which resulted in new virtual machines that were successfully created, their contextualization was performed, user tasks were started, and the results were sent to the storage element. No special actions were required to run tasks on different cloud resources. At the moment, the program code of DIRAC is being finalized, because not all the necessary functionality is present in the basic version of the system.

At present, the integration of the JINR Member State organizations clouds into DIRAC-based distributed platform is at different stages. Their technical integration has been fulfilled, work on testing and debugging is in progress for the Astana branch of the Institute of Nuclear Physics — the private entity "Nazarbayev University Library and IT Services" (Astana, Kazakhstan) [12], the Scientific Research Institute for Nuclear Problems of Belarusian State University (Minsk, Belarus), Yerevan Physical Institute (Yerevan, Armenia), the Institute of Physics of the National Academy of Sciences of Azerbaijan (Baku, Azerbaijan), and Plekhanov Russian University of Economics (Moscow, Russia). In the process of integration are the clouds of the Institute for Nuclear Research and Nuclear Energy of BAS (Sofia, Bulgaria), Sofia University "St. Kliment Ohridski" (Sofia, Bulgaria), Georgian Technical University (Tbilisi, Georgia), and the Institute of Nuclear Physics (Tashkent, Uzbekistan). Negotiations are in progress with the University "St. Kliment Ohridski" (Bitola, Macedonia). Figure 4 maps the location of the organizations listed above.

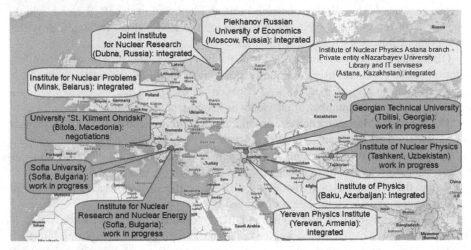

Fig. 4. The geographical location of cloud infrastructures of organizations from JINR Member States involved in the integration of cloud resources.

5 Training

Trainings on how to build local cloud or grid infrastructures, integrate them into distributed environment and use them for own purposes are held on a regular basis or upon requests from the JINR Member State organizations.

A set of training events was organized and conducted for specialists from various countries in creating cloud platforms based on OpenNebula and using resources of distributed information and computing environments (the information on conducted trainings are shown in the Table 1).

The purpose of the training courses is to provide information to university students, employees of various organizations in the form of easy-to-understand and use in their everyday needs, both personal and organizations.

The training includes the following aspects:

- providing information about the main cloud services;
- providing information on the use of virtualization, advantages and disadvantages;
- hands-on tutorial with access to cloud infrastructures and the opportunity to get practical experience in VM management: its creation, deployment, suspending, resuming, making VM disk snapshots, terminating, etc.).

The Joint Institute for Nuclear Research is actively working on the organization and conduct of schools, conferences, round tables, schools at conferences.

Table 1. The information on conducted trainings.

Organization/Event	Organization location	Training dates	Number of trainees	Training type	Training location
Internship of specialists from Uzbekistan	Uzbekistan	08.06-06.07.2018	2	usage and administration	JINR, Dubna, Russia
Internship of young scientists from CIS countries	CIS countries	24.05.2018	20	usage	JINR, Dubna, Russia
The course of cloud services and virtual environments	Dubna University, Dubna, Russia	01.09.-29.12.2017	22	usage	Dubna University, Dubna, Russia
Internship of young scientists from CIS countries	CIS countries	17-18.07.2017	6	usage	JINR, Dubna, Russia
L.N. Gumilyov Eurasian National University	Astana, Kazakhstan	22.07.2017	5	usage	JINR, Dubna, Russia
Kazakhstan, Georgia, Bulgaria scientific organizations	Kazakhstan, Georgia, Bulgaria	05-09.06.2017	7	usage and administration	JINR, Dubna, Russia
Internship of young scientists from CIS countries	CIS countries	02.11.2016	20	usage (demo)	JINR, Dubna, Russia
Institute for Nuclear Problems of Belarusian State University	Minsk, Belarus	31.10-03.11.2016	3	usage and administration	JINR, Dubna, Russia
Grid'2016 school	JINR	05.07.2016	5	usage	JINR, Dubna, Russia
Egyptian scientific organizations	Egypt	06-08.06.2016	4	usage	JINR, Dubna, Russia
Institute of Experimental and Applied Physics, Czech Technical University	Prague, Czech Republic	07-10.07.2015	2	usage	JINR, Dubna, Russia
Egyptian scientific organizations	Egypt	05-09.06.2015	3	usage	JINR, Dubna, Russia
JINR	Dubna, Russia	26-27.01.2015	11	usage	JINR, Dubna, Russia
Gdansk university of technologies	Gdansk, Poland	06.10-12.12.2014	1	usage and administration	JINR, Dubna, Russia

From 2010 to 2016, under support of the Institute, the AIS-GRID information technology school "GRID and administrative and management systems of CERN" had been held annually [13–19]. The aim of the school was to acquaint students with issues of managing complex scientific complexes and information systems in such areas as web, grid technologies, distributed, cloud computing, administrative information systems. Leading specialists from JINR and CERN gave lectures during AIS-GRID schools.

From September 25 to 29, 2017, Montenegro, Budva the 2nd International School on Heterogeneous Computing Infrastructure within the framework of the XXVI International Symposium on Nuclear Electronics and Computing NEC'2017 was held [20]. The main topics of the school conference were big data analytics, distributed and cloud computing, high-performance and high-speed computing systems, machine learning. The school was attended by leading scientists from Russia, USA, Italy, UK, JINR staff, SIC KI, CERN and DESY.

From September 10 to 14, 2018 at the Laboratory of Information Technologies (LIT) of the Joint Institute for Nuclear Research (JINR), Dubna in frames of the Conference "Distributed Computing and Grid-technologies in Science and Education" International school "Scientific computing, Big Data analytics and machine learning technology for megascience projects" was held [21]. The aim of the school was to attract young scientists, graduate students and students to solve IT problems related to various aspects of megaprojects in the field of high-energy physics, as well as acquaintance with modern methods of big data analytics, machine learning technologies on high-performance computing systems used to solve these problems. The proposed lecture and training program of the School allowed participants to familiar with all aspects of research related to big data using the example of the NICA mega-project and experiments at the Large Hadron Collider as the main sources of big data in high-energy physics. Within the school, training courses are organized on distributed systems for collecting, processing, managing and storing information; the use of high-performance and high-speed computing systems (supercomputers, computer clusters, cloud computing) for processing and modeling data from physical experiments, including methods of machine learning. The school participants had the opportunity to listen to the plenary reports of leading world scientists and specialists in the field of grid technologies and distributed computing presented at the GRID'2018 conference.

From 24 to 26 September 2018, Baku hosted the "International Conference and School dedicated to the 100th anniversary of Academician G. B. Abdullayev" [22]. The school program covered various aspects of information technologies applications in such areas as solid-state physics, high-energy physics, nuclear physics, mathematics, particle detectors and photoconverters, virtual learning systems.

In addition to organizing schools and conferences, LIT has tight cooperation with universities from Russia and other JINR Member States. Especially close cooperation with the University "Dubna", where the laboratory staff conduct semester courses in various areas of information technology, including such courses as "Distributed computing and cloud technologies", "Cloud services and virtual environments".

As part of these courses, students are introduced to the concepts of "distributed computing", "cloud technologies", and the main cloud services:

- SaaS (Software as a Service) - applications running in the cloud, access to which end users receive through a web interface;
- PaaS (Platform as a Service) - a set of tools and services that facilitate the development and deployment of cloud applications;
- IaaS (Infrastructure as a Service) - computing infrastructure (servers, data storage, networks, operating systems), which is provided to customers to run their own software solutions.

The advantages and disadvantages of each service learn the basics of virtualization, work with different hypervisors (VMware, KVM). Students use various cloud-based software during the learning process, from personal use programs to creating their own virtual machine in the cloud. University students have the opportunity to work both in the JINR cloud, creating virtual machines based on OpenNebula open source software, and in the university cloud, creating virtual machines based on the Virtual Computing Laboratory platform.

The Dubna University's Virtual Computing Lab software platform is based on VMware vSphere software, which consists of vSphere ESXi hypervisors with specific enhancements and optimizations for specific hardware that process all virtual machine computing work, as well as vCenter Server central management servers.

The vCenter Server consists of the following key components:

- vCenter Single Sign-On. This component is critical to the whole environment, since it provides secure authentication services for many vSphere components. Single Sign-On creates an internal secure domain in which the various components and solutions that are included in the vSphere ecosystem are registered during the installation or upgrade process, and subsequently they will be assigned basic infrastructural resources. Within the VCL architecture this component is responsible not only for internal authentication services, but it is also used to authenticate users from the university's internal domain who have Microsoft Active Directory accounts at the university.
- vCenter Server. The vCenter Server component is a central component that is used to manage the vSphere environment. This module provides management and monitoring interfaces for a number of vSphere nodes, and it also enables the use of such technologies as VMware vSphere vMotion and VMware vSphere High Availability.
- vCenter Inventory Service. Approximately ninety percent of vSphere Web Client requests to the server are just requests to read the current configuration of the system and its state. The Inventory Service is a component that caches most of the information about the current state of the environment in order to respond to vSphere Web Client requests thus reducing the load on vCenter basic processes.
- vSphere Server for Web Client (vSphere Web Client). vSphere Web Client is the main interface that is used to manage the environment in centralized manner. It can be divided into two parts: the first server part which serves requests from the second part which is the end user's Adobe Flex compatible browser with support for NPAPI-plugins. It is worth noting that the VCL may also be managed using the vCenter Server Desktop Client that is installed on the end user's computer.

- vCenter Server Database. The database is one of the key modules in the vCenter Server stack architecture. Almost every request sent to the vCenter Server entails communicating with the database. This database is the main storage location for vCenter Server parameters, and it is also a repository of statistical data. Saved statistical data make it possible to optimize system performance during subsequent analysis.
- The NVidia Kepler graphics card is used for 3D virtualization, and VMware Horizon Suite is used for remote VDI connections as well as for creating images of virtual servers and workstations that are separated into layers using VMware ThinApp and for managing these images. This solution is very important for machine learning due to a significant increase in the speed of learning of neural networks.

A centralized management portal as well as a knowledge management system were created in order to manage the virtual computer laboratory. The need to create such a system was conditioned by the fact that students are able to learn about distributed information systems remotely, so it is important to create a social network between all participants as well as to create an environment that provides for pupils the opportunity to independently engage in such processes as the identification, acquisition, presentation, and use (distribution) of knowledge without the direct involvement of the instructor [23–31].

6   Conclusion

When working at a research institute and developing new technologies, it is imperative that you pass on your knowledge, since the exchange of experience is one of the engines of progress. Attending conferences, organizing round tables, conducting and attending seminars and master classes is a necessary criterion for the successful development of an organization. Conducting courses at universities, in turn, not only improves the level of theoretical and practical knowledge of students, but also prepares qualified future personnel for the further development of information technology.

References

1. Ursul, A.D.: Informatization of society. Introduction to social informatics. AON at the Central Committee of CPSU, Moscow (1990). (in Russian)
2. Multifunctional Information and Computing Complex Homepage. https://micc.jinr.ru
3. Baranov, A.V., Balashov, N.A., Kutovskiy, N.A., Semenov, R.N.: JINR cloud infrastructure evolution. Phys. Part. Nucl. Lett. **13**(5), 672–675 (2016). https://doi.org/10.1134/S1547477116050071
4. Moreno-Vozmediano, R., Montero, R.S., Llorente, I.M.: IaaS cloud architecture: from virtualized datacenters to federated cloud infrastructures. IEEE Comput. **45**, 65–72 (2012). https://doi.org/10.1109/MC.2012.76
5. The Raft Consensus Algorithm Homepage. https://raft.github.io. Accessed 18 Dec 2018
6. Ongaro, D., Ousterhout, J.: In search of an understandable consensus algorithm. In: Gibson, G., Zeldovich, N. (eds.) Proceedings of the 2014 USENIX Conference on USENIX Annual Technical Conference (USENIX ATC'14), pp. 305–320. USENIX Association, Berkeley (2014)

7. Sage, A.W., et al.: Ceph: a scalable, high-performance distributed file system. In: Proceedings of the 7th Symposium on Operating Systems Design and Implementation, pp. 307–320. USENIX Association (2006). https://www.usenix.org/legacy/event/osdi06/tech/full_papers/weil/weil.pdf

8. Balashov, N., Baranov, A., Mazhitova, Ye., Kutovskiy, N., Semenov, R.: JINR member states cloud infrastructure. In: CEUR Workshop Proceedings, vol. 2023, pp. 202–206 (2017). http://ceur-ws.org/Vol-2023/202-206-paper-31.pdf

9. Baranov, A.V., et al.: Approaches to cloud infrastructures integration. Comput. Res. Model. **8**(3), 583–590 (2016). https://doi.org/10.20537/2076-7633-2016-8-3-583-590

10. Tsaregorodtsev, A.: DIRAC distributed computing services. J. Phys: Conf. Ser. **513**(Track 3), 032096 (2014). https://doi.org/10.1088/1742-6596/513/3/032096

11. Source code of VMDIRAC module Homepage. https://github.com/DIRACGrid/VMDIRAC/tree/integration/VMDIRAC. Accessed 18 Dec 2018

12. Balashov, N.A., Baranov, A.V., Kutovskiy, N.A., Mazhitova, Ye., Semenov, R.N.: Integrated cloud infrastructure of the LIT JINR, PE "NULITS" and INP's Astana branch. In: EPJ Web of Conferences, vol. 177, p. 05002 (2018). https://doi.org/10.1051/epjconf/201817705002

13. AIS-GRID school Homepage. http://ais-grid-2010.jinr.ru. Accessed 18 Dec 2018

14. AIS-GRID school Homepage. http://ais-grid-2011.jinr.ru. Accessed 18 Dec 2018

15. AIS-GRID school Homepage. http://ais-grid-2012.jinr.ru. Accessed 18 Dec 2018

16. AIS-GRID school Homepage. http://ais-grid-2013.jinr.ru. Accessed 18 Dec 2018

17. AIS-GRID school Homepage. http://ais-grid-2014.jinr.ru. Accessed 18 Dec 2018

18. AIS-GRID school Homepage. http://ais-grid-2015.jinr.ru. Accessed 18 Dec 2018

19. AIS-GRID school Homepage. http://ais-grid-2016.jinr.ru. Accessed 18 Dec 2018

20. The 2nd International School on Heterogeneous Computing Infrastructure Homepage. http://schoolnec2017.jinr.ru. Accessed 18 Dec 2018

21. International school "Scientific computing, Big data analytics and machine learning technology for megascience projects" Homepage. http://school-grid2018.jinr.ru. Accessed 18 Dec 2018

22. Academician G. B. Abdullayev Centenary International Conference and School Homepage. http://physics.gov.az/mtcmp/index_ru.html. Accessed 18 Dec 2018

23. VMware Homepage. https://www.vmware.com/products/vsphere.html. Accessed 18 Dec 2018

24. Belov, M., Kryukov, Yu., Lupanov, P., Mikheev, M., Cheremisina, E.: The concept of cognitive interaction with a virtual computer laboratory based on visual models and expert systems. Modern Science: actual problems of theory and practice. Natural and Technical Sciences, vol. 10, pp. 27–35 (2018). (in Russian). https://elibrary.ru/item.asp?id=36403665

25. Belov, M.A., Cheremisina, E.N., Potemkina, S.V.: Distance learning through distributed information systems using a virtual computer lab and knowledge management system. J. Emerg. Res. Solut. in ICT **1**(2), 39–46 (2016). https://doi.org/10.20544/ERSICT.02.16.P04

26. Belov, M.A., Cheremisina, E.N., Tokareva, N.A., Lupanov, P.E.: The experience of deploying a virtual computer lab in education – running failover clusters in a virtualized environment. In: Distributed Computing and Grid-technologies in Science and Education (GRID 2016), JINR, Dubna, Russia (2016)

27. Lishilin, M.V., Belov, M.A., Tokareva, N.A., Sorokin, A.V.: Conceptual model of knowledge management system for forming professional competence in the field of it in a Virtual Computer Lab. Fundam. Res. **11**(5), 886–890 (2015). (in Russian). https://elibrary.ru/item.asp?id=25097628

28. Belov, M.A., Cheremisina, E.N., Tokareva, N.A.: Virtual computer laboratory 2.0. 3D graphics as service. Methodological aspects of the use in research and education. In: Nuclear Electronics & Computing, XXV International Symposium (NEC'2015), Budva, Montenegro (2015)

29. Belov, M.A., Tokareva, N.A., Lishilin, M.V.: Implementation of knowledge control elements into educational environment of "Dubna" university. Experiences and perspectives – International Scientific. In: Practical Conference Innovative Information Technologies, Prague (2014)
30. Antipov, O.E., Belov, M.A.: Development and implementation of the software and hardware platform of a virtual computer laboratory in the educational process of higher education. Sci. Mod. (7-2), 8–11 (2010). (in Russian). https://elibrary.ru/item.asp?id=21084205
31. Liebowitz, M., Kusek, C., Spies, R.: VMware vSphere Performance: Designing CPU, Memory, Storage, and Networking for Performance-Intensive Workloads, Sybex (2014)

Implementing Interactive Information Technologies When Learning Integral Calculus in Teaching Further Mathematics

Nadezhda Eyrikh[1] , Ruslan Bazhenov[1] , Tatiana Gorbunova[2]([✉]) ,
and Vasilii Masyagin[3]

[1] Sholom-Aleichem Priamursky State University, Shirokaya Str. 70,
679015 Birobidzhan, Russia
nadya_eyrikh@mail.ru, r-i-bazhenov@yandex.ru
[2] Moscow State University of Civil Engineering, Yaroslavskoe Shosse 26,
129337 Moscow, Russia
tngorbunova@yandex.ru
[3] Omsk State Technical University, Mira Ave. 11, 644050 Omsk, Russia
masaginvb@mail.ru

Abstract. The article observes the effectiveness of various strategies and methods of organizing classes using IT, while studying the section *Integration* of Further mathematics course. The Fundamental theorem of integral and differential calculus offers 1st-year students a learning platform to study vocational courses. Many students do not cope with the subject, though. An active use of information technologies available in the educational process enable them refine the course successfully. The students learn certain definitions using original interactive computer games. Individual work is arranged using various applications of LearningApps.org. web service. The students learn geometric applications of integrals via Maple graphical capabilities. The educational experiment was run at Sholom-Aleichem Priamursky State University, Moscow State University of Civil Engineering, and Omsk State Technical University. The participants are the students of the Institute of Electrical Engineering, Electrical Engineering, Information Systems and Technology, Applied Mathematics and IT. There were 60 students in the control group, whereas there were 65 students in the experimental group. The survey resulted in a qualitative student academic performance in the experimental group larger by 17%. This confirms an assumption that using interactive technologies in the learning process enhances cognitive performance, stimulates students' self-study, and guides them to acquire real, not by-the-book knowledge.

Keywords: Integrating · Educational computer games · LearningApps.org · Computer algebra system Maple

1 Introduction

The proficiency in differential and integral calculus integrated in the standard course of further mathematics at university ensures a basis for studying numerous vocational

© Springer Nature Switzerland AG 2020
V. Sukhomlin and E. Zubareva (Eds.): SITITO 2018, CCIS 1201, pp. 163–172, 2020.
https://doi.org/10.1007/978-3-030-46895-8_13

subjects majoring in technical curricula. It is impossible to succeed in an engineering career for those who do not have the required skills.

It is necessary to use a mathematical apparatus in order to solve a variety of applied issues. A mathematical apparatus is connected to differential and integral calculus with functions of single or several real variables. However, lots of freshmen are not good at Advanced Mathematics course and find it one of the most difficult to learn. The reasons for this belief are a lower number of class hours and a much-decreased level of mathematical proficiency among secondary school leavers. In addition, specific research approaches used in the course ('the calculus of infinitesimals', or 'infinitesimal calculus', 'limiting transition'), require students' well-developed abstract thinking for comprehending and practicing. In the authors' point of view, regular use of modern information technologies in the learning process allows to overcome these difficulties.

Many scholars explore the potential for using current information and communications technologies (ICT) in higher education institutions for training. They actually observe advantages and disadvantages of e-learning in teaching in higher education institutions [1]. They evaluate educational resource quality presented on numerous online computing platforms: GeoGebra Materials, LearningApps, I2Geo [2]. The scientists examine the capacity of ICT for learning, and search for the crucial factors that contribute to use digital technologies in education successfully [3].

The authors believe that educational mobile applications that specialize in different contents of studying [4] have really high potential. Mobile learning, aimed at achieving double-subject educational outcomes, encourage the ability "learning for life" [5].

In mathematical education, the practice of using various computer algebra systems (CAS) becomes more widespread. These systems significantly improve the educational impact of teaching aids due to their excellent drawing utilities and symbolic computing techniques [6].

Computer algebra systems Maple and GeoGebra are considered to be the excellent means for performing geometric constructions of the objects observed. The visualization makes solving problems easier [7].

Students are better equipped with animated images designed in computer algebra system (CAS) Maple, in learning the material when studying discrete mathematics [8], and numerical analysis [9].

The visualization capabilities provided by Maple let a learner to choose from several methods for solving a given problem [10]. Integration of Maple software into teaching the topic *Integral Calculus* at the university enables students to enhance understanding of integral calculus technology [11].

The use of specialized software in educational process makes it possible to apply programming as a modern method of getting mathematical skills, since the algorithm for solving typical problems can serve as an instrument for cognition, control, and development of one's own knowledge of mathematics [12].

In addition, Maple TA software can be used for a catalogue of exam questions, maintain automatic point scoring. Thus, it makes the exam more convenient, as well as reduces examiners' work.

The authors also report on the positive effect of using computer games in training [14]. The game influences concentration, logical thinking positively, and suggests problem-solving skills [15]. Students are taught competences and skills when playing games [16]. All these factors are intended to improve their views on academic performance [17].

2 Methods

When giving classes, lecturers used a specially developed teaching and methodological materials, including workbooks and dynamic presentations. Students were learning the basic integration methods, practising and mastering their computing skills while doing assignments in workbooks. The lecturer used original interactive computer games to give some definitions. The lecturer also arranged individual work through LearningApps.org web service. The study of geometric applications of double integrals was guided by Maple graphical capabilities.

2.1 Original Computer Learning Games

Students learn the definition and geometric value of a certain integral using the interactive computer game Find the cross-section area of the river. First, a player selects the number of depth measurements, and computer displays the depth of the river at the selected points. Then, a student needs to calculate the cross-sectional area of the river according to the formulas of the left, right and middle rectangles. If the correct value is entered, the corresponding step figure is displayed on the screen (see Fig. 1). The program checks the entered answers and evaluates the results. The game is available at https://constructortest. 000webhostapp.com/gamePixel/river.php.

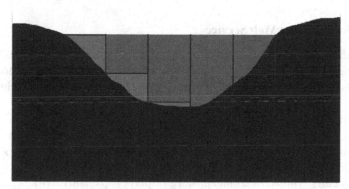

Fig. 1. The game for calculating the cross-section area of the river with left rectangles for 5 measurements.

Students learn the squarable figures, the Jordan inner and outer measure using
Find the area of shadow computer game (https://constructortest.000webhostapp. com/gamePixel/game.php).

Students are asked to calculate an approximation of the area of the shadow of different animals, flowers and other images. To do this, the shadow of the figure is split by means of graphical depiction or cell complex (the size of the cells is 1 cm or 0.5 cm for the game). A player can see two similar shadows of the selected picture via cellular decomposition on the screen. A student selects only those cells that are completely of the shadow of this figure in the left picture. And only those cells are selected that has at least one point of the shadow in the right picture (see Fig. 2). The program counts the marked cells. Having selected all the cells, a student enters the value of the area, and the computer checks the result. Wrong cells are highlighted in red. The computer shows the points and a final grade.

Fig. 2. The game to calculate the area of rabbit's shadow (the side of the cell is 1 cm).

2.2 LearningApps.org Web Service

Students' individual work is arranged through LearningApps.org web service. The developers designed various types of self-check assignments. They used this application template to assess students' competence and skills, and test the integration technique (see Fig. 3, 4).

To test priori knowledge, the authors choose the following templates:

- "Crossword" (https://learningapps.org/display?v=p2ak9zz2v18),
- "Hangman" (https://learningapps.org/display?v=paefvchbn18),
- "Matching Pairs" (https://learningapps.org/display?v=pxgismv3t18).

Students are offered to assess the solving antiderivatives skills (integration). The templates are given below:

- "Freetext input" (https://learningapps.org/watch?v=pjn9neqrk18),
- "Multiple-Choice Quiz" (https://learningapps.org/display?v=pnk2vewe218),
- "Horse race" (https://learningapps.org/watch?v=p8hvc5n5n18).

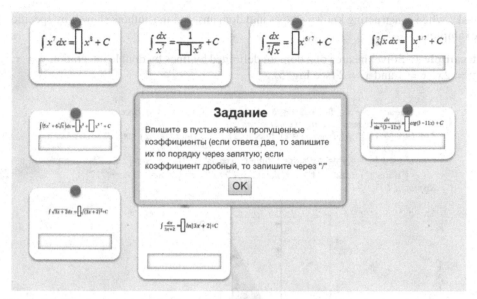

Fig. 3. Freetext input – The task: Enter the missing coefficients in the empty cells (if there are two answers, write them in order separated by commas, if the fractional coefficient, write through '/').

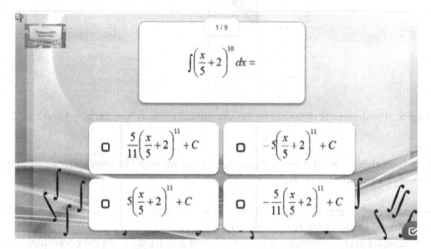

Fig. 4. Multiple-Choice Quiz – Testing the skill to find indefinite integrals.

2.3 Maple Computing Software

The authors use a computer algebra system Maple when studying geometric applications of integrals. The graphical capabilities of this mathematical software visualize plain domains and space shapes. The areas and volumes of them have to be found through the use of an integral. Finally, students face particular problems with solving similar tasks when constructing known shapes and domains. Let the authors show it by specific examples.

Example 1. Solve the area of a domain delimited by lines by double integration $y = x$, $y = 2x$, $x = 1$ and $x = 2$ (see Fig. 5).

$d :=$ *inequal*($\{y - x \geq 0, y - 2 \cdot x \leq 0, x \geq 1, x \leq 2\}$, $x = 0..3$, $y = 0..5$, *color*
   $=$ "DarkMagenta", *scaling = constrained*) :
$l :=$ *line*($[0, 1]$, $[1, 1]$, *linestyle* $= 2$), *line*($[0, 2]$, $[2, 2]$, *linestyle* $= 2$), *line*($[0, 4]$, $[2, 4]$,
   linestyle $= 2$) :
$t :=$ *textplot*($[2.5, 4.3, y = 2x$', *font'* $=$ ["times", "roman", 17]]), *textplot*($[2.5, 2.2, y = x$', *font'*
   $=$ ["times", "roman", 17]]), *textplot*($[1.5, 2.2, \Omega$', *font'* $=$ ["times", "roman", 17]]) :
display(d, l, t);

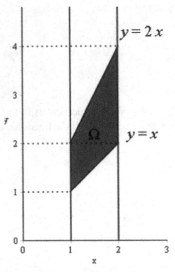

Fig. 5. The domain Ω delimited by the straight lines $y = x$, $y = 2x$, $x = 1$ and $x = 2$.

Let the authors describe the commands used from the additional software of graphic extensions plots and plot tools:

– unequal creates a graphic object where d is an area delimited by the known inequalities and marks this area with the proper color;
– line creates a graphic object where l are dotted graphs showing the coordinates of the cross point of the given curves.

Example 2. Find the volume of a shape delimited by given surface areas by double integration: the paraboloid of revolution $z = x^2 + y^2$, Cartesian planes and the plane $x + y = 1$.

First, it is necessary to understand that what the integrand function $f(x, y)$ is in order to 'see' the shape, as well as what the integration domain is, i.e. on which planar domain the integrand function is given.

The first thing the authors begin with is depicting the known surfaces in order to answer all these questions. But each time they choose the best values of boundaries of coordinate changes. They make it possible to design a more informative image (see Fig. 6).

$$implicitplot3d\left(\left[z = x^2 + y^2, x + y = 1\right], x = -1.7 .. 1.7, y = -1.7 .. 1.7, z = 0 .. 2.5, color = [blue, green], scaling = constrained, axes = normal\right)$$

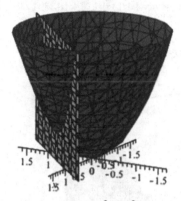

Fig. 6. The paraboloid of revolution $z = x^2 + y^2$ and the plane $x + y = 1$.

As it is seen from Fig. 6, the known shape is delimited by the paraboloid of revolution $z = x^2 + y^2$ from above, and there is a triangle with the lines $x + y = 1$, $x = 0$ and $y = 0$ in the bottom base. The authors draw the lower and upper bases of a cylinder parallelepiped (see Fig. 7).

```
> d := plot3d(0, x = 0 .. 1 − y, y = 0 .. 1, color = "BlueViolet") :
  f := plot3d(x² + y², x = 0 .. 1 − y, y = 0 .. 1, color = blue, scaling = constrained, axes
     = boxed) :
  display(d, f);
```

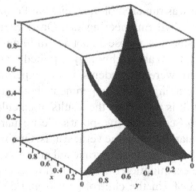

Fig. 7. Upper and lower bases of a cylinder parallelepiped.

To add a lateral surface, they draw a collection of lines parallel to Z-axis, and connecting the corresponding points of the lower and upper bases (see Fig. 8).

```
>  N := 200 :
   for i from 1 to N do x[i] := i/N; y2[i] := i/N; y3[i] := (1 − x[i]); z1[i] := (x[i])²; z2[i]
           := (y2[i])²; z3[i] := (x[i])² + (y3[i])²;
           l1[i] := line([x[i], 0, 0], [x[i], 0, z1[i]], linestyle = 1, thickness = 2);
           l2[i] := line([0, y2[i], 0], [0, y2[i], z2[i]], linestyle = 1, thickness = 2);
           l3[i] := line([x[i], y3[i], 0], [x[i], y3[i], z3[i]], linestyle = 1, thickness = 2) od:
   bp1 := seq(l1[i], i = 1 ..N) :
   bp2 := seq(l2[i], i = 1 ..N) :
   bp3 := seq(l3[i], i = 1 ..N) :
   display(d, f, bp1, bp2, bp3, view = [0 ..1, 0 ..1, 0 ..1])
```

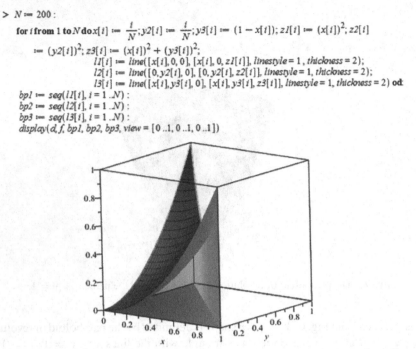

Fig. 8. Cylinder parallelepiped delimited by the paraboloid of revolution $z = x^2 + y^2$, by the coordinate planes and the plane $x + y = 1$.

3   Results and Discussion

The educational experiment was run at Sholom-Aleichem Priamursky State University, Moscow State University of Civil Engineering, and Omsk State Technical University. The participants were the students whose major is Building Engineering, Electrical Engineering, Information systems and technology, Applied mathematics and IT.

In the control group there were 60 students, in the experimental group there were 65 students. Before the beginning of the experiment, both groups showed the same proficiency level in general. It is proved by the results of calculus exam during the first examination time (see Fig. 9). Scores on a five-point scale are marked along the horizontal axis. Number of students is marked along the vertical axis. Qualitative achievement in the control group is 37%, and 38.5% is in the experimental group. According to the results of the exam during the second examination time (in a half a year) (see Fig. 10) qualitative academic performance is 35% (in the control group) and 52% (in the experimental group). In the experimental group, qualitative academic performance is higher by 17%.

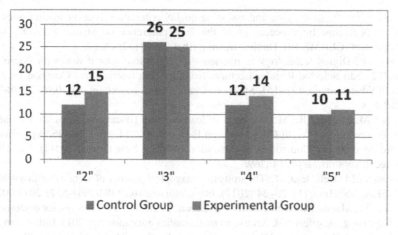

Fig. 9. The exam results at the first session (before experiment).

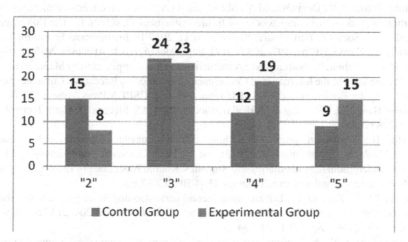

Fig. 10. The exam results at the second session (after experiment).

4 Conclusion

The research has proved a positive influence of interactive technologies on the educational process. Interactive educational process stimulates students' cognitive activity, contributes to their independent work, and directs them to understand the material they have been studying thoroughly.

References

1. Arkorful, V., Abaidoo, N.: The role of e-learning, advantages and disadvantages of its adoption in higher education. Int. J. Instruct. Technol. Dist. Learn. **2**(12), 397–410 (2015). https://www.ijern.com/journal/2014/December-2014/34.pdf

2. Kimeswenger, B.: Identifying and assessing quality criteria for dynamic mathematics materials on platforms. In: Proceedings of the 7th Conference on Mathematical Knowledge Management (CERME 10), Dublin, Ireland. ffhal-01942132f (2017)
3. Drijvers, P.: Digital technology in mathematics education: why it works (or doesn't). In: Cho, S.J. (ed.) Selected Regular Lectures from the 12th International Congress on Mathematical Education, pp. 135–151. Springer, Cham (2015). https://doi.org/10.1007/978-3-319-17187-6_8
4. Beutner, M., Pechuel, R.: Modern ways of learning with educational Apps. In: Bastiaens, T. (ed.) Proceedings of World Conference on E-Learning 2014, pp. 188–196. Association for the Advancement of Computing in Education (AACE), New Orleans (2014). https://www.learntechlib.org/primary/p/148769/
5. Goryunova, M., Lebedeva, M.: The study of pedagogical practice of mobile learning in Russia. EUREKA: Soc.Hum. (1), 20–24 (2017). https://doi.org/10.21303/2504-5571.2017.00242
6. Kaneko, M., Maeda, Y., Hamaguchi, N., Nozawa, T., Takato, S.: A scheme for demonstrating and improving the effect of CAS use in mathematics education. In: 2013 13th International Conference on Computational Science and Its Applications, Ho Chi Minh City, 2013, pp. 62–71 (2013). https://doi.org/10.1109/iccsa.2013.19
7. Gainutdinova, T.Y., Denisova, M.Y., Shirokova, O.A.: Innovative teaching methods in formation of professional competencies of future mathematics teachers. In: The European Proceedings of Social & Behavioural Sciences. IFTE 2017 III International Forum on Teacher Education, Kazan, RF, pp. 197–205 (2017). https://doi.org/10.15405/epsbs.2017.08.02.24
8. Alharbi, A., Tcheir, F., Siddique, M.: A mathematics e-book application by Maple animations. In: Proceedings of the International Conference on Frontiers in Education: Computer Science and Computer Engineering (FECS 2016), pp. 148–151. CSREA Press, Athens (2016)
9. Perjési-Hámori, I.: Teaching numerical methods using CAS. Electron. J. Math. Technol. 9(3), 229–238 (2015)
10. Blyth, B.: Maximum problems without calculus: design, teaching and assessment using Maple. In: Lighthouse Delta 2013: The 9th Delta Conference on Teaching and Learning of Undergraduate Mathematics and Statistics, Kiama, Australia, pp. 12–29 (2013). http://deltaconference.org/documents/program/1B-4-Blyth2013.pdf
11. Salleh, T.S.A., Zakaria, E.: Enhancing students' understanding in integral calculus through the integration of maple in learning. Procedia Soc. Behav. Sci. 102, 204–211 (2013). https://doi.org/10.1016/j.sbspro.2013.10.734
12. Semenikhina, E.V.: Programming as a method of forming mathematical knowledge in conditions of informatization of education. In: Proceedings of Francisk Scorina Gomel State University, vol. 2, no. 89, pp. 42–45 (2015)
13. Wu, L.: Maple and Maple T.A. in teaching college mathematics. J. Shanghai Second Polytech. Univ. 2, 130–134 (2013)
14. Mateos, M.J., Muñoz-Merino, P.J., Kloos, C.D., Hernández-Leo, D., Redondo-Martínez, D.: Design and evaluation of a computer based game for education. In: 2016 IEEE Frontiers in Education Conference (FIE), Erie, PA, USA, 2016, pp. 1–8 (2016). https://doi.org/10.1109/fie.2016.7757356
15. De Aguilera, M., Mendiz, A.: Video games and education: education in the face of a "Parallel School". Comput. Entertain. 1(1), 1–14 (2003). https://doi.org/10.1145/950566.950583
16. Prensky, M.: Don't Bother Me Mom – I'm Learning!. Paragon House, St. Paul (2006)
17. Blumenfeld, P.C., Kempler, T.M., Krajcik, J.S.: Motivation and cognitive engagement in learning environments. In: Sawyer, R.K. (Ed.) The Cambridge Handbook of: The Learning Sciences, pp. 475–488. Cambridge University Press, Cambridge (2006)

Intellectual Analysis of the Education System of the Region with the Use of Lean-Technologies and Soft Models of Assessment Situations

Aleksey Karataev[✉] ⓘ

Surgut State University, Lenin Ave. 1, KMAO-Yugra, 628403 Surgut, Russia
karataev86@mail.ru

Abstract. The article is devoted to the introduction into practice of education management in the region of elements of artificial intelligence, in particular, in the areas called "data mining in active systems", "lean production", "soft computing". It is shown that the concept of "soft estimation of situations" is the development of the methodology of "soft" measurements. Practical approaches, which are based on fuzzy logic in the whole, fuzzy clustering and semantic triangulation, subjective probability and evolutionary algorithms.

Keywords: Active systems · Lean-technologies · Digitalization of education · Non-factors · Soft models and measurements

1 Introduction

The concept of Lean-production originated in industries with discrete production [1, 2] and was successfully adapted to the real application in many activities: trade, services, public administration and etc. The basic scientific and educational center for training and research in the field of Lean-technologies was established as part of the implementation of this concept in Surgut State University. The tasks of the center include the search and adaptation to the conditions of the district of advanced international and domestic practices of implementation and maintenance of Lean-technologies in public administration, educational and health organizations. Considering the activities of educational and scientific-educational organizations from the position of bringing (or not bringing) additional value (usefulness) in the final results, it is possible to identify the main production (educational and educational) processes, scientific process and ensuring processes that are necessary and consume resources, but do not create visible value for the consumer-accounting, personnel records, legal support and etc.

The discussion on the use of Lean-technologies in the main "production educational" processes is conducted both within the framework of the discussion of their applicability and the content of the terms. So far, the authors have different interpretations of the term "overproduction" in the educational process: "overproduction - unnecessary duplication of information, the overload of students not meeting his needs of information" [4 p. 74]; "when the proposal on the profession exceeds demand, there is an overproduction" [5 p. 48]. This approach, from the point of view of the authors of this article, is dangerous

© Springer Nature Switzerland AG 2020
V. Sukhomlin and E. Zubareva (Eds.): SITITO 2018, CCIS 1201, pp. 173–185, 2020.
https://doi.org/10.1007/978-3-030-46895-8_14

because it can reduce education to "training" on the solutions of actual at the moment, specific problems, incompatible with the national concept of the fundamental nature of higher education. And yet there are works with the description of successful (from our point of view) specific examples of the use of Lean-technologies in the main educational (production) processes. It is quite interesting, in our opinion, the practice of mapping the educational process in the Kazan State Energy University [6], the practice of stretching (CANBAN [7]) in relation to the organization of the educational process in the network interaction of the University and the College at the National Research Tomsk Polytechnic University [8] and the implementation of the agreed curricula of secondary and higher professional education in at Shadrinsk State Pedagogical Institute [9] and etc. In other words, Lean-technologies are certainly justified when there is a bunch of College (College) – University. As for auxiliary (supporting) processes, they are currently the first and the main source of saving opportunities by reducing losses.

Let us consider in more detail the main processes, as they are the subject of research in this paper.

1.1 Analysis of the Practices of Modern Technologies in the Main Processes of Educational Institutions

There are [10, 18] the following main trends, both in the external environment and in the universities themselves:

1. Increase in the number of higher education institutions.
2. Globalization and increased competition in educational sphere.
3. Introduction of new technologies in higher education.
4. Changing demand for skills and competencies.
5. Changing students' values and expectations.

While the first two trends have been discussed over the past few decades, the last three are fairly new and are classified as key trends for the first time. Therefore, we will focus on them.

Introduce New Technologies

Traditional learning is gradually transforming under the influence of student expectations and relatively cheap (or free) access to virtually any information.

Expected results:

– development of online-tools (in 2013, the market for distance learning products amounted to 42.7 billion, currently exceeding $ 50 billion);
– widespread adoption of mobile devices;
– introduction of virtual reality systems, games and simulators in teaching of various disciplines;
– using the capabilities of artificial intelligence (as a coach, mentor and partner).

The general conclusion of the authors of the report: "Digital technologies have changed the media industry, the sphere of retail sales, the entertainment industry and many other industries – the next step is higher education. Campuses will remain, but digital technology will change the way we create "value" in education".

With regard to the consequences of the development of this trend, associated with the development of online learning technologies, with the power of regional conservatism, they have clearly not manifested itself, but in the near future we should expect a significant outflow of students and the emergence in the regions of the new wave branches – the so-called "access points" through which leading universities will implement blended learning. And it is good if such an "access point" would be a regional University, but for this regional universities need to do a lot.

Changing Demand for Skills and Competencies

Let's step back a little from the text of the report and give an example. Today the whole world is talking about the "digital economy". According to our President, the development of the digital economy is an unprecedented project in its scale and impact:

"It (the project of digital economy) is really compared with the breakthrough transformations that at different historical stages allowed Russia to make a serious step forward, to strengthen its position in the world. Among them - the construction of Railways in the end of XIX century or electrification of the country in the first half of the XX century" [10]. In accordance with the Presidential Decree, the Government of the Russian Federation, when implementing the national program "Digital economy of the Russian Federation" together with the state authorities of the constituent entities of the Russian Federation [11], should ensure by 2024 the solution of the problem of providing training of highly qualified personnel for the digital economy. Can anyone say what skills and competencies should have a specialist for the digitalization of the region's economy in all areas – public administration, medicine, education, small and medium-sized business… And training of such specialists should be started in the next academic year.

The situation is no better with the formation of competencies aimed at supporting and developing the clustering of regional economies. And these are only two particular examples. There are professional standards, but there is no digital economy and clustering.

Changing Values and Expectations of Students

"The number of students who doubt the practical value of education and do not show interest in learning is growing". Here is such a disappointing conclusion the authors of the report [10]. It seems to us that this conclusion contradicts the first trend, and the authors themselves as a result of the analysis of this trend come to the conclusion that "we need an interesting and effective education that has a practical orientation". It seems to us that the trend is to increase the demand for practice-oriented, based on modern methodological approaches and technologies of training, which coincides with the general conclusion of the authors of the report: the considered trends indicate the need to introduce new models of education that effectively use modern technology and meet the requirements of the economy and society.

We are cautiously optimistic about this trend. Where, if not at a regional University, the needs of regional business and the needs of regional management should be known, where, if not at a regional University, the most active representatives of business and management of the region can teach – these are opportunities that leading universities do not have. It is these opportunities, combined with new learning and management technologies, that give Russian regional universities a chance to compete in the already formed, whether we like it or not, educational services market.

Thus, the world is gradually abandoning the compulsory model of higher education, in which the University (and in the case of our country – the state through educational standards) decided what and how to teach. The compulsory model is replaced by a new, individually oriented model in which the needs of the labor market will determine the content of education, and the student will choose a convenient form of education.

Whether regional universities will find a place in this new model of education depends on their current activity.

In these circumstances, it is very important to analyze the practice of using new technologies in higher education by Russian universities.

2 Modern Learning Models

Individualization of education as a principle is stated in the first edition of the "Law of education" of 1992. However, due to the difficult economic situation, the fall of state and citizens ' incomes in the 1990s, this situation remained practically unrealized.

Individualization (personalization) of educational programs, of course, increases the quality of education, and the size of the human capital formed by it.

At the same time, it is obvious that the requirements for individualization of education and taking into account the personal characteristics of the student in full may not be feasible. The implementation of such requirements is not enough any resources. This is also a hidden reason for refusing individualization, even where it is appropriate, in the public interest. It is here that digital technologies are creating a revolution. The education system is the "bridge" that should provide not only the Russian economy, but also the whole society with a confident transition to the digital age, associated with new types of work and a sharp increase in the creative capabilities of man, the rise of his productivity.

The changes will begin with the fact that education will use the same digital resources (tools, sources and services) that are used today in professional and daily human activities. Already existing technologies allow to overcome the traditional, familiar to all restrictions, for example, the impossibility or limited choice of a teacher at the University. Digital technologies for the first time in history make it possible to provide individualization for each student of the educational trajectory, methods (forms) and pace of development of educational material. The President of Russian Federation noted in his Address of 1st of March, 2018: "we need to move to fundamentally new, including individual learning technologies… to creative search, to teach teamwork, which is very important in the modern world, the skills of life in the digital age".

Successful work to achieve the goals of education facing the modern general education and vocational school requires an appropriate model of education, as well as its consistent implementation in practice. Such a model should, first of all, provide students with systematic, solid and at the same time operational knowledge, and, equally important, provide conditions that facilitate the implementation of the already known requirement: to teach students to learn on their own. The first feature of the defined model is the dialectical unity of teaching and learning, linking and mutually determining the course of both these processes.

The knowledge acquired by students ensures the realization of not only cognitive and educational, but also educational tasks. Thanks to the cognitive function creates conditions for better knowledge of different areas of human life. The educational function determines the development of students' interests and abilities. The educational function of the knowledge acquired during the learning process is related to the formation of students' scientific view of the world, value beliefs and civic attitudes, correspondence between behavior and theoretically accepted ethical standards, habits of cooperation, etc. Thus, the second feature of the modern model of education is the dialectical unity of educational and educational influences. This means that the teacher in his work should strive to solve certain, pre-set tasks in the field of education of students. The practice of the best schools and teachers has proved that good results are obtained by such planning of educational work, which involves simultaneous and consistent solution during each lesson of specific educational tasks and substantially related tasks of educational nature.

The modern model of the learning process should also be adapted to a variety of educational tasks, including:

- self-acquisition by students of certain knowledge and skills through both individual and collective work;
- students acquire knowledge by direct cognition, for example as a result of observations, experiments, conversations, etc., while providing them with the conditions and means that ensure the enrichment of existing knowledge and skills with indirect knowledge;
- students of systematic implementation of monitoring and evaluation of the results of our study, with the simultaneous inclusion of these actions in an organized school system of monitoring and evaluation of the final results of educational work, etc.

It can be considered that an important feature of the modern model of the learning process is its versatility. It can be considered that an important feature of the modern model of the learning process is its versatility. It is thanks to this feature that it is possible to establish the connection of education organized in the school with out-of-school education; combining school education with industrial and social activities; carrying out educational activities at a level adapted to the capabilities of students, to the characteristics of individual subjects, as well as to special educational tasks, the expression of which, in particular, is the differentiation of education into elementary and scientific, verbal and based on observation and experiment, systematic and based on examples, etc.; finally, the solution of a wide range of educational tasks. From this point of view, this model is fundamentally different from the Herbart and progressive models, which, as we remember, were aimed primarily at informing students of ready knowledge (Herbart model) or their acquisition by students in the course of independent research, based mainly on direct knowledge (model progressives).

The next feature of the modern model of education characterizes the possibility of coverage of educational activities of children and young people, close in age, but with different initial volume of knowledge, i.e. with different levels of training in the subject, with qualitative and quantitative differences in the abilities and pace of training. Because of this the model software provides each student the necessary minimum knowledge and skills, simultaneously creating capable students opportunities for significant excess of this minimum. It is not intended that those who are more capable complete their studies faster, for example in a given class or school, which should also be taken into account in the future - the task is to give them the opportunity to study the program material more fully. This feature of the modern model of learning is becoming increasingly visible. We owe this primarily to programmed learning, and especially to the ways and means of implementing the principle of individualization of learning promoted by its proponents.

Another feature of the described model of the learning process relates to its methodological and organizational flexibility. In order to implement it, it is proposed to use different methods and organizational forms of education, selected, however, each time in accordance with the content of the tasks to be solved, as well as taking into account the age of students. Thus, from this point of view of modern model differs from the models to cultivate or search methods (progressivism), or reporting (herbalism); the study, organized almost exclusively in the school and class (herbalism) or outside of school (some variant of progressivism).

2.1 Problem Block

Features of the modern model of the learning process:

1. Unity of teaching and teaching;
2. Unity of didactic and educational influences;
3. Comprehensiveness, the ability to solve a wide range of didactic problems;
4. Individualization of the teaching, taking into account the abilities of individual students, the pace of their work and the degree of advancement in learning;
5. Methodological and organizational flexibility, and above all the conformity of teaching methods with the objectives of training and education.

Using the materials collected during the lesson, give examples that illustrate each of these features of the learning process. Discuss them with friends.

To this end, the education system must learn to use new technological tools and virtually unlimited information resources. Below is a brief description and features of the most common modern models of learning, based on different approaches. A more detailed description of the most common approaches to learning is presented in [9, 11, 17].

Project-based learning is a dynamic personality-oriented approach in which students gain knowledge and skills in the design, planning and implementation of the project, exploring and solving complex and interesting problems or tasks.

The project approach in training is characterized by distinctive and important elements:

1. The need to identify the present problem or situation. The problem should be provocative, open to multiple interpretations, complex and related to the main concepts, theories or practices being studied.

2. Establishment of the project implementation period and schedule of intermediate goals.
3. The need to develop the skills of teamwork, communication and critical thinking, the use of special technologies and tools for the professional implementation of the project.
4. The definition of educational objectives, provision of teacher feedback, the use of ratings of performance for self and peer analysis of the processes and outcomes of the project along with direct feedback.

Problem-based learning assumes that attention is paid to a key problem, situation, or case from practice. It is characterized by:

1. Identification of a real, complex problem related to the studied concepts, theories or practices.
2. The inclusion of different solutions.
3. Conducting brainstorming sessions or discussions to identify issues on the issue.
4. Giving students time to interact, and involving all students in the problem-solving process.
5. Regular assessment of progress.
6. Feedback exchange between students is necessary for the learning process and informed assessment.

Competency-based learning is an approach to education aimed at presenting students with the desired learning outcomes, which are a key element of the learning process. Within the framework of this approach, much attention is paid to the development of educational programs by students at a convenient pace, in a convenient degree for them, etc. A key feature of competency-based learning is the emphasis on subject ownership. In the system of competence-based learning students are unable to continue working as long as they do not demonstrate the possession of certain professional knowledge (i.e. required to demonstrate the desired learning outcomes).

Blended Learning and the "Flipped Classroom" Methodology
This is an approach to teaching that combines the effectiveness and socialization of the classroom with the technologically rich possibilities of active learning in an online environment. The approach consists of two parts: interactive group classes in the classroom and direct individual training outside the classroom using computer technology. Using this method implies that students are first introduced to new material outside the classroom, usually while reading or watching video lectures, and then use the study time to make an effort to acquire knowledge, perhaps through problem solving, discussion or debate.

Individualized Learning
It includes [15, 17] educational programs, activities, learning approaches, and teaching methods that take into account the different learning needs, interests, aspirations, or cultural backgrounds of each student.
The characteristic features of Individualized (personalized) learning are:

1. Teaching methods that take into account the individual needs of students, so that everyone can adapt the learning process to their interests.
2. The dynamics of teaching may vary according to individual needs.
3. Educators use real-time assessment procedures and student feedback to adapt teaching methods and provide effective impact and support to ensure that each student follows an education plan.

3 Modeling Methods of Education Quality Assessment in the Framework of Digital Technologies

Depending on the level and purpose for which the model of organization of the education system (further - OES) is intended, it may include very different elements as components [13, 15, 17]. For example, for OES modeling, the model elements are technical (computer) and ergatic (involving personnel) elements of the manual and execution elements. To simulate the state of a person in the OES model elements are the level of performance, level of fatigue, emotional state, etc. To ensure the tasks of ergatic design, i.e. the processes of selection of such organizational and design solutions in the education system as the human-machine system (HMS), which provide high efficiency of the OES and the necessary working conditions for a person, the models should contain the components of the "labor process - labor results". Let us consider in more detail the last type of OES models (we will call them functional-pragmatic models, further - FPM), since they are the most often the object of study. In contrast to mechanized production, the effectiveness of OES is determined not only by human actions, but also depends on the characteristics of the whole complex "human − means of labor − the process of functioning of HMS".

To clarify the object of modeling, you need to specify a specific OES in the form of a tuple: $S_i = \langle E_i, F_i, R_i, Q_i \rangle$, where E_i - the set of elements forming the system; F_i - the set of functions performed by this system; R_i - the set of interrelations (between elements, functions), existing really in this system; Q_i - the set of indicators of the quality of the system, as well as its individual elements and functions. In those cases when several variants of the same HMS different in structure or quality are modeled, the object of modeling is a generalized (multivariate) image of the OES $S = \langle S_i \rangle$. Included in the definition of the tuple S_i set can be clarified as follows: $S_i = \{E_1, E_2, E_3, E_4, E_5, E_6\}$, where E_1 – the set of organizational elements (set of goals U and tasks Z), determining the purpose and functionality of the system; E_2 – the set of personnel (dispatchers, operators, production workers, repairmen, etc.); E_3 – the set of the tools (technological equipment, automation equipment, computing equipment, instruments, tools, means of technological equipment, etc.); E_4 – the set of subjects of work (for example, pieces of information modules, initial information, etc.); E_5 – the set of products of labor (finished products, solved problems, marriage, waste (expelled students), etc.); E_6 – the set of tools support (energy, protection and habitability, etc.).

$F = \{F_1, F_2, F_3, F_4\}$, where F_1 – the set of the processes of functioning of OES (determined on the basis of the sets U and Z); F_2 – the set of technological operations, which consist of the processes of operation of the OES (from the set F_1); F_3 – the set of personnel actions within a technological operation (from the set F_2); F_4 – the set of machine operations included in the technological operations (from the set F_3); $R = \{R_E, R_F, R_{EF}\}$, where R_E – the set of component and morphological element structures-relations defined on the Cartesian product of the sets $E \times F$, displays the composition of the elements involved in the functions, displaying all types of relationships between the elements (part-whole, energy and information links, organizational relationships); RF – the set of functional structures – the set of logical-time relations defined on the component sets of $F \times F$, displaying the relationship of functional units; R_{EF} - the set of morphological element-functional structures defined on the Cartesian product of the sets of $E \times F$, representing the composition of the elements involved in the performance of functions.

$Q = \{Q_E, Q_F, Q_R, Q_S\}$, where Q_E – the set of characteristics of the quality of the elements (on set of E); Q_F – the set of characteristics of the quality of functions (from set of F); Q_R – the set of characteristics of the quality of the relationships (from set of R); Q_S – the set of system-wide characteristics of the OES as a whole, including not only attribute, but also pragmatic characteristics such as the effectiveness and quality of the HMS. One of the forms of complex accounting can be a generalized model of OES. When assessing the quality of the OES some subset of the characteristics N is selected from the set Q_S depending on the study objectives. When $N = 1$ (for determining part is taken, for example, only the effectiveness of the HMS) we have a scalar estimate, and for $N \geq 2$ – vector one. The more N, as a rule, the more complex the process of modeling the HMS. It is advisable to carry out a reasonable selection of the estimated parameters of the HMS.

With the recommended pragmatic approach [15–17], the selection of the evaluation parameters of the OES should be carried out at a minimum of characteristics that determine the effectiveness of the HMS. In many applications, we can limit ourselves to the vector $qS = (tS, hS, CS)$, where ts is a generalized characteristic of performance OES (for example, performance or timeliness of the task); hs – generalized characteristics of reliability (for example, the probability of defect-free manufacturing of products or the probability of error-free solution of the problem); Cs – generalized cost measure (cost of solving the problem or making a product).

The nomenclature of the estimated indicators. In accordance with the functional-pragmatic approach [17], [19] and the principles of functional-structural theory of OES, the indicator of the highest rank, evaluating the OES as a whole, is its effectiveness, i.e. the degree of achievement of the goals by the system, characterized by the vector $\ni S = (\ni_1, \ni_2, ..., \ni_n)$, where $\ni S$- the effectiveness of the OES as a whole; $\ni_i$- the effectiveness of the OES in i-th objective; $i = (1 \ldots n) \in U$, specified in the object model.

Efficiency depending on the depth of consideration may be:

- pragmatic – when limited to the consideration of only the result, without taking into account the effects;
- specific (medical, technical) – when taken into account not only the results, but also the effects obtained from them;
- specific-economic, if additional costs are taken into account to achieve the result.

When solving ergatic problems, as a rule, it is enough to limit the consideration of only pragmatic efficiency. For pragmatic effectiveness, the key indicator is the likelihood of achieving i-th target $Э_i = ПЦ_i$ i.e., the effectiveness of multipurpose OES in this case $ЭS = (ПЦ_1, ПЦ_2, \ldots, ПЦ_i)$.

But in addition to the effectiveness in achieving the goal of the researcher may also be interested in the characteristics of the process of achieving the goal-the vector of performance indicators KS ; $КЦ_i = (ТЦ_i, \overline{СЦ_i})$, where $ТЦ_i$, $СЦ_i$ average time and cost of achieving the i-th goal. Thus, the set of system-wide characteristics of the OES is a tuple of the above indicators $QS = \langle ЭS, KS \rangle$. To achieve each goal, it is necessary to solve a number of problems (from the set Z given in the model). The solution of each problem Z_i is carried out by performing the function F, belonging to the set F_1, given in the model. Indicators of the quality of the task in common are:

$$K_{Zi} = \left(\Pi_{Zi(t)};\ TZ_i;\ D_{(tzi)};\ \overline{C}_{zi} \right),$$

where $\Pi_{Zi(t)}$ - the probability of error-free and timely (for a time less than a given t) execution of the task; T_{Zi} and $D_{(tzi)}$ mathematical expectation and variance of execution time of tasks; C_{zi} - mathematical expectation of costs. In particular cases, the composition of indicators can be selected from this set (often one $K_{zi(t)}$ is sufficient). Indicators at the level of the Q_s system are determined through the K_{zi} indicators based on logical functions that link the tasks to be solved with the goal. For example, if a logical function has the form of a conjunction ("the purpose is reached, if will be solved and the task Z_{i1}, and the tasks Z_{i2}, $\ldots$, Z_{in}"), that the probability of achieving of ith target: $P_{Цi} = P_{zi1}P_{zi2}\ldots P_{zi\,Ki}$. The function $Lc - {}_3Ui$ must be specified in the model as part of the set of Rf. To determine the indicators included in the K_{zi}, it is necessary to present each function of F_{zi} in the form of a functional network consisting of technological operations f_i (see the set of F2 in the HMS model) and set quality indicators for each of them:

$$K_{oj} = \left(\Pi_{oj}, \bar{T}_{oj}, D(T_{oj}), \bar{C}_{oj} \right),$$

Where Π_{oj} - probability of correct execution of the j-th technological operation; $\bar{T}_{oj}$ - and $D(T_{oj})$ - expectation and dispersion of the j-th technological operation execution time; $\bar{C}_{oj}$ - the expectation of the cost of performing the j-th technological operation. In cases where the technological operation consists only of human actions Π_{oj} is the probability of error-free human operation and its value is taken as the source of the directories. In cases where the technological operation is performed only by a person, it is recommended to calculate the indicators of stereotyping and logical complexity of the algorithm, which do not give a pragmatic assessment, but complement its characteristics of human conditions. Quality indicators at the task level are determined through the quality indicators of technological operations $Kzi = f(L_3 - oF, K_{oj})$, with the help of mathematical dependencies obtained in the functional-structural theory. At each level of evaluation, the quality indicators depend on many factors, which can be divided into the following groups: X – a set of controlled factors used in the ergatic design to improve performance indicators, V – perturbations that affect the quality of the functioning process.

Consider the possible composition of X and V on levels.

At the level of operations: Xo - options for changing the design of individual organs and their mutual location, working conditions in the performance of operations; Vo - human errors and equipment failures, structural and organizational failures of the HMS. At the level of formation of the structure of the task of operations: X_{3-0} - changing the structure of the activity algorithm (introduction of control, parallelization of operations, etc.), workplace organization, distribution of functions between man and technology; V_{3-0} - limitations (physical, intellectual, time) on task execution. At the task level: X_3 - level of professional training, discipline, motivation; V_3 - conditions of activity (monotonic, operational tension, etc.), causing errors at the level of the task. At the level of achieving the goal in solving a set of problems of X_{c-3} distribution of functions between specialists, the organization of work and rest; V_{c-3} - psychophysiological restrictions on the duration of continuous work, health (the possibility of physiological failures due to illness, injuries, etc.).

At the system level: X_c - professional selection of specialists, change of payment standards; V_c - conditions and effects on the system as a whole (influence of atmospheric and geomagnetic factors on all specialists; electromagnetic and radiation). Ten years after the introduction of such technologies, the role of the teacher will undergo a global rethinking [18]. But, even more seriously, the student in the event of such textbooks will no longer need a school class, therefore, in the school itself. He will sit at home and study, and the teacher-controller will remotely check whether the student has passed the material, how much time it took, what difficulties he had in the process of studying different topics. But then there will not be what we call the skills of the XXI century: the ability to communicate with other people, to work in a team and the like. If we want to get these skills, we will have to create an environment in which these competencies will be developed, in addition to the learning process itself. For example, a school will be a sports ground or a theater studio, or a choir, or something else. We will have to take children away from the digital environment and put them in the human environment. Thus, the tasks of the school can change significantly. The digital environment will really provide us with individual learning, and the school will have to build practices of collective (non-digital) action.

4 Conclusion

According to the data presented in the report of the Center for Strategic Research and Higher school of Economics "Twelve solutions for new education" [11] in 2016, the volume of the Russian market of online education amounted to 20,7 billion rubles, or 1,1% of the global market, while online University programs are less than a quarter. Today in Russia, the commercial educational market in the field of online higher education programs is almost not formed. There are no relatively large private providers specializing in this sector. Most market participants do not have their own resources to invest in promising technologies and even in promising resources and services based on existing technologies. There are a number of interesting initiatives (for example, projects "Netology group" or SkyEng, included in the top 20 most expensive companies Runet [Forbes rating]), but they specialize mainly in school and additional education.

Acknowledgments. The article is performed under the grant of The Russian Foundation for Basic Research (the project № 18-410-860008 p_a).

References

1. Womack, J.P., Jones, D.T., Roos, D.: The Machine That Changed the World: The Story of Lean Production. Free Press, New York (1991)
2. Ohno, T.: Taiichi Ohno's Workplace Management. Gemba Press (2007)
3. Order of the government of the Khanty-Mansiysk Autonomous Okrug – Ugra of August 19, 2016, № 455-RP On approval of The Concept of "Lean Region" in the Khanty-Mansiysk Autonomous Okrug – Ugra. https://leanregion.admhmao.ru/kontseptsiya/760256/rasporyazheniya-pravitelstva-khanty-mansiyskogo-avtonomnogo-okruga-yugry-ot-19-avgusta-2016-g-455-rp. Accessed 10 Nov 2018. (in Russian)
4. Shakirova, A.K.: Introduction of technology "lean-production" in the organization of the educational process. In: The System of Education and Technology of Lean Production: Materials of Part-Time Regional Scientific-Practical Conference, pp. 72–79. Publishing House of Nizhnevartovsk State University, Nizhnevartovsk (2017). http://konference.nvsu.ru/konffiles/323/Sistema%20obrazovaniya%20i%20tehnologii%20berezhlivogo%20proizv-va%20-%20Mat%20konf%20-%202017.pdf. Accessed 10 Nov 2018. (in Russian)
5. Sokolkin, A.V.: Overproduction production in vocational education. In: The System of Education and Technology of Lean Production: Materials of Part-Time Regional Scientific-Practical Conference, pp. 49–51. Publishing House of Nizhnevartovsk State University, Nizhnevartovsk (2017). (in Russian)
6. Khusainova, L. Sh., Nigmatzyanov, A.R.: The application of Lean manufacturing principles in the educational process. In: Grani nauki-2014, KPFU, Kazan (2014). (in Russian)
7. Chuchalin, A.I., Petrovskaya, T.S., Chernova, O.S.: Net interaction of institutions of higher education and vocational education while implementing programmes of "applied baccalaureat". High. Educ. Russia (11), 3–10 (2013). https://elibrary.ru/item.asp?id=20744853. Accessed 10 Nov 2018. (in Russian)
8. Burnasheva, E.P.: Use of lean production instruments in designing the educational process. Integr. Educ. **20**(1), 105–111 (2016). https://doi.org/10.15507/1991-9468.082.020.201601.105-111. (in Russian)
9. Official site of the International Bank for reconstruction and development. http://www.vsemirnyjbank.org/ru/who-we-are/ibrd. Accessed 10 Nov 2018. (in Russian)
10. The Center for Strategic Research of Higher School of Economics. Report: Twelve solutions for new education. https://kai.ru/documents/10181/6946092/Доклад_образование.pdf. Accessed 10 Nov 2018. (in Russian)
11. Program "Digital Economy of the Russian Federation". http://static.government.ru/. Accessed 10 Nov 2018. (in Russian)
12. Kramarov, S.O., Sakharov, L.V., Khramov, V.V.: Soft computing in management: control of complex multi-factor systems based on fuzzy analog controllers. Sci. Bull. South. Inst. Manage. (3), 42–51 (2017). https://elibrary.ru/item.asp?id=30280910. Accessed 10 Nov 2018
13. Khramov, V.V.: Information aggregation as a problem of personal self-organization. Russ. Psychol. J. **4**(4), 9–21 (2007). https://elibrary.ru/item.asp?id=16974213. Accessed 10 Nov 2018. (in Russian)
14. Khramov, V.V.: The principle of intelligence and its use in recognition tasks. In: The Collection: Thematic Scientific and Technical Collection of Pushchino, pp. 62–66 (1994) https://elibrary.ru/item.asp?id=32838003. Accessed 10 Nov 2018. (in Russian)

15. Khramov, V.V., Vitchenko, O.V., Tkachuk, E.O., Golubenko, E.V.: Intellectual methods, models and algorithms of educational process organization in Modern University. Rostov State Transport University, Rostov-on-Don (2016) https://elibrary.ru/item.asp?id=28322733. Accessed 10 Nov 2018. (in Russian)
16. Khramov, V.V., Gvozdev, D.S.: Intelligent information systems: data mining. Rostov State Transport University, Rostov-on-Don (2016) https://elibrary.ru/item.asp?id=32762296. Accessed 10 Nov 2018. (in Russian)
17. Khramov, V.V.: Method of aggregation of several sources of fuzzy information. Izvestiya TRTU 3(21), 52–53 (2001) https://elibrary.ru/item.asp?id=12886331. (in Russian)

Algorithm for Optimization of the Content of the Training Course Practical Part Using the Artificial Immune System

Irina Astachova[1]([⊠]) [iD] and Ekaterina Kiseleva[2] [iD]

[1] Voronezh State University, University Square 1, 394036 Voronezh, Russia
astachova@list.ru
[2] Voronezh State Pedagogical University, Lenin Street 86, 394024 Voronezh, Russia
ekaterkisel@mail.ru

Abstract. The article presents a model of a training system using the artificial intelligence methods for optimization of certain educational process components. The training system allows the teacher to create and optimize training courses based on the accumulated statistical information. For development of the training system, a hybrid system was chosen combining the advantages of various technologies that allow solving each problem in the optimal way. An algorithm for optimization of the content of the training course practical part using the artificial immune system has been considered. A set of the class's practical tasks is divided into classes of tasks of similar complexity aimed at achieving similar objectives of the course. The objective function and problem limitations are formulated using H. Markowitz's model. One of the problem's objective functions minimizes the correlation between the complexity of tasks of different classes, which allows excluding presence of many single-type tasks in the collection of practical tasks; another objective function maximizes the effectiveness (notion "effectiveness" is introduced in the article) of the collection of tasks. The model's variables are shares of the total number of tasks selected from each class. For optimization of the given model, a set of Pareto-optimal solutions of a bicriterial problem is found, which allows selecting the optimal relation between the tasks diversity and their effectiveness. The work offers an algorithm for finding the solution of this problem, modified for the artificial immune system. The algorithm suggested in the problem allows obtaining, in a relatively short time, a satisfactory approximation of the Pareto-optimal set for solution of the problem.

Keywords: Training program structural model · Optimization of the training course practical part · Artificial immune system

1 Introduction

Presently, various training systems based on the information-communication technologies have gained acceptance. They differ in many parameters: in the degree of the function allocation between the user and the system (in some of them, the user may independently choose the trajectory of his movement inside the system, while in others this function

V. Sukhomlin and E. Zubareva (Eds.): SITITO 2018, CCIS 1201, pp. 186–195, 2020.
https://doi.org/10.1007/978-3-030-46895-8_15

is partly or fully laid on the computer); in the degree of combination of theoretical and practical components; in the presence or absence of the controlling function [1]. The creators of various systems selected the combination of parameters corresponding to the system's destination. However, all the information technology training systems, in the process of their using, have a potential to accumulate statistical information about the trainees' movement along the complex, about their mistakes made in the working process, about the success when passing the control tasks etc., which can be used for optimization of the complex's functioning [2].

One of the modern computer-assisted training means are online stores of practical tasks, which are widely used when preparing pupils for Basic State Examinations and Uniform State Examinations. However, the solution of all the tasks contained in such a store is very time-consuming because of a great number of single-type task. Thus, there is a need for an algorithm for choosing the optimal collection of tasks sufficient for achieving the set goals.

2 Purpose of Work

The work intended to optimize the content of the course practical part within the training system that uses the artificial intelligence technologies and allows the user to apply the accumulated statistical data for optimization of the target and content components of training. In order to achieve the purpose, the following tasks were set: creating a mathematical model of the training system; selecting the means for realization and optimization of the obtained model, and development of the optimization algorithm. For the development of the training system, a hybrid system was chosen, since it combines the advantages of various technologies that allow solving each problem in the optimal way. A hybrid system is a system that combines two or more various computer technologies [3, 4].

3 Problem Solving Methods

The basis for creation of the training system structural model (Fig. 1) was the training process model. The target component determines the teacher's activity in the system, which is expressed in constructing the training content and methods [5]. The content component includes theoretical and practical materials that comprise the content of the courses within the system. The control component allows determining whether the training goals have been achieved. The statistics collection and analysis component allows storing the information about the trainees' work within the educational system [6].

Among the topical modern areas of research in the field of artificial intelligence are artificial immune systems. Methods of artificial immune systems belong to the class of bioinspired algorithms and are based on the human immune system functioning principles. The artificial system algorithms have much in common with the classical genetic algorithms, and their advantage is the ability to learn and the availability of memory.

Presently, a lot of models have been created using artificial immune systems, which are successfully applied in the process of optimization, classification and compression

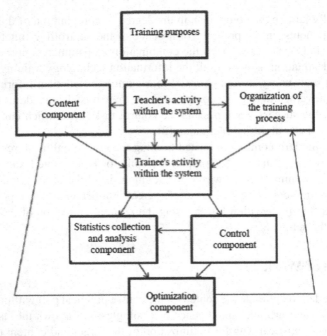

Fig. 1. Structural model of a computer training system.

of information, clustering [7], abnormality search [8], computer-aided learning [9], data processing [10], computer security [11] and adaptive management [12].

Artificial immune systems present a collection of B-antibodies that can be subject to cloning and mutation operations.

Application of artificial immune systems in education is limited since this field of research is relatively new as compared to the classical genetic algorithm and neural network technologies.

In work [13], the immune system is used for managing the distance education process. The distance education technology created by the author includes creation of effective algorithms for training of artificial immune systems based in the factor data analysis; the errors in evaluation of the artificial immune system are eliminated based on the properties of homologous proteins [14].

The suggested technology is the basis for the operation of the intelligent expert system capable of real-time processing of multidimensional data. The input characteristic of an artificial immune system is the time series composed of the trainee's characteristics determined during the input testing. The evaluation of the trainee's intellectual potential based on the initial data allows the artificial immune system to develop an individual training program. The system's output data are the comprehensive assessment of the trainees' knowledge, their grouping, and prediction of the training quality. The peculiarities of an artificial immune systems allow taking into account quite a great number of indicators when organizing the adaptive learning, which in turn allows using individual approach to each trainee.

The content of the obtained courses can be optimized using an artificial immune system.

An artificial immune system is based on the biological principle of the natural human immune system. Just like natural immune systems, artificial immune systems use the model for recognition of alien structures – antigens, by special receptors – antibodies. An artificial immune system represents an idealized version of a natural analog and reproduces the key components of the natural process: selection of the best antibodies of the population depending on the degree of their affinity (closeness) to the antigen, cloning of antibodies and mutation of antibodies.

The algorithm of functioning of the artificial immune system may be presented as follows.

1. Determining the antigen.
2. Formation of the initial population of antibodies of size N.
3. Calculation of affinity Aff of each antibody of the current population to the antigen.
4. Selecting from the current population the antibodies that have the best affinity values and obtaining a number of their copies (cloning).
5. Mutation of the antibodies' clones consisting in modification of their structure in a random way.
6. Calculation of affinity Aff of the antibodies' clones.
7. Formation of a new population via the antibody clones' joining the current population. Finding the current solution – the antibody with the best affinity value.
8. Removing some antibodies with the worst affinity values.
9. Generating new randomly formed antibodies and their joining the population until its size N is restored.
10. The condition for the algorithm completion is stabilization of the population over some number of cycles. If the condition is met, the solution is the antibody with the best affinity value; otherwise proceed to step 3.

According to the classical testing theory, each practical task of the training course is characterized by the following parameters:

Task weight is calculated by the formula:

$$\mu k = n/m, \tag{1}$$

where n is the number of the training course competences whose achieving is facilitated by successful fulfillment of the given task; m is the total number of competences of the given training course.

Task complexity is calculated by the formula:

$$\delta = Ne/Nt, \tag{2}$$

where Ne is the number of trainees that fulfilled the task correctly, Nt is the number of trainees that dealt with the task.

The set of the classes practical tasks can be subjected to discrete clustering. In the same class are included the tasks aimned at formation of the same course competences. Then, inside each class, interval clustering can be performed based on the task complexity value. Upon completion of these procedures, the set of tasks will be divided into classes of tasks of similar complexity aimed at the achievement of similar course objectives.

Each class is characterized by:

1. number of tasks k,
2. weight of tasks μ_i, calculated by formula (1)–(2),
3. average task complexity coefficient determined by the formula:

$$\delta_{imid} = \frac{1}{k} \sum_{1}^{k} \delta_i, \tag{3}$$

where k is the number of tasks of the given class; δ_i is the complexity of task i of this class, calculated by formula (3).

The target function and task limitations are formulated using the model suggested by H. Markowitz. It is necessary to determine the share of the tasks of each class in the total number of practical tasks offered to the trainee and meeting the following conditions:

$$R(X) = \sum_{i=1}^{N2} \sum_{j=1}^{N2} \sigma_{ij} x_i x_j \rightarrow min, \tag{4}$$

$$D(X) = \sum_{i=1}^{N2} \mu_i x_i \rightarrow max, \tag{5}$$

$$\sum_{i=1}^{N2} x_i = 1, \ x_i^{min} \leq x_i \leq x_i^{max}, i = 1, \ldots N2,$$

where N is the number of task classes available in the training course; μ_i – the weight of the tasks of class i; σ_{ij} – the covariance of the coefficients of average task complexity of classes i and j; x_i^{min} – the lower limitation for the share of the tasks selected from class i, x_i^{max} – the upper limitation for the share of the tasks selected from class i, x_i – the share of the total volume of tasks selected from given class i.

The variables of the model are share of the total number of tasks, selected from class i.

The target function (4) minimizes the correlation between the complexity of tasks of different classes, which allows excluding presence of many single-type tasks in the collection of practical tasks; the target function (5) maximizes the effectiveness of the collection of tasks.

For optimization of the given model, a set of Pareto-optimal solutions of a bicriterial problem [15] should be found, which will allow selecting the optimal relation between the tasks diversity and their effectiveness. The work [16] offers an algorithm for finding the solution of this problem. In this work, the suggested algorithm is modified for the artificial immune system [17].

1. Definition of antigen. Antigen is a vector $(R^*(X), D^*(X))$, whose components are optimal values of the respective functions (4), found separately, when transferring the second function to the limitations.
2. Formation of a population of antobodies of size N. The antibody in this problem is vector $X = (x_1, x_2, \ldots, x_n)$, containing a share of tasks of each class in the collection suggested to the trainee, which meets the conditions. The antibody population has a user-defined size. The population is formed as follows: each vector component is assigned an acceptable minimal value, and then, m of various components is randomly selected, whose value increases by $\frac{1}{m}\left(1 - \sum_{1}^{n} x_i\right)$.
3. Evaluation of the affinity of the antibodies to the antigen [12] is carried out as follows.

For each solution X in the population, a vector $(R(X), D(X))$, is calculated. A ranking procedure is applied to the obtained set in the following way:

- in the current population are found and temporarily excluded from consideration all the solutions nondominated by Pareto;
- the procedure is repeated until all the elements of the initial set are excluded;
- the elements belonging to the last considered set receive rank 1; those belonging to the last but one set – rank 2. The nondominated solutions excluded by the first ones receive the highest rank k, respectively equal to the number of the exclusion procedures carried out.

Then, each antibody receives the evaluation of affinity to the antigen. For each antibody X, Euclidean distance d from vector $(R(X), D(X))$, to vector $(R^*(X), D^*(X))$, is calculated. Each antibody receives evaluation

$$Aff = k + 1/d, \tag{6}$$

where k – rank of the set to which this antibody belongs, d – Euclidean distance from the antibody to the antigen.

Such a method of evaluation sets the algorithm up for search for nondominated solutions closest to the optimal values calculated by each criterion separately.

1. The antibody with the best affinity value is determined, which is deemed the current solution of the problem [13, 14]. $P(P < N)$ of antibodies is selected with the best affinity values, to which the cloning operator (creation of copies) is applied.
2. The mutation operator is applied to the obtained antibody clones. The selected realization of the mutation operator implies random selection of two positions i and j

and exchanging their values. If in this case the limitations for the maximum share size are violated, for example $x_j > x_i^{max}$, then

$$x_i = x_i^{max}, x_j = x_j + x_i - x_i^{max}. \tag{7}$$

Table 1 shows the example of mutation when the second and the ninth positions changed places.

Table 1. Mutation of antibodies.

Antibody	Antibody after mutation
0.12	0.12
0.34	**0.04**
0.17	0.17
0.15	0.15
0.08	0.08
0.05	0.05
0.14	0.14
0.03	0.03
0.04	**0.34**
0.01	0.01

3. Affinity of the antibody clones is calculated.
4. A new population is formed via the antibody clones' joining the current population.
5. Some antibodies with the worst affinity values are removed from the population and changed with new randomly generated antibodies.
6. Starting from the third step, the process is repeated until the population stabilization is obtained over some user-defined number of cycle repetitions.

The problem's solution is the current solution obtained during the last algorithm iteration. The current population of antibodies is the sought-for set of Pareto-optimal solutions of the bicriterial problem.

The suggested algorithm allows obtaining a satisfactory approximation of Pareto-optimal set for the solution of the problem in a relatively short time.

4 Interface of the Training System User

The main page is common for all users and is the linking node between various system sections. Two log-on blocks are available on the page: log-on through the teacher's account and log-on through the students account. It is also possible to register a new student's account (Fig. 2).

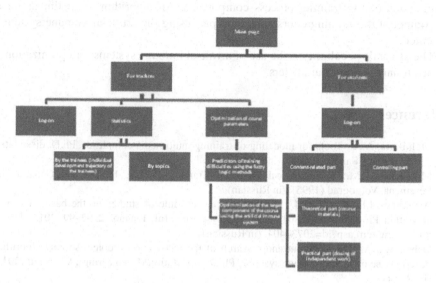

Fig. 2. Interface of the training system user

The new student's account registration page prompts the user to enter the personal information to set up the trainee's profile in the training system. The user also enters login and password that will be used to obtain access to the personal account.

Upon registration as a trainee, the user immediately enters the personal account. This page is the linking node – in the personal account one can view the current list of training courses, fulfill the theoretical and practical parts in each course, pass tests, view all his or her results with the complete information about the tests passed, and change the personal data. At the first visit of the personal account, the user is offered to read the system operation rules.

Page "Results" provides all the cumulative information about the test results in each course. Apart from the grade and the execution date, the user is also provided with the answer mask, which shows correct and incorrect answers to the questions of a certain test. Following the link for each test, the user can see the questions of this test. However, it is not possible to change the answers.

After entering login and password into the main page form, the user enters the user's personal account. The user is offered pages "Statistics" and "Optimization". Page "Statistics" is a cumulative table with the information about the students and the tests they have passed in each course created by the teacher. Viewing the test results, the teacher can see what questions were asked to the student in this test. Page "Optimization" allows optimizing the course content and the system of practical tasks of the course for each training course created by him.

5 Conclusion

The present work describes the system using the artificial intelligence methods for optimization of the training process components. An algorithm for optimization of the content of the training course practical part using the artificial immune system is presented.

The system's peculiarity is the use of artificial immune systems for optimization of various training course parameters.

References

1. Melnikova, A.A.: Tools for modeling of training multimedia complexes. Ph.D. dissertation (Engineering), Samara (2004). (in Russian)
2. Monakhov, V.M.: Technological Bases of Training Process Design and Construction. Peremena, Volgograd (1995). (in Russian)
3. Astakhova, I.F., Firas, A.M.: Drawing up the schedule of studies on the basis of genetic algorithm. Proc. Voronezh State Univ. Ser. Syst. Anal. Inf. Technol. **2**, 93–99 (2013). https://elibrary.ru/item.asp?id=20734404. (in Russian)
4. Ushakov, S.A.: Development and research of the recognition problem solving algorithms based on the artificial immune systems. Ph.D. dissertation (Engineering), Voronezh (2015). (in Russian)
5. Vasekin, S.V.: Technological optimization procedures when designing the training process in mathematics: abstract of thesis. Ph.D. dissertation (Pedagogy), Moscow (2000). (in Russian)
6. Astakhova, I.F., Shashkin, A.I., Korobkin, E.A.: Fuzzy logic design system of the prediction stability of ground mass. Proc. Voronezh State Univ. Ser. Syst. Anal. Inf. Technol. **1**, 98–106 (2015). https://elibrary.ru/item.asp?id=23441770. (in Russian)
7. Stankevich, L.A., Kazanskii A.B.: Immunological security system of a humanoid robot. In: Topical Problems or Protection and Security: Proceedings of the 9th All-Russian Scientific and Practical Conference, Voronezh, no. 5, pp. 145–152 (2006). (in Russian)
8. Garret, S.M.: How do we evaluate artificial immune systems? Evol. Comput. **13**(2), 145–177 (2005). https://doi.org/10.1162/1063656054088512
9. Hunt, J.E., Cooke, D.E.: Learning using an artificial immune system. J. Netw. Comput. Appl. **19**(2), 189–212 (1996). https://doi.org/10.1006/jnca.1996.0014
10. Knight, T., Timmis, J.: AINE: an immunological approach to data mining. In: Proceedings 2001 IEEE International Conference on Data Mining, San Jose, CA, USA, pp. 297–304 (2001). https://doi.org/10.1109/icdm.2001.989532
11. Kim, J., Bentley, P.J.: Towards an artificial immune system for network intrusion detection: an investigation of clonal selection with a negative selection operator. In: Proceedings of the 2001 Congress on Evolutionary Computation (IEEE Cat. No.01TH8546), Seoul, South Korea, vol. 2, pp. 1244–1252 (2001). https://doi.org/10.1109/cec.2001.934333
12. Kalmanje, K.K., Neidhoefer, J.: Immunized adaptive critic for an autonomous aircraft control application. In: Dasgupta, D. (eds.) Artificial Immune Systems and Their Applications. Springer, Berlin, Heidelberg, pp. 221–241 (1990). https://doi.org/10.1007/978-3-642-59901-9_12

13. Tarakanov, A.O.: Formal peptide as a basic agent of immune networks: from natural prototype to mathematical theory and applications. In: Proceedings 1st International Workshop of Central and Eastern Europe on Multi-Agent Systems (CEEMAS 1999). St. Petersburg, Russia, pp. 281–292 (1999)
14. Samigulina, G.A.: Development of a distance educational technology based on artificial immune systems. Open Educ. (6), 52–58 (2008). https://elibrary.ru/item.asp?id=11693391. (in Russian)
15. Deb, K.: Multi-Objective Optimization Using Evolutionary Algorithms. Wiley, Hoboken (2001)
16. Kashirina, I.L., Ivanova, K.G.: Managing the securities portfolio using a neural network committee. In: System Modeling of Socio-Economic Processes: Proceedings of the 31st International Scientific Workshop School, VSU, Voronezh, Part III, pp. 131–135 (2008). https://elibrary.ru/item.asp?id=28316806. (in Russian)
17. Thompson, P.W.: Mathematical microworld and intelligent computer assisted instruction. In: Kearsley, G.E. (ed.) Artificial Intelligence and Instruction: Applications and Methods, pp. 83–109. Addison-Wesley, New York (1987)

Integration and Development
of Professionally-Oriented Social Network
in the Context of the Evolution
of the Information Landscape

Andrey Lytchev[1]($\boxtimes$) (iD), Aleksei Rozhnov[1,2] (iD), Igor Lobanov[2] (iD),
and Sergei Pronichkin[3] (iD)

[1] National University of Science and Technology "MISIS",
Leninskij Avenue, 4, 119049 Moscow, Russia
lytchev@mail.ru
[2] V. A. Trapeznikov Institute of Control Sciences of Russian Academy of Sciences,
Profsoyuznaya Street 65, 117997 Moscow, Russia
[3] Federal Research Center "Computer Science and Control" of Russian Academy of Sciences,
Institute for Systems Analysis, 60-Letiya Oktyabrya Avenue, 9, 9117312 Moscow, Russia

Abstract. The report implements the discussions on the theme "Convergence of professional, scientific and educational network communities and prerequisites for its implementation: a collaboration of intellectual processes and investigations of advanced technology precursors". The target setting corresponds to an initiative focused on a comprehensive discussion of issues of formation of digital socio-economic environments and assessment of the quality of processes on the basis of conceptual models of integration, collective expertise, and convergence of professional, scientific and educational network communities. In this regard, interdisciplinary research and development in its fundamental basis are directly aimed at the implementation of effective management of the socio-economic environment of professional, scientific and educational network communities in the transition to digital, intelligent production technologies, new materials, by creating original tools for search, collection, storage and processing of pertinent information resources in modern conditions of rapid development of artificial neural network, cognitive and other bio-inspired technologies.

Keywords: Professionally Oriented Social Network · Information landscape · System integration · Data Envelopment Analysis · Bio-inspired technologies

1 Introduction

One of the main reasons for the lag in the technological development of some regions is that progressive ideas and innovations of the world community remain on the periphery of the information landscape and priorities of socio-economic development. In this regard, for regions, it is relevant to consider the problematic issues of transferring the economy to an innovative development path. A key factor in shifting the region's economy to the

V. Sukhomlin and E. Zubareva (Eds.): SITITO 2018, CCIS 1201, pp. 196–207, 2020.
https://doi.org/10.1007/978-3-030-46895-8_16

innovative path of development is the formation and effective use of the innovation potential. The innovative potential of a region depends on the level of innovation development and the innovation readiness of business entities located on its territory, the innovation infrastructure created and the existing opportunities for innovation development.

The target setting corresponds to an initiative focused on a comprehensive discussion of issues of formation of digital socio-economic environments and assessment of the quality of processes on the basis of conceptual models of integration, collective expertise, and convergence of professional, scientific and educational network communities. In this regard, interdisciplinary research and development in its fundamental basis are directly aimed at the implementation of effective management of the socio-economic environment of professional, scientific and educational network communities in the transition to digital, intelligent production technologies, new materials, by creating original tools for search, collection, storage and processing of pertinent information resources in modern conditions of rapid development of artificial neural network, cognitive and other bio-inspired technologies.

Development on such a methodological basis and improvement of economic and mathematical models for analyzing the innovative potential of a region are particularly relevant when developing a scientifically based regional innovation policy and creating regional development programs with due account for the effective use of regional information (innovation) landscape in terms of evolution advanced Professionally-Oriented Social Networks.

In the report, along with the use of some well-known possibilities of Data Envelopment Analysis (DEA) [14], e.g., two-stage evaluation of efficiency using DEA [24] and target setting [20], it is proposed to pay a little more attention to the phased selection of variables and the justification of procedures (e.g., stepwise selection of variables in DEA [36]) in a visual representation of generalized models [32] in the interest of creating Professionally-Oriented Social Networks.

This paper presents the context and the following primary accents for Integration and Development of Professionally-Oriented Social Network [21, 23]:

- Integration in the Context of the Evolution of the Region Information Landscape;
- Convergence of Professional, Scientific, and Educational Network Communities and Prerequisites for its Implementation; and others [12, 19].

2   Integration in the Context of the Evolution of the Region Information Landscape

2.1   Innovative Potential of the Region

The innovation potential of the region is a complex economic category, which is formed under the influence of many factors. Among the publications devoted to the analysis of the innovation potential of the region, there are a lot of interesting and profound papers that study the bottlenecks and imperfections of regional innovation systems, see [4, 7, 10, 22, 33, 34] among others. In these papers, we can find a description and analysis of the infrastructural and institutional failures of regional innovation systems. In the works of Borrás and Edquist [2], Hekkert and Negro [11], Elzen and Wieczorek [8], authors try to identify the functional determinants of regional innovation systems, the failure of which leads to system failures. Some approaches were developed to definition and formation of the innovative potential of the region.

The resource approach considers the innovative potential as an interrelated system of labor, information, material and technical, organizational and managerial resources, the joint use of which ensures the effective innovative development of economic entities. Another approach examines the innovation potential as the result of innovation, i.e., the real product obtained in the innovation process. In this case, the innovation potential is presented as a possible future innovative product.

There are different approaches in the scientific literature to determining the structure of the innovation potential. It should be noted that most of the authors focus on the resource component when determining the structure of the innovative potential. In our opinion, this is a necessary but not sufficient condition, since the innovative development of the region is ensured through the innovative activities of economic entities. This study uses a generalized approach to the definition of innovation potential, which considers the innovation potential as the ability and readiness of the regional innovation system to ensure a continuous and sustainable innovation process. In our opinion, such an approach is preferred, since when analyzing the innovation potential, it is necessary to comprehensively explore the resources and outcome, reflecting, respectively, the readiness and ability of the region for innovative development. At the same time, when analyzing the innovation potential, it is necessary to take into account that the innovative development of the region is carried out in a quite predetermined environment.

2.2 The Information Landscape and Data Envelopment Analysis

Data Envelopment Analysis (DEA) is a powerful analytical research tool for measuring the relative efficiency of a homogeneous set of Decision-Making Units (DMUs) by obtaining empirical estimates of relations between multiple inputs and multiple outputs related to the DMUs [5]. DEA models are widely used throughout the world to analyze the behavior of complex socio-economic systems, such as financial and industrial companies, banks branches, municipalities, public organizations, universities, etc. Thousands of DEA-related articles were published in international journals [9].

Our experience shows that sometimes traditional DEA models can produce inconsistent results that contradict expert opinion: some DMUs were efficient, while experts believed that these units should have less efficiency score. So we need to modify models in order to take into account expert judgment. For this reason, an original approach based on dominance cones was used. Currently, two special cases of cones are widely known in the literature and applied in practice: the assurance region method and cone-ratio method. Both of these approaches are reduced to the construction and subsequent addition of cones in the multiplier space that is dual to the input-output space. Therefore, the considered models may cause difficulties in their application in practice.

The paper discusses a model for analyzing the innovative potential of a region based on a generalized DEA model [17]. This model uses constructive methods to improve the adequacy of the model in the input-output space of the regions innovative potential, which will also significantly expands the range of capabilities of decision makers resulting in the better and faster decision-making process in professionally-oriented social networks.

2.3 DEA Background

Since DEA was first introduced in 1978, there have been a large number of papers written on DEA or applying DEA on various sets of problems. Emrouznejad and Yang [9] give a survey and analysis of the 40 years of scholarly literature in DEA up to the year 2016. According to this study, more than 10,000 DEA-related articles were published in the literature. There are about 2,200 articles published as working paper, book chapter or conference proceedings which they did not include in the study. A number of international conferences devoted to this subject are held regularly, e.g. DEAIC2018, NAPW2018, DEA40, EWEPA2017, DEA2018 etc.

Next, we briefly describe the main DEA models and its underlying technologies. Suppose there are a set of n Decision Making Units (DMUs) to be assessed. Each observed DMU_j, $j = 1, \ldots, n$ is represented by the pair (X_j, Y_j), where $X_j = (x_{1j}, \ldots, x_{mj}) \geq 0$, $j = 1, \ldots, n$ is the vector of inputs, and $Y_j = (y_{1j}, \ldots, y_{rj}) \geq 0$, $j = 1, \ldots, n$ is the vector of outputs. All data are assumed to be nonnegative, but at least one component of every input and output vector is positive.

The production technology T is defined as $T = \{(X, Y)| \text{ outputs } Y \text{ can be produced from inputs } X\}$, i.e., it contains the set of all feasible input-output vectors.

The generalized formulation of convex and non-convex DEA technologies under different returns to scale assumptions can be written in the following form [3]

$$T^{\Lambda,\Gamma} = \left\{ (X, Y)|X \geq \sum_{j=1}^{n} X_j \delta \lambda_j, \quad Y \leq \sum_{j=1}^{n} Y_j \delta \lambda_j, \quad \lambda_j \in \Lambda, \ \delta \in \Gamma \right\},$$

where $\lambda = (\lambda_1, \ldots, \lambda_n)^{\mathrm{T}}$ is called the intensity vector, $\delta \in \mathbb{R}_+$ is the scaling factor, $\Lambda \in \{NC, C\}$, NC and NC represent non-convexity and convexity, respectively,

$$NC = \left\{ \sum_{j=1}^{n} \lambda_j = 1, \ \lambda_j \in \{0, 1\} \right\} \quad \text{and} \quad C = \left\{ \sum_{j=1}^{n} \lambda_j = 1, \ \lambda_j \geq 0, \ \lambda_j \in \mathbb{R}_+ \right\},$$

set Γ contains specific assumptions regarding the returns to scale [13, 14, 25] of technology T and defined as $\Gamma \in \{VRS, CRS, NDRS, NIRS\}$, with

$$VRS = \{\delta|\delta = 1\}, \qquad CRS = \{\delta|\delta \geq 0\},$$
$$NIRS = \{\delta|0 \leq \delta \leq 1\}, \ NDRS = \{\delta|\delta \geq 1\}.$$

Taking convexity and assuming variable returns to scale we derive technology $T^{C, VRS}$ of the traditional BCC model; $T^{C, CRS}$ represents the technology of classical CCR model [5]; the non-convex FDH technology [6] is generated using $T^{NC, VRS}$. The rest combinations of Λ and Γ produce other well-known convex and non-convex DEA reference technologies.

In order to visualize the frontier in a multidimensional space of inputs and outputs we can construct two- and three-dimensional sections of the frontier. Parametric optimization algorithms for the construction of sections for convex technologies are described in [18, 35]. For non-convex models, algorithms of the frontier visualization using enumeration and optimization methods are developed in [15, 16]. Visual representation in this form is more convenient for perception and analysis; it strengthens the performance analysis and the intuitive decision making.

For the purpose of implementation the multilayer hierarchical structures in the DEA framework, we apply a generalized Multiple Layer Data Envelopment Analysis (MLDEA) model [32]. Following MLDEA approach, we use the mathematical deduction process for substantiation the weights in each layer of the hierarchy, and extract different types of possible weight restrictions.

2.4 Prototype of Optimization Modeling System

In order to apply the DEA models described in the previous section to various production units, the optimization modeling system is developed [19]. It implements a number of algorithms for efficiency analysis and frontier visualization with the help of construction of two- and three-dimensional sections. The functional diagram of the modeling system is shown in Fig. 1.

The external data source is connected to the system and contains raw information about the units under investigation. Depending on the research task (level of detail, model parameters, size of the entire task) the data is aggregated and converted into the internal data format of the modeling system; then it is recorded in the internal database.

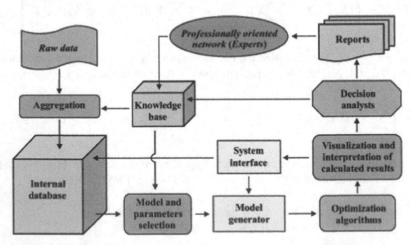

Fig. 1. The functional diagram of the optimization modeling system.

The purpose of the research and application area determines the choice of DEA models and a set of parameters. Based on the information stored in the internal data-base the model generator produces the optimization problems and store it in a special format.

Essentially, the generator creates a whole family of optimization tasks that are needed to build the cut of the frontier. The output of the model generator is transmitted to the input of the solver, and then calculated results are presented for data analysts in the form of tables, diagrams, and visualized in the form of two-and three-dimensional sections. The model optimizer was developed on the basis of recent advances in the theory and methods of solving problems of high dimensionality and is capable of solving problems with tens and hundreds of thousands of variables and constraints.

The knowledge base accumulates information about the tasks studied (aggregation rules, model parameters, objects dynamics, their efficiency scores, different cuts of the frontier, etc.) for subsequent use and construction of new models based on the knowledge gained.

Based on the approach described above, the prototype of optimization modeling system was developed for modeling and visualization the behavior of complex systems. It is designed for supporting strategic decision making or data analysis, evaluating various scenarios, forecasting the development of complex systems. It can be used both in daily analytical work and in the operational mode for the analysis of critical situations. In order to enhance effect from financial systems analysis, a projection system was developed where 3D sections of the frontier are generated using virtual reality. To create a visual stereo effect, two projectors with polarizing filters are used. On a special screen, two images for the left and right eyes are simultaneously formed. The screen has a special metallic surface that preserves the polarization of the images to be presented to each eye, see Fig. 2 and Fig. 3.

Fig. 2. The projection system for visualization of three-dimensional sections of the frontier.

3 Convergence of Professional, Scientific and Educational Network Communities and Prerequisites for Its Implementation

3.1 A Collaboration of Intellectual Processes and Investigations of Advanced Technology Precursors

The report implements the initiative round table on the theme "Convergence of professional, scientific and educational network communities and prerequisites for its implementation: a collaboration of intellectual processes and investigations of advanced technology precursors". The target setting corresponds to a new project focused on a comprehensive discussion of issues of formation of digital socio-economic environments and assessment of the quality of life of the Russian population on the basis of conceptual models of integration, collective expertise, and convergence of professional, scientific and educational network communities. The aim of the new project is to ensure interdisciplinary interaction of groups of researchers in the interrelated fields of socio-humanitarian and natural sciences. The conception consists of the formation of digital formation of digital socio-economic environments based on conceptual models of integration, collective expertise, and convergence of professional, scientific and educational network communities in the conditions of the digital economy of Russia and the evolutionary self-organization of the information landscape.

Fig. 3. Visualization of the three-dimensional section of six-dimensional DEA frontier.

The main content of the project is the development of an original digital platform. In this regard, interdisciplinary research and development in its fundamental basis are directly aimed at the implementation of effective management of the socio-economic environment of professional, scientific and educational network communities (professional social network of research teams) in the transition to digital, intelligent production technologies, new materials, by creating original tools for search, collection, storage and processing of pertinent information resources in modern conditions of rapid development of bio-inspired technologies. At the same time, the complex studies (in the presented problematic issues of the initiated project) are determined by the internal logic of the development of socio-humanitarian and natural sciences. This work described by the context of the problem of ensuring the humanity readiness for big challenges, taking into account the interaction of man and technology, social institutions at the present stage of global development.

In this section, the problem-based learning systems and integration of its intellectual components (advanced precursors) into expert systems are investigated using data envelopment analysis approach. Accelerated staff training is a factor of future effectiveness of mixed groups of robotic systems created from these basic components. Also, effectiveness achieved by taking into account the information on the latest developments, and using the high quality software and training facilities on the test bench, i.e. by improving training and material support of universities. An implementation of the original problem-oriented system on the basis of pertinent search algorithms for processing of information resources is invited to consider for the further comprehensive study of the conditions and interaction information. Simulation the activity of mixed robotic groups is performed by using the knowledge base on bionic technology. Moreover, a number of substantiated proposals for the development of operational processing technology and pertinence of information resources under the International Charter on Space and Major Disasters has a significant effect in the present conditions. The innovative potential of the virtual environment in the long term can be used for developing an unmanned vehicle as a component of an intelligent city. Another application of the proposed approach is 3D-visualization software and hardware solutions and integration of its components in the simulation of mixed (space) robotics groups and even game applications [1, 26–31].

3.2 Knowledge Extraction for the Optimization Modeling System

The concepts and methods of scientometrics, theoretical linguistics, and decision-making theory will be used as the main methods and approaches for conducting scientific research within the framework of this project, allowing for a comprehensive analysis of the problems of extracting knowledge from scientific publications. In addition, when conducting research, it is planned to use general scientific methods of cognition: the dialectical method; comparison methods and comparative analysis; empirical data analysis methods.

The proposed project will theoretically explore the concept of a scientific result as a type of knowledge using the approaches of the science of science. The scientific results of various types will be studied. Along with this, the introduction in scientific publications of new concepts and categories will be investigated. For the study of linguistic means of expressing results and new concepts in scientific publications using the example of the Russian language, approaches of theoretical linguistics will be used.

Also in the proposed project, based on the results of theoretical studies, knowledge extraction methods will be developed, in particular, descriptions of results and new concepts introduced in scientific publications. For the analysis of scientific publications, the method of relational analysis based on semantic-syntactic analysis of texts will be applied. To represent the semantics of the scientific text necessary for the effective extraction of knowledge, a relational-situational model of the text will be used, which describes the semantics of each sentence as a set of components bearing an elementary sense, connected by semantic situational relations.

To extract knowledge from scientific publications, it is proposed to use approaches and methods of machine learning for marked corpuses of texts. This implies the creation within the framework of a project of a corpus of scientific texts with manual marking, highlighting in the text wording containing the results and new concepts. The process of marking packages is a time-consuming task, so it is proposed to use the principles of hybrid active machine learning, involving interactive user interaction to obtain teaching examples and using the technique of incremental (adaptive) learning.

As basic learning strategies, it is proposed to use compositions of learning algorithms and iterative self-improvement approaches that provide an increase in the quality of education in small training samples. The composition of learning methods will be logical methods based on the generation of rules, and statistical methods based on conditional random fields. The quality of the developed methods will be assessed on a specially created verification markup corpus of publications in the humanities, natural and mathematical sciences. The fundamental difference between scientific publications and other sources of knowledge is the presence of feedback that allows us to accept or not accept new knowledge. To assess the reliability of the results obtained, they will be evaluated based on the expertise of the scientific community.

The novelty of the proposed methods and approaches consists in the application of the relational-situational analysis to the processing of scientific texts, the application of active learning to the extraction of scientific results and new concepts from scientific publications, the use of a composition of logical and statistical learning models.

The prospect of development of knowledge extraction for the optimization modeling system is the elaboration of the approach from An index to quantify an individual's scientific leadership [12], which is currently being compared and analyzed to apply.

3.3 Application of the Economic-Mathematical Models of Regional Innovative Potential Analysis

The current stage of history puts forward the need for system analysis and understanding of the level of a country's development, assessing the future prospects of its regions as parts of a single state, taking into account the characteristic features of each region. One of the key factors for the development of the region is the formation and effective use of regional innovation potential. In existing works, when analyzing the innovative potential of a region, the focus is on the resource component, using unreasonable transformations of the initial data, as a rule, traditionally using subjective quantitative characteristics, averages, and weights. The work is devoted to the development of DEA models for analyzing the innovative potential of a region, which will allow a comprehensive study of the resource and productive components, reflecting, respectively, the readiness and ability of the region to innovate. It is proposed to use direct methods for constructing an economic-mathematical model of the region's innovative potential based on a methodology for analyzing the functioning environment, and also to use methods for transforming the efficient frontier in the space of inputs and outputs to adjust the model. Using this model, recommendations for the development of regions will be developed taking into account the effective use of innovative resources.

The research results will solve many theoretical problems of the innovation development economy, for example, problems of identifying and researching failures of the regional innovation system, identifying an interconnected effective system of control actions aimed at eliminating and mitigating these failures.

4 Conclusion

The report presents a discussion on the thematic area "Convergence of professional, scientific and educational network communities and prerequisites for its implementation: the collaborative nature of intellectual processes and investigations of advanced technology precursors." The research is in line with the new original project, focused on a comprehensive discussion of the problematic issues of creating digital socio-economic environments and assessing the quality of life of the population based on conceptual models of integration, collective expertise, and convergence of professional, scientific and educational network communities.

Acknowledgments. This work was partially supported by the Russian Science Foundation, project No. 17-11-01353 (implementation of DEA approach). Partially financial support from the RFBR according to the research projects No. 17-06-00237 (investigation of innovative potential of the region), and No. 18-311-00267 (knowledge extraction for the optimization modeling system) is also gratefully acknowledged.

References

1. Abrosimov, V., Ryvkin, S., Goncharenko, V., Rozhnov, A., Lobanov, I.: Identikit of modifiable vehicles at virtual semantic environment. In: 2017 International Conference on Optimization of Electrical and Electronic Equipment (OPTIM) and 2017 International Aegean Conference on Electrical Machines and Power Electronics (ACEMP), Brasov, pp. 905–910 (2017). https://doi.org/10.1109/optim.2017.7975085
2. Borrás, S., Edquist, C.: The choice of innovation policy instruments. Technol. Forecast. Soc. Chang. **80**(8), 1513–1522 (2013). https://doi.org/10.1016/j.techfore.2013.03.002
3. Briec, W., Kerstens, K., Eeckaut, P.V.: Non-convex technologies and cost functions: definitions, duality and nonparametric tests of convexity. J. Econ. **81**(2), 155–192 (2004). https://doi.org/10.1007/s00712-003-0620-y
4. Carlsson, B., Jacobsson, S., Holmén, M., Rickne, A.: Innovation systems: analytical and methodological issues. Res. Policy **31**(2), 233–245 (2002). https://doi.org/10.1016/s0048-7333(01)00138-x
5. Cooper, W.W., Seiford, L.M., Tone, K.: Data Envelopment Analysis, 2nd edn. Springer, Boston (2007). https://doi.org/10.1007/978-0-387-45283-8
6. Deprins, D., Simar, L., Tulkens, H.: Measuring labor efficiency in post offices. In: Marchand, M., Pestieau, P., Tulkens, H. (eds.) The Performance of Public Enterprises: Concepts and Measurements, Chap. 10, pp. 243–268. North Holland, Amsterdam (1984)
7. Edquist, C., Zabala-Iturriagagoitia, J.M.: Public procurement for Innovation as mission-oriented innovation policy. Res. Policy **41**(10), 1757–1769 (2012). https://doi.org/10.1016/j.respol.2012.04.022

8. Elzen, B., Wieczorek, A.: Transitions towards sustainability through system innovation. Technol. Forecast. Soc. Chang. **72**(6), 651–661 (2005). https://doi.org/10.1016/j.techfore.2005.04.002
9. Emrouznejad, A., Yang, G.-L.: A survey and analysis of the first 40 years of scholarly literature in DEA: 1978-2016. Socio-Econ. Plann. Sci. **61**, 4–8 (2018). https://doi.org/10.1016/j.seps.2017.01.008
10. Gregersen, B., Johnson, B.: Learning economies, innovation systems and european integration. Reg. Stud. **31**(5), 479–490 (1997). https://doi.org/10.1080/00343409750132270
11. Hekkert, M.P., Negro, S.O.: Functions of innovation systems as a framework to understand sustainable technological change: empirical evidence for earlier claims. Technol. Forecast. Soc. Chang. **76**(4), 584–594 (2009). https://doi.org/10.1016/j.techfore.2008.04.013
12. Hirsch, J. E.: hα: An index to quantify an individual's scientific leadership. arXiv e-prints p. arXiv:1810.01605 (2018)
13. Krivonozhko, V.E., Førsund, F.R., Lychev, A.V.: Measurement of returns to scale in radial DEA models. Comput. Math. Math. Phys. **57**(1), 83–93 (2017). https://doi.org/10.1134/s0965542517010080
14. Krivonozhko, V.E., Førsund, F.R., Rozhnov, A.V., Lychev, A.V.: Measurement of returns to scale using a non-radial DEA model. Dokl. Math. **85**(1), 144–148 (2012). https://doi.org/10.1134/s1064562412010322
15. Krivonozhko, V.E., Lychev, A.V.: Algorithms for construction of efficient frontier for nonconvex models on the basis of optimization methods. Dokl. Math. **96**(2), 541–544 (2017). https://doi.org/10.1134/s1064562417050337
16. Krivonozhko, V.E., Lychev, A.V.: Frontier visualization for nonconvex models with the use of purposeful enumeration methods. Dokl. Math. **96**(3), 650–653 (2017). https://doi.org/10.1134/s1064562417060047
17. Krivonozhko, V.E., Utkin, O.B., Safin, M.M., Lychev, A.V.: On some generalization of the DEA models. J. Oper. Res. Soc. **60**(11), 1518–1527 (2009). https://doi.org/10.1057/jors.2009.64
18. Krivonozhko, V.E., Utkin, O.B., Volodin, A.V., Sablin, I.A., Patrin, M.V.: Constructions of economic functions and calculations of marginal rates in DEA using parametric optimization methods. J. Oper. Res. Soc. **55**(10), 1049–1058 (2004). https://doi.org/10.1057/palgrave.jors.2601759
19. Krivonozhko, V., Rozhnov, A., Lychev, A.: Construction a hybrid intelligent information framework and components of expert systems using the generalized data envelopment analysis model [in Russian]. Neurocomputers **6**, 003–012 (2013). https://elibrary.ru/item.asp?id=19118083
20. Lovell, C.A.K., Pastor, J.T.: Target setting: an application to a bank branch network. Eur. J. Oper. Res. **98**(2), 290–299 (1997). https://doi.org/10.1016/s0377-2217(96)00348-7
21. Lychev, A. V., Rozhnov, A. V.: Advanced analytics software for performance analysis and visualization of financial institutions. In: Proceedings of the 11th IEEE International Conference on Application of Information and Communication Technologies (AICT 2017), Moscow, Russia, pp. 1–5 (2017). https://doi.org/10.1109/icaict.2017.8687039
22. Malerba, F., Orsenigo, L., Peretto, P.: Persistence of innovative activities, sectoral patterns of innovation and international technological specialization. Int. J. Ind. Organ. **15**(6), 801–826 (1997). https://doi.org/10.1016/s0167-7187(97)00012-x
23. Nechaev, V., Goncharenko, V., Rozhnov, A., Lytchev, A., Lobanov, I.: Integration of virtual semantic environments components and generalized data envelopment analysis (DEA) model [in Russian]. In: CEUR Workshop Proceedings: Selected Papers of the XI International Scientific-Practical Conference Modern Information Technologies and IT-Education (SITITO 2016), Moscow, Russia, vol. 1761, pp. 339–347 (2016). http://ceur-ws.org/Vol-1761/paper44.pdf

24. Paradi, J.C., Rouatt, S., Zhu, H.: Two-stage evaluation of bank branch efficiency using data envelopment analysis. Omega **39**(1), 99–109 (2011). https://doi.org/10.1016/j.omega.2010.04.002
25. Podinovski, V.V.: Returns to scale in convex production technologies. Eur. J. Oper. Res. **258**(3), 970–982 (2017). https://doi.org/10.1016/j.ejor.2016.09.029
26. Rozhnov, A., Lychev, A.: System integration of research activities and innovations in distributed computer and telecommunication networks using data envelopment analysis [in Russian]. In: Vishnevskiy, V., Samouylov, K. (eds.) Distributed computer and communication networks: control, computation, communications (DCCN-2018), vol. 1, pp. 273–280. Peoples' Friendship University of Russia, Moscow, Russia (2018)
27. Rozhnov, A.V., Lobanov, I.A.: Investigation of the joint semantic environment for heterogeneous robotics. In: 2017 Tenth International Conference Management of Large-Scale System Development (MLSD), Moscow, Russia, pp. 1–5 (2017). https://doi.org/10.1109/mlsd.2017.8109678
28. Rozhnov, A.V., Melikhov, A.A.: Vectorizing textual data sources to decrease attribute space dimension. In: 2017 Tenth International Conference Management of Large-Scale System Development (MLSD), Moscow, Russia, pp. 1–4 (2017). https://doi.org/10.1109/mlsd.2017.8109662
29. Ryvkin, S., Rozhnov, A., Lobanov, I.: Convergence of technologies of the evolving prototype of an energy efficient large-scale system. In: 2018 20th International Symposium on Electrical Apparatus and Technologies (SIELA), pp. 1–4 (2018). https://doi.org/10.1109/siela.2018.8447067
30. Ryvkin, S., Rozhnov, A., Lobanov, I., Chemyshov, L.: Investigation of the stratified model of virtual semantic environment for modifiable vehicles. In: 2018 20th International Symposium on Electrical Apparatus and Technologies (SIELA), pp. 1–4 (2018). https://doi.org/10.1109/siela.2018.8447069
31. Ryvkin, S., Rozhnov, A., Lychev, A., Lobanov, I., Fateeva, Y.: Multiaspect modeling of infrastructure solutions at energy landscape as virtual semantic environment. In: 2017 International Conference on Optimization of Electrical and Electronic Equipment (OPTIM) and 2017 International Aegean Conference on Electrical Machines and Power Electronics (ACEMP), pp. 935–940 (2017). https://doi.org/10.1109/optim.2017.7975090
32. Shen, Y., Hermans, E., Ruan, D., Wets, G., Brijs, T., Vanhoof, K.: A generalized multiple layer data envelopment analysis model for hierarchical structure assessment: a case study in road safety performance evaluation. Expert Syst. Appl. **38**(12), 15262–15272 (2011). https://doi.org/10.1016/j.eswa.2011.05.073
33. Smith, D.J.: The politics of innovation: why innovations need a godfather. Technovation **27**(3), 95–104 (2007). https://doi.org/10.1016/j.technovation.2006.05.001
34. Soete, L., Verspagen, B., ter Weel, B.: Chapter 27 - systems of innovation. In: Hall, B.H., Rosenberg, N. (eds.) Handbook of the Economics of Innovation, Volume 2, Handbook of the Economics of Innovation, vol. 2, pp. 1159–1180. North-Holland (2010). https://doi.org/10.1016/s0169-7218(10)02011-3
35. Volodin, A.V., Krivonozhko, V.E., Ryzhikh, D.A., Utkin, O.B.: Construction of three-dimensional sections in data envelopment analysis by using parametric optimization algorithms. Comput. Math. Math. Phys. **44**(4), 589–603 (2004)
36. Wagner, J.M., Shimshak, D.G.: Stepwise selection of variables in data envelopment analysis: Procedures and managerial perspectives. Eur. J. Oper. Res. **180**(1), 57–67 (2007). https://doi.org/10.1016/j.ejor.2006.02.048

Research and Development in the Field of New IT and Their Applications

Different Approaches to Solving the Problem of Reconstructing the Distance Matrix Between DNA Chains

Boris Melnikov[1]([✉]) [iD], Marina Trenina[2] [iD], and Elena Melnikova[1] [iD]

[1] Russian State Social University, Wilhelm Pieck Str. 4, 129226 Moscow, Russia
bf-melnikov@yandex.ru, ya.e.melnikova@yandex.ru
[2] Togliatti State University, Belorusskaya Str. 14, 445020 Togliatti, Russia
trenina.m.a@yandex.ru

Abstract. In this paper, we consider one of the tasks of biocybernetics, i.e. the problem of reconstructing the distance matrix between DNA sequences. In this problem, not all the elements of the matrix under consideration are known at the input of the algorithm (usually 50% or less elements). The basis for the development of the algorithm for reconstructing such a matrix is the method of comparative evaluation of the algorithms for calculating distances between DNA sequences developed and investigated by us earlier. In this analysis, the badness of each of the triangles of the matrix determined by us was applied.

The restoration of the matrix occurs as a result of several computational passes. Estimates of unknown matrix elements are averaged in a special way using the risk function, and the result of this averaging is considered as the received value of the unknown element. To optimize the algorithm for solving this problem, we consider the use of the branch and bound method in it.

Keywords: DNA sequences · Metric · Distance matrix · Partially filled matrix · Recovery · Branch and bound method

1 Introduction

In practice, quite often there is a need to calculate a specially defined distance between sequences of different nature. Such algorithms are often used in bioinformatics, they are a separate, very important kind of problem of finding the distance between the given genetic sequences [1–5]. The main difficulty that arises when calculating the distance between genetic sequences is a very long length of such a sequence.

Because of this, algorithms that calculate the exact value of the distance between two sequences are inapplicable, and to estimate the distance between such chains we have to use heuristic algorithms that give approximate results [6].

There are various similar algorithms, but their obvious disadvantage is to obtain several different results when using different heuristic algorithms applied to the calculation of the distance between the same pair of DNA strings. Therefore, there is a problem of assessing the quality of the used metrics (distances) and the results obtained in solving

© Springer Nature Switzerland AG 2020
V. Sukhomlin and E. Zubareva (Eds.): SITITO 2018, CCIS 1201, pp. 211–223, 2020.
https://doi.org/10.1007/978-3-030-46895-8_17

this problem; we can some conclusions about the applicability of a specific algorithm for calculating distances to various applied studies.

In addition, one of the problems considered in biocybernetics is the problem of restoring the distance matrix between DNA sequences (below, simply DNA matrix), in which not all the elements of the considered matrix are known at the input of the algorithm [7]. In this regard, there exists another problem: to use the developed method of comparative evaluation of algorithms for calculating distances between sequences for a completely different purpose, namely, i.e., for the problem of restoring the distance matrix between DNA sequences described below.

We have considered a method of comparative analysis for the resulting work of any algorithm for calculating the distances between the genomes of the matrix is based on the consideration of all possible triangles. In this case, we assume that ideally they should be acute isosceles [8]. To answer the question, how "correct" is the matrix obtained as a result of some heuristic algorithm is, we propose to use the "departure characteristic" of the obtained triangles from the "elongated isosceles" the above value of badness.

In this approach (i.e., when the application of the method for comparative evaluation of algorithms for calculating the distance to the recovering of matrices), the recovering is the implementation of multiple computational passes. On each of the passes, for some yet empty (unknown) elements of the matrix, the different estimates are obtained; these estimates are averaged in a special way and the averaging result is taken as the value of the unknown element. From the physical point of view, the applied averaging gives the position of the center of gravity of a one, i.e. dimensional system of bodies whose mass is given by a special risk function [9].

In addition, we consider the possibility of optimizing this algorithm, since the calculation of the unknown elements of an incomplete matrix based on the use of the value of the badness index is carried out on the basis of the fact that it should ideally be equal to zero, and the definition of the elements "left-to-right and top-down", i.e. in a strictly defined sequence, can lead to the fact that for previously defined triangles the value of the badness index will increase significantly. One form of smoothing out this situation is the use of the risk function.

Continuing to improve the algorithms for solving this problem, we consider the application of the branch and bound method in it. To do this, for some known sequence of empty elements, we apply the algorithms described above; however, the sequence we select using a specially developed variant of the branch and bound method.

In our interpretation of this method, we perform the following actions.

- All possible sequences of unknown elements of the upper triangular part of the matrix are taken as the set of feasible solutions.
- In each current subproblem, the matrix elements that have not yet been filled are taken as possible separating elements.
- The boundary is the sum of the badness values for all triangles that have already formed by the time this subproblem is considered.
- An auxiliary algorithm for selecting the separating element is that among the possible separating elements we choose one for which the boundary between the formed right and left subproblems is obtained in the most possible way.

Thus, the determination of the elements of an incomplete matrix occurs in such a sequence, in which the final value of the badness for all triangles is selected using a greedy heuristics, which fully fits into the framework of the classical variants of the description of the branch and bound method.

2 Preliminaries

This section presents one of the methods of comparative analysis of different algorithms for calculating the distances between DNA sequences, and on its basis, a method for restoring an incomplete matrix is developed.

In order to carry out this comparative analysis, we propose to consider all possible triangles for the resulting algorithm for calculating the distances between genomes, because ideally they should be acute isosceles.

To answer the question of how "correct" is the matrix obtained as a result of some heuristic algorithm, we propose to use the "characteristic of the departure" of the obtained triangles from the "elongated isosceles" triangles, i.e., the index of badness.

The formula can be used to calculate the badness index

$$\sigma = \frac{\alpha - \beta}{\alpha}, \tag{1}$$

here, α, β and γ are the angles of the triangle, and we assume that $\alpha \geq \beta \geq \gamma$ [4].

The sides can also be used in the formula to calculate the value of badness instead of the angles of the triangle:

$$\sigma = \frac{a - b}{a}, \tag{2}$$

where a, b, c side of triangle, and $a \geq b \geq c$ [6].

When calculating the badness of the entire matrix for each recovering option, we can:

- either summing the corresponding badness over all possible triangles of the considered matrices;
- or take the maximum badness for these triangles.

However, when calculating this indicator (the badness of the whole matrix), there may be some (in practice, very small) number of triangles for which the value of badness may differ significantly from others. In particular, you can get triangles where the value of badness is 1.

Based on all this, we use a special averaging to calculate the value of the badness of the whole matrix. From the physical point of view, the applied averaging gives the position of the center of gravity of a one-dimensional system of bodies whose mass is given by a special function of the so-called risk function [7]. Badness for all triangles determines the coordinates of bodies, and the risk function of their mass, while the larger the coordinate, the less its mass (i.e., the greater the value of badness, the less its contribution).

So, as already noted above, we believe that in a properly filled matrix of distances between DNA sequences, all possible constructed triangles should be as close to the isosceles sharp-angled, and then on the basis of this conclusion it is possible to restore the matrix of distances between the rows of DNA, which first has a number of unknown elements. We will continue to fill in such matrices.

3   Strictly Description of the Recovering Algorithm

To determine the unknown element, we consider all the possible triangles formed from elements of this matrix for which one of the sides is unknown. For each such triangle, given the condition that it is an isosceles acute-angled triangle, we obtain one of the possible values of this unknown side.

Next, we calculate the final value of this side (unknown element) in a special way.

Namely, to calculate it on the basis of all the estimates obtained, the element is assumed to be equal to the arithmetic mean of all the values obtained; or, as an alternative, we can exclude the largest and the smallest of the values obtained.

With a large number of missing elements of the triangle matrix with two known sides will be small, so the restoration of the matrix in one pass is usually impossible.

When restoring the matrix on the second and subsequent passes, you can either use only the elements of the matrix of the last pass, or use all the matrices obtained on the previous passes.

In the second case, with each subsequent passage in the matrix, there are more elements calculated approximately. Therefore, when evaluating an unknown element, it is possible to use an analogue of the risk function, which will adjust the weight of the elements depending on the number of the passage.

When using the so-called static risk function, the weight of the elements with each pass decreases with the same coefficient, and the formula is used to estimate the unknown element of the matrix

$$E = \frac{c_0 E_0 + c_1 E_1 + \ldots + c_k E_k}{c_0 + c_1 + \ldots + c_k},\tag{3}$$

where: E_i are the values of elements of the matrix, received on i-th pass; $c_0, c_1, \ldots, c_k$ are some specially selected coefficients. In practice [8], the good results are achieved when the next formula for coefficients is used: $c_0 = 1$, $c_i = p \cdot c_{i-1}$.

According to [7], the risk function can be *dynamic*: using the last one, we take averaging, depending on the "rough estimate" of the final value: whether it is "good", "average" or "bad". Also, we can consider a *sequence* of dynamic risk functions, where at each stage, we rely on the value obtained in the previous step. In our case, to evaluate the unknown element of the matrix of distances between DNA strings, we use the formula

$$\frac{\sum\limits_{i=1}^{k} a_i f(a_i)}{\sum\limits_{i=1}^{k} f(a_i)},\tag{4}$$

where $f(x)$ is a special manner selected decreasing function.

Algorithm 1 *(Restoring the DNA matrix using a static risk function)*
Input: Incomplete definite matrix $A = a_{ij}$.

The following *auxiliary variables* are used: b_i is the array of unknown item ratings.

Description of the algorithm

Step 1: Set $s := 1$; it is the number of the pass.

Step 2: Calculate h, i.e. the number of elements of the top triangle, equal to 0.

Step 3:

if $a_{ij} = 0$ and $i \neq j$ then begin

 count := 0; {we consider the number of triangles built on an unknown element}

 for $k := 0$ to n do begin

  if $k \neq I$ and $k \neq j$ and $a_{ki} \neq 0$ and $a_{kj} \neq 0$ then begin

  count := *count* + 1; $c_0 := 1$; $c_s := c_{s-1} \cdot p$;

$$E_{ki} = \frac{c_0 E_{ki}^0 + c_1 E_{ki}^1 + \ldots + c_k E_{ki}^s}{c_0 + c_1 + \ldots + c_s}; \quad E_{kj} = \frac{c_0 E_{kj}^0 + c_1 E_{kj}^1 + \ldots + c_k E_{kj}^s}{c_0 + c_1 + \ldots + c_s};$$

  if $E_{kj} > E_{ki}$ then $b_{kol} := E_{ki}$ else $b_{kol} := E_{kj}$.

  end;

 end;

end;

$$a_{ij} = \frac{b_0 + \ldots + b_{kol}}{kol}.$$

Step 4: Calculate h_1, i.e. the number of elements of the top triangle, equal to 0 after the next pass.

Step 5:

If $h_1 = 0$ then output 1;

if $h_1 = h$ then output 2;

$s := s + 1$;

go to step 2.

Output 1: The filled (restored) matrix A.

Output 2: The matrix A cannot be restored. □

For performing a comparative analysis of the results of the reconstruction of the matrix (after the execution of the algorithm), we use such an indicator as the discrepancy, it characterizes the deviation of the resulting matrix from the original matrix. Namely, we calculate the discrepancy on the basis of the natural metric.

$$d = \frac{1}{n(n-1)} \sqrt{\sum_{i=1}^{n-1} \sum_{j=i+1}^{n} (a_{ij} - \tilde{a}_{ij})^2}, \tag{5}$$

where: $\tilde{a}_{ij}$ are elements of the matrix obtained as a result of applying some algorithm for calculating the distances between a pair of genomes (in our case, for Needleman-Wunsch algorithm); a_{ij} are the elements of the matrix, restored at the result of the above algorithm.

4   The Branch and Bound Method in the Problem of Recovering DNA Matrix

The branch and bound method is designed to develop algorithms for solving optimization problems, and we consider its interpretation close to [9]. It refers to the method of developing algorithms, known as *backtracking programming* and explores a tree-like model of the space of feasible solutions. The purpose of applying the branch and bound method in our case, i.e. to restore the matrix, is finding the optimal *sequence* of calculation of unknown elements; in the end of such calculation, the discrepancy would be minimal (or close to the minimum, i.e., pseudo-minimal). Minimizing the residual is directly related to minimizing the badness value of the entire matrix, so the problem of applying the branch and bound method for matrix recovering is to minimize the badness value of the entire matrix.

Always when using the branch and bound method, the following auxiliary algorithms should be described:

- the branching procedure for the set of feasible solutions;
- the procedure for finding the lower and upper bounds of the goal function.

In the problem we are solving, the space of admissible solutions is all possible sequences for determining the unknown elements of the upper half of the matrix. Branching occurs according to the separating elements known from the very beginning of the algorithm operation, which in our case coincide with the unfilled elements of the matrix. Branching on the set of admissible solutions will be performed as follows: for the selected element, all the sequences are divided into two sequences:

- starting with this element;
- and not starting with it.

One of the important auxiliary heuristics is the heuristic for the selection of the separating element $a_{ij}(i < j)$. It consists in:

- to find all possible k, for which a_{ki} and a_{kj} are known, $k \neq i$ and $k \neq j$;
- to calculate the difference

$$\left| a_{ki} - a_{kj} \right|. \tag{6}$$

We first select the elements for which k takes the largest value, and then among them, we choose the one for which the difference (6) is greatest; we consider this element as the separating one.

The boundaries, as noted above, are formed as a sum of the badness values for all triangles that are already formed in the matrix. It follows that the filling of the matrices with new elements leads to an increase (or rather, not a decrease) of this value.

Given the large number of triangles formed and for clarity of calculations, we move from the index of badness for the triangle to the same indicator, but for the elements of the matrix. For each element above the main diagonal, we consider all the triangles built on it and calculate the value of the exponent σ of each triangle. And the element $a_{ij} (i < j)$ put in the corresponding value

$$\sigma_{ij} = \max_{1 \leq k \leq n} \sigma_k, \tag{7}$$

where σ_k is the badness of a triangle built on elements a_{ij}, a_{ki}, a_{kj}.

For the entire DNA matrix, we determine the sum of the values of badness for all elements, i.e.

$$\sigma = \sum_{i=1}^{n-1} \sum_{j=j+1}^{n} \sigma_{ij}, \tag{8}$$

The goal of matrix reconstruction is to minimize the index (8).

The developed algorithm 1 in a slightly modified form will be used as an auxiliary for the algorithm for restoring the incomplete matrix of distances between DNA chains by the branch and bound method.

Algorithm 2 (Auxiliary algorithm for assigning a value to the selected element)
Input: 1. Incomplete definite matrix $= a_{ij}$.

2. Selected unknown item a_{ij}.

Description of the algorithm.
  for $k := 0$ to n do begin
    if $k \neq i$ and $k \neq j$ and $a_{ki} \neq 0$ and $a_{kj} \neq 0$ then
      if $a_{ki} > a_{kj}$ then $a_{ij} := a_{ij} + a_{ki}$
      else $a_{ij} := a_{ij} + a_{kj}$
  end;
  $a_{ij} := a_{ij} / kol_{ij}$.
Output: Value of the element a_{ij}. $\square$

Algorithm 3. (Recovering matrix by the branch and bound method)

Input: 1. Incomplete definite matrix $= a_{ij}$.

Description of the algorithm.

Step 1: Initialization: "zeroing" of the list of subproblems and the current pseudo-optimal solutions.

Step 2: Adding to the list of subproblems of the problem corresponding to the source matrix.

Step 3: If the list of subproblems is empty, output 1.

Step 4: If the algorithm time is over, then output 1.

Step 5: Select a new subproblem from the list of subproblems and delete it.

Step 6: The "best" of the unknown element.

1) if $a_{ij} = 0$ then

  begin $kol_{ij} := 0$ {consider the number of triangles, built on an unknown element}

    $mas\_m_{ij} := 0$ { calculate the maximum difference }

    for $k := 0$ to $n - 1$ do begin

      if $k \neq i$ and $k \neq j$ and $a_{ki} \neq 0$ and $a_{kj} \neq 0$ then

      begin

        $kol := kol + 1$; $m := |a_{ki} - a_{kj}|$;

        If $m > mas\_m_{ij}$ then $mas\_m_{ij} := m$;

      end;

    end;

2) Determine the largest value of the array kol_{ij} : $maxk = \max\limits_{\substack{1 \leq i \leq n \\ 1 \leq j \leq n}} kol_{ij}$.

3) if $maxk = 0$, then output 2.

4) Among the elements for which $kol_{ij} = maxk$, we find the one with the largest mas_m_{ij} value.

Step 7: Call algorithm 2 to calculate the selected item.

Step 8: Calculate the value of the badness metric for it:

  for $k := 0$ to n do begin

    if $k \neq i$ and $k \neq j$ and $a_{ki} \neq 0$ and $a_{kj} \neq 0$ then

    sort in descending order a_{ki}, a_{kj}, and a_{ij}

    and denote them accordingly a, b, c;

    $\sigma_k = \dfrac{a - b}{c}$;

  end;

  $\sigma_{ij} := \max\limits_{1 \leq k \leq n} \sigma_k$

Step 9: The formation of the left and the right subproblems based on the comparison of the values of the indicator of badness for the selected item. The left one is the one for which this value is less.

Step 10: Check if the left problem is valid, otherwise go back to step 6.

Step 11: If the value of the badness index of the obtained matrix for the left sub-problem is less than the corresponding value of the current pseudo-optimal solution, this subproblem becomes the current one and go to step 2. Otherwise go to step 5)

Output: 1: Current pseudo-optimal solution (if any).

Output 2: The matrix A cannot be restored.□

5   Some Results of Computational Experiment

This section presents the results of a computational experiment. We selected one genome from 28 mammalian orders [14]. The results of applying the considered algorithms (particularly algorithm of Needleman-Wunsch) are typically expressed in "percent of close". According to our previous works ([9, 15], etc.), we need a similar characteristic ("relative distance") resulting by subtracting the "proximity percentage" of 100 and dividing by 100, the data for convenience in the tables will be indicated by integers formed by the first three significant digits of these values.

So, in the original distance matrix (Table 1 of the application) we removed about 63% of the element pairs (left about 37% of the pairs; we remove some element of the upper triangle together with the corresponding element of the lower one). The resulting matrix is shown in Table 2 of the Appendix. The Appendix is available here [16].

For the comparative analysis, we first made the restoration of the matrix using only the elements of the matrix that was formed on the last pass. As noted in the previous section, two approaches are possible. The results of the restoration using the first approach, where the arithmetic mean was calculated by all estimates obtained from all the regular triangles constructed on this element with two other known sides, are presented in Table 3 of the Appendix. At Table 4 of the Appendix, the matrix obtained using the second approach is given: from all the plurality of the estimates, if some are allowed, we excluded the largest and the smallest elements, and the remaining was calculated arithmetic mean.

On the basis of the analysis of Table 4, obtained by applying the second approach, it can be concluded that this approach is insufficient for the restoration of the DNA matrix. Moreover, this inadequate efficiency is manifested, despite the fact that this approach should give a relatively better option: in fact, we exclude the "extreme situations". However, in matrices of large dimensions, a large number of identical elements are obtained; this fact explained, that an unknown element is formed small number of triangles with two other known sides, so the exception highest and lowest estimates leads to the fact, that the calculation of the average made for a very small number of estimates.

The number of passes necessary to restore the entire matrix depends on the percentage of missing elements. As the results of computational experiments showed, if the percentage of missing elements is less than about 55%, then the entire matrix is restored in 1 pass. If this number exceeds about 64%, it usually required more than 2 passes are. In addition, in this case the number of passes will depend on the location of the missing elements. When absence of all the elements of some row (column), the restoration of the matrix is completely impossible, and therefore, with increasing the percentage of zeroing the matrix, the probability of its restoration certainly decreases.

To perform a comparative analysis of the various methods of matrix reconstruction, we calculated the discrepancy, and also identified the greatest deviation. The results of the calculations are presented in Table 1.

Table 1. Comparison of discrepancies in the different approaches to matrix reconstruction.

	1st approach		2nd approach	
	max d_{ij}	d	max d_{ij}	d
1st pass	0.214	0.00194	0.214	0.00332
2nd pass	0.236	0.00279	0.350	0.00394

The use of the second approach on the first pass gives a smaller value of the maximum deviation, but, in general, the residual is greater, and the greatest deviation of this residual from the residual obtained for the first approach occurs at the second iteration, when the number of triangles with two other known vertices becomes larger. Thus, in calculating the arithmetic mean of all the "preliminary values" of the element, the value of the residual is much smaller.

The results are obtained by reconstructing the matrix using only the elements of the matrix of the last pass. However, in this case, the larger the pass number, the less accurate the matrix elements.

Next, we present the results obtained by applying both static and dynamic risk functions. For the static risk function, the best result was obtained for the coefficient $p = 0.9$. And for the dynamic risk function we chose a decreasing function

$$f(x) = 1 - \sqrt{0.1x} \tag{9}$$

The use of risk functions has made it possible to reduce the significance of the discrepancy, especially with the second and further passes (Table 2).

Table 2. Comparison of the discrepancy recovering matrix with the use of static and dynamic risk functions.

	Restoration of the matrix using a static risk function, $p = 0.95$		Recovering the matrix using a dynamic risk function $f(x) = 1 - \sqrt{0.1x}$	
	max d_{ij}	d	max d_{ij}	d
1st pass	0.1852	0.001715	0.1414	0.001689
2nd pass	0.1852	0.001851	0.1414	0.001801

Thus, the use of the risk function in restoring the matrices makes it possible to reduce the value of the discrepancy, especially with a large number of passes. Tables 5 and 6 of the Appendix show the recovered matrices using the static and dynamic risk functions of the matrix.

The summary Table 3 shows the number of passes that were required in the computational experiment for a different percentage of the excluded matrix elements, as well as the residual values after the matrix reconstruction, using the risk function and without it.

Table 3. The summary table of calculations.

%	Number of passes	Matrix recovery based only on the matrix of the last pass		Restoration of the matrix using a static risk function, $p = 0.95$		Recovering the matrix using a dynamic risk function, $f(x) = 1 - \sqrt{0.1x}$	
		max d_{ij}	d	max d_{ij}	d	max d_{ij}	d
50	1	0.193	0.00198	0.186	0.00173	0.158	0.00168
62	2	0.214	0.00279	0.185	0.00185	0.141	0.00180
65	3	0.203	0.00293	0.175	0.00203	0.156	0.00200

Further, we recovered the same matrix by the branch and bound method. The resulting matrix is presented in Table 7 of the Appendix.

When restoring matrix algorithm 1 the value of the indicator of badness of the matrix equal to $\sigma = 57.7$, and the value of the discrepancy amounted to $d = 0.00185$, and when the restoration branch and bound method $\sigma = 45.3$ and $d = 0.00145$.

Thus, as a result of applying the branch and bound method, the value of the indicator of badness of the matrix has decreased by 21%, the residual error decreased by 20%. A comparison of the results of different methods for the reconstruction of the matrix of distances between DNA chains is given in Table 4.

It is important to note that a significant improvement in the main characteristics of the matrix recovering practically did not affect the increase in the time of the algorithm: it increased only by about 10%.

Table 4. Comparison of the discrepancy of reconstruction of one matrix using the branch and bound method and without it

	σ	max d_{ij}	d
Without the branch and bound method	57.7	0.141	0.00185
Branch and bound method	45.3	0.106	0.00145
Improvement, %	21.4	24.8	21.6

6 Conclusions

So, in the basis of the proposed method of reconstruction of the matrix of distances between DNA sequences, we propose to use an approach that was previously developed and applied in practice for the comparative evaluation of other algorithms of algorithms for calculating distances between such sequences; simplifying, we can say that we are trying to achieve the property of acute isosceles for all the resulting triangles.

Application of the described method to fill the matrix of distances between DNA sequences will significantly reduce the time of its filling: for example, to build a matrix of the order of 50 × 50, which recorded the distance calculated by the algorithm Needlman-Wunsch, it takes about 28 h, and when using the proposed method about 1 h.

At the same time, the application of the branch and bound method made it possible to determine the unknown elements of the matrix in the sequence that minimizes the value of the matrix badness index and, as a consequence, the discrepancy.

As one of the directions of the future improvement of the heuristic algorithm described here (first of all, reducing the time of its operation), we assume the use of clustering of situations, the application of which is described in [17]. In applying this approach, we try to select the same separating element in different subproblems (situations) obtained on different branches of the tree of the branch and bound method, which (subproblems) correspond to some close ones by some "natural" matrix metric. Such use (if possible) requires virtually no time despite the fact that the time spent on the choice of element is most of the time work branch and bound method.

References

1. Toppi, J., et al.: A new statistical approach for the extraction of adjacency matrix from effective connectivity networks. In: 2013 35th Annual International Conference of the IEEE Engineering in Medicine and Biology Society (EMBC), Osaka, pp. 2932–2935 (2013). https://doi.org/10.1109/embc.2013.6610154
2. Torshin, I.Yu.: Bioinformatics in the Post-Genomic Era: The Role of Biophysics. Nova Biomedical Books, New York (2006)
3. Van der Loo, M.P.J.: The stringdist package for approximate string matching. R J. 6(1), 111–122 (2014). https://doi.org/10.32614/RJ-2014-011
4. Pages, H., Aboyoun, P., Gentleman, R., DebRaoy, S.: Biostrings: string objects representing biological sequences and matching algorithms. R package version 2.10.1 (2009)
5. Morgan, M., Lawrence, M.: ShortRead: base classes and methods for high-throughput short-read sequencing data. R package version 1.0.6 (2009)
6. Melnikov, B., Radionov, A., Gumayunov, V.: Some special heuristics for discrete optimization problems. In: Proceedings of 8th International Conference on Enterprise Information Systems, ICEIS 2006, Paphos, pp. 360–364 (2016). https://elibrary.ru/item.asp?id=15292060
7. Eckes, B., Nischt, R., Krieg, T.: Cell-matrix interactions in dermal repair and scarring. Fibrogenesis Tissue Repair 3, 4 (2010). https://doi.org/10.1186/1755-1536-3-4
8. Midwood, K.S., Williams, L.V., Schwarzbauer, J.E.: Tissue repair and the dynamics of the extracellular matrix. Int. J. Biochem. Cell Biol. 36(6), 1031–1037 (2004). https://doi.org/10.1016/j.biocel.2003.12.003

9. Melnikov, B., Pivneva, S., Trifonov, M.: Comparative analysis of the algorithms of calculating distances of DNA sequences and some related problems. In: Proceedings of the III International Conference "Information Technology and Nanotechnology (ITNT 2017)", pp. 1640–1645 (2017). https://elibrary.ru/item.asp?id=29267020
10. Melnikov, B.: Heuristics in programming of nondeterministic games. Program. Comput. Softw. **27**(5), 277–288 (2001). https://doi.org/10.1023/A:1012345111076
11. Melnikov, B., Melnikova, E.: Approach to programming nondeterministic games (Part I: description of general heuristics). In: Proceedings of Higher Educational Institutions, Volga Region. Physics and Mathematics, vol. 4, no. 28, pp. 29–38 (2013). https://elibrary.ru/item.asp?id=21392713. (in Russian)
12. Needleman, S., Wunsch, Ch.: A general method applicable to the search for similarities in the amino acid sequence of two proteins. J. Mol. Biol. **48**(3), 443–453 (1970). https://doi.org/10.1016/0022-2836(70)90057-4
13. Hromkovič, J.: Algorithmics for Hard Problems: Introduction to Combinatorial Optimization, Randomization, Approximation, and Heuristics. Springer, Heidelberg (2004). https://doi.org/10.1007/978-3-662-05269-3
14. Ayala, F.J., Kayger, J.: Modern Genetics. V. 1. Benjamin/Cummings Pub., Menlo Park (1980)
15. Melnikov, B., Pivneva, S., Trifonov, M.: Various algorithms, calculating distances of DNA sequences, and some computational recommendations for use such algorithms. In: CEUR Workshop Proceedings, vol. 1902, pp. 43–50 (2017). https://doi.org/10.18287/1613-0073-2017-1902-43-50
16. Appendix A. Matrices 28 × 28 and Additional Information. https://yadi.sk/i/JxAfi8jm3aEtEY
17. Melnikov, B., Radionov, A., Moseev, A., Melnikova, E.: Some specific heuristics for situation clustering problems. In: ICSOFT, Technologies, Proceedings 1st International Conference on Software and Data Technologies, pp. 272–279 (2006). https://elibrary.ru/item.asp?id=15292004

Development of the Tools for Research of Transformation of Digital Objects Based on Generative Adversarial Networks

Alexander Kadan[1](✉) [iD] and Maria Kadan[2] [iD]

[1] Yanka Kupala State University of Grodno, Elizy Ozheshko Street 22, 230023 Grodno, Belarus
kadan@mf.grsu.by
[2] Instinctools Ltd., Lermontova Street 29/2, 230029 Grodno, Belarus
maria.kadan@gmail.com

Abstract. Generating models are a modern, rapidly developing direction of research in the application of neural network technologies. Its currently known applications include, in particular, image visualization, drawing, image resolution improvement, structured prediction, research in the field of training and data pre-processing for neural networks in cases where the production of test data is an unacceptably expensive process. They are actively discussing their capabilities in the tasks of providing information and computer security, tasks of computer technical expertise, tasks of transforming and restoring objects by fragments or when the information is extremely noisy.

Generating models are a modern rapidly developing field of research in neural network technologies. Its applications include image visualization, drawing, image resolution improvement, structured prediction, research in the field of providing information security, tasks of computer technical expertise, tasks of transforming and restoring fragmented or is extremely noisy objects. The aim of the study is to create a software product that tests the hypothesis of the successful use of generative adversarial networks (GAN) to improve the characteristics of images. The use of GAN allows solving the problem of correcting distorted digital objects not by traditional adjustment of their individual parameters, but by generating undistorted objects that are "indistinguishable" from the original ones.

The article presents and analyzes the method of building a neural network that is capable to remove noise from images, preventing them from being too blurred and retaining clarity (in comparison with the original), which proves its ability to generalize. The experiment showed that GAN with sufficient efficiency not only removes noise from images with a distorting signal on which it was trained, but also in the case of noise unknown to the etymology network. The success of training to suppress specific distortions of digital graphic objects makes it possible to assume that by training a neural network to work with other types of distortion, one can achieve successful results for solving a wider class of problems.

Keywords: Generating models · Noise reduction · Generative adversarial networks · Neural networks · Machine learning

© Springer Nature Switzerland AG 2020
V. Sukhomlin and E. Zubareva (Eds.): SITITO 2018, CCIS 1201, pp. 224–237, 2020.
https://doi.org/10.1007/978-3-030-46895-8_18

1 Introduction

The amount of information in the digital world has overstepped all previously conceivable limits. However, the characteristics of the initial information often do not allow using it in full without prior adjustment. In particular, the most common problem associated with the use of visual information is the poor quality of images (static photos or selective video frames). Traditionally, we can use various technologies to adjust the quality of images, based on the setting of specific image parameters, such as sharpness, contrast, etc. Or a variety of algorithms to improve the structure of the image (its transformation), its statistical characteristics or its individual characteristics.

An alternative approach to the task of transformation of digital images is the use of generating models that are based on their own perception of the statistical characteristics of the image, which makes it possible to synthesize image without undesirable distortions. Generating models are usually based on neural networks that allow the use of non-obvious characteristics of the structure of processed images [1]. Variational autoencoders (VAE) [2, 3] and generative adversarial networks (GAN) [4] are among the generating models.

The task of the autoencoder is to form, on the basis of the input data, a compressed informative presentation of this data with subsequent restoration of the original sample on its basis. This is achieved through network training to extract significant features from the input data [5, 7, 15, 16].

Generative adversarial networks propose an approach that focuses on the theoretical aspects of the antagonistic game to train the image synthesis model. A number of researchers have shown that GAN can create realistic image samples in datasets with low variability and low resolution [8, 9]. GANs, however, attempt to create high-resolution, globally-coherent samples, in particular, from high-variability datasets. Currently, the theoretical understanding of GAN is a very popular research topic [10, 11]. In addition, the problems of training the models for image processing were considered in [18, 19].

Modern achievements in machine learning make it possible to significantly improve the quality of image models. Improved image models significantly advance modern progress in noise reduction [13], compression [14], painting [15, 16] and super-resolution [3, 17].

The possibilities of GAN in the tasks of providing information and computer security, tasks of computer technical expertise, object recognition with a minimum of errors, tasks of transforming and restoring objects by fragments or in tasks of restoring extremely noisy information are actively discussed.

1.1 Autoencoders

The autoencoder usually consists of two neural networks - an encoder and decoder. The task of the first network is to compress the original data vector into a smaller dimension vector. The second network is a mirror copy of the first and performs the transformation of the vector obtained at the output of the first network to the initial dimension vector (i.e., tries to restore the original data from compressed) [2, 12, 20–22]. The scheme of the autoencoder is shown in Fig. 1.

The input signal is restored with errors due to coding losses, but in order to minimize them, the network has to train to select the most important features. More formally, autoencoders consist of two parts: the g encoder and the f decoder. The encoder, based on the input signal x forms its code: $h = g(x)$, and the decoder recovers the signal by its code: $\bar{x} = f(h)$. The autoencoder, changing g and f, seeks to obtain the identity function $x = f(g(x))$, while minimizing the error functional $L(\bar{x}, f(g(x)))$.

The concept of autoencoding is widely used to study generative data models. The most important thing is not just the ability of autoencoders to compress data, but the ability to distinguish between the useful properties of the input signal. Autoencoders with a large number of layers can detect of more complex nonlinear input data, which, as you would expect, will allow you to restore noisy test images. For this, it is necessary to input noisy $\ddot{x}$ data at the input and to compare the output with the noise-free data $L(x, f(g(\ddot{x})))$. An example of the operation of such a network is presented in Fig. 1c.

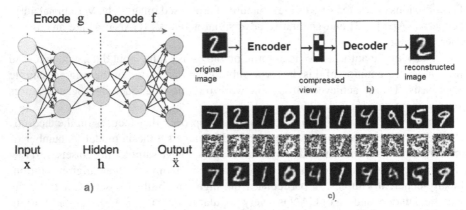

Fig. 1. (a) Autoencoder neural network scheme, (b) Operation scheme of the autoencoder, (c) Example of processing noisy data

A variational autoencoder (VAE) is a generative algorithm that adds additional restrictions on the encoding of input data, namely, the hidden representations are normalized [5, 6]. Variational autoencoders can both compress data (like autoencoders) and synthesize data (like generative adversarial networks). However, while generative adversarial neural networks generate clear and detailed data, images created by variational autoencoders tend to be more blurry and less clear.

1.2   Generative Adversarial Networks

A generative adversarial network is an algorithm of machine learning built on a combination of two neural networks, one of which (generative model, network G) generates samples, and the other (discriminative model, network D) tries to distinguish right ("genuine") samples from incorrect ones ("generated"). Networks G and D have opposite goals—to create samples and reject samples. Therefore, their interaction can be considered as an antagonistic game [4].

In other words, the generative adversary network is a technique for teaching a pair of models (see Fig. 2a):

1. Generative G, which generates data by random noise that is subject to a certain probability distribution;
2. Discriminative D, which attributes the incoming data to its input, the probability that they are obtained from the training dataset (they are "real") or generated by the model G (are "fake").

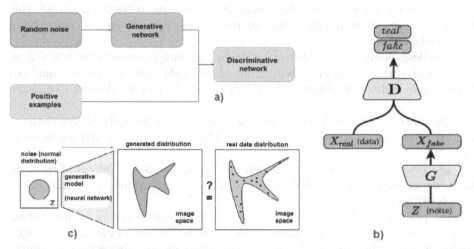

Fig. 2. (a) GAN operation scheme; (b) The formal scheme of the GAN; (c) Representation of the GAN work process in terms of distributions

The generator G accepts a random noise vector z at the input and synthesizes the image X fake $= G(z)$. The discriminator D receives either the original or the synthesized image as an input signal and forms the probability distribution $P(S|X) = D(X)$, where $S = \{$real, fake$\}$ are possible sources of the image (see Fig. 2b). To evaluate the performance of the generative-competitive network, the likelihood functions

$$L = M\left[\log P\left(S = \text{ real } | X \text{ real}\right)\right] + M\left[\log P\left(S = \text{ fake } | X \text{ fake}\right)\right]$$

are used. Moreover, the discriminator should maximize its first term, and the generator should minimize its second term.

As a result, the model G is trained to maximize the probability that model D is false. And model D is trained to distinguish real data substitution of from those generated by the model G.

In a generative adversarial network, images can be interpreted as patterns from a multidimensional probability distribution (see Fig. 2c) that extends to image pixels. This distribution is used to determine whether the synthesized samples will be identified as "real" or "fake". The true probability distribution of real images is not known in advance and too complex to be formally described; therefore, it can only be determined by analyzing test data and selecting the parameters and weights of the neural network. The complexity of selecting weights depends in part on complex conditional dependencies, since the value of a single pixel depends on the values of other pixels in the image.

2   Description of the Experiment

2.1   The Task of Correcting Distortion in Digital Graphic Objects

Based on the foregoing, it can be argued that the problem of transformation of distorted images is actual since the time when visual information has become widespread. This has led to a constant search for tools to improve the quality of distorted images to bring them to the etalon.

The description and characterization of the structure of natural images is still an actual area of research activity. Natural images are subject to internal invariants and demonstrate multi-scale statistical structures that are historically difficult to measure [1].

The aim of the research is to create a software product that tests the hypothesis of the use of generative adversarial networks (GAN) in improving the characteristics of images.

The object of this research are neural network technologies. Subject of research: methods of transformation of distorted objects using generative adversarial neural networks.

The practical significance of the research lies in the field of writing and using of the software product based on the ideas of GAN, solving the task of correcting distorted digital objects not by adjusting their individual parameters, but by generating undistorted objects that are "indistinguishable" from the original ones. Successful solution of such task be used not only in education, but also in other areas, in particular, in computer security, in solving tasks related to transformation and restoration of objects.

2.2   Features of the Experiment

Requirements to the Initial Data

Further, under the graphic object we will understand some raster image. Its size can be set as the number of pixels along the length and width, and the total number of pixels. It follows from this that the pixel representation of the graphic object can be specified by both the matrix and the vector of the total length.

We assume that the images use a color depth equal to three, i.e. eight-bit color. We consider the image from the standard digital camera has three channels - red, green and blue, which can be represented as three two-dimensional arrays superimposed on each other, each containing pixel values ranging from 0 to 255 or normalized values ranging from 0 to 1. Thus, each pixel can be represented by a tuple of three elements (r, g, b), where r, g and b are the intensity (in the range of 0 to 255, or, in case of normalized data, of 0 to 1), respectively, red, green and blue pixel colors.

As already mentioned, we interpret images (their representation in the form of vectors) as samples of complex probability distributions. By distortions in graphic objects we mean the deviation of their characteristics from the etalon probability distributions. In particular, in this article we consider the noise of images of different percentage.

The main problem with using GAN in cases of image restoration is the difficulty of predicting the values of adjacent pixels by this type of networks, rather than restoration from a fixed distribution of the entire data vector in which GAN certainly succeed.

Certainly, we had to apply various modifications to the classical concept of generative adversarial networks in order to achieve satisfactory results in solving the problems of eliminating distortion. This is due to the fact that in order to correct a specific noise pixel in the image, it is necessary to specify various attributes of the image adjacent to the given pixel, and then decide, based on these characteristics, what this noise pixel should be filled with.

Training and Testing Datasets

The hypothesis on the possibility of adjusting graphic objects by means of GAN was tested on images of Latin symbols. In order to teach the designed network, we decided to use a dataset consisting of uppercase and lowercase letters of the English alphabet of computer fonts. For these purposes, we have selected "Chars74K dataset", containing 67,956 images of lowercase and uppercase letters in English, normal, bold and italics. Each image is a graphic object of non-fixed size. Therefore, for further use in training and testing the model, the images were converted to a size of 80×80 pixels with a color depth of 3. For some of them, this transformation caused a loss of quality, but for the given task it is not critical. For each image class in the training dataset 1016 different examples were used. The number of classes was 52, i.e. the sum of the number of uppercase and lowercase letters of the English alphabet.

Artificially distorted images were used to test the neural network operation. To test the noise elimination hypothesis, random noise was added to the images, i.e. random pixels have been replaced by pixels in shades of gray. We used the dataset that consists of images having replaced pixels in a different percentage of the total number of pixels, namely 5%, 15%, 25%, and 35%. Examples of the data used are shown in Fig. 3.

Used Software

During the experiment, we used the Keras library at the top of the TensorFlow framework, which allowed us to combine the convenience and the possibility of fast implementation with the wide capabilities of the mathematical apparatus used at work. We also used the idea of implementing of Image Denoising GAN.

Network Topology for the Experiment

For visual recognition tasks, the depth of the network is crucial. The deeper the network, the better the result. Although deep network learning is an extremely difficult task, some solutions [17, 24] based on residual networks (Residual nets, ResNets) [24] have been proposed to solve this problem. ResNets are networks that can reach 152 layers of depth due to heavy use of missed connections and batch normalization.

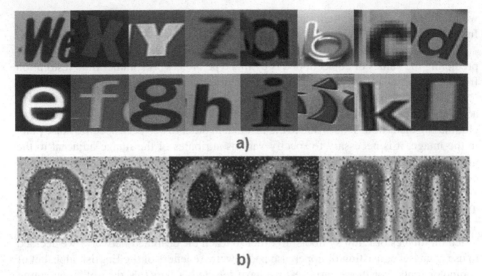

Fig. 3. (a) Sample data from the training set "The Chars74K dataset"; (b) Example of test data from right to left: pairwise noisy images with a noise percentage of 15% and 25%.

In the implemented system, the ResNet block is a complex layer of the neural network that consists of two convolution layers. In addition, the output of the last convolution layer is added as the input of this block. This is done so that the signal properties included in the ResNet block are available for the subsequent layers. Thus, the output of this block will not differ much from the original input vector. Otherwise, the characteristics of the original images will not be saved after processing by this block, and the result of its work will be too different from the input data.

Based on the above justification, in order to achieve this goal, we chose a deep residual network architecture, which is a GAN-based network. The network of generator learns to create indistinguishable from real patterns. In this way, it tries to deceive the discriminator network with the recovered images. Similarly, the discriminator learns to distinguish reconstructed images from real images.

To implement the distortion correction system, we chose the GAN network topology, where the discriminator D is a standard convolutional neural network, and the G generator is a combination of two networks: convolutional and "reverse convolution" where the sequence of layers of the standard convolutional neural network is inverted, i.e. reverse operations of conventional convolution networks are performed, which means that images are recreated from the sequence of feature maps. This is due to the need to use a specific image as the discriminator's input for its further adjustment, rather than a random vector, as in the classical GAN representation. Then at the first stage of the generative network, the main features will be highlighted from the desired image, the appropriate transformations will be applied, and the image will be converted to the initial dimensions. With a properly trained GAN input image will retain its main features and will be free from distortion at the output of the generative unit.

The purpose of the generator is to convert the input image into an equivalent image, which contains no noise. The generator should be able to fill image noise with the values of nearby pixels, while preserving the features of the original image as much as possible. This means that the main success of the entire image correction system depends on a well-designed generative network.

Each of the elementary units of both generative and discriminatory network consists of convolution layer, batch normalization and function of nonlinearity. Basically this is Leaky ReLU (LReLU) [23]. The only exceptions are the blocks at the ends of both networks, where instead of LReLU in the generator and discriminator, the hyperbolic tangent and sigmoid are used (to derive the probability response). The step in each convolution is 1.

The generator network is a convolutional network with a symmetric structure, which is presented in Table 1:

Table 1. Generative network topology.

Layer	Activation	Kernel	Feature cards
Convolution	LReLU	9×9	10
Convolution	LReLU	3×3	20
Convolution	LReLU	3×3	40
ResNet	LReLU	3×3	40
ResNet	LReLU	3×3	40
ResNet	LReLU	3×3	40
Deconvolution	LReLU	3×3	20
Deconvolution	LReLU	3×3	10
Deconvolution	th	3×3	3

1. Three convolutional blocks of elementary units;
2. Three ResNet blocks of elementary units, but with two convolutional layers instead of one, as well as the subsequent summing data obtained during the calculations with input data;
3. Three units of reverse convolution of elementary units.

In addition, the result of the first convolutional block is summed with the penultimate layer of the reverse convolution, and the result of the last block calculations (after applying the hyperbolic tangent to the obtained image) is summed with the input image.

The discriminator network is represented by four elementary blocks (see Table 2).

Table 2. Discriminative network topology.

Layer	Activation	Kernel	Feature cards
Convolution	LReLU	4×4	48
Convolution	LReLU	4×4	96
Convolution	LReLU	4×4	192
Convolution	Sigmoid	4×4	1

Features of network training. During the training, 10,000 iterations were performed with the size of image sampling for the test iteration equal to 3 (although originally scheduled 8) due to the limits of computing power.

The preliminary analysis of the features of the training process revealed the following necessary aspects:

1. As an activation function of neurons LReLU with a coefficient of 0.0002 was chosen. In the course of training a neural network, depending on the success of the choice made, the coefficient can be changed to a more appropriate one;
2. As an optimization algorithm instead of the classical method of stochastic gradient descent, Adam [25] (abbreviated as "adaptive assessment") was used—an optimization algorithm for updating of network iterations weights based on training data;
3. Instead of optimizing (error propagation) after generation and discrimination of each single image at once, the gradient was updated based on the average N value of loss gradients calculated for N different images. The gradient estimated using the data batch is closer to the true gradient by the training data than the gradient calculated from a single image;
4. Reducing the dimension of feature maps was achieved by using a larger step in the convolutional layers instead of using sub-discretization layers;
5. The data were normalized during the network training (by introducing layers of batch normalization);
6. The generator and the discriminator were trained in stages, and it was not known in advance how many training cycles each component should perform. The indicator of the transmission of training rights to the opponent were the error values in the calculations;
7. We used the "exclusion method" or "dropout" to prevent retraining. The exclusion of the neuron corresponds to the returning by them at any input signal value of "zero". Excluded neurons do not contribute to network training at any stage of the optimization algorithm (Adam, in our case). At the same time, the exclusion of at least one neuron is equivalent to training a new neural network.

The training of the developed network model on a 2.5 GHz Intel Core i5 processor took 180 h of continuous performing. The training of the model on a computer equipped with two NVidia 1080 RAM 8 GB graphics cards takes much less time, but all other aspects of the training remain the same.

3   Implementation of the Distortion Correction System

3.1   Dataset Formation

Noisy images from various shaped sets were fed to the generator input. The sets were generated in several ways: the first was a Salt & Pepper noise modification image, the second was a Gaussian additive monochrome noise.

In the classic version, the Salt & Pepper noise is the distortion of the image by random black or white pixels. In our case, we used grayscale as noise units. Thus, the dataset was generated by replacing random pixels with pixels in grayscale on the original images.

The second set was generated using noise with a normal distribution—Gaussian additive noise. This was done by software: a single-channel image containing noise was created. Then it expanded to standard for three RGB channels and summed with the original image from the set. As indicators for the normal distribution, namely mathematical expectation and standard deviation (the exponent of dispersion of the values of a random variable in relation to its mathematical expectation), 15 and 5, respectively, were chosen.

To generate more reliable data, in addition to the randomness of the distribution, we also used the multiplication of both mathematical expectation and standard deviation by a random value in the range from 1 to 2.5. The obtained samples are shown in Fig. 4.

The first and second methods have transformed half of the existing dataset. 30% of the remaining images without additional noise were used to train the discriminator along with the images modeled by the generating unit. The remaining images were used to test the success of the training.

To test the model in different conditions, different classes of noisy images were generated. One of the sets of images included both images with noise used in the research, and with noise that the constructed model has not encountered. This was done to test the hypothesis of the need to train the network on specific data for their successful processing in the future. Examples of used images are shown in Fig. 4c).

We also decided to evaluate the effectiveness of the model on the data with which it did not encounter at all. Gaussian noise was applied to the images seen in Fig. 4d).

3.2   Analysis of the Results

As a result of network training, we were able to achieve positive results in removing monotone noise from test images. The assessment of the effectiveness of the model from the point of view of success for the person was carried out by visual means. Figure 5a shows successful examples of the work of the developed model on data that have additive Gaussian monochrome noise as distortions.

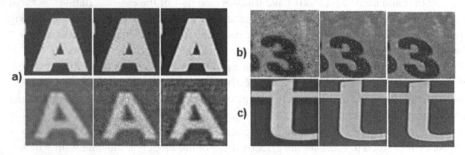

Fig. 4. (a) Example of images noisy with Salt & Pepper modification; (b) An example of images noisy using a Gaussian distribution; (c) Examples of images used to validate the model (from top to bottom: color noise, high-intensity noise, similar to the test noise); (d) Test images from third-party sampling (from left to right: original, images with less and more noise).

In the case of noise, which consists of monochrome pixels that replace and not just affect the real ones, things were worse. Approaching the recent network iterations, it was possible to approximate the data, but not enough to consider this approach as successful in this particular case (see Fig. 5b).

In the case of additive Gaussian noise, it has been possible in most cases of the generative adversarial network to successfully replace noise pixels with suitable adjacent pixels. The network training process is shown in Fig. 5c.

Fig. 5. (a) Two examples of the operation of a neural network in additive Gaussian noise; (b) The process of learning a neural network on the noise of Salt & Pepper. Image step: 2000 iterations; (c) The process of learning a neural network in Gaussian noise. Image Step: 5000 iterations

Figure 6 shows the dynamics of discriminator and generator error changes during the training process. Despite instability of the generative network error, there is a tendency to reduce it during the training process. The green graph shows the average probability with which the discriminator is not mistaken in recognizing "authentic" images. Blue - the probability with which it recognizes "fake" images as "real." If the discriminator were not mistaken, these probabilities would always be equal to 0.0 and 1.0. The orange graph shows the probability that the discriminator $D(t)$, where t is the number of the epoch, determines the "fake" images as "real" after updating the generator to $G(t + 1)$.

The fact that the orange graph is above the blue graph indicates progress in GAN training. That is, the generator version $G(t + 1)$, built in the next epoch, synthesizes more realistic images than its previous version $G(t)$, built in the current epoch.

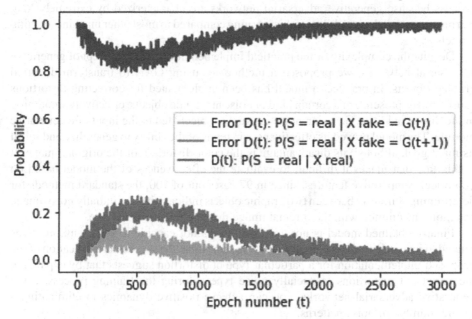

Fig. 6. Change in error functions during the learning process (Color figure online)

The obvious problem (disadvantage) of the model is the fact that if they were trained on one type of noise (monochrome), when trying to remove color noise, it does not show equivalent effectiveness.

As can be seen from the results of the experiment, the constructed model has another global disadvantage - the change of the original colors during image correction. It is possible to solve this problem only by modifying the error function in consideration of the larger number of image indicators.

4 Conclusion

During the experiment, it was shown that the generative adversarial neural network most effectively removes noise from images with a distorting signal of the same type on which it was trained. In the case of the noise of unknown etymology to the network, the results can be both successful and moderately satisfactory. However, the ability to train a network to suppress a specific signal in graphical objects makes it possible to assume that by training a neural network to work with another noise source, successful results can be achieved for solving a wider class of problems.

Theoretically, generative adversarial networks are a powerful mechanism of learning without a teacher, able to find dependencies even in unmarked data without outside interference. In practice, the stability of training of generative adversary networks is difficult to achieve and requires careful tuning and a fine understanding of the principles of the training organization.

The selection of parameters when using generative adversarial networks is a complex process because generative adversarial networks are characterized by extremely long learning time and the instability of this learning compared to most other machine learning models.

Despite the complexity of the practical implementation of the concept of generative adversarial networks, we proposed a method for using GAN to transform distorted graphic objects. In practice, a model has been implemented for correcting distortions caused by the presence of a certain kind of noise in graphic objects, effectively smoothing monochrome additive Gaussian noise in graphic objects fed to the input of a generative module. The model proved its effectiveness in terms of the ability to generalize and fulfill its main goal, although its disadvantage is the color distortion of the original image. It is this fact that makes it difficult to evaluate the effectiveness of the model based on numerical comparative features, since in 97 cases out of 100, the standard methods for determining similarity between two graphic objects indicate that the initially noisy image has more in common with the original image than the reconstructed one.

Finally obtained model is not universal and is not capable to solve any problems related to image distortions correction. At the same time, the successful application of the proposed implementation for a particular type of distortion suggests that by expanding the variety of distortions (especially noise types) during the training process, using generative adversarial networks, you can achieve positive dynamics in eliminating a greater number of noise patterns.

References

1. Simoncelli, E., Olshausen, B.: Natural image statistics and neural representation. Ann. Rev. Neurosci. **24**, 1193–1216 (2001). https://doi.org/10.1146/annurev.neuro.24.1.1193
2. Kingma, D.P., Welling, M.: Auto-Encoding Variational Bayes. arXiv: 1312.6114 (2014). https://arxiv.org/abs/1312.6114. Accessed 25 Sept 2018
3. Rezende, D., Mohamed, S., Wierstra, D.: Stochastic Backpropagation and Approximate Inference in Deep Generative Models. arXiv: 1401.4082 (2014). https://arxiv.org/abs/1401.4082. Accessed 25 Sept 2018
4. Goodfellow, I.J., et al.: Generative Adversarial Networks. arXiv: 1406.2661 (2014). https://arxiv.org/abs/1406.2661. Accessed 25 Sept 2018
5. Rezende, D., Mohamed, S.: Variational Inference with Normalizing Flows. arXiv: 1505.05770 (2015). https://arxiv.org/abs/1505.05770. Accessed 25 Sept 2018
6. Kingma, D.P., Salimans, T., Welling, M.: Improving variational inference with inverse autoregressive flow Flows. arXiv: 1606.04934 (2016). https://arxiv.org/abs/1606.04934. Accessed 25 Sept 2018
7. Dinh, L., Sohl-Dickstein, J., Bengio, S.: Density estimation using real NVP. arXiv: 1605.08803 (2016). https://arxiv.org/abs/1605.08803. Accessed 25 Sept 2018
8. Denton, E.L., Chintala, S., Szlam, A., Fergus, R.: Deep generative image models using a laplacian pyramid of adversarial networks. arXiv: 1506.05751 (2015). https://arxiv.org/abs/1506.05751. Accessed 25 Sept 2018
9. Radford, A., Metz, L., Chintala, S.: Unsupervised representation learning with deep convolutional generative adversarial networks. arXiv: 1511.06434 (2015). https://arxiv.org/abs/1511.06434. Accessed 25 Sept 2018

10. Uehara, M., Sato, I., Suzuki, M., Nakayama, K., Matsuo, Y.: Generative Adversarial Nets from a Density Ratio Estimation Perspective. arXiv: 1610.02920 (2016). https://arxiv.org/abs/1610.02920. Accessed 25 Sept 2018
11. Mohamed, S., Lakshminarayanan, B.: Learning in implicit generative models. arXiv: 1610.03483 (2016). https://arxiv.org/abs/1610.03483. Accessed 25 Sept 2018
12. Odena, A., Olah, C., Shlens, J.: Conditional Image Synthesis with Auxiliary Classifier GANs. arXiv: 1610.09585 (2016). https://arxiv.org/abs/1610.09585. Accessed 25 Sept 2018
13. Balle, J., Laparra, V., Simoncelli, E.P.: Density modeling of images using a generalized normalization transformation. arXiv: 1511.06281 (2015). https://arxiv.org/abs/1511.06281. Accessed 25 Sept 2018
14. Toderici, G., et al.: Full resolution image compression with recurrent neural networks. arXiv: 1608.05148 (2016). https://arxiv.org/abs/1608.05148. Accessed 25 Sept 2018
15. van den Oord, A., Kalchbrenner, N., Kavukcuoglu, K.: Pixel recurrent neural networks. arXiv: 1601.06759 (2016). https://arxiv.org/abs/1601.06759. Accessed 25 Sept 2018
16. van den Oord, A., Kalchbrenner, N., Vinyals, O., Espeholt, L., Graves, A., Kavukcuoglu, K.: Conditional image generation with pixelcnn decoders. arXiv: 1606.05328 (2016). https://arxiv.org/abs/1606.05328. Accessed 25 Sept 2018
17. Ledig, C., et al.: Photo-Realistic Single Image Super-Resolution Using a Generative Adversarial Network. arXiv: 1609.04802 (2016). https://arxiv.org/abs/1609.04802. Accessed 25 Sept 2018
18. Kingma, D.P., Rezende, D.J., Mohamed, S., Welling, M.: Semi-supervised learning with deep generative models. arXiv: 1406.5298 (2014). https://arxiv.org/abs/1406.5298. Accessed 25 Sept 2018
19. Blundell, C., et al.: Model-Free Episodic Control. arXiv: 1606.04460 (2016). https://arxiv.org/abs/1606.04460. Accessed 25 Sept 2018
20. Liou, C.-Y., Cheng, C.-W., Liou, J.-W., Liou, D.-R.: Autoencoder for words. Neurocomputing 139, 84–96 (2014). https://doi.org/10.1016/j.neucom.2013.09.055
21. Hinton, G.E., Salakhutdinov, R.R.: Reducing the dimensionality of data with neural networks. Science 313(5786), 504–507 (2006). https://doi.org/10.1126/science.1127647
22. Zhu, J., Park, T., Isola, P., Efros, A.A.: Unpaired Image-to-Image Translation using Cycle-Consistent Adversarial Networks. arXiv: 1703.10593 (2017). https://arxiv.org/abs/1703.10593. Accessed 25 Sept 2018
23. Maas, A. L., Hannun, A.Y., Ng. A.Y.: Rectifier nonlinearities improve neural network acoustic models. In: Proceedings of the 30th International Conference on Machine Learning, Atlanta, Georgia, USA, JMLR: W&CP, vol. 28 (2013). https://ai.stanford.edu/~amaas/papers/relu_hybrid_icml2013_final.pdf. Accessed 25 Sept 2018
24. He, K., Zhang, X., Ren, S., Sun, J.: Deep residual learning for image recognition. In: 2016 IEEE Conference on Computer Vision and Pattern Recognition (CVPR), Las Vegas, NV, pp. 770–778 (2016). https://doi.org/10.1109/cvpr.2016.90
25. Kingma, D.P., Ba, J.: Adam: A Method for Stochastic Optimization. arXiv: 1412.6980 (2014). https://arxiv.org/abs/1412.6980. Accessed 25 Aug 2018

Genesis of Information Technologies as a Marker of the Genesis of Hierarchies in the Humankind's System: A Model Representation

Sergey Grinchenko[1,2]($\boxtimes$) ⓘ and Julia Shchapova[1,2] ⓘ

[1] Federal Research Center "Computer Science and Control" of Russian Academy of Sciences, Institute of Informatics Problems, Vavilova Str. 44/2, 119333 Moscow, Russia
sgrinchenko@ipiran.ru
[2] Lomonosov Moscow State University, Leninskie Gory, 1, GSP-1, 119991 Moscow, Russia

Abstract. According to the informatics-cybernetic model of the Humankind's hierarchical system, information technologies (IT) appear historically: 1) IT signal poses/sounds/movements: the characteristic size (radius of the same area circle) is ~64 m, the anthropogenic impact accuracy is ~28 cm, start ~28.23, culmination ~9.26 million years ago, carrier of pre-humans *Hominoidea*; 2) IT mimics/gestures: ~1 km and ~1.8 cm, ~1.86 and ~0.612 million years ago, *Homo archaeo-paleolithicus* and *Homo mezo-paleolithicus*; 3) IT speech/language: ~15 km, production technology accuracy ~1.8 mm, ~123 and ~40 thousand years ago (near the IT-initiated Upper Paleolithic revolution), *Homo sapiens'* (*H.s. paleolithicus superior* and *H.s. neolithicus*); 4) IT writing: ~222 km and 80 μm, ~6100 and ~700 years BC (near the Urban revolution of "axial" time), *Homo sapiens"* (*H. paleometallicus* and *H.s. neometallicus*); 5) IT replicating texts: ~3370 km and 5 μm, ~1446 and ~1806 years AD (near the industrial revolution), *Homo sapiens"'*; 6) IT computer: ~51 thousand km (planetary) and 0.35 μm, ~1946 and ~1970 (near the computer revolution – the creation of microprocessors), *Homo sapiens " "*; 7) IT network: ~773 thousand km (Near Cosmos) and 23 nm, ~1979 and ~2003 (about the revolution of mobile telephony, Internet, etc.), *Homo sapiens""'*; 8) nano-IT (possibly, nano-hardware supported selective telepathy): ~11.7 million km (Intermediate Cosmos) and 1.5 nm, ~1981 and ~2341, *Homo sapiens""""* (*H.s. informaticus*, according to the extrapolation of the archaeological epoch "Fibonacci's" model). This list reflects **the genesis of IT** – part of **the genesis of hierarchies** (subsystems) in the Humankind's system. The main components of the genesis of hierarchies include anthropo-, psycho-, techno-, culture-, socio-, ideal-genesis, etc. Thus, the genesis of IT, which has quantitative (model) estimates of the characteristic times of its course, can act as a marker both for the genesis of hierarchies in general and for its components.

Keywords: The genesis of information technologies · The genesis of hierarchies · Cybernetic model of the self-controlling hierarchical system of humankind · "Fibonacci's" model of the archaeological epoch · Homo sapiens technologicus · Homo sapiens informaticus

© Springer Nature Switzerland AG 2020
V. Sukhomlin and E. Zubareva (Eds.): SITITO 2018, CCIS 1201, pp. 238–249, 2020.
https://doi.org/10.1007/978-3-030-46895-8_19

1 On the Genesis of Information Technologies

According to the informatics-cybernetic model (ICM) of the hierarchical system of Humankind [1–4], the full list of information technologies (IT), which people use to communicate with each other, successively arising in its historical development, is as follows [5, 6]:

1. IT of signaling poses/sounds/movements owned by animals, especially herd, including pre-humans *Hominoidea*, in areas with a characteristic size (radius of the same area circle) up to 64 m, increasing the accuracy of anthropogenic impacts to 28 cm, starting with about 28.23 million years ago – with the culmination of this process speed about 9.26 million years ago;
2. IT of mimics/gestures with which the very distant human ancestors of *Homo archaeo-paleolithicus* (*Homo ergaster, Homo erectus, Homo heidelbergensis*, etc.), in areas with a characteristic size up to 1 km, increasing the accuracy of anthropogenic influences to 1.8 cm, began to take hold about 1.86 million years ago – with a culmination of speed about 612 thousand years ago; further IT mimics/gestures continued to develop by *Homo mezo-paleolithicus* (*Homo neanderthalensis, Homo helmei, Homo sapiens africaniensis, Homo sapiens orientalensis, Homo sapiens altaiensis* [7], etc.);
3. IT of speech/language that *Homo sapiens'* began to master: *Homo sapiens paleolithicus superior*, in areas with a characteristic size up to 15 km, increasing the accuracy of production technologies to 1.2 mm, about 123 thousand years ago – with a culmination of speed about 40 thousand years ago (near the Upper Paleolithic revolution initiated by this IT), as well as *Homo sapiens neolithicus*, who continued to develop this IT;
4. IT of writing, the history of which began *Homo sapiens"*: *Homo sapiens paleometallicus*, in areas with a characteristic size up to 222 km, increasing the accuracy of production technologies to 80 microns, about 6.1 thousand years BC – with a culmination of speed around 670 BC (near the urban revolution of the "axial" time initiated by this IT) and continued *Homo sapiens neometallicus*;
5. IT of texts replication, or typography, which *Homo sapiens"'* actively developed in areas with a characteristic size up to 3,370 km, increasing the accuracy of production technologies to 5 microns, from ~1446 – with a culmination of speed about 1806 (near the industrial revolution, initiated by this IT);
6. Computer IT, the timing of which began *Homo sapiens " "*, in the territory with a characteristic size up to 51 thousand km (planetary size), increasing the accuracy of production technologies to 0.35 microns, approximately in 1946 – with a culmination of speed about 1970 (near the computer revolution initiated by this IT – the creation of microprocessors);
7. Network (telecommunication) IT, which *Homo sapiens"""* began to develop, on a territory with a characteristic size up to 773 thousand km (Near Cosmos), increasing the accuracy of production technologies to 23 nm, approximately in 1979 – with a culmination of speed about 2003 (near the network revolution of the peak speed of the spread of mobile telephony, the Internet, etc., initiated by this IT);

8. Perspective nano-IT (possibly, "IT of nano-hardware-supported selective telepathy" [8]), which *Homo sapiens*"""" began to develop, in an area with a characteristic size up to 11.7 million km (Intermediate Cosmos), increasing the accuracy of production technologies to 1.5 nm, approximately in 1981 – with the predicted, according to model calculations, the culmination of speed about 2341 years.

The proposed sequence expresses a unified process of development and complexity of IT, which is naturally called **the genesis of information technologies**.

The proximity of the proposed estimates to the empirical data available in the literature is quite acceptable for a given area of archaeological and historical knowledge.

The time estimates given above were obtained as a result of calculations on informatics-cybernetic model (ICM) of Humankind's self-governing system (Fig. 1), based on the fact that the time intervals between the starts of new IT, as well as the delays of IT culminations in relation to their starts, are subject to a simple mathematical pattern: each of them is shorter than the previous one in $e^e = 15, 15426...$(the calculation of the culmination dates of network and nano-IT, the pattern of the appearance of which is changing, is an exception). (This geometric progression was revealed in the study of biological systems by A.V. Zhirmunsky and V.I. Kuzmin [9]. S.N. Grinchenko applied it to the description of social systems, in a generalized form). In other words, ICM time is presented on a logarithmic scale, with the base of the logarithm 15,15 ....

The convergence point of the time series of IT starts is around 1981, marking the end of the "childhood-adolescence-youth" stage of Humanity and the beginning of its "maturity" stage [10]. The last statement is based on the fact that the emergence of each new IT is associated with the emergence of a new subsystem in the self-governing system of Humankind (Fig. 1), the appearance of which, of course, does not cancel the existence of the previous one – there is a cumulative effect. This is schematically represented in Fig. 2.

2   On the Genesis of Anthropo-, Psycho-, Techno-, Culture-, Socio-Genesis, and the Genesis of the Ideal

In addition to informational-technological, we will consider other, well-known, examples of the manifestation of consistency in the processes of human development. Among the latter, we highlight the following:

- **Anthropogenesis** – the historical and evolutionary formation of the anatomical and physiological (physical) type of person (including its ancestral forms). According to the Great Russian Encyclopedia, "Anthropogenesis (from anthropo ... and ... genesis), the doctrine of the formation of the modern type human (*Homo sapiens*). The general model A. and the factors influencing on it *are still far from clear* (our emphasis – S.G., J.Sh.). A. is part of the evolution of the Universe – the genesis of systems that are in constant motion towards complication and ordering" [11];
- **Psychogenesis** – "the emergence and development of mental life (feelings, speech, volitional and mental activity) in humans" [12]. In addition to this, we note that the existence of the psyche is not only in humans, but also in animals – and, therefore, of their psychogenesis! – recognized since the days of Aristotle;

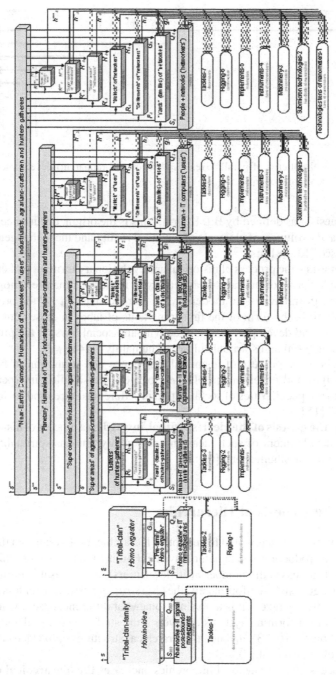

Fig. 1. Scheme of a hierarchical self-governing (according to random search optimization algorithms of target criteria of an energy nature with restrictions such as equality and inequality) of a system of personal-production-social nature (Humanity) [4].

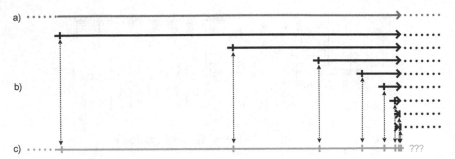

Fig. 2. Conditional patterns of parallel (real) and sequential (apparent) development of natural systems hierarchical components.

- **Technogenesis** – as defined by B.I. Kudrin, "this is the origin, occurrence, process of formation and evolution of elements of technical reality and the technogenic world as a whole" (see [13: 281]);
- **Culturegenesis** – the process of historical and evolutionary formation of culture (a set of sustainable forms of human social activity in its various manifestations and their results) from primitiveness to modernity. In a broad sense, it is "the process of the birth of culture in the form of the first stone tools of labor in close connection with the formation and development of tool activity and social laws … the process of the birth of the material and spiritual culture of humanity" [14];
- **Sociogenesis** – the process of historical emergence and formation of human society, "the origin and development of consciousness, personality, interpersonal relations, due to the peculiarities of socialization in different cultures and socio-economic formations" [15];
- And finally, **the genesis of the ideal (spiritual, inward)** is a process of historical emergence and development of such ideas and personality traits as spirituality, intellect, morality, ethics, aesthetics, etc. [6].

3   About the Genesis of Hierarchies

To reflect the process of sequential formation of hierarchical subsystems in the hierarchy of the personal-production-social natural system (Humankind), each of which is meta-evolved (i.e., it increases the number of its levels/tiers), it is advisable to introduce the term "hierarchy genesis". (Unfortunately, the term *stratogenesis*, more or less appropriate in this case, is already taken: it is used (in a somewhat different sense) by geologists as "the mechanism for forming systems of layers – the studied and correlated sections of the geological past" [16: 83], and not as hierarchical structures embedded each other on the principle of "matryoshka").

In the process of the genesis of hierarchies, increases **the hierarchical complexity** of such subsystems, defined as the number of levels/tiers in the system hierarchy, where it varies in the range of 3–19 (according to the formula $N = 1 + 2n$, with: $n = 1 \div 9$). Hierarchical complexity is manifested (in concrete) through various processes, in a certain sense, conjugate (Fig. 3):

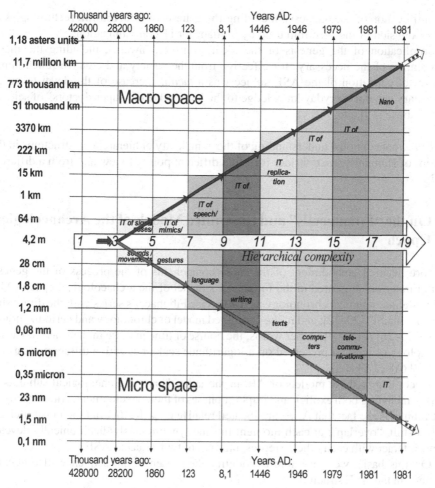

Fig. 3. Spatio-temporal characteristics and IT trend in the process of the genesis of hierarchies (according to ICM).

- growth of typical spatial sizes of social and infrastructural objects (in macrospace) [17];
- increasing the typical accuracy of the human impact on the human environment (in microspace) [ibid];
- complication of the anatomical and physiological parameters of a human during his anthropogenesis;
- complication of the parameters of the human psyche during psychogenesis, including the meta-evolution of the psyche *substrate* as a *tactful* reduction of the spatial dimensions of its elementary units from tissue and eukaryotic cell to macromolecules and organic molecules [18];
- complication of the process, tools and results of technogenesis;
- complication of the process, tools and results of culturegenesis;

- complication of sociogenesis, including **the genesis of information technologies** as an extension of the spectrum used by humans for IT communication;
- complication of the genesis of the ideal (spiritual, inward), including the meta-evolution of the necessary (for effective from the society and creative functioning) level of education of the ASE subjects as a *tactful* increase of this level from the primary general everyday knowledge to the knowledge of "super-doctors" of science and above [19], etc.

For a more detailed understanding of the complexity of hierarchical structures in the system of Humanity, we consider it from a different point of view and from a different angle.

4   On the "Fibonacci's" and the United Models of the Archaeological Epoch

A more detailed embodiment of the main components of the process of the genesis of hierarchies is presented in the Fibonacci's model of the archaeological epoch (AE), which defines its nodal chronology as the inverse Fibonacci's series with the dimension of millennia BC [20–22], and in the combined model of chronology and periodization of AE [6, 23–26] (Fig. 4). In other words, the course of time in these models, as well as the chronology of ICM, is presented on a logarithmic scale, but with a different logarithm basis: 0.618 …

According to these models of AE, in the latter there are archeological sub-epochs (ASE), including both explicit and implicit phases of their development. Another important feature is the fact that ASEs are located relative to each other in time in parallel and with a shift, "overlap": at each moment in time synchronously/diachronically develop – and interact with each other – representatives of two adjacent ASE.

On this basis, we were able to identify the presence and sequence of *dominant* changes in the ASE structure:

1. anthropogenesis and closely related psychogenesis (the first periods of each of the ASE – archeolith, divisions of Paleolith, Neolith, Bronze and Iron Ages);
2. technogenesis (the second periods for the Paleolith and Neolith);
3. culturegenesis (the third periods for the Paleolith and Neolith);
4. sociogenesis (the fourth periods for the Paleolith and Neolith);
5. the genesis of the ideal (the fifth periods – for the Middle and Upper Paleolith, the fourth – for the Neolith, the third – for the Bronze and Iron);
6. involution of all components of the ASE (their last periods).

Note that, according to the unified model, the beginning of each of the above ASE is preceded by key moments of IT formation – information coups (starts) and information revolutions (culminations of speed). The only exception (one of eight) from this pattern is the culmination of IT writing, somewhat late in relation to the beginning of the Iron Age. This may be explained by the transition of the ratio of the values of adjacent members

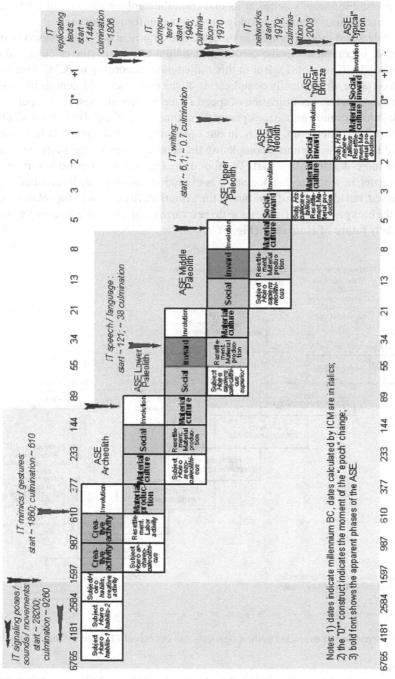

Fig. 4. Combined model of chronology and periodization of AE: "Fibonacci's" model of AE + chronological scale of ICM [6].

of the reverse Fibonacci's series at its end from the "golden section" of 0.618 … to 1 (i.e. the "harmonious" series smoothly turns into a uniform sequence).

The calculated model, as well as the available empirical data, give reason to believe that the AE is completed in the second millennium of our era (the calculated dates of AD: either ~1446 or ~1981). But in this millennium, according to ICM, three pairs of events took place, dramatically complicating all the processes of IT genesis in the system of Humanity: start and culmination of speed IT replication of texts, IT computer and IT network (telecommunication) took place (the culmination of speed of the last ~2003 goes beyond second millennium, which, in our opinion, in such a context is not essential). They fall into one millennium, completing the combined model, naturally initiating the need for more detail in this part. We found it expedient to propose a variant of the unified model, in which anthropogenesis is expanded (i.e., not only its dominant periods are reflected, but all ranges of variants of the evolutionarily complicating *Homo sapiens*) against the background of IT genesis with their carriers, also extended, according to ICM, in the likely future of Humanity (Fig. 5).

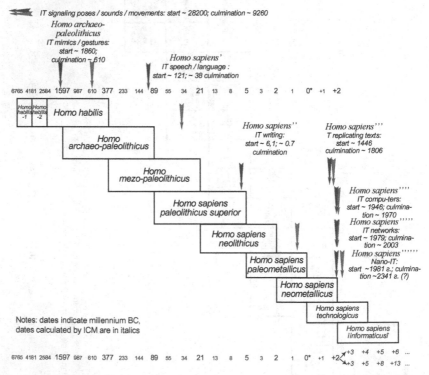

Fig. 5. Comparison of extended anthropogenesis and genesis of IT in the system of Humankind.

Extrapolation of the development trend of all previous ASEs to a relatively near future suggested, within the framework of the Fibonacci's AE model, the appearance of a new "technological" civilization near the moment of changing "eras" of the sub-epochs of a new "technological" civilization, whose subject we called *Homo sapiens technologicus* [6]. According to the unified model, this subject is the carrier of three, successively emerging, information technologies: IT replicating texts of *Homo sapiens"'*, IT computers *Homo sapiens""* and IT networks *Homo sapiens""'*. The lack of meaningful data prevents us from estimating the moment of the supposed completion of this sub-epoch. Let us fill in the missing, referring to the principle of extrapolation of the AE model representation.

The problem lies in the determination of the time scale of the Humankind's development after 2000. The first version is that it is an inertial uniform sequence, with steps of 2-3-4-5-6- ... millennia AD (which the reverse Fibonacci's series shows, starting from the 3rd millennium BC). The second version is that it is a revolutionary logarithmic time scale with steps of 2-3-5-8-13- ... (when the inverse Fibonacci's series is replaced by its direct version). Both of these versions seem to us equally probable, and we bring them together (Fig. 5).

Designations (Fig. 1): 1) ascending arrows (having the "many-to-one" structure) reflect the first of the three main components of the search optimization circuit – the search activity of the representatives of the corresponding tiers in the hierarchy; 2) downward continuous (having the "one-to-many" structure) arrows reflect the second component – the target criteria for search optimization of the energy system of Humankind; 3) downward dotted ("one to many") arrows reflect the third component – the system memory of the personal-production-social (the result of the adaptive influences of the representatives of the overlying hierarchical tiers on the structure of the underlying under them).

Notation (Fig. 2): a) the development scheme of the living hierarchical system, the structure of which for the last ~540 million years has not changed; b) a set of schemes of real parallel development of hierarchical subsystems of the personal-production-social (from ~28.2 million years to our days and further into the future); c) a line that reflects the apparent projections on it of the beginning moments of the personal-production-social subsystems formation, rather than a real process (the increase in labels on it is related with the convergence of the time series of subsystem starts around 1981, and thus in no way means "end of history", etc.).

Continuing this extrapolation, we received another hypothetical, emerging since 2000 AD, a sub-epoch, which it would be logical to call an "informatic" civilization, and the subject of which is *Homo sapiens "informaticus"*. He seems to be the main carrier of the predicted nano-IT *Homo Sapiens""""* (*Homo sapiens technologicus* appears to be involved in the creation of this IT only sporadically: in the same way as *Homo mezo-paleolithicus* participated in creating IT speech/language).

As in the archaeological epoch, *Homo sapiens technologicus* and *Homo sapiens "informaticus"* coexist nowadays in parallel and interacting with each other.

Finally, the same extrapolation points to a hypothetical possibility of appearing in the future, perhaps around 4,000 or 5,000 years, the next sub-epoch of the development of Humanity – "civilization ***", the discussion of the details of which and the characteristics of its subject is now clearly premature.

5   Findings

1. A unified sequence of permanently complicating IT in their immanent connection with the increasing new hierarchical subsystems of Humankind of increasing sizes, in itself necessarily indicates the genesis of hierarchies – a unified systemic process of the Humankind's formation, which historians pay attention to (see, for example, [27]).
2. Comparing the sequence of moments of appearance/ peaks in the development of information technologies of communication and the stages of complication of the AE human subject, we extended the history of the subject of Civilization beyond the limits of the existence of *Homo sapiens neometallicus* and suggested the emergence of such forms of *Homo sapiens* like *Homo sapiens technologicus* and *Homo sapiens "informaticus"*.
3. We determined the chronology and ranges of the predicted emergence of new subjects of Civilization, based on mathematical-informatics-cybernetic model concepts and a quantitative approach. It is the latter that makes it possible to use the genesis of IT as a marker both for the genesis of hierarchies as a whole and for its components: anthropogenesis, psychogenesis, technogenesis, culturegenesis, sociogenesis, ideal genesis, etc.

References

1. Grinchenko, S.N.: Social meta-evolution of Mankind as a sequence of steps to form the mechanisms of its system memory. Invest. Russia **145**, 1652–1681 (2001). (in Russian)
2. Grinchenko, S.N.: System Memory of the Life (as the basis of its meta-evolution and periodic structure). IPIRAN, Mir, Moscow (2004). (in Russian)
3. Grinchenko, S.N.: Meta-evolution of the nature system - the framework of history. Soc. Evol. Hist. **5**(1), 42–88 (2006). (in Russian). https://elibrary.ru/item.asp?id=9304647
4. Grinchenko, S.N.: Metaevolution (of Inanimate, Animate and Social-Technological Nature Systems). IPIRAN, Moscow (2007). (in Russian)
5. Grinchenko, S.N., Shchapova, Yu.L.: Paleoanthropology, chronology and periodization of the archaeological epoch: numerical model. Space Time **1**(27), 72–82 (2017). (in Russian). https://elibrary.ru/item.asp?id=29065435
6. Shchapova, Yu.L., Grinchenko, S.N.: Introduction to the Theory of the Archaeological Epoch: Numerical Modeling and Logarithmic Scales of Space-Time Coordinates. MSU, FRC CSC, Moscow (2017). (in Russian)
7. Derevyanko, A.P.: Formation of a human modern anatomical species and its behavior in Africa and Eurasia. Archeol. Ethnograph. Anthropol. Eurasia **3**(47), 2–31 (2011). (in Russian). https://elibrary.ru/item.asp?id=16547999
8. Grinchenko, S.N.: Afterword. Materials of the report at the Joint Scientific Seminar of the Institute for Informatics Problems of the Russian Academy of Sciences and the Institute of Scientific Information on Social Sciences of the Russian Academy of Sciences "Methodological Problems of Information Sciences". Moscow, pp. 5–8 (2012). (in Russian). http://legacy.inion.ru/files/File/MPNI_9_13_12_12_posl.pdf
9. Zhirmunsky, A.V., Kuzmin, V.I.: Critical Levels in the Development Processes of Biological Systems. Nauka, Moscow (1982). (in Russian)

10. Grinchenko, S.N.: The Pre- and Post-History of Humankind: What is it? Problems of Contemporary World Futurology, pp. 341–353. Cambridge Scholars Publishing, Newcastle-upon-Tyne (2011)

11. Zubov, A.A.: Anthropogenesis. The Great Russian Encyclopedia, vol. 2. Moscow, pp. 83–85 (2005). (in Russian)

12. A Large Dictionary of Foreign Words. Publishing House "IDDK" (2007). (in Russian)

13. Popov, M.: Terminological Dictionary on Tehnetike. Cenological Research, vol. 42. Tehnetika, Moscow (2009). (in Russian)

14. Flier, A.Ya.: Culturology XX century. Encyclopedia, Moscow (1996). (in Russian)

15. Brief Psychological Dictionary. In: Karpenko, L.A., Petrovsky, A.V., Yaroshevsky, M.G. (eds.) PHOENIX, Rostov-on-Don (1998). (in Russian)

16. Zhukov, R.A., Pinsky, E.M.: Regional geology: genesis. Reg. Geol. Metallogeny **74**, 78–89 (2018). (in Russian). https://elibrary.ru/item.asp?id=35249200

17. Grinchenko, S.N., Shchapova, Yu.L.: Space and time in archeology. Part 3. About the metric of humankind basic spatial structure in archaeological epoch. Space Time **1**(15), 78–89 (2014). (in Russian)

18. Grinchenko, S.N.: On the evolution of mind as a hierarchical system (a cybernetic approach). Hist. Psychol. Soc. **5**(2), 60–76 (2012). (in Russian). https://elibrary.ru/item.asp?id=18749871

19. Grinchenko, S.N.: Homo eruditus (an educated person) as an element of the system of humankind. Open Educ. **2**, 48–55 (2009). (in Russian). https://elibrary.ru/item.asp?id=11992835

20. Shchapova, Yu.L.: Chronology and periodization of ancient history as a numerical sequence (Fibonacci series). Inf. Bull. Assoc. "Hist. Comput." **25**, 197–205 (2000). (in Russian). https://elibrary.ru/item.asp?id=23230771

21. Shchapova, Yu.L.: Archaeological Epoch: Chronology, Periodization, Theory, Model. KomKniga, Moscow (2005). (in Russian)

22. Shchapova, Yu.L.: Material Production in the Archaeological Epoch. Aleteya, St. Petersburg (2011). (in Russian)

23. Grinchenko, S.N., Shchapova, Yu.L.: Periodization models of the humanity history. Bull. Russ. Acad. Sci. **80**(12), 1076–1084 (2010). (in Russian). https://elibrary.ru/item.asp?id=16367086

24. Grinchenko, S.N., Shchapova, Yu.L.: Human history periodization models. Herald Russ. Acad. Sci. **80**(6), 498–506 (2010). https://doi.org/10.1134/S1019331610060055

25. Grinchenko, S.N., Shchapova, Yu.L.: Information technology in the history of humankind. Inf. Technol. **S8**, 1–32 (2013). (in Russian). https://elibrary.ru/item.asp?id=20154191

26. Grinchenko S.N., Shchapova, Yu.L.: Archaeological epoch as the succession of generations of the evolutive subject-carrier archaeological sub-epoch. In: Philosophy of Nature in Cross-Cultural Dimensions. The Result of the International Symposium at the University of Vienna. Komparative Philosophy und Interdisziplinäre Bildung (KoPhil), Band 5. Hamburg: Verlag Dr. Kovač, pp. 423–439 (2017)

27. The History of Humankind. Volume I. Prehistoric Times and the Beginnings of Civilization. In: De Laat Z.Ya.(ed.) Foreword. Sakharov A.N. The history of Humankind is unified. Relatively. C. VIII-X. Publishing House MAGISTR-PRESS (2003). (in Russian)

Information Technologies of Evolutionarily Stable Behavior Recognition

Oleg Kuzenkov$^{(\boxtimes)}$ (iD)

Lobachevsky State University of Nizhni Novgorod, Gagarina Avenue 23,
603950 Nizhny Novgorod, Russia
kuzenkov_o@mail.ru

Abstract. A software package was developed to find the quantitative and qualitative characteristics of evolutionarily stable vertical migrations of aquatic organisms according to the observed dynamical characteristics of the environment. The
mathematical basis for solving the problem of predicting evolutionarily stable
behavior is the maximum fitness principle. The method of deriving this function
relies on the study of the population density dynamics over the space of hereditary
elements. Evolutionally stable behavior is found by solving the classical problem
of the calculus of variations, in which the fitness function is taken as the target
functional. The software is built in the form of two interconnected complexes. The
first complex provides a numerical solution of the problem of the calculus of variations to maximize the analytically defined fitness function of aquatic organisms
under certain environmental conditions. This allows us to find evolutionarily stable
behavior for a number of characteristic cases as the solution of the optimization
problem. As a result, a training set of comparison samples is formed. It contains
known precedents of the dynamic states of the environment and the corresponding
strategies of evolutionarily stable vertical migrations of aquatic organisms. It is
used for the recognition process. The second subsystem recognizes the qualitative
characteristics of evolutionarily stable vertical migrations according to approximately given characteristics of the environment on the basis of using the formed
base of the comparison samples.

Keywords: Software · Diel vertical migration · Evolutionarily stable behavior ·
Hereditary strategy · Zooplankton · Fitness function · Calculus of variations ·
Numerical algorithm · Pattern recognition

1 Introduction

Currently, information technologies are actively used in researches of various subject
areas, for example, to study the multicomponent ecological systems dynamics or complex adaptive strategies. In particular, they are used to predict the evolutionary stable
behavior of living organisms, i.e. the behavior which is formed in the population during
the evolution in conditions of struggle for existence. Studying the mechanism of diel
migrations of aquatic organisms is one of important applied problems that require the
effective use of artificial intelligence methods [1].

© Springer Nature Switzerland AG 2020
V. Sukhomlin and E. Zubareva (Eds.): SITITO 2018, CCIS 1201, pp. 250–257, 2020.
https://doi.org/10.1007/978-3-030-46895-8_20

The first data on diel vertical migrations of freshwater zooplankton was published by Cuvier in 1817 [1]. He observed the accumulations of Daphnia near the water surface in the morning and evening and under a cloudy sky and moving them to the depth in bright daylight. Subsequently, it was found that a wide variety of freshwater and marine zooplankton make regular vertical movements during the day [1–3]. Such movements are the most significant synchronous movement of biomass on Earth [3, 4]. As a result, they are the significant factor influencing the Earth's climate [5, 6]. Observation of such phenomena, identification of the causes and mechanisms of their formation is the actual problem of modern ecology.

Environmental factors affecting the behavior of zooplankton include the saturation density of the water layer with food (phytoplankton), the density of predators (fish) in the water layer, the predator activity depending on the time of day, temperature, radiation and oxygen saturation of the water layer, etc. [1.7–12]. All these factors mathematically are functions from the vertical coordinate or time. The evolutionarily stable behavior of zooplankton is continuous periodic (with the period one day) function of the vertical position of zooplankton depending on time. The complexity of the problem is aggravated with the fact that it is really never impossible to measure directly these functions. Only their approximate estimates are always available in some range.

Various mathematical models describing the effect of daily migrations of zooplankton were considered by a wide range of researchers [7–16]. One of effective approaches to finding the evolutionarily stable behavior is based on methods of adaptive dynamics [17, 18]. This approach involves linearization of the considered system in a neighborhood of the equilibrium point in the space of hereditary elements (strategies of hereditary behavior). Other more general approach is based on consideration of the population distribution dynamics over the space of hereditary elements [19–22]. Such approaches give the opportunity to develop a numerical algorithm for finding evolutionarily stable strategy under the known factors of the environment by means of calculus of variations [23, 24]. Thus, these methods are a mathematical basis of the effective convenient information support development for carrying out researches in the applied area.

But, of course, the developed software cannot be limited only to the exact solution of the optimizing problem. Such mathematical solution has limited value in the conditions of approximate, inexact basic data. From the point of view of a researcher, finding key qualitative characteristics of zooplankton movement is more important than the exact solution. For example, one of these qualitative characteristic is expressed oscillations existence. Therefore, it is necessary to create the means of evolutionarily stable behavior recognition adapted to the specific empirically obtained incomplete and inexact initial information. In this case it is useful to apply pattern recognition algorithms and learning neural networks for solving the problem. Now there are a number of the effective algorithms for solving the problem of qualitative characteristic recognition [25]. The problem of pattern recognition can be reduced to the sequence of the making decision problems. These problems are considered on the base of hybrid intellectual systems, based on knowledge, and neural network technologies of making decision [26, 27]. There is also well developed methodology of automated researching system creation. These systems have broad applications in various subject areas, in particular, in biology when modeling biological evolution. Existence of such theoretical base provides development of an intellectual system for modeling of evolutionarily stable behavior.

2 Purpose

The purpose of the work is the convenient computer means creation for finding quantitative and qualitative characteristics of evolutionarily stable vertical migrations of water organisms under observed dynamical characteristics of the environment.

The created software has to solve two main interconnected objectives. The first objective is a numerical maximizing of the analytical fitness function by calculus of variations under the known conditions of the environment. It has to find the evolutionarily stable behavior for a number of characteristic cases. Solving the first problem, it is possible to form the training set of comparison models. This training set has to contain the known precedents of environment dynamical conditions and corresponding evolutionarily stable vertical migrations of water organisms. It provides a possibility of their recognition. The second objective is to recognize qualitative characteristics of evolutionarily stable vertical migrations under the set of environment characteristics using the created base of comparison models.

3 Research Methods

The evolutionarily stable behavior of zooplankton is found on the base of the fitness maximum principle. This principle is the mathematical formalization of Darvin's idea "survival of fittest" [15, 28]. The fitness function reflects selective advantages of each hereditary element of the considered population, in particular the strategy of diel vertical migrations. Only that hereditary element (corresponding to observed behavior) remains eventually in a population for which the fitness functions has the greatest value.

The technique of deriving such function involves a research of dynamics of the population density distribution over the population hereditary elements space [20]. Studying the density dynamics allows us to introduce the ranking order reflecting selective advantages in the space of hereditary elements and to find the fitness function corresponding to the introduced order [22]. Arguments of the fitness function are functionals depending on the hereditary behavior and the known factors of the environment [15].

There are analytical expressions of the fitness function for a number of relevant ecosystem models describing zooplankton dynamics [15, 29]. The evolutionarily stable behavior can be found solving the classical problem of calculus of variations in the case when the fitness function is known. Here the target functional is the fitness function.

It is impossible to be limited only to the exact solution of the problem because information on environment factors can be never presented in the form of exact functional and analytical dependences. Our knowledge of these factors is always approximate and has discrete selective character. Moreover the evolutionarily stable synchronous movement of the population is only its statistical property. The accidental dispersion takes always place in the behavior of certain individuals. From this point of view, the most productive approach is not finding the exact function of the movement, but only recognition of its main qualitative characteristics. For example, it can be the recognition of existence or lack of the expressed vertical oscillations against the background of accidental fluctuations of individuals in the population. This problem was solved using the algorithm of recognition. The base of the samples generated by the first complex was used as the training set.

The basis of this recognition is the method of the split-up standards. The algorithm is based on creation of a system of the hyperspheres in the space of the training sample. Every hypersphere contains all objects of the training set of one known class. If the hyperspheres corresponding to different classes of objects are crossed, then the second level hyperspheres are generated. These hyperspheres cover the objects of the training set of each class in the field of the first level hyperspheres intersection. This procedure repeats until hyperspheres of the last level are disjoint or don't contain objects of different classes. Recognition of a new object is the process of including it in one of the constructed hyperspheres. If a recognizable object does not get only to one of the constructed hyperspheres, then it is necessary the action of "teacher" to specify solving rule. For example, it is possible to make the decision to include the object to a class and to correct the system of the dividing hyperspheres. The last decisive action forms a basis for training of the distinguishing system [25].

4 Results of a Research

The software for mathematical modeling of evolutionarily stable vertical migrations of zooplankton is implemented in the form of the system of two interconnected complexes.

The first complex provides finding diel migrations under the set of exact functions of the external environment. Basic data for work of this complex are the functions describing the dynamical state of environment: density of saturation of food (phytoplankton) depending on the water layer, density of predators (fishes) in the water layer, activity of a predator depending on time of day and temperature. Input of these functions is provided both in the form of analytical expressions and graphically. It is also provided by possibility of analytical interpolation of these functions on separate points (corresponding to data of observation) in the form of curves of the third order. Besides, the coefficients reflecting extent of influence of the specified factors on fitness are set. Further the known function of fitness corresponding to the ecosystem model is used. Arguments of this function are calculated as integrated functionals from initial functions of the environment and the possible strategy of behavior. The algorithm of calculus of variations for maximizing the specified function of fitness is developed and is programmatically realized. The solution of this problem is the evolutionarily stable strategy of vertical migrations of zooplankton in these environmental conditions. A tabular and graphic output of this function is provided.

The base of comparison models corresponding to the exact evolutionarily stable behavior is formed as the result of work of the first complex. It is used further as the training set. The studied precedents are considered on existence or lack of the expressed vertical oscillations. The threshold value of the amplitude of the oscillation is set. It allows us to identify expressed oscillations against the background of accidental fluctuations of depth of zooplankton. Formation of the training set is carried out as follows:

a series of four initial functions is serially set, the amplitude of corresponding evolutionarily stable strategy is found using the first complex, and then found amplitude is compared with the threshold value. If the value of the amplitude is higher threshold, then this precedent is considered as a case of existence of the expressed oscillation. If it is not, then it is considered that the oscillation is not expressed against the background of constant accidental hindrances. The logical value "yes/no" - existence/lack of the expressed oscillations is put in compliance to each four of external factors. Respectively, the fours of external factors break into two not crossed classes.

The second complex allows distinguishing qualitative characteristics of the strategy under the really observed characteristics of the environment. At the same time the created training set is used. Input of the values of environmental factors is provided for separate points with some admissions (dispersion). Then entered data is compare with the precedents in base using the chosen algorithm of recognition. The method of the split-up standards is used. The result of recognition is affiliation of the corresponding evolutionarily stable behavior to one of two classes – absence or existence of the expressed oscillations. Output information of the second complex is the answer about existence/lack of the oscillation of zooplankton under the considered environment conditions. The second complex also provides the possibility of replenishment of the base of comparison models – addition of information on those precedents which the system could not identify and also a possibility of system learning.

Work on selection of test tasks is carried out for forecasting of qualitative characteristics of behavior of a multicomponent water ecosystem on observed visual data. Models of comparison according to visual data of the movement are collected.

5 Summary

A program complex was created as a result of this work. The program complex allows determining the presence or absence of pronounced hereditary daily migrations of aquatic organisms depending on the proposed graphic (observable) information about environmental factors (distribution of food and predators in water layers, predator behavioral responses, temperature distribution of water). The algorithm of recognition presence or absence of predetermined characteristics in the studied system on the available base of models of comparison is developed. Program providing for realization of the offered algorithm is created and approbated.

Also, it should be noted that results of work are introduced in educational process of Institute of Information Technology, Mathematics and Mechanics of Lobachevsky State University of Nizhni Novgorod. Results are used within studying of a training course "Mathematical modeling of selection processes" for students of a bachelor degree of studied areas "Fundamental Informatics and Information Technologies" and "Applied Mathematics and Informatics". They are used for the implementation of term and final qualification work of bachelors and masters and when passing the professional practice. Therefore the important applied problem of intellectual information support creation for real subject area is involved in the educational process. It is coordinated with the purposes and the principles of modern educational approaches of the higher education [30, 31]. Such introduction corresponds to a methodology of attraction of results of scientific research in educational process. It provides the close connection of science and education which traditionally develops in UNN [32]. It corresponds to the trends of modernization of training of graduates existing in UNN in the field of information and communication technologies [33–35] and to the best educational practices of UNN [36–40].

Acknowledgements. The work was supported by Ministry of education and science of the Russian Federation (Project No. 14.Y26.31.0022).

References

1. Clark, C.W., Mangel, M.: Dynamic State Variable Models in Ecology: Methods and Applications. Oxford Series in Ecology and Evolution. Oxford University Press, Oxford (2000)
2. Ohman, M.: The demographic benefits of diel vertical migration by zooplankton. Ecol. Monogr. **60**(3), 257–281 (1990). https://doi.org/10.2307/1943058
3. Hays, G.: A review of the adaptive significance and ecosystem consequences of zooplankton diel vertical migrations. Hydrobiologia **503**(1–3), 163–170 (2003). https://doi.org/10.1023/B:HYDR.0000008476.23617.b0
4. Kaiser, M.J., et al.: Marine Ecology: Processes, Symptoms and Impacts. Oxford Univercity Press, Oxford (2005)
5. Ducklow, H., Steinberg, D., Buesseler, K.: Upper ocean carbon export and the biological pump. Oceanography **14**(4), 50–58 (2001). https://doi.org/10.5670/oceanog.2001.06
6. Buesseler, K.O., Lamborg, C.H., Boyd, P.W., et al.: Revisiting carbon flux through the ocean's twilight zone. Science **316**(5824), 567–570 (2007). https://doi.org/10.1126/science.1137959
7. Fiksen, O., Giske, J.: Vertical distribution and population dynamics of copepods by dynamic optimization. ICES J. Mar. Sci. **52**(3–4), 483–503 (1995). https://doi.org/10.1016/1054-3139(95)80062-X
8. Bollens, S.M., Frost, B.W.: Predator-induced diel vertical migration a planktonic copepod. J. Plankton Res. **11**(5), 1047–1065 (1989). https://doi.org/10.1093/plankt/11.5.1047
9. McLaren, I.: Effects of temperature on growth of zooplankton, and the adaptive value of vertical migration. J. Fish. Res. Board Can. **20**(3), 685–727 (1963). https://doi.org/10.1139/f63-046
10. Pearre Jr., S.: Eat and run? The hunger/satiation hypothesis in vertical migration: history, evidence and consequences. Biol. Rev. **78**(1), 1–79 (2003). https://doi.org/10.1017/S146479310200595X
11. Ringelberg, J.: Changes in light intensity and diel vertical migration: a comparison of marine and freshwater environments. J. Mar. Biol. Assoc. UK **75**, 15–25 (1995). https://hdl.handle.net/11245/1.116358
12. Iwasa, Y.: Vertical migration of zooplankton: a game between predator and prey. Am. Nat. **120**(2), 171–180 (1982). https://doi.org/10.1086/283980
13. Wilfried, G., Bernhard, T.H.: Vertical migration of zooplankton as an evolutionarily stable strategy. Am. Nat. **132**(2), 199–216 (1988). https://doi.org/10.1086/284845
14. Morozov, A.Yu., Arashkevich, E.G.: Towards a correct description of zooplankton feeding in models: taking into account food-mediated unsynchronized vertical migration. J. Theor. Biol. **262**(2), 346–360 (2009). https://doi.org/10.1016/j.jtbi.2009.09.023
15. Morozov, A.Y., Kuzenkov, O.A.: Towards the construction of a mathematically rigorous framework for the modelling of evolutionary fitness. Bull. Math. Biol. **81**, 4675–4700 (2019). https://doi.org/10.1007/s11538-019-00602-3

16. Lindemann, C., Aksnes, D.L., Flynn, K.J., Menden-Deuer, S.: Editorial: modeling the plankton – enhancing the integration of biological knowledge and mechanistic understanding. Front. Mar. Sci. **4**, 358 (2017). https://doi.org/10.3389/fmars.2017.00358

17. Dieckmann, U., Heino, M., Parvinen, K.: The adaptive dynamics of function-valued traits. J. Theor. Biol. **241**(2), 370–389 (2006). https://doi.org/10.1016/j.jtbi.2005.12.002

18. Parvinen, K., Dieckmann, U., Heino, M.: Function-valued adaptive dynamics and the calculus of variations. J. Math. Biol. **52**, 1–26 (2006). https://doi.org/10.1007/s00285-005-0329-3

19. Gorban, A.N.: Selection theorem for systems with inheritance. Math. Model. Nat. Phenom. **2**(4), 1–45 (2007). https://doi.org/10.1051/mmnp:2008024

20. Kuzenkov, O.A.: Investigation of a dynamic system of Radon probability measures. Diff. Equ. **31**(4), 591–596 (1995). (in Russian)

21. Kuzenkov, O.A., Novozhenin, A.V.: Optimal control of measure dynamic. Commun. Nonlinear Sci. Numer. Simul. **21**(103), 159–171 (2015). https://doi.org/10.1016/j.cnsns.2014.08.024

22. Kuzenkov, O.A., Ryabova, E.A.: Limit possibilities of solution a hereditary control system. Diff. Equ. **51**(4), 523–532 (2015). https://doi.org/10.1134/S0012266115040096

23. Kuzenkov, O., Ryabova, E.: Variational principle for self-replicating systems. Math. Model. Nat. Phenom. **10**(2), 115–128 (2015). https://doi.org/10.1051/mmnp/201510208

24. Kuzenkov, O.A., Ryabova, E.A., Sokolov, M.S.: Determination of robust-optimal periodic migrations of aquatic organisms on the basis of the variational selection principle. In: Stability and Oscillations of Nonlinear Control Systems (Pyatnitsky's Conference). Proceedings of the XIII International Conference, Moscow, Russia, pp. 226–228 (2016). https://elibrary.ru/item.asp?id=28299619. (in Russian)

25. Mestetsky, L.M.: Mathematical Methods of Pattern Recognition. MSU, Moscow (2004). (in Russian)

26. Basalin, P.D., Bezruk, K.V.: Hybrid intellectual decision making support system architecture. Neurocomputers (8), 26–35 (2012). https://elibrary.ru/item.asp?id=17997728. (in Russian)

27. Basalin, P.D., Timofeev, A.E.: Product type hybrid intelligent educational environment. Educ. Technol. Soc. **21**(1), 396–405 (2018). https://elibrary.ru/item.asp?id=32253182. (in Russian)

28. Kuzenkov, O.A., Ryabova, E.A.: Mathematical Modeling Selection Processes. UNN, Nizhny Novgorod (2007). (in Russian)

29. Kuzenkov, O.A., Kuzenkova, G.V.: Optimal control of self-reproduction systems. J. Comput. Syst. Sci. Int. **51**(4), 500–511 (2012). https://doi.org/10.1134/S1064230712020074

30. Kuzenkov, O.A., Tihomirov, V.V.: Using the tuning methodology in the development of national ICT competence frameworks. Mod. Inf. Technol. IT Educ. **9**, 77–87 (2013). https://elibrary.ru/item.asp?id=23020512. (in Russian)

31. Zakharova, I., Kuzenkov, O.: Experience in implementing the requirements of the educational and professional standards in the field if ICT in Russian education. In: CEUR Workshop Proceedings. Selected Papers of the 11th International Scientific-Practical Conference Modern Information Technologies and IT-Education, SITITO 2016, pp. 17–31. MSU, Moscow (2016). http://ceur-ws.org/Vol-1761/paper02.pdf. (in Russian)

32. Gergel, V.P., Kuzenkov, O.A.: Development of independently installed educational standards of the Nizhny Novgorod State University in the field of information and communication technologies. Sch. Future (4), 100–105 (2012). https://elibrary.ru/item.asp?id=17926157. (in Russian)

33. Bedny, A., Erushkina, L., Kuzenkov, O.: Modernising educational programmes in ICT based on the tuning methodology. Tuning J. High. Educ. **1**(2), 387–404 (2014). https://doi.org/10.18543/tjhe-1(2)-2014pp387-404

34. Soldatenko, I., et al.: Modernization of math-related courses in engineering education in Russia based on best practices in European and Russian universities. In: Proceedings of the 44th SEFI Annual Conference 2016 - Engineering Education on Top of the World: Industry University Cooperation (SEFI 2016), 12–15 September 2016, Tampere, Finland (2016)
35. Zakharova, I., et al.: Using SEFI framework for modernization of requirements system for mathematical education in Russia. In: Proceedings of the 44th SEFI Annual Conference 2016 - Engineering Education on Top of the World: Industry University Cooperation (SEFI 2016), 12–15 September 2016, Tampere, Finland (2016)
36. Basalin, P.D., Belousova, I.I.: Interactive learning forms in the educational process. Vestnik of Lobachevsky University Nizhni Novgorod (3–4), 18–21 (2014) https://elibrary.ru/item.asp?id=22862959. (in Russian)
37. Basalin, P.D., Kumagina, E.A., Nejmark, E.A., Timofeev, A.E., Fomina, I.A., Chernyshova, N.N.: IT-education using intelligent learning environments. Mod. Inf. Technol. IT Educ. 13(4), 105–111 (2017). https://elibrary.ru/item.asp?id=30725852. (in Russian)
38. Makarov, E.M.: Using Java to test competencies on geometric modeling. Educ. Technol. Soc. 21(1), 494–505 (2018). https://elibrary.ru/item.asp?id=32253190. (in Russian)
39. Grezina, A.V., Panasenko, A.G.: A course in physics at the Institute of Information Technologies, Mathematics and Mechanics of the UNN on the basis of the e-learning system. Educ. Technol. Soc. 21(1), 487–493 (2018). https://elibrary.ru/item.asp?id=32253189. (in Russian)
40. Grezina, A.V., Panasenko, A.G.: The use of modern technologies in the teaching of physics in the preparation of bachelors. Mod. Inf. Technol. IT Educ. 14(1), 293–303 (2018). https://doi.org/10.25559/SITITO.14.201801.293-303. (in Russian)

On the Problem of Correctness and Stability of Composite Indices of Complex Systems

Tatyana Zhgun$^{(\boxtimes)}$, Aleksandr Lipatov , and German Chalov

Yaroslav-the-Wise Novgorod State University, Bolshaya St. Petersburg Str. 41,
173003 Velikiy Novgorod, Russia
Tatyana.Zhgun@novsu.ru

Abstract. The construction of the integral characteristic of the system can be considered as a problem signal-to-noise discrimination. The signal in this case is the weight coefficients of the linear convolution of indicators. Composite index weights should reflect the structure of the system being evaluated. The successful application of principal component analysis in different systems structure description allows us to suggest that the method will also provide adequate results for social systems description. However, principal component analysis and factor analysis determine the structure of principal components and principal factors differently for different observations. The reason for this may be the presence of inevitable errors in the used data. As a method of avoiding this, a modification of the principal component analysis method is proposed, taking into account the presence of errors in the data used. A solution of the problem requires a detailed understanding of input data errors' influence on the calculated model's parameters. Therefore, the question of the problem correctness is essential. A clarification of the concept of computation a system's quality changes composite index problem correctness is proposed. The consequence of the stability is on average a slight change (increment) of objects Rank for different measurements. This increment can be estimated a posteriori using a number of observations of the proposed variance criterion. The results of different composite index evaluation stability according to this criterion are presented. The integral indicators calculated using the author's method have a good stability.

Keywords: Composite index · Data error · Principal component analysis · Correctness and stability of composite index · Rank robustness tests

1 Introduction

Perception indicators are often aggregated in composite indices such as the annual Corruption Perceptions Index, published by Transparency International, and the World Bank governance indicators, which also measure, among other things, the ability of countries to control corruption.

The task of determining the composite index of complex systems arises both in the study of physical phenomena, technical systems, and in solving problems of management of socio-economic systems. In the description of stochastic dynamic systems in

© Springer Nature Switzerland AG 2020
V. Sukhomlin and E. Zubareva (Eds.): SITITO 2018, CCIS 1201, pp. 258–279, 2020.
https://doi.org/10.1007/978-3-030-46895-8_21

the problems of hydrodynamics, magnetic hydrodynamics, astrophysics, plasma physics, radio physics, the composite quantities characterizing such systems are their main characteristics. For example, all conservation laws in mechanics and electrodynamics of continuous media are written for composite quantities. Composite characteristics describe the dynamics as a whole, allowing to distract from the side effects associated with the randomness of the parameters distorted by noise and are the key to understanding the structure formation in stochastic dynamic systems [1].

The construction of composite indexes introduces order relations on a multidimensional set of objects and allows comparing the quality of objects. Comparison of the composite indexes of the objects under consideration and their ratings, which are determined by the composite characteristics, allows us to judge the degree of achievement of the management goal. International organizations, analytical centers and social sciences at the turn of the millennium significantly increased the number of integral indicators used to measure a variety of latent characteristics of socio-economic systems: social capital, human development, quality of life, quality of management, etc. According to the UN, by 2011 there were 290 indices developed for ranking or comprehensive assessment of countries. A review of the phenomenal growth in the number of composite indices used for the integrated assessment of countries conducted by Bandura [2–4] showed that only 26 of them (9%) were formed before 1991, 132 (46%) – from 1991 to 2006, and 130 composite indices were formed between 2007 and 2011. A huge number of methods used to assess the latent characteristics of social systems indicates dissatisfaction with the results and the need for further research in this area.

The rapid increase in the number of composite indices is a clear sign of their importance in politics and the economy as a whole. All major international organizations, such as the Organization for economic cooperation and development (OECD), the European Union, the world economic forum or the international Monetary Fund, construct composite index in a variety of areas [4, 5]. The overall goal of most of these indicators is to rank the objects (countries) and their comparative analysis [4, 6–8]. The use of a single indicator for administrative, managerial and political purposes that characterizes complex, poorly formalized processes (quality of life, financial stability, market policy, etc.) is an extremely attractive idea. Therefore, improving the quality of such indicators is a very important research issue from both theoretical and practical points of view.

Despite the huge number of composite indices, unsolved methodological problems in the development of integrated indicators, problems of incompleteness and reliability of most statistical indicators, lead to the fact that often the calculated composite indices raise more questions than give answers. Discussion of the pros and cons of composite indicators is given in [5, 6].

The organization for economic cooperation and development (OECD) is continuously working to improve the methods of constructing composite indices [5, 7, 9, 10]. In 2008, OECD together with the Joint research Centre (Joint Research Centre European Commission) prepared a Handbook [11], which was the result of many years of research in this area [5, 7, 9, 10, 12], which sets out a set of technical principles for the formation of composite indicators. The main method of data aggregation, the authors choose a linear convolution of indicators, and the main tool for constructing summary indicators—multivariate analysis.

The organization for economic cooperation and development (OECD) is continuously working to improve the methods of constructing composite indices [5, 7, 9, 10]. In 2008, OECD together with the Joint research Centre (Joint Research Centre European Commission) prepared a Handbook [11], which was the result of many years of research in this area [5, 7, 9, 10, 12], which sets out a set of technical principles for the formation of composite indicators. The main method of data aggregation, the authors choose a linear convolution of indicators, and the main tool for constructing summary indicators – multivariate analysis.

The principal difference in the definition of composite indices for socio-economic systems is the uncertainty of the quality of the data used, in contrast to the characteristics of technical and physical systems for which the measurement error is known in advance. Nevertheless, it is the statistical data containing irreparable errors that currently represent the best estimates of the available real values in social systems [5].

Multivariate statistical data analysis, namely factor analysis and principal component analysis (PCA), is a tool for working with multivariate data. The application of this technique to the characteristics of physical, biological, technical systems gives meaningful and reliable results. It is therefore obvious that this tool should also be used to describe social systems. For the first time factor analysis was used to combine a set of indicators into a single index in the development of the health index in the work of Hightower in 1978 [13], and is now widely used for these purposes [5, 9, 12]. The principal component analysis was chosen as the standard method of construction in the calculation of Socioeconomic status indicators (Socio-Economic Status Indices, SES), and the calculated index determined the projection on the first principal component [14, 15]. The same methodology was used by Lindman and Sellin to create the environmental sustainability Index [16], Somarriba and Pena to measure the quality of life in Europe [17]. Among the local studies should be noted the work of S. A. Ayvazyan [18] to determine the index of quality of life using the first main component.

However, the first principal component well approximates the simulated situation if the maximum eigenvalue of the covariance matrix gives a significant contribution (at least 70%) to the sum of all eigenvalues. In this case, the structure of the system is satisfactorily described by the first main component. This condition is satisfied if the system is described by a small number of features (no more than five), and one of the properties of the system obviously dominates over the others. When describing socioeconomic systems, the structure of the system does not allow a simple approximation. As a way out of this situation is considered according to [18] lowering the threshold of informativeness to 55%, and the division of the original system into subsystems described by fewer variables. In the above studies [13–15, 17], the contribution of the largest eigenvalue ranged from 13% to 38%, except for the work [17], which considered a model example, where this figure was 56%. The authors followed the recommendations [17], which stated that the first principal component gives satisfactory weight coefficients when calculating the integral index even in cases where the largest eigenvalue makes a small contribution to the sum of all eigenvalues. However, this statement cannot be called indisputable.

Researchers of the Organization for economic cooperation and development hold a different view. To form a composite indicator, factor analysis is used, where the principal component analysis is used exclusively to extract factors so that the number of extracted factors would explain more than 50% of the total variance. The composite index value in this case is determined only by the significant loads of the selected principal factors after rotation. Actually, this method becomes the standard for composite indices calculating [5, 9, 12]. Although the authors [5] note that different methods of extracting the principal components and different methods of rotation imply different significant variables, and hence different weights of variables in the calculation of the composite index, and therefore different values of the calculated integral indicator. In addition, factor analysis assumes that there is a sufficient correlation between the initial variables, which in some sense contradicts the idea of a complete description of the phenomenon under study by a set of independent quantities.

Another circumstance should also be noted. The method of determining the weight coefficients using factor analysis (as well as the principal component analysis) cannot be used to compare the characteristics of the described objects in dynamics, since even with fixed methods of extracting factors and the method of rotation, factor analysis for different observations of the system differently determines the structure of the principal factors (significant loads), which makes it meaningless to compare objects in dynamics [19]. The reason for this phenomenon may be the insufficient quality of the data used, namely, the presence of irreparable errors in the statistical data used, which the researcher cannot estimate. The influence of these errors can be the cause of unsatisfactory solution of the problem of ranking objects on the basis of the calculated integral characteristics.

The purpose of the proposed work is to consider the correctness and stability of the solution of the problem of calculating the integral characteristics of the system, which is considered as the problem of signal isolation against noise, exactly:

- The rationale for the use of weight coefficients of linear convolution, which determines the integral characteristic as characteristics reflecting the structure of the system;
- The substantiation of the possibility of modification of the principal components analysis used to identify the structure of the system for a noisy signal – a series of consecutive measurements;
- The analysis of the specifics of the study of the correctness of the problems of calculating the integral characteristics of the system in the conditions of insufficient quality information;
- The research of stability of the solution of the problem of calculation of the integral indicator by quantitative methods.

2 A Problem Definition

Let us consider the construction of an integral evaluation of a system of m objects, for which the tables of object descriptions for a number of observations are known – a matrix of dimension $m \times n$, $t = 1, \ldots, T$. Matrix element - a value of the j-th index of the i-th object, vector - description of the i-th object at the T moment. For each moment t the vector of composite index (integral indicators) has the form

$$q^t = A^t \cdot w^t, \tag{1}$$

Or, for the i-th object at time t

$$q_i^t = \sum_{j=1}^{n} w_j^t \cdot a_{ij}^t, \tag{2}$$

where $q^t = \left(q_1^t, q_2^t, \ldots, q_m^t\right)^T$ – the vector of integral indicators of the moment t, $w^t = \left(w_1^t, w_2^t, \ldots, w_m^t\right)^T$ – the vector of weights of indicators for the moment t, A^t – the matrix of preprocessed data for the moment t.

The numerical characteristics of the system are previously subjected to unification – bringing the values of variables to the interval [0, 1] on the principle: "the more, the better". If the initial indicator is associated with the analyzed integral quality property monotonic dependence, then the initial variables x_{ij} for each moment of observation are transformed according to the rule when the initial indicators are unified:

$$a_{ij}^t = s_j + (-1)^{s_j} \cdot \frac{x_{ij}^t - m_j}{M_j - m_j}$$

where $s_j = 0$, if the optimal value of the j-th indicator is the maximum and $s_j = 1$, if the optimal value of the j-th indicator is the minimum, m_j – the lowest value of the j-th indicator for the entire sample (global minimum), M_j—the highest value of the j-th indicator for the entire sample (global maximum).

If the initial indicator is associated with the analyzed integral quality property by non-monotonic dependence (i.e. within the range of change of this indicator there is a value x_j^{opt}, at which the highest quality is achieved), the value of the corresponding unified indicator is calculated by the formula:

$$a_{ij}^t = \left(1 - \frac{\left|x_{ij}^t - x_j^{opt}\right|}{\max\left\{\left(M_j - x_j^{opt}\right), \left(x_j^{opt} - m_j\right)\right\}}\right).$$

In further reasoning, the data to which the necessary transformations have been applied are used as input data. In particular, the principal component analysis involves, in addition to unification, also pre-centering of data. Each element of the centered data matrix is calculated by the formula:

$$z_{ij} = \frac{a_{ij} - \overline{a_j}}{s_j},$$

where $\overline{a_j} = \frac{1}{m} \sum_{i=1}^{m} a_{ij}$—the sample mean, $s_j^2 = \frac{1}{m} \sum_{i=1}^{m} (a_{ij} - a_j)^2$—the sample variance. Centered data is used to calculate weights w^t.

The estimated object is considered as a complex (not amenable to satisfactory formalization), large (the number of states above modern computing capabilities) system. Such systems are both every biological object and any social system. The system is available for observation, and we know a finite, sufficiently large number of recorded with some accuracy of the numerical characteristics of this system at different times.

The significance of the recorded indicators for the functioning of the system is generally unknown. To solve the control problem, it is required to give a motivated assessment of each observed object over the entire period of observations, i.e. to calculate the dynamics of the integral characteristic of the quality of the system. To build the desired integral indicator of the quality of the system, it is required to find the weights of the indicators for each moment of time that adequately reflect the properties of the system under consideration. That is, the determined weight coefficients should reflect the structure of the estimated system. This interpretation of the weights eliminates one of the main uncertainties in the design of the composite indices.

The estimated object is considered as a complex (not amenable to satisfactory formalization), large (the number of states above modern computing capabilities) system. Such systems are both every biological object and any social system. The system is available for observation, and we know a finite, sufficiently large number of recorded with some accuracy of the numerical characteristics of this system at different times. The significance of the recorded indicators for the functioning of the system is generally unknown. To solve the control problem, it is required to give a motivated assessment of each observed object over the entire period of observations, i.e. to calculate the dynamics of the integral characteristic of the quality of the system. To build the desired integral indicator of the quality of the system, it is required to find the weights of the indicators w^t for each moment of time that adequately reflect the properties of the system under consideration. That is, the determined weight coefficients should reflect the structure of the estimated system. This interpretation of the weights eliminates one of the main uncertainties in the design of the composite index.

When using the methods of calculation of integral characteristics "supervised learning" [20, 21] weight coefficients (1–2) are assigned by experts and reflect the importance (or importance) of variables in the system from the point of view of experts. The main objection to this method is the fact that the services of experts are a commodity and very expensive, therefore, expert evaluation will inevitably reflect the opinion of the customer of the study. On the other hand, the importance of the variable on the part of the expert Advisor may not coincide with the properties of the system, which reflect the weights of the variables.

Formal methods of constructing composite indexes (methods "unsupervised learning») do not use subjective preferences to determine the weight coefficients. One of the simplest methods of analyzing the structure of the system under study is the principal component analysis (PCA). The principal component space is optimal for modeling the internal data structure.

In the research [22] PCA is used to analyze the structure of the relief, in [23] to study the structural properties of carbon nanotubes, in [24] to analyze the geometric properties of chemical compounds, in [25] to analyze the spectrum of drugs. In [26], PCA is used to analyze the structures of biomolecular objects. Among the advantages of the principal components method for the analysis of data flow (x-ray images), the authors [26] note the high efficiency of the method for the problem of noise filtering and for finding the most characteristic features in the data. The successful application of PCA to describe the structure of systems of various types suggests that the method will also provide adequate results for the description of social systems.

While calculating the composite indexes by the met, the projections of objects on a new coordinate system, called the principal components, are constructed. The sum of the squares of the distances from the objects to their projections on the first principal component is minimal. Consider the orthogonal matrix W in the linear combination $Z^T = A^T \cdot W$ of the row vectors of the matrix A such that the columns of the matrix Z have the maximum sum of the variances.

$$\sum_{j=1}^{n} \sigma^2(z_i) \rightarrow \max,$$

where $\sigma^2(z) = \frac{1}{m} \sum_{i=1}^{m} (z_i - \bar{z})^2$ and $\bar{z} = \frac{1}{m} \sum_{i=1}^{m} z_i$.

It is shown in [27, 28] that the column vectors of the matrix W are eigenvectors of the covariance data matrix $\Sigma = A^T \cdot A$. This matrix can be found by a singular value decomposition of the matrix $A^T \cdot A$. As $\Sigma = A^T \cdot A = W \Lambda^2 W^T$ (in the singular value decomposition of the matrix are orthogonal and the matrix Λ is diagonal with non-increasing non-negative elements), then $\Sigma W = WA$ is the eigenvalue system of the matrix ΣW.

Typically, the vector of integral indicators $q_{PCA} = A \cdot w$ is calculated as a projection of vectors – rows of the unified data matrix A on the first *principal* component, where the eigenvector w is the first row of the matrix W. This vector corresponds to the maximum eigenvalue of the covariance matrix. This method is used to estimate static systems if the first principal component approximates the simulated situation well, i.e. the maximum eigenvalue of the covariance matrix contributes at least 70% to the sum of all eigenvalues. This ratio is performed if a small number of features are considered n is small, usually no more than five, and one of the properties of the system clearly dominates the others. In describing socio-economic systems, this assumption is not fulfilled: the number of variables is much more than five, and the structure of the system does not allow a simple approximation. As a way out of this situation is considered according to [29, 30] lowering the threshold of informativeness to 55% and dividing the source system into blocks-subsystems described by fewer variables in which the necessary condition of informativeness is fulfilled. Dispersion informativeness is used as a criterion of informativeness. If the projection on the first component cannot be considered a good estimate, the situation can be corrected if instead of one component choose l such component to the relative share of the spread γ_l falling on the first l ($l \leq n$) principal components:

$$\gamma_l = \frac{\lambda_1 + \lambda_2 + \ldots + \lambda_l}{\lambda_1 + \lambda_2 + \ldots + \lambda_n} \geq \theta \tag{3}$$

was not less than a certain value. The selected components are columns of the W matrix. When using PCA, the selected principal components form a matrix W and for each feature the effect of the selected components is summarized and thus the weights in (2):

$$w_j^t = \sum_{i=1}^{l} w_{ij}^t$$

When factor analysis is used, the selected components are rotated to determine significant and insignificant loads. Typically, loads greater than 0.5 are considered significant. Minor loads are reset. The criterion for a satisfactory solution is usually the possibility of a clear meaningful interpretation of the resulting factors. The obtained factors also form a matrix W and for each feature the effect of the selected factors is summarized in the same way.

3 The Correctness of the Problem of Calculating the Composite Index of the System

Thus, the vector of integral indicators is calculated as a weighted sum, i.e. a linear combination of columns of the data matrix A and the weight vector W, which is determined by the eigenvalues calculated from the correlation data matrix and eigenvectors $q = A \cdot W$. The Problem of this approach is that even a small perturbation of the original data can cause a significant change in the weight coefficients when using multivariate analysis methods. In this case, the objectivity of the integral indicator characterizing the entire sample will be violated.

The use of the most modern technologies in solving applied problems requires a detailed understanding of the influence of the degree of error of the observed parameters on the degree of certainty of the calculated parameters of the model. Therefore, the question of whether the task is correct is very important. Most computational problems can be reduced to an equation of the form:

$$A \cdot x = y, \quad x \in X, \quad y \in Y, \tag{4}$$

in which the given, not necessarily linear operator A, acting from space X to space Y and a given element $x \in X$ is required to determine the solution $y \in Y$. We give a definition according to [31, 32].

Definition. *We call the problem (4) correct Hadamard on the Y set if, for any fixed set of initial data $x \in X$, the solution:*

- *exists in space Y;*
- *unique in Y;*
- *stable in Y.*

Using the norms of the corresponding spaces, we can write the stability condition. It assumes that for any $\varepsilon > 0$ it is possible to specify such $\delta(\varepsilon) > 0$ that from inequality $\|\hat{x} - x\| \leq \delta(\varepsilon)$ the inequality $\|\hat{y} - y\| \leq \varepsilon$ follows, where $\hat{y}$ - an approximate solution corresponding to an approximate set of input data $\hat{x}$, y – is an unknown exact solution for an exact set of x data. If at least one of the conditions is not met, the task is called incorrect.

The idea of finding a solution not on the whole set Y, but on some subset of $Y^* \subset Y$, which is a narrowing of the original solution space, belongs to A.N. Tikhonov. The narrowing of the set of possible solutions is made on the basis of a priori information about the properties of the solution. Consciously or intuitively, the introduction of a priori information (in one form or another) into the algorithm for solving incorrect problems allows us to obtain reasonable results. The reliability of the a priori information used significantly affects the accuracy of the solutions.

If there is a continuous dependence of the solution on the initial data, then the inverse operator A^{-1} exists and it is continuous, and, consequently, limited, and the set $X^* = A^{-1} \cdot Y^*$ is limited.

Definition. *Let's call the problem (4) correct according to Tikhonov [32, 33]. On the set $Y^* \subset Y$, and the set itself Y^* – he set of correctness (the set of admissible solutions), if for any admissible set of initial data $x^* \in X^*$ from the prototype of the set of admissible solutions $X^* = A^{-1} \cdot Y^*$:*

- *there is a solution $y^* \in Y^*$;*
- *y^* is only in Y^*;*
- *y^* is stable in Y^*.*

The meaning of determining the correctness of Tikhonov is that the correctness can be achieved by narrowing the considered set of solutions to the set of correctness.

We consider the problem of correctness of the problem of calculating the composite indexes. When calculating the integral characteristic of the system according to the formula (1–2), the existence and uniqueness of the solution are obvious. The question of the stability of the obtained solution remains open. If at the turn of the Millennium the attention of researchers was focused on the design of integrated indicators [10–17], at the beginning of the third Millennium the focus of researchers is on the quality of composite indices, their correctness and stability [34–36].

In the study of the stability of composite indexes, the behavior of models is considered on a single n - dimensional cube $[0, 1]^n \subset R^n$ for each object. The values of unified variables fill a subset of this cube, but it is incorrect to assume that for each object any of the unified variables runs through all possible values in the interval. For example, when describing the quality of life of the subjects of the Russian Federation, it is unreasonable to believe that any variable describing this category can take the same values for Mordovia and Tuva as for Moscow or Kaliningrad.

For a single observation, the permissible values of the j-th variable characterizing the i-th object lie in some neighborhood from the observed values of a_{ij}. If the values of the j-th variable characterizing the i-th object for a number of observations a_{ij}^t, $t = 1, \ldots, T$ are known, the values of this variable are limited by the interval $[m_{ij}, M_{ij}]$, where $m_{ij} = \min\limits_{t} a_{ij}^t$, $M_{ij} = \max\limits_{t} a_{ij}^t$. Then the whole set of variables fills a subset of the unit cube for object i

$$[m_{ij}, M_{ij}]^n = [m_{i1}, M_{i1}] \times \ldots \times [m_{in}, M_{in}] \subset [0, 1]^n.$$

This subset is the set of valid values for the given problem (1–2)

$$X^* = \bigcup_{i=1}^{m} [m_{ij}, M_{ij}]^n.$$

Since the operator of calculation of the integral index is continuous, we can say that the set of correctness in the calculation of the integral index is the image of the set of feasible solutions

$$Y^* = A(X^*) = A\left(\bigcup_{i=1}^{m} [m_{ij}, M_{ij}]^n\right).$$

The problem of calculating the integral indicator will be correct if its solution is stable on the set of admissible input data measured with some error.

4 The Use of Principal Components Analysis for Creating an Composite Indexes for a Series of Observations

Any measurement, including statistical measurement, is related to the accuracy of the measuring device, so the measurement result inevitably contains a fatal error. The construction of the integral characteristic of the system can be considered as the problem of isolation of a useful signal against the background of noise. Obtaining the exact characteristics of the object (and weights of composite indices as well) on the basis of a single measurement, inevitably containing an unknown error, is not possible. However, for a series of such measurements, the calculation of an unknown characteristic is quite likely. Such a task, in particular, is successfully solved by astrophotometry, which determines the basic numerical parameters of astronomical objects not by a single observation (image), but by a series of noisy images.

The task of finding the best method of signal recognition in the presence of interference is one of the main and complex problems in measuring technology, radar, astronomy, optical communication, location, navigation, television automation and many other fields of science and technology. The ideal reception of signals in conditions of noise and interference is based on simple and deep ideas presented in the most consistent and clear form by F.M. Woodward [37]. Following this idea, the task of an ideal device, the input of which is a mixture of signal with noise, is the complete destruction of unnecessary information contained in the mixture, and the preservation of useful information about the parameters of the signal that are of interest to the user of the system. In any communication system, the most important parameter characterizing the noise level is the ratio of the signal level to the noise level (S/N). This value most fully describes the quality of signal reproduction in television systems, in mobile communication systems, in astrophotometry. The acceptable quality of the reproduced signal is determined by the signal-to-noise ratio set by the standard.

Using the basic ideas underlying the astrophotometry, it is possible to consider the construction of integral characteristics of the quality change of a complex system as the solution to the problem of allocation of a useful signal in a series of observations, containing a description of the unknown parameter (in multidimensional noisy data array) in the conditions of a priori uncertainty about the properties of the useful signal on the basis of the commanded ratio signal/noise. The algorithm is given in [38, 39]. The determined signal in this case is the weight coefficients determined by the set of matrices $A^t = \left\{ a_{ij}^t \right\}_{i,j=1}^{n,m}$. This task is similar to the problem of restoring digital images distorted by Gaussian noise.

The technique of multivariate analysis, which works perfectly for the evaluation of technical systems, gives an unsatisfactory result in the construction of an integral characteristic of social systems for a number of consecutive observations. In particular, the calculated integral indicators are extremely unstable, the ratings determined by these indicators have a large spread. The way out of this situation will be a modification of the principal components analysis, taking into account the presence of errors in the data used. Principal component analysis (PCA) allows to allocate structure in high noised dataset and, in particular, has been successfully applied to noise reduction for image recognition, that allows to hope for successful application of this method for construction of integral characteristics of poorly formalized systems.

Table 1. The determination of the empirical eigenvalues.

Year	Eigenvalues								
	1	*2*	*3*	*4*	*5*	*6*	*7*	*8*	*9*
2007	3.27	2.17	1.14	0.78	0.63	0.46	0.32	0.21	0.02
2008	3.32	2.19	1.05	0.8	0.68	0.46	0.32	0.17	0.02
2009	3.11	2.21	1.08	0.85	0.71	0.51	0.31	0.21	0.02
2010	3.08	2.14	1.17	0.83	0.72	0.47	0.31	0.25	0.03
2011	3.04	2.22	1.2	0.75	0.68	0.52	0.32	0.23	0.04
2012	3.11	2.24	1.23	0.73	0.7	0.47	0.29	0.2	0.03
2013	3.14	2.18	1.21	0.81	0.62	0.52	0.28	0.19	0.03
2014	3.2	2.29	1.25	0.65	0.56	0.53	0.29	0.2	0.03
2015	3.2	2.3	1.26	0.62	0.56	0.5	0.3	0.21	0.04
2016	3.32	2.29	1.32	0.6	0.51	0.43	0.29	0.2	0.03
Empirical eigenvalues	*3.18*	*2.22*	*1.19*	*0.74*	*0.64*	*0.49*	*0.3*	*0.21*	*0.03*

If the composite index of the system is determined for a number of consecutive observations, the change in data over time is caused by both a change in the situation and random errors. The principal component analysis describes the invariant structure of the system based on the eigenvectors and eigenvalues different for different moments. Therefore, it is the undistorted values of eigenvalues and eigenvectors that will characterize the structure of the system under consideration and will be the signal that should be isolated from noisy data according to available implementations. Averaging works on the assumption of absolutely random nature of noise and gives stable results for technical systems. For example, it is the averaging of values used in astrophotography to suppress noise in the image.

For eigenvalues, this signal will be the average value for all observations. The average values of the obtained values are called empirical eigenvalues. An example of finding empirical eigenvalues from ten observations is given in Table 1.

The eigenvectors of the PCA are defined up to the direction, in contrast to the eigenvalues determined uniquely. The average value of the factor loads of variables depends on the selected direction of the main components and can not uniquely characterize the signal. For Fig. 1 the choice of eigenvectors direction for the fourth principal component is presented.

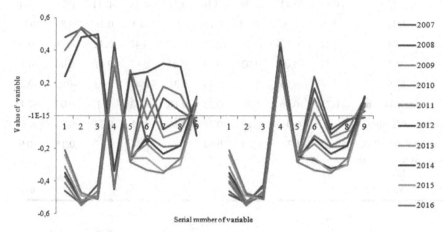

Fig. 1. Coordination of eigenvector directions in determining the fourth empirical principal component. On the left – the initial directions of eigenvectors, on the right – the choice of the eigenvectors direction, which maximizes the signal level.

On the basis of eigenvectors calculated for different observations (ordered in descending order of eigenvalues), it is necessary to recognize random and non-random components of these vectors. The presence of a nonrandom (significant) contribution of the variable to the structure of the main components will be considered not greater than the value of the factor load after rotation, and the invariance of the factor load with perturbations, a sign of which is the calculated signal-to-noise ratio, determined by the ratio of the mean value of the factor load (signal) to the standard deviation (noise). If this ratio is higher than the threshold value, then such a variable is not considered accidental. Otherwise, the variable characterizes the noise component of the signal and does not participate in further consideration. The criterion for choosing the direction of eigenvectors will be the maximization of the signal level – the sum of the calculated SNR values in significant variables. The resulting principal component will be called the empirical principal component (EPC).

The significant EPC variables, as in the factor analysis, will participate in the further consideration, and the insignificant variables are reset. Tables 2a, 2b and 2c shows an example of determining significant EPC loads from five observations. The first, second and sixth variables proved to be significant (the computed value of the SNR above the threshold value of 2.2) and the value of the loads, these variables will be non-zero loadings in the EPC.

Table 2a. The determination of the empirical principal component: approval of directions for the 1st, 2nd and 6th variables.

Year	Variables								
	1	2	3	4	5	6	7	8	9
2012	0.19	-0.11	-0.36	-0.16	0.22	-0.43	-0.11	0.74	-0.01
2013	0.19	-0.06	-0.12	0.15	-0.1	-0.7	0.33	0.56	0.01
2014	0.22	-0.02	0.25	0.39	0.25	-0.42	0.42	-0.49	-0.28
2015	0.43	-0.09	0.02	0.36	0.23	-0.67	0.41	0.03	-0.12
2016	0.3	-0.04	0.09	0.35	0.31	-0.43	0.43	-0.42	-0.37
Mean value, m	0.27	-0.06	-0.02	0.22	0.18	-0.53	0.3	0.09	-0.15
Standard deviation, s	0.1	0.04	0.23	0.23	0.16	0.14	0.23	0.56	0.17
Calculated SNR	**2.63**	1.73	0.11	0.94	1.14	**3.84**	1.27	0.15	0.9
Sum of SNRs for the line									12.72
Active (Valid) SNR									6.47

A qualitative description of the structure of the system requires either all the main components or a sufficiently large number of them. It may be that the information that is valuable for a particular task is contained in areas with less variance. For example, when creating a digital elevation model, which is based on digitized images, the required relief

Table 2b. The determination of the empirical principal component: approval of directions for the 1st, 2nd and 6th variables the 3rd variables.

Year	Variables								
	1	2	3	4	5	6	7	8	9
2012	-0.19	0.11	0.36	0.16	-0.22	0.43	0.11	-0.74	0.01
2013	-0.19	0.06	0.12	-0.15	0.1	0.7	-0.33	-0.56	-0.01
2014	0.22	-0.02	0.25	0.39	0.25	-0.42	0.42	-0.49	-0.28
2015	0.43	-0.09	0.02	0.36	0.23	-0.67	0.41	0.03	-0.12
2016	0.3	-0.04	0.09	0.35	0.31	-0.43	0.43	-0.42	-0.37
Mean value, m	0.11	0	0.17	0.22	0.13	-0.08	0.21	-0.44	-0.15
Standard deviation, s	0.29	0.08	0.14	0.23	0.21	0.6	0.33	0.29	0.17
Calculated SNR	0.4	0.04	1.23	0.98	0.63	0.13	0.63	1.52	0.93
Sum of SNRs for the line									6.48
Active (Valid) SNR									0

Table 2c. The determination of the empirical principal component: approval of directions for the 4th and 7th variables.

Year	Variables								
	1	2	3	4	5	6	7	8	9
2012	-0.19	0.11	0.36	0.16	-0.22	0.43	0.11	-0.74	0.01
2013	0.19	-0.06	-0.12	0.15	-0.1	-0.7	0.33	0.56	0.01
2014	0.22	-0.02	0.25	0.39	0.25	-0.42	0.42	-0.49	-0.28
2015	0.43	-0.09	0.02	0.36	0.23	-0.67	0.41	0.03	-0.12
2016	0.3	-0.04	0.09	0.35	0.31	-0.43	0.43	-0.42	-0.37
Mean value, m	0.19	-0.02	0.12	0.28	0.1	-0.36	0.34	-0.21	-0.15
Standard deviation, s	0.23	0.08	0.19	0.12	0.24	0.46	0.13	0.51	0.17
Calculated SNR	0.83	0.26	0.63	**2.4**	0.4	0.78	**2.58**	0.41	0.86
Sum of SNRs for the line									9.16
Active (Valid) SNR									4.98

is given by the eighth and ninth main components, and the main components 12 and 13 in the Caterpillar method indicate the presence of periodicals with a fractional period in the analyzed data [40].

Approaches to estimating the number of principal components by the required fraction of the explained variance are formally always applicable, but implicitly they assume that there is no separation of "signal" and "noise" in the data, and any predetermined accuracy makes sense. And if the signal is considered with superimposed noise, the specified accuracy loses its meaning and you want to redefine the concept of informativeness. Similarly to the dispersion informativeness according to (3) it is possible to determine SNR-informativeness for the selected number of empirical principal components N, determined by the given signal-to-noise ratio (SNR):

$$\gamma_{SNR} = \frac{S_{11} + S_{12} + \ldots + S_{1N}}{S_{21} + S_{22} + \ldots + S_{2N}} \tag{5}$$

where S_{1k} – the sum of the SNR values of the selected active changes k of EPC, S_{2k} – the sum of the SNR of all variables of this EPC. SNR-informativeness, characterizes the noise level in the signal (in the main component), In contrast to the dispersion informativeness, SNR-informativeness cannot reach 100% according to the logic of construction. This informative is the signal in the absence of noise, but in this case, the SNR-the information content is not considered. Full and detailed information of the selected system of signs is determined by the variance and SNR-informative:

$$\gamma = \gamma_\sigma \cdot \gamma_{SNR} \tag{6}$$

Number of selectable EPC involved in the calculation of the composite index must maximize the total information content of the solution, defined as the traditional variance of the accumulated information and the accumulated SNR – informative, characterizing the signal level of the EPC relative to the background level. Dispersion informativeness increases with the number of used EPC, and SNR-informativeness – decreases, since the younger components carry more noise. The SNR- informativeness of the EPC as defined in Table 2a is $6.47/12.72 = 0.509$. The algorithm implementing the above is given in [39].

We further evaluate the stability of the results obtained using this algorithm and other techniques.

5   The Assessment of Stability of Integrated Indicators

The main application area of composite indexes is object ranking. Researchers who calculate integral indicators for practical application often finish their research at the stage of calculation and consideration of the obtained ratings without analyzing the quality problems of the obtained results [12–18, 41, 42]. It is the position of the object relative to other objects that is the basis for attracting public attention and for making political decisions. If small changes in the input data in the calculation of the integral indicators radically change the ranking of objects produced on the basis of the integral indicators, such an integral indicator cannot be considered reliable. A necessary feature of the reliability of the composite index is the stability with respect to the perturbations of the initial rating data determined by the integral characteristics.

Foreign researchers believe that ratings are a function of weights, and if there is uncertainty about the correct weights, there is uncertainty about the validity of these ratings. Therefore, the stability analysis of integral indices is reduced to the rank robustness tests generated by composite indices with equal weights [43] or alternative weights [44].

If the weights are not determined arbitrarily, and there is no doubt in their reliability, it is necessary to consider the stability of composite indices with respect to changes in the characteristics of objects over time. The observed parameters of changes in the characteristics of the system will determine the set of permissible values of variables and it is possible to study the behavior of integral characteristics when the change in the input data does not leave the area of permissible values and, therefore, the solutions under consideration do not leave the area of correctness. The consequence of the stability of the integral characteristic, in particular, is a slight (average) change in the rating of objects for different moments of time.

For example, the ranks of the 25 countries members of the European Union for the period 2009–2011, exhibited on the basis of the values of the Index of Human Development (HDI), which calculates the indicator value of HDI using a linear convolution of variables with equal weights, gives the average change in rating for the year of 7.7% [45]. Rating change of more than 15% is 14% of cases, more than 30%–2%. This behavior of the rating gives reason to call a stable composite indicators of the HDI.

In the study, which determines the quality of life of the population of the Russian Federation by the method proposed by S.A. Ayvazyan, the author of the method [18, 30], the ratings of the subjects of the Russian Federation were set by two methods: in one case, the weights of indicators in the linear convolution for each year were determined by experts, in the other – were determined by the method proposed by the author. Cases where a change in the rating amounted to more than 15% in the case of expert weights 18, in the case of the calculated weights is one. The average rating change for the first method is 3.6%, for the second – 1.6%. I.e. the proposed method showed the excellent quality of the composite index.

However, with careful application of this technique by other authors, the results are quite different. For example, in work [41] composite indicators of quality of life of municipalities of the Tyumen region for 2005–2008 were calculated. In this case, a rating change of more than 15% of the maximum possible is 48.9% of the total number of cases. In 17.9% of cases this value exceeds 30%. The average rating change is 16.9%. In work [42] the values of ratings of municipalities of the Samara region calculated by the same technique are given. A one-time rating change of more than 15% of the maximum possible is 45% of the total number of cases. In 21.6% of cases this value exceeds 30%. The average rating change is 16.9%. In this case, we should talk about the instability of the integral indicator.

If small changes in the input data in the calculation of the composite index radically change the ranking of objects, then such an integral indicator can not be considered reliable. A necessary sign of the reliability of the composite index is the stability with respect to the perturbations of the original data. In particular, the consequence of this is a slight (average) change in the rating of objects for different measurements. Schemes for determining weights using factor analysis or the principal component analysis do not have such a property. Next, we define a measure to assess the smallness of changes in the rating of objects.

Accept $R_t = (r_{t1}, r_{t2}, \ldots, r_{tm})$ – ratings of the m objects for t moment. The values of the R_t rating sets are known for moments $t = 1, \ldots, T$ that are uniformly distributed on the interval $[1, m]$ random variables with numerical characteristics corresponding to a uniform distribution:

$$M(R_t) = \frac{(m+1)}{2}, \quad D(R_t) = \frac{(m-1)^2}{12}, \quad t = 1, \ldots, T. \tag{7}$$

The values of expectation and variance of R_t values defined by (7) are constant for all observations of t. Note that the values of the ratings for object t at successive moments of time $r_{ti}, r_{t+1,i}, \ldots, r_{t+2,i}$ represent a numerical implementation of a complex functional dependence reflecting the properties of the system under study. It is not possible to find a formal description of this dependence. The degree of linear relationship between the sets of ratings R_t, R_{t+1} is high, the correlation coefficients of Pearson and Spearman are close to one and do not allow to draw conclusions about the quality of ratings.

For more informative descriptions of the quality ratings of the magnitude of the increments of ratings. Changes in ratings over time are dictated mainly by the properties of the system and – to a lesser extent – by random factors. The extent of this accident can be assessed. The smaller the share of randomness for the magnitude of the difference of the ratings, the better described the structure of the system in the selection of weighting coefficients and the higher the quality of the integral indicator. We propose a method for assessing the stability of the composite index based on the analysis of the difference in ratings.

If the ratings of objects for successive observations do not reflect the properties of the system and are set absolutely randomly, the random values of ratings R_t, R_{t+1} for successive moments of time are independent, and the variance of the difference of independent random variables $D(R_{t+1} - R_t)$ is maximum and equal to the sum of the variances of R_t, R_{t+1}, uniformly distributed over the interval $[1, m]$.

$$D_{\max} = D(R_{t+1} - R_t) = D(R_{t+1}) + D(R_t) = \frac{(m-1)^2}{6}, \tag{8}$$

where m is the number of objects.

It is possible to assess the stability of the integral characteristic by estimating the randomness (randomness) of the difference in the ratings Δ_t. This assessment of randomness is the proportion of the variance of the realization of the magnitude $\Delta_t = R_{t+1} - R_t$ of the relative variance (8), which reaches a maximum if the ratings of R_t, R_{t+1} for two consecutive points in time are completely independent from each other and exposed completely by accident.

$$k = \frac{D(R_{t+1} - R_t)}{D_{\max}} \cdot 100\% \tag{9}$$

Since randomness is not the main reason for the rating change, this share should be small. Table 3 shows the results of the evaluation of the quality of different composite indices by comparing the share of the variance of the difference between the ratings relative to the maximum possible values of such dispersion. As a conventional unit of resistance, we can consider the rating of the integral indicator, the HDI, which is approximately 7%. The value of the estimate, comparable to this value, will indicate a good stability of the composite index from the input data. Values that significantly exceed this value characterize the instability of the composite indicators and, consequently, its poor quality. In the table, these studies [44] and [45]. Integrated indicators calculated by the author's method show good stability.

Table 3. The comparison of quality indicators of integral characteristics.

Complex index	Weights source	Period	Number			Evaluation
			Observations	Variables, n	Objects, m	
HDI of the EU countries [45]	Expert	2009–2011	3	5	25	6.9
Quality of life of the Russia [18]	Expert	1997, 1999	2	9	79	6.3
Quality of life of the Russia [18]	Expert	1997, 2000	2	9	79	1.2
Quality of life in the Samara Region [42]	PCA	2002–2004	3	11	37	31.5
Quality of Life of the Tyumen Region [41]	PCA	2005–2008	2	17	26	22.7
Quality of life of the Russian Federation [38]	PCA	2007–2014	8	37	83	1.7
Quality of life of the Russia (*)	PCA	2007–2016	10	37	85	1.6
Sustainable Society Index. Human Wellbeing [46]	Expert	2006–2016	6	9	154	1
Sustainable Society Index. Environmental Wellbeing [46]	Expert	2006–2016	6	8	154	3.5
Sustainable Society Index. Economic Wellbeing [46]	Expert	2006–2016	6	5	154	4.5
Environmental Performance Index [47, 48]	Expert	2016, 2018	2	19	176	11.5

Note: Composite index (*) are calculated by the author's method.

6 Conclusion

The construction of the composite indicators of the system can be considered as the problem of isolation of a useful signal against the background of noise. The signal in this case is the weight coefficients of the linear convolution of indicators. The weights to be determined should reflect the structure of the system being evaluated. The successful application of PCA to describe the structure of systems of different types suggests that the method will also provide adequate results for the description of social systems. However, principal component analysis and factor analysis (even with fixed factor extraction and rotation methods) determine the structure of principal components and principal factors differently for different observations. Hence, the method of determining the weight coefficients using multivariate analysis cannot be used to compare the characteristics of objects in dynamics.

The reason for this may be the presence of fatal errors in the data used. Even a small perturbation of the original data can cause a significant change in the weight coefficients when using multivariate analysis methods. As a way out of the situation, a modification of the principal component analysis is proposed, taking into account the presence of errors in the data used. The algorithm uses a new approach to the choice of the number of main components, to the determination of the weights of the subsystems under consideration and to the determination of the information content of the obtained characteristics on the basis of the selected signal-to-noise ratio parameter.

The solution of the problem requires a detailed understanding of the impact of the errors of the data used on the calculated parameters of the model. Therefore, the question of the correctness of the problem is essential. Proposed clarification of the notion of correctness of a problem of calculation of composite indexes of changes in the quality system. Correctness can be achieved by narrowing the considered set of solutions to the set of correctness based on a priori information about the properties of the solution. The problem of calculating the integral indicator will be correct if its solution is stable on the set of valid input data determined by the observed measurements. The consequence of stability is, on average, a slight change (increment) in the rating of objects for different measurements. This increment can be posteriori estimated from a number of observations by the proposed variance criterion. The results of stability evaluation of different composite indexes by this criterion are presented. The stability estimates of different composite indicators according to the dispersion criterion are given. Composite indicators calculated using the proposed modification of the principal component analysis, taking into account the presence of errors in the data used, show good resistance to changes in the input data.

References

1. Klyatskin, V.I.: Integral characteristics: a key to understanding structure formation in stochastic dynamic systems. Phys. Usp. **54**(5), 441–464 (2011). https://doi.org/10.3367/UFNe.0181.201105a.0457
2. Bandura, R., del Campo, C.: Indices of National Performance: A Survey. Office of Development Studies, United Nations Development Programme, New York (2016)

3. Bandura, R.: A survey of composite indices. Measuring country performance: 2008 update. Technical report, Office of Development Studies, United Nations Development Programme (UNDP), New York (2008)
4. Bandura, R.: Composite indicators and rankings: inventory 2011. Technical report, Office of Development Studies, United Nations Development Programme (UNDP), New York (2011)
5. Nardo, M., Saisana, M., Saltelli, A., Tarantola, S. (eds.): Tools for composite indicators building. Ispra, Italy: Joint Research Centre – European Commission (2005)
6. Foa, R., Tanner, J.C.: Methodology of the Indices of Social Development. ISD Working Paper Series, vol. 4, pp. 1–66 (2012). http://hdl.handle.net/1765/50510
7. Saltelli, A., Munda, G., Nardo, M.: From complexity to multidimensionality: the role of composite indicators for advocacy of EU reform. Tijdschrift vor Economie en Management L1(3), 221–235 (2006)
8. Sharpe, A.: Literature Review of Frameworks for Macro-indicators. CSLS Research Reports 2004-03. Centre for the Study of Living Standards, Ottawa, Canada (2004). http://www.csls.ca/reports/LitRevMacro-indicators.pdf
9. Nicoletti, G., Scarpetta, S., Boylaud, O.: Summary indicators of product market regulation with an extension to employment protection legislation. Economics department working papers No. 226, ECO/WKP(99)18 (2000). https://www.oecd.org/eco/outlook/1880867.pdf
10. Saltelli, A.: Composite Indicators between analysis and advocacy. Soc. Indic. Res. 81(1), 65–77 (2007). https://doi.org/10.1007/s11205-006-0024-9
11. Nardo, M., Saisana, M., Saltelli, A., Tarantola, S., Hoffman, A., Giovannini, E.: Handbook on Constructing Composite Indicators: Methodology and User Guide. OECD Publication, Paris (2008)
12. Tarantola, S., Saisana, M., Saltelli, A.: Internal Market Index 2002: Technical details of the methodology. JRC European Commission. Institute for the Protection and Security of the Citizen Technological and Economic Risk Management Unit I-21020 Ispra (VA), Italy (2002). https://www.ec.europa.eu/internal_market/score/docs/score11/im-index-2002_en.pdf
13. Hightower, W.L.: Development of an index of health utilizing factor analysis. Med. Care 16(3), 245–255 (1978). https://doi.org/10.1097/00005650-197803000-00006
14. McKenzie, D.J.: Measuring inequality with asset indicators. J. Popul. Econ. 18(2), 229–260 (2005). https://doi.org/10.1007/s00148-005-0224-7
15. Vyas, S., Kumaranayake, L.: Constructing socio-economic status indices: how to use principal components analysis. Health Policy Plann. 21(6), 459–468 (2006). https://doi.org/10.1093/heapol/czl029
16. Lindman, C., Sellin, J.: Measuring Human Development. The Use of Principal Component Analysis in Creating an Environmental Index. University essay from Uppsala universitet, Uppsala (2011). http://www.diva-portal.org/smash/get/diva2:464378/FULLTEXT03
17. Somarriba, N., Pena, B.: Synthetic indicators of quality of life in Europe. Soc. Indic. Res. 94(1), 115–133 (2009). https://doi.org/10.1007/s11205-008-9356-y
18. Ajvazjan, S.A.: Empirical analysis of the population's life quality synthesized categories. Econ. Math. Methods 39(3), 19–53 (2003). https://elibrary.ru/item.asp?id=17299169. (in Russian)
19. Zhgun, T.V.: Constructing the integral characteristic of the system quality changes on the basis of statistical data as a solution to the problem of signal allocation under conditions of prior uncertainty. Vestnik Yaroslav Wise Novgorod State Univ. (81), 10–16 (2014). https://elibrary.ru/item.asp?id=22777430. (in Russian)
20. Strizhov, V.V., Shakin, V.V.: Coordination of expert assessments. In: Proceedings of 10th Russ. Simp. Mathematical Methods of Pattern Recognition, Moscow, pp. 137–138 (2001). http://strijov.com/papers/mmro10.pdf. (in Russian)

21. Kuznetsov, M.P., Strijov, V.V.: Integral indicator construction using rank-scaled design matrix. In: Proceedings of the International conference "Intelligent Information Processing" IIP-9, Montenegro, Budva, pp. 130–132 (2012). http://strijov.com/papers/Kuznetsov2012IOI.pdf. (in Russian)
22. Puzachenko, Yu.G., Onufrenia, I.A., Aleshcenko, G.M.: Multidimentional analyses of relief structure (principle components method). Izvestiya RAN (Akad. Nauk SSSR). Seriya Geograficheskaya (1), 26–36 (2004). https://elibrary.ru/item.asp?id=17636361. (in Russian)
23. Oddershede, J., Nielsen, K., Stahl, K.: Using X-ray powder diffraction and principal component analysis to determine structural properties for bulk samples of multiwall carbon nanotubes. Zeitschrift für Kristallographie - Crystalline Materials **222**(3–4), 186–192 (2007). https://doi.org/10.1524/zkri.2007.222.3-4.186
24. da Silva, J.P.B., Ramos, M.N.: Principal component analysis of molecular geometries of cis- and trans-C2H2X2. J. Braz. Chem. Soc. **15**(1), 43–49 (2004). https://doi.org/10.1590/s0103-50532004000100009
25. Li, W., Zhong, Y., Yu, D., Qu, D., Sun, B., Li, M., Liu, J.: Application of principal component analysis for identification of drugs packed in anthropomorphic phantom. ARPN J. Eng. Appl. Sci. **7**(7), 915–921 (2012). https://arpnjournals.com/jeas/research_papers/rp_2012/jeas_0712_740.pdf
26. Teslyuk, A.B., Senin, R.A., Ilyin, V.A.: Applying principal component analysis for macromolecular objects diffraction images sorting. Math. Biol. Bioinform. **8**(2), 708–715 (2013). https://doi.org/10.17537/2013.8.708. (in Russian)
27. Rao, C.R.: Linear Statistical Inference and Its Applications, 2nd edn. Wiley, Hoboken (1973)
28. Isenmann, A.J.: Modern Multivariate Statistical Techniques. Regression, Classification and Manifold Learning. Springer, New York (2008). https://doi.org/10.1007/978-0-387-78189-1
29. Ajvazjan, S.A.: Integrated Indicators of the Quality of Life: Their Construction and Use in Social and Economic Management and Interregional Comparisons. CJeMI RAN, Moscow (2000). (in Russian)
30. Ajvazjan, S.A.: Towards a methodology of measuring of the population's life quality synthesized categories. Econ. Math. Methods **39**(2), 33–53 (2003). https://elibrary.ru/item.asp?id=17293598. (in Russian)
31. Hadamard, J.: Le probleme de Cauchy et les eguations aux derives particlee lineaires hyperbolique. Hermann, Paris (1932)
32. Tikhonov, A.N., Arsenin, V.Ya.: Methods for Solving Ill-Posed Problems. Nauka, Moscow (1986). (in Russian)
33. Tikhonov, A.N., Goncharsky, A.V., Stepanov, V.V., Yagola, A.G.: Regularizing Algorithms and A Priori Information. Nauka, Moscow (1988). (in Russian)
34. Saltelli, A., Ratto, M., Andres, T., Campolongo, F.: Global Sensitivity Analysis: The Primer. Wiley (2008). https://doi.org/10.1002/9780470725184
35. Huergo, L., Münnich, R., Saisana, M.: Robustness Assessment for Composite Indicators with R. The second international conference useR! Vienna, Austria (2006). https://www.r-project.org/conferences/useR-2006/Abstracts/Huergo+Munnich+Saisana.pdf
36. Saltelli, A., Annoni, P., Azzini, I., Campolongo, F., Ratto, M., Tarantola, S.: Variance based sensitivity analysis of model output. Design and estimator for the total sensitivity index. Comput. Phys. Commun. **181**(2), 259–270 (2010). https://doi.org/10.1016/j.cpc.2009.09.018
37. Woodward, P.M.: Probability and Information Theory with Applications to Radar. Pergamon Press, London (1955)
38. Zhgun, T.V.: Building an integral measure of the quality of life of constituent entities of the Russian Federation using the principal component analysis. Econ. Soc. Changes Facts Trends Forecast **10**(2), 214–235 (2017). https://doi.org/10.15838/esc/2017.2.50.12. (in Russian)

39. Zhgun, T.V.: An algorithm for constructing integral quality indicator of complex systems for a sequence of observations. Bull. South Ural State Univ. Ser. Comput. Math. Softw. Eng. **6**(1), 5–25 (2019). https://doi.org/10.14529/cmse170101. (in Russian)
40. Golyandina, N.E., Usevich, K.D., Florinsky, I.V.: Singular spectrum analysis for filtering of digital terrain models Geodesy Cartography (5), 21–28 (2008). https://elibrary.ru/item.asp?id=11516739. (in Russian)
41. Gaydamak, I.V., Khokhlov, A.G.: Modelling of integral indexes of life quality for the south of Tyumen region. Tyumen State Univ. Herald. Phys. Math. Model. Oil Gas Energy (6), 176–186 (2009). https://elibrary.ru/item.asp?id=13287475. (in Russian)
42. Ajvazjan, S.A., Stepanov, V.S., Kozlova, M.I.: Measurement of synthetic categories of quality of life of the population of the region and identify key areas of improvement in socio-economic policy (in the Samara region and its municipalities an example. Appl. Econ. **2**(2), 18–84 (2006). https://elibrary.ru/item.asp?id=9482361
43. Foster, J.E., McGillivray, M., Seth, S.: Rank Robustness of Composite Indices: Dominance and Ambiguity. OPHI Working Papers 26b. University of Oxford (2012)
44. Seth, S., McGillivray, M.: Composite Indices, Alternative Weights, and Comparison Robustness. OPHI Working Paper 106. University of Oxford (2016)
45. Human Development Reports 1990–2014. United Nations Development Programme (1990–2014). http://hdr.undp.org/en/reports/. Accessed 7 Sept 2018
46. Sustainable Society Index. http://www.ssfindex.com/data-all-countries. Accessed 20 May 2019
47. Environmental Performance Index. http://epi.yale.edu/reports/2016-report. Accessed 6 June 2019
48. Environmental Performance Index. https://epi.envirocenter.yale.edu/downloads/epi2018policymakerssummaryv01.pdf. Accessed 6 June 2019

DDoS-Attacks Identification Based on the Methods of Traffic Dynamic Filtration and Bayesian Classification

Andrey Krasnov$^{(\boxtimes)}$ (iD), Evgeniy Nadezhdin (iD), Dmitri Nikol'skii (iD), and Petr Panov (iD)

Federal State Autonomous Educational Establishment of Additional Professional Education
"Center of Realization of State Educational Policy and Informational Technologies",
Golovinskoe shosse 8, korp. 2a, 125212 Moscow, Russia
krasnovmgutu@yandex.ru

Abstract. An approach to the problem of DDoS attacks identifying is considered, it includes: formation of network traffic's secondary informative features of its temporal structure, based on the observed primary characteristics (header of data packets), detection of attacks, and classification of attack types. The first task is solved by the method of dynamic filtering, the second – by estimating of changes in the statistic of traffic secondary informative features by the minimum set of their observations, and the third – by the Bayesian classification. For traffic dynamic filtering, it is suggested to use: the causal transformation operator, the evolution operator, and median and correlation operators. For attacks detection, Wald's sequential analysis is applied. Experimental studies were conducted on the test stand with special software complex for simulating DDoS attacks and software complex for their detection and identification. The results that our software complex for DDoS attacks detection and identification achieves are: detection of network attacks of various types based on joint consideration of probabilistic statistics generated separately by the values of parameters of address and load fields of data packet headers; using the obtained statistics to detect attacks with a priori specified values of errors of the 1st and 2nd type; the choice of an adequate method of protection against DDoS-attacks, taking into account its type.

Keywords: Network traffic · DDoS attack · Identification · Detection · Classification · Dynamic filtering · Causal · Evolution · Median · Correlation · Sequential analysis · Bayesian classification · Experimental study · Test stand

1 Introduction

Currently, the development of promising means of countering DDoS attacks is carried out on the basis of various data mining methods [1]. Over the past decade, dozens of papers on this subject have been published. The work [2] describes the main stages in the preparation and conduct of DDoS attacks, proposes a set of actions to ensure the protection of an organization's network infrastructure, prevent an attack or minimize its potential consequences. In [3], protection methods used in real time for high-speed data transmission in a broadband communication channel are described; various approaches

© Springer Nature Switzerland AG 2020
V. Sukhomlin and E. Zubareva (Eds.): SITITO 2018, CCIS 1201, pp. 280–294, 2020.
https://doi.org/10.1007/978-3-030-46895-8_22

to managing network services during a DDoS attack are reflected. In [4], the features of network protocols and their vulnerability to DDoS attacks are considered, and attention is focused on packet analysis issues, which makes it possible to present the most likely attacker's strategy. In [5], the features of various types of DDoS attacks and their methods of implementation are considered, the main stages and mechanisms for creating botnets are analyzed. At the same time, special attention is paid to the description of statistical analysis and machine learning methods used to detect and prevent DDoS attacks. Practical experience of creating and applying test stands for emulating various types of DDoS attacks in the interests of evaluating the effectiveness of detection and detection methods is presented. Features of the organization of DDoS attacks on cloud resources and existing methods of their protection are reflected in the review [6].

Traditionally, the detection of traffic anomalies is carried out according to the results of determining the deviation of its current state from the patterns of normal states, using various methods of intellectual analysis, including: the principal component analysis [7], wavelet analysis [8], histogram analysis [9], support vectors machines [10, 11], detection of shifts in the space-time traffic patterns [12]. For more in-depth analysis, secondary informative features are used that are formed as: logical fingerprints for various network protocols [13], entropy [14], correlation [15] and structural [16] functions of the primary informative characteristics of network traffic. Various measures and metrics are used to discriminate DDoS attacks from high-volume legitimate traffic (including "flash crowds" effect) [17, 18].

The use of signatures to detect DDoS attacks requires the accumulation of a significant amount of data for all types of attacks and is similar to the methods of virus detection [19]. Neural networks are widely used as part of complex systems for detecting and protecting against DDoS attacks. The ability to identify hidden patterns in traffic and create a reliable recognition system makes them promising and attractive to researchers. However performing characteristics of systems using neural networks depend significantly on the relevance of the training set. In [20], an algorithm is presented that determines with sufficiently high accuracy the actions of users or the influence of illegitimate traffic based on the Turing test and neural network. In [21], neural networks were successfully applied for estimation of the potential size of an attacking botnet. In [22], an algorithm is presented that is based on the use of neural networks for detecting attacks using the TCP, UDP and ICMP protocols based on the analysis of traffic patterns.

Another approach is based on identifying group abnormal behavior, which is characteristic of botnets and differs from the usual actions of legitimate users. The IP addresses of the traffic originator [23] and the packet identification numbers [24] can also be used to detect DDoS attacks. In [25], a detection system was proposed that effectively identifies the anomalous state of the system using group activity patterns of network nodes. The system uses a two-level correlation analysis to identify sets of nodes with the same communication pattern for a long time. This allows you to detect malicious traffic generated by even a small number of infected sites with unique behavior. In [26–29], known clustering methods were used to detect malicious packets in traffic and to detect botnets.

It should be noted that in the field of network security there are no publications that set out the formation and productive use of the space of traffic secondary informative features from the standpoint of statistical dynamics. In the works mentioned above, network traffic is considered as a set of static data (for example, the number of packets per second) without taking into account their dynamical structure, which is determined by the statistics of time following and the corresponding stable connections of the primary features. However, in fact, any network channels and traffic passing through them are dynamical systems [29]. For their adequate description, it is necessary to take into account the rate of change in traffic, and not just the instantaneous values of network loads. It should also be noted that it is quite rare to find algorithms that automatically adjust the threshold values of secondary informative features to determine the anomalous behavior of the system. In practice, this leads to the need for constant manual adjustment of these thresholds and, as a result, to errors in the identification of types of attacks. Very rarely there are works devoted to algorithms that ensure the achievement of given probabilities of errors of the first and second types when attacks are detected.

The purpose of the proposed work is to summarize the results of theoretical and experimental research by authors on the analysis of network traffic [16, 30, 31] and justify the method for identifying DDoS attacks (their detection and classification) based on dynamic filtering and Bayesian classification.

1.1 Statement of Research Tasks

From the engineering point of view, the conducted research consisted in solving three main tasks: the formation of observable primary characteristics of traffic (header parameters of its data packets) secondary informative features of its temporal structure as a stochastic dynamical system; attack detection; classification of types of attacks.

In terms of the control theory, the first task is to form the vectors $F_n = (F_{1n}, \ldots, F_{Kn})^T$ of the finite set of $K (k = 1, 2, \ldots, K)$ secondary informative features (phase coordinates) by current observations of the vectors $P_n = (P_{1n}, P_{2n}, \ldots, P_{Mn})^T$, including M parameters P_{mn} $(m = 1, 2, \ldots, M)$; $(n = 1, 2, \ldots, N)$ of network traffic packet headers removed from the border router at discrete points in time $t_n \in (t_0, t_N]$ in some fixed dynamical ("sliding") window $w_{n, \Delta N}$ with aperture ΔN.

The second task is related to the attack detection by using the disorder method, which consists in estimating for each n-th window position of the moments $n + n^*$ deviations of the traffic statistics from the statistics of its normal state St_0 with a predetermined probability (for given values of errors of the first and second kind) according to the minimal set $F_n, F_{n+1}, \ldots, F_{n+n^*}$ of its secondary features.

The third task is to estimate belonging probabilities $(St_r | F_n, F_{n+1}, \ldots, F_{n+n^*})(r = 1, 2, \ldots, R - 1)$ of the current traffic state to subsets of states $\{St_1, \ldots, St_{R-1}\}$, characterizing the state of $R - 1$ types of attacks.

1.2 DDoS Attacks Identification

The functional-structural scheme of the proposed method for identifying DDoS attacks is shown in Fig. 1.

Let us consider in more detail used identification methods.

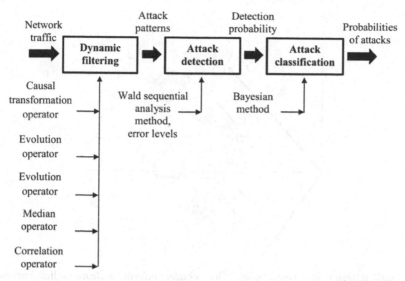

Fig. 1. Functional-structural scheme of the identification of DDoS attacks.

1.3 Dynamic Traffic Filtering. Filtration Methods and Experimental Results

Dynamic filtering is performed by scanning the vector $P_n = (P_{1n}, P_{2n}, \ldots, P_{Mn})^T$ of the stream of M header parameters $P_{mn}(m = 1, 2, \ldots, M; n = 1, 2, \ldots, N)$ of network traffic data packets with a dynamical window $w_{n,\Delta N}$ with aperture ΔN. At each n-th window position, the vector $F_n = (F_{1n}, \ldots, F_{Kn})^T$ of K secondary informative features of network traffic is formed. In the general case, each k-th secondary informative feature is formed by the action of the corresponding functional or operator F_k:

$$F_{kn} = F_k(P_n, P_{n-1}, \ldots, P_{n-\Delta N+1}), \quad k = 1, 2, \ldots, K \tag{1}$$

on the set of parameter's vectors of headers of the network traffic data packets included in the window $w_{n,\Delta N}$.

The formation of vectors of secondary informative features is necessary to take into account the statistical relationship of the ΔN vectors of primary informative features in order to take into account the temporal structure of its behavior. For a stable description of such a relationship, we used normalized frequency distributions $\omega(F_1, \ldots, F_K | r)$, formed from a set of N observations of vectors F_n in different states $St_r (r = 0, 1, \ldots, R - 1)$ of the traffic. The normalized frequency distributions were considered as conditional probabilities of the values of traffic secondary informative features in given states. In this formulation of the dynamic filtering problem, a certain trajectory in the phase space of its secondary informative features corresponds to the traffic (Fig. 2). The trajectory passes through various subspaces corresponding to different traffic's states $St_r (r = 0, 1, \ldots, R - 1)$. In this case, the subspaces can overlap, which is typical for real network traffic containing a mixture of attacking packets. Therefore, the detection of the fact that the traffic trajectory enters into any subspace and the classification of the subspace type are probabilistic procedures.

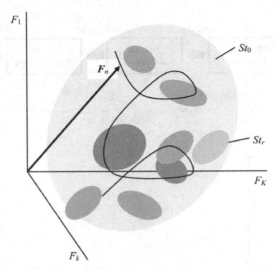

Fig. 2. Traffic trajectory in the phase space of its secondary informative features (light background is a subspace of the normal state of traffic, dark background is a subspace of anomalous traffic conditions).

Due to the multidimensionality of the phase space of secondary informative features in these procedures, the following factorization models of normalized multidimensional frequency distributions $\omega(F_1, \ldots, F_K | r)$ were used:

$$\omega(F_k, F_l | r) = \omega(F_K | r)\omega(F_l | r) \tag{2}$$

for statistically independent features F_k, F_l $(k, l = 1, \ldots, K)$ and

$$\omega(F_k, F_l | r) = \omega(F_K | r) + \omega(F_l | r) - \omega(F_K | r)\omega(F_l | r) \tag{3}$$

for statistically dependent features F_k, F_l $(k, l = 1, \ldots, K)$
In the latter case, the recursion is obvious:

$$\omega(F_k, F_l, F_s | r) = \omega(F_k, F_l | r) + \omega(F_s | r) - \omega(F_k, F_l | r)\omega(F_s | r), \tag{4}$$

where $k, l, s = 1, \ldots, K$.
The following operators were used for dynamic filtering.

1.4 Causal Transformation Operator

This operator converts auxiliary features X_{mn}, calculated by the primary informative features P_{mn} $(m = 1, \ldots, M)$ of the traffic, into its intermediate signs Y_{mn}. For the conversion, the FIR-filter of Hilbert with finite impulse response h_n is used [30]:

$$Y_{mn} = h_1\big(X_{m,n+1} - X_{m,n-1}\big) + h_3\big(X_{m,n+3} - X_{m,n-3}\big)$$
$$+ h_s\big(X_{m,n+s} - X_{m,n-s}\big) + \ldots + h_{\Delta N}\big(X_{m,n+\Delta N} - X_{m,n-\Delta N}\big). \tag{5}$$

The coefficients $h_n \in \left(1, \ 1/3, \ 1/5, \ldots, \ 1/\Delta N\right)$ of the FIR-filter ensure the orthogonality of the sequences X_{mn} and Y_{mn}:

$$\sum_n X_{mn} Y_{mn} = 0, \quad \text{for} \quad \forall m = 1, 2, \ldots, M. \tag{6}$$

Intermediate traffic's features describe the generalized rates of its change, since they depend on the derivatives of higher ΔN-th orders of auxiliary features that correspond to generalized coordinates. For linear independence of intermediate features in (5), odd central differences should be used so that each Y_{mn} does not depend on X_{mn} $\forall n = 1, 2, .., N$.

The combination of intermediate and auxiliary features of the traffic allows us to consider the functioning of the network data transmission channel as the behavior of a multidimensional dynamical system of ΔN-th order with generalized coordinates X_m and generalized speeds Y_m. For practice, it suffices to use $\Delta N = 7 \ldots 13$.

The states of a multidimensional dynamical system with generalized coordinates X_m and generalized velocities Y_m are described by a family of phase portraits which do not contain time explicitly, but describe the change in the system states $\{X, Y\}_m$ [30, 31]. The representation of traffic states in the space of its generalized phase coordinates is similar to Fig. 2.

In a computer experiment, a traffic dump was collected from the mirror port containing the traffic of a certain Web service. Removal was carried out by the program dumpcap for half an hour. An irregular time series (time; Octets (bytes): ...; 0.000000, 70; 0.000201, 70; 0.002205, 70; 0.002333, 70; 0.059672, 66; 0.059864, 15; 0.059919, 90; 0.061212, 64; 0.095265, 70; 0.099552, 70; ...) was extracted from this dump.

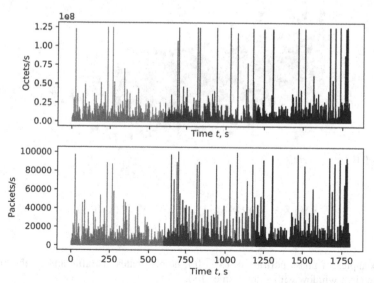

Fig. 3. An example of time series composed of characteristics (Octets/s and Packet/s) of the traffic load part (aggregation in a window with a duration of 0.01 s). (Color figure online)

For an irregular time series, an aggregation was performed with a window of 0.01 s. Regular time series (time; Octets (bytes); Packets: …0.000000, 28000.000000, 400.000000; 0.010000, 0.000000, 0.000000; 0.020000, 0.000000, 0.000000; 0.030000, 0.000000, 0.000000; …) were obtained as the change the number of octets and the number of packets per unit of time (Fig. 3).

All graphics are marked with colors. In the first part (red), from 0 to 10 min, we observe normal traffic (NORMAL-I) without anomalies. The second part (green) from the 10th to the 20th minute contains anomalous traffic corresponding to the TCP Connection Flood attack (TCPCON-II). The third part (blue) from the 20th to the 30th minute contains normal traffic (NORMAL-III) without anomalies.

Figure 3 shows that the TCP Connection Flood attack is noticeable in a slightly increased number of packets transmitted per unit of time. On the Octets/s graph, the anomaly is not visually distinguishable.

Examples of phase portraits $W(X, Y|r)$ corresponding to the normal state of the traffic and its abnormal state (a case of TCP Connection Flood attack) are shown in Fig. 4. As a generalized coordinate X, the ratio of the parameters (Octets/Packets) of the load part of the traffic data packet headers received from the mirror network port is taken. In this example, the packages were aggregated for 1 s. Each of marked phase portraits was formed along the stream of aggregated data packets received within 10 min: the first 10 min showed normal traffic (NORMAL-I); the second 10 min was observed attack (TCPCON-II); the third 10 min normal traffic was observed (NORMAL-III).

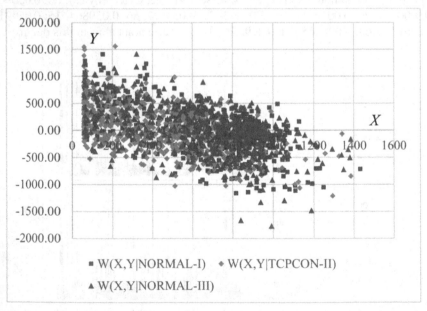

Fig. 4. Examples of phase portraits $W(X, Y|r)$: normal states of traffic and its abnormal state (aggregation in a window with a duration of 1 s).

1.5 Hash Statistical Distributions

When describing traffic conditions in the form of phase portraits, it is rather difficult to carry out the numerical calculations necessary for detecting attacks with a predetermined probability. Therefore, to simplify the calculations, the generalized coordinates and pulses were transferred to one-dimensional secondary informative features using hashing [30]:

$$F_{mn} = X_{mn} + Y_{mn}, \, m = 1, 2, \ldots, M; \, n = 1, 2, \ldots, N. \tag{7}$$

For these hash functions, their normalized frequency distributions were formed. An example of normalized one-dimensional frequency distributions $\omega(F|r)$, formed with respect to the parameters (Octets/Packets) of the load part of the traffic for $N = 3000$ observations in different states $r \in$ {NORMAL-I;TCPCON-II; NORMAL-III} shown in Fig. 5. In this example, the packages were aggregated for 0.2 s. Each of marked distributions was formed along the stream of aggregated data packets received within 10 min.

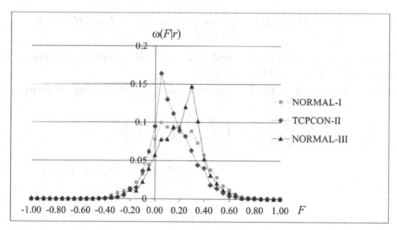

Fig. 5. An example of patterns for three traffic states accordance with causal operator ($N = 3000$, $\Delta N = 11$).

As can be seen from Fig. 5, frequency distributions of abnormal and normal traffic states differ at various intervals (-0.1–0.15 and 0.25–0.60) of values F.

1.6 Evolution Operator

When forming this operator, it is considered that the continuous vector $P(t) = [P_1(t), \ldots, P_M(t)]^T$ of M traffic's characteristics $P_m(t)$ ($m = 1, \ldots, M$) is described by the differential equation [16, 32]:

$$\frac{dP(t)}{dt} = \frac{1}{\Delta t} H(t) P(t), \tag{8}$$

the dynamic operator $H(t)$ of which is not known, and only the values of the components of the vector P of the parameters of the traffic data packet headers observed at various discrete points in time $t_n \in (t_0, t_N]$ are known. In (8), the time interval Δt is introduced for dimensional considerations. It is also considered that for $H(t)$ there exists an operator $S(t, \tau)$, which gives a solution to Eq. (8):

$$P(t) = S(t, \tau) P(\tau), \quad S(t, t) = E. \tag{9}$$

In mathematics, the operator $S(t, \tau)$ is called the matriciant or the Cauchy matrix [33], and in physics it is called the evolution operator or the time shift operator [34]. The connection of the evolution operator $S(t, \tau)$ of a dynamic system with its dynamic operator $H(t)$ was first introduced by the Italian mathematician Peano as a series [35]:

$$S(t, \tau) = E + \frac{1}{\Delta t} \int_\tau^t H(t_1) dt_1 + \left(\frac{1}{\Delta t}\right)^2 \int_\tau^t H(t_1) dt_1 \int_\tau^{t_1} H(t_2) dt_2 + \ldots . \tag{10}$$

Currently in physics, a series is used in the Dyson representation [36]:

$$S(t, \tau) = E + \frac{1}{\Delta t} \int_\tau^t H(t_1) dt_1 + \frac{1}{2!} \left(\frac{1}{\Delta t}\right)^2 \int_\tau^t dt_1 \int_\tau^t dt_2 \Im[H(t_1) H(t_2)] + \ldots, \tag{11}$$

where $\Im$ is the operator of chronological ordering $\Im[H(t_1) H(t_2)] = H(t_1) H(t_2)$, if $t_1 > t_2$ and $\Im[H(t_1) H(t_2)] = H(t_1) H(t_2)$, if $t_1 < t_2$.

The solution's estimate of the Eq. (9) with respect to $S(t, \tau)$ has the form [32]:

$$S(t, \tau) = \frac{P(t) P^T(\tau)}{P^T(\tau) P(\tau)} = \left(\sum_{m=1}^M P_m(\tau) P_m(\tau)\right)^{-1}$$

$$\times \begin{bmatrix} P_1(t) P_1(\tau) & \cdots & P_1(t) P_M(\tau) \\ \vdots & \ddots & \vdots \\ P_M(t) P_1(\tau) & \cdots & P_M(t) P_M(\tau) \end{bmatrix}. \tag{12}$$

Secondary informative features of traffic were formed by solving an equation derived from the third-order approximation of the Eq. (11) [31, 37]:

$$1 + F(t, \tau) + \frac{1}{2} F^2(t, \tau) + \frac{1}{6} F^3(t, \tau)$$

$$= \left\langle \frac{\left\{\sum_{m=1}^M \rho_{mm} P_m(t) P_m(\tau) + \sum_{m \neq n}^M \sum_n^M \rho_{mm} \rho_{nn} P_m(t) P_n(\tau)\right\}}{\sum_{m=1}^M P_m(\tau) P_m(\tau)} \right\rangle, \tag{13}$$

Where $\rho_{mm} \left(\sum_{m=1}^M \rho_{mm} = 1\right)$ are the values of significance of traffic's characteristics P_m ($m = 1, \ldots, M$), and $\langle \ldots \rangle$ is means averaging over the window ΔN.

The normalized frequency distributions $\omega(F|r)$ for different states $St_r (r = 0, 1, 2, \ldots, R)$ of traffic were formed by observing all of its N samples.

For an example, the normalized frequency distributions $\omega(F|r)$ formed by two parameters (X as the ratio the number P_1 of octets to the number P_2 of packets, and Y from (5)) of the loading part of the traffic for $N = 60000$ samples of observations as a result of solving the Eq. (13) for neighboring t and τ at different states $r \in \{$NORMAL-I; TCPCON-II; NORMAL-III$\}$ are shown in Fig. 6. In this example, the packages were aggregated for 0.01 s.

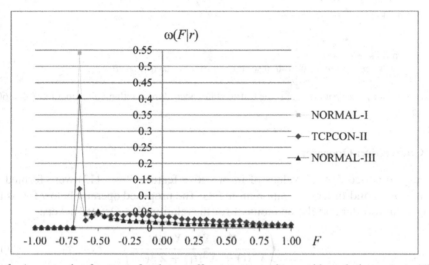

Fig. 6. An example of patterns for three traffic states accordance with evolution operator ($N = 60000$, $\Delta N = 7$).

As can be seen from Fig. 6, the frequency distributions of normal and abnormal traffic states differ at different intervals (-0.70–-0.40 and -0.35–0.60) of values F.

Normalized frequency distributions $\omega(F|r)$, formed by any known dynamic filtering method, are peculiar images (patterns) of states $St_r (r = 0, 1, 2, \ldots, R)$ of the traffic.

1.7 Median Operator

This operator is the easiest to form traffic secondary informative features, however, compared to the previous two, it is less selective for the variety of forms of temporary structures of the traffic load. At the same time, as experiments have shown, with a small variety of these forms, it is most efficient to use the values of medians of traffic parameters determined in a dynamical window with aperture $\Delta N = 3, 5$.

An example of patterns formed using normalized medians of load parameters ($F =$ Octets/Packets) of headers of data packets for $N = 600$ observations is presented in Fig. 7. In this example, the packages were aggregated for 1 s. Each of marked distributions was formed along the stream of aggregated data packets received within 10 min.

As can be seen from Fig. 7, the frequency distributions of abnormal and normal traffic states differ at different intervals (-0.10–0.55 and 0.70–0.90) of values F.

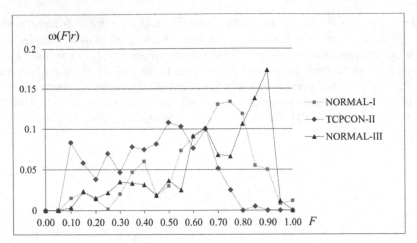

Fig. 7. An example of patterns for three traffic states accordance with median operator ($N = 600$, $\Delta N = 5$).

1.8 Correlation Operator

It is easy to notice that the values of informative features from (13) were formed on the basis of second-order correlation moments. The proposed operator below forms the averaged third-order correlation moment for the relation $X = $ Octets/Packets:

$$F(t) = \left\langle \frac{3X(t)X(t_1)X(t_2)}{X^3(t) + X^3(t_1) + X^3(t_2)} \right\rangle, \tag{14}$$

where t, t_1, t_2 three adjacent time points, and $\langle \ldots \rangle$ is means averaging over the window ΔN.

An example of patterns formed using normalized correlation moment for $N = 60000$ observations is presented in Fig. 8. In this example, the packages were aggregated for 0.01 s. Each of marked distributions was formed along the stream of aggregated data packets received within 10 min.

As can be seen from Fig. 7, the frequency distributions of normal and abnormal traffic states differ at different intervals (0.00–0.10 and 0.15–1.00) of values F.

1.9 Attack Detection

Detection of the instants $n + n^*$ of the attack was carried out by the method of sequential Wald analysis based on recurrent computation using discrete moments $(n, n + 1, \ldots, n + n^*)$ observations of likelihood ratios [37]:

$$Lik_{n+n^*} = \frac{\omega(F_{n+n^*}|r)}{\omega(F_{n+n^*}|0)} Lik_{n+n^*-1}, r = 1, \ldots, R - 1, \tag{15}$$

where n^* is the number of consecutive observations (traffic's packets or aggregates) from the moment n at which the given probabilities of errors of the first and second kind are

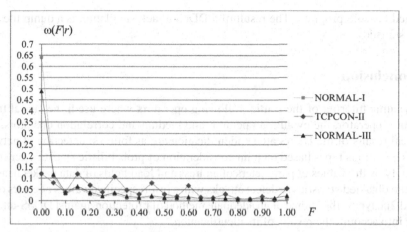

Fig. 8. An example of patterns for three traffic states accordance with correlation operator ($N = 60000$, $\Delta N = 7$).

realized. Usually, when detecting DDoS attacks, a 95% probability of detection is used at significance levels (probabilities of errors of the first and second kind) of 5%.

In (15), in the case of using the feature vector all likelihoods $\omega(F_{n+n^*}|r)$ and $\omega(F_{n+n^*}|0)$ were calculated by models (2–4).

1.10   Bayesian Attack's Types Classification

To classify the detected attacks, the Bayesian method of static decision-making was used by calculating the a posteriori probabilities of attack's types under the assumption of their equal prior probabilities:

$$\omega(S_r|F_n, F_{n+1}, \ldots, F_{n+n^*}) = \frac{\omega(F_{n+n^*}|r)\omega(F_{n+n^*-1}|r) \ldots \omega(F_n|r)}{\sum_{r=1}^{R-1} \omega(F_{n+n^*}|r)\omega(F_{n+n^*-1}|r) \ldots \omega(F_n|r)}. \quad (16)$$

The determination of these probabilities is necessary for the formation of priorities when choosing protective countermeasures.

1.11   Test Stand

For experimental studies, a test stand was created containing the «DDoS Attacks simulator» software complex, which is designed to simulate DDoS attacks, and a software complex for detecting and identifying DDoS attacks [38]. The «DDoS Attacks simulator» complex includes simulators of legitimate and abnormal traffic, as well as utilities for intercepting network traffic and collecting statistics. To store the results of a computer experiment, a specially designed relational database (DB) is used. The complex is a set of console programs designed to run under the control of the SLURM service. To simulate a specific DDoS attack or a group of attacks during a specific period of time, the user assigns tasks through the SLURM service. Each of the tasks starts and stops the specified console program. The result of a DDoS attack simulation is a dump file with attack statistics.

2 Conclusion

For dynamic filtering of the traffic, following operators where used: the causal transformation operator, the evolution operator, and median and correlation operators. The technical results of the DDoS attack identification are as follows: detection of network attacks of various types based on joint consideration of probabilistic statistics generated separately by the values of parameters of address and load fields of data packet headers; using the obtained statistics to detect attacks with a priori specified values of errors of the 1 st and 2nd types; the choice of an adequate method of protection against DDoS-attacks, taking into account the results of its identification.

All proposed methods were tested experimentally. The number of octets and the number of packets were used as the initial parameters of the traffic received from the mirror port of a Web service as characteristics of its aggregation at different time intervals (0.01 s–1 s). Secondary informative features of traffic were calculated as the ratio of the number of octets to the number of packets. It is shown that for traffic aggregated in the 1s interval, causal transformation operator and median operator work well. At the intervals of 0.01 s–0.1 s, the evolution operator works better, based on the second-order correlation moments of the secondary informative traffic's features, and the correlation operator based on the third-order correlation moments of the secondary informative traffic's features. Apparently, this is due to the fact that the correlation moments of the second and third order of the secondary informational traffic's signs take into account not only the values of their amplitudes, but also the values of the derivatives of the first and second orders. A distinctive feature of the proposed methods is their applicability to the identification of both high-frequency and low-frequency attacks.

References

1. Mirkovic, J., Reiher, P.: A taxonomy of DDoS attack and DDoS defense mechanisms. ACM SIGCOMM Comput. Commun. Rev. **34**(2), 39–53 (2004). https://doi.org/10.1145/997150. 997156
2. Sindhu Arumugam, D.V., Sumathi, M.V.P.: Detection of botnet using fuzzy C-means clustering by analyzing the network traffic. Int. J. Sci. Eng. Res. **6**(4), 475–479 (2015)
3. Raghavan, S.V., Dawson, E. (eds.): An Investigation into the Detection and Mitigation of Denial of Service (DoS) Attacks: Critical Information Infrastructure Protection, 1st edn. Springer, New Delhi (2011). https://doi.org/10.1007/978-81-322-0277-6
4. Sanders, C.: Practical Packet Analysis: Using Wireshark to Solve Real-World Network Problems, 2nd edn. No Starch Press Inc, San Francisco (2011)
5. Bhattacharyya, D.K., Kalita, J.K.: DDoS Attacks. Evolution, Detection, Prevention, Reaction and Tolerance. Taylor and Francis, Boca Raton (2016)
6. Bonguet, A., Bellaiche, M.: A survey of denial-of-service and distributed denial of service attacks and defenses in cloud computing. Future Internet **9**(3), 43 (2017). https://doi.org/10. 3390/fi9030043

7. Liu, Y., Zhang, L., Guan, Y.: Sketch-based streaming PCA algorithm for network-wide traffic anomaly detection. In: 2010 IEEE 30th International Conference on Distributed Computing Systems, pp. 807–816. Department of Electrical and Computer Engineering Iowa State University, Ames (2010). https://doi.org/10.1109/icdcs.2010.45

8. Srihari, V., Anitha, R.: DDoS detection system using wavelet features and semi-supervised learning. In: Mauri, J.L., Thampi, S.M., Rawat, D.B., Jin, D. (eds.) SSCC 2014. CCIS, vol. 467, pp. 291–303. Springer, Heidelberg (2014). https://doi.org/10.1007/978-3-662-44966-0_28

9. Kind, A., Stoecklin, M.P., Dimitropoulos, X.: Histogram-based traffic anomaly detection. IEEE Trans. Netw. Serv. Manage. 6(2), 110–121 (2009). https://doi.org/10.1109/TNSM.2009.090604

10. Catania, C.A., Bromberg, F., Garino, C.G.: An autonomous labeling approach to support vector machines algorithms for network traffic anomaly detection. Expert Syst. Appl. 39(2), 1822–1829 (2012). https://doi.org/10.1016/j.eswa.2011.08.068

11. Ye, J., Cheng, X., Zhu, J., Feng, L., Song, L.: A DDoS attack detection method based on SVM in software defined network. Secur. Commun. Netw. 2018 (2018). Article no. 9804061. http://doi.org/10.1155/2018/9804061

12. Yuan, J., Mills, K.: Monitoring the macroscopic effect of DDoS flooding attacks. IEEE Trans. Dependable Secure Comput. 2(4), 324–335 (2005). https://doi.org/10.1109/TDSC.2005.50

13. Crotti, M., Dusi, M., Gringoli, F., Salgarelli, L.: Traffic classification through simple statistical fingerprinting. ACM SIGCOMM Comput. Commun. Rev. 37(1), 5–16 (2007). https://doi.org/10.1145/1198255.1198257

14. Reddy, V.S., Rao, K.D., Lakshmi, P.S.: Efficient detection of DDoS attacks by entropy variation. IOSR J. Comput. Eng. 7(1), 13–18 (2012). https://doi.org/10.9790/0661-0711318

15. Yu, S., Zhou, W., Jia, S., Guo, W., Xiang, Y., Tang, F.: Discriminating DDoS attacks from flash crowds using flow correlation coefficient. IEEE Trans. Parallel Distrib. Syst. 23(6), 1073–1080 (2012). https://doi.org/10.1109/TPDS.2011.262

16. Galayev, V.S., Krasnov, A.E., Nikol'skii, D.N., Repin, D.S.: The space of structural features for increasing the effectiveness of algorithms for detecting network attacks, based on the detection of deviations in traffic of extremely large volumes. Int. J. Appl. Eng. Res. 12(21), 10781–10790 (2017)

17. Ke, L., Wanlei, Z., Ping, L., Jianwen, L.: Distinguishing DDoS attacks from flash crowds using probability metrics. In: 2009 IEEE Third International Conference on Network and System Security, pp. 9–17. School of Engineering and Information Technology Deakin University, Shanghai (2009). https://doi.org/10.1109/nss.2009.35

18. Chawla, S., Sachdeva, M., Behal, S.: Discrimination of DDoS attacks and flash events using pearson's product moment correlation method. Int. J. Comput. Sci. Inf. Secur. 14(10), 382–389 (2016)

19. Malina, L., Dzurenda, P., Hajny, J.: Testing of DDoS protection solutions. In: Security and Protection of Information 2015, Brno, Czech, pp. 113–128 (2015)

20. Chen, J.H., Zhong, M., Chen, F.J., Zhang, A.D.: DDoS defense system with turing test and neural network. In: IEEE International Conference on Granular Computing, Hangzhou, China, pp. 38–43 (2012) https://doi.org/10.1109/grc.2012.6468680

21. Gupta, B.B., Joshi, R.C., Misra, M.: ANN based scheme to predict number of zombies in a DDoS attack. Int. J. Netw. Secur. 14(2), 61–70 (2012)

22. Saied, A., Overill, R.E., Radzik, T.: Detection of known and unknown DDoS attacks using Artificial Neural Networks. Neurocomputing 172(C), 385–393 (2016). https://doi.org/10.1016/j.neucom.2015.04.101

23. Baishya, R.C., Hoque, N., Bhattacharyya, D.K.: DDoS attack detection using unique source IP deviation. Int. J. Netw. Secur. 19(6), 929–939 (2017). https://doi.org/10.6633/IJNS.201711.19(6).09)

24. Thang, T.M., Nguyen, V.K.: Synflood spoof source DDoS attack defence based on packet ID anomaly detection - PIDAD. Information Science and Applications (ICISA) 2016. LNEE, vol. 376, pp. 739–751. Springer, Singapore (2016). https://doi.org/10.1007/978-981-10-0557-2_72

25. Chen, C.M., Lin, H.C.: Detecting botnet by anomalous traffic. J. Inf. Secur. Appl. **21**, 42–51 (2015). https://doi.org/10.1016/j.jisa.2014.05.002

26. Dietrich, C.J., Rossow, C., Pohlmann, N.: CoCoSpot: clustering and recognizing botnet command and control channels using traffic analysis. Comput. Netw. **57**(2), 475–486 (2013). https://doi.org/10.1016/j.comnet.2012.06.019

27. Terzi, D.S., Terzi, R., Sagiroglu, S.: Big data analytics for network anomaly detection from net flow data. In: 2017 IEEE International Conference of Computer Science and Engineering (UBMK), Antalya, Turkey, pp. 592–597 (2017) https://doi.org/10.1109/ubmk.2017.8093473

28. Lu, W., Rammidi, G., Ghorbani, A.A.: Clustering botnet communication traffic based on n-gram feature selection. Comput. Commun. **34**(3), 502–514 (2011). https://doi.org/10.1016/j.comcom.2010.04.007

29. Wang, K., Huang, C.-Y., Lin, S.-J., Lin, Y.-D.: A fuzzy pattern-based filtering algorithm for botnet detection. Comput. Netw. **55**(15), 3275–3286 (2011). https://doi.org/10.1016/j.comnet.2011.05.026

30. Krasnov, A.E., Nadezhdin, E.N., Galayev, V.S., Zykova, E.A., Nikol'skii, D.N., Repin, D.S.: DDoS attack detection based on network traffic phase coordinates analysis. Int. J. Appl. Eng. Res. **13**(8), 5647–5654 (2018)

31. Nolte, D.D.: The tangled tale of phase space. Phys. Today **63**(4), 31–33 (2010). https://doi.org/10.1063/1.3397041

32. Krasnov, A.E., Nadezhdin, E.N., Nikol'skii, D.N., Repin, D.S., Galayev, V.S.: Detecting DDoS attacks by analyzing the dynamics and interrelation of network traffic characteristics. Bull. Udmurt Univ. Math. Mech. Comput. Sci. **28**(3), 407–418 (2018). [in Russian]. https://doi.org/10.20537/vm180310

33. Demidovich, B.P.: Lectures on the Mathematical Theory of Stability. Nauka, Moscow (1967). [in Russian]

34. Sitenko, A.G.: Scattering Theory (Lecture Course), 2nd edn. Viwa shkola, Kiev (1975). [in Russian]

35. Peano, G.: Intégration par séries des équations différentielles linéaires. Math. Ann. **32**, 450–456 (1888). https://doi.org/10.1007/BF01443609

36. Dyson, F.J.: The *S* matrix in quantum electrodynamics. Phys. Rev. **75**(11), 1736–1755 (1949). https://doi.org/10.1103/PhysRev.75.1736

37. Wald, A.: Sequential Analysis. Wiley, New York (1947)

38. Krasnov, A.E., Nadezhdin, E.N., Nikol'ski, D.N., Repin, D.S.: Concept of the DDoS-attack detection database complex on the basis of intellectual analysis of network traffic. In: Kolesnikov, A.V. (ed.) Proceedings of the IV All-Russian Pospelovsky Conference with International Participation "Hybrid and Synergetic Intellectual Systems", pp. 349–354. Immanuel Kant Baltic Federal University, Kaliningrad (2018). [in Russian]. https://elibrary.ru/item.asp?id=34914854&

Source Code Authorship Identification Using Tokenization and Boosting Algorithms

Sergey Gorshkov[ID], Maxim Nered[ID], Eugene Ilyushin[✉][ID], Dmitry Namiot[ID], and Vladimir Sukhomlin[ID]

Lomonosov Moscow State University, Leninskie gory 1, 119991 Moscow, Russia
serggorsar@yandex.ru, freepvps@gmail.com,
eugene.ilyushin@gmail.com, dnamiot@gmail.com, sukhomlin@mail.ru

Abstract. Each programmer has his unique coding style. Identification source code authorship solves the problem of determining the most likely creator of the source code, in particular, for plagiarism and disputes about intellectual property violations, as well as to help in finding the creators of malware. Extraction a unique style helps to maintain the uniformity of code in repositories, considering the different influence of programmers. Currently, methods based on random forests and abstract syntax trees, short n-grams for structure preservation and Bayes classifier and others are proposed. We present a new model, called StyleIndex, based on tokenization and tools for analyzing the semantics of programming languages and context of tokens in the program text, and extraction unique author's style Index. The algorithm applies to various programming languages and shows very high classification accuracy. Moreover, our algorithm is able not only to correlate the source code and its creator, examples of programs which are available for training, but also to divide the program into categories by the alleged authors and have trained on other authors, thereby extraction the components define the style as a global concept, independent from specific authors. The main factors that determine the style are also identified.

Keywords: Computational stylometry · NLP · Tokenization · Boosting · Style index · Word embedding

1 Introduction

The coding style concept is intuitively clear to every developer. There are some "etiquette rules" that need to be followed for the code to be more readable and understandable, to provide it with comments, the names of the variables to reflect their essence, and so on. However, there is much more to programming style, and it is much more complex. In many studies, for example, in [1, 2] it was hypothesized that each programmer has his unique style of writing programs, which uniquely identifies him or her, like, for example, a fingerprint. Indeed, there are certain patterns and stylistic features that each programmer uses, without going beyond the guidelines for writing code in a specific programming language. Naturally, the problem of determining the authorship of programs arises, which may be due to many practical issues. Firstly, with increasing Internet access, the

© Springer Nature Switzerland AG 2020
V. Sukhomlin and E. Zubareva (Eds.): SITITO 2018, CCIS 1201, pp. 295–308, 2020.
https://doi.org/10.1007/978-3-030-46895-8_23

problem of software plagiarism will become increasingly important. Secondly, it is a matter of defining copyright. It can be either borrowing someone else's code or litigation related to the theft of an employee's code with no relevant labor agreement, as well as ghostwriting (when the "author" of the code in fact contracted/hired someone actually to write the code). In this case, it is necessary to select the author of the disputed code from a very limited number of people. Thirdly, this is an examination of malicious software, when it is necessary to determine the author with the highest probability among a wide range of candidates based on samples of software collected by analysts. Knowing which developer created the malicious code helps not only to find the culprit but also facilitates the process of neutralizing the virus since it is very likely that the approach used in this software is similar to the one used in the studied malware of this author or group of authors. Another interesting task of analyzing style is related to work of a team (group) of programmers on a project, when the style of writing code is set, for example, by general corporate rules or a specific set of rules (style guide) for a given group (project). Accordingly, all separate parts of the project (new releases, corrections, etc.) need to be analyzed for compliance with the general style (deviations from the general style need to be found). This task can be noted particularly since it says that style analysis can become a tool for everyday use for a group of developers in a corporate environment (in a formalized project).

The task of identifying programming style can be viewed as a subtask of NLP, in which some serious limitations are imposed on the text and the methods of computational stylometry can be applied. Currently, many methods have been developed that solve the problem of identifying the source code authorship, largely using machine learning methods. Section 2 is devoted to their description. In this paper, we propose a method based on the word2vec models [3] and using the TensorFlow library [4]. Description of the method with necessary explanations of the algorithms used will be given in Sect. 3. In Sect. 4, we describe the testing of this algorithm and present the results of the work. In Sect. 5, we discuss the results of the algorithm work and compare them with the other studies results. Section 6 will conclude on the work done and describe further research plans.

2   Related Work

Most of the research on the program authorship definition is based on machine learning methods, and the algorithm can be divided for our purpose into the extracting metrics stage and model training using the selected metrics. Types of metrics and their selection are described in detail in [5].

In [6], the SCAP method is used, based on the analysis of 1500 most frequent n-grams found in Java programs of each author and the intersection size of the most frequently encountered n-grams sets is considered as the similarity metric. This approach is quite reliable with a small number of authors (6–8), with 30 authors and the best selection of parameters, accuracy reaches 96.9%. Also, the idea of representing the code as n-grams at the byte level is used in [14].

In [7], style metrics were distinguished, as well as distribution metrics in the text. To filter the metrics, it was determined which values of the metrics are characteristic for each developer. For this, the Shannon entropy was calculated for each metric and each developer as well as for each metric and the entire code set, and their ratio was optimized. Next, the top 50 metrics were selected based on the most optimal metric selection criteria. The Bayes classifier and the Voting Feature Intervals classifier were used for prediction. At best, the classification accuracy reached 76%.

Layout metrics, style metrics, and structure metrics were used in [15]. With the help of the statistical control, 86% of the metrics were selected as having an influence on the coding style for estimating their contribution. In [16], metrics associated with various distributions were added, complementing the metric system used in [15]. This approach was also developed in [17]. A large number of papers use a combination of layout and lexical metrics, for example, in [18–20]. Such set of metrics can be considered classical for the task of attributing source code authorship at the early stages of development of this scientific field.

To determine the source code authorship, an abstract syntax tree is often used. For example, in [8], about 120000 syntactic (this group includes syntactic tree properties and use of keywords), lexical (various metrics related to distribution of various features in the program text) and layout metrics (characteristics associated with indents, the use of spaces and tab characters in the source code, empty lines, etc.) using AST, then about 1000 are selected for further training using the WEKA toolkit [9]. Random scaffolding is used as a machine learning model, the prediction accuracy of 250 authors is 98.04%. However, this study analyzes the problem-solving in the Google Code Jam competition, which is a bit detached from reality.

The AST analysis is also applied in [10]. A depth-first traversal of the tree is done, and vector representation for its leaves is generated. Next, each subtree is encoded using vector representation with the help of recurrent neural networks. For 70 authors, the best accuracy is 88.86% for Python programs and 85.00% for ten authors writing in C++.

In [11], feature metrics are retrieved at a lexical, layout, structural, and syntactic levels, and then backpropagation (BP) neural network based on particle swarm optimization (PSO) is used. For 40 Java-programmers, accuracy was 91.1%.

3 Proposed Method

In this study, we present the StyleIndex method. In it, we first distinguish lexical, layout, and style metrics by splitting the text into tokens, each of them belongs to a group. Next, we associate each token with a vector based on the context proximity of tokens. Then we compose a matrix of distances between the vectors and weigh the signs. As a result, each author will be associated with an index (or several indices) defining his style. All programs of each author are divided into groups by a certain number of files (regarding datasets characteristics described in Sect. 4.1, we chose 40), and an index is built for each group. Based on the indices proximity, we will evaluate which author is most likely to have written the program. The metrics by which we will evaluate the indices proximity are described in Sect. 3.4.

3.1 Tokenization of Program Source Code

To parse the text of the program, we will use the methods of lexical analysis. We will distinguish the following tokens categories, in each of them we will specify the tokens types:

1. Whitespaces - spaces, tabs, line feeds, carriage returns
2. Brackets, namely opening and closing curly, square and round brackets
3. Punctuation marks - dot, comma, semicolon, colon
4. Special characters - @, #, mathematical operations, logical operations. Separately, we single out multiple-meaning operations, for example, * in C++.
5. Keywords of the language. These are branch operators, loops, exception mechanisms, class options, macro notations (in C++), type conversions and smart pointers (C++), data type names or their notations (for languages with dynamic typing) and other words, often found in programs in the chosen language
6. Also, we select whether the entity is an integer or a floating-point number
7. Naming features - names written in capital letters, small letters, in CamelCase or snake_case, the use of underscores in the name, as well as very short words (one or two characters), short words (from 3 to 7 characters long) and long words (no less than eight characters in the title)
8. Long and short comments

These categories of metrics, except for the language keywords of the, do not depend on the selected programming language. Technically, this is implemented as several parsers through which the program text passes. Tokens that do not belong to any of the above categories are ignored. As a result of this step, the resulting source code of the program will be converted into a sequence of tokens, which can be further analyzed.

At the same time, we do not consider words frequently encountered in programs, which depend on the purpose of the program and are used strictly in this type of file. For example, constructions related to the use of Google Test [13], as well as words that are encountered frequently, but that are part of popular packages and are used directly in certain types of tasks.

3.2 word2vec Algorithm

word2vec is an algorithm developed by a group of Google researchers in 2013, based on distributive semantics and the vector representation of words. As we can guess from the name, each word will be associated with a certain vector. Besides, the tokens occurring next to the same tokens (and therefore, having a similar meaning) will have close coordinates in the vector representation. There are two basic learning algorithms in word2vec - CBOW (Continuous Bag of Words) and Skip-gram. The first model predicts the current word based on its surrounding context, and the second uses the current word to predict the words surrounding it. Both methods use artificial neural networks as classification algorithms. In our StyleIndex method, we apply the CBOW algorithm to the sequence of tokens obtained in the first step and build a word2vec model with the following parameters: vector length 30, context size (the window in question) is 50. We find it convenient to use this model to solve the problem of identifying the source code author since it formally describes the mutual arrangement of tokens, which is one of the programming style characteristics. So, at this step, we got a set of numerical vectors, which can be used to compile further the index of the author, which will be his "fingerprint". In this article, we will use the implementation of this algorithm as part of a package for thematic modeling gensim for the Python language.

3.3 Compiling the Author's Style Index

Then, for each set of 40 (or fewer) files, a distance matrix is constructed between all pairs of vectors using the Euclidean distance. For the pairs of objects that did not participate in the training set, the distance is defined as 0, for pairs, in which exactly one object did not participate, the distance was defined as infinity. Then, on the basis of distances pairs for the objects of the training set, the dispersion is calculated, which is then used when converting the distance into the metric of object similarity. Each row of the distance matrix is translated into a vector-row of the similarity matrix by the following formula:

$$a[i] = softmax\left(-\frac{v^2}{\sigma^2}\right), \tag{1}$$

where σ is distances dispersion, and the function SoftMax is defined as follows:

$$softmax = \frac{e^{z_i}}{\sum_{k=1}^{K} e^{z_k}}. \tag{2}$$

This is the logistical function generalization to a set of vectors. The resulting matrix is called the ordinary index. At this stage, we must enter the distance metric between the two indices, but this is impossible until the importance of the various components of the given index is determined (or, in other words, the weights of its components are not calculated).

3.4 Description of Finding Weights and Theoretical Aspects of Model Training

We define the weights matrix of the index W components in the space of real numbers. To find it, it is necessary to apply an optimization algorithm to a certain loss function loss, which would contain weighted indices (ordinary indices multiplied by a matrix of component weights, i.e., $I \circ W$), and would also reflect whether the indices are code indices of one author. Here, the Hadamard product was used to multiply the matrices:

$$(A \circ B)_{i,j} = (A)_{i,j} \cdot (B)_{i,j} \tag{3}$$

We use it here since to find the weighed components in each matrix element, it is necessary to multiply the weight of the component by its actual weight, obtained from the matrix W.

We describe some nontrivial formulas and introduce the concepts that are necessary to derive the loss function:

$$\|X\|_1 = \sum_{i,j} |X_{i,j}| \qquad (4)$$

L_1-norm (Manhattan distance) - will be used to find the norm of the weighted indices difference. This norm is used for convenience in calculating the gradient.

$$\sigma(x) = \frac{1}{1 + e^{-x}} \qquad (5)$$

Logistical sigmoid - will be used to translate the shifted norm into a real number in the range from 0 to 1.

For two indices, we introduce the function of predicting the match of authors by their indices:

$$Predict(I_1, I_2) = 1 - \sigma(\|(I_1 - I_2) \circ W_1\| + bias), \qquad (6)$$

Where *bias* is an error resulting from an erroneous assumption in the learning algorithm. As a result of a large bias, the algorithm may be undertrained, which cannot be allowed. Specifically, in the task in question, it will be a threshold value for the function. The target loss function will be as follows:

$$loss(W, bias) = \sum_{i,j} \left(Predict(I_1, I_2) - a_{i,j}\right)^2, \qquad (7)$$

where $a_{i,j} = 1$, if I_1, I_2 - are single author indices, else $a_{i,j} = 0$.

We define as a goal for the optimization algorithm minimization of the loss function derived above.

For training the model, we can use an arbitrary optimization algorithm. In our work, we use the AdamOptimizer algorithm from the library for machine learning TensorFlow [12].

4   Testing StyleIndex Model and Evaluating Algorithm Accuracy

This section presents the experimental results of the study. Testing was conducted for programs in Java, C++, and JavaScript. First, the principles of dataset formation and their characteristics are described. The following are specific accuracy values when testing in two different ways and the most significant types of tokens, which largely determine the development style in a particular language. The training was performed on an NVIDIA Tesla P100 GPU with 16 GB GDDR with the performance of 9.3 teraflops with a learning rate of 0.1 and 10,000 iterations.

4.1 Dataset Creation

To determine the source code authorship, it is very important to choose a representative sample that can reveal the style of writing the code and at the same time will not be artificially created. For example, there is an approach using problem solutions from international competitions in sports programming. However, in our opinion, this situation is detached from real life, since it is often necessary to determine authorship by programs that have completely different subjects and solve various practical problems. Also, a solution of one problem of Olympiad programming is often given in one file, which can exclude from consideration signs related to the work of a project that consists of several files and directories. As a result, it was decided to take the open source repositories from GitHub (accessible at https://github.com). Only repositories written by one author were selected (however, it is impossible to guarantee that some parts of the code were not written by someone else, which may cause some incoherent data). Further, repositories containing too few training files were discarded. The uses of external libraries, plug-ins that are in the public domain and were not written by the author of the repository in question were removed from these repositories. As a result, 40 repositories were selected for each programming language. To better compare the results of the programs in the Java language, we used the repository used in [11]; for C++ and JavaScript, we compiled a dataset ourselves, based on the same considerations. In the set of programs in C++, the number of files ranged from 10 to 366, in JavaScript - from 20 to 360, in Java - from 11 to 712. Histograms of the number of files distribution for each author are shown in Fig. 1, 2 and 3 for C++, JavaScript, Java, respectively.

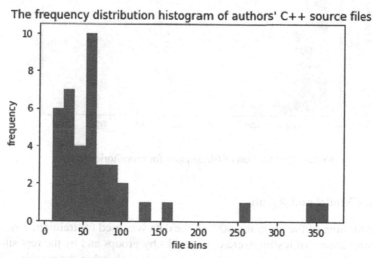

Fig. 1. Distribution of file amount for repositories in C++.

The frequency distribution histogram of authors' JavaScript source files

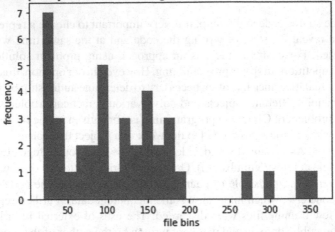

Fig. 2. Distribution of file amount for repositories in JavaScript.

The frequency distribution histogram of authors' Java source files

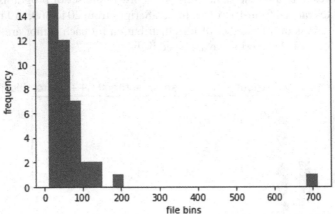

Fig. 3. Distribution of file amount for repositories in Java.

4.2 Testing Model and Results

During the running of the program, 60% of the data was used for training, 40% as a test sample. Two variants of testing were conducted - by groups and by the repository. The first one is a classic for research on the source code authorship determining: for each author we select a certain percentage of files (in our case 60%) in which the model is trained, and the remaining files of each author fall into the test sample. The second one is as follows: for the training sample, a certain percentage of authors are selected (in our case, also 60%), and training takes place on all the files written by them, and all other developers' files fall into the test sample. That is, predicting the author the program breaks the test sample into several sets, the programs in each of those are written by one developer, and the programs in different sets by different developers. This means that it is not only the style of certain authors that is distinguished but also style as an indicator inherent to all authors and extrapolated to all developers based on the style of a very limited number of developers from the training sample. Like in other papers, as accuracy metric we considered accuracy:

$$accuracy = \frac{TP + TN}{TP + TN + FP + FN}, \tag{8}$$

where TP = true positive, FP = false positive, TN = true negative, FN = false negative. During the algorithm running, the dispersion was insignificant (less than 0.01%).

Cross-validation was used in the testing. In Table 1, we present the average values for accuracy and program runtime for repositories written in Java, C++, and JavaScript when testing by groups. In Table 2, we give corresponding figures when testing the algorithm by the repository.

Table 1. Results of the algorithm when testing by a group.

Language	Accuracy	Time
C++	97.25%	155.84
JavaScript	97.45%	158.32
Java	98.89%	124.66

Table 2. Results of the algorithm when testing by the repository.

Language	Accuracy	Time
C++	94.20%	153.91
JavaScript	94.16%	159.70
Java	95.18%	133.63

For testing by repositories, being the best at distinguishing characteristics that determine the style of writing code, we give a list of the top 15 features that have the greatest contribution to the prediction for Java, C++ and JavaScript languages (Table 3).

The main contribution is made by features, the use of which is the author's prerogative. For example, use of; in JavaScript characterizes the author. In fact, a feature set from Table 3 is synthesized style.

We allot the main purposes of the characteristics groups that have a significant contribution to the programming style. The results are listed in Table 4 in the following format: the name of some characteristics groups and the highest place of the corresponding type of tokens for each programming language.

Table 3. Top 15 most significant characteristics for C++, JavaScript, Java languages.

	C++	JavaScript	Java
1	Word longer than seven letters, written in uppercase	Use of keyword indexOf	Use of keyword package
2	Use of keyword auto	Use of;	Lowercase word starting with _
3	Use of keyword iterator	Use of keyword private	Use of keyword assert
4	Use of *	Use of keyword while	Use of keyword interface
5	Use of keyword namespace	Use of @	Uppercase word
6	Use of keyword nullptr	Use of &, |, ^, !	A word that is a number
7	Use of @	Use of keyword interface	Use of keyword public
8	Use of keyword static	Use of keyword class	Use of;
9	Use of keyword protected	Uppercase word	Word not longer than two letters
10	Use of keyword public	Use of keyword public	Variable type name
11	Use of keyword typedef	Use of keyword for	The floating point number designation
12	Use of keyword while	Word longer than seven letters, written in lowercase	Use of keyword import
13	Use of keyword void	Use of keyword extends	Use of $+, -, *, /, \%$
14	Use of keyword export	Use of keyword static	Use of @
15	Use of keywords ifdef, ifndef, endif	The floating-point number designation	Word not longer than seven letters

5 Discussion

5.1 The Correctness of Algorithm Use

Determining the source code authorship is a difficult task not only regarding the statement, but also regarding data for testing. It is quite difficult to find a repository with code written entirely by one person (or extract the code of a single developer from a repository) since a developer often uses someone else's code without corresponding remarks. At the same time, we should not forget about the fact of developer skills evolution that influences the style of writing code. With the growth of programmer's level from beginner to expert, the quality of the code written by him will grow, including the programming style. He may have his practices, patterns, which the author will use for his convenience starting from a certain point in time. This progress is quite difficult to track, therefore, within one developer's works, over time, the style may differ slightly, which will create additional noise and some difficulties in identifying the developer StyleIndex. However, according to the model construction, there should be no retraining as well as

Table 4. Impact degree of some groups of factors on coding style.

Groups of factors	C++	JavaScript	Java
Phrases having an obvious alternative in the language syntax	2	1	3
Characteristics of variable naming	1	9	2
Variable length	1	12	9
Characteristics related to multi-modular projects	5	29	1
Constructs related to work with class type	10	3	7
Use of symbols of arithmetic and binary operations, having various uses besides directly arithmetic and logical	4	6	13

no undertraining, which is indirectly confirmed by the logical nature of selecting the most significant features that identify the author's style.

For example, in the Java language, among the most popular types of tokens are language keywords, such as package, import, which explicitly depend on breaking the code into various files and directories, as well as assert, which is one of the alternatives for working with exceptions within the language syntax. Some recommendations for naming are documented in coding standards (for example, https://google.github.io/styleguide/javaguide.html) and implemented in various IDEs (for example, IntelliJ IDEA from JetBrains), therefore naming features are to a significant extent, will of a programmer and determine his style.

In C++, factors such as the pointer dereference (in many cases it has alternatives), use of keywords auto (can often be replaced by iterators), export and namespace (which depend on splitting the project into several files), spelling the word in capital letters (in some coding standards, constants are called like that), etc. have a big influence.

In JavaScript, such keywords as indexOf, keywords related to work with classes, use of for/while loops, and some naming features of variables and functions make a great contribution. Expectedly a very large contribution is made by the use of a semicolon, since putting it in some cases is not at all necessary and this is a programmer's prerogative.

Summarizing these differences, it can be noted that the keywords of the language responsible for the connection between project files and work with scopes, elements of syntactic sugar (as well as elements of program code that can be implemented in several ways), and naming features which are associated with coding standards adopted in some places have a significant impact on the programmer's style.

5.2 Comparing Research Results with Results of Other Works

In Table 5, we present the comparison results of the algorithms presented in the articles described in Sect. 2. Within this comparison, we choose the best result in the presented articles for accuracy for any language. The results of this study are presented with the note "This work" with a breakdown by programming languages. For the results of this work, we still consider the average accuracy value.

Table 5. Comparison results of the algorithms.

Related work	# of Programmers	Results
Ding, Samadzadeh [15]	46	67.2%
Lange, Mancoridis [16]	20	75.0%
Kothari et al. [7]	12	76.0%
Yang et al. [11]	40	91.1%
Alsulami et al. [10]	25	96.0%
Frantzeskou et al. [6]	30	96.9%
Caliskan-Islam et al. [8]	250	98.0%
This work, C++	40	97.2%
This work, JavaScript	40	97.4%
This work, Java	40	98.9%

6   Conclusion and Plans for Further Research

This article introduced the StyleIndex algorithm for identifying source code authorship. Programs were reviewed in the C++, JavaScript, Java languages, the algorithm was tested on them, and the most significant features were affecting the coding style were shown. The test results were as follows: 97.25% for C++, 97.45% for JavaScript, 98.89% for Java.

The most important groups of features are language keywords, which are responsible for the connection between project files and work with scopes, use of syntactic sugar elements, as well as naming features. Accuracy was higher than in most of the works on this topic.

The results of the repository testing confirmed that each programmer has his style, and the style is a combination of some characteristics that are not dependent on the author. Within the model testing, the results were as follows: 94.20% for C++, 94.16% for JavaScript, 95.18% for Java.

In the future, it is planned to increase the number of languages, and try to identify more global groups of tokens and mark out factors that will make it possible to move beyond language dependence. Particular attention should also be paid to language constructs that are similar in use or interchangeable or are syntactic sugar. There are plans to allocate features depending on the programming paradigm used. It is also planned to test this algorithm not only for solving the problem of identifying the authorship of the source code but also for other NLP tasks. Also, it is planned to investigate the correctness of the algorithms use depending on the source data and programming languages.

References

1. Holmes, D.I.: Stylometry. Encyclopedia of Statistical Sciences. Wiley, Hoboken (2006)
2. Daelemans, W.: Explanation in computational stylometry. In: Gelbukh, A. (ed.) CICLing 2013. LNCS, vol. 7817, pp. 451–462. Springer, Heidelberg (2013). https://doi.org/10.1007/978-3-642-37256-8_37
3. word2vec introduction. https://code.google.com/archive/p/word2vec/
4. TensorFlow. https://www.tensorflow.org
5. Gorshkov, S., Nered, M., Ilyushin, E., Namiot, D.: Using machine learning methods to establish program authorship. Int. J. Open Inf. Technol. 7(1), 115–119 (2019). https://elibrary.ru/item.asp?id=36694876
6. Frantzeskou, G., Stamatatos, E., Gritzalis, S., Katsikas, S.: Effective identification of source code authors using byte-level information. In: Proceedings of the 28th International Conference on Software (ICSE 2006), pp. 893–896. ACM, New York (2006). https://doi.org/10.1145/1134285.1134445
7. Kothari, J., Shevertalov, M., Stehle, E., Mancoridis, S.: A probabilistic approach to source code authorship identification. In: Fourth International Conference on Information Technology (ITNG 2007), Las Vegas, NV, pp. 243–248 (2007). https://doi.org/10.1109/itng.2007.17
8. Caliskan-Islam, A., et al.: De-anonymizing programmers via code stylometry. In: Jung, J. (ed.) Proceedings of the 24th USENIX Conference on Security Symposium (SEC 2015), pp. 255–270. USENIX Association, Berkeley (2015)
9. Quinlan, J.: Induction of decision trees. Mach. Learn. 1(1), 81–106 (1986). https://doi.org/10.1007/BF00116251
10. Alsulami, B., Dauber, E., Harang, R., Mancoridis, S., Greenstadt, R.: Source code authorship attribution using long short-term memory based networks. In: Foley, S.N., Gollmann, D., Snekkenes, E. (eds.) ESORICS 2017. LNCS, vol. 10492, pp. 65–82. Springer, Cham (2017). https://doi.org/10.1007/978-3-319-66402-6_6
11. Yang, X., Xu, G., Li, Q., Guo, Y., Zhang, M.: Authorship attribution of source code by using back propagation neural network based on particle swarm optimization. PLoS ONE 12(11), e0187204 (2017). https://doi.org/10.1371/journal.pone.0187204
12. AdamOptimizer explanation. https://www.tensorflow.org/api_docs/python/tf/train/AdamOptimizer
13. Google Test. https://github.com/google/googletest
14. Burrows, S., Tahaghoghi, S.: Source code authorship attribution using n-grams. In: Proceedings of the 12th Australasian Document Computing Symposium, pp. 32–39 (2007)
15. Ding, H., Samadzadeh, M.: Extraction of Java program fingerprints for software authorship identification. J. Syst. Softw. 72(1), 49–57 (2004). https://doi.org/10.1016/S0164-1212(03)00049-9
16. Lange, R.C., Mancoridis, S.: Using code metric histograms and genetic algorithms to perform author identification for software forensics. In: Proceedings of the 9th Annual Conference on Genetic and Evolutionary Computation (GECCO 2007), pp. 2082–2089. ACM, New York (2007). https://doi.org/10.1145/1276958.1277364
17. Burrows, S., Uitdenbogerd, A.L., Turpin, A.: Comparing techniques for authorship attribution of source code. Softw. Pract. Exp. 44(1), 1–32 (2014). https://doi.org/10.1002/spe.2146
18. Elenbogen, B.S., Seliya, N.: Detecting outsourced student programming assignments. J. Comput. Sci. Coll. 23(3), 50–57 (2008)

19. Krsul, I., Spafford, E.H.: Authorship analysis: identifying the author of a program. Comput. Secur. **16**(3), 233–257 (1997). https://doi.org/10.1016/S0167-4048(97)00005-9
20. Macdonell, S.G., Gray, A.R., MacLennan, G., Sallis, P.J.: Software forensics for discriminating between program authors using case-based reasoning, feedforward neural networks and multiple discriminant analysis. In: ICONIP 1999, ANZIIS 1999 & ANNES 1999 & ACNN 1999, 6th International Conference on Neural Information Processing, Proceedings (Cat. No. 99EX378), Perth, WA, Australia, vol. 1, pp. 66–71 (1999). https://doi.org/10.1109/iconip. 1999.843963

Methodology of Formation of Unite Geo-Informational Space in the Region

Sergey Kramarov[1]([⊠]) [iD] and Vladimir Khramov[2] [iD]

[1] Surgut State University, Lenin Avenue 1, 628412 Surgut, KMAO-Yugra, Russia
maoovo@yandex.ru
[2] Southern University (IMBL), M. Nagibin Avenue 33a/47, 344068 Rostov-on-Don, Russia

Abstract. The paper considers and studies the methods of a complex approach to the formation of unite geo-informational space of territories on the basis of a digital plan-scheme as an elementary semantic object of the image of the underlying surface, the choice of approaches to the use for this purpose of intellectual analysis of fuzzy data stored in virtual data warehouses of target objects. The directions of theoretical research on the construction, structure, methods and algorithms of formation and functioning of a unite geo-informational space (further - UGIS) as a system of systems on the principles of geo-interoperability are specified.

Keywords: Knowledge base · Digital plan diagram · Information layer · Complex systems · System analysis · Soft models and methods · Geoinformation space · Geo-interoperability

1 Introduction

Currently, both theoretical and applied issues of geo-informational space and geo-interoperability have been developed at the level of simple (linear) interaction of various information systems [1–5] (for example, the technical specification of interoperability is already the basic informational basis for the construction of high-speed Railways in Europe). However, to describe the complex, dynamically developing other systems is necessary more accurate and effective way of describing the base, which foundation may be the theory of fuzzy sets and other applications fuzzy mathematics. Over the past 5 years, within the framework of the SMART project, the complex of research work, directed to the study of the properties of geo-informational objects [7–9] was carried out, where the capabilities and quality of information sources were evaluated to improve the accuracy and reliability of data on complex information systems for a wide range of applications (issues of agricultural land monitoring, GLONAS and GPS systems, development of transport corridors, etc.). Methods of their practical realization are developed [10–13]. The basis of the ideology of the project initiated the concept of cognitive space that implements the methodology of multidimensional soft open complex systems involves the operational, self-generating and self-regulatory(ting) of system of systems (further - SoS) [1, 14–17], in which the communicative experience of decision makers is being formed, developed and transformed. The concept of cognitive space is applied

V. Sukhomlin and E. Zubareva (Eds.): SITITO 2018, CCIS 1201, pp. 309–316, 2020.
https://doi.org/10.1007/978-3-030-46895-8_24

in order to ensure cognitive interoperability in the informational environment. The concept of cognitive information space allows us to take into account the multifactorial interaction of information layers, in particular, with fuzzy (and/or not fully consistent) systems of terms or lack of definitions of key (critical) concepts. In such interactions, the concept of cognitive interoperability (the ability to interact associated with situational response) becomes important. Intelligent systems [2–5] are interoperable in this sense, if intelligent agents (a person, an object of the intelligent system) in two different systems perceive consistent images of the presented information. This concept was introduced by Buddenberg in 2006. It complements the concept of cognitive space with the aspect of situational response and emphasizes the ability of agents to find consistent images of the information they operate in the course of their activities.

2   Problem State

The purpose of the research carried out by the authors is the development of theoretical foundations of construction, structure and algorithms of functioning of the system of systems of UGIS [7, 9, 18–20, 22] using an open set of information sources of different physical nature.

The objectives of these studies are following:

1. Development of methods, way and algorithms for the formation and development of an open information system of UGIS for the rapid production of problem-oriented digital plan-schemes (further - DPS) in the interests of various sectors of the economy, business, social and cultural development of the territories.
2. Selection, development and validation of criteria and estimates the information content available to measure and study the properties of geo-informational objects, assessment of the sources and tools of obtaining of the original data.
3. Formation of an open multidimensional model of UGIS for stationary and dynamic options as a complex information system systems.
4. Carrying of computer and natural modeling (based on satellite information), comparison of results, assessment of model adequacy and determination of its development directions.

The fundamentally new scheme of the integral multidimensional information system of UGIS systems is developed, the components of which one have interoperable properties that improve the accuracy and reliability of the assessment of the current state and dynamics of development of territories. It will, in turn, automatically generate DPS [9–12, 19] territories focused on specific applications and/or users (legal entities and individuals).

To ensure the necessary accuracy and reliability of the DPS it is planned to develop analytical models of connectivity of existing and developing subsystems included in UGIS, supported by a distributed knowledge base and associated with the global project "Digital Earth".

To achieve the announced objectives and tasks re-designed and refined:

1. The concept of construction and structure of the new system of information systems "Unite geo-informational space";
2. Heuristic approaches to the formation of a new methodology for the construction and self-organization of a Unite geo-informational space, based on the use of space monitoring tools, principles of geo-interoperability and fuzzy logic research;
3. New architectural solutions in specialized knowledge bases for generation of digital plan schemes of territories formed with the use of satellite navigation systems;
4. Methods of fuzzy triangulation and new ways of contour coding of informational objects in the system of technical vision in combination with neural network methods and means of recognition of images of objects, including the use of non-traditional rasters;
5. Elements of a universal mathematical apparatus for identifying and describing invariant characteristics of geoinformation space, fuzzy triangulation and interoperability;
6. Nonlinear fuzzy model of a complex information system of systems, invariant to the features of the properties and structure of individual measurements in multidimensional UGIS.

The methods of lexico-semantic modeling of cognitive structures of knowledge, which allow to take into account the peculiarities of the geoinformation environment, were identified among the studied methods. The structure of intellectual analysis proposed in the study is based on hybrid forms of knowledge representation: a combination of hierarchical classification with the possibility of establishing and adaptive modification of several types of thesaurus - semantic relations [23]. Methods and approaches of fuzzy lexical-semantic modeling, which are currently widely used in various subject areas, are used in the design of informational support architecture of geo-informational space (further - GISp), formation of the structure of intellectual analysis of geodata in geo-informational system (GIS) and integration of linguistic support of thesaurus type in UGIS. This approach, which actively uses the concepts of "cognitive geospace" and "cognitive geointerability", is designed to coordinate the work of experts from different subject areas, in informational system in automatic/semi-automatic mode; study of methods and approaches of computer linguistics and their adaptive applications to create a new IT generation of geoinformation orientation.

Hypotheses and axioms by which the system is represented by the corresponding model, as a rule, do not take into account a number of their properties, which leads to uncertainty in the description of the control object. Here it is appropriate to recall the principle of incompatibility L. Zadeh: "As the complexity of the system increases, our ability to formulate precise, meaningful statements about its behavior decreases to a certain threshold beyond which one accuracy and meaning become mutually exclusive [5]." The results of the analysis of scientific and technical sources to determine the existing theoretical base and the formation of the research thesaurus allowed to assess the conditions of invariance in the model of GISp as a multidimensional fuzzy system (structure, architecture, geophysical, socio-economic and other aspects) to theoretically justify this choice. The classification of the fuzziness that characterize the particular district of the South Federal region.

In the course of the primary rapid analysis of available data and information links of regional properties by means of data mining, a set of methods for detecting previously unknown, non-trivial, practically useful and accessible interpretations of knowledge necessary for decision-making in the interests of economic and social development of territories in the existing data is highlighted.

To implement the concept of construction and structure of a unite geo-informational space, methods for detecting interoperability of territory properties based on semantic triangulation of information sources of different physical nature were developed. The developed multidimensional nonlinear model of UGIS was used, which is invariant to the features of the structures of individual measurements, the type of their stochastic characteristics, the complex of non-factors and the type of fuzziness; mathematical modeling of semantic interoperability and triangulation of many available sources of information.

The synthesis of analytical models for object-oriented cross-sections of UGIS in different coordinate systems (CS) allowed with the required accuracy to identify the required in the study of the objects or scenes on the digital electronic map.

The development and simulation modelling of procedures for semantic triangulation of the properties of informational objects in UGIS, provided a stable assessment of all the parameters of the state and development of UGIS as a System of Systems at long intervals of time. The development of a method for dynamic assessment of the location and condition of the informational object of UGIS on triangular and hexagonal rasters using Delaunay triangulation, built on the information of electronic maps of various physical fields and the use of satellite and/or full-scale measurements, allowed to implement numerical simulation of semantic triangulation procedures based on fuzzy analog-controllers of minimum dimension. The choice and justification of methods and algorithms for coordination subsystems UGIS provided adequate synthesis and simulation of nonlinear dynamic algorithm aggregation characteristics of measurements of informational objects UGIS, including satellite information. The developed working structure of UGIS with the use of both full-scale measurements and satellite monitoring systems with spatially distributed reception of satellite data of different resolutions and frequency zones, allowed to form a working mechanism for the development of the architecture of the knowledge base of UGIS in the process of changes in the source data and their dynamics.

The formation of the knowledge base of UGIS, including its constantly updated mathematical image, invariant and time (dynamic) components, known and revealed patterns and interdependence of the properties of this space, including the issues of socio-economic development of the territories ensures their relevance in the foreseeable future.

The formation of a single information space of agricultural areas includes the construction of a complex of technical and software tools for data processing, providing automated formation and replenishment of a special knowledge base for the recognition of images of these areas and their analysis. The analysis is carried out in the form of a search - oriented by various criteria ordered set of information arrays-blocks of tasks implemented in the form of a virtual data warehouse. Each of these blocks is a structured description of the task of forming a specific type of DPS using a hierarchical classification of analysis, processing and image recognition tasks. he blocks also include a thesaurus for the analysis, processing and recognition of images, as well as thematic mapping of agricultural objects. The procedure for the formation of DPS facilities for agricultural purposes can be represented by diagrams of the algorithms and main procedures of implementation and includes 8 stages [12, 13]. The method of creation of basic DPS is based on the thematic processing of space survey data, the direct preparation of the GIS-project and geocoding in the coordinate system PZ 90.02, which is the basis of the GLONASS satellite navigation system, that allows the use of basic GPS for integration into satellite navigation maps, as well as for the collection of coordinate data. The use of GIS-design on the basis of basic DPS allows to create thematic maps of any content (land reclamation, fertility, crop rotation, agrometeorology, purpose, processing, etc.) as output forms. Construction of thematic CPS of agricultural land allows to have a layer-by-layer organization: each information layer contains data of the same type (by object type: point, line, polygon, etc.). Since data of different types and formats can be used as a layer, this property assumes the use of virtual data storage and provides the widest possibilities of analysis and processing of different types of data. The automated system of processing of initial information for formation of DPS of various level, their storage and delivery to the user in the form of the corresponding report, is carried out in the form of knowledge base.

The knowledge base [7, 9, 20] can be characterized by the fact that:

- the central control unit of data processing and transmission contains interconnected search and control subsystems;
- modules included in the complex subsystem of organized storage and replenishment of knowledge, made in the form of data warehouse;
- the module, which is part of the subsystem of knowledge replenishment includes a device for obtaining scientifically based integral features of images invariant to image transformations such as shift and rotation [15, 16].

The criteria and evaluations of the information content available to study the properties of geographic information objects are being selected and justified, sources and tools for obtaining the original data are being selected. In this case, the issues of informativeness are solved on the basis of a fuzzy approach. In particular, in a number of applied tasks of digital processing of monitoring information describing the physical object (land use) or its components there is a need to carry out functional scaling [17, 18] and aggregation of data obtained from several observers (sensors), characterized by limited clarity and, consequently, reliability.

3 The Solution of Problem

Let us consider a way of aggregating indicators and criteria for such data on the example of a system of technical vision, but without restrictions on the generality of the approach.

Let $b_{i,j}^{k}$ - digital information about the satellite image element with coordinates (i, j), $i = \overline{1, n}$ and $j = \overline{1, m}$, received from source with number $k = \overline{1, l}$. In the special case, if the k-th source corresponds to the wavelength λ_k of probe signal, can be formed normalized image in the form of a matrix $\left\| I_{ij}^{\lambda_k} \right\|$, where

$$I_{I_{uo}}^{\lambda_k} = \frac{b_{ij}^{k} - b_{\min}^{\lambda_k}}{b_{\max}^{\lambda_k} - b_{\min}^{\lambda_k}} \tag{1}$$

As a standard prepared in advance, the most probable value of the image element obtained at the wavelength is taken λ_k: $I_3^{\lambda_k}$. Turning to the problem image of the object under study, we will form a matrix $\left\| \mu_{ij}^{\lambda_k} \right\|$, the elements of which are calculated as the values of the membership function formed by the experts [4]. In relation to the images of objects in the visible part of the electromagnetic wave spectrum, several analytical expressions can be used to describe the membership functions (further - MF) [5, 21]. The following expression has relative universality:

$$\mu_{ij}^{\lambda_k} = \exp\left\langle -\alpha \left| I_{ij}^{\lambda_k} - I_3^{\lambda_k} \right|^\beta \right\rangle \tag{2}$$

where α and β are the membership function parameters set by the experts.

Since MF is continuous on $I_{ij}^{\lambda_k} \in (0, \infty)$, then to evaluate the image element by means of majority transformations, replace the disjunction and conjunction operations with the operations of selecting the maximum and minimum values of the membership function, respectively.

By theorem [18]: Let $\{\mu_A^i\}$, $i = \overline{1, 2k+1}$. Then the logical sample m from $2k+1$ corresponds to the m-th element in the ordered variation series $\mu^1 \le \mu^2 \le \ldots \le \mu^m \le \ldots \le \mu^{2k+1}$.

An important special case is the majority sample $k+1$ from $2k+1$, implemented through the function of the median:

$$\overset{\Lambda}{\mu} = med\left\langle \mu^1, \mu^2, \ldots, \mu^{2k+1} \right\rangle = med\left\langle \mu_1, \mu_2, \ldots, \mu_{k+1}, \ldots, \mu_{2k+1} \right\rangle = \mu_{k+1} \tag{3}$$

Recent estimate $\overset{\Lambda}{\mu}$ provides a minimum of the sum of absolute deviations:

$$\sum_{i=1}^{2k+1} \left| \overset{\Lambda}{\mu} - \mu^i \right| = \min. \tag{4}$$

The described method of aggregation, in addition to improving the image quality in vision systems, provides increased reliability in decision-making systems with fuzzy and incomplete source data.

4 Conclusion

Using the tools developed earlier by the authors of the project to analyze the characteristics of macroscopic properties of solids on the basis of microstructural analysis data, as well as methods for creating UGIS using earth surface monitoring data (aerospace data), a complex open information multidimensional connectivity model of UGIS is developed for both stationary and dynamic options. The model developed in the project is based on the basic correlation scheme of analysis of characteristics of complex objects of research. The order parameters of this model are determined and justified. Thus, conducted research, including computer and full-scale modelling (based on satellite information), allowed to compare the results, assess the adequacy of stochastic and fuzzy models and determine the direction of their development. The assessment of the applicability of the research results was made in the interests of geodesy, geology, forestry, agriculture, ecology, transport, etc.

References

1. Kramarov, S., Temkin, I., Khramov, V.: The principles of formation of united geo-informational space based on fuzzy triangulation. Procedia Comput. Sci. **120**, 835–843 (2017). https://doi.org/10.1016/j.procs.2017.11.315
2. Gurevich, L.: Cognitive Space of Metacommunication. ISLU, Irkutsk (2009). (in Russian)
3. Dulin, S., Rosenberg, I.: About development of methodological bases and concepts of geoin-formatics. Syst. Means Inform. **16**(3), 201–256 (2006). (in Russian). https://elibrary.ru/item.asp?id=13060522. Accessed 21 Nov 2018
4. Dulin, S.K., Dulina, N.G., Kozhunova, O.S.: Cognitive interoperability of expert activity and its application in geoinformatics. In: Proceedings of the 13th National Conference on Artificial Intelligence with International Participation (KII-2012), vol. 1, pp. 351–357. Publishing House of BSTU. V.G. Shukhov, Belgorod (2012). (in Russian)
5. Zadeh, L.A.: Outline of a new approach to the analysis of complex systems and decision processes. IEEE Transactions on Systems, Man, and Cybernetics **SMC-3**(1), 28–44 (1973). https://doi.org/10.1109/tsmc.1973.5408575
6. Kramarov, S., Mityasova, O., Khramov, V.: Analysis of prospects of application of the concept of geoinformation space on the basis of fuzzy methods and algorithms of satellite monitoring data processing. In: Proceedings of the XV all-Russian Open Conference "Modern problems of remote sensing of the Earth from space", pp. 97. IKI RAS, Moscow (2017). (in Russian). https://elibrary.ru/item.asp?id=32863380. Accessed 21 Nov 2018
7. Kramarov, S., Khramov, V., Nebaba, A., Mityasova, O., Pruss, M., Romanchenko, V.: Technologies satellite monitoring for generating digital plan schemes of environmental status of territories. Technol. Technosp. Saf. **1**(71), 255–258 (2017). (in Russian). https://elibrary.ru/item.asp?id=29871104. Accessed 21 Nov 2018
8. Lindenbaum, M., Lukasevich, V., Khramov, V.: Method of description of supporting orients with use of triangulations to delona. In: Proceedings of the International Scientific-Practical Conference on Transport: Science, Education, Production, pp. 120–124 (2017). (in Russian). https://elibrary.ru/item.asp?id=32625134. Accessed 21 Nov 2018
9. Akperov, I.G., Kramarov, S.O., Khramov, V.V., Mitjasova, O.Y., Povh, V.I.: Method of identification of extended objects of the Earth's surface. Patent RF, no. 2640331 (2017)
10. Akperov, I., Kramarov, S., Kovtun, O.G., Khramov, V.V., Lukasevich, V.: A method of improving the accuracy of the location of the ground moving object and the device for its implementation. Patent RF, no. 2638358 (2017)
11. Radchevsky, A., Kramarov, S., Povh, V., Lukasevich, V., Khramov, V., Akperov, I.: Method of formation of the digital plan-scheme of objects of agricultural purpose and system for its realization. Patent RF, no. 2612326 (2017)
12. Kramarov, S., Khramov, V., Sakharova, L., Mityasova, O.: Ecologization of adaptive landscape land use on the basis of geoinformation technologies and soft computing systems. In: Proceedings of the XV All-Russian Open Conference "Modern Problems of Remote Sensing of the Earth from Space", pp. 369. IKI RAS, Moscow (2017). (in Russian). https://elibrary.ru/item.asp?id=32863651. Accessed 21 Nov 2018
13. Akperov, I., Khramov, V., Lukasevich, V., Mityasova, O.: Fuzzy methods and algorithms in data mining and formation of digital plan-schemes in earth remote sensing. Procedia Comput. Sci. **120**, 120–125 (2017). https://doi.org/10.1016/j.procs.2017.11.218

14. Cordón, O., Herrera, F.: A general study on genetic fuzzy systems. In: Periaux, J., Winter, G., Galán, M., Cuesta, P. (eds.) Genetic Algorithms in Engineering and Computer Science, pp. 33–57. Wiley, New York (1995)
15. Jamshidi, M.M.: A system of systems framework for autonomy with big data analytic and machine learning. Procedia Comput. Sci. **120**, 6 (2017). https://doi.org/10.1016/j.procs.2017. 11.202
16. Jamshidi, M.: System-of-systems engineering-a definition. In: 2005 IEEE International Conference on Systems, Man and Cybernetics, SMC 2005 (2005)
17. Khramov, V.: Method of aggregation of several sources of fuzzy information. Izvestiya of TRTU **3**(21), 52–53 (2001). (in Russian). https://elibrary.ru/item.asp?id=12886331. Accessed 21 Nov 2018
18. Cvetkov, V.: Informatization, innovative processes and geoinformation technologies. In: Proceedings of the Higher Educational Institutions. Izvestia vuzov "Geodesy and aerophotosurveying" **4**, 112–118 (2006). (in Russian). https://elibrary.ru/item.asp?id=25115047. Accessed 21 Nov 2018
19. Khramov, V.: The principle of intelligence and its use in recognition problems technologies. In: Thematic Scientific and Technical Collection of Pushchino, pp. 62–66 (1994). (in Russian). https://elibrary.ru/item.asp?id=32838003. Accessed 21 Nov 2016
20. Lindenbaum, M., Sakharova, L., Khramov, V.: Management of complex multi-factor systems based on fuzzy analog controllers. In: Proceedings of the all-Russian National Scientific and Practical Conference "Modern Development of Science and Technology (Science-2017)", Publishing of Rostov State Transport University, Rostov-on-Don, pp. 65–69 (2017). (in Russian). https://elibrary.ru/item.asp?id=32629668. Accessed 21 Nov 2016
21. Kramarov, S., Sakharova, L., Khramov, V.: Soft Computing in management: management of complex multivariate systems based on fuzzy analog controllers. Sci. Bull. Southern Inst. Manage. **3**, 42–51 (2017). (in Russian). https://elibrary.ru/item.asp?id=30280910. Accessed 21 Nov 2016
22. Grozdev, D.S., Khramov, V., Golubenko, E., Kovalev, S.: Applied methods of identification in automated transport systems. Rostov State Transport University, Rostov-on-Don (2015). (in Russian). https://elibrary.ru/item.asp?id=27492569. Accessed 21 Nov 2016
23. Zacman, I.M.: Semiotic model of interrelations of concepts, information objects and computer codes. Inform. Appl. **3**(2), 65–81 (2009). (in Russian). https://elibrary.ru/item.asp?id= 13027102

Scientific Software in Education and Science

Comparison of Neural Network and Multilayered Approach to the Problem of Identification of the Creep and Fracture Model of Structural Elements Based on Experimental Data

Alexander Vasilyev[1]([✉])[iD], Evgenii Kuznetsov[2][iD], Sergey Leonov[2][iD], and Dmitry Tarkhov[1][iD]

[1] Peter the Great St. Petersburg Polytechnic University, Politekhnicheskaya Str. 29, 195251 St. Petersburg, Russia
a.n.vasilyev@gmail.com, dtarkhov@gmail.com
[2] Moscow Aviation Institute (National Research University), Volokolamskoe shosse 4, 125993 Moscow, Russia
kuznetsov@mai.ru, powerandglory@yandex.ru

Abstract. The paper considers the solution of one class of coefficient inverse problems connected with the identification of models describing the process of inelastic deformation of structural elements under creep conditions up to fracture moment. Systems of ordinary differential equations are used to describe the creep process. Some structural materials, such as metals, concrete and composite materials have creep properties at high and moderate temperatures. Wherein, the non-consideration of material creep can lead to significant errors in the structures deformation-strength characteristics determining, that leads to the emergencies. However, creep modeling involves some difficulties. There is no general creep theory describing all or most of the observed phenomena. Dozens of different creep theories have been developed applied to specific narrow classes of problems. Moreover, constitutive equations of each theory contain sets of material constants determined by the results of the experiment. Traditional methods of creep models identification depend both on the type of constitutive equations, and the conditions under which construction works. For identification of creep models parameters, the authors proposed a general unified method, which is based on the technique and principles of neural network modeling. A new multilayered method is developed in addition to using the traditional neural network approximations with activation functions of a special type. In the new approach, the problem is preliminarily discretized using known numerical schemes on a segment with a variable right boundary. The advantages of the proposed approaches compared with the traditional ones are shown by the example of creep model identification for a uniaxial tension of steel 45 cylindrical samples under creep conditions. The reliability of the obtained data is confirmed by a comparison with the experimental data and the results of other authors.

© Springer Nature Switzerland AG 2020
V. Sukhomlin and E. Zubareva (Eds.): SITITO 2018, CCIS 1201, pp. 319–334, 2020.
https://doi.org/10.1007/978-3-030-46895-8_25

Keywords: Creep · Fracture · Parameter identification · The Cauchy problem · Ordinary differential equations · Artificial neural networks · Multilayered neural networks

1 Introduction

In recent years, there is an increasing need for the description of deformation and fracture processes in complex temperature-power regimes for materials with complicated rheological characteristics including viscosity. These problems find wide application in different fields of science and technology, e.g. mechanical engineering and aerospace industry. Special attention is paid to the possibility of creep accounting at high and moderate temperatures for metal and composite structures. However, up to now, there has been no common approach to the description of this phenomenon, and there are dozens various creep theories (e.g. the aging theory, the hardening theory, the heredity theory and the Rabotnov theory of structural parameters) and their modifications. It is not usually possible to reliably determine which of the theories is better to use in a particular case. Applying equations of any theory may be a very complex process, as equations used usually contain several material constants (creep characteristics), which complicated to obtain. In other words, these parameters can be determined by using information about a deformation process. A primary source of information is an experiment. Creep characteristics may depend on the type of used material and its condition, regime of loading, temperature, type of anisotropy, and other factors. Problems of their identification are very complicated. All these reasons indicate the need for a common approach to determining parameters of models for various equation types. This paper provides a unified method for identifying parameters of models describing creep and fracture processes of structures. The method considered involves the use of experimental data. The principles and the techniques of neural network modeling are adopted as a basis for the approach developed in the work. The results of the neural network method proposed in the paper [1] are compared with the results of the method of creating multilayer models, which allows building an approximate solution of the differential equation in the form of a function that more accurately satisfies the experimental data than the exact solution of the differential equation.

2 Neural Network Methodology

Neural networks are flexible and convenient apparatus, successfully applied to the solution of differential equations [2–16]. They are quite effectively applied to the solution of inverse problems [17–25]. By using the methodology and some results of the papers [12–16], we consider the construction of a neural network for the system of N ordinary differential equations (ODEs) of order r with p unknown scalar parameters given by a vector $\alpha = \left(\alpha_1, \alpha_2, \ldots, \alpha_p\right)^T$

$$\mathbf{F}(t, \mathbf{y}, \mathbf{y}', \ldots, \mathbf{y}^{(r)}, \boldsymbol{\alpha}) = 0, \quad t \in [t_0, t_*] \tag{1}$$

with initial conditions

$$\mathbf{y}(t_0) = \mathbf{y}_0, \ldots, \mathbf{y}^{(r-1)}(t_0) = \mathbf{y}_{r-1}. \tag{2}$$

The following notations are introduced here

- $F(t, y, y', \ldots, y^{(r)}, \alpha)$ is a vector function of vector arguments with components
  $f_1(t, y, y', \ldots, y^{(r)}, \alpha), \ldots, f_N(t, y, y', \ldots, y^{(r)}, \alpha)$;
- $f_i(t, y, y', \ldots, y^{(r)}, \alpha)$ are scalar functions of vector arguments, $i = 1, \ldots, N$;
- $y(t) = (y_1(t), y_2(t), \ldots, y_N(t))^T$ is the desired solution, which is a vector function of argument t, and also implicitly depends on the parameters $\alpha_1, \alpha_2, \ldots, \alpha_p$;
- $y_j = (y_{j1}, y_{j2}, \ldots, y_{jN})^T$ are vectors of values of $y(t)$ and its $r - 1$ derivatives at the point t_0, $j = 0, \ldots, r - 1$;
- $y^{(j)}(t) = \frac{d^j y(t)}{dt^j}$, $y^{(0)}(t) = y(t)$.

While solving physical problems, certain restrictions must be imposed on ranges of values of the parameters $\alpha_1, \alpha_2, \ldots, \alpha_p$

$$\alpha_s \in A_s \subseteq \mathbb{R}, \quad s = 1, \ldots, p. \tag{3}$$

Suppose that the problem (1)–(2) also satisfies the Cauchy existence theorem.

Moreover, we assume there is a set of additional data on the behavior of the function $y(t)$ at points $t_1, t_2, \cdots, t_l$

$$y(t_q) = y_q^e, \quad t_q \in (t_0, t_*], \quad q = 1, \ldots, l, \tag{4}$$

where $y_q^e = (y_{q1}^e, y_{q2}^e, \ldots, y_{qN}^e)^T$ are vectors of $y(t)$ values at points $t_1, t_2, \ldots, t_l$.

We are going to approximate each component of the vector function $y(t)$ via an artificial neural network

$$\hat{y}_i(t, w_i) = \sum_{j=1}^{N_i} c_{ij} v_j(t, a_{ij}), \quad i = 1, \ldots, N. \tag{5}$$

We use the notations here:

- $w_i = (w_{i1}, w_{i2}, \ldots, w_{iN_i})$ are matrices of parameters to be determined (neural network coefficients);
- $w_{ij} = (c_{ij}, a_{ij})$;
- c_{ij} are linear input parameters;
- $a_{ij} = (a_{ij}^1, a_{ij}^2)$ are nonlinear input parameters;
- N_i are numbers of neuron units in the expansion (5).

The type of a neural network basis element $v_j(t, a_{ij})$ is determined by a scalar function of the scalar argument, so-called activation function, of the form

$$v_j(t, a_{ij}) = \varphi_j(x), x = \psi(t, a_{ij}),$$

where $\psi(\cdot)$ is some given function (for example, linear regression $\psi(t, a_{ij}) = a_{ij}^1 t + a_{ij}^2$). The activation function may be given in the form of the hyperbolic tangent $\varphi(x) = th(x)$, the Cauchy function $\varphi(x) = (1 + x^2)^{-1}$, the Gaussian function $\varphi(x) = \exp(-x^2)$ or in another sophisticated form.

Using relations (1), initial conditions (2), and additional data (4), as well as the neural network approximations (5), we obtain a normalized error functional in the discrete form [12–16]

$$J(\alpha, \mathbf{w}_1, \ldots, \mathbf{w}_N)$$
$$= \left(\sum_{i=1}^{N} (\beta_i M + \gamma_i r + \delta_i l)\right)^{-1} \cdot \sum_{i=1}^{N} \left(\beta_i \sum_{j=1}^{M} \left|f_i(\xi, \hat{\mathbf{y}}, \hat{\mathbf{y}}', \ldots, \hat{\mathbf{y}}^{(r)}, \alpha)\right|^2\right.$$
$$\left. + \gamma_i \sum_{j=0}^{r-1} \left|\hat{y}_i^{(j)}(t_0, \mathbf{w}_i) - y_{ji}\right|^2 + \delta_i \sum_{q=1}^{l} \cdot \left|\hat{y}_i(t_q, \mathbf{w}_i) - y_{qi}^e\right|^2\right)$$

$$(6)$$

where

- $\hat{\mathbf{y}}(t, \mathbf{w}_1, \ldots, \mathbf{w}_N) = \left(\hat{y}_1(t, \mathbf{w}_1), \ldots, \hat{y}_N(t, \mathbf{w}_N)\right)^T$ is a vector of the neural network approximations (5);
- $\beta_i, \gamma_i, \delta_i, i = 1, \ldots, N$ are positive penalty coefficients.

The components of the vector function $\mathbf{F}(t, \hat{\mathbf{y}}, \hat{\mathbf{y}}', \ldots, \hat{\mathbf{y}}^{(r)}, \alpha)$ are calculated at test point (point of reference) ensemble $\{\xi_j\}_{j=1}^{M}$ [12–16]; the random components of the ensemble are supposed to be uniformly distributed on the segment $[t_0, t_*]$.

We obtain model parameters and neural network coefficients while solving the error functional (6) minimization problem within the constraints (3)

$$J(\alpha, \mathbf{w}_1, \ldots, \mathbf{w}_N) \xrightarrow{\mathbf{w}_1, \ldots, \mathbf{w}_N, \alpha_1, \alpha_2, \ldots, \alpha_p} \min. \tag{7}$$

Note that the process of the error functional minimization (7) is being conducted not up to a global minimum, but up to the moment when the functional value is less than the preassigned value of a permissible error $\eta > 0$, i.e. $J < \eta$. And this functional value J_* is taken as an approximation to the error functional global minimum. To avoid interruption of the minimization process at points of the local minimum we periodically make some regeneration of the test point set $\{\xi_j\}_{j=1}^{M}$ after a few iterations of the minimization algorithm [12–16].

In the paper, this approach is used for the solution to the creep model parameter identification problem for uniaxial tension of isotropic aviation steel 45 cylindrical specimens at the constant temperature $T = 850\,^\circ\mathrm{C}$.

3   Uniaxial Tension Problem

To describe the behavior of metals under creep conditions up to the fracture moment we will use the constitutive equations of the Yu. Rabotnov theory of the structural parameters [26, 27] in the form of a system of two ODEs

$$\frac{d\varepsilon}{dt} = \frac{f_1(\sigma)}{\omega^\alpha (1 - \omega^{\alpha+1})^m},$$
$$\frac{d\omega}{dt} = \frac{f_2(\sigma)}{\omega^\alpha (1 - \omega^{\alpha+1})^m}, \tag{8}$$

where ε is creep strain, ω is scalar damage parameter, σ is stress, t is time, T is temperature, α and m are model parameters that can depend on the temperature T in general case.

Functional relationships are determined by experimental data. As in the work [27], we choose the functions $f_1(\sigma)$ and $f_2(\sigma)$ in a power form

$$f_1(\sigma) = B_\varepsilon \sigma^n, \quad f_2(\sigma) = B_\omega \sigma^k,$$

where $B_\varepsilon, B_\omega, n, k$ are creep characteristics.

As the initial conditions for the system (8) we use

$$\omega(0) = 0, \, \varepsilon(0) = 0. \tag{9}$$

If $\sigma = \sigma_0 = \text{const}$, we can also get the solution of the Cauchy problem (8)–(9) in the same way as it is done in the work [28]

$$\omega(t) = \left(1 - \left(1 - (\alpha + 1)(m + 1)B_\omega \sigma_0^k t\right)^{\frac{1}{m+1}}\right)^{\frac{1}{\alpha+1}}, \tag{10}$$

$$\varepsilon(t) = \frac{B_\varepsilon \sigma_0^n}{B_\omega \sigma_0^k} \omega(t). \tag{11}$$

Taking into account that the damage parameter is equal to unity at the fracture moment, from the Eq. (10) we obtain the value of long-term strength t^* of this construction

$$t^* = \left[(\alpha + 1)(m + 1)B_\omega \sigma_0^k\right]^{-1}. \tag{12}$$

Further, we assign this value t^* as the parameter t_* from the previous section.

4 Model Parameter Identification Problem

We can solve the parameter identification problem for the system (8), by using the neural network approach described above. As an additional data about the behavior of the solution we use the results of the experiment on uniaxial tension of cylindrical aviation steel 45 specimens for a stress level σ_0 at constant temperature $T = 850\,°C$, given in the article [27]

$$\varepsilon(t_q) = \varepsilon_q, \quad \omega(t_q) = \omega_q, \quad t_q \in (0, t^*], \quad q = 1, \ldots, l, \tag{13}$$

where

- t_q is the moment when the experimental value with the number q was obtained;
- ε_q is the experimental value of the creep strain at the moment t_q;
- ω_q is the experimental value of the damage parameter at the moment t_q;
- l is the number of the experimental points.

For the neural network approximation (5) we choose the neural network basis elements of a special form

$$\hat{\varepsilon}(t, \mathbf{c}, A) = \sum_{j_1=1}^{N_1} c_{j_1} \frac{\text{th}(a_{1j_1}t + a_{2j_1})}{(1 + a_{3j_1}t + a_{4j_1})},$$

$$\hat{\omega}(t, \mathbf{b}, D) = \sum_{j_2=1}^{N_2} b_{j_2} \frac{\text{th}(d_{1j_2}t + d_{2j_2})}{(1 + d_{3j_2}t + d_{4j_2})},$$

(14)

where

- $\mathbf{c} = \{c_{j_1}\}$, $\mathbf{b} = \{b_{j_2}\}$ are vectors of linear input parameters;
- $A = \{a_{ij_1}\}$, $D = \{d_{ij_2}\}$ are matrices of nonlinear input parameters, $i = 1, \ldots, 4$.

Using the neural network approximation (14) along with the equations of the system (8), the initial conditions (9), and the experimental data for a certain stress value σ_0 (13) we get the error functional J in the discrete form

$$J(B_\varepsilon, B_\omega, n, k, \alpha, m, \mathbf{c}, A, \mathbf{b}, D)$$

$$= R_1 \cdot \left\{ \delta \sum_{j=1}^{M} \left[\left| \frac{d\hat{\varepsilon}}{dt} - \frac{B_\varepsilon \sigma_0^n}{\hat{\omega}^\alpha (1 - \hat{\omega}^{\alpha+1})^m} \right|^2 + \left| \frac{d\hat{\omega}}{dt} - \frac{B_\omega \sigma_0^k}{\hat{\omega}^\alpha (1 - \hat{\omega}^{\alpha+1})^m} \right|^2 \right]_{t=\xi_j} \right.$$

$$+ \delta_1 |\hat{\varepsilon}(0, \mathbf{c}, A)|^2 + \delta_2 |\hat{\omega}(0, \mathbf{b}, D)|^2$$

$$\left. + \delta_3 \sum_{q=1}^{l} |\hat{\varepsilon}(t_q, \mathbf{c}, A) - \varepsilon_q|^2 + \delta_4 \sum_{q=1}^{l} |\hat{\omega}(t_q, \mathbf{b}, D) - \omega_q|^2 \right\}.$$

(15)

Here

- $\{\xi_j\}_{j=1}^{M}$ is a set of random test points uniformly distributed on the segment $[0, t^*]$;
- M is a number of the test points;
- $R_1 = (2 \cdot \delta \cdot M + \delta_1 + \delta_2 + (\delta_3 + \delta_4) \cdot l)^{-1}$;
- $\delta_1, \delta_2, \delta_3, \delta_4$ are positive penalty coefficients.

Terms of the first sum in the expression (15) are calculated at $t = \xi_j$.

We find values of the model parameters B_ε, B_ω, n, k, α, m by minimization of the error functional (15)

$$J(B_\varepsilon, B_\omega, n, k, \alpha, m, \mathbf{c}, A, \mathbf{b}, D) \xrightarrow{B_\varepsilon, B_\omega, n, k, \alpha, m, \mathbf{c}, A, \mathbf{b}, D} \min.$$

(16)

Additionally, taking into account a deformation process at creep conditions, one must restrict ranges of the model parameter values by the following constraints

$$B_\varepsilon > 0, \quad B_\omega > 0, \quad n > 0, \quad k > 0, \quad \alpha > 0, \quad m > 0.$$

(17)

So we obtain the minimization problem with inequality constraints (17). As a result, we find the model parameters B_ε, B_ω, n, k, α, m and the neural network coefficients $\mathbf{c}^*$, A^*, $\mathbf{b}^*$, D^*. Substituting these coefficients in the expansion (14), we get the neural network approximation for the creep strain and the damage parameter.

5 Neural Network Parameters and Experimental Data

We find the ODE system (8) parameters for the constant stress $\sigma_0 = 35;\ 40;\ 45$ MPa.

The experimental data for the creep strain are taken from the paper [27], the experimental data for the damage parameter are calculated by the formula $\omega = \frac{\varepsilon}{\varepsilon_*}$, where ε_* is the creep strain value at the fracture moment. All the experimental data are shown in Tables 1, 2 and 3.

Table 1. Experimental data for steel 45, stress $\sigma_0 = 35$ MPa.

	1	2	3	4	5	6	7
t, h	0 51	0.98	1.461	1.918	2.441	2.935	3.433
ε	0.044	0.081	0.109	0.141	0.163	0.175	0.195
ω	0.084	0.157	0.211	0.273	0.316	0.34	0.378
	8	9	10	11	12	13	14
t, h	3.902	4.445	4.898	5.327	5.837	6.531	6.706
ε	0.211	0.234	0.249	0.264	0.287	0.379	0.516
ω	0.41	0.454	0.482	0.512	0.557	0.735	1

Table 2. Experimental data for steel 45, stress $o_0 = 40$ MPa.

	1	2	3	4	5
t, h	0.286	0.51	0.735	0.906	1.429
ε	0.05	0.111	0.155	0.187	0.24
ω	0.0808	0.18	0.253	0.303	0.39
	6	7	8	9	10
t, h	2	2.429	2.714	2.947	2.98
ε	0.3	0.366	0.412	0.505	0.616
ω	0.487	0.595	0.67	0.82	1

Table 3. Experimental data for steel 45, stress $\sigma_0 = 45$ MPa.

	1	2	3	4	5	6
t, h	0.088	0.273	0.392	0.527	0.637	0.739
ε	0.007	0.072	0.134	0.183	0.232	0.273
ω	0.012	0.113	0.211	0.29	0.366	0.431
	7	8	9	10	11	12
t, h	0.857	0.996	1.061	1.163	1.184	1.224
ε	0.318	0.368	0.413	0.468	0.541	0.633
ω	0.503	0.581	0.652	0.738	0.854	1

Table 4 presents the number of neuron units in approximation, the number of test and experimental points, the penalty coefficient values and other neural network parameters.

Table 4. Neural network parameters.

σ_0, MPa	δ	δ_1	δ_2	δ_3	δ_4	N_1	N_2	M	l	η
35	10	10	10	10	10	3	3	30	14	$5 \cdot 10^{-4}$
40	1	1	1	1	1	4	3	20	10	$5 \cdot 10^{-4}$
45	10^4	10^5	10^5	10^5	10^5	4	3	20	12	$5 \cdot 10^{-4}$

6 Numerical Results

The minimization problem (16)–(17) is solved by the conjugate gradient method [29]. The results of the paper [27] and the parameters of the ODE system (8) obtained are shown in Table 5.

Table 5. Model parameters.

σ_0, MPa	$B_\varepsilon \sigma_0^n, h^{-1}$	$B_\omega \sigma_0^k, h^{-1}$	α	m
Results of paper [27]				
35	0.0115297	0.0201714	0.849	2.83
40	0.0340058	0.0511611		
45	0.0882853	0.1162713		
Results of problem (16)–(17) solving				
35	0.0079387	0.0156534	0.9468	3.8725
40	0.0382844	0.061904	0.806	1.966
45	0.1602613	0.2551528	0.2971	1.4793

The basic data on the deformation process are shown in Table 6, where δt^*, $\delta \varepsilon_*$ are relative errors of long-term strength and creep deformation at the fracture moment, t_n is computational time.

The graphs of the creep strain and the damage parameter with respect to time are shown in Fig. 1, where

- dots denote the experiment data;
- solid lines are the results obtained in the paper [27];
- dashed lines denote curves (10)–(12) corresponding to the parameters obtained in this work.

Table 6. Basic data on the deformation process.

	Parameters [27]			Problem (16)–(17)			Experimental data [27]		
	Pressure, MPa								
	35	40	45	35	40	45	35	40	45
t^*, h	7.0005	2.7601	1.2145	6.7348	3.0158	1.2187	6.7061	2.9796	1.2245
ε_*	0.5716	0.6647	0.7593	0.5072	0.6185	0.6281	0.5161	0.6155	0.6333
δt^*, %	4.39	7.37	0.82	0.43	1.21	0.47	–	–	–
$\delta \varepsilon_*$, %	10.77	7.98	19.9	1.73	0.47	0.82	–	–	–
$J_* \cdot 10^5$	–	–	–	4.691	12.517	17.16	–	–	–
t_n, s	–	–	–	934	762	973	–	–	–

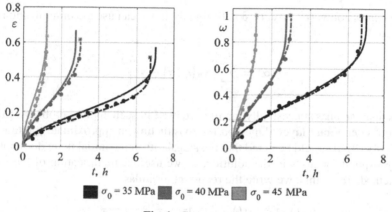

$\sigma_0 = 35$ MPa $\sigma_0 = 40$ MPa $\sigma_0 = 45$ MPa

Fig. 1. Creep curves.

Graphs of the obtained neural network solutions of the problem (8)–(9) are shown in Fig. 2, represented by a dashed line.

7 Multilayered Methodology

Classical methods of numerical solution of the Cauchy problem (1)–(2) consist in the partition of the interval $[t_0, t_*]$ into n parts: $t_0 < t_1 < \ldots < t_k < t_{k+1} < \ldots < t_n = t_* = t_0 + a$, and in the application of an iterative formula of the form $y_{k+1} = A(\mathbf{f}, y_k, y_{k+1}, h_k, t_k)$, where $h_k = t_{k+1} - t_k$; y_k – approximation to the exact value of the desired solution, A – a function that determines the method used. Our approach [30] is to use this iterative formula (with a function A, corresponding to the chosen method) for constructing an approximate solution of the problem (1)–(2) on a variable-length interval $[t_0, t], t \in [t_0, t_*]$. In this case $h_k = h_k(t), y_k = y_k(t), y_0(t) = y_0$. As an approximate solution, it is proposed to use $y_n(t)$. Problem parameters $\boldsymbol{\alpha}$ are explicitly included in the

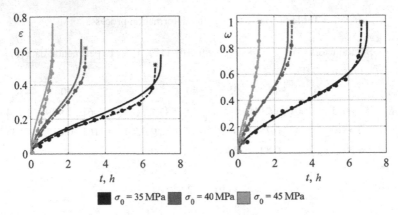

$\sigma_0 = 35\,\mathrm{MPa}$ $\sigma_0 = 40\,\mathrm{MPa}$ $\sigma_0 = 45\,\mathrm{MPa}$

Fig. 2. Neural network solutions of the problem (8)–(9).

solution expression $\mathbf{y}_n(t) = \mathbf{y}_n(t, \boldsymbol{\alpha})$. To find them, we can use the minimization of the functional

$$J(\boldsymbol{\alpha}) = \sum_{q=1}^{l} \left\| \mathbf{y}_n\big(t_q, \boldsymbol{\alpha}\big) - \mathbf{y}_q^e \right\|^2.$$

This approach has successfully manifested itself in such applied problems [31–34].

We consider a multilayered method for constructing an approximate solution to the problem (8)–(9). It should be noted that the singularity at the initial point does not allow applying explicit methods in the solution, so we use our modification of the implicit Euler method. To do this, we write the recurrent formulas

$$\begin{aligned}
\varepsilon_i(t) &= \varepsilon_{i-1}(t) + h_i(t)\frac{f_1(\sigma)}{\omega_i^{\alpha}(t)\left(1-\omega_i^{\alpha+1}(t)\right)^m}, \\
\omega_i(t) &= \omega_{i-1}(t) + h_i(t)\frac{f_2(\sigma)}{\omega_i^{\alpha}(t)\left(1-\omega_i^{\alpha+1}(t)\right)^m},
\end{aligned} \tag{18}$$

here $i = 1, \ldots, N$. Initial functions are defined according to initial conditions $\varepsilon_0(t) = 0$, $\omega_0(t) = 0$. We will select steps from the condition $\varepsilon_i(t) = \frac{i \cdot \varepsilon_N(t)}{N}$, $\omega_i(t) = \frac{i \cdot \omega_N(t)}{N}$. As an approximate solution to the problem, we will use $\varepsilon = \varepsilon_N(t)$ и $\omega = \omega_N(t)$. From formulas (18) we find

$$\begin{aligned}
\varepsilon &= N \cdot h_i(t) \cdot \frac{f_1(\sigma) \cdot N^{\alpha+m+\alpha m}}{i^{\alpha} \cdot \omega^{\alpha}\left(N^{\alpha+1} - i^{\alpha+1} \cdot \omega^{\alpha+1}\right)^m}, \\
\omega &= N \cdot h_i(t) \cdot \frac{f_2(\sigma) \cdot N^{\alpha+m+\alpha m}}{i^{\alpha} \cdot \omega^{\alpha}\left(N^{\alpha+1} - i^{\alpha+1} \cdot \omega^{\alpha+1}\right)^m}.
\end{aligned} \tag{19}$$

Hence, from formulas (19) we get

$$\begin{aligned}
h_i(t) &= \frac{\varepsilon \cdot i^{\alpha} \cdot \omega^{\alpha}\left(N^{\alpha+1} - i^{\alpha+1} \cdot \omega^{\alpha+1}\right)^m}{f_1(\sigma) \cdot N^{\alpha+m+\alpha m+1}}, \\
h_i(t) &= \frac{i^{\alpha} \cdot \omega^{\alpha+1}\left(N^{\alpha+1} - i^{\alpha+1} \cdot \omega^{\alpha+1}\right)^m}{f_2(\sigma) \cdot N^{\alpha+m+\alpha m+1}}.
\end{aligned}$$

Summing by $i = 1, \ldots, N$, we obtain

$$
t = a \cdot \varepsilon \cdot \omega^{\alpha} \sum_{i=1}^{N} i^{\alpha} \cdot \left(N^{\alpha+1} - i^{\alpha+1} \cdot \omega^{\alpha+1}\right)^{m},
$$
$$
t = b \cdot \omega^{\alpha+1} \sum_{i=1}^{N} i^{\alpha} \cdot \left(N^{\alpha+1} - i^{\alpha+1} \cdot \omega^{\alpha+1}\right)^{m},
$$

(20)

here $a = (f_1(\sigma))^{-1} \cdot N^{-(\alpha+m+\alpha m+1)}$, $b = (f_2(\sigma))^{-1} \cdot N^{-(\alpha+m+\alpha m+1)}$.

The constants α, m, a, and b are determined by experimental data on the least squares method

$$
J = \sum_{q=1}^{l} \left[t_q - a \cdot \varepsilon_q \cdot \omega_q^{\alpha} \sum_{i=1}^{N} i^{\alpha} \left(N^{\alpha+1} - i^{\alpha+1} \cdot \omega_q^{\alpha+1}\right)^{m} \right]^{2}
$$
$$
+ \sum_{q=1}^{l} \left[t_q - b \cdot \omega_q^{\alpha+1} \sum_{i=1}^{N} i^{\alpha} \left(N^{\alpha+1} - i^{\alpha+1} \cdot \omega_q^{\alpha+1}\right)^{m} \right]^{2} \rightarrow \min.
$$

The advantage of this approach in comparison with the neural network one is that the same parameters as for the exact solution of the equation are selected.

We present the results of calculations for $\sigma_0 = 35$ MPa, $N = 3$.

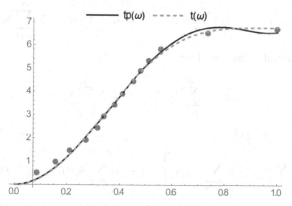

Fig. 3. A graph of the exact solution of the Cauchy problem $t(\omega)$ and the approximate solution $tp(\omega)$ (20) with the coefficients found by the least squares method; the points correspond to the experimental values.

The values of the error functional are $J = 0.665$ for the exact solution, $J = 0.630$ for the approximate solution, i.e. the approximate solution corresponds to the experimental data slightly better than the exact one. The analysis of the graphs shows that this is true for all experimental points except the last two.

It is possible to build a solution starting from the end of the interval, but the implicit Euler method was not effective enough. We apply a more accurate method of trapezoids.

To do this, we invert the equations (8)

$$\frac{dt}{d\varepsilon} = \frac{\omega^\alpha \left(1 - \omega^{\alpha+1}\right)^m}{f_1(\sigma)},$$

$$\frac{dt}{d\omega} = \frac{\omega^\alpha \left(1 - \omega^{\alpha+1}\right)^m}{f_2(\sigma)}. \qquad (21)$$

Application of the trapezoid method for system (21) gives the following recurrent formulas

$$\begin{cases} t_i(\varepsilon, \omega) = t_{i-1}(\varepsilon, \omega) + \frac{(\varepsilon_i - \varepsilon_{i-1})}{2 f_1(\sigma)} \cdot \left[\omega_{i-1}^\alpha \left(1 - \omega_{i-1}^{\alpha+1}\right)^m + \omega_i^\alpha \left(1 - \omega_i^{\alpha+1}\right)^m \right], \\ t_i(\omega) = t_{i-1}(\omega) + \frac{(\omega_i - \omega_{i-1})}{2 f_2(\sigma)} \cdot \left[\omega_{i-1}^\alpha \left(1 - \omega_{i-1}^{\alpha+1}\right)^m + \omega_i^\alpha \left(1 - \omega_i^{\alpha+1}\right)^m \right]. \end{cases}$$

We will choose the steps from the condition $\varepsilon_i = \varepsilon_* + \frac{i \cdot (\varepsilon - \varepsilon_*)}{N}$, $\omega_i = 1 + \frac{i \cdot (\omega - 1)}{N}$, whence

$$t_i(\varepsilon, \omega) = t_{i-1}(\varepsilon, \omega) + a \cdot (\varepsilon - \varepsilon_*) \cdot S_i(\omega), \quad t_i(\omega) = t_{i-1}(\omega) + b \cdot (\omega - 1) \cdot S_i(\omega),$$

where

$$S_i(\omega) = (N + (i - 1) \cdot (\omega - 1))^\alpha \left(1 - (N + (i - 1)(\omega - 1))^{\alpha+1}\right)^m$$

$$+ (N + i \cdot (\omega - 1))^\alpha \left(1 - (N + i(\omega - 1))^{\alpha+1}\right)^m.$$

Summing by $i = 1, \ldots, N$, we obtain

$$t = t_* + a \cdot (\varepsilon - \varepsilon_*) \sum_{i=1}^N S_i(\omega), \quad t = t_* + b \cdot (\omega - 1) \sum_{i=1}^N S_i(\omega). \qquad (22)$$

Substituting the initial values, we have

$$t_* = a \cdot \varepsilon_* \sum_{i=1}^N S_i(0), \quad t_* = b \sum_{i=1}^N S_i(0).$$

Excluding t_* and ε_*, we get

$$t = a \cdot \varepsilon + b \left[\sum_{i=1}^N S_i(0) - \sum_{i=1}^N S_i(\omega) \right], \quad t = b \left[\sum_{i=1}^N S_i(0) + (\omega - 1) \sum_{i=1}^N S_i(\omega) \right].$$

As before, the constants α, m, a, and b are determined by experimental data on the least squares method. We present the results of calculations for $N = 3$, thus we will analyze the second dependence, for the first one the results are similar.

The second term of the error functional for the exact solution is 0.333, for the approximate solution it is 1.317. Note that the solution constructed from the starting point has a small error at the beginning of the interval, and the solution constructed from the end point has a small error at the end of the interval. Let's make a weighted average approximate solution by multiplying the first by $2x^3 - 3x^2 + 1$, and the second by $3x^2 - 2x^3$.

The second term of the error functional for the weight-average solution is 0.248, which is significantly less than for the exact solution.

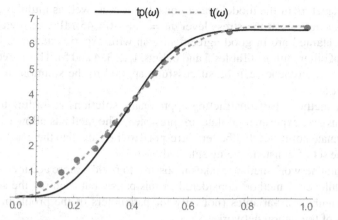

Fig. 4. A graph of the exact solution of the Cauchy problem $t(\omega)$ and the approximate solution $tp(\omega)$ (22) with the coefficients found by the least squares method; the points correspond to the experimental values.

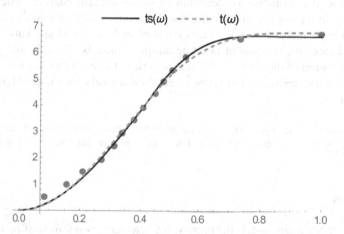

Fig. 5. A graph of the exact solution of the Cauchy problem $t(\omega)$ and the weighted average solution $ts(\omega)$ with the coefficients found by the least squares method; the points correspond to the experimental values.

8 Conclusion

The following results were obtained:

1. The process of the Cauchy problem solution constructing for ODEs system of order r with unknown parameter set is described with the use of the neural network technique and new multilayered method;
2. These developed approaches were used to solve the creep model parameter identification problem for uniaxial tension of steel 45 specimens at the constant stress and constant temperature;

3. The parameters of the model under consideration, as well as multilayer and neural network solutions at the stress level $\sigma_0 = 35; \ 40; \ 45$ MPa, are determined. The results obtained are in good agreement both with experimental data and with the results of other authors (Tables 5 and 6, Figs. 1, 2, 3, 4 and 5). This agreement shows that these approaches can be successfully applied to the solution of this class of problems;

4. Flexible methods for constructing approximate solutions according to differential equations and experimental data are presented. The methods allow us to construct approximate solutions that better correspond to the data than the exact solution with the same set of constants being selected;

5. The neural network method makes it possible to build a more accurate solution than the multilayered method considered in this paper, but requires the selection of a larger number of variables (not only the parameters of the problem, but also the weights of the neural network).

Further studies will consider the application of the proposed approaches to solving planar and spatial creep problems, as well as viscoelastic problems. Special attention will be paid to the problems of determining strain-strength characteristics of structural elements in a complex stress state. Such problems are often found in engineering practice, but experimental data for them is not enough or not at all. This fact significantly complicates the process of building adequate models. Thus, before proceeding to the consideration of the above tasks, it is important to investigate the use of different neural network architectures and types of error functionals for the problem of model identification.

Acknowledgments. The article was prepared on the basis of scientific research carried out with the financial support of the Russian Science Foundation grant (project No. 18-19-00474).

References

1. Vasilyev, A.N., Kuznetsov, E.B., Leonov, S.S.: Neural network method of identification and analysis of the model of deformation of metal structures under creep conditions. Mod. Inf. Technol. IT-Educ. **11**(2), 360–370 (2015). https://elibrary.ru/item.asp?id=26167516. (in Russian)
2. Yadav, N., Yadav, A., Kumar, M.: An Introduction to Neural Network Methods for Differential Equations. SpringerBriefs in Applied Sciences and Technology. Springer, Dordrecht (2015). https://doi.org/10.1007/978-94-017-9816-7
3. Lagaris, I.E., Likas, A., Fotiadis, D.I.: Artificial neural networks for solving ordinary and partial differential equations. IEEE Trans. Neural Netw. **9**(5), 987–1000 (1998). https://doi.org/10.1109/72.712178
4. Dissanayake, M.W.M.G., Phan-Thien, N.: Neural-network-based approximations for solving partial differential equations. Commun. Numer. Methods Eng. **10**(3), 195–201 (1994). https://doi.org/10.1002/cnm.1640100303
5. Fasshauer, G.E.: Solving differential equations with radial basis functions: multilevel methods and smoothing. Adv. Comput. Math. **11**(2–3), 139–159 (1999). https://doi.org/10.1023/A:1018919824891

6. Fornberg, B., Larsson, E.: A numerical study of some radial basis function based solution methods for elliptic PDEs. Comput. Math Appl. **46**(5–6), 891–902 (2003). https://doi.org/10.1016/S0898-1221(03)90151-9

7. Galperin, E., Pan, Z., Zheng, Q.: Application of global optimization to implicit solution of partial differential equations. Comput. Math Appl. **25**(10–11), 119–124 (1993). https://doi.org/10.1016/0898-1221(93)90287-6

8. Li, J., Luo, S., Qi, Y., Huang, Y.: Numerical solution of elliptic partial differential equation using radial basis function neural networks. Neural Netw. **16**(5–6), 729–734 (2003). https://doi.org/10.1016/S0893-6080(03)00083-2

9. Kansa, E.: Multiquadrics – a scattered data approximation scheme with applications to computational fluid dynamics I: surface approximations and partial derivative estimates. Comput. Math Appl. **19**(8–9), 127–145 (1990). https://doi.org/10.1016/0898-1221(90)90270-T

10. Kansa, E.: Multiquadrics – a scattered data approximation scheme with applications to computational fluid dynamics II: solutions to parabolic, hyperbolic and elliptic partial differential equations. Comput. Math Appl. **19**(8–9), 147–161 (1990). https://doi.org/10.1016/0898-1221(90)90271-K

11. Mai-Duy, N., Tran-Cong, T.: Numerical solution of differential equations using multiquadric radial basis function networks. Neural Netw. **14**(2), 185–199 (2001). https://doi.org/10.1016/S0893-6080(00)00095-2

12. Tarkhov, D., Vasilyev, A.: New neural network technique to the numerical solution of mathematical physics problems. I: Simple problems. Opt. Mem. Neural Netw. (Inf. Opt.) **14**, 59–72 (2005)

13. Tarkhov, D., Vasilyev, A.: New neural network technique to the numerical solution of mathematical physics problems. II: Complicated and nonstandard problems. Opt. Mem. Neural Netw. (Inf. Opt.) **14**, 97–122 (2005)

14. Vasilyev, A., Tarkhov, D.: Mathematical models of complex systems on the basis of artificial neural networks. Nonlinear Phenom. Complex Syst. **17**(3), 327–335 (2014). https://elibrary.ru/item.asp?id=29102291

15. Budkina, E.M., Kuznetsov, E.B., Lazovskaya, T.V., Leonov, S.S., Tarkhov, D.A., Vasilyev, A.N.: Neural network technique in boundary value problems for ordinary differential equations. In: Cheng, L., Liu, Q., Ronzhin, A. (eds.) ISNN 2016. LNCS, vol. 9719, pp. 277–283. Springer, Cham (2016). https://doi.org/10.1007/978-3-319-40663-3_32

16. Lazovskaya, T.V., Tarkhov, D.A., Vasilyev, A.N.: Parametric neural network modeling in engineering. Recent Patents Eng. **11**(1), 10–15 (2017). https://doi.org/10.2174/1872212111666161207155157

17. Li, Z., Mao, X.-Z.: Least-square-based radial basis collocation method for solving inverse problems of Laplace equation from noisy data. Int. J. Numer. Methods Eng. **84**(1), 1–26 (2010). https://doi.org/10.1002/nme.2880

18. Gorbachenko, V.I., Lazovskaya, T.V., Tarkhov, D.A., Vasilyev, A.N., Zhukov, M.V.: Neural network technique in some inverse problems of mathematical physics. In: Cheng, L., Liu, Q., Ronzhin, A. (eds.) ISNN 2016. LNCS, vol. 9719, pp. 310–316. Springer, Cham (2016). https://doi.org/10.1007/978-3-319-40663-3_36

19. Lozhkina, O., Lozhkin, V., Nevmerzhitsky, N., Tarkhov, D., Vasilyev, A.: Motor transport related harmful PM2.5 and PM10: from on-road measurements to the modeling of air pollution by neural network approach on street and urban level. IOP Conf. Ser. J. Phys. Conf. Ser. **772**(1), 012031 (2016). https://doi.org/10.1088/1742-6596/772/1/012031

20. Kaverzneva, T., Lazovskaya, T., Tarkhov, D., Vasilyev, A.: Neural network modeling of air pollution in tunnels according to indirect measurements. IOP Conf. Ser. J. Phys. Conf. Ser. **772**(1), 012035 (2016). https://doi.org/10.1088/1742-6596/772/1/012035

21. Kainov, N.U., Tarkhov, D.A., Shemyakina, T.A.: Application of neural network modeling to identification and prediction problems in ecology data analysis for metallurgy and welding industry. Nonlinear Phenomena Complex Syst. **17**(1), 57–63 (2014). https://elibrary.ru/item. asp?id=29102259

22. Bolgov, I., Kaverzneva, T., Kolesova, S., Lazovskaya, T., Stolyarov, O., Tarkhov, D.: Neural network model of rupture conditions for elastic material sample based on measurements at static loading under different strain rates. IOP Conf. Ser. J. Phys. Conf. Ser. **772**(1), 012032 (2016). https://doi.org/10.1088/1742-6596/772/1/012032

23. Egorchev, M.V., Tiumentsev, Y.: Learning of semi-empirical neural network model of aircraft three-axis rotational motion. Opt. Mem. Neural Netw. (Inf. Opt.) **24**(3), 201–208 (2015). https://doi.org/10.3103/S1060992X15030042

24. Kozlov, D.S., Tiumentsev, Y.: Neural network based semi-empirical models for dynamical systems described by differential-algebraic equations. Opt. Mem. Neural Netw. (Inf. Opt.) **24**(4), 279–287 (2015). https://doi.org/10.3103/S1060992X15040049

25. Gorbachenko, V.I., Zhukov, M.V.: Solving boundary value problems of mathematical physics using radial basis function networks. Comput. Math. Math. Phys. **57**(1), 145–155 (2017). https://doi.org/10.1134/S0965542517010079

26. Rabotnov, Y.: Creep Problems in Structural Members. North-Holland Publishing Company, Amsterdam/London (1969)

27. Gorev, B.V., Zakharova, T.E., Klopotov, I.D.: On description of creep and fracture of the materials with non-monotonic variation of deformation-strength properties. Phys. Mesomech. J. **5**(2), 17–22 (2002). https://elibrary.ru/item.asp?id=12912517. (in Russian)

28. Gorev, B.V., Lyubashevskaya, I.V., Panamarev, V.A., Iyavoynen, S.V.: Description of creep and fracture of modern construction materials using kinetic equations in energy form. J. Appl. Mech. Tech. Phys. **55**(6), 1020–1030 (2014). https://doi.org/10.1134/S0021894414060145

29. Polak, E.: Computational Methods in Optimization: A Unified Approach. Academic Press, New York (1971)

30. Lazovskaya, T., Tarkhov, D.: Multilayer neural network models based on grid methods. IOP Conf. Ser. Mater. Sci. Eng. **158**(1), 012061 (2016). https://doi.org/10.1088/1757-899X/158/1/012061

31. Lazovskaya, T., Tarkhov, D., Vasilyev, A.: Multi-layer solution of heat equation. In: Kryzhanovsky, B., Dunin-Barkowski, W., Redko, V. (eds.) NEUROINFORMATICS 2017. SCI, vol. 736, pp. 17–22. Springer, Cham (2018). https://doi.org/10.1007/978-3-319-66604-4_3

32. Vasilyev, A.N., Tarkhov, D.A., Tereshin, V.A., Berminova, M.S., Galyautdinova, A.R.: Semi-empirical neural network model of real thread sagging. In: Kryzhanovsky, B., Dunin-Barkowski, W., Redko, V. (eds.) NEUROINFORMATICS 2017. SCI, vol. 736, pp. 138–144. Springer, Cham (2018). https://doi.org/10.1007/978-3-319-66604-4_21

33. Zulkarnay, I.U., Kaverzneva, T.T., Tarkhov, D.A., Tereshin, V.A., Vinokhodov, T.V., Kapitsin, D.R.: A two-layer semi-empirical model of nonlinear bending of the cantilevered beam. IOP Conf. Ser. J. Phys. Conf. Ser. **1044**, 012005 (2018). https://doi.org/10.1088/1742-6596/1044/1/012005

34. Bortkovskaya, M.R., et al.: Modeling of the membrane bending with multilayer semi-empirical models based on experimental data. In: CEUR Workshop Proceedings. Proceedings of the II International Scientific Conference "Convergent Cognitive Information Technologies" (Convergent 2017), vol. 2064, pp. 150–156. MSU, Moscow (2017). http://ceur-ws.org/Vol-2064/paper18.pdf

Arc Length and Multilayer Methods for Solving Initial Value Problems for Differential Equations with Contrast Structures

Evgenii Kuznetsov[1] (ID), Sergey Leonov[1] (ID), Dmitry Tarkhov[2](✉) (ID),
Ekaterina Tsapko[1] (ID), and Anastasia Babintseva[2] (ID)

[1] Moscow Aviation Institute (National Research University), Volokolamskoe Shosse 4, 125993 Moscow, Russia
kuznetsov@mai.ru, powerandglory@yandex.ru
[2] Peter the Great St. Petersburg Polytechnic University, Politekhnicheskaya Street 29, 195251 St. Petersburg, Russia
dtarkhov@gmail.com

Abstract. In this paper, we investigate the features of the numerical solution of Cauchy problems for nonlinear differential equations with contrast structures (interior layers). Similar problems arise in the modeling of certain problems of hydrodynamics, chemical kinetics, combustion theory, computational geometry. Analytical solution of problems with contrast structures can be obtained only in particular cases. The numerical solution is also difficult to obtain. This is due to the ill-conditionality of the equations in the neighborhood of the interior and boundary layers. To achieve an acceptable accuracy of the numerical solution, it is necessary to significantly reduce the step size, which leads to an increase of a computational complexity. The disadvantages of using the traditional explicit Euler method and fourth-order Runge-Kutta method, as well as the implicit Euler method with constant and variable step sizes are shown on the example of one test problem with two boundary and one interior layers. Two approaches have been proposed to eliminate the computational disadvantages of traditional methods. As the first method, the best parametrization is applied. This method consists in passing to a new argument measured in the tangent direction along the integral curve of the considered Cauchy problem. The best parametrization allows obtaining the best conditioned Cauchy problem and eliminating the computational difficulties arising in the neighborhood of the interior and boundary layers. The second approach for solving the Cauchy problem is a semi-analytical method developed in the works of Alexander N. Vasilyev and Dmitry A. Tarkhov their apprentice and followers. This method allows obtaining a multilayered functional solution, which can be considered as a type of nonlinear asymptotics. Even at high rigidity, a semi-analytical method allows obtaining acceptable accuracy solution of problems with contrast structures. The analysis of the methods used is carried out. The obtained results are compared with the analytical solution of the considered test problem, as well as with the results of other authors.

Keywords: Contrast structures · Method of solution continuation · The best argument · Ill-conditionality · Cauchy problem · Ordinary differential equations · Semi-analytical methods

© Springer Nature Switzerland AG 2020
V. Sukhomlin and E. Zubareva (Eds.): SITITO 2018, CCIS 1201, pp. 335–351, 2020.
https://doi.org/10.1007/978-3-030-46895-8_26

1 Introduction

In this paper, we consider solution of Cauchy problem for n-th order ordinary differential equations with small parameter ε

$$\varepsilon \frac{d^n u}{dt^n} = F\left(t, u, \frac{du}{dt}, \ldots, \frac{d^{n-1} u}{dt^{n-1}}\right), \quad \varepsilon > 0 \tag{1}$$

with initial conditions

$$u(0) = u_0, \quad \frac{d^k u}{dt^k}(0) = u_0^k, \quad k = 1, \ldots, n - 1. \tag{2}$$

In works of A. N. Tikhonov [1] differential equations type (1) have been called the equation with small parameter at the senior derivative. Subsequently, they have been known as singularly perturbed equations. The feature of this type problem is that the integral curves have one or more rapidly changing parts.

When there are rapidly changing parts in either one or both boundary points, problem (1)–(2) is commonly referred to as boundary layers problem. One of the first man who noted the effect of boundary layers was L. Prandtl in 1905 [2]. He regarded the viscous liquid movement with small friction. It was described by Navier-Stokes equations. Since the 1940s, certain techniques had been developed in works of A. N. Tikhonov [1, 3, 4], A. B. Vasil'yeva and V. F. Butuzov [5, 6], S. A. Lomov [7]. These techniques are used for solving singularly perturbed equations in form of asymptotic series in powers of a small parameter.

Besides boundary layers, interior layers can arise in singularly perturbed problems. In works of A. B. Vasil'yeva, V. F. Butuzov and N. N. Nefedov these structures are known as contrast structures. These problems arise in the modeling of certain problems of hydrodynamics, chemical kinetics, catalytic reactions theory, combustion theory, in differential geometry problems, and in planning nuclear power reactor [8]. Despite the fact, that this type of problem is relevant and significance, scientists are facing with computing difficulties, while solving problems.

It is difficult to find an analytical solution when the function of the right-hand side of an equation (1) is nonlinear. The use of asymptotic methods developed for problems with contrast structures in articles by A. B. Vasilyeva, V. F. Butuzov and N. N. Nefedov [9–12] is effective only for small values of the ε parameter. As the value of the ε parameter increases, the number of summands of the asymptotic series which must be taken into account also increases. The use of numerical methods also involves a number of difficulties due to the fact that within the adjacency of boundary and inner layers the explicit schemes [13] lose their stability. Even a significant reduction in the integration step does not always give a result. While using implicit schemes and special methods for solving stiff problems [14], the problem of loss of stability is extincted, but new problems associated with solving nonlinear equations and their systems appear. At the same time, computational complexity when using implicit schemes increases with the dimension of a system of equations. Moreover, a number of implicit schemes can not overcome the interior layers.

A method of solution continuation with respect to parameter and its modification [15–17] is developed in the works by V. I. Shalashilin, E. B. Kuznetsov and their students.

The idea of this method is replacing the original argument of the Cauchy problem by a new one that is measured at a tangent direction along its integral curve. It is proved that the obtained argument makes the problem best conditioned. It is shown that the transformation to the best argument allows to obtain several advantages over the traditional numerical methods for ill-conditioned Cauchy problems [17].

Besides, it is applied the semi-analytic method suggested in the article [18], the main point of which is to apply the formulas of traditional explicit and implicit methods of numerical solution for intervals with a variable right boundary. This method has been successfully applied to a number of practical interest problems [19–25]. In particular, with the help of this method some approximate solutions better corresponding to the experimental data than the exact solutions of the original differential equations were obtained in the works [19–21].

2 Purpose of the Study

A number of stiff Cauchy problems with contrast structures and methods for their solution were considered in the works by N. N. Kalitkin and A. A. Belov [26, 27]. Since traditional numerical methods for solving the Cauchy problem are ineffective for problems with contrast structures, as indicated in the works [26, 27], the solution is based on the arc length method (the method of solution continuation with respect to the best argument) with a variable step that varies according to the Runge rule and the curvature of the integral curve [28]. But there is no comparison of the arc length method with traditional explicit and implicit methods in works of N. N. Kalitkin and A. A. Belov. The purpose of this work is a comparative analysis of methods for solving problems with contrast structures and the development of a new method of solution based on a semi-analytical approach. A number of explicit and implicit methods for solving the Cauchy problem with constant and variable step will be considered, as well as the method of solution continuation with respect to the best argument. All the obtained results will be compared with each other, as well as with the analytical solution and known results of other authors.

3 Formulation of the Problem

We consider the following Cauchy problem suggested by A. A. Belov and N. N. Kalitkin [26, 27]

$$\frac{du}{dt} = -\frac{\xi(t)\left(u^2 - a^2\right)^2}{\left(u^2 + a^2\right)}, \quad u(0) = 0, \quad t \in [0; 2\pi]. \tag{3}$$

The problem can be integrated analytically if $\xi(t) = \xi_0 \cos t$

$$u(t) = -\frac{2a^2\xi_0 \sin t}{1 + \sqrt{1 + 4a^2\xi_0^2 \sin^2 t}}. \tag{4}$$

The stiffness of a problem (3) is determined by the value of the ξ_0, factor that stands for a periodic function. As the cosine approaches zero, the rate of change of the solution also tends to zero regardless of the ξ_0 value. However, as the cosine value approaches unity, the rate of change of the solution will reach its maximum. When ξ_0 values are large, a sharp change occurs in the adjacency of maximum and minimum cosine points. Thus, the problem can be conditionally divided into three classes [27]: the problem is non-stiff if $\xi_0 < 10$, it is stiff if $\xi_0 \geq 10$, and it is super-stiff if $\xi_0 \geq 1000$. Figure 1 shows the integral curves of problem (3) for various ξ_0 values. Hereinafter we assume $a = \pi$.

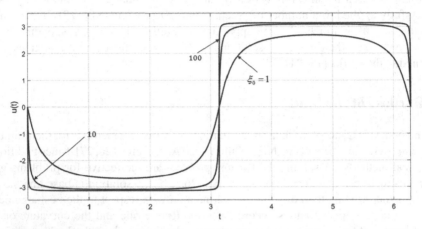

Fig. 1. The analytical solution of the problem (3) with $\xi_0 = 1, \xi_0 = 10, \xi_0 = 100$.

4 Traditional Numerical Methods with a Constant Step

We consider the application of traditional explicit and implicit schemes with a constant step of integration for solving initial problems with contrast structures. The simplest traditional methods include explicit methods of Euler and Runge-Kutta of the fourth order of accuracy. Table 1 shows the mean absolute error of the numerical solution ε, obtained using the analytical solution (4), and the computational time t_c for the problem (3). It can be seen that the Runge-Kutta method, due to a higher order of accuracy, makes it possible to obtain a solution with a smaller error, but takes much more time than the explicit Euler method. We should note that the maximum size of the integration step cannot exceed the value ξ_0^{-1}. Table 1 shows that this fact is reflected in the impossibility of constructing a solution for $\xi_0 = 10$ when $h = 0.1$ and for $\xi_0 = 100$ when $h = 0.01$.

The obtained results are due to the limited stability region of explicit methods. Numerical solutions for stiff problems often use implicit methods which have a much larger area of stability. It can be expected that implicit methods will not require a strong reduction of the integration step.

Table 2 shows the results of applying the implicit Euler method with a constant step for solution of the problem (3). The nonlinear equation obtained during the solution is solved by the fixed point iteration method (FPIM) and the Newton method (NM) [29]. In comparison with the explicit Euler method (see Table 1), it can be noticed that the

Table 1. The mean absolute error ε and the computational time t_c for the problem (3), explicit methods with a constant step.

Parameters		Explicit Euler method		Explicit Runge-Kutta method	
ξ_0	h	ε	t_c, s	ε	t_c, s
1	0.1	0.4548	0.009	$2.1332 \cdot 10^{-4}$	0.0081
	0.01	0.0361	0.0095	$2.2776 \cdot 10^{-8}$	0.0656
	0.001	0.0035	0.0255	$2.1461 \cdot 10^{-12}$	0.1732
10	0.1	–	–	–	–
	0.01	0.0826	0.0109	$2.3893 \cdot 10^{-5}$	0.0168
	0.001	0.008	0.0301	$2.5136 \cdot 10^{-9}$	0.0759
100	0.1	–	–	–	–
	0.01	–	–	–	–
	0.001	0.0127	0.0381	$2.4843 \cdot 10^{-6}$	0.1011

Table 2. The mean absolute error ε and the computational time t_c for the problem (3), implicit Euler method with a constant step.

Parameters		Implicit Euler method			
		FPIM		NM	
ξ_0	h	ε	t_c, s	ε	t_c, s
1	0.1	0.3137	0.0662	0.3138	0.0255
	0.01	0.034	0.1774	0.0345	0.1457
	0.001	$8.6629 \cdot 10^{-4}$	1.188	0.0035	0.6134
10	0.1	–	–	–	–
	0.01	0.074	0.1864	0.0787	0.0878
	0.001	0.0029	1.1653	0.008	0.7302
100	0.1	–	–	–	–
	0.01	–	–	–	–
	0.001	0.0078	0.9977	0.0126	1.5954

implicit Euler method makes it possible to obtain a result with slightly less error, but it spends much more computational time (by an order or more).

The aforementioned results show that the traditional explicit and implicit methods make it possible to obtain the solution of the problem (3) only for the values $\xi_0 \leq 100$. For large ξ_0 values, the integration step must be reduced considerably, which leads to an increase in the computational time by orders of magnitude. More effective method for solving problems with contrast structures is solution continuation with respect to the best argument.

5   The Method of Continuation of the Solution with the Best Argument

We use the method of solution continuation with respect to the best argument [15]. We introduce a new argument λ, measured to the tangent along the integral curve of the original problem (3), in the form

$$d\lambda^2 = du^2 + dt^2.$$

Using this argument, we obtain the following transformed Cauchy problem for a system of differential equations

$$
\begin{cases}
\dfrac{du}{d\lambda} = \dfrac{-\xi_0 \cos t \left(u^2 - a^2\right)^2}{\sqrt{\left(u^2 + a^2\right)^2 + \xi_0^2 \cos^2 t \left(u^2 - a^2\right)^4}}, & u(0) = 0, \\[4mm]
\dfrac{dt}{d\lambda} = \dfrac{\left(u^2 + a^2\right)}{\sqrt{\left(u^2 + a^2\right)^2 + \xi_0^2 \cos^2 t \left(u^2 - a^2\right)^4}}, & t(0) = 0.
\end{cases}
\tag{5}
$$

Table 3 shows the results of solving problems (3) and (5) by the explicit Runge-Kutta method with a constant step. The l step along the λ argument was fixed, and the h step along the t argument was chosen in such a way that the orders of the mean error ε coincided for both problems. It can be seen that for a transformed problem (5) can be used a larger integration step (up to several orders) than for the problem (3). This can significantly reduce the computational time for large ξ_0 values. Similar results are obtained for the explicit Euler method.

Table 3. The mean absolute error ε and the computational time t_c for the parametrized and non-parametrized problems by the fourth-order Runge-Kutta method with a constant step.

ξ_0	Parametrized			Non-parametrized		
	l	ε	t_c, s	h	ε	t_c, s
1	0.1	$5.4369 \cdot 10^{-7}$	0.0213	0.02	$3.6307 \cdot 10^{-7}$	0.0418
	0.01	$2.9799 \cdot 10^{-11}$	0.183	0.002	$3.6427 \cdot 10^{-11}$	0.2405
	0.001	$5.0522 \cdot 10^{-14}$	0.5505	0.0002	$6.4592 \cdot 10^{-13}$	2.0987
10	0.1	$2.4647 \cdot 10^{-4}$	0.0236	0.02	$3.0375 \cdot 10^{-4}$	0.0422
	0.01	$3.2723 \cdot 10^{-9}$	0.0969	0.001	$2.5136 \cdot 10^{-9}$	0.4414
	0.001	$3.7533 \cdot 10^{-12}$	0.5886	0.0002	$3.662 \cdot 10^{-12}$	2.2979
100	0.1	0.3525	0.0289	0.004	0.0012	0.1303
	0.01	$4.834 \cdot 10^{-6}$	0.1178	0.001	$2.4843 \cdot 10^{-6}$	0.4484
	0.001	$5.0063 \cdot 10^{-11}$	0.5289	0.00005	$1.7076 \cdot 10^{-11}$	8.2501
1000	0.1	–	–	–	–	–
	0.01	0.0047	0.2086	0.00047	0.0012	0.9134
	0.001	$4.0885 \cdot 10^{-8}$	0.5288	0.00007	$5.9638 \cdot 10^{-8}$	5.9466

6 Variable Step of Integration

In practice, a variable step is often used instead of a constant integration step. There are many methods for constructing nonuniform grids [30], but the procedure for changing the integration step with accuracy control according to the Runge rule [31] is traditionally used. Table 4 shows the results obtained with a variable step of integration, which is varies according to the Runge rule. The accuracy of the solution θ was fixed for the transformed problem (5) and equaled 10^{-12}. Then the accuracy for the original problem (3) was selected from the condition of equality of the orders of the mean error ε for both problems.

We could have expected that the implicit Euler method with variable step would give better results, but the results in Table 5 are not much different from those represented in Table 2.

We should note that the order of the mean error of the initial problem (3) depends on the initial step for fixed accuracy, whereas for the transformed problem this dependence is not observed. In addition, the use of the method of solution continuation with respect to the best argument allows to significantly reduce the computational time while maintaining the accuracy.

Table 4. The mean absolute error ε and the computational time t_c for parametrized and non-parametrized problems by the fourth-order Runge-Kutta method with a variable step.

Parameters		Parametrized			Non-parametrized		
ξ_0	h	θ	ε	t_c, s	θ	ε	t_c, s
1	0.1	10^{-12}	$1.1561 \cdot 10^{-10}$	0.2388	10^{-10}	$2.1774 \cdot 10^{-10}$	0.4892
	0.01		$1.6079 \cdot 10^{-10}$	0.2592	$3 \cdot 10^{-10}$	$1.1338 \cdot 10^{-10}$	0.571
	0.001		$1.7008 \cdot 10^{-10}$	0.1889	10^{-10}	$2.1458 \cdot 10^{-12}$	1.3038
10	0.1		$2.365 \cdot 10^{-9}$	0.2065	10^{-7}	$1.5164 \cdot 10^{-9}$	1.6533
	0.01		$2.2218 \cdot 10^{-9}$	0.2812	$4 \cdot 10^{-8}$	$1.1642 \cdot 10^{-9}$	2.025
	0.001		$1.6625 \cdot 10^{-9}$	0.2691	10^{-7}	$2.5134 \cdot 10^{-9}$	1.3089
100	0.1		$3.497 \cdot 10^{-8}$	0.2982	10^{-4}	$5.8346 \cdot 10^{-8}$	3.2128
	0.01		$3.1933 \cdot 10^{-8}$	0.3346	10^{-5}	$2.3953 \cdot 10^{-8}$	4.0536
	0.001		$3.0792 \cdot 10^{-8}$	0.3015	$3 \cdot 10^{-5}$	$2.3106 \cdot 10^{-8}$	4.7691
1000	0.1		$4.2953 \cdot 10^{-7}$	0.2729	–	–	–
	0.01		$3.2001 \cdot 10^{-7}$	0.2318	10^{-3}	$9.1802 \cdot 10^{-8}$	15.794
	0.001		$8.7845 \cdot 10^{-7}$	0.1772	10^{-2}	$6.4254 \cdot 10^{-7}$	9.8967

Table 5. The mean absolute error ε and the computational time t_c for problem (3), the implicit Euler method with variable step, chosen according to Runge rule with $\theta = 10^{-4}$ accuracy.

Parameters		Implicit Euler method, FPIM	
ξ_0	h	ε	t_c, s
1	0.1	0.005	0.6852
	0.01	0.034	0.6912
	0.001	0.0031	0.6395
10	0.1	–	–
	0.01	0.0803	0.9471
	0.001	0.043	1.0648
100	0.1	–	–
	0.01	–	–
	0.001	1.45	0.9754

7 Semianalytical Multilayer Methods

We write down the equation of the problem (3) in the form of

$$\begin{cases} \frac{du}{dt} = F(t, u), \\ F(t, u) = -\frac{\xi(t)(u^2 - a^2)^2}{(u^2 + a^2)}. \end{cases} \quad (6)$$

Then we apply the trapezoid method [29] to the solution of Eq. (6)

$$u_{k+1} = u_k + 0.5 \cdot h_k \cdot (F(t_k, u_k) + F(t_{k+1}, u_{k+1})), \quad h_k = t_{k+1} - t_k. \quad (7)$$

Equation (7) can be solved by one step of Newton's method, linearizing it by $u_{k+1} - u_k$:

$$u_{k+1} = u_k + 0.5 \cdot h_k \cdot \left(F(t_k, u_k) + F(t_{k+1}, u_k) + F'_u(t_{k+1}, u_k) \cdot (u_{k+1} - u_k) \right),$$

whence

$$u_{k+1} = u_k + \frac{h_k \cdot (F(t_k, u_k) + F(t_{k+1}, u_k))}{2 - h_k F'_u(t_{k+1}, u_k)}. \quad (8)$$

According to [18], we apply this formula to an interval of variable length, choosing $h_k = \frac{t - t_0}{n}$, $t_k = t_0 + k\frac{t - t_0}{n}$, $u_0(t) = u_0$. Here $u_0 = u_0(t_0)$ is a certain starting value which is initially considered unknown. In the particular case $t_0 = 0$ we have $u_0 = 0$ from the initial condition. The solution of the problem is obtained by blending such solutions constructed from several initial t_0 points. We demonstrate the results of this procedure for $t_0 = 0$ and $t_0 = \frac{\pi}{2}$, since these are the closest characteristic points of the right-hand side of Eq. (3).

It would be desirable to blend solutions smoothly (for functions and derivatives to coincide), but real calculations showed that this is not possible, so the following procedure was implemented:

1. An approximate $v(t) = u_n(t)$ solution was constructed with $t_0 = 0$;
2. The blending point was defined as a point with a minimum derivative;
3. A $w(t) = u_n(t)$ solution with $t_0 = \frac{\pi}{2}$ and $u\left(\frac{\pi}{2}\right) = u_0$ was built
4. The u_0 value was chosen in such a way that $v(t) = w(t)$ congruence was accomplished at the blending point.

We denote the blending approximate solution by $s(t)$.

8 The Results of Computational Experiments for Semianalytic Multilayer Methods

We represent some results of calculations for $\xi_0 = 10$ (Figs. 2, 3 and 4).

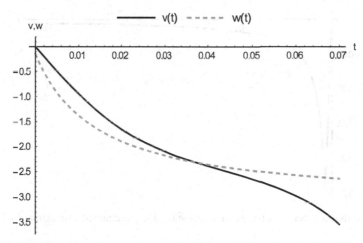

Fig. 2. Blending of the approximate solution $v(t)$ with the initial point $t_0 = 0$ and the approximate solution $w(t)$ with the starting point $t_0 = \frac{\pi}{2}$ for $n = 2$.

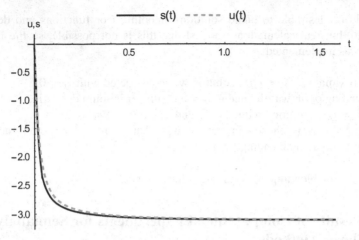

Fig. 3. The exact solution (4) and the blended approximate solution $s(t)$ for $n = 2$.

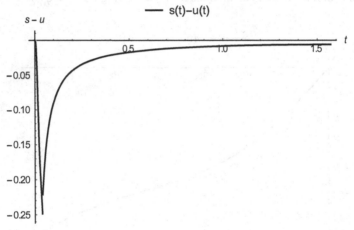

Fig. 4. The difference between the exact solution (4) and the coupled approximate solution $s(t)$ for $n = 2$.

The error decreases with an increase in the number of layers (Figs. 5 and 6):

Next, we build a new approximate solution by taking $t_0 = \pi$ as a starting point and looking for the $v(\pi)$ value in such a way as to ensure the most smooth blending with $w(t)$. Because of the symmetry of $w(t)$ regarding $\frac{\pi}{2}$, this does not lead to a significant increase in the error. In the future, we continue this procedure for the time period of our interest.

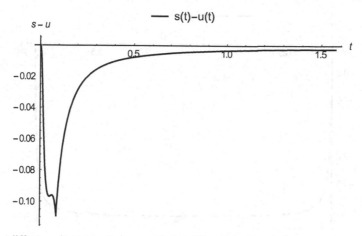

Fig. 5. The difference between the exact solution (4) and the blended approximate solution $s(t)$ for $n = 4$.

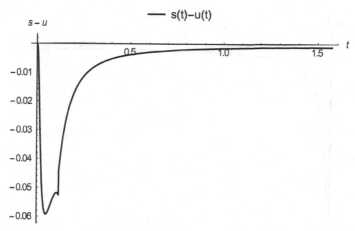

Fig. 6. The difference between the exact solution (4) and the blended approximate solution $s(t)$ for $n = 6$.

Another approach is not to use the approximate $v(t) = u_n(t)$ solution with $t_0 = 0$, but to select u_0 in such a way that the initial $w(0) = 0$ condition is met. This method is simpler, but the errors larger in comparison with the first method (Figs. 7, 8, 9 and 10).

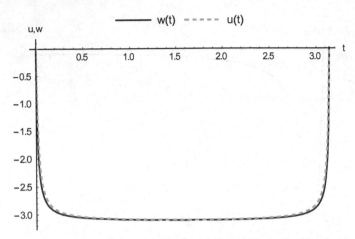

Fig. 7. The exact solution (4) and the approximate solution $w(t)$ obtained by the second way for $n = 2$.

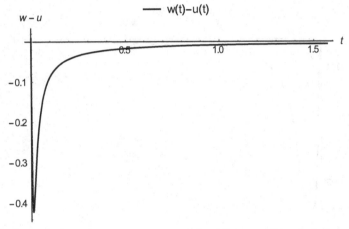

Fig. 8. The difference between the exact solution (4) and the approximate solution $w(t)$ obtained by the second method for $n = 2$.

Next, we build a new approximate solution, taking $t_0 = \frac{3\pi}{2}$ as the starting point and looking for the value at the point $\frac{3\pi}{2}$ in such a way as to ensure the most exact match of $w(t)$ with $t = \pi$. Because of the $w(t)$ symmetry regarding $\frac{\pi}{2}$, this does not lead to an increase in the error. In future, we continue the procedure for the period of time of our interest.

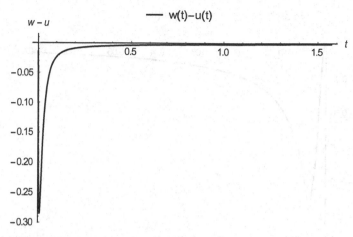

Fig. 9. The difference between the exact solution (4) and the approximate solution $w(t)$ obtained by the second method for $n = 4$.

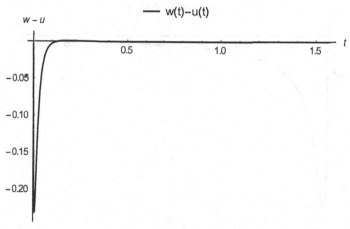

Fig. 10. The difference between the exact solution (4) and the approximate solution $w(t)$ obtained by the second method for $n = 6$.

We could have expected that an increase in the ξ_0 parameter would require a significant increase in the number of layers n to maintain acceptable accuracy, but this was not so, which is confirmed by the results given below (Figs. 11, 12, 13 and 14).

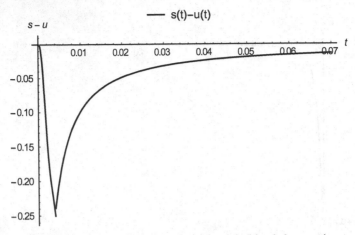

Fig. 11. The difference between the exact solution (4) and the blended approximate solution $s(t)$ for $n = 2$ and $\xi_0 = 100$.

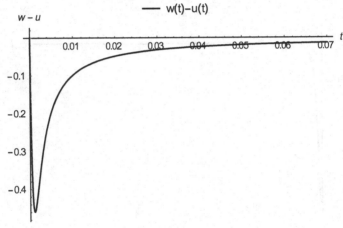

Fig. 12. The difference between the exact solution (4) and the approximate solution $w(t)$ obtained by the second method for $n = 2$ and $\xi_0 = 100$.

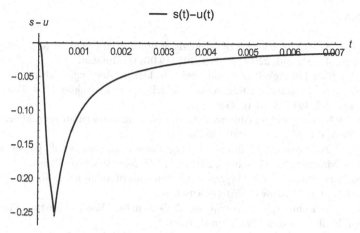

Fig. 13. The difference between the exact solution (4) and the blended approximate solution $s(t)$ for $n = 2$ and $\xi_0 = 1000$.

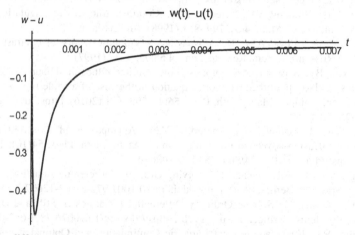

Fig. 14. The difference between the exact solution (4) and the approximate solution $w(t)$ obtained by the second method for $n = 2$ and $\xi_0 = 1000$.

9   Conclusion

In this article we suggested and tested methods applicable to a wide range of stiff problems, in particular, to problems of modeling contrast structures. The work of the methods was tested using the example of the Cauchy problem (3) suggested by A. A. Belov and N. N. Kalitkin [26, 27]. The results of our computational experiments have showed high efficiency of the suggested approaches in stiff and super-stiff cases.

Acknowledgments. The article was prepared on the basis of scientific research carried out with the financial support of the Russian Science Foundation grant (project No. 18-19-00474).

References

1. Tikhonov, A.N.: On dependence of solutions of differential equations on small parameter. Matematicheskii Sbornik **22**(64), 2, 193–204 (1948). (in Russian)
2. Prandtl, L.: über Flüssigkeitsbewegung bei sehr kleiner Reibung. Verhandlungen des III. Internationalen Mathematiker Kongresses, Heidelberg, 8–13 August 1904. B. G. Teubner, Leipzig, pp. 485–491 (1905). (in German)
3. Tikhonov, A.N.: On systems of differential equations containing parameters. Matematicheskii Sbornik **27**(69), 1, 147–156 (1950). (in Russian)
4. Tikhonov, A.N.: Systems of differential equations containing small parameters in the derivatives. Matematicheskii Sbornik **31**(73), 3, 575–586 (1952). (in Russian)
5. Vasil'eva, A.B., Butuzov, V.F.: Asymptotic Expansions of Solutions of Singularly Perturbed Equations. Nauka, Moscow (1973). (in Russian)
6. Vasil'eva, A.B., Butuzov, V.F.: Asymptotic Methods in the Theory of Singular Perturbations. Vysshaya shkola, Moscow (1990). (in Russian)
7. Lomov, S.A.: Introduction to the General Theory of Singular Perturbations. American Mathematical Society (1981)
8. Chang, K.W., Howes, F.A.: Nonlinear Singular Perturbation Phenomena: Theory and Application. Springer, New York (1984). https://doi.org/10.1007/978-1-4612-1114-3
9. Vasil'eva, A.B., Butuzov, V.F., Nefedov, N.N.: Contrast structures in singularly perturbed problems. Fund. Appl. Math. **4**(3), 799–851 (1998). (in Russian)
10. Butuzov, V.F., Vasil'eva, A.B., Nefedov, N.N.: Asymptotic theory of contrast structures (review) [in Russian]. Autom. Remote Control **58**(7), 4–32 (1997)
11. Butuzov, V.F., Bychkov, A.I.: Asymptotics of the solution of the initial boundary value problem for a singularly perturbed parabolic equation in the case of a triple root of the degenerate equation. Comput. Math. Math. Phys. **56**(4), 593–611 (2016). https://doi.org/10.1134/S0965542516040060
12. Antipov, E.A., Levashova, N.T., Nefedov, N.N.: Asymptotics of the front motion in the reaction-diffusion-advection problem. Comput. Math. Math. Phys. **54**(10), 1536–1549 (2014). https://doi.org/10.1134/S0965542514100029
13. Hairer, E., Norsett, S.P., Wanner, G.: Solving Ordinary Differential Equations I: Nonstiff Problems. Springer, Berlin (1987). https://doi.org/10.1007/978-3-662-12607-3
14. Hairer, E., Wanner, G.: Solving Ordinary Differential Equations II: Stiff and Differential-Algebraic Problems. Springer, Berlin (1996). https://doi.org/10.1007/978-3-642-05221-7
15. Shalashilin, V.I., Kuznetsov, E.B.: Parametric Continuation and Optimal Parametrization in Applied Mathematics and Mechanics. Kluwer Academic Publishers, Dordrecht (2003). https://doi.org/10.1007/978-94-017-2537-8
16. Kuznetsov, E.B., Leonov, S.S.: Parametrization of the Cauchy problem for systems of ordinary differential equations with limiting singular points. Comput. Math. Math. Phys. **57**(6), 931–952 (2017). https://doi.org/10.1134/S0965542517060094
17. Kuznetsov, E.B., Leonov, S.S.: Examples of parametrization of the cauchy problem for systems of ordinary differential equations with limiting singular points. Comput. Math. Math. Phys. **58**(6), 914–933 (2018). https://doi.org/10.1134/S0965542518060076
18. Lazovskaya, T., Tarkhov, D.: Multilayer neural network models based on grid methods. IOP Conf. Ser. Mater. Sci. Eng. **158**(1), 012061 (2016). https://doi.org/10.1088/1757-899x/158/1/012061
19. Vasilyev, A.N., Tarkhov, D.A., Tereshin, V.A., Berminova, M.S., Galyautdinova, A.R.: Semi-empirical neural network model of real thread sagging. In: Kryzhanovsky, B., Dunin-Barkowski, W., Redko, V. (eds.) NEUROINFORMATICS 2017. SCI, vol. 736, pp. 138–144. Springer, Cham (2018). https://doi.org/10.1007/978-3-319-66604-4_21

20. Zulkarnay, I.U., Kaverzneva, T.T., Tarkhov, D.A., Tereshin, V.A., Vinokhodov, T.V., Kapitsin, D.R.: A two-layer semi-empirical model of nonlinear bending of the cantilevered beam. IOP Conf. Ser. J. Phys. Conf. Ser. **1044**, 012005 (2018). https://doi.org/10.1088/1742-6596/1044/1/012005

21. Bortkovskaya, M.R., et al.: Modeling of the membrane bending with multilayer semi-empirical models based on experimental data. In: CEUR Workshop Proceedings. Proceedings of the II International Scientific Conference "Convergent Cognitive Information Technologies", Convergent 2017, vol. 2064, pp. 150–156. MSU, Moscow (2017). http://ceur-ws.org/Vol-2064/paper18.pdf

22. Vasilyev, A., Tarkhov, D., Shemyakina, T.: Approximate analytical solutions of ordinary differential equations. In: CEUR Workshop Proceedings. Selected Papers of the XI International Scientific-Practical Conference Modern Information Technologies and IT-Education, SITITO 2016, vol. 1761, pp. 393–400. MSU, Moscow (2016). http://ceur-ws.org/Vol-1761/paper50.pdf. (in Russian)

23. Vasilyev, A., et al.: Multilayer neural network models based on experimental data for processes of sample deformation and destruction. In: CEUR Workshop Proceedings. Proceedings of the I International Scientific Conference "Convergent Cognitive Information Technologies", Convergent 2016, vol. 1763, pp. 6–14. MSU, Moscow (2016). http://ceur-ws.org/Vol-1763/paper01.pdf. (in Russian)

24. Tarkhov, D., Shershneva, E.: Approximate analytical solutions of mathieu's equations based on classical numerical methods. In: CEUR Workshop Proceedings. Selected Papers of the XI International Scientific-Practical Conference Modern Information Technologies and IT-Education, SITITO 2016, vol. 1761, pp. 356–362. MSU, Moscow (2016). http://ceur-ws.org/Vol-1761/paper46.pdf. (in Russian)

25. Lazovskaya, T., Tarkhov, D., Vasilyev, A.: Multi-layer solution of heat equation. In: Kryzhanovsky, B., Dunin-Barkowski, W., Redko, V. (eds.) NEUROINFORMATICS 2017. SCI, vol. 736, pp. 17–22. Springer, Cham (2018). https://doi.org/10.1007/978-3-319-66604-4_3

26. Belov, A.A., Kalitkin, N.N.: Features of calculating contrast structures in the Cauchy problem. Math. Models Comput. Simul. **9**(3), 281–291 (2017). https://doi.org/10.1134/S2070048217030048

27. Belov, A.A., Kalitkin, N.N.: Numerical methods of solving Cauchy problems with contrast structures. Model. Anal. Inf. Syst. **23**(5), 529–538 (2016). https://doi.org/10.18255/1818-1015-2016-5-529-538. (in Russian)

28. Belov, A.A., Kalitkin, N.N.: Curvature-based grid step selection for stiff Cauchy problems. Math. Models Comput. Simul. **9**(3), 305–317 (2017). https://doi.org/10.1134/S207004821703005X

29. Verzhbitskiy, V.M.: Numerical Methods (Mathematical Analysis and Ordinary Differential Equations). Vysshaya shkola, Moscow (2001). (in Russian)

30. Kalitkin, N.N., Alshin, A.B., Alshina, Ye.A., Rogov, B.V.: Calculations on Quasi-Equidistant Grids. Fizmatlit, Moscow (2005). (in Russian)

31. Arushanyan, O.B., Zaletkin, S.F.: Numerical Solution of Ordinary Differential Equations Using FORTRAN. Moscow State Univ, Moscow (1990). (in Russian)

Analytical Risks Prediction. Rationale of System Preventive Measures for Solving Quality and Safety Problems

Andrey Kostogryzov[1,2](✉) ⓘ, Andrey Nistratov[3] ⓘ, and George Nistratov[4] ⓘ

[1] Federal Research Center "Computer Science and Control" of the Russian Academy of Sciences, Vavilova Street 44/2, 119333 Moscow, Russia
Akostogr@gmail.com
[2] Main Research Scientific and Probatory Center of Robotics at the Ministry of Defense of Russian Federation, Seregin Street 5/1, 125167 Moscow, Russia
[3] The Russian Power Agency of Ministry for the Power Generating Industry, Shchepkin Street 40, 1129110 Moscow, Russia
[4] Research Institute of Applied Mathematics and Certification, Myasnikovskaya 1-ya Street 3, 1075641 Moscow, Russia

Abstract. The approach for building new probabilistic models which is intended to predict risks for complex intellectual structures under different threats and to solve quality and safety problems in system life cycle, is proposed. The approach includes: selection of models for every system element allowing to estimate probability to lose integrity during given prognostic period; the approach to build probability distribution functions (PDF) by the models selected to predict probability and risks to lose integrity for different scenarios of threats; the approach to integrate PDF for structure from two elements united by serial and/or parallel connection and generalization for complex structure; the approach to form input for modeling and to solve quality and safety problems in application to complex intellectual structures; applications, which can prove efficiency in different areas. The approach is applicable for the analysis of the reliability of complex systems built from unreliable components, estimations of increasing expected reliability and safety for intelligent manufacturing, modeling of robotic and automated systems operating in cosmic space, optimization of a centralized heat supply system, estimating the mean residual time before the next parameters abnormalities for monitored critical systems, control of information quality, estimation of human factor, analysis of vulnerability of sea oil and gas systems etc. Effects are demonstrated by practical examples.

Keywords: Analysis · Model · Operation · Probability · Prediction · Quality · Risk · Safety · System

1 Introduction

Today the serious discrepancy in the information and technical progress, connected with objective necessity of digital transformation and aspiration to keep useful possibilities of the existing equipment, technologies and skills, is observed. This discrepancy is aggravated because of increasing complexity of the intellectual equipment interfaced to "smart" systems and vulnerabilities, caused by "human factor» and threats from purposeful negative influence on the information and software. As a result different uncertainties generate threats to system in life cycle. Without an adequate estimation of these threats processes of providing quality and safety of system elements and whole system are badly controlled. Importance of efficient risks control is required at level of the international standards of system engineering - for example, ISO/IEC/IEEE 15288, ISO 13379, ISO 13381, ISO 17359, IEC 61508, etc. However, now there is no enough universal effective approach to risks predictions and rationale of preventive measures. Considering an actuality of different system engineering views, the approach for building new probabilistic models which is intended to predict risks for complex intellectual structures under different threats and to solve quality and safety problems in system life cycle, is proposed. The approach is based on author's models applicable to complex intellectual structures and develops the existing approaches [1–19]. The ideas of approach can be applied also by using another probabilistic models which supported by software tools and can predict on a level of probability distribution functions.

   Note.

1. System is combination of interacting elements organized to achieve one or more stated purposes (according to ISO/IEC/IEEE 15288).
2. Risk is defined as effect of uncertainty on objectives considering consequences. An effect is a deviation from the expected — positive and/or negative (according to ISO Guide 73).

2   The Essence of Approach

After defining problems in system life cycle which should be solved by risks prediction the proposed approach for building new probabilistic models includes:

- selection of models for every system element (presented as "black box") allowing to estimate probability to lose integrity during given prognostic period;
- the approach to build probability distribution functions (PDF) by the models selected to predict probability and risks (considering consequences) to lose integrity for different scenarios of threats;
- the approach to integrate PDF for structure from two elements united by serial or parallel connection with built PDF for every element and generalisation of this approach for complex structure;
- the approach to form input for modeling and to solve quality and safety problems in application to complex intellectual structures;
- applications, which can prove practical effects in different areas.

   Note. System (or system element) integrity is defined as such system (system element) state when system (system element) purposes are achieved with the required quality and/or safety.

The application of approach allows to predict risks for complex intellectual structures under different threats and to solve different quality and safety problems in system life cycle.

2.1   Problems which Should be Solved by Risks Prediction

The problems formulated to be solved by risks predictions in system life cycle are defined according to standard requirements (for example to ISO/IEC/IEEE 15288, ISO 13379, ISO 13381, ISO 17359, IEC 61508) considering system specificity. For example, there may be problems devoted to:

- system analysis of uncertainty factors (including "human factor"), reliability, expected quality, capabilities of operation in real time, information gathering and processing, protection from authorized access and dangerous influences;
- definition of system requirements to conditions for effective operation;
- rationale of measures for customer satisfaction;
- system analysis and optimization in architectural design including functional components with the functions of serving, gathering, control, analysis, monitoring, counteraction against threats;
- optimization of different processes;
- comparative estimations of efficiency and profits;
- prognostic estimations of real system quality, safety, interaction "user-system", conditions for effective system operation, stakeholder satisfaction etc.

The foundation for solving all these problems is the creation of more adequate probability distribution functions (PDF) for modeling and predictions in connection with time line.

Why the creation of PDF is important? As an answer the researches quantitatively proved, that the popular today the mode for risks prediction based on uses of frequencies of failures (and corresponding exponential PDF) is a rough and unpromising engineering way. Its application deforms very essentially probabilistic estimations of risks and can't be useful for scientific search of effective counteraction measures against different threats. Deviations from more adequate PDF estimations are very high: more than thousand percent. On Fig. 1 the limitations to admissible risks, fragment of exponential and an adequate PDF of time between losses of system integrity with identical frequency of system integrity losses are illustrated. Example when all requirements to admissible risk are met is presented on Fig. 2. It means more adequate PDF allows more right understanding of probabilistic vision of events prediction with scientific interpretation considering situations in time line.

Comparison at identical frequency of system integrity losses has shown, that for more adequate PDF (considering proactive periodical diagnostics, monitoring between diagnostics, recovery of the lost system integrity) the level of risk may be less in hundred-thousand times and the real period of effective system operation (without losses of integrity) is more in tens-hundreds times against the exponential PDF approximation [7, 8].

P(t)- probability P(τ ≤ t), τ is random value of time between neighboring losses of system integrity

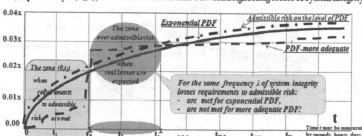

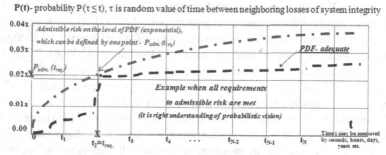

Fig. 1. The possible variants of correlations of the limitations to admissible risks, exponential and an adequate PDF of time between losses of system integrity with identical frequency of system integrity losses.

P(t)- probability P(τ ≤ t), τ is random value of time between neighboring losses of system integrity

Fig. 2. All requirements to admissible risk are met for an adequate PDF of time between losses of system integrity.

3 Selected Models for "Black Box"

Selected models for every system element, presented as "black box", should allow to estimate to lose integrity during given prognostic period considering consequences. A probabilistic space (Ω, B, P) for estimation of system operation processes should be clear, where: Ω - is a limited space of elementary events; B – a class of all subspace of Ω- space, satisfied to the properties of σ- algebra; P – a probability measure on a space of elementary events Ω. Such space (Ω, B, P) is built [1–5] and proposed for using.

Not considering specificity in general case intellectual operation of system element aims to provide reliable and timely producing complete, valid and, if needed, confidential information – see Fig. 3. And later information is used for its proper specificity. And models should allow to estimate intellectual operation processes on a level of a probability of "success" in provision of used information quality (information may be used by technical devices, "smart" elements, robotics, users etc.).

The proposed analytical models ("The model of functions performance by a complex system in conditions of unreliability of its components", "The models complex of calls processing for the different dispatcher technologies", "The model of entering into system current data concerning new objects of application domain", "The model of information gathering", "The model of information analysis", "The models complex of dangerous

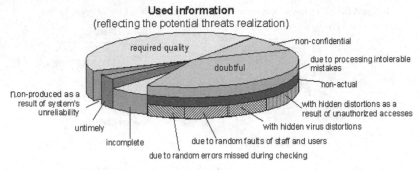

Used information
(reflecting the potential threats realization)

Fig. 3. An abstraction of used information.

influences on a protected system", "The models complex of an authorized access to system resources") allow to estimate probability of "success" and risks to lose quality of intellectual operation during given prognostic period considering consequences.

These models, supported by different versions of software Complex for Evaluation of Information Systems Operation Quality, patented by Rospatent №2000610272 (CEISOQ +), may be applied and improved for solving quality and safety problems, connected with intellectual system element or intellectual system presented as "black box" [1, 2].

For system element allowing prediction of risks to lose its integrity during given prognostic period there are proposed two general technologies of providing protection from critical influences on system: technology 1 - periodical diagnostics of system integrity (without the continuous monitoring between diagnostics) and technology 2 – continuous monitoring between periodical diagnostics is added to technology 1 – see Fig. 4.

Technology 1 is based on periodical diagnostics of system integrity, that are carried out to detect danger sources penetration from threats (destabilizing factors) into a system or consequences of negative influences. The lost system integrity can be detect only as a result of diagnostics, after which system recovery is started. Dangerous influence on system is acted step-by step: at first a danger source penetrates into a system and then after its activation begins to influence. Penetration time is random value which can be distributed by PDF of time between neighboring occurrences of danger

$$\Omega_{penetr}(t) = P(\tau_{penetration} \le t) = 1 - \exp(t/T_{penetr}),$$

T_{penetr} – is mathematical expectation and activation time is random value which can be distributed by PDF of activation time of occurred danger

$$\Omega_{activ}(t) = P(\tau_{activation} \le t) = 1 - \exp(t/T_{activ}),$$

T_{activ} – is mathematical expectation or mean time). System integrity can't be lost before a penetrated danger source is activated. A danger from threats (destabilizing factors) is considered to be realized only after a danger source has influenced on a system.

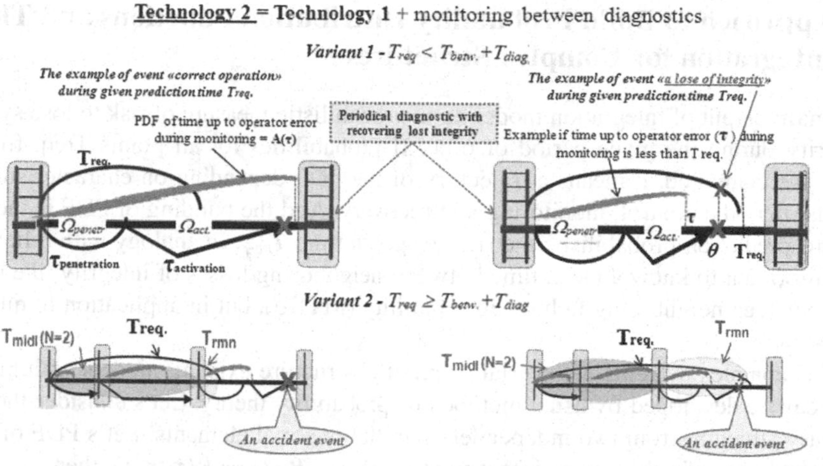

Technology 2 = Technology 1 + monitoring between diagnostics

Variant 1 - $T_{req} < T_{betw.} + T_{diag}$

Fig. 4. Some events to lose integrity during given time.

Technology 2, unlike the previous one, implies that operators alternating each other trace system integrity between diagnostics (operator may be a man or special device or their combination). In case of detecting a danger source an operator recovers system integrity. The ways of integrity recovering are analogous to the ways of technology 1. Faultless operator's actions provide a neutralization of a danger source trying to penetrate into a system. When operators alternate a complex diagnostic is held. A penetration of a danger source is possible only if an operator makes an error but a dangerous influence occurs if the danger is activated before the next diagnostic. Otherwise the source will be detected and neutralized during the next diagnostic.

It is supposed for technologies 1 and 2 that the used diagnostic allows to provide necessary system integrity recovery after revealing danger sources penetration into a system or consequences of influences. Assumption: for all time input characteristic the probability distribution function (PDF) exists. Thus the probability of correct system operation within the given prognostic period (i.e. probability of success) may be computed as a result of use the models. For the identical damages risk to lose integrity is an addition to 1 for probability of correct system operation $R = 1 - P$ [1, 2, 5, 18, 19].

There are possible the next variants for technology 1 and 2: variant 1 – the given prognostic period T_{req} is less than established period between neighboring diagnostics $(T_{req} < T_{betw} + T_{diag})$; variant 2 – the assigned period T_{req} is more than or equals to established period between neighboring diagnostics $(T_{req} \geq T_{betw} + T_{diag})$. Here T_{betw} – is the time between the end of diagnostic and the beginning of the next diagnostic, T_{diag} – is the diagnostic time.

Selected models, supported by different versions of software tools may be applied and improved for solving quality and safety problems, connected with monitored system element or system presented as "black box" [1, 2, 5, 18, 19].

4 Approach to Build Probability Distribution Functions and Their Integration for Complex Structures

The main output of integration modeling is probabilistic measure of risk to lose system integrity during the given period of time. If probabilities for all points Treq. from 0 to ∞ are computed, it means a trajectory of the PDF depending on characteristics of threats, periodic control, monitoring and recovery. And the building of PDF is the real base to prediction probabilistic metrics for given time T_{req}. In analogy with reliability it is important to know a mean time between neighboring losses of integrity like mean time between neighboring failures in reliability (MTBF), but in application to quality, safety etc.

For complex systems with serial or parallel structure existing models with known PDF can be developed by usual methods of probability theory. Let's consider the elementary structure from two independent parallel or serial elements. Let's PDF of time between losses of i-th element integrity is $B_i(t)$, i.e. $B_i(t) = P(\tau_i \le t)$, then:

1. time between losses of integrity for system combined from serial connected independent elements is equal to a minimum from two times τ_i: failure of 1st or 2nd elements (i.e. the system goes into a state of lost integrity when either 1st, or 2nd element integrity is lost). For this case the PDF of time between losses of system integrity is defined by expression

$$B(t) = P(\min(\tau_1, \tau_2) \le t) = 1 - P(\min(\tau_1, \tau_2) > t) =$$
$$= 1 - P(\tau_1 > t)P(\tau_2 > t) = 1 - [1 - B_1(t)][1 - B_2(t)]; \quad (1)$$

2. time between losses of integrity for system combined from parallel connected independent elements (hot reservation) is equal to a maximum from two times τ_i: failure of 1st and 2nd elements (i.e. the system goes into a state of lost integrity when both 1st and 2nd elements have lost integrity). For this case the PDF of time between losses of system integrity is defined by expression

$$B(t) = P(\max(\tau_1, \tau_2) \le t) = P(\tau_1 \le t)P(\tau_2 \le t) = B_1(t)B_2(t). \quad (2)$$

Applying recurrently expressions (1)–(2), it is possible to build PDF of time between losses of integrity for any complex system with parallel and/or serial structure.

For example integrated complex system, combined from complex intellectual structures 1 and 2 for modeling interested system (see Fig. 5), can be analyzed by the formulas (1)–(2) and probabilistic models described above and allowing to form PDF for (1)–(2). The correct operation of this complex system during the given period means: during given period of prediction both the 1-st and the 2-nd systems (described by intellectual structures 1 and 2) should operate correctly according their destinations. I.e. integrity of complex system is provided if "AND" integrity of 1-st system left "AND" integrity of 2-nd system right are provided.

All these ideas for analytical modeling operation processes are supported by the software tools "Mathematical modeling of system life cycle processes" – "know how" (registered by Rospatent №2004610858), "Complex for evaluating quality of production processes" (registered by Rospatent №2010614145) and others [1, 2, 5, 18, 19].

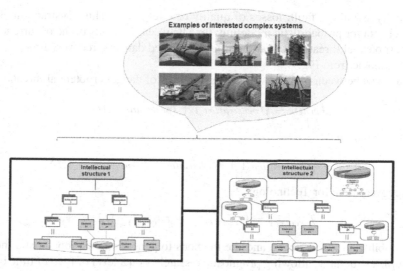

Fig. 5. Integrated complex system of two different systems (serial combination).

5 Approach to Form Input for Modeling and to Solve Quality and Safety Problems

We demonstrate the approach to form input for modeling on example of form mean time T_{penetr} for $\Omega_{penetr}(t)$ and mean time T_{activ} for $\Omega_{activ}(t)$ from random values $\tau_{penetration}$ and $\tau_{activation}$ on practice proper for intelligent manufacturing (see Figs. 4, 5 and 6).

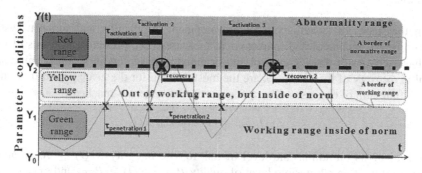

Fig. 6. The universal elementary ranges for traced parameters.

For the beginning the elementary ranges for monitired parameters from quality or safety point of view should be set. For each parameter the ranges of possible values of conditions are set: "Working range inside of norm", "Out of working range, but inside of norm", "Abnormality", interpreted similarly light signals – "green", "yellow", "red" – see Fig. 6. The condition "Abnormality" characterizes a threat to lose system integrity after danger influence (on the logic level this range "Abnormality" may be interpreted analytically as failure, fault, losses of quality or safety etc.). This construction allows to extract data for probabilistic modeling: time between moments of the occurrences of dangers (potential threats), activation time of occurred dangers, recovery time.

For example from Fig. 6:

mean time between moments of the occurrences of dangers (potential threats)

$$T_{penetr} = \left(\tau_{penetration\_1} + \tau_{penetration\_2}\right)/2,$$

mean activation time

$$T_{activ} = \left(\tau_{penetration\_1} + \tau_{penetration\_2} + \tau_{penetration\_3}\right)/3,$$

mean recovery time for Technology 2

$$T_{recovery} = \left(\tau_{recovery\_1} + \tau_{recovery\_2}\right)/2.$$

Probabilistic models above and the methods to generate new probabilistic models for complex structures, allowing prognostic researches on a level of PDF of time before the next abnormality for one element, subsystem, system are selected.

For optimization admissible risks are defined. For rationale of system preventive measures to provide quality and safety it is necessary to know and predict system behavior in time line at various influences.

The statement of problems for system analysis includes definition of conditions, threats and estimation a level of admissible risk established by precedent principle. Thus the final choice of integrated measures is allocated on a payoff to the customer in view of specificity of created or maintained system.

For solving problems of optimization there are used the next general formal statements:

1. on the stages of system concept, development, production and support: system parameters, technical and management measures (Q), presented in terms of time characteristics of threats, control and-or monitoring of conditions and comprehensible recovery of lost integrity, are the most rational for the given period if on them the minimum of expenses (Z_{dev}) for creation of system is reached:

$$Z(Q_{rational}) = \min_Q Z_{dev}(Q),$$

at limitations on admissible level of risk to lose integrity $R(Q) \leq R_{adm}$ and/or probability of an admissible level of quality $P_{quality}(Q) \geq P_{adm}$ and expenses for operation $C_{oper}(Q) \leq C_{adm}$ and under other development, operation or maintenance conditions;

2. on operation stage: system parameters, technical and management measures, presented in terms of time characteristics of threats, control and-or monitoring of conditions and comprehensible recovery of lost integrity, are the most rational for the given period of operation if on them the minimum of risk to lose system integrity is reached:

$$R(Q_{rational}) = \min_Q R_{oper}(Q),$$

at limitations on admissible level of risk to lose integrity for i-th subsystem (element) $R_i(Q) \leq (R_{adm})_i$ and/or probability of an admissible level of quality $P_{quality}(Q) \geq P_{adm}$ and expenses for operation $C_{oper}(Q) \leq C_{adm}$ and under other operation or maintenance conditions.

There may be combination of these formal statements in system life cycle.

6 Examples of Applications

Applications of proposed models cover: analysis of reliability of complex systems built from unreliable components; estimations of increasing expected reliability and safety for intelligent manufacturing, modeling of robotic and automated systems operating in cosmic space, optimization of a centralized heat supply system, analysis of the possibilities to keep "organism integrity" by continuous monitoring, estimating the mean residual time before the next parameters abnormalities for monitored critical systems, control of timeliness, completeness and validity of used information; comparison of information security in networks; estimation of effectiveness of technologies for revealing bugs in tested software; resource management and prediction of quality for information systems operation; choice of rational ways to build and develop heat supply systems, Estimation of human factor, analysis of vulnerability of sea oil and gas systems in conditions of terrorist threats, development of recommendations to increase security of the important land objects, researches of effectiveness of measures to increase flights safety, estimation of technology clements for elections [1, 2, 5–19].

6.1 Example to Rationale Residual Time Before Abnormalities

The models for risks prediction are implemented in remote monitoring system (RMS) by the Joint-Stock Company "Siberian Coal Energy Company" ("SUEK" is the leading coal producer in Russia and one of the world's largest coal companies). Effects are reached on the basis of gathering and analytical processing in real time the information on controllable parameters of objects monitored. RMS is intended for a possibility of prediction and the prevention of possible emergencies, minimization of a role of human factor regarding control and supervising functions. Used models for providing safety allow to estimate mean residual time before abnormalities for traced parameters of equipment – see Fig. 6, 7.

6.2 Example of Pragmatic Effects

The Complex (as a part of global system) of risks predictions for technogenic safety support on the objects of oil & gas distribution has been awarded by Award of the Government of the Russian Federation in the field of a science and technics for 2014. The created peripheral posts are equipped additionally by means of Complex to feel vibration, a fire, the flooding, unauthorized access, hurricane, and also intellectual means of the reaction, capable to recognize, identify and predict a development of extreme situations – see engineering decisions on Fig. 6.

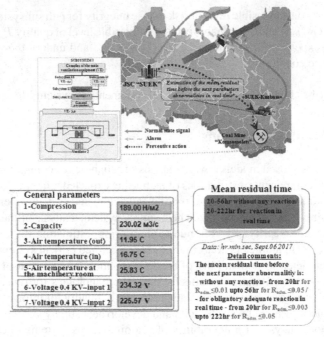

Fig. 7. Example of reaction in real time.

The applications of Complex for 200 objects in several regions of Russia during the period 2009–2014 have already provided economy about 8, 5 Billions of Roubles. The economy is reached at the expense of effective implementation of the functions of risks prediction and processes optimization [7].

References

1. Kostogryzov, A., Nistratov, G.: Standardization, mathematical modelling, rational management and certification in the field of system and software engineering. Armament. Policy. Conversion, Moscow (2004)
2. Kostogryzov, A.I., Stepanov, P.V.: Innovative management of quality and risks in systems life cycle. Armament. Policy. Conversion, Moscow (2008)
3. Zio, E.: An Introduction to the Basics of Reliability and Risk Analysis: Series in Quality, Reliability and Engineering Statistics, vol. 13, World Scientific Publishing Co. Re. Ltd. (2006)
4. Kolowrocki, K., Soszynska-Budny, J.: Reliability and Safety of Complex Technical Systems and Processes. Springer, London (2011). https://doi.org/10.1007/978-0-85729-694-8
5. Kostogryzov, A., Nistratov, G., Nistratov, A.: Some applicable methods to analyze and optimize system processes in quality management. In: Total Quality Management and Six Sigma, InTech, pp. 127–196 (2012). https://doi.org/10.5772/46106
6. Grigoriev, L., Guseinov, Ch., Kershenbaum, V., Kostogryzov, A.: The systemic approach, based on the risks analysis and optimization, to research variants for developing hydrocarbon deposits of Arctic regions. J. Polish Saf. Reliabil. Assoc. Summer Saf. Reliabil. Seminars 5(1–2), 71–78 (2014)

7. Akimov, V., Kostogryzov, A., Mahutov, N., et al.: Security of Russia [in Russian]. In: Mahutov, N.A. (ed.) Legal, Social & Economic and Scientific & Engineering Aspects. The Scientific Foundations of Technogenic Safety. Znanie, Moscow (2015)
8. Kostogryzov, A., Nistratov, A., Zubarev, I., Stepanov, P., Grigoriev, L.: About accuracy of risks prediction and importance of increasing adequacy of used adequacy of used probabilistic models. J. Polish Saf. Reliabil. Assoc. Summer Saf. Reliabil. Seminars **6**(2), 71–80 (2015)
9. Artemyev, V., Kostogryzov, A., Rudenko, J., Kurpatov, O., Nistratov, G., Nistratov, A.: Probabilistic methods of estimating the mean residual time before the next parameters abnormalities for monitored critical systems. In: Proceedings of the 2nd International Conference on System Reliability and Safety (ICSRS), Milan, Italy, pp. 368–373 (2017). https://doi.org/10.1109/icsrs.2017.8272850
10. Kostogryzov, A., Stepanov, P., Nistratov, A., Nistratov, G., Klimov, S., Grigoriev, L.: The method of rational dispatching a sequence of heterogeneous repair works. Energetika **63**(4), 154–162 (2017). https://doi.org/10.6001/energetika.v63i4.3624
11. Kostogryzov, A., Stepanov, P., Nistratov, A., Atakishchev, O.: About probabilistic risks analysis during longtime grain storage. In: Zhang, H. (eds.) Proceedings of the 2nd Internationale Conference on the Social Science and Teaching Research (ACSS-SSTR), vol. 18, Advances in Social and Behavioral Science. Management and Sports Science Institute, PTE.Ltd., Singapore, pp. 3–8 (2017)
12. Kostogryzov, A., Stepanov, P., Grigoriev, L., Atakishchev, O., Nistratov, A., Nistratov, G.: Improvement of existing risks control concept for complex systems by the automatic combination and generation of probabilistic models and forming the storehouse of risks predictions knowledge. In: Proceedings of the 2nd International Conference on Applied Mathematics, Simulation and Modelling (AMSM 2017), pp. 279–283. DEStech Publications, Inc., Phuket, Thailand (2017). https://doi.org/10.12783/dtctr/amsm2017/14857
13. Kostogryzov, A., Atakishchev, O., Stepanov, P., Nistratov, A., Nistratov, G., Grigoriev, L.: Probabilistic modelling processes of mutual monitoring operators actions for transport systems. In: Proceedings of the 4th International Conference on Transportation Information and Safety (ICTIS), Banff, AB, pp. 865–871 (2017). https://doi.org/10.1109/ictis.2017.8047869
14. Kostogryzov, A., Panov, V., Stepanov, P., Grigoriev, L., Nistratov, A., Nistratov, G.: Optimization of sequence of performing heterogeneous repair work for transport systems by criteria of timeliness. In: Proceedings of the 4th International Conference on Transportation Information and Safety (ICTIS), Banff, AB, pp. 872–876 (2017). https://doi.org/10.1109/ictis.2017.8047870
15. Kostogryzov, A., Nistratov, A., Nistratov, G., Atakishchev, O., Golovin, S., Grigoriev, L.: The probabilistic analysis of the possibilities to keep "Organism Integrity" by continuous monitoring. In: Proceedings of the 2018 International Conference on Mathematics, Modelling, Simulation and Algorithms (MMSA 2018). Advances in Intelligent Systems Research, vol. 159, pp. 432–435 (2018). https://doi.org/10.2991/mmsa-18.2018.96
16. Kostogryzov, A., Grigoriev, L., Golovin, S., Nistratov, A., Nistratov, G., Klimov, S.: Probabilistic modeling of robotic and automated systems operating in cosmic space. In: Proceedings of the 2018 International Conference on Communication, Network and Artificial Intelligence (CNAI 2018), pp. 298–303. DEStech Publications, Inc., Beijing (2018)
17. Kostogryzov, A., Grigoriev, L., Kanygin, P., Golovin, S., Nistratov, A., Nistratov, G.: The experience of probabilistic modeling and optimization of a centralized heat supply system which is an object for modernization. In: International Conference on Physics, Computing and Mathematical Modeling (PCMM), pp. 93–97. DEStech Publications, Inc., Shanghai (2018). https://doi.org/10.12783/dtcse/pcmm2018/23643

18. Artemyev, V., Rudenko, Ju., Nistratov, G.: Probabilistic methods and technologies of risks prediction and rationale of preventive measures by using "Smart Systems": applications to coal branch for increasing industrial safety of enterprises. In: Kostogryzov, A. (ed.) Probabilistic Modeling in System Engineering, pp. 23–51 (2018). https://doi.org/10.5772/intechopen. 75109
19. Kershenbaum, V., Grigoriev, L., Kanygin, P., Nistratov, A.: Probabilistic modeling processes for oil and gas. In: Kostogryzov, A. (ed.) Probabilistic Modeling in System Engineering, IntechOpen, pp. 55–79 (2018). https://doi.org/10.5772/intechopen.74963

Predictive Analytics in Mining. Dispatch System Is the Core Element of Creating Intelligent Digital Mine

Igor Temkin[1]([✉]) [ID], Dmitry Klebanov[2] [ID], Sergey Deryabin[1] [ID], and Ilya Konov[1] [ID]

[1] National University of Science and Technology "MISiS", Lenin Avenue 4, 119049 Moscow, Russia
temkin.io@misis.ru

[2] VIST Group, Dokuchaev Per. 3s1, 107078 Moscow, Russia

Abstract. The following article is devoted to using prediction analytics methods in controlling a mining and logistics complex of an open-pit mine. The possibilities of using telemetric information for solving a wide variety of important technological tasks, that are then reduced to data interpretation, object identification, parameter and condition diagnostics and control of robotized interaction. Described are the possibilities of on-board monitoring systems that are currently equipped on BELAZ heavy trucks. It is shown which new tasks in predictive maintenance can be solved using machine learning. Approaches to creating a universal instrument for automatic suggestion and checking hypotheses are reviewed, using heavy truck's tire durability prediction.

Keywords: Intelligent control systems · Predictive analytics · Digital mine · Transport systems

1 Introduction

The prevailing trend of the global mining industry in the short term is deemed to be an open-pit mining method as it provides the best economic performance. The open-pit mining accounts for over 80% of the world mining production, in the USA it accounts for 83%, in CIS (Commonwealth of Independent States) countries - about 70%. In Russia 91% of iron ore, over 70% of non-ferrous metal ores, over 60% of coal are produced using the open-pit mining method.

Despite the use of more powerful and high-performance equipment, the mining cost inevitably increases mainly due to increased quantity of cut and transportation of overburden rock. The expenses of mining enterprises for utility vehicles during open pit deepening increase in faster pace than the expenses for ore extraction. Currently, 80% of the total volume of transported minerals during open pit mining is transported by dump trucks, and costs of vehicles account for 60– 65% of total costs, at further deepening of pits costs of motor vehicles may be three to four times the mining costs. High operating costs include the most expensive components, such as fuel, oil, tires, interchangeable assemblies, maintaining of the quality of roads, and so on. At most open pits performance

© Springer Nature Switzerland AG 2020
V. Sukhomlin and E. Zubareva (Eds.): SITITO 2018, CCIS 1201, pp. 365–374, 2020.
https://doi.org/10.1007/978-3-030-46895-8_28

indicators of the rock mass transportation decrease with increase of the depth of the open pit.

The most important component of the effective operation of the mining enterprise is the automated monitoring of dump trucks condition, their redistribution between the loading equipment and offloading points, as well as the calculation of their optimal number at the routes.

With increasingly complex mining and geological conditions and increased safety requirements, the effective use of mining equipment can be ensured by exclusion of people from hazardous areas, in addition, it is possible to improve the efficiency of open pit mining by optimum operation of equipment and automatic optimization of cargo traffic.

All these tasks are performed by modern Mine Fleet Management System, which later may include an autonomous vehicles.

2 Dispatching of Heavy Trucks in Modern Open-Pit Mines

The modern Mine Fleet Management System shall ensure prompt receipt of real time information about the work of mining, transport and auxiliary equipment, as well as on-board technology systems. It is required to monitor the execution time of all operations during the transportation of rock mass, number of trips, cargo weight, fuel level in the tank, quality of driving of dump trucks and other performance indicators of dump trucks. Currently, a persistent trend of introduction of perspective unmanned operation based on remotely controlled equipment and robotic dump trucks for open-pit mining emerged in some countries. As compared to the existing technologies of mining and transportation of minerals, robotic dump trucks can provide a higher efficiency of open-pit mining, equipment performance and level of personnel and industrial safety, they can reduce operating costs by reducing equipment downtime due to human factor and errors. According to expert estimates, automated operation of dump trucks can improve its performance by more than 20% [3, 12].

In 2010, VIST Group company (one of the world leading manufacturer of Mine Fleet Management Systems) and the Belarusian manufacturer of BELAZ dump trucks, one of the three world leading manufacturers of heavy-duty and extra heavy-duty dump trucks first developed and presented in the framework of the scientific and technical conference "Prospects for further development of open-pit transport" remote-control BELAZ dump truck with a cargo-carrying capacity of 130 tons and equipped with a DC drive. The developed remote control system for BELAZ dump trucks was an important step towards creation of the fully autonomous dump truck [9].

Modern BELAZ dump trucks are already equipped with on-board equipment, allowing efficient on-route use of the machine: a system for video surveillance, remote monitoring and diagnostic of the machine based on the unification of onboard equipment, use of common control and software algorithms. This approach allows you to gradually move to the robotization of dump trucks and offer modern robotic dump trucks. The main feature of dump trucks is the capability of monitoring and remote control of multiple components and assemblies of the dump truck, in addition, hundreds of gigabytes of information received and stored by the modern dispatch system open up great opportunities for mining enterprises to increase their effectiveness.

The main feature of robotic BELAZ dump truck, unlike its predecessor – remotely controlled dump truck, is the capability to move along a predetermined route. During the movement of dump truck to the controller all necessary information about road conditions, as well as the condition of control systems is received wirelessly. The movement of the dump truck to the loading or unloading point in the autonomous mode is provided by a high-precision GPS/GLONASS satellite navigation system. An optoelectronic system installed on the dump truck ensures the safety of the driving in all weather and climatic conditions, as well as at any time of the day. This solution is designed to reduce the risk to humans when working in places with hazardous operating conditions, as well as to eliminate the effect of harmful environmental factors on the body of the driver. An experienced operator during the continuous process cycle can successfully operate four or five robotic dump trucks while in office.

For the further development in the field of implementation of electronic control systems and more efficient design of robotic machinery BELAZ took another step forward, completing the development of the multi-functional diagnostic system, representing a multi-channel digital net-work of the dump truck, which brings together different systems of the machine into a single information space.

Implementation of the multi-functional diagnostic system has the following advantages:

1. Flexibility of control due to the added functions: by means of the software configuration of electronic equipment units and a digital information network under specific operating conditions.
2. Improvement of the diagnostics and control efficiency: by means of electrical systems integration, load control, hydraulics, video surveillance and decentralized structure.
3. Material consumption is a principle of distributed control (local input/output modules, arranged by function on the chassis and in the cab) reduces the number of contact connections and the length of electrical wires.
4. Effective service is an access to quite extensive diagnostic functions (event logs, black box, guided help in fault finding and more) will enable to diagnose and correct faults more efficiently and quicker, as well as to predict their occurrence and to prevent outages of expensive components and assemblies.
5. Hazardous behavior warning to the driver.
6. Human-machine interface, built in a display module.

Now let's consider some of the possible solutions for remote monitoring, control and automated management of the mining equipment and dump trucks. VG Service System allows to control the work of mining and transport equipment via WEB interface and solves the following tasks [9, 12]:

- increase in performance of the mining and transport complex by means of reduction of all types of downtime, load control;
- reduction of fuel and lubricants consumption per ton of transported rock mass by means of reduction of inter-shift downtime, rational planning on the basis of objective information on fuel consumption for each piece of equipment;

- reliable information on the number of runs and transported rock mass, actual work of excavators, dump trucks, other vehicles;
- increase in the operating time of machine assemblies by means of the automated load control and monitoring of speed limits, control of other types of equipment;
- automated reporting by types of work, operating time, analysis of the service factors of mining and transport equipment (equipment utilization ratio, technical availability, specific fuel consumption, plan/actual comparison, operational analysis for dump trucks ton/kilometer, etc.).

This system is designed for mining enterprises, which do not still use the modern Mine Fleet Management Systems or decided to introduce the dispatch control in phases, as well as for open pits with a small equipment fleet, where it is important to control the operating conditions and statistics in the first phase. The main task of the Karier Mine Fleet Management Systems in addition to the recording, monitoring the KPIs is automated dispatch control and optimization based on a set of criteria (ore quality management, performance parameters, plan targets, etc.), i.e. automatic distribution of dump trucks in the beginning of the shift (static optimization) and d shift (dynamic optimization).

There is the opportunity to apply various optimization criteria for the different complexes of "excavator - dump trucks" (for example, stripping and mining), control the last run. Moreover, the system allows to quickly classify downtimes using an on-board computer, optimize the load, transmitting real-time information about each loaded bucket to the excavator operator, control the optimal fuel consumption, increase machine performance and avoid overload of dump trucks (Fig. 1).

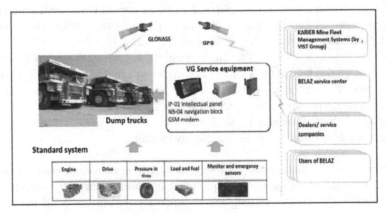

Fig. 1. The architecture of the dispatch system and remote monitoring of BELAZ equipment.

The efficient use of dump trucks and the whole mining and transport complex is particularly relevant for managers of companies exploiting several open pits. The objective of such companies is to bring performance to the best practice of the results, achieved by the company, and to achieve the world's best performance, while maximizing cost savings and ensuring a high rate of return on investment. Thus, mining companies need an effective system for operation of open pit machinery and capabilities of performance data analysis, equipment utilization factor, technical availability, operating conditions, equipment repairs.

In this regard, based on the accumulated statistics on the enterprise performance, historical data and the integration of information from various sources (the machinery diagnostic system and Mine Fleet Management Systems, MES, ERP, logs of failures) it is possible to find dependencies of downtime and operating factors for equipment on its operating conditions, analyze actual events, that has already occurred, and also predict the performance of equipment in the future.

3 Development of the Intelligent Dispatch Control Platform

Worth mentioning that on the current stage, development of Mine Fleet Management System suggests creation of an intelligent software platform that is based on step by step expansion of system's capabilities in context of robotized machinery integration and usage of modern technologies of data analyzing and processing (geological, operating, technological, sensor and expert data). These steps, characterizing system's capabilities are sorted by control reactions speed and increasing autonomy of technological machinery and "pilotlessness" level of the control process:

- centralized supervisor control, based on operative planning models and mining-transport machinery;
- supervisor control based on sensory data of partially robotized mining equipment's;
- complex functioning control of robotized units with wide variety of functions (diagnostics, interpretation, identification, predicting);
- remote control of robotized equipment's;
- remote control and interaction of partially-autonomous trucks. The system can be viewed as a complex of interacting intellectual agents, that have varying behavior models and basic parameters. Intellectual agents is a complex of software modules that exchange input and output information [1–3]. Thus several agent classes are defined;
- operator agent. Basically, a self-educating agent, capable of forming a situational model without human interaction by collecting, accumulating and sorting various facts, events and situations from other agents and interacting with them, capable of choosing the best strategy for fulfilling its objective;
- infrastructural agent units, that act as static technological environment elements: loading bays, roads, traffic intersections, etc. Each of this agents are described by an array of parameters, and other agent's interaction with them is followed by a corresponding set of rules;
- reflective autonomous agents are system elements whose behavior is based on environmental conditions and information from other agents. All robotized units, such as heavy trucks, excavators, conveyor belts, maintenance vehicles are considered this class.

Autonomous functioning and agent's interaction is based on two baseline models: cognitive, that are used for describing agent behavior and strategy selection conditions;

and processing, that are used for agent condition and technological situations interpretation, agent planning optimization, identification as well as data base parameters optimization [4, 10, 11].

The system's functioning is mainly dependent on information data base that is formed using every control system set up in an open-pit mine and all of the available telemetric data. The most developed element nowadays, as was stated before, is heavy truck on-board computing devices. Constant moving of select heavy trucks on an industrial site allows for data collection of not only the unit itself, but of its surrounding environment as well. Depending on the current objective the data collected can be processed by on-board computers in real-time and transferred to remote servers for more detailed analyses.

The telemetric data collected by the mobile units' on-board computers can be sorted into several segments considering its role, that is represented by varying parameters in the control system:

- data regarding mobile unit's positioning;
- parameters, characterizing mobile object's functioning data (fuel levels, load, movement speed, suspension load, etc.);
- integral indicators, reacting to precise unit's movements – unit's vector acceleration sensors;
- parameters, describing unit's position relative to static units in the environment;

Figure 2 shows how system's components interact mobile agents with the data base while managing the movement.

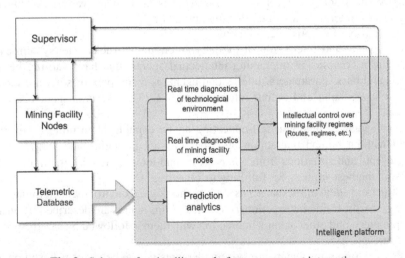

Fig. 2. Scheme of an intelligent platform component interaction.

Here are example scenarios of predictive analytics, which can be followed, analyzing information in the Karier Mine Fleet Management System and other information systems of the mining enterprise. The mine planning system has a plan for excavators per each shift, resulting from division of monthly plans by the number of shifts. This plan takes into account the economy, calculated in ERP, that is, a plan of shipments, according to which the production and stripping volumes are planned. Machines with their costs and technical availability factors shall be distributed according to these volumes.

However, as Mine Fleet Management System receive information on real situation with utility vehicles, created at the current shift – vehicle utilization, conditions in the work faces in the form of coefficients reducing or to the contrary increasing performance, then upon completion of the shift actual data for shift are obtained, on the basis of actual telemetry data received from dump trucks and other mining equipment. Mining companies can analyze causes of performance decrease in Mine Fleet Management System and understand what has induced such causes.

It should be noted that Karier Mine Fleet Management System do not simply extrapolate results of a shift over a longer period, they can determine the causes and trends in order to analyze the enterprise management.

4   An Example of the Predictive Analytics Application

Predictive analytics is able to identify the causes of risks, repeated violations, including during operation of BELAZ machinery. An example, relating to identification of the causes of failures during equipment operation, is based on predictive analytics. Let's assume that dump trucks equipped only with pressure and temperature sensors in the tires work in an open pit. This information is transmitted to the dispatch system. Eventually one, then another tire break occurs, or in the end of the shift it is evident that some tires are worn more than others. Information accumulated only in the sensors installed in these tires is not enough. For predictive analytics it is required to know runs of each tire, roads (angles of roads, radii, formation on roads, etc.), environment where these tires ran, who drove these dump trucks from the date the tires were installed. It is necessary to analyze all possible relevant data on the life of tires. So, when all the main and auxiliary data are analyzed for making forward-looking decisions on a subject of evaluation (in this case the tires) and an incident occurs, the mathematical model of predictive analytics binds all the data to the incident.

Brief description of formal mechanisms used to predict tire durability is as follows. Source data for predictive analytics can be accumulated during a continued period of time (months, a year, several years). Elements of such a table are records e_1, e_2, ..., e_n (~700000 in this example) contain information about tires workload (tire model, ID) installed on a specific heavy truck (truck model, truck ID, driver ID) during a specific shift on a specific mining facility. In our research task data from several open pit mines (in our case – 7) is analyzed. The initial table also contains information about tire condition by the end of the shift. Possible variants: {normal condition, replace by order, exploded, repairing due to puncture, incision and other damage}. Source table can then be converted into several integral tables, that are used to check hypothesizes related to various factor-parameters influence on tire condition. Table structure is represented in Fig. 3 as a semantic network with key variables declared.

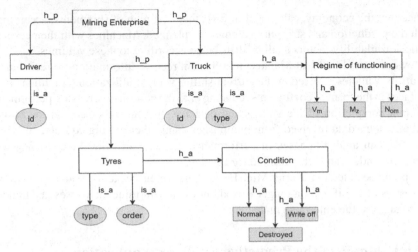

Fig. 3. Structure of tire data base in semantic net forms.

Three types of connections are used in the scheme has part:

h_p – has a part of notion;
h_a – has certain ability;
is_a – be an example of class.
V_m, M_Z, N_{om} – integral parameters that characterize tire strain during a certain period of work: average speed, total transported cargo, amount of rides while overloaded, etc.

Suggested scheme is considered a base for creating an automated mecha-nism for introducing hypothesizes that are further approved or disapproved dur-ing table processing. In the initial group of factors $S_1, S_2, \ldots, S_{m_2}$ picked out are a group of quality and identification parameters $I_1, I_2, \ldots, I_{m_1}$, predictive type $I_1(A_1), I_2(A_2), \ldots, I_{m_1}(A_{m_1})$, where $A_1, A_2, \ldots, A_{m_1}$ – object variables and $a_{11}, \ldots, a_{1k_1}, a_{21}, \ldots, a_{2k_2}, a_{m_1 1}, \ldots, a_{m_1 k_{m_1}}$ their values.

$X_1, X_2, \ldots, X_{m_2}$ – quantitative parameters that describe operation modes, that act as observable parameters (nominal symptoms) that create the processing base for predictive models.

$D = \{d_1, d_2, \ldots, d_{m_3}\}$ – a set of possible diagnostic conditions of tires.

Initial information data base can be represented as follows:

$$W \subseteq I_1 * \ldots * I_{m_1} * X_1 * \ldots * X_{m_2} * D \tag{1}$$

Further exposition will be given with consideration of the following assumptions:

H_1: A possibility and relevant toolkits for creating classification rules exist. They provide a stable object classification by tire failure types, based on analyzing operational characteristics:

$$H_1 : \exists F(x_1, x_2, \ldots, x_p) = \tilde{y} : \begin{Bmatrix} y < \delta_F \to D_i \\ y \geq \delta_F \to \overline{D_i} \end{Bmatrix} \tag{2}$$

where D_i – one of tire failure types.

H_2: There exists a model that allows interconnecting tire operation modes and its operation duration for a specific subject (truck model, tire model, driver):

$$H_2 : \widehat{X_i} = \varphi\{x_1, x_2, \ldots, x_{i-1}, x_i, \ldots, x_{m_2}, P(I_1, \ldots, I_{m_1})\}, \tag{3}$$

where $P(I_1, \ldots, I_{m_1})$ is a procedure for forming (setting up) a learning table, relevant to the tested hypothesis.

This procedure starts the first stage of processing and hypothesis testing mechanism – an automated generation of learning samples.

For example, testing every of the below stated "tire endurance" (duration of tire operation without failure) hypothesis depends on:

h_1 – tire model;
h_2 – specific driver;
h_3 – specific drivers that controlled the truck this tire was installed on;
...
h_k – tire install position on the truck;

and implies that a specific learning table will be generated:

$$P(I_1, \ldots, I_{m_1}) : W \to W_i, i = \overline{1, k} \tag{4}$$

The second stage of the mechanism's operation is checking the hypothesizes, including the selection of optimal model structure with use of statistic and entropy criteria.

An automated hypothesis checking procedure W, P, K_S, K_E {LPA} is implemented with open-source resources with use of libraries containing over 150 basic tools for different tasks of predictive analytics – {LPA}.

5 Brief Conclusion

Currently researches are conducted to adapt the suggested mechanism for solving a wide variety of diagnostic and prediction tasks that can occur during control and supervision of a robotized open-pit mine.

Very important is that one case and a dozens of cases are not enough for "prediction", for predictive analytics and understanding of the trends in the future, it is required to maintain statistics, based on the condition and on incidents that occurred in the past. The same approach can be applied not only for dump trucks, but also for excavators, which are equipped with a number of diagnostic system sensors.

At last, we would like to note that today it is difficult even to imagine the work of modern mining enterprises without the use of Mine Fleet Management System for monitoring and control of operation of dump trucks and other equipment.

Due to the fact that BELAZ dump trucks are provided with on-board equipment allowing to quickly connect the machinery to the dispatch systems and to analyze the effectiveness of the use of dump trucks, mining companies achieve significant economic effects and increase the performance of their main facilities and mining equipment, and the use of this information for prediction of production activity is the key to the competitiveness of mining enterprises.

Acknowledgments. The study was carried out at the expense of a grant from the Russian Foundation for Basic Research (RFBR) (project № 16-07-01197).

References

1. Dadhich, S., Bodin, U., Anderson, U.: Key challenges in automation of earth-moving machines. Autom. Constr. **68**, 212–222 (2016). https://doi.org/10.1016/j.autcon.2016.05.009
2. Yan, Z., Jouandeau, N., Cherif, A.A.: A survey and analysis of multi-robot coordination. Int. J. Adv. Robot. Syst. **10**(12) (2013). https://doi.org/10.5772/57313
3. Vennapusa, P.K.R., White, D.J., Jahren, C.T.: Impacts of automated machine guidance on earthwork operations. In: Civil, Construction and Environmental Engineering Conference Presentations and Proceedings, vol. 34, pp. 207–216 (2015). https://lib.dr.iastate.edu/ccee_conf/34
4. Jiang, B., Fei, Y.: Vehicle speed prediction by two-level data driven models in vehicular networks. IEEE Trans. Intell. Transp. Syst. **18**(7), 1793–1801 (2017). https://doi.org/10.1109/TITS.2016.2620498
5. Zhu, Q., Hu, J., Cai, W., Henchen, L.: A new robot navigation algorithm for dynamic unknown environment based on dynamic path re-computation and an improved scout ant algorithm. Appl. Soft Comput. **11**, 4667–4676 (2011)
6. Kammoun, H.M., Kallel, I., Casillas, J., Abraham, A., Alimi, A.M.: *Adapt-Traf*: an adaptive multiagent road traffic management system based on hybrid ant-hierarchical fuzzy model. Transport. Res. Part C Emerg. Technol. **42**, 147–167 (2014). https://doi.org/10.1016/j.trc.2014.03.003
7. Ghifari, N.T.A., Jati, A.N., Saputra, R.: Coordination control for simple autonomous mobile robot. In: 2017 5th International Conference on Instrumentation, Control and Automation (ICA), Yogyakarta, Indonesia, pp. 93–98 (2017). https://doi.org/10.1109/ica.2017.8068420
8. Nowakowski, C., Shladover, S.E., Tan, H.-S.: Heavy vehicle automation: human factors lessons learned. Procedia Manuf. **3**, 2945–2952 (2015). https://doi.org/10.1016/j.promfg.2015.07.824
9. Temkin, I.O., Deryabin, S.A., Konov, I.S., Klebanov, D.A.: Method for determining the status of quarry technological roads when controlling the interaction of robotic elements of the mining transport [in Russian]. Gornyi Zhurnal **1**, 78–82 (2018). https://doi.org/10.17580/gzh.2018.01.14
10. Temkin, I.O., Goncharenko, A.N.: Interaction modeling problems of intellectual agents at the mining enterprise [in Russian]. St. Petersburg Polytechnic Univ. J. Eng. Sci. Technol. **183**(4–2), 252–258 (2013). https://elibrary.ru/item.asp?id=21252948
11. Temkin, I., Deryabin, S., Konov, I.: Soft computing models in an intellectual open-pit mines transport control system. Procedia Comput. Sci. **120**, 411–416 (2017). https://doi.org/10.1016/j.procs.2017.11.257
12. Temkin, I.O., Klebanov, D.A.: Intellectual control systems in open pit mines transport system: comprehensive state, objects and mechanisms of decision [in Russian]. Gorny Informatsionno-Analiticheskiy Byulleten (nauchno-teknicheskii zhurnal) S1, pp. 257–266 (2014). https://elibrary.ru/item.asp?id=22486663

The Use of Irregular Precise Observations for Parametric Adaptation of a Discrete Stochastic Filter

Sergey Sokolov[1] , Sergey Kramarov[2(✉)] , Elena Chub[3] ,
and Marianna Polyakova[3]

[1] Rostov State University of Economics, Bol'shaya Sadovaya Str. 69,
344002 Rostov-on-Don, Russia
[2] Surgut State University, Lenin Ave. 1, 628412 Surgut, Russia
maoovo@yandex.ru
[3] Rostov State Transport University, ploshchad' Rostovskogo Strelkovogo polka 2,
344038 Rostov-on-Don, Russia

Abstract. The estimation of the state of dynamic stochastic systems using the methods of filtration theory assumes the exact a priori setting of the parameters of the equation of the system and the probabilistic characteristics of its noises, which in practice are known approximately or change in time randomly. In this regard, the algorithm of adaptive estimation of one of the most critical parameters of the discrete stochastic filter - the dispersion matrix of noises acting on the system is considered for measuring and information systems that use, in addition to continuous noisy observations, also accurate observations at random times. The advantage of the proposed algorithm is the possibility of analytical determination of this dispersion matrix based on current precise observations and, as a consequence, a significant increase in the overall accuracy of the evaluation of the perturbed state vector of the system. A numerical example illustrating the possibility of effective practical use of the developed algorithm is given.

Keywords: Discrete stochastic filter · Adaptive estimation · Dispersion matrix · Irregular precise observations

1 Introduction

The estimation of the state of dynamic stochastic systems using the methods of the stochastic filtration theory and, in particular, the Kalman filter, assumes the exact a priori setting of the parameters of the equation of the system and the probabilistic characteristics of the perturbing effects for the system. But often in practice, the parameters of the system and its noise or are known approximately, or change in time randomly. In this regard, a large number of different measurement and information systems (further - MIS) as the main option of their operation use the correction of the current estimates of the state vector on the exact observations formed with some arbitrary time interval. This is the MIS of robots, where the zero speed of the robot's foot (or the lower point of the wheel) at the time of touching the earth's surface is taken into account when evaluating the robot's orientation parameters [1],

V. Sukhomlin and E. Zubareva (Eds.): SITITO 2018, CCIS 1201, pp. 375–383, 2020.
https://doi.org/10.1007/978-3-030-46895-8_29

– and inertial-satellite navigation systems (further - NS), in which the correction of inertial NS indications, which errors grow with time, is made by measurements of satellite NS, which act as reference [2, 3],
– and MIS of various transport systems (marine, railway, etc.), in which the correction of the orientation and navigation parameters of the object is carried out at the time of passing the base (reference) points with exactly known coordinates [4–6],
– and combined NS, providing navigation inside the premises and enclosed spaces on the basis of inertial sensors [7], etc.

Currently, such correction is performed mainly by direct replacement of the current estimates of phase coordinates with their corresponding precise observations without correction of the parameters of the estimation algorithm [8–10]. It is obvious that with this approach, the growth of errors in the estimation of phase coordinates on the time interval determined by the moment of the next precise observation will not decrease (which occurs in the above-mentioned MIS).

In this regard, there is a need for adaptive formation of the parameters of the estimation algorithm directly from the obtained precise observations, which will allow to significantly improve the accuracy of the estimation of the vector of the state of the system as a whole at the time intervals between them.

As one of the most critical from the point of view of accuracy of estimation filter parameters is the variance matrix of noise of the system, directly determines the value coefficient of gain filter, and, as a consequence, the rate (and even the fact) of convergence of the estimation process, then below we consider the possibility of improving the accuracy of the Kalman filtering process on the basis of its adaptive evaluation.

2 Problem Formulation

As precise observations are made at irregular discrete moments of time, to solve this problem, we consider the discrete version of the most commonly used in solving the problems of estimation algorithm – Kalman filter, in which the evaluation of the state vector of the system X_{k+1} in $k + 1$-th moment of time determines in accordance with the equation [11]:

$$\hat{X}_{k+1} = \Phi_k \cdot \hat{X}_k + K_k \cdot (Z_k - H_k \cdot \hat{X}_k) \tag{1}$$

where $\hat{X}_k$ - estimation of the state vector of the system at the kth time;
Φ_k - the transition matrix of the system state; Z_k - measurement vector:

$$Z_k = H_k \cdot X_k + V_k,$$

H_k- a measurement matrix representing the space of system state vectors in the space of measurement vectors;
V_k- centered Gaussian sequence with dispersion matrix R_k,
K_k- coefficient of gain filter, defined as:

$$K_k = P_{k/k-1} \cdot H_k^T \cdot (H_k \cdot P_{k/k-1} \cdot H_k^T + R_k)^{-1} \tag{2}$$

$$P_{k/k-1} = \Phi_k \cdot P_{k-1} \cdot \Phi_k^T + Q_k \tag{3}$$

where $P_{k/k-1}$ - extrapolated covariance matrix; Q_k - the required diagonal dispersion matrix of the Gaussian noise of the system.

Based on the presented form of the filter gain, the problem of estimating the dispersion noise matrix of the object by precise observations is formulated as the problem of finding the matrix Q_k from the condition of coincidence at the corresponding time of the vector of estimates $\hat{X}_{k+1}$ (1) with the precise state vector of the system X_{k+1} (precise observations).

3 Problem Solution

To solve this problem, we will use the full expression of the Kalman gain obtained by substituting (3) into (2):

$$K_k = (\Phi_k \cdot P_{k-1} \cdot \Phi_k^T + Q_k) \cdot H_k^T \cdot \left[H_k \cdot (\Phi_k \cdot P_{k-1} \cdot \Phi_k^T + Q_k) \cdot H_k^T + R_k \right]^{-1}$$

where to make your future decisions, we will introduce the designation $(\Phi_k \cdot P_{k-1} \cdot \Phi_k^T + Q_k) \cdot H_k^T = \gamma$ and we write the coefficient expression in the following way:

$$K_k = \gamma \cdot (H_k \cdot \gamma + R_k)^{-1} \tag{4}$$

In this case, Eq. (1) takes the form:

$$\hat{X}_{k+1} - \Phi_k \cdot \hat{X}_k = \gamma \cdot (H_k \cdot \gamma + R_k)^{-1} \cdot (Z_k - H_k \cdot \hat{X}_k) \tag{5}$$

and with respect to the matrix Q_k, included in the matrix γ, it is a nonlinear vector equation, the solution of which by traditional numerical methods requires multiple application of a very expensive matrix reversal procedure. For the possibility of analytical solution of Eq. (5), we draw the following constructions.

Because the conditions of the problem is $\hat{X}_{k+1} = X_{k+1}$, then, introducing the notation $X_{k+1} - \Phi_k \cdot \hat{X}_k = X_*$, $Z_k - H_k \cdot \hat{X}_k = Z_*$, let's present the Eq. (5) as:

$$X_* = \gamma \cdot (H_k \cdot \gamma + R_k)^{-1} \cdot Z_* \tag{6}$$

Multiplying both parts of Eq. (6) by the inverse matrix $\left[\gamma (H_k \gamma + R_k) \right]^{-1}$, have:

$$(H_k \cdot \gamma + R_k) \cdot \gamma^{-1} \cdot X_* = Z_*, \text{ or}$$

$$R_k \cdot \gamma^{-1} \cdot X_* = Z_* - H_k \cdot X_* \tag{7}$$

Continuing further multiplying both parts of Eq. (7) by the matrix $\gamma \cdot R_k^{-1}$, we bring it to the form, linear with respect to γ, and, consequently, with respect to Q_k:

$$X_* = \gamma \cdot R_k^{-1} \cdot (Z_* - H_k \cdot X_*) \tag{8}$$

For the final solution of this equation with respect to Q_k solve the expression $\gamma = (\Phi_k \cdot P_{k-1} \cdot \Phi_k^T + Q_k) \cdot H_k^T$ and receive:

$$X_* = (\Phi_k \cdot P_{k-1} \cdot \Phi_k^T \cdot H_k^T \cdot R_k^{-1} + Q_k \cdot H_k^T \cdot R_k^{-1}) \\ \times (Z_* - H_k \cdot X_*) \tag{9}$$

Introducing to simplify the subsequent withdrawal of the designation $\Phi_k \cdot P_{k-1} \cdot \Phi_k^T \cdot H_k^T \cdot R_k^{-1} = \Delta_{k,k-1}$, let's present the Eq. (9) in the form:

$$X_* = \Delta_{k,k-1}(Z_* - H_k \cdot X_*) + Q_k H_k^T R_k^{-1}(Z_* - H_k \cdot X_*) \tag{10}$$

Denoting vectors $\Delta_{k,k-1} \cdot (Z_* - H_k \cdot X_*) = \Delta_*$, $H_k^T R_k^{-1}(Z_* - H_k \cdot X_*) = U_*$, we give the Eq. (10) to the following form:

$$X_* - \Delta_* = Q_k U_* \tag{11}$$

Equation (11) easily admits an analytical solution with respect to all elements of the diagonal matrix Q_k, if we consider the possibility of presenting the work $Q_k U_*$ in form $U_{*diag} Q_{k\ vect}$, where

$$U_{*diag} = \begin{vmatrix} U_{*1} & 0 & 0 & ....0 \\ 0 & U_{*2} & 0 & ....0 \\ & \multicolumn{2}{c}{............} \\ 0 & 0 & 0 & .....U_{*n} \end{vmatrix}, \quad Q_{k\ vect} = \begin{vmatrix} Q_{k1} \\ Q_{k2} \\ \vdots \\ Q_{kn} \end{vmatrix},$$

U_{*i}, Q_{ki}, $i = 1, \ldots, n$ — elements, correspondingly, of vector U_* and matrix Q_k. In this case, we have the desired expression of the vector of the elements of the dispersion matrix of the object perturbation in the form

$$U_{*diag}^{-1}(X_* - \Delta_*) = Q_{k\ vect} \tag{12}$$

where U_{*diag}^{-1} - inverse matrix, easily computed due to its diagonality:

$$U_{*diag}^{-1} = \begin{vmatrix} \frac{1}{U_{*1}} & 0 & 0 & .... & 0 \\ 0 & \frac{1}{U_{*2}} & 0 & .... & 0 \\ & \multicolumn{3}{c}{............} \\ 0 & 0 & 0 & .....\frac{1}{U_{*n}} \end{vmatrix}.$$

Thus, the found solution of the nonlinear vector Eq. (5) in the form (12) allows analytically solving the problem of adaptive estimation of the dispersion matrix of the system noise from the obtained exact observations, which, in turn, will allow for the time intervals between them to significantly improve the accuracy of the evaluation of the state vector of the system as a whole.

Let us consider an example illustrating the effectiveness of the proposed approach.

4 Example

The simplified Eular-Krylov equations are used to test the gyrostabilized platform (GSP) and to determine its random drift in the inertial coordinate system (ICS) at small time intervals (tens of minutes) when describing the rotation of the GSP [6]:

$$
\begin{vmatrix} \dot{\alpha} \\ \dot{\beta} \\ \dot{\gamma} \end{vmatrix} = \begin{vmatrix} \omega_x \\ \omega_y \\ \omega_z \end{vmatrix},
$$

$$
\alpha(0) = \alpha_0, \ \beta(0) = \beta_0, \ \gamma(0) = \gamma_0,
$$

(13)

where α, β, γ - angles of Eular-Krylov, determining the orientation GSP in ICS, $\begin{vmatrix} \omega_x & \omega_y & \omega_z \end{vmatrix}^T$ random vector of absolute angular velocity of rotation of GSP, described by white Gaussian noise with unknown intensity matrix. With an interval of 20, 25 and 30 from the optical monitoring system based on spatially distributed mirror do the measuring of angles α, β, γ, considered accurate, and at other times with tact $\tau = 0.05c$ are used appropriately prepared the readings of the accelerometers [6], forming noisy linear measurements on channels α, β, γ.

The discrete filter constructed according to the equations of the object (13), in the accepted designations has the form:

$$
\hat{X}_{k+1} = \Phi_k \hat{X}_k + K_k (Z_k - H_k \hat{X}_k),
$$

(14)

where

$$
\hat{X}_k = \begin{vmatrix} \hat{\alpha} \\ \hat{\beta} \\ \hat{\gamma} \end{vmatrix}, \quad \Phi_k = \begin{vmatrix} 1 & 0 & 0 \\ 0 & 1 & 0 \\ 0 & 0 & 1 \end{vmatrix}, \quad H_k = \begin{vmatrix} 80 & 0 & 0 \\ 0 & 70 & 0 \\ 0 & 0 & 155 \end{vmatrix},
$$

$$
R_k = \begin{vmatrix} 4.2 \cdot 10^{-7} & 0 & 0 \\ 0 & 3.5 \cdot 10^{-7} & 0 \\ 0 & 0 & 9.5 \cdot 10^{-7} \end{vmatrix}.
$$

The true dispersion matrix Q was chosen constant and equal

$$
Q = \begin{vmatrix} (\tau \cdot 3 \cdot 10^{-9})^2 & 0 & 0 \\ 0 & (\tau \cdot 1,2 \cdot 10^{-9})^2 & 0 \\ 0 & 0 & (\tau \cdot 2 \cdot 10^{-9})^2 \end{vmatrix},
$$

but since the dispersion matrix Q of the random perturbation of the object is unknown under the conditions of the problem, the Euler angles were estimated for two cases: the classical Kalman filter (1), when the value Q is given with an error on the entire modeling interval

$$Q = \begin{vmatrix} (\tau \cdot 3 \cdot 10^{-5})^2 & 0 & 0 \\ 0 & (\tau \cdot 1,2 \cdot 10^{-5})^2 & 0 \\ 0 & 0 & (\tau \cdot 2 \cdot 10^{-5})^2 \end{vmatrix},$$

and adaptive filter, when the value of Q is estimated according to the proposed scheme.

Graphs of angle estimation errors α, β, γ, obtained in the direct implementation of the filter (14) are shown in Fig. 1, 2 and 3, where there is a significant instability of the

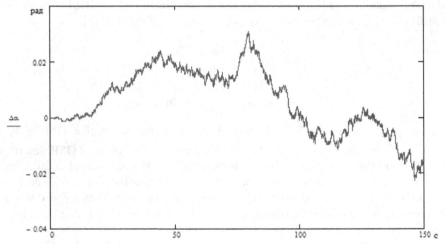

Fig. 1. The graph of estimation error of angle α, obtained in implementations of the classical Kalman filter.

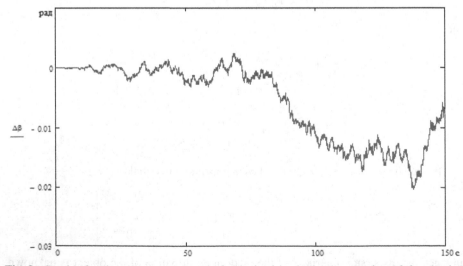

Fig. 2. Graph of estimation error of angle β, obtained in the implementation of the classical Kalman filter.

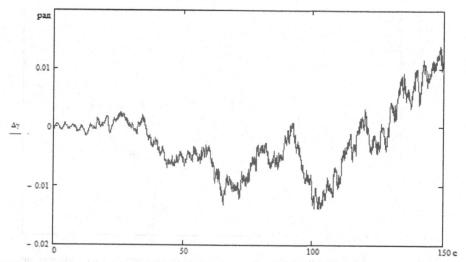

Fig. 3. Graph of estimation error of angle γ, obtained in the implementation of the classical Kalman filter.

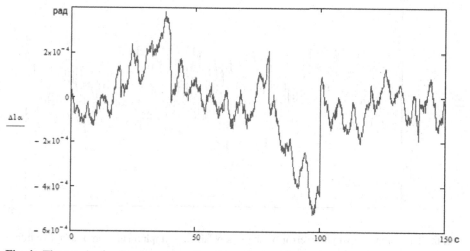

Fig. 4. The graph of estimation error of angle α, obtained in implementation of adaptive filter.

filtration process with significant errors of evaluation at all three angles (up to 0.02 rad (1 deg) for 150th second).

When organizing the filter according to the above adaptive algorithm, the estimation errors have the following form, shown in Fig. 4, 5 and 6. In this case, in first, the estimation process is stable throughout the interval of simulation for all three corners, and second, the estimation error after 100-th seconds does not exceed $5 \cdot 10^{-4}$ rad (100 angles/sec), that provides high accuracy of calibration of drift of GSP.

Thus, it can be concluded from the comparison of the results of modeling of traditional and adaptive filtering schemes that the proposed estimation algorithm using

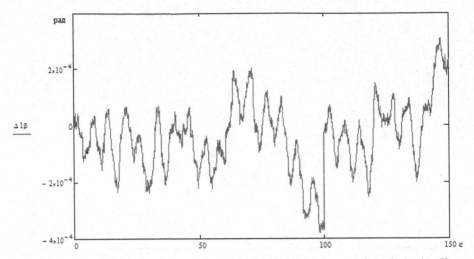

Fig. 5. The graph of estimation error of angle β, obtained in implementation of adaptive filter.

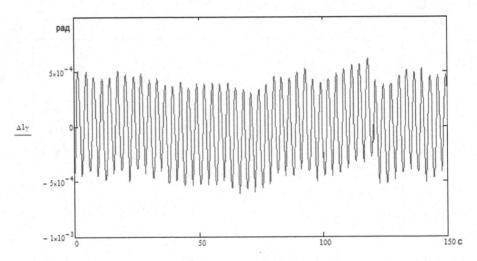

Fig. 6. The graph of estimation error of angle γ, obtained in implementation of adaptive filter.

irregular accurate observations allows for a relatively small increase in computational costs to significantly improve the accuracy of the estimation of the vector of the state of the stochastic dynamic system operating under perturbation conditions with unknown statistical parameters.

5 Conclusion

The considered approach to the synthesis of adaptive estimation algorithms, using the possibility of obtaining irregular accurate observations, can be effectively used in measurement and information systems operating under random disturbances with unknown probabilistic characteristics, when traditional filtration schemes are inoperable. At the same time, a slight increase in computational costs caused by the need for adaptive calculation of the filter parameters is compensated by a significant increase in the overall accuracy of the perturbed state vector estimation MIS.

Acknowledgments. The work is supported by the grant of Russian Foundation for Basic Research №18-07-00126. The results of the work are used in the performance of the state task №1.11772.2018/11.12.

References

1. Looney, M.: Optimization of navigation characteristics of a mobile robot. Comp. Technol. **1**(126), 48–50 (2012). (in Russian). https://elibrary.ru/item.asp?id=17344352
2. Litvin, M.A., Malyugina, A.A., Miller, A.B., Stepanov, A.N., Chickrin, D.E.: Error classification and approximation in inertial navigational systems. Inf. Process **14**(4), 326–339 (2014). (in Russian). https://elibrary.ru/item.asp?id=22800358
3. Velikanova, E.P., Voroshilin, E.P.: Adaptive estimation of maneuvering object position in changeable radio channel transmission gain. Proc. TUSUR **2–1**(26), 29–35 (2012). (in Russian). https://elibrary.ru/item.asp?id=18814279
4. Reznichenko, V.I., Maleev, P.I., Smirnov, Yu.M.: The satellite correction of orientation parameters for marine objects, vol. 27, pp. 25–32 (2008). (in Russian). https://elibrary.ru/item.asp?id=15565357
5. Jwo, D.-H., Chung, F.-C., Weng, T.-P.: Adaptive Kalman filter for navigation sensor fusion. In: Thomas, C. (ed.) Sensor Fusion and its Applications, pp. 65–90. IntechOpen (2010). https://doi.org/10.5772/9957
6. Sokolov, S.V., Pogorelov, V.A.: Stochastic Assessment, Management and Identification of High Precision Navigation Systems. Fizmatlit Publication, Moscow (2016). (in Russian)
7. Shilina, V.A.: Inertial sensor system for indoor navigation. Youth Sci. Tech. Bull. **4**, 39 (2015). (in Russian)
8. Tsyplakov, A.: An introduction to state space modeling. Quantile **9**, 1–24 (2011). http://quantile.ru/09/09-AT.pdf
9. Sung, W., Choi, S., You, K.: TDoA based UGV localization using adaptive Kalman filter algorithm. In: 2008 Second International Conference on Future Generation Communication and Networking Symposia, Sanya, pp. 99–103 (2008). https://doi.org/10.1109/fgcns.2008.126
10. Mohamed, A.H., Schwarz, K.P.: Adaptive Kalman filtering for INS/GPS. J. Geodesy **73**(4), 193–203 (1999). https://doi.org/10.1007/s001900050236
11. Tikhonov, V.I., Kharisov, V.N.: Static analysis and synthesis of radio engineering devices and communication systems. Radio i svyaz', Moscow (2004). (in Russian)

On Information Technology Development for Monitoring of Air Pollution by Road and Water Transport in Large Port Cities (St. Petersburg, Vladivostok and Sevastopol)

Vladimir Lozhkin[1]([⊠]) [iD], Olga Lozhkina[1] [iD], Gleb Rogozinsky[2,3] [iD],
and Igor Malygin[4] [iD]

[1] Saint Petersburg University of State Fire Service of EMERCOM of Russia,
Moskovskij Avenue 149, 196105 Saint Petersburg, Russia
vnlojkin@yandex.ru, olojkina@yandex.ru
[2] The Bonch-Bruevich Saint-Petersburg State University of Telecommunications,
Prospect Bolshevikov 22/1, 193232 Saint Petersburg, Russia
gleb.rogozinsky@gmail.com
[3] St. Petersburg State University of Film and Television,
Pravda Street 13, 191119 Saint Petersburg, Russia
[4] Solomenko Institute of Transport Problems of the Russian Academy of Sciences,
12-th Line VO, 13, 199178 Saint Petersburg, Russia
malygin_com@mail.ru

Abstract. The paper presents an information technology based on the modified multi-domain infocommunications model, which allows describing the interaction between the objects of the physical, informational (cybernetic) and cognitive levels in the field of environmental monitoring and forecasting of road and water transport impact though the set of unified terms. The effectiveness of the suggested approach is illustrated with the development of calculation model for the air pollution control and predicting in the areas of simultaneous impact of motor and water transport in large port cities like St. Petersburg, Vladivostok and Sevastopol.

Keywords: Information technologies · Port cities · Urban transport · Air pollution monitoring · Calculation model

1 Introduction

Air pollution in the large city area remains a significant problem not only for developing regions, but also for well-developed areas. The informational telecommunications, i.e. ubiquitous sensor networks, cyber-physical and embedded systems provide a novel approach for the environmental monitoring development and applications, though the utilization of the novel technologies demands their adaptation to the complex of existing theoretical and practical knowledge, and models of interactions between various elements of the monitoring system. Those elements may include both humans and machines, physical and cybernetic entities, pre-infocom components and state-of-art technologies.

V. Sukhomlin and E. Zubareva (Eds.): SITITO 2018, CCIS 1201, pp. 384–396, 2020.
https://doi.org/10.1007/978-3-030-46895-8_30

Below, we give first a theoretical modeling approach to be used as a meta-modeling medium for the set of a various domain- and study specific methods.

2 Multi-domain Model as a Core Approach

The outbreak of the Cyber-Physical Systems (or CPS) conceptualizes the integration of the physical objects and their digital twins or virtual models. Joined together, the two domains of Cyber-Physical objects existence form a Cyber-Physical Space. Above it lays the Cognitive Domain, where the human beings are able to extract knowledge from the information they receive through their bio-sensory systems, and make decisions to control the systems. Thus, we separate an interaction between physical objects, software entities and humans into the three intersecting domains, which are Physical Domain, Informational Domain, and Cognitive Domain. Such approach is known as Multi-Domain Model (MM), first described by Sotnikov [1, 2]. Later, Rogozinsky and Sotnikov [3] did a modification of the MM for the tasks of polymodal monitoring. Here we use the term of both models as a core approach for the informational technology development in the field of transport ecological monitoring.

According to the MM, the Physical Domain is concerned with the energy processes and the interaction between physical objects. The intellectual system analysis and cognitive activities are the products of mental and psychic activity of the Cognitive Domain. The Informational Domain is the domain of the abstractions and data flow between models of physical objects and human-machine interfaces.

At the domain borders, the corresponding interfaces perform the information interaction between various elements of the system. The finite number of states, represented by its own thesaurus, can characterize each object/subject of the system.

Thus, the mapping onto the set of informational representations $\langle A \rangle^{\xi_A}$ of the thesaurus ξ_A object A of a Physical Domain with the corresponding thesaurus states, can be described as (1):

$$\langle A \rangle^{\xi_A} \overset{Signal}{\Rightarrow} \left(\langle A \rangle^{\xi_A} \right)^{\xi_B}. \tag{1}$$

Thus, we assume an information to be transferred, when the signal transmitting some image (notion) from the varifold thesaurus of the source system A into the varifold thesaurus of the target system B is changed.

The information is received when a new image of the source is formed within the varifold thesaurus of the target system.

$$\langle A \rangle^{\xi_A} \overset{Q_1}{\longrightarrow} \langle C \rangle^{\xi_C} \overset{Q_2}{\longrightarrow} \left(\left(\langle A \rangle^{\xi_A} \right)^{\xi_C} \right)^{\xi_B}, \tag{2}$$

where Q_1, Q_2 are mapping operators between different domains, ξ_C, ξ_B – thesauri of a target signal and a source signal.

In details, we can write (2) as following:

$$\langle A \rangle^{\xi_A} \overset{Q^{\xi_A}\xi_S}{\longrightarrow} \left(\langle A \rangle^{\xi_A} \right)^{\xi_S} \overset{Q^{\xi_S}\xi_U}{\longrightarrow} \left\lfloor \left(\langle A \rangle^{\xi_A} \right)^{\xi_U} \right\rfloor, \tag{3}$$

Thus the mapping between the corresponding domains is actually the operation of information impact between entities of the domains, expressed in the discovery of maximum conformity between elements of thesauri ξ_A, ξ_B, ξ_U.

In the generalized case of the polymodal representation, we will use an array operator $\overline{Z}$. The elements of $\overline{Z}$ are thesauri transform operators, which describe the translation from Informational Domain to the human-machine interface for each mode available. Thus, for the 4-modal case, i.e. visual Q^V, auditory Q^A, tactile Q^T and olfactory Q^O modalities, we have [4]:

$$\overline{Z} = \left\{ Q^A; Q^V; Q^O; Q^T \right\} \tag{4}$$

Upon applying of $\overline{Z}$ to some object of the Informational Domain we have:

$$\langle C \rangle^{\xi \tilde{C}} \xrightarrow{\overline{Z}} \left\{ \left(\langle C \rangle^{\xi \tilde{C}} \right)^{\xi M_i} \right\}_{i=1...M_{max}} \tag{5}$$

where M_i is the modality i, M_{max} is the maximum number of modalities in the given system.

According to (3), the Informational Domain – Cognitive Domain translation for the human sensory analysis will be described by (6):

$$\left[\left(\langle C \rangle^{\xi \tilde{C}} \right)^{\xi M_i} \right]_{i=1...M_{max}} \xrightarrow{Q_i^N} \left[\left\langle \left(\langle C \rangle^{\xi \tilde{C}} \right)^{\xi M_i} \right\rangle^{\xi U_i} \right]_{i=1...M_{max}}, \tag{6}$$

where ξ^{U_i} – human operator thesauri in the Cognitive domain.

E.g., the visual modality translation will be described by (7):

$$\left| \langle C \rangle^{\xi C} \xrightarrow{Q^\downarrow} \langle C \rangle^{\xi \tilde{C}} \xrightarrow{Q^V} \left\langle \langle C \rangle^{\xi \tilde{C}} \right\rangle^{\xi V} \right\rangle_{ID} \xrightarrow{Q_V^N} CD \left\langle \left\langle \left(\langle C \rangle^{\xi \tilde{C}} \right)^{\xi V} \right\rangle^{\xi U_V} \right|, \tag{7}$$

where ID – Information (Cyber) Domain, CD – Cognitive Domain; $Q^\downarrow$ – thesauri reduction operator, thus $\xi^C \subset \xi^{\tilde{C}}$.

The above terms give the formalized description for the processes, existing in the multiple domains of any complex system. The proposed abstractions provide a unified symbolic description, which is important for the further development of methods and theoretical models.

In the research below, we mainly focused on Physical and Information Domains, leaving Cognitive Domain for the future research. Next to the development of the thesauri specific for each domain, based on domain-specific classes of methods, we will be able to integrate domain-specific thesauri into the meta-domain level using proposed Multi-Domain Model approach. Figure 1 concretizes our research objects and medium.

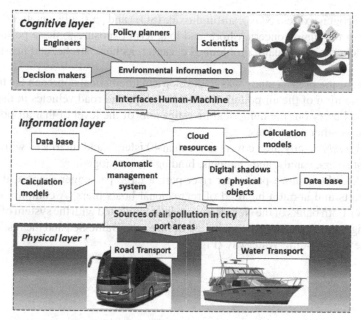

Fig. 1. The elements of Multi-Domain Model in the air pollution information technology development.

3 Application Study of the Developed Approach for the Monitoring and Forecasting of Air Pollution by Road and Water Transport in Three Large Port Cities (St. Petersburg, Vladivostok and Sevastopol)

3.1 Description of the Areas Examined

This work illustrates the proposed approach through the numerical investigations of road and water transport-related air pollution in the three large port cities, namely St. Petersburg, Vladivostok, and Sevastopol.

The analysis shows that the main air pollution sources in a port area located in a city center are the passenger ships and vehicles. The typical harbor operations include ship movements in the area, ship discharges, loading and unloading of passengers or goods. Whereas numerous studies on the road traffic-related air pollution have been conducted in the past [5–8], only little known about the magnitude and effects of air pollution caused by the river and marine vessels [9, 10]. Few studies deal with the simultaneous impact of the road and water transport across the urban areas.

The main difference between the vessels and the vehicles is that the engines are designed not only for the movement of the ship, but also for the other needs like waste utilization, heat and electric energy generation, etc. Though the usage of the ship diesel or heavy fuel oil for the vessels is much cheaper comparing to the petrol (mostly used for road transportation in this country), it also does a high pollution [11, 12].

Toxic nitrogen oxides (NO_X), sulfur dioxide (SO_2) and particulate matter (PM_{10} and $PM_{2.5}$) are of the main concern. Short- and long-term exposure to these pollutants can contribute to a range of health problems, i.e. cancer, asthma, stroke, and heart diseases [13, 14].

The aim of the present study was to develop a mathematical approach for the simultaneous estimation of the air pollution caused by ships and road vehicles in the areas of city ports and carry out the numerical investigations of the level of that air pollution at the adverse weather conditions.

Saint Petersburg city area covers more than 40 islands and interlaces with complex networks of rivers, canals, and channels, binding the city together.

Saint Petersburg has a passenger river port, a large passenger seaport, three large cargo seaports and about a hundred of recreational boats piers. A complex system of river ports on both banks of the Neva River are interconnected with the system of seaports, thus making Saint Petersburg the main link between the Baltic Sea and the rest of Russia through the Volga-Baltic Waterway (Fig. 2).

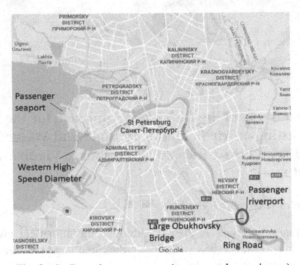

Fig. 2. St. Petersburg area map (www.google.com/maps)

The passenger seaport of Saint Petersburg is the largest one in the Baltic Region. It is a modern port constructed in 2011 and located in the city center on the reclaimed territories of Vasilievsky Island (Fig. 3). The port complex includes seven berths with the total length of 2171.06 m, three cruise terminals, and one combined cruise-ferry terminal. Passenger seaport of Saint Petersburg can host cruise ships of up to 340 m. The passenger turnover is about one million people per year. The city navigation lasts from the end of April to the beginning of October.

Three main piers of the passenger river port are located in the water area of the Neva River between Volodarsky Bridge and Bol'shoy Obukhovsky Bridge (Fig. 3). The passenger turnover is about 100 000 people per navigation season. The number of ships is 550–600 units. The St. Petersburg passenger river port and the passenger sea port are

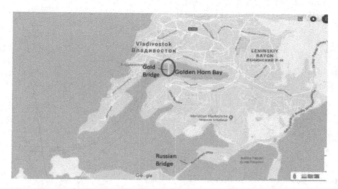

Fig. 3. Vladivostok area map (www.google.com/maps)

located in the densely populated areas with a highly intensive road traffic. The exhaust emissions from ships may cause an additional impact on people's health.

Vladivostok is a port city located in the Far East of Russia on the shore of the Sea of Japan, on the Muraviev-Amursky Peninsula and several islands of the Peter the Great Bay. Vladivostok is also known as the last stop of the world-famous Trans-Siberian railway. The port of Vladivostok is ice-free and operates all year round. The infrastructure of the city was considerably renovated and improved in 2012. There are two vast cable-stayed bridges, namely Gold Bridge over the Golden Horn Bay in the city center, and the Russian Bridge from the mainland to the Russian Island (Fig. 3).

High level of air and water pollution is a big problem of Vladivostok. E.g. Golden Horn Bay was recognized as the dirtiest water area of Russia 2013. The increased level of air pollution is typical for this city. The annual concentration of nitrogen dioxide is approximately 1.5–2.0 times higher the Standard Limit Value (40 $\mu g/m^3$). Poor air condition is mainly due to the high exhaust emissions from vehicles.

Sevastopol is the largest port city on the Crimean Peninsula. It is also one of the main seaport of the Black Sea. The population is approximately 393 300 living mostly near the Sevastopol Bay and its surroundings. Sevastopol maintains a large port facility in the Sevastopol Bay and smaller bays around. The port handles traffic from passengers (local transportation and cruise), cargo, and commercial fishing. The port infrastructure is fully integrated with the city of Sevastopol.

A distinctive feature of Sevastopol is that it is located around a fairly long Sevastopol Bay, crashing into the coastline for many kilometers (Fig. 4). Therefore, people need to go about 40 km around to get from the Southern (most populated) side to the North. Unlike many cities, where water transport is mostly a touristic attraction, passenger boats and ferries operate as a regular public transport here.

The urban public transport includes 101 bus lines, 14 trackless trolley lines, 52 light commercial bus lines, 6 boat lines and 1 ferry line.

The Nakhimov Avenue and the Lenin Street circle the Central Hill and both lead to the Passenger Port in the City Center. There are three regular boat lines departing from the City Center, namely City Center – North, City Center – Inkerman, City Center – Holland. The busiest is the City Center – North line. The boats are scheduled every 10–15 min. The boats carry 10–11 thousand people daily in low season and up to 25

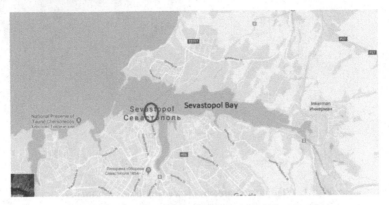

Fig. 4. Sevastopol area map (www.google.com/maps)

Fig. 5. Passenger boat in Sevastopol, vessel type 1438.

thousand passengers in high season. The overall annual passenger turnover is about 7.5 million people. During 1980–1984, over 26 boats were specially built for such needs at the Ilyichevsky shipyard. Fourteen of them operate in Sevastopol, 7 in Vladivostok and the rest in the other port cities of Russia (Fig. 5).

Technical specifications are following: unit's length 28.7 m, beam 6.35 m, depth 1.62 m, tonnage 149.3 t, installed engines 2 × 12 CSP 15/18 3D6S, forward propulsion 150 kW, reverse gear nor less 99 kW, rotational speed 1500 rpm, fuel consumption 224 g/kWh, speed 12 knots, capacity 250 passengers, crew 3 persons.

3.2   Description of the Calculation Model

A bottom-up mathematical model was developed on the base of the Russian methodology for the calculation of the dispersion of harmful substances in the atmospheric air.

The methodology is based on the analytical approximation of the results of joint numerical integration of the equation of atmospheric diffusion and the system of equations of hydro thermodynamics for the atmospheric boundary layer [15, 16]. According to Berlyand [17] such parameters as instant concentrations of the pollutant pulsed deviations from these values and the velocity of its diffusion should be taken into consideration while developing an emission model. The problem is simplified by the application of the turbulent diffusion model:

$$\frac{\partial q}{\partial t} + u\frac{\partial q}{\partial x} + v\frac{\partial q}{\partial y} + w\frac{\partial q}{\partial z} = \frac{\partial}{\partial x}k_x\frac{\partial q}{\partial x} + \frac{\partial}{\partial y}k_y\frac{\partial q}{\partial y} + \frac{\partial}{\partial z}k_z\frac{\partial q}{\partial z} - \alpha q, \qquad (8)$$

where q is the concentration of pollutant (g/m^3); x and y are the horizontal axis (m); z is the vertical axis (m); t is the time (s); u, v, w are the components of the wind speed in the direction of the axes x, y, z, respectively, (m/s); k_x, k_y, k_z are the components of the coefficient of turbulent diffusion along the Cartesian coordinate axes; α is the coefficient taking into account probable metabolism of a pollutant in the atmosphere.

Using this approach, also known as K-theory, together with some approximations and assumptions, there was established that the concentration of a pollutant emitted from an unregulated point source, such as a ship, is as follow:

$$C_M = \frac{AMFnD\eta}{8H^{4/3}V_1}, \qquad (9)$$

and from an unregulated line source, like a traffic flow, is as follow:

$$C_M = \frac{AMFn\eta 2LV_1}{8H^{4/3}V_1\left(L^2W_0 + V_1\right)}, \qquad (10)$$

where C_M is the concentration of pollutant (g/m^3); A is the coefficient considering the temperature stratification of the atmosphere; M is the emission of a pollutant from a ship or a traffic flow (g/s), F is the dimensionless coefficient considering the velocity of gravitational sedimentation of particulate matter; $m' = 0{,}9$; η is the dimensionless coefficient considering the influence of the terrain relief; H is the source height (m), L is the length of the road, D is the diameter of the pipe, V_1 is the exhaust volume emitted in 1 s (m^3/s), W_0 is the pollutant emission rate (g/s).

The authors of the present paper have a positive experience of the application of this model (K-theory) for the estimation and the forecast of transport and fire-related air pollution [18–22].

4 Mathematical Modeling and Computer Simulation of Air Pollution Caused by Ships and Vehicles in Port Areas

4.1 Input Data for the Model

Emissions from traffic flow were calculated using the software Maghistral (Integral Co Ltd., St. Petersburg, Russia) with emission factors of major pollutants (CO – carbon oxide, CH – hydrocarbons, NO$_2$ – nitrogen dioxide, PM – particle matter, SO$_2$ – sulfur dioxide, CO$_2$ – carbon dioxide; formaldehyde, benzpyrene) specified for the local vehicle fleet of each city port examined (St. Petersburg, Vladivostok, Sevastopol).

Emission factors for vessels were determined on the base of the analysis of literature data [23]. They are summarized in Table 1.

Table 1. Vessels exhaust emission rates at different operational mode.

Vessel type	Engine	Power, kW	Mode of operation							
			25%		50%		75%		100%	
			Exhaust emission rates, g/s							
			NO_X	CO	NO_X	CO	NO_X	CO	NO_X	CO
1438	12CSP15/183D6S	150	n/a	n/a	0.47	0	0.34	0	n/a	n/a
588	6NVD48	294	11.11	2.61	2.07	0.46	1.27	0.22	n/a	n/a
301, 302	6CRN36/45 (EG70-5)	742	n/a	n/a	3.0	0	2.66	0	2.10	2.22
342E	12CNS18/20	992	6.92	0.80	6.59	0.41	5.51	0.88	4.57	1.40

Note: n/a – not available.

The information on the fleet composition, engine type and fuel used for each vessel, the frequency of visits, the average time spent at berth were also taken in consideration.

The dispersion of pollutants from ships (or boats) and traffic flow in the port area was estimated by means of the Ecolog-3 software (Integral Co Ltd., St. Petersburg, Russia) based on the modeling approach described in Item 3.2.

There were examined three port areas (marked with red color oval on Figs. 2, 3 and 4):

1. St. Petersburg: the area near the Passenger Riverport and Large Obukhvsky Bridge (Fig. 2).
2. Vladivostok: the area near Gold Bridge (Fig. 3).
3. Sevastopol: the area near the City Center Pier (Count's Wharf), Lenin street and Nakhimov avenue (Fig. 4).
4. The results of traffic examinations are summarized in Table 2.

Table 2. Average traffic at evening rush hours.

Road	Traffic flow, vehicle/h					
	Cars	LDV	Buses	HDV < 12 t	HDV > 12 t	Total
Large Obukhovsky Bridge (St. Petersburg)	7845	1619	72	331	1833	11700
Golden Bridge (Vladivostok)	1828	28	13	15	8	1892
Lenin street (Sevastopol)	1188	114	90	–	–	1392
Nakhimov avenue (Sevastopol)	1052	132	120	–	–	1304

Note: LDV – Light Duty Vehicles, HDV – Heavy Duty Vehicles.

It was found that the average traffic flow on Large Obukhovsky Bridge, where St. Petersburg Ring Road runs, is close to 12000 vehicles per hour at rush hours in summer season. It is the busiest road in St. Petersburg. The average traffic flow on Golden Bridge in Vladivostok and on Lenin street and Nakhimov avenue in Sevastopol are much lower, 1892, 1392 and 1304 vehicle per hour, respectively.

4.2   Results of Computer Simulation of Air Pollution Caused by Ships and Traffic Flow in Port Areas in St. Petersburg, Vladivostok and Sevastopol

It should be taken into account that all the areas examined are very close to housing estates. That means that adjacent residential area may be exposed to high air pollution related to road and water transport, especially, at adverse meteorological conditions, including calm, temperature inversion and high photochemical activity of the atmosphere, which is essential for $NO-O_3-NO_2-O_2$ chemical transformations.

In fact, there are mostly favorable weather conditions minimizing negative effects of transport-related air pollution in St. Petersburg, Vladivostok and Sevastopol.

At the same time, the results of computer simulation of potential air pollution, caused by road vehicles and vessels in city port areas at intensive traffic and unfavorable weather conditions, gives an idea about significant concentrations of nitrogen oxides, particulate matter, and sulfur dioxide in the air.

We have developed three scenarios:

1. St. Petersburg: traffic volume on Large Obukhovsky Bridge as in Table 1; three large river vessels, namely vessel type 301, vessel type 302, vessel type 588 (Table 2), preparing for departure; air temperature 22 °C; wind speed 0.5–1 m/s; high insolation.
2. Vladivostok: traffic volume on Gold Bridge as in Table 1, two speedy boats (vessel type 342E, Table 2) running under the bridge, air temperature 25 °C, wind speed 1.0–2 m/s, high insolation.
3. Sevastopol: traffic volume on Lenin street and Nakhimov avenue as in Table 1, three boats (vessel type 1438, Table 2): one loading, one departing, one berthing; air temperature 28 °C, wind speed 1.0–2 m/s, high insolation.

The calculations on ground level (at a height of 2 m) predict that the area of the Passenger riverport in St. Petersburg may be exposed to the enhanced levels of NO_2 and PM_{10} exceeding National Day Limit Value by 5–10 times and by 1.1–3.0 times, respectively. Figure 6 demonstrates the maps of predicted air pollution by NO_2.

Graphical results are presented not in terms of concentrations but in terms of limit value units, in other words, as the ratio of the calculated concentration to the limit value.

Regarding the evaluation of NO_2 and PM concentrations near Gold Bridge in Vladivostok, it is clear that there are zones, where the concentration of NO_2 may exceed more than 2–4 times Limit Value of 40 $\mu g/m^3$, and the concentration of PM10–1.1–1.5 times Limit Value of 50 $\mu g/m^3$.

Concerning Sevastopol, it is expected the daily NO_2 increase by 1.2–3.5 times Legal Limit Value at periods of high traffic emissions in combination with stable meteorological conditions, thermal inversion and low wind speed.

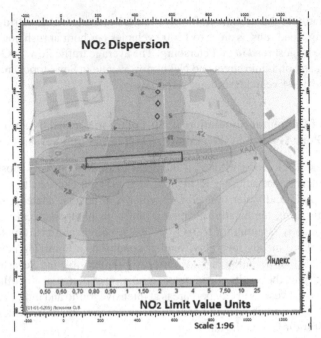

Fig. 6. Air pollution by transport-related NO$_2$ in the area of Large Obukhovsky Bridge in St. Petersburg.

5 Conclusion

Application of a bottom-up pollution model is important for a detailed assessment and prediction of air pollution on city scale and for the identification of problem areas with excessive contamination of the urban air. Obviously, this kind of approaches aimed at the calculation of pollutant concentrations in port and coastal areas depends on the structure of vehicles and vessels traffic flows and on the conditions of emissions dispersion, including meteorological factors (temperature, wind velocity and direction) and characteristics of buildings and roads etc., requires a detailed routine determination of all input data, and supposes the involving of a great number of human operators.

This problem may be solved by the implementation of intellectual transport systems, GIS-technologies, and modern informational systems. Multimodal human-machine interfaces find their application in various technical systems and allow formal description of the interaction between objects of physical, informational (cybernetic) and cognitive domains. Its extension on monitoring subsystems, particularly in cyber-physical systems, gives a formalization of processes, which take place in different domains, and provides the basis for a set of methods of multimodal representation of data and corresponding interfaces design.

Acknowledgements. The study was partially supported by the Russian Foundation for Basic Research within the framework of the project № 18-410-920016 p_a "Research of socio-economic and ecological processes of Sevastopol with the growth of industrial, traffic, transit and tourist potentials".

References

1. Sotnikov, A.: Principles of the applied area analysis in healthcare infocommunication systems. Proc. Telecommun. Univ. **171**, 174–183 (2004). [in Russian]
2. Sotnikov, A.: Classification and models of applied infocommunication systems. Proc. Telecommun. Univ. **169**, 149–162 (2003). [in Russian]
3. Sotnikov, A., Rogozinsky, G.: The multi domain infocommunication model as the basis of an auditory interfaces development for multimedia informational systems. T-Comm-Telecommun. Transp. **11**(5), 77–82 (2017). https://elibrary.ru/item.asp?id=29320338
4. Rogozinsky, G., Komashinsky, V.: Modified multi domain model of cyber-physical systems monitoring. Mar. Intellect. Technol. **3**(4), 177–182 (2017). [in Russian]. https://elibrary.ru/item.asp?id=32466817
5. Alves, C.A., Lopes, D.J., Calvo, A.I., Evtyugina, M., Rocha, S.: Emissions from light-duty diesel and gasoline in-use vehicles measured on chassis dynamometer test cycles. Aerosol Air Qual. Res. **15**(1), 99–116 (2015). https://doi.org/10.4209/aaqr.2014.01.0006
6. Requia, W.J., Ferguson, M., et al.: Spatio-temporal analysis of particulate matter intake fractions for vehicular emissions: hourly variation by micro-environments in the greater Toronto and Hamilton area, Canada. Sci. Total Environ. **599–600**, 1813–1822 (2017). https://doi.org/10.1016/j.scitotenv.2017.05.134
7. Shahbazi, H., Ganjiazad, R., Hosseini, V., Hamedi, M.: Investigating the influence of traffic emission reduction plans on Tehran air quality using WRF/CAMx modeling tools. Transp. Res. Part D Transp. Environ. **57**, 484–495 (2017). https://doi.org/10.1016/j.trd.2017.08.001
8. Sun, S., Jiang, W., Gao, W.: Vehicle emission trends and spatial distribution in Shandong Province, China, from 2000 to 2014. Atmos. Environ. **147**(C), 190–199 (2016). https://doi.org/10.1016/j.atmosenv.2016.09.065
9. Jalkanen, J.-P., Johansson, L., Kukkonen, J.: A comprehensive inventory of the ship traffic exhaust emissions in the Baltic Sea from 2006 to 2009. AMBIO **43**(3), 311–324 (2014). https://doi.org/10.1007/s13280-013-0389-3
10. Jalkanen, J.-P., Brink, A., Kalli, J., Pettersson, H., Kukkonen, J., Stipa, T.: A modelling system for the exhaust emissions of marine traffic and its application in the Baltic Sea area. Atmos. Chem. Phys. **9**(23), 9209–9223 (2009). https://doi.org/10.5194/acp-9-9209-2009
11. Kozarev, N., Stoyanov, S., Ilieva, N.: Air pollution in port areas (2014). https://www.researchgate.net/publication/266875796
12. Kirby, M.F., Law, R.J.: Accidental spills at sea – risk, impact, mitigation and the need for co-ordinated post-incident monitoring. Mar. Pollut. Bull. **60**(6), 797–803 (2010). https://doi.org/10.1016/j.marpolbul.2010.03.015
13. Pope III, C.A.: Review: epidemiological basis for particulate air pollution health standards. Aerosol Sci. Technol. **32**(1), 4–14 (2000). https://doi.org/10.1080/027868200303885
14. Beelen, R., Hoek, G., van den Brandt, P.A., et al.: Long-term effects of traffic-related air pollution on mortality in a Dutch cohort (NLCS-AIR study). Environ. Health Perspect. **116**(2), 196–202 (2008). https://doi.org/10.1289/ehp.10767
15. Genikhovich, E.L., Gracheva, I.G., Onikul, R.I., Filatova, E.N.: Air pollution modelling at an urban scale – Russian experience and problems. Water Air Soil Pollut. Focus **2**(5–6), 501–512 (2002). https://doi.org/10.1023/A:1021336829300
16. Genikhovich, E.L., Sciermeier, F.A.: Comparison of United States and Russian complex terrain diffusion models developed for regulatory applications. Atmos. Environ. **29**(17), 2375–2385 (1995). https://doi.org/10.1016/1352-2310(95)00053-2
17. Berlyand, M.E.: The main principles of atmospheric diffusion modelling for regulatory purposes in Russia. Int. J. Environ. Pollut. **5**(4–6), 508–517 (1995). https://doi.org/10.1504/IJEP.1995.028397

18. Lozhkin, V.N., Lozhkina, O.V., Ushakov, A.: Using K-theory in geographic information investigations of critical-level pollution of atmosphere in the vicinity of motor roads. World Appl. Sci. J. Probl. Archit. Constr. **23**(13), 96–100 (2013). https://doi.org/10.5829/idosi.wasj.2013.23.pac.90020
19. Lozhkina, O.V., Lozhkin, V.N.: Estimation of nitrogen oxides emissions from petrol and diesel passenger cars by means of on-board monitoring: effect of vehicle speed, vehicle technology, engine type on emission rates. Transp. Res. Part D Transp. Environ. **47**, 251–264 (2016). https://doi.org/10.1016/j.trd.2016.06.008
20. Lozhkin, V.N., Lozhkina, O.V., et al.: Adaptation of the European traffic pollution monitoring process to Saint Petersburg, Russia. Pollut. Res. **35**(4), 897–901 (2016)
21. Vasilyev, A., Tarkhov, D., Lozhkin, V., Lozhkina, O., Timofeev, V.: Neural network approach in information process for predicting highway area air pollution by peat fire [in Russia]. In: CEUR Workshop Proceedings (CEUR-WS.org): Selected Papers of the XI International Scientific-Practical Conference Modern Information Technologies and IT-Education (SITITO 2016), Moscow, Russia, vol. 1761, pp. 386–392 (2016). http://ceur-ws.org/Vol-1761/paper49.pdf
22. Lozhkina, O.V., Lozhkin, V.N.: Information technology forecast the emergency of air pollution exhaust gases of ships and vehicle. Mod. Inf. Technol. IT-Educ. **13**(1), 222–227 (2017). https://doi.org/10.25559/SITITO.2017.1.426. [in Russian]
23. Ivanchenko, A.A.: Complex decrease of harmful exhaust emissions by diesel engines of river vessels: dis. … Dr.Sci. (Technology), Saint Petersburg (1998). [in Russian]

Complex Design of Granulation Units with Application of Computer Simulation and Software Modeling: Case "Vortex Granulator"

Artem Artyukhov$^{(\boxtimes)}$ ⓘ and Nadiia Artyukhova ⓘ

Sumy State University, Rimskogo-Korsakova Str. 2, Sumy 40000, Ukraine
a.artyukhov@pohnp.sumdu.edu.ua

Abstract. The article is devoted to the description of the complex method to design granulation unit, which is based on the joint use of the computer modeling results on the simulation models and software modeling based on author's software products. The description of the software package Granulation Unit© to carrying out the structural and technological calculations for the granulation unit is given. The role of computer and software modeling in the general design algorithm of the granulation unit is shown. The optimization criteria are selected and an algorithm of design optimization for granulation unit is described using the example of the "Vortex Granulator" case. A general method of granulation unit designing "turnkey" with the use of automated design elements is presented. The results of automated calculations form the base to design an industrial granulation unit for the porous ammonium nitrate production. On the example of a specific product of the granulation unit (porous ammonium nitrate), the author's software product is presented to determine the quality of the porous surface in the granule.

Keywords: Granulation unit · Computer simulation · Software · Optimization calculation

1 Introduction

Development of the current chemical industry under conditions of the severe competition at the market of various chemicals production, puts new strict demands for project designers to the technology of heat-mass transfer processes implementation, to the ecological and economic properties of the chemical apparatuses design in production [1].

The optimal decision regarding the chemical apparatuses design of the chemical unit and technological principles of its operation can be made only on the basis of the complex design using modern means of the automated calculation [2]. Under conditions of the multifactorial simulation experiment, such an approach lets to avoid systematical errors at the stage of the unit design. Therefore, combining various methods to carry out the simulation multifactorial experiment (computer simulation, use of the author's software packages) enables strictly to follow the optimization criterion, set by the designer thanks to the possibility for customer to take in excess the definite number of the initial

© Springer Nature Switzerland AG 2020
V. Sukhomlin and E. Zubareva (Eds.): SITITO 2018, CCIS 1201, pp. 397–414, 2020.
https://doi.org/10.1007/978-3-030-46895-8_31

parameters in the chemical and technological system, controlling actions and necessary final features of the unit (process, production) [3].

The project is based on the idea to investigate the small-sized granulation modules (units) using the equipment with active (intensive) hydrodynamic modes. Due to the turbulence of the flow, multistage phase contact implementation (and combination of such methods) and the specific power growth of the equipment, it is possible to increase the energy and ecological efficiency of the granulation processes and other secondary stages. The proposed Complex approach to creating small-sized granulation modules has to take into account the hazardous waste disposal processes (with the possibility of their repeated return to the process) and heat and moisture recovery with further use of this potential within the module. This thesis forms another idea of the project, which is to use separate waste heat and moisture recovery unit, and to use elements, built into the main equipment of elements for hazardous waste disposal, in the granulation module.

Conceptions and models, which are used in the project:

– conception regarding the ecological and economic objectivation of reasonability to implement changes in the organization of the flow motion forms in the granulation units applying devices with active hydrodynamic modes from the viewpoint of evaluation of specific emissions into the atmosphere (per unit of specific weight or per unit of the granulation unit productivity) and specific cost of the production unit;
– conception regarding the full disposal of material flows (dust, unconditioned granules, harmful components of the waste gases) owing to the disposal units implementation;
– the concept of energy (heat) resources recovery through the use of modern refrigeration compressor cycles;
– theoretical and computer models for the integrated assessment of the impact, made by hydro and thermodynamic factors of the granulation module equipment work, on the heat-mass transfer processes intensity.

In this paper, *the object of the research* is a granulation unit, in which the devices with intensive hydrodynamics (with active hydrodynamic modes) are used.

The aim of the study is to introduce a comprehensive algorithm to design granulation units based on the combined simulation modeling methods.

Methodology
The project consists of the following interconnected structural elements:

– ecological and economic objectivation regarding the introduction of the devices with intensive hydrodynamics into the granulation unit;
– theoretical block – mathematic device and author's software package to calculate the hydrodynamic and heat-mass transfer indicators in the implementation of the target and related process in the granulation unit;
– experimental block – to check the adequacy of the created mathematic device using the software package: to study hydrodynamic and heat-mass transfer features of the processes, carried out in the granulation unit, to define the impact made by the constructive and technological parameters of the main equipment in the unit on the intensity and efficiency of the granulation process;

- block of analysis and comparison of the study results;
- block of evaluation of the energy efficiency and ecological safety of the stated technology and equipment for its implementation;
- block of investigation of the engineering calculation methods regarding the main technological equipment of the granulation unit.

Results
The example of the case "Vortex granulator" shows the main stages of the industrial equipment sample creation with a description of all designing stages, based on the simulation modeling.

Scientific Novelty
The complex approach to the simulation modeling, which combines author's theoretical models (software products) and multifactorial computer simulation models of the hydro-dynamic and heat-mass transfer features with intensive hydrodynamics are represented for the first time.

Practical Significance
The complex design instruments of the chemical industry units let to perform the optimization design of the unit at the pre-design preparation stage without using the expensive experimental base for physical modeling. Theoretical and experimental blocks of the project are described in more detail.

2 Software Complex Granulation Unit© - Short Description and Principles of Work

The software complex Granulation Unit© is used for the complex design of the small-size granulation units, technological calculations of the granulation process and constructive calculations of the main equipment. The software complex is based on the software package, theoretical fundamentals of creation and detailed description of which are given in [4–21]. The cluster Granulation Unit© is designed for the technological and constructive calculation of the vortex granulator to produce granules from solutions or fusions and to form the porous structure on the granule surface and in the near-surface layers of the granule through humidification with further heat treatment. The user applies to the separate sub-programmes, implemented in the form of individual blocks of the general algorithm regarding engineering calculation of the vortex granulator. The consistent calculations determine the main technological parameters to carry out the granulation process, peculiarities of the constructive design and concrete sizes of the vortex granulator. Since it is necessary to investigate Rich Internet Application (RIA), the decision has been made to create a cluster and its components in the Java language. JavaFX, which lets to construct unified applications with the rich graphical interface of the user, was chosen as a platform for RIA development. JavaFX contains a set of utilities, with the help of which programmers can quickly create programs for desktops, mobile devices, etc.

Short description of every software product is shown in Table 1.

Java is a multiplatform programing language, and that is why it does not depend on the operational system, on which the program will run. The developers have created a special software - JVM (Java Virtual Machine), which is downloaded to a computer, mobile phone or another electronic device. As soon as the program is written in Java language, it is compiled into byte-code, which is interpreted by the virtual machine for the concrete platform.

Table 1. Short description of the software products in the software complex Granulation Unit©

Theoretical fundamentals (references for a short description of the theoretical model)	Computed value	The software product
System of the Reynolds differential equations and flow continuity equations [4, 5]	The average velocities field (vertical, circular, radial) of the gas flow in the workspace with the height-variable cross-sectional area	Conical channel© [22]
System of the Navier-Stokes differential equations and flow continuity equations [6]	The instant velocity field (vertical, circular, radial) of the gas flow in the workspace with the height-variable cross-sectional area	Vortex Flow© [23]
System of the granule motion differential equations, kinetic equations of heating and drying of the capillary-porous body [7–12]	• the instant velocity field (vertical, circular, radial) of granules in the workspace with the height-variable cross-sectional area; • trajectories of the granules motion; • "hydrodynamic" time the granule stays in the vortex granulator; • field of temperatures and humidities of the granule; • time for heating and drying of granules; • "thermodynamic" time the granule stays in the vortex granulator	Vortex Granulator© [24]
Force analysis of the dispersed phase motion, the dispersed phase balance in the swirling gas flow [13–15]	• distribution of granules of various size (mass) along the height of the vortex granulator's workspace; • range of the vortex granulator's stable operation; • separation of the small fraction granules and dust	Classification in vortex flow© [25]
Force analysis of the dispersed phase motion [16–19]	Time, the granule stays in the sectioned workspace of the device	Multistage Fluidizer© [26]
Force analysis of the solid and dispersed phase motion [20, 21]	The trajectory of the gas flow and liquid film motion in the mass-transfer-separation element	Vortex Tray© [27]

Since the creation of Java, a number of libraries and add-ons have been developed, which extend the functionality of the programs, written in this language. One of such libraries, which was used, for example, during the investigation of the Vortex Granulator and Classification in vortex flow programs, is Apache POI library. Thanks to this library, the program has the opportunity to save the results in a spreadsheet format.

Operation of all the above software products is united in the cluster Granulation Unit© through separate structural blocks (Fig. 1).

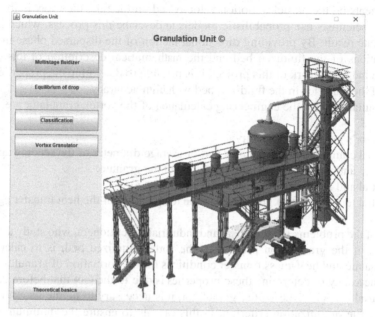

Fig. 1. The interface of the software complex Granulation Unit©

3 Case "Vortex Granulator"

The detailed analysis and patent review of the fluidized-bed granulation device show that the essence of most security documents comes down to the constructive improvement of the current equipment (in addition, in most cases without theoretical substantiation of the proposed constructive solution), and not to a new form of flow motion organization. All these tendencies prove the definite disadvantage of the reliable theoretical principles for calculating devices of such type. The proposed constructions of devices are definitely effective (in relation to the qualitative granulation production). The efficiency at this stage satisfies producers, but in future, they can lose competition due to the low energy efficiency and poor environmental safety. Besides, devices with classical fluidized bed (which do not have the regulated directional motion of the dispersed particles by installation of various guiding (accelerating) elements and inserts of various configuration; they make the main equipment park of the granulation unit), unlike the functional and multistage devices with directional fluidized bed (vortex, gravitational and others), have well-known calculation methods and due to constructive improvement, there is no need to observe such methods. In most cases, equipment, using the fluidized bed, has been patented by large industrial enterprises, which can carry out experimental research, because theoretical base to calculate such devices has not been highlighted in the scientific literature yet and is limited by basic knowledge of hydrodynamics and heat-mass transfer.

Additional interest in the project implementation is the study of the dispersed phase motion in the dense (constrained) flow mode, when it is necessary to take into account the mutual influence of the dispersed phase particles (particle ensembles) and granulator's elements on the particles motion velocity and on the time they stay in the device. Currently, scientists use probabilistic models to describe this process, which gives an approximate result. By providing directional motion of the dispersed phase in various configurations of the fluidized bed and the mathematical description of this process, created in the framework of this project, it is possible to determine the properties of the motion of the particles in the fluidized bed with high accuracy.

The initial data for the engineering calculation of the vortex granulator are:

– granulator's production capacity;
– fractional composition of granules and/or average diameter of the seeding agent;
– the initial and necessary final humidity rate of the granule;
– the initial and necessary final humidity rate of the air;
– the initial temperature of granules and the temperature of the heat transfer agent.

One of the problems for scientists and industrial practitioners, who study theoretical principles of the granulation process in the vortex fluidized bed, is to calculate the hydrodynamic and heat-mass transfer conditions for the formation of granules.

The necessity to determine these properties is due to the fact that before designing an industrial model of the vortex granulator, it is necessary to define its optimal construction. The optimization criterion, in this case, is to ensure the minimum required time; the granule stays in the granulator workspace, which will let to form a complete crystal structure of the granule with certain hardness indicators and the monodispersity degree of the commodity fraction. It is especially important when designing the vortex granulators to obtain granules with special properties, particularly, porous ammonium nitrate. In addition to the above indicators of the final product quality, the porous ammonium nitrate granules must have regulatory specific indicators, for example, retentivity and absorptivity towards diesel fuel [28, 29]. In this case, it is important to follow the condition, when "hydrodynamic" time, the granule stays in the workspace of the device, should be no less than "thermodynamic" time (this parameter is defined by the kinetics of the dehydration process in the granule) [30, 31]. Therefore, in order to keep the core hardness of the granule, "hydrodynamic" time has not to exceed "thermodynamic" time more than by 5–10%. Optimal design of the vortex granulator, which satisfies the requirements of the optimization criterion, is achieved through regulation of the hydrodynamic features of the flows motion.

The authors propose the following algorithm (case) to calculate the vortex granulator, based on the above structural elements.

1. Hydrodynamic calculation – computer simulation (Fig. 2).
2. Thermodynamic calculation – software modeling (Figs. 3, 4).

3. Technological calculation – software modeling (Figs. 5, 6).
4. Constructive calculation – software modelling, creation of the solid-state models granulator's units and its construction, based on the optimization calculation results, granulator's layout as a part of the granulation unit (Figs. 7, 8, 9, 10, 11, 12 and 13).

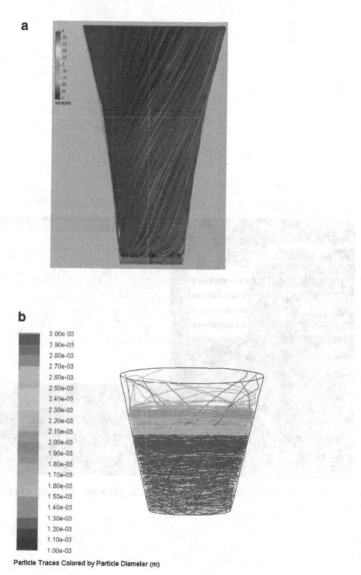

Particle Traces Colored by Particle Diameter (m)

Fig. 2. **a.** Hydrodynamic calculation – stages of the computer simulation – a selection of the rational construction of the workspace and swirler. **b.** Hydrodynamic calculation – stages of the computer simulation – calculation of the granules classification process. **c.** Hydrodynamic calculation – stages of the computer simulation – calculation of the granules motion trajectory in the constrained mode.

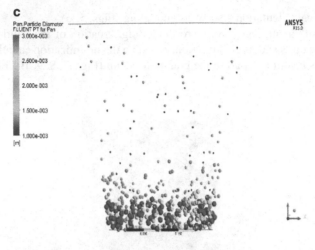

Fig. 2. (*continued*)

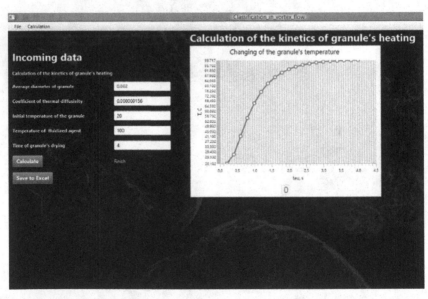

Fig. 3. Thermodynamic calculation – stages of the software modeling: calculation of the granule heating process.

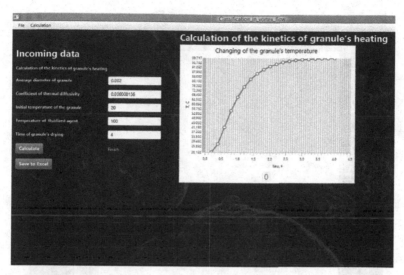

Fig. 4. Thermodynamic calculation – stages of the software modeling: calculation of the granule mass changes.

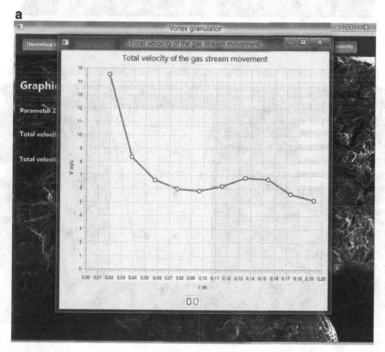

Fig. 5. a. Technological calculation – stages of the software modeling – determination of the gas flow velocity. **b.** Technological calculation – stages of the software modeling – determination of the granules velocity.

b

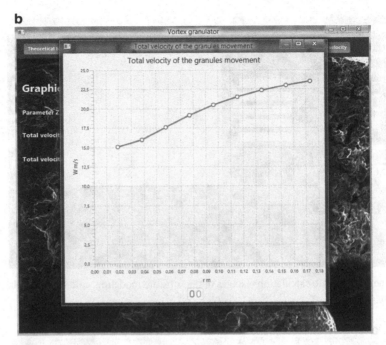

Fig. 5. (*continued*)

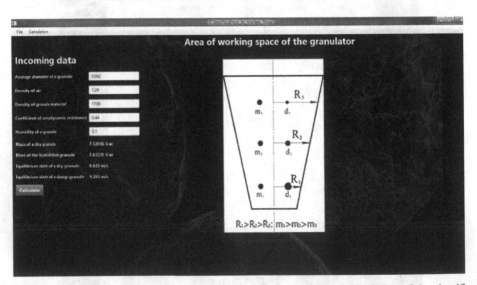

Fig. 6. Technological calculation – stages of the software modelling: calculation of the classification process.

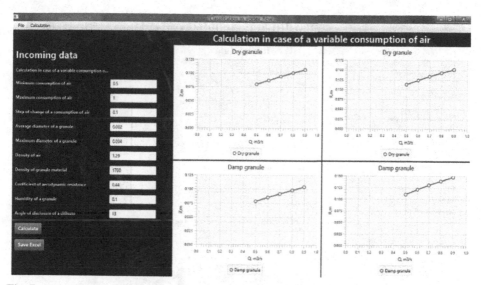

Fig. 7. Constructive calculation – stages of the software modeling: calculation of the workspace size in the vortex granulator under various initial conditions.

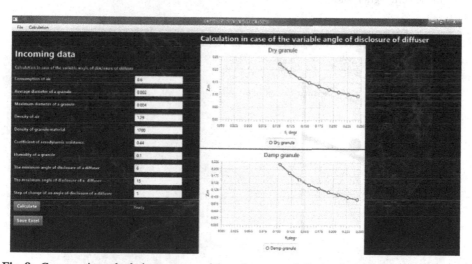

Fig. 8. Constructive calculation – stages of the software modeling: calculation of the workspace size and classification processes and granule separation.

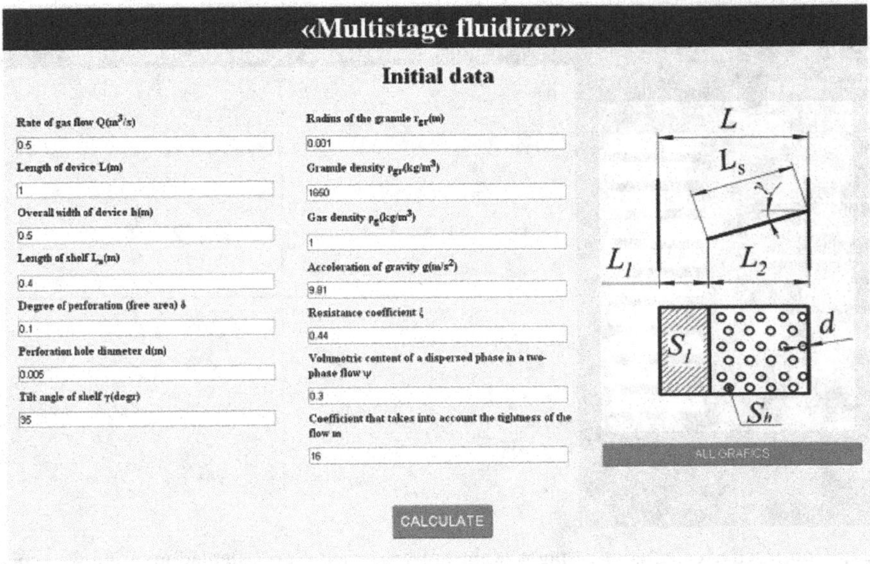

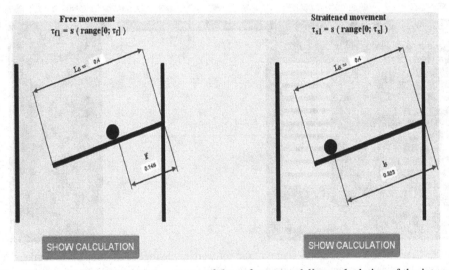

«Multistage fluidizer»

Initial data

Rate of gas flow Q(m³/s)
0.5

Length of device L(m)
1

Overall width of device h(m)
0.5

Length of shelf L_n(m)
0.4

Degree of perforation (free area) δ
0.1

Perforation hole diameter d(m)
0.005

Tilt angle of shelf γ(degr)
35

Radius of the granule r_{gr}(m)
0.001

Granule density ρ_{gr}(kg/m³)
1950

Gas density ρ_g(kg/m³)
1

Acceleration of gravity g(m/s²)
9.81

Resistance coefficient ξ
0.44

Volumetric content of a dispersed phase in a two-phase flow ψ
0.3

Coefficient that takes into account the tightness of the flow m
16

CALCULATE

Fig. 9. Constructive calculation – stages of the software modeling: calculation of the annular space in the vortex granulator.

Free movement
$\tau_{f1} = s (\text{range}[0; \tau_f])$

Straitened movement
$\tau_{s1} = s (\text{range}[0; \tau_s])$

$L_6 = 0.4$

l
0.146

$L_6 = 0.4$

l_6
0.323

SHOW CALCULATION   SHOW CALCULATION

Fig. 10. Constructive calculation – stages of the software modeling: calculation of the internal circulation of the seeding agent.

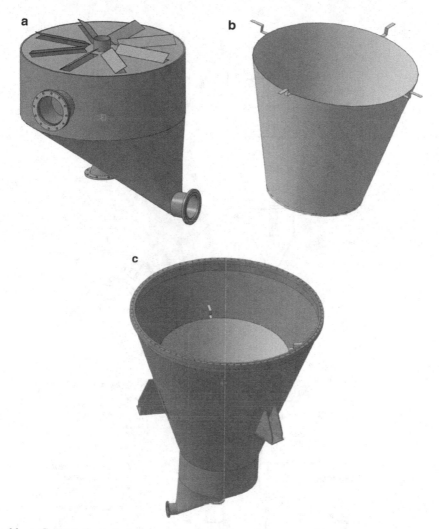

Fig. 11. a. Constructive calculation – formation of the solid-state models of the granulator's units: gas-distributing device. **b.** Constructive calculation – formation of the solid-state models of the granulator's units: internal cone. **c.** Constructive calculation – formation of the solid-state models of the granulator's units: the body of the granulator.

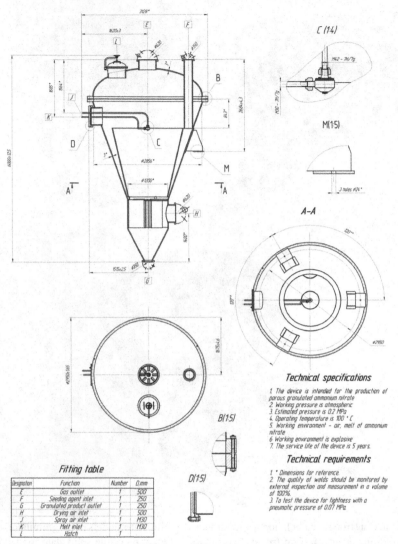

Fig. 12. Constructive calculation – the creation of the granulator's solid-state model and obtaining of the working drawings.

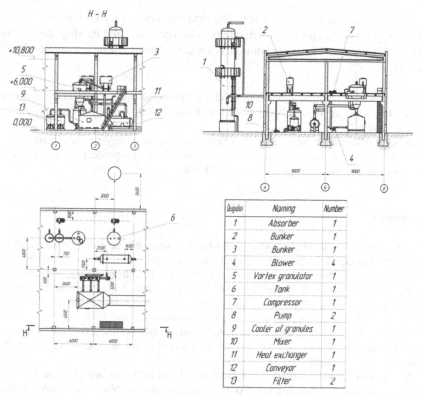

Позиция	Naming	Number
1	Absorber	1
2	Bunker	1
3	Bunker	1
4	Blower	4
5	Vortex granulator	1
6	Tank	1
7	Compressor	1
8	Pump	2
9	Cooler of granules	1
10	Mixer	1
11	Heat exchanger	1
12	Conveyor	1
13	Filter	2

Fig. 13. Constructive calculation – the layout of granulator as a part of the granulation unit.

4 Conclusions and Recommendations

For the first time, based on the ecological and economic justification (particularly, SWOT and PESTEL-analysis) of reasonability to introduce new types of the equipment to the granulation unit, the possibility to substitute or to modernize the current units under conditions of the industrial capacity and specific intensity (efficiency) increase at the industrial enterprises, was evaluated.

As a result of the original idea implementation to create compact and mobile granulation plants using technologies that reuse the drying agent potential, the ability to dispose harmful substances and heat and energy recovery, a scientific method has been developed for calculating small-sized and mobile energy-efficient and environmentally friendly modules based on the author's results of theoretical and experimental studies.

The obtained results of the project will enable to solve the following perspective tasks:

– to carry out further development of the convection drying conception in the multistage shelf dryers with heat and energy recovery within the drying unit;
– to study the influence of the shelf contacts construction and method to create various forms of the directional motion of the dispersed phase on the heat transfer processes intensity;

– to define the complex influence of hydro- and thermodynamic conditions to perform the convection drying process on the dehydration process from the dispersed particles with peculiar features (porous ammonium nitrate, capsulated by the organic fertilizer shell etc.).

Acknowledgments. The author thanks researchers of Processes and Equipment of Chemical and Petroleum Refinery Department, Sumy State University, for their valuable comments during the article preparation.

This work was carried out under the project «Small-scale energy-saving modules with the use of multifunctional devices with intensive hydrodynamics for the production, modification and encapsulation of granules», project No. 0119U100834.

References

1. Song, J., Han, B.: Green chemistry: a tool for the sustainable development of the chemical industry. Natl. Sci. Rev. **2**(3), 255–256 (2015). https://doi.org/10.1093/nsr/nwu076
2. Chemical Market Reports 2018. Chemical Industry (2018). https://www.reportlinker.com
3. Sarathy, V., Gotpagar, J., Morawietz, M.: The next wave of innovation in the chemicals industry. In: Strategy+Business, 5 June (2017). https://www.strategy-business.com/article/The-Next-Wave-of-Innovation-in-the-Chemicals-Industry?gko=25f38
4. Artyukhov, A., Sklabinskyi, V.: Hydrodynamics of gas flow in small-sized vortex granulators in the production of nitrogen fertilizers. Chem. Chem. Technol. **9**(3), 337–342 (2015). https://doi.org/10.23939/chcht09.03.337
5. Artyukhov, A.E., Sklabinskyi, V.I.: Experimental and industrial implementation of porous ammonium nitrate producing process in vortex granulators. Naukovyi Visnyk Natsionalnoho Hirnychoho Universytetu **6**, 42–48 (2013). http://nvngu.in.ua/index.php/ru/component/jdownloads/finish/44-06/727-2013-6-artyukhov/0. (in Russian)
6. Artyukhov, A., Sklabinskyi, V.: Theoretical analysis of granules movement hydrodynamics in the vortex granulators of ammonium nitrate and carbamide production. Chem. Chem. Technol. **9**(2), 175–180 (2015). https://doi.org/10.23939/chcht09.02.175
7. Artyukhov, A.: Application software products for calculation trajectories of granules movement in vortex granulator. In: CEUR Workshop Proceedings (CEUR-WS.org): Selected Papers of the XI International Scientific-Practical Conference Modern Information Technologies and IT-Education (SITITO 2016), Moscow, Russia, vol. 1761, pp. 363–373 (2016). http://ceur-ws.org/Vol-1761/paper47.pdf
8. Artyukhov, A.E., Sklabinskyi, V.I.: 3D nanostructured porous layer of ammonium nitrate: influence of the moisturizing method on the layer's structure. J. Nano Electron. Phys. **8**(4–1), 04051 (2016). https://doi.org/10.21272/jnep.8(4(1)).04051
9. Artyukhov, A.E., Voznyi, A.A.: Thermodynamics of the vortex granulator's workspace: the impact on the structure of porous ammonium nitrate. In: 2016 International Conference on Nanomaterials: Application & Properties (NAP), Lviv, Ukraine, pp. 02NEA01-1–02NEA01-4 (2016). https://doi.org/10.1109/nap.2016.7757296
10. Artyukhov, A.E.: Kinetics of heating and drying of porous ammonium nitrate granules in the vortex granulator. In: 2016 International Conference on Nanomaterials: Application & Properties (NAP), Lviv, Ukraine, pp. 02NEA02-1–02NEA02-3 (2016). https://doi.org/10.1109/nap.2016.7757297
11. Artyukhov, A.E., Sklabinskyi, V.I.: Thermodynamic conditions for obtaining 3D nanostructured porous surface layer on the granules of ammonium nitrate. J. Nano Electron. Phys. **8**(4), 04083 (2016). https://doi.org/10.21272/jnep.8(4(2)).04083

12. Artyukhov, A.E., Sklabinskyi, V.I.: Investigation of the temperature field of coolant in the installations for obtaining 3D nanostructured porous surface layer on the granules of ammonium nitrate. J. Nano Electron. Phys. **9**(1), 01015 (2017). https://doi.org/10.21272/jnep.9(1).01015. (in Russian)
13. Artyukhov, A., Sklabinskiy, V., Ivaniia, A., Moskalenko, K.: Software for calculation of vortex type granulation devices. In: CEUR Workshop Proceedings (CEUR-WS.org): Selected Papers of the XI International Scientific-Practical Conference Modern Information Technologies and IT-Education (SITITO 2016), Moscow, Russia, vol. 1761, pp. 374–385 (2016). http://ceur-ws.org/Vol-1761/paper48.pdf
14. Artyukhov, A.E., Obodiak, V.K., Boiko, P.G., Rossi, P.C.: Computer modeling of hydrodynamic and heat-mass transfer processes in the vortex type granulation devices. In: CEUR Workshop Proceedings (CEUR-WS.org): Proceedings of the 13th International Conference on ICT in Education, Research and Industrial Applications. Integration, Harmonization and Knowledge Transfer, Kyiv, Ukraine, vol. 1844, pp. 33–47 (2017). http://ceur-ws.org/Vol-1844/10000033.pdf
15. Artyukhov, A.E., Fursa, A.S., Moskalenko, K.V.: Classification and separation of granules in vortex granulators. Chem. Pet. Eng. **51**(5-6), 311–318 (2015). https://doi.org/10.1007/s10556-015-0044-x
16. Artyukhova, N.A., Shandyba, A.B., Artyukhov, A.E.: Energy efficiency assessment of multi-stage convective drying of concentrates and mineral raw materials. Naukovyi Visnyk Natsionalnoho Hirnychoho Universytetu **1**, 92–98 (2014). http://nvngu.in.ua/index.php/ru/component/jdownloads/finish/42-01/701-2014-1-artyukhova/0. (in Russian)
17. Artyukhova, N.O.: Multistage finish drying of the N_4HNO_3 porous granules as a factor for nanoporous structure quality improvement. J. Nano Electron. Phys. **10**(3), 03030 (2018). https://doi.org/10.21272/jnep.10(3).03030
18. Artyukhov, A.E., Artyukhova, N.O., Ivaniia, A.V.: Creation of software for constructive calculation of devices with active hydrodynamics. In: 2018 14th International Conference on Advanced Trends in Radioelectronics, Telecommunications and Computer Engineering (TCSET 2018), Slavske, Ukraine, pp. 139–142 (2018). https://doi.org/10.1109/tcset.2018.8336173
19. Artyukhov, A., Ivaniia, A., Artyukhova, N., Gabrusenoks, J.: Multilayer modified NH_4NO_3 granules with 3D nanoporous structure: effect of the heat treatment regime on the structure of macro- and mezopores. In: 2017 IEEE International Young Scientists Forum on Applied Physics and Engineering (YSF 2017), Lviv, Ukraine, pp. 315–318 (2017). https://doi.org/10.1109/ysf.2017.8126641
20. Artyukhov, A.E.: Optimization of mass transfer separation elements of columnar equipment for natural gas preparation. Chem. Pet. Eng. **49**(11), 736–741 (2014). https://doi.org/10.1007/s10556-014-9827-8
21. Prokopov, M.G., Levchenko, D.A., Artyukhov, A.E.: Investigation of liquid-steam stream compressor. Appl. Mech. Mater. **630**, 109–116 (2014). https://doi.org/10.4028/www.scientific.net/AMM.630.109
22. Certificate of authorship No. 66782. Computer program Conical Channel©
23. Certificate of authorship No. 52659. Computer program Vortex Flow©
24. Certificate of authorship No. 65140. Computer program Vortex Granulator©
25. Certificate of authorship No. 67472. Computer program Classification in vortex flow©
26. Certificate of authorship No. 79141. Computer program Multistage Fluidizer©
27. Certificate of authorship No. 55360. Computer program Vortex Tray©
28. Artyukhov, A.E., Gabrusenoks, J., Rossi, P.C.: Obtaining of the modified NH_4NO_3 granules with 3-D nanoporous structure: impact of humidifier type on the granule's structure. In: Springer Proceedings in Physics, vol. 214, pp. 395–405 (2018). https://doi.org/10.1007/978-3-319-92567-7_25

29. Artyukhov, A.E., Gabrusenoks, J.: Phase composition and nanoporous structure of core and surface in the modified granules of NH_4NO_3. In: Springer Proceedings in Physics, vol. 210, pp. 301–309 (2018). https://doi.org/10.1007/978-3-319-91083-3_21

30. Artyukhov, A., Artyukhova, N.: Utilization of dust and ammonia from exhaust gases: new solutions for dryers with different types of fluidized bed. J. Environ. Health. Sci. **16**(2), 193–204 (2018). https://doi.org/10.1007/s40201-018-0307-5

31. Artyukhov, A.E., Sklabinskiy, V.I., Goncharov, A.G.: Development of technology for obtaining N_4HNO_3 multilayer granules with nanostructured porous layers. J. Nano Electron. Phys. **10**(5), 05013-1–05013-4 (2018). https://doi.org/10.21272/jnep.10(5).05013

School Education in Computer Science and ICT

Implementation of Complex Enumeration Computational Problems: An Approach for "Advanced" Junior Students

Boris Melnikov⬚, Elena Melnikova⬚, and Svetlana Pivneva(✉)⬚

Russian State Social University, Wilhelm Pieck Str. 4, 129226 Moscow, Russia
bf-melnikov@yandex.ru, ya.e.melnikova@yandex.ru,
tlt-swetlana@yandex.ru

Abstract. This paper deals with some issues related to the training of students of junior courses (approximately 14–19 years). At least two objectives are set. Firstly, we focus on potential participants of the programming Olympiads: according to our calculations, at least one third of the tasks of high-level Olympiads can be called exhaustive-searched. Secondly (which, apparently, is more important), mastering the proposed approach to the implementation of hard exhaustive-searched problems can (and should) serve as an "advanced" student as a first step into the "big science": the tasks themselves, and the approach we propose to implement them, are closely connected with the set of directions of modern artificial intelligence, the analysis of large data, and similar subject areas. Several of the problems we are considering are related to different subjects. Among these problems (subjects areas) are, first, the tasks previously given at different levels of the ACM Olympiads, including at the final stage of this Olympiad. The solutions we offer for these tasks are no more complicated than the original ones, and considering that they can be quickly implemented using the approach we proposed (described in this article), we can say that they are much easier to learn by the trainees. In the article, we describe some classes implemented in C++, intended for the quick generation of programs for solving a variety of enumeration tasks. We give also some specific programming techniques for such tasks.

Keywords: Complex enumeration problems · An approach to the implementation · Olympiads problems · The first step in the science

1 Introduction and Motivation

This paper deals with some issues related to the training of students of junior courses (approximately 14–19 years). These questions are related to the approach to the implementation of programming algorithms for solving brute-force problems. In the opinion of the authors of the paper, the proposed approach can even be considered as a possible standard designed to develop and design algorithms for solving exhaustive problems. To note that, of course, the paper deals with the generalization of "advanced" high school students and junior students. At the same time, the following objectives are set.

© Springer Nature Switzerland AG 2020
V. Sukhomlin and E. Zubareva (Eds.): SITITO 2018, CCIS 1201, pp. 417–426, 2020.
https://doi.org/10.1007/978-3-030-46895-8_32

Firstly, we focus on potential participants of the programming Olympiads. We present an easily realizable method for solving an entire class of enumeration problems. It can be called an approach to the implementation of a set of algorithms based on the method of branches and bounds, which includes many additional similar heuristics; this uniformity lies in the fact that the heuristics themselves do not practically change when passing from one task to another.

Therefore, according to [1, 2] etc., we called this method a *multi-heuristic approach*. The complexity of the tasks we solve using this approach is very different: from "student Olympiad" problems to large software projects, often representing a complex of heuristic algorithms for the *practical* solution of some NP-difficult problem. It should be noted that despite this, the setting and *implementation* of our proposed tasks is available to a 16–17 year old "advanced" student.

In our previous publications, almost nothing was said on the implementation of algorithms; and in this paper, we try to eliminate this defect. According to the authors, in many scientific publications devoted to the descriptions of algorithms, as well as in various textbooks, the actual implementation of programs is often "overlapping taboo". Moreover, there is often a much worse situation, the next one. The very texts of the programs, given in very good books (like [3, 4]), seem somewhat "unfinished", simply because the authors practically do not pay attention to "purely programming" questions. Among these issues, we first of all note the allocation and release of dynamic memory, etc., but not only them. And for the implementation of the programs described by us, it seems that quite enough knowledge of a small subset of C++; it should be a small one, but a "good" subset, a self-sufficient one.

Secondly (which, apparently, is more important), mastering the proposed approach to the implementation of hard exhaustive-searched problems can (and should) serve as an "advanced" student as a first step into the "big science": the tasks themselves, and the approach we propose to implement them, are closely connected with the set of directions of modern artificial intelligence, the analysis of large data, and similar subject areas.

Several of the problems we are considering are related to different subjects. Among these problems (subjects areas) are, first, the mentioned before tasks previously given at different levels of the ACM Olympiads, including at its final stage. The solutions we offer for these tasks are no more complicated than the original ones, and considering that they can be quickly implemented using the approach we proposed (described in this article), we can say that they are much easier to learn by the trainees. The second class of subject areas is various classical hard-to-solve brute-force problems, usually NP-difficult; as examples, we assume to result in the continuation article a very similar program applied to much more complex problems: the traveling salesman problem in the classical formulation, the problems of computing certain invariants of a graph, and the problem of state minimization for nondeterministic finite automata. We shall set one more goal to consider a concrete example of one of such problems. This analysis will include the basics of the necessary mathematical theory.

In the current paper, we describe some classes implemented in C++, intended for the quick generation of programs for solving a variety of enumeration tasks. Examples of programs that are accessible for understanding by an "advanced" junior student of

14–15 years who owns the very basics of object-oriented programming are given. The following different things should be noted (sometimes once again):

- perhaps in our case, the implementation does not provide the fastest solution, but it provides *a method* for solving several Olympiad problems of different levels;
- some programming subtleties are explained in the comments to the programs; this is why we present the texts of the programs in more or less detail;
- our approach to such implementation constitutes an essential part of the subject of this paper; greatly simplifying the situation, it is *the first step on the way to science*;
- the MFC class library used by us (and perhaps a little "outdated") has exact analogues for a "much more modern" API interface library (its description is given, e.g., in [5]).

2   One Problem of the ACM 2007 Finals

Let us start with one of the problems of the 2007 ACM finals, namely, from task F, see [6] etc. This is the problem of the finals of the most prestigious international student's world championship (even one of the simplest tasks offered there), but its level is approximately such that when solving "off-line", its complexity is quite accessible to the "advanced" high school student. As already noted above, when we consider it, we actually get a method for solving similar search problems.

So, we give the condition of the problem. (And we will note in advance that we have slightly simplified the formulation of the condition when deciding. For example, we will consider only the case $N = 4$. Besides, we did not replace the word "blue" in the wording: even in the case of a black-and-white picture, the meaning is obvious.)

A Marble Game is played with M marbles on a square board. The board is divided into N N unit squares, and M of those unit squares contain holes. Marbles and holes are numbered from 1 to M. The goal of the Marble game is to roll each marble into the hole that has the same number. A game board may contain walls. Each wall is one unit long and stands between two adjacent unit squares. Two squares are considered adjacent if and only if they share a side.

At the beginning of the game, all marbles are placed on the board, each in a different square. A "move" consists of slightly lifting a side of the game board. Then all marbles on the board roll downward toward the opposite side, each one rolling until it meets a wall or drops into an empty hole, or until the next square is already occupied by another marble. Marbles roll subject to the following restrictions:

- *Marbles cannot jump over walls, other marbles, or empty holes.*
- *Marbles cannot leave the board. (The edge of the board is a wall.)*
- *A unit square can contain at most a single marble at any one time.*
- *When a marble moves into a square with a hole, the marble drops into that hole. The hole is then filled, and other marbles can subsequently roll over the hole. A marble in a hole can never leave that hole.*

The game is over when each marble has dropped into a hole with the corresponding number.

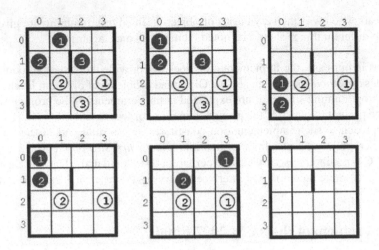

Fig. 1. The figure illustrating the condition of the problem.

Figure 1 illustrates a solution for a game played on a 4 × 4 board with three blue marbles, three holes and a wall. The solution has five moves: lift the east side, lift the north side, lift the south side, lift the west side, lift the north side.

The program should determine the fewest number of moves to drop all the marbles into the correct holes – if such a move sequence is possible.

Before discussing the solution, it should be noted that instead of the term "game" it is more accurate to use the word "puzzle", which is more in line with the terminology used in the literature on artificial intelligence ([7, 8] etc.; see also [9, Sect. 5.5, 10]). However, when considering the condition of the problem, we left the terminology of the original. And since this is a puzzle, then we can apply the usual method of solving them, i.e. a complete search in the state space. But, as it was mentioned in the introduction, our approach to solving similar problems, to organizing the search in them (more precisely, the search with returns, backtracking) can be applied to other, much more complex problems. In Fig. 2, we give only the "beginning" of the search tree (each vertex is a position): its bush, which refers to the root (i.e. the starting position).

So, the full search (the brute force method) is considered. At the same time, we must:

– firstly, prevent possible loops (in the search tree, i.e. in this case, in the tree of positions);
– secondly, find the optimal solution (minimum in the number of moves);
– and thirdly, be able to find situations in which there is no solution.

All this leads to the idea of using a search in breadth - which we will do. We will not save the entire search tree. Here - and more importantly, that *everywhere in such situations* - it is enough (and desirable!) to store only the leaves of this tree; and since we decided to organize a search in width, then it is desirable to store the leaves in the form of a queue, see [3] etc. (And in the case of searching the most convenient version of the data in depth, it appears that the stack is also conveniently organized on the basis

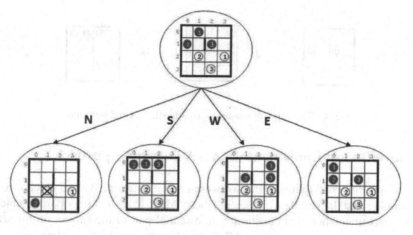

Fig. 2. The "beginning" of the search tree.

of an array or list.) We implement the queue using the simplest array (pointers to the vertices-positions). In the next program, each such vertex will be of type **MyBoard**. And we will be the easiest way to prevent possible looping: we will remember all the positions that we met. (Let us note in advance, that in more complex problems, this path is certainly unacceptable. Therefore, it is necessary to look for other methods).

So, in our program there will be even 2 arrays: in one we will store the positions not yet considered, and in the other is already considered. At the beginning of the work, the first one (the main one) consists of a single element (corresponding to the starting position), the second one is generally empty. Next, we sequentially delete the first element of the main array, the current position (adding it simultaneously to the second array), and instead write to it at the end of the main array (queue!) three positions, each of which can be obtained from the current one in 1 move. (More precisely, no more than 3 positions. But not 4 positions, because the same move is meaningless to do two times in a row; by the way, for this purpose we are lower in class MyBoard using field nLast. The only possible exception is that the 4 positions can be added for the first time, i.e. when processing the root of the search tree. And, of course, we do not record in the arrays any "bad" positions (similar to the left bottom in Fig. 2), nor those who meet again). The values of the main array (list) after the first and second iterations are shown in Fig. 3 and 4 respectively.

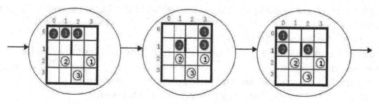

Fig. 3. The value of the main list after the first iteration.

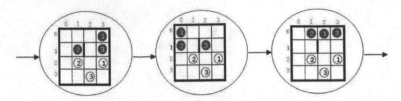

Fig. 4. The value of the main list after the second iteration.

3   The Software Implementation – A Possible Approach

Let us turn to the description of the software implementation. We use object-oriented programming and the simplest classes of library MFC [11]. It is important to note that it is this implementation that constitutes an essential part of the subject of this article. Also, let us note once again, that the MFC class library used by us (and perhaps a little "outdated") has exact analogues for a "much more modern" API interface library.

So, the following description of the class-position (`MyBoard`) is possible:

```
class MyBoard {
private:
int nDim; //dimension
int Board [4] [4];
bool WallRight [4] [3]; //the wall is to the right of //this cell
bool WallDown [3] [4]; //the wall is from below of this //cell
int nDeep;
//level, depth of search (the number of moves already //made)
int nLast;
//the last made move:
//0 we do not know; 1 nord; etc.
public:
MyBoard ();
MyBoard (MyBoard& copy); //copy constructor
int GetDim () {return nDim; }
int Get (int i, int j) {return Board[i][j]; }
int GetDeep () {return nDeep; }
int GetLast () {return nLast; }
friend istream& operator >> (istream& is, MyBoard& board);
friend ostream& operator << (ostream& os, MyBoard& board);
bool Empty ();
//is everything already good? is the board already emp- //ty?
bool North ();
//to raise the board from the north;
//returns true if none of the balls hit the other's //hole;
//else returns false
bool South (); //to raise the board from the south
bool West (); //to raise the board from the west
bool East (); //to raise the board from the east
};
bool operator == (MyBoard& board1, MyBoard& board2);
```

```
//compares only the arrays of the Board
//of the objects under consideration
}
```

Some comments have already been given in the class description itself. Implementation of the methods, apparently, is unlikely to cause interest; here, it is purely technical work.

To store arrays of positions (more precisely, pointers to positions), it is convenient to use a specially written successor of the class CPtrArray; it is important to note that this approach is desirable very often, when considering an array (or list) of pointers to a variety of data structures. So, the following description of the derived class CPtrArray is possible:

```
class MyArray : public CPtrArray {//of MyBoard*
public:
bool Exists (MyBoard* pBoard);
void MyAdd (MyBoard* pBoard);
};
```

And already now, when considering a not very complicated problem, it is worth noting the following circumstance. An array (or list) of positions (and in more complex situations, of subtasks) can be ordered according to different criteria – and not only by the distance from the root in the search tree, as in our case, i.e. when searching in width. Even in our example, we could apply other criteria of ordering, for example, by increasing the number of remaining balls, which somehow characterizes the "closeness of position to the solution". We also note that such an ordering can be connected with the solution of another problem of [6], namely Problem B.

Unlike the previously discussed MyBoard class, we shall introduce here the implementation of these methods.

```
bool MyArray::Exists (MyBoard* pBoard) {
for (int i = 0; i <GetSize(); i++) {
MyBoard* pN = (MyBoard*)GetAt(i);
if (*pN ==*pBoard) return true;
}
return false;
}
void MyArray::MyAdd (MyBoard* pBoard) {
if (Exists(pBoard)) delete pBoard; else Add(pBoard);
}
```

Here, the Exists() method, by the simplest linear search, gives an answer to the question of the presence in the array of some element-position (for the possibility of such a search, we have previously reloaded the comparison operator of the MyBoard class) and the MyAdd() method adds a new position to the end of the array. If the position in question is already present in the array, then we do not add it; moreover, we call the destructor for it. Note that this approach requires accuracy (since the establishment of the object occurs at one level of the program, and its removal occurs at the other one), but it is possible. Now consider the most important class MyTask defining our main construction, i.e. *the whole task*. It is very important to note that it is desirable to use *almost the same class* in a lot of more complicated discrete optimization problems.

```
class MyTask {
private:
MyArray Current; //positions not yet considered
MyArray Old; //positions already considered
public:
MyTask (MyBoard& board);
friend ostream& operator << (ostream& os, MyTask& task);
int Step ();
//returned value:
//−1 the array of subtasks is empty;
//0 this situation requires the continuation of the //work;
//>0 the answer
int Run ();
//returned value:
//−1 there is no answer;
//>=0 the answer
};
```

The Run() method is of no interest: it consists of sequential calls to the Step() method; the implementation of the last one is given below.

```
int MyTask::Step () {
if (this -> Current.GetSize() <=0) return −1;
MyBoard* pOld = (MyBoard*)Current.GetAt(0);
if (pOld -> Empty()) return pOld -> GetDeep(); //the "rein-
//surance"
this -> Current.RemoveAt(0);
int nLast = pOld -> GetLast();
if (nLast! = 1) {//we can lift the board from the north side
MyBoard* pN = new MyBoard(*pOld);
if (!pN -> North()) delete pN;
else if (pN -> Empty()) {
int n = pN -> GetDeep();
delete pN;
return n;
}
else if (Old.Exists(pN)) delete pN;
else this -> Current.MyAdd(pN);
}
//...
//similar challenges of lifting the board from 3 other //sides;
//the texts of such calls are omitted
//...
```

```
Old.Add(pOld);
return 0;
}
```

Let us note, that it is possible to simplify the full search (that is, to reduce the number of positions considered) in different ways; we mean not only not reviewing the same move twice consecutively (i.e., using the `nLast` field). However, we will not discuss this point in more detail, we hope to return to it in the paper-continuation.

4 Conclusion

In the next publication, we are going to cite the continuation of this material, and to complicate it both from the point of view of the problems under consideration and from the point of view of algorithms.

As problems of discrete optimization solved by the same approach, we propose to consider the traveling salesman problem in its classical formulation ([9] etc.), and also the problem of minimization of nondeterministic finite automata ([12] etc.). Among our publications, devoted to this topic, we note once again [1, 2] and also [13, 14]. These problems (of the article-continuation) should be available to the "advanced" student. And as the algorithms that develop this topic, we propose to consider the following. First, we note that in the above problem, we can actually not separate the matrix and the subtask that includes it; however, in more complex cases this can not normally be done. The discussion of such an implementation (let us repeat, also available to the "advanced" young student) is assumed in the collapsing publication. One of the auxiliary algorithms necessary for this is the division of the task into two subtasks; this division is one of the most important parts of the branch and boundary method (see also [9] etc.). We carry out this division as a method of the subtask class (in our notation, `MySubTask`): this method changes the owner (the object of the class `MySubTask`), making from it the so-called "right subtask", [1]. As an output, it gives a pointer to the created "left" subtask, to which the constructor was previously applied.

Acknowledgements. The research was partially supported by Russian State Social University.

References

1. Melnikov, B.: Multiheuristic approach to discrete optimization problems. Cybern. Syst. Anal. **42**(3), 335–341 (2006). https://doi.org/10.1007/s10559-006-0070-y
2. Melnikov, B., Melnikova, E., Pivneva, S., Churikova, N., Dudnikov, V., Prus, M.: Multi-heuristic and game approaches in search problems of the graph theory. In: Information Technology and Nanotechnology Proceedings (ITNT-2018), pp. 2884–2894. Samara, Russia (2018). https://elibrary.ru/item.asp?id=34895071&
3. Cormen, T., Leiserson, Ch., Rivest, R., Stein, C.: Introduction to Algorithms. MIT Press, Boston (2009)
4. Lipski, W.: Combinatorics for Programmers. Polish Sci. Publ. (PWN), Warsaw (1982). (in Polish)

5. Java Platform, Standard Edition 8, API Specification. https://docs.oracle.com/javase/8/docs/api/overview-summary.html
6. The 2007 ACM Programming Contest World Finals. https://icpc.baylor.edu/regionals/finder/world-finals-2007
7. Russell, S., Norvig, P.: Artificial Intelligence: A Modern Approach. Prentice Hall, NJ (2002)
8. Luger, G.: Artificial Intelligence: Structures and Strategies for Complex Problem Solving. Addison-Wesley, Boston (2003)
9. Hromkovič, J.: Theoretische Informatik: Formale Sprachen, Berechenbarkeit, Komplexitts-theorie, Algorithmik, Kommunikation und Kryptographie. Springer Verlag, Berlin (2011). (in German). https://doi.org/10.1007/978-3-8348-9853-1
10. Melnikov, B., Melnikova, E.: Some competition programming problems as the beginning of artificial intelligence. Inf. Educ. 6(2), 385–396 (2007). https://www.mii.lt/informatics_in_education/htm/INFE110.htm
11. MFC classes, https://msdn.microsoft.com/ru-ru/library/bk77x1wx.aspx
12. Polák, L.: Minimizations of NFA using the universal automaton. Int. J. Found. Comput. Sci. 16(5), 999–1010 (2005). https://doi.org/10.1142/S0129054105003431
13. Melnikov, B.: The complete finite automaton. Int. J. Open Inf. Technol. 5(10), 9–17 (2017). https://elibrary.ru/item.asp?id=30101608
14. Makarkin, S., Melnikov, B., Trenina, M.: Approach to Solve a Pseudogeometric Version of the Traveling Salesman Problem. University proceedings. Volga region. Phys. Math. Sci. 2(34), 135–147 (2015). (in Russian). https://elibrary.ru/item.asp?id=24254294

Economic Informatics

The Role of Controlling in Process Management

Igor Fiodorov[1]([✉]) [iD] and Alexander Sotnikov[2] [iD]

[1] Plekhanov Russian University of Economics, Stremyannyj per. 36, 115093 Moscow, Russia
Igor.Fiodorov@mail.ru
[2] Joint Supercomputer Center of the Russian Academy of Sciences, Leninskij Ave. 14, 119991 Moscow, Russia
ASotnikov@jscc.ru

Abstract. Processes are the core of organizations. Business Process Management (BPM) helps organizations gain a competitive advantage by improving and innovating their processes through a holistic process-oriented view. We argue that interpretation of process management as pure process model re-design, limit our capability of process control. A model modification is essential but not the only way of process management. It is possible to manage a process without model modification. We introduce three levels of process controlling.

Keywords: Business Process Management · Business Process Management Systems · Business process controlling

1 Introduction

Business processes are among today's hottest topics in the science and practice of information systems. In recent years, several organizations have made significant investments in a multitude of Business Process Management (BPM) initiatives. Business Process Management Systems support the execution of business processes through the automated coordination of activities and resources according to a formally defined model of the business process. Recent publications on business process management consider the entire spectrum from theoretical aspects, application scenarios and implementation issues. In our opinion the business processes controlling deserves more attention than it has received so far.

The theoretical and practical issues of how to control business processes have been neglected in the past. A group of experts from BPM.com and ABPMP forums, led by K. Swenson, agreed a comprehensive definition of Business Process Management as «a discipline involving any combination of modeling, automation, execution, control, measurement and optimization of business activity flows, in support of enterprise goals, spanning systems, employees, customers and partners within and beyond the enterprise boundaries» [1]. Compared to a known definition by Gartner [2] one can find a new word here - a control. Experts explain - «a control means that there is some aspect of making sure that the process follows the designed course» [1]. Being formally correct, this definition of a term «control» doesn't explain what a practician should do in order to maintain process normal execution. Moreover, experts see process management as «the act of improving those processes» [1]. We argue that it would not be correct to limit a Business Process Management to a change of the process model only. Such interpretation of management as of sole process model redesign limits our capability of process control. A model modification is essential but not the only way of process management. As we will show, it is possible to control a process without modification of its model.

Unfortunately, it is difficult to find a clear distinction between process controlling, management and improvement. According to M. Hammer, processes could fail to meet performance requirements either due to defective design or due to faulty execution. Pervasive performance shortcomings generally indicate a design flaw, while occasional ones are usually the result of execution difficulties. To resolve problems of both kinds he suggests using Deming's PDCA cycle, with the addition of the attention to process design [7]. In most cases controlling is understood in connection to process improvement. For example, P. Kueng and P. Kawalek understand a process controlling, as a part of Business Process Management and deem that measuring, analyzing, and improving processes represents a loop that coordinates process execution [3]. But they did not explain how this loop works. D. Heckl and J. Moormann suppose that Business Process Management includes three categories of controlling: normative, strategic, and operational process control [4]. The first two categories should be seen as a process improvement rather than a process controlling. The last one is a process controlling, but it relies on a manual reaction of a «process manager who searches for short-term improvements that immediately influence process performance results». M. zur Muehlen gives a better definition of process controlling and its levels. He declared that «the strategic level of process controlling has to ensure that all organizational processes cooperatively support the organization's goals. At the operative level, process controlling has to ensure the efficient execution of individual processes and the proper utilization of the resources required for process execution. Operative process controlling overlaps with operative process management, since both have the same purpose» [5]. Unfortunately, there is no explanation of how business process controlling should be implemented. A-W. Scheer and E. Brabaender state that «the business process controlling phase involves measurement of the efficiency of the business processes implemented with the help of IT systems and the implementation of internal control systems to monitor compliance with a wide range of regulations» [6]. So they suggest performing a measurement to check if a process improvement has a positive impact. They suppose that process controlling allows companies to introduce proactive process management but doesn't explain how to do it. Today Business Process Management is often implemented with a help of BPMS. This type of IT systems not only automate a process execution and helps to measure process performance but also allow process controlling and a proactive business process management. Unfortunately, there is no clear understanding of how to proceed with business process controlling.

The goal of this article is to describe possible options of process controlling and analyze various management decisions. In conclusion, we show that this interpretation of control has the practical application and is able to provide companies with significant business advantages.

2 Process Management vs. Process Controlling

In this article, we suggest distinguishing between the management of an enterprise with the help of business processes and the management of business processes themselves. The first is a holistic management approach focused on aligning all aspects of an organization with the wants and needs of clients [7]. M. Hammer claims that through process management, an enterprise can create high-performance processes, which operate with lower costs, faster speeds, greater accuracy, reduced assets, and enhanced flexibility. This kind of management has a general name - a process approach, it is described in detail in different paperwork [8], so we will not consider it in this paper.

On the other hand, we can also manage business processes themselves. Individual processes can execute with a deviation of a process indicators. M. Hammer calls it a faulty execution. But a process will not fail, if a special activity, compensating deviation will return a specific process indicator to its normal value.

We define a process controlling as an activity directed at overcoming consequences of the deviations that can arise during a process execution. The analyst sees the «ideal» process without anomalies and with consistent quality at the output. In the reality, runtime deviations occur. Processes controlling includes the actions to detect the deviations and work out the compensating signal to change some process inputs in such a way that the process stays at its set point despite disturbances.

In order to distinguish between a process management and a process controlling we identify an object of administration. In the first case, it is entire organization, in the second – the inside of the processes. Thus, a process management and a process controlling are two different but complementary approaches to administer the organization and its performance. In this article, we will discuss the levels of a business process controlling, try to analyze the difference between a controlling a management, give a recommendation on a design of a proactive BPM.

3 Three Levels of Process's Controlling

Let us discuss the three levels of process controlling. The first level is an operational, aimed to control the individual process instances on a short-term planning horizon. For example, it is naive to assume that all process exemplars are executed at regular speed, as details on a conveyor. Individual process instances may outrun or lag behind the schedule for a variety of reasons. In the latter case, a process manager should take such an action, that lagging instances could catch up a schedule. In this way, we can eliminate the random deviations of process parameters.

The second level controls the group of processes instances on a midterm timing interval. If process manager observes some systematic deviations, he can take an action that influences a collection of processes. First of all, a process manager can reallocate resources in order to eliminate different bottlenecks. Secondly, by changing business rules he can alter process policies. In both cases, the logic of the process remains unchanged.

The third level of controlling implies a change of the process map in the case of radical changes in business environment. It is used for a long-term planning horizon so we call it a strategic management. The modification of the process map should be done only when the operational and tactical levels of business process controlling are no longer able to compensate runtime deviations. We shall discuss the techniques used to control process execution at these three levels.

3.1 Operational Level Controlling

Controlling the individual process instances assumes the measurement of the execution parameters of each process exemplar in order to identify those that are performed with deviations and elaborate a reaction that can compensate the deflection so the business process instance will stay at its set-point despite disturbances. That means a process's logic should include a pattern to measure the deviations of execution parameters and proactively produce countermeasures to correct the deviation. That means a process indicators are a key factor of the controlling, while the product indicators are left out of analyses.

Let us discuss what can be done, when a deviation of a process indicator is detected? For the sake of brevity, we will focus on an elapsed time, because it indirectly influences many other process characteristics, for example, a cost of process execution. The time allocated for a completing a particular task consists of waiting time before a performer starts a task and of execution time to fulfill a task. If a particular process instance is out of a schedule we can consider following patterns of operational control:

1. Change a priority of a process instance task. Normally an actor takes the topmast task from his work list, so the oldest entry will be processed first. By changing the priority we can rearrange the work list so that a task with the highest priority will be located on the top and will be taken first.
2. Remind an employee appointed to this task that the allowed time expires so he should start doing a task. This prompt should be sent beforehand, leaving enough time to accomplish a task.
3. Escalate a task to a manager if an executor does not react to a reminder. In this case, a manager can fulfill a task himself or delegate it another employee.
4. Limit a time allowed for proceedings a task. Normally a participant can suspend the task execution and resume it later. By restricting the duration of a task we deny any interruptions.
5. A strong process delay could even cancel process exception. Let us imagine a case where the execution of the process's instance after a certain period of time is considered inadmissible and that instance should be terminated. When the time limit expires, an exception occurs, the process terminates.
6. In addition to monitoring of process' indicators, it is necessary to provide the process manager with a capability to intervene in the work of their subordinates. For example, consider the situation when an employee who was appointed to the task is absent from the workplace. In this case, the manager must be able to intercept the corresponding process instance in order to transfer the task to another actor or do it himself. The process's developer should build an interception's hierarchy so that the manager could seize the job of his staff. In addition, the process owner can intercept a task from managers.

7. Finally, the lagging process can be executed in a manual mode outside the business process management system. In order to avoid violations of the process's rules, it is recommended to provide an opportunity for a "manual" process execution to the process manager only.

Our practice shows that before the introduction of the operational control over 20% of business process instances were lagging of the schedule. After the implementation of operational control, the number of delays has reduced to 5%. As a result, the customer satisfaction increases. As we can see this level of business process controlling doesn't require any changes to a process logic, so it doesn't entail any modifications of the process model. We can also see that it helps in avoiding random fluctuations in process execution.

3.2 Tactical Level

The tactical level of business process controlling implies a control of a group of processes instances on a mid-term planning horizon. We analyze the possible management actions aiming to keep a business process in a manageable state. We identify two mechanisms of business process controlling at this level: reallocation of resources in order to eliminate different bottlenecks and change of business rules that modify runtime policies.

Resource Management
Usually, a performance of a process is limited by some bottlenecks. Often happens that one of business process tasks takes much longer than others thus limiting the performance of the whole chain. Let assume that employees are participating in one process only. To find a bottleneck a process manager can investigate a size of a work list for all operations of the process. If at one process step the number of instances waiting for execution is significantly higher than on others, it is a sign of a bottleneck. If the owner finds a bottleneck of the process, he can provide additional human resources for that operation and raise the productivity. However, after exceeding a certain threshold the performance ceases to increase because the bottleneck moves to another location. If we would like to know the upper limit of resources that can be added to a particular operation, we can use the process performance simulation in BPMS. Figure 1 shows the result of the process's performance simulation. The green number shows the number of processes that are processed to the moment, the yellow number indicates the number of processes waiting for processing. Steps that are highlighted in red denote the operations where the queue length exceeds some critical value and where the process owner intervention is required.

Thus, by manipulating the resources it is possible to achieve optimum balance and harmony of the process execution. Today managers allocate more resources to the process than it is really necessary in order to secure a process in a case of unexpected deviations [9]. These additional reserves decrease process efficiency so there is a discussion on its usage [10]. Using tactical controlling we can allocate additional reserves only to operations, with a high risk of a bottleneck. Thus reserves are minimal so efficiency increases.

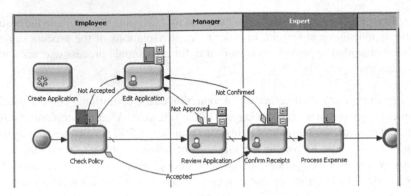

Fig. 1. The result of process simulation. (Color figure online)

Business Rules

Now let's discuss how one can manage the business process with the help business rules. Under the business rule we understand the statement defining or limiting some aspects of the business [11]. In contrast to the procedural description, the business rules postulate the limitations of the execution of the business process but do not specify how to achieve the expected result. R. Ross defines the following classification of business rules [12]:

1. Behavioral Rule: defines the need of the appropriate action. They are about what actors must or must not do.
2. Definitional Rules: establishes a criterion for the applicability of a business concept. They are about what actors can know, are divided into:

- Computation rules help find the values of the unknown quantities, which are called facts.
- Classification rules provide decision logic needed to verify the truth of the facts.

Behavioral rules play a role of logic in a control flow. The branching of the process is done based on the Behavioral Rules which takes on input True or False and switches the route accordingly. But what is true and what is false, is defined in the Classification Rule. In turn, the latter should receive the input value, which can be obtained by using the Calculation Rule. For example, consider the following sequence: calculate the discount as a function of the size of the current order (calculation Rule), classify the size of the discounts as: large, medium, low (classification Rule) and, and, finally, send the transaction for the approval by the supervisor with the appropriate authority (behavioral rule). The behavioral and computation rules usually remain constant through the process lifecycle, while classification rules can change. For example, a banking "approve a credit" process includes a scoring procedure, which is a computation rule. If the score exceeds a particular threshold a credit can be approved otherwise a request is denied. That is a classification rule that compares a score with a threshold. If a bank wishes to decrease its risk he increases a barrier. That mean, by changing classification business rules we can adapt a process to temporal changes on a market. We also recommend keeping classification and computation rules separately, that will help the analyst to clearly locate the appropriate logic. By changing the business rules, we manipulate the value of the threshold, without changing the process template and thus change the way of process execution.

By separating three types of business rules we can make a process model variable. For example, depending on the economic situation, the bank can decide on the transition to expansion or contraction of credit. Changing the rules of lending is realized by changing the threshold of a scoring system: by lowering the threshold, the bank decreases the requirements for the borrower and by raising the threshold, the bank increases lending. Thus, the threshold is a parameterized variable. If the bank can dynamically react to the environment changes by modifying its rules, he will be able to effectively manage risk.

All described methods of tactical control will influence a group of processes instances that are launched after changes have been deployed to BPMS and will be applicable until new changes will be deployed. The methods of tactical process control help avoiding systematic deviations in process execution.

3.3 Strategic Level of Management

We understand the strategic management as the change of the business process map, caused by the need to meet new business requirements or in response to changing in the business environment. This level of control is applied if the operational and tactical levels of a process controlling are no longer able compensate deviations or there was a radical change in business. This type of controlling involves the administration of process indicators on the long-term interval.

In "traditional" understanding, process controlling, imply a purposeful change of the process model aimed at improving the methods of work execution. It is also important to note that the process improvement is objective only if it is implemented on the basis of direct measurements of process indicators. It allows using only those changes that lead to objective process improvements and discard other that did not prove its viability in practice. We will not dwell on the process improvement, because they are well described in the literature, but we will discuss the ability of BPM to manage process's versions. The process controlling at the strategic level is not limited to the replacement of one model with another, but also includes the administration of process migration from the «old» map on the "new" one. IT managers are aware of the difficulties associated with the «parallel» operation of an old and a new systems and migration between them. An important feature of the industrial BPMS is the support of the business processes model versioning.

Processes Model Versioning
Business processes model versioning means that after the new process diagram is deployed, BPMS can simultaneously run in parallel old and new processes versions.

We distinguish between versioning of an executable model and source code versioning and discuss only the first one. When faced with the task to translate the "old" process on a "new" track, it is necessary to determine the level of differences between old and new processes maps to assess their degree of compatibility. If the differences are slightly, we can automatically convert the "old" process on the «new» track, otherwise, the process diagrams are incompatible, automatic transformation is impossible. In this case, the administrator shall separately transfer processes one by one in a manual mode. For example, a process developer removes the interactive operation from the process template. If some instance of the "old" process currently executes the operation that was removed in a new model, then transfer to a new model will result in the loss of this process instance, which is unacceptable. This transfer is possible in manual mode only: the administrator must first ensure that the process instance currently not execute the specified interactive operation and only after that he can manually transfer the instance on the process to the new template. It should be noted that the source of incompatibilities can be in data structures and in the program code. Certainly, the use of means of a source code versioning facilitates the comparison of both schemes, but unfortunately, the developers forget to use the tools necessary to support source code versioning. The full list of changes that lead to the incompatibility of the process models can be found in the vendor's BPMS documentation.

The financial benefits derive from the rapidity of the changes and from the cost reductions for parallel operation of the "old" and "new" systems. We can roughly estimate the time required to change the process template. At medium and small changes that amount of time rarely exceeds 5–10 man-days. It is unlikely that such changes can be implemented in a comparable time, using alternative methods of developing systems for managing business processes. For the traditional IT systems the cost of the parallel operations of an old and new system includes the cost of additional hardware and software platforms, the cost of administration and migration of applications and data. In the case of BPMS the costs are limited to the cost of administration, i.e., are negligible.

4 Conclusions

In this article, we suggest distinguishing between the management of an enterprise with the help of business processes and the controlling of business processes. The main difference between both is in the object of administration. In the case of an enterprise management it is an entire organization, in case of business processes controlling – individual processes instances. We conclude that the process management and the process controlling are two different but complementary approaches to administer the organization and its performance.

We also introduce three levels of business process controlling. The first level is aimed to control the individual process instances on a short-term planning horizon. The second level controls the group of processes instances on a midterm timing interval. The third level of controlling implies a change of the process map in the case of radical changes in a business environment. It is used for a long-term planning horizon so we call it a strategic management. The modification of the process map should be done only when the operational and tactical levels of business process controlling are no longer able to compensate runtime deviations. Table 1 summarizes the analyses of a process controlling.

The analysts and developers of the BPMS need to be aware of these levels of process controlling and include necessary patterns to the process model. This way they make a process map variable, reduce the need for model modification. By calculation of a minimum necessary number of reserves, a process owner can eliminate human resources allocated to the process and thus increase efficiency.

Table 1. Three levels of process controlling.

	Object	Deviation	Responsible	Focus	Horizon	Type of management
Strategic level	Organization	Systematic	Process owner	Goals	Family of processes	Manual
Tactic level	A department participating in a process	Systematic	Process manager	Resources	Group of processes	Manual and automatic
Operational level	Line of a business	Random	Process manager	Norms	Process instance	Automatic

We assume that this recommendation can help a developer making an executable process model a controllable and can help your organization achieve high productivity and efficiency with a minimal change to their process model.

References

1. Swenson, K.: One common definition for BPM. Thinking Matters, K. Swenson's blog (2014). http://social-biz.org/2014/01/27/one-common-definition-for-bpm/
2. Gartner. Business Process Management: Technology Defined IT Glossary (2011). http://www.gartner.com/it-glossary/business-process-management-bpm-standards
3. Kueng, P., Kawalek, P.: Goal-based business process models: creation and evaluation. Bus. Process Manage. J. **3**(1), 17–38 (1997). https://doi.org/10.1108/14637159710161567
4. Heckl, D., Moormann, J.: Process performance management. In: vom Brocke, J., Rosemann, M. (eds.) Handbook on Business Process Management 2. International Handbooks on Information Systems, pp. 115–135. Springer, Heidelberg (2010). https://doi.org/10.1007/978-3-642-01982-1_6
5. zur Muehlen, M.: Workflow-Based Process Controlling (2002)
6. Scheer, A.W., Brabänder, E.: The process of business process management. In: vom Brocke, J., Rosemann, M. (eds.) Handbook on Business Process Management 2. International Handbooks on Information Systems International Handbooks on Information Systems, pp. 239–265. Springer, Heidelberg (2010). https://doi.org/10.1007/978-3-642-01982-1_12
7. Hammer, M.: What is business process management? In: vom Brocke, J., Rosemann, M. (eds.) Handbook on Business Process Management 1. IHIS, pp. 3–16. Springer, Heidelberg (2015). https://doi.org/10.1007/978-3-642-45100-3_1
8. Harmon, P.: The scope and evolution of business process management. In: vom Brocke, J., Rosemann, M. (eds.) Handbook on Business Process Management 1. IHIS, pp. 37–80. Springer, Heidelberg (2015). https://doi.org/10.1007/978-3-642-45100-3_3
9. Thomas, P.R.: Competitiveness Through Total Cycle Time. McGraw-Hill, New York (1990)
10. Oviatt, B.M.: Agency and transaction cost perspectives on the manager-shareholder relationship: incentives for congruent interests. Acad. Manag. Rev. **13**(2), 214–225 (1988). https://doi.org/10.5465/amr.1988.4306868
11. March, J.G., Simon, H.A.: Organizations. Wiley, New York (1958)
12. Ross, R.: Principles of the Business Rule Approach. Addison-Wesley Professional, Boston (2003)
13. Ross, R.: Business Rule Concepts: Getting to the Point of Knowledge. Business Rule Solutions, LLC, Houston (2009)

Author Index

Printed in the United States
By Bookmasters